Standardized Service Contract (693)
"Services within the same service inventory are in compliance with the same contract design standards."

Service Loose Coupling (695)
"Service contracts impose low consumer coupling requirements and are themselves decoupled from their surrounding environment."

Service Abstraction (696)
"Service contracts only contain essential information and information about services is limited to what is published in service contracts."

Service Reusability (697)
"Services contain and express agnostic logic and can be positioned as reusable enterprise resources."

Service Autonomy (699)
"Services exercise a high level of control over their underlying runtime execution environment."

Service Statelessness (700)
"Services minimize resource consumption by deferring the management of state information when necessary."

Service Discoverability (702)
"Services are supplemented with communicative meta data by which they can be effectively discovered and interpreted."

Service Composability (704)
"Services are effective composition participants, regardless of the size and complexity of the composition."

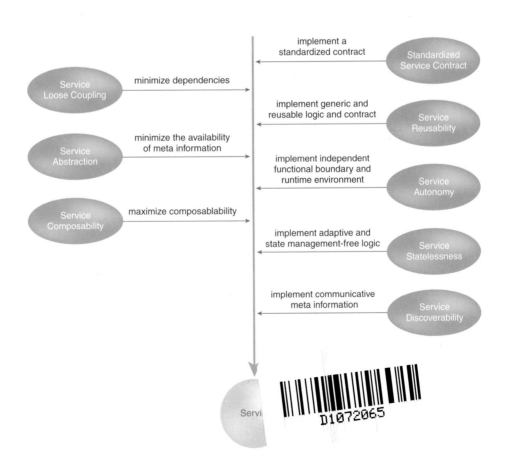

Agnostic Capability [709] How can multi-purpose service logic be made effectively consumable and composable?

 Agnostic Context [710] How can multi-purpose service logic be positioned as an effective enterprise resource?

 Agnostic Sub-Controller [711] How can agnostic, cross-entity composition logic be separated, reused, and governed independently?

 Asynchronous Queuing [712] How can a service and its consumers accommodate isolated failures and avoid unnecessarily locking resources?

 Atomic Service Transaction [713] How can a transaction with rollback capability be propagated across messaging-based services?

 Brokered Authentication [714] How can a service efficiently verify consumer credentials if the consumer and service do not trust each other or if the consumer requires access to multiple services?

 Canonical Expression [715] How can service contracts be consistently understood and interpreted?

 Canonical Protocol [716] How can services be designed to avoid protcol bridging?

 Canonical Resources [717] How can unnecessary infrastructure resource disparity be avoided?

 Canonical Schema [718] How can services be designed to avoid data model transformation?

Canonical Schema Bus [719]

 Canonical Versioning [720] How can service contracts within the same service inventory be versioned with minimal impact?

 Capability Composition [721] How can a service capability solve a problem that requires logic outside of the service boundary?

 Capability Recomposition [722] How can the same capability be used to help solve multiple problems?

 Compatible Change [723] How can a service contract be modified without impacting consumers?

 Compensating Service Transaction [724] How can composition runtime exceptions be consistently accommodated without requiring services to lock resources?

 Composition Autonomy [725] How can compositions be implemented to minimize loss of autonomy?

 Concurrent Contracts [726] How can a service facilitate multi-consumer coupling requirements and abstraction concerns at the same time?

 Contract Centralization [727] How can direct consumer-to-implementation coupling be avoided?

 Contract Denormalization [728] How can a service contract facilitate consumer programs with differing data exchange requirements?

 Cross-Domain Utility Layer [729] How can redundant utility logic be avoided across domain service inventories?

 Data Confidentiality [730] How can data within a message be protected so that it is not disclosed to unintended recipients while in transit?

 Data Format Transformation [731] How can services interact with programs that communicate with different data formats?

 Data Model Transformation [732] How can services interoperate when using different data models for the same type of data?

 Data Origin Authentication [733] How can a service verify that a message originates from a known sender and that the message has not been tampered with in transit?

 Decomposed Capability [734] How can a service be designed to minimize the chances of capability logic deconstruction?

 Decoupled Contract [735] How can a service express its capabilities independently of its implementation?

(pattern list continued on inside back cover)

Praise for this Book

"Microsoft's diverse product line has long supported the service-oriented enterprise, but putting it all together into a cohesive whole can be daunting. From more established products, like Windows Communication Foundation, Windows Workflow Foundation, Microsoft Office SharePoint Server, and BizTalk Server, to newer offerings like Windows Azure and AppFabric, the experts assembled here expose the sweet spots for each technology, talk through the high-level trade-offs, and offer a roadmap to a unified Microsoft SOA story."

—*Kevin P. Davis, Ph.D.*
Software Architect

"This book excels in giving hands-on and in-depth expertise on the SOA architecture style with the .NET framework and the Azure cloud platform. It's a practical guide for developers, architects, and SOA implementers. A must read!"

—*Ricardo P. Schluter*
ICT Architect, Parnassia Bavo Group

"While the industry overall may have hyped 'the cloud' to the level it often seems to cure world hunger, *SOA with .NET and Windows Azure* helps cut through the questions and hype and more clearly discusses the benefits and practical techniques for putting it to work in the real world. This book helps you understand the benefits associated with SOA and cloud computing, and also the techniques for connecting your current IT assets with new composite applications and data running in the cloud. This book will help you understand modern middleware technologies and harness the benefits of the cloud both on and off premises."

—*Burley Kawasaki*
Director of Product Management, Microsoft

"The authors have a combined SOA and .NET experience of several decades—which becomes obvious when reading this book. They don't just lead you down one path with a single descriptive solution. Instead, the sometimes nasty trade-offs that architects face in their design decisions are addressed. These are then mapped to the Microsoft .NET platform with clear code examples. A very refreshing look at this major contender in the SOA space and a definite must for the .NET SOA practitioner!"

—*Dr. Thomas Rischbeck*
IT Architect, Innovation Process Technology

"In order to evolve as a software craftsman one must read excellent books that will help you grow and evolve in your profession. One of those books that every software craftsman interested in good design and best practices should read is *SOA with .NET and Windows Azure*. With this book, you will learn which design patterns will provide the best solution for the kinds of software design problems you, as a developer or designer, face every day. This book has everything that software architects, software designers, and programmers need to know when building great quality software with Microsoft technologies.

"This will undoubtedly be one of those books that you reference repeatedly when starting new SOA projects. There is plenty of information that even those not working with typical service-oriented architecture will find very useful. With plenty of real-life examples (code, design, and modeling), readers see in a practical manner how they could use SOA patterns to solve everyday software problems and be more productive. *SOA with .NET and Windows Azure* will fit in my top three books and will definitely be one of those that I will use in my everyday work."

—*Arman Kurtagic*
Consultant at Omegapoint AB

SOA with .NET
and Windows Azure™

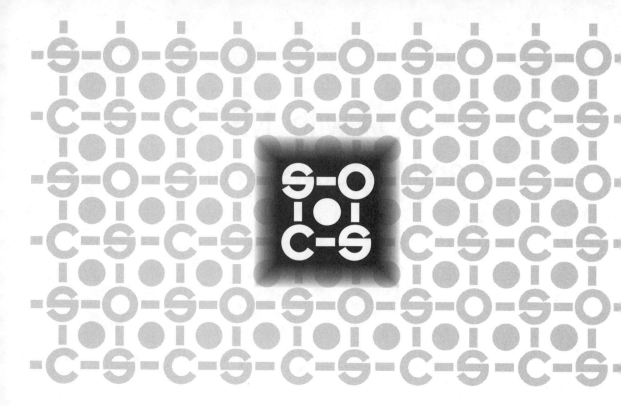

The Prentice Hall Service-Oriented Computing Series
from Thomas Erl aims to provide the IT industry with
a consistent level of unbiased, practical, and
comprehensive guidance and instruction in the areas
of service-oriented architecture, service-orientation,
and the expanding landscape that is shaping
the real-world service-oriented computing platform.

For more information, visit www.soabooks.com.

SOA with .NET
and Windows Azure™

Realizing Service-Orientation with the Microsoft Platform

David Chou, John deVadoss, Thomas Erl,
Nitin Gandhi, Hanu Kommapalati, Brian Loesgen,
Christoph Shittko, Herbjörn Wilhelmsen,
Mickie Williams

With contributions from
Scott Golightly, Daryl Hogan, Jeff King, Scott Seely

With additional contributions by members of the
Microsoft Windows Azure and AppFabric teams

PRENTICE HALL

PRENTICE HALL

UPPER SADDLE RIVER, NJ • BOSTON • INDIANAPOLIS • SAN FRANCISCO

NEW YORK • TORONTO • MONTREAL • LONDON • MUNICH • PARIS • MADRID

CAPETOWN • SYDNEY • TOKYO • SINGAPORE • MEXICO CITY

Many of the designations used by manufacturers and sellers to distinguish their products are claimed as trademarks. Where those designations appear in this book, and the publisher was aware of a trademark claim, the designations have been printed with initial capital letters or in all capitals.

The authors and publisher have taken care in the preparation of this book, but make no expressed or implied warranty of any kind and assume no responsibility for errors or omissions. No liability is assumed for incidental or consequential damages in connection with or arising out of the use of the information or programs contained herein.

The publisher offers excellent discounts on this book when ordered in quantity for bulk purchases or special sales, which may include electronic versions and/or custom covers and content particular to your business, training goals, marketing focus, and branding interests. For more information, please contact:

U.S. Corporate and Government Sales
(800) 382-3419
corpsales@pearsontechgroup.com

For sales outside the United States please contact:

International Sales
international@pearson.com

Visit us on the Web: informit.com/ph

The Library of Congress Cataloging-in-Publication Data is on file.

Copyright © 2010 SOA Systems Inc.

ISBN-13: 978-0-13-158231-6
ISBN-10: 0-13-158231-3
Text printed in the United States on recycled paper at Edward Brothers in Ann Arbor, Michigan.
First printing May 2010

Editor-in-Chief
Mark L. Taub

Development Editor
Christina Erl-Daniels

Managing Editor
Kristy Hart

Project Editor
Betsy Harris

Senior Indexer
Cheryl Lenser

Proofreaders
Williams Woods Publishing
Amy Chou

Publishing Coordinator
Kim Boedigheimer

Cover Designers
Thomas Erl
Ivana Lee

Compositor
Bumpy Design

Photos
Thomas Erl

Diagram Designer
Christina Erl-Daniels

To my family for their unconditional love and support.
And to everyone who encouraged and granted me opportunities to grow.
—David Chou

A big thank you to my wife and my two kuttis, Dipu and Gitu,
for their support and for giving me time to work on this book.
—John deVadoss

To Nikolas, who joined our team last June and has proven himself an expert
in the functional decomposition of anything he can get his hands on.
—Thomas Erl

Dedicated to my kids Tanay and Tanisha.
—Nitin Gandhi

I dedicate this book to my wife Vijayalakshmi and our daughters
Ajitha and Akshatha for putting up with me when I worked long hours
on this project while at the same time keeping a day job!
I would also like to mention the hard work of my parents
Yanadaiah and Anasuyamma but for whose help I would still be
a farmer in rural South India.
—Hanu Kommalapati

I'd like to dedicate my contribution to this book to my wife Miriam and children
Steven and Melissa, and thank them for their continual support and understanding.
—Brian Loesgen

To Alex.
—Christoph Schittko

To my son and wife.
—Herbjörn Wilhelmsen

Contents

Foreword by S. Somasegar . . . . **xxxi**

Foreword by David Chappell . . . . **xxxiii**

Acknowledgments . . . . **xxxv**

CHAPTER 1: Introduction **1**

    1.1 About this Book 2

    1.2 Objectives of this Book 3

    1.3 Who this Book is For 4

    1.4 What this Book Does Not Cover 4

    1.5 Prerequisite Reading 4

    1.6 How this Book is Organized 6

        Part I: Fundamentals 7

            Chapter 3: SOA Fundamentals 7

            Chapter 4: A Brief History of Legacy .NET Distributed Technologies . . 7

            Chapter 5: WCF Services 7

            Chapter 6: WCF Extensions 7

            Chapter 7: .NET Enterprise Services Technologies 7

            Chapter 8: Cloud Services with Windows Azure 8

        Part II: Services and Service Composition 8

            Chapter 9: Service-Orientation with .NET Part I:
            Service Contracts and Interoperability 8

            Chapter 10: Service-Orientation with .NET Part II:
            Coupling, Abstraction, and Discoverability 8

            Chapter 11: Service-Orientation with .NET Part III:
            Reusability and Agnostic Service Models 8

            Chapter 12: Service-Orientation with .NET Part IV:
            Service Composition and Orchestration Basics 9

            Chapter 13: Orchestration Patterns with WF. 9

            Chapter 14: Orchestration Patterns with BizTalk Server 9

Part III: Infrastructure and Architecture. 9
   Chapter 15: Enterprise Service Bus with BizTalk Server and
   Windows Azure 9
   Chapter 16: Windows Azure Platform AppFabric Service Bus. 10
   Chapter 17: SOA Security with .NET and Windows Azure 10
   Chapter 18: Service-Oriented Presentation Layers with .NET 10
   Chapter 19: Service Performance Optimization 10
   Chapter 20: SOA Metrics with BAM 10
Part IV: Appendices 10
   Appendix A: Case Study Conclusion 10
   Appendix B: Industry Standards Reference. 11
   Appendix C: Service-Orientation Principles Reference 11
   Appendix D: SOA Design Patterns Reference 11
   Appendix E: The Annotated SOA Manifesto. 11
   Appendix F: Additional Resources 11

1.7 How Principles and Patterns are Used in this Book 11
   Sources 11
   Reference Notation 12

1.8 Symbols, Figures, and Style Conventions. 13
   Symbol Legend. 13
   How Color is Used 13
   Additional Information 13
   Updates, Errata, and Resources (www.soabooks.com) 13
   Master Glossary (www.soaglossary.com) 13
   Referenced Specifications (www.soaspecs.com). 13
   SOASchool.com™ SOA Certified Professional (SOACP) 14
   The SOA Magazine (www.soamag.com) 14
   Notification Service 14

CHAPTER 2: Case Study Background 15

2.1 How Case Studies Are Used. 16
2.2 Case Study Background #1: Standard Mold 16
   History 16
   Technical Infrastructure. 16
   Business Goals and Obstacles. 17

2.3 Case Study Background #2: Superior Stamping 18

    History 18

    Technical Infrastructure 18

    Business Goals and Obstacles 19

PART I: FUNDAMENTALS

CHAPTER 3: SOA Fundamentals 23

3.1 Basic SOA Terminology 24

    Service-Oriented Computing 25

    Service-Orientation 25

    Service-Oriented Architecture (SOA) 27

    Services 28

        Services as Components 29

        Services as Web Services 30

        Services as REST Services 31

    Service Models 31

        Agnostic Logic and Non-Agnostic Logic 32

    Service Composition 33

    Service Inventory 34

    Service-Oriented Analysis 34

    Service Candidate 35

    Service-Oriented Design 35

    Service Contract 36

    Service-Related Granularity 37

    SOA Design Patterns 38

3.2 Service-Oriented Computing Goals 40

    Increased Intrinsic Interoperability 40

    Increased Federation 40

    Increased Vendor Diversification Options 40

    Increased Business and Technology Domain Alignment 41

3.3 Further Reading 41

CHAPTER 4: A Brief History of Legacy .NET Distributed Technologies 43

4.1 Distributed Computing 101 44

    Client-Server 44

    Distributed Architecture 45

    Service-Oriented Architecture 47

4.2 .NET Enterprise Services 48

    It All Began with COM (and DCOM) 48

    COM+ Services 49

    .NET Assemblies 51

    Distributed Transaction Coordinator 51

    .NET Enterprise Services and Service-Orientation 53

4.3 .NET Remoting 54

    .NET Remoting Architecture 54

        Serializable Classes 56

        Remotable Classes 56

        Ordinary Classes 56

    Hosting .NET Remoting Components 56

        Windows Service 56

        IIS Hosting Under ASP.NET 57

        Hosting a .NET Remoting Component in a Console Application 57

        .NET COM+ Services 57

    .NET Remoting Configurations 57

        Activation Types 58

        Message Formats 60

        Communication Protocols 60

        Object Lifetime Management 61

    .NET Remoting and Service-Orientation 61

4.4 Microsoft Messaging Queue (MSMQ) 63

    The Queues 64

    Sending and Receiving Messages 65

    MSMQ and Service-Orientation 66

4.5 System.Transactions 67

    Distributed Resource Transactions 67

    Explicit and Implicit Programming Models 68

    Ambient Transactions 69

4.6 Web Services (ASMX and WSE) 70

XML Web Services (ASMX) 71

The WebService Attribute 71

The WebMethod Attribute 72

Web Service Enhancements (WSE) 73

4.7 REST Service Processing with IHttpHandler 74

CHAPTER 5: WCF Services **75**

5.1 Overview 76

5.2 Service Contracts with WCF 78

WCF Terminology 78

WCF Service Contract 78

Interface Contract 78

Operation Contract 78

Data Contract 78

Message Contract 79

Service Endpoint 79

The ServiceContract and OperationContract Attributes 79

Data Models and the DataContract Attribute 82

Messaging and the MessageContract Attribute 83

Service Endpoints and the endpoint Element 86

Address 88

Bindings 89

Contract 92

REST Service Classes and Attributes 92

The WebGet Attribute 93

The WebInvoke Attribute 95

WCF UriTemplate Attribute 96

Faults and the FaultContract Attribute 98

MEX Endpoints 100

Versioning Considerations 102

5.3 Service Implementation with WCF 104

Behaviors 104

Instancing 105

A Sample Implementation 106

5.4 Service Hosting with WCF. 108

Self-Hosted Services. 110

Managed Windows Services. 112

IIS Process Boundary 113

Windows Activation Services (WAS) 114

Hosting REST Services 115

5.5 Service Consumers with WCF. 116

Using the Service Metadata Tool 117

Writing the Proxy Class for a Service 118

Using the ChannelFactory Class. 119

CHAPTER 6: WCF Extensions 121

6.1 WCF Security. 122

Security Modes 123

Authorization 125

Federated Identity 126

6.2 WCF Transactions 127

Operation Attributes for Transactions 127

TransactionScopeRequired *128*

TransactionAutoComplete *128*

TransactionFlow *128*

Service Attributes for Transactions 129

TransactionIsolationLevel *129*

TransactionAutoCompleteOnSessionClose *130*

TransactionTimeout *130*

Durable Services. 131

6.3 WCF Router. 132

The RoutingService Class. 133

Routing Contracts 134

Routing Configuration 135

Step 1: Define Endpoints *135*

Step 2: Configure Service Behavior *136*

Step 3: Enumerate Target Endpoints *136*

Step 4: Define Message Filters *137*

Step 5: Create a Filter Table *138*

Fault Tolerance 139

6.4 WCF Discovery 140
    Discovery Modes 141
    Locating a Service Ad Hoc 143
    Sending and Receiving Service Announcements. 144
    Discovery Proxies for Managed Discovery 146
        Discovering from a Discovery Proxy *146*
    Implicit Service Discovery 147

6.5 WCF Extensibility. 148
    WCF Layers 149
    Layered Extensibility 149
    Channel Layer Extensibility 150

6.6 WCF Management Tools 151
    Administration 151
    Troubleshooting 151
    Logging Messages 153

**CHAPTER 7: .NET Enterprise Services
Technologies 155**

7.1 SQL Server 156
    Native XML Web Services Support 157
    Service Broker (SSB) 160
    Query Notification 165
    XML Support in SQL Server 165

7.2 Windows Workflow Foundation (WF). 166
    WF Architecture 167
    Workflows 168
        Sequential Workflows *169*
        State Machine Workflows *169*
    Workflow Designer 169
    Workflow Persistence (with WF) 170
    Communicating with the Host Container 171
    Activities 172
    Workflow Runtime Environment 175
    WF Programming Model 176
    Passing Parameters into a Workflow Instance 178

Returning Parameters from a Workflow Instance 178
Workflow-Enabled Services. 179
Versioning Orchestrations 180
WF Extensibility 180
Business Rules 180

7.3 Application Blocks and Software Factories 181
Application Blocks 182
Software Factories. 184
  Guidance Toolkits 184
  Web Services Software Factory 184

7.4 Windows Server AppFabric 187
Configurable Hosting Environment 188
Workflow Persistence (with AppFabric) 189
In-Memory Application Cache Platform 190
Manageability Extensions 192
Application Server Event Collector 192

7.5 BizTalk Server 193
BizTalk Server Architecture 194
Messaging 196
  Pipelines 197
  Pipeline Components 198
  Ports and Locations 199
Adapters 199
Context Properties. 200
Itineraries 201
Unified Exception Management 202

CHAPTER 8: Cloud Services with Windows Azure 205

8.1 Cloud Computing 101. 206
Cloud Deployment Models 208
  Public Cloud 208
  Private Cloud 208
  Community Cloud 209
  Other Deployment Models 209
  The Intercloud (Cloud of Clouds) 209
  Deployment Models and Windows Azure. 210

Service Delivery Models 210

Infrastructure-as-a-Service (IaaS) *210*

Platform-as-a-Service (PaaS) *211*

Software-as-a-Service (SaaS) *211*

Other Delivery Models *211*

IaaS vs. PaaS *211*

8.2 Windows Azure Platform Overview 213

Windows Azure (Application Container) 216

SQL Azure 217

Windows Azure Platform AppFabric 218

8.3 Windows Azure Roles 219

Web Roles and Worker Roles *220*

Virtual Machines *220*

Input Endpoints *221*

Inter-Role Communication *222*

8.4 Hello World in Windows Azure 223

1. Create a Cloud Service Project 224

2. Choose an ASP.NET Web Role 224

3. Create the Solution 225

4. Instantiate the Service 226

8.5 A Web Service in Windows Azure 227

1. Create a Host Service and Storage Service 233

2. Create and Deploy a Service Package 233

3. Promote the Service to Production 234

8.6 A REST Service in Windows Azure 235

REST Service Addressing 235

Creating a Windows Azure REST Service 236

8.7 Windows Azure Storage 239

Tables 240

Entities and Properties *240*

Data Access *241*

Queues 241

Blobs 242

Block Blobs *242*

Page Blobs *243*

Windows Azure Drive 243

PART II: SERVICES AND SERVICE COMPOSITION

CHAPTER 9: Service-Orientation
with .NET Part I: Service Contracts
and Interoperability 247

9.1 Standardized Service Contract 250
Contract-First 250
1. Create or Reuse Data Contract 251
2. Create Message Contract 251
3. Create Interface Contract 252
Standardized Service Contract and Patterns 252

9.2 Canonical Schema 253
Creating Schemas with Visual Studio 254
Generating .NET Types 258
Using the DataContract Library 264

9.3 Data Model Transformation 267
Object-to-Object 269
LINQ-to-XML 271
XSLT Transformation 272

9.4 Canonical Protocol 274
Web Service 275
REST Service 277
Component 278
Another WCF Option: Named Pipes 279
Dual Protocols with WCF 279

9.5 Canonical Expression 280
Service Naming Conventions 280
Service Capability Naming Conventions 281

CHAPTER 10: Service-Orientation
with .NET Part II: Coupling, Abstraction,
and Discoverability 283

10.1 Service Loose Coupling 285
Service Loose Coupling and Patterns 286

10.2 Decoupled Contract 288

    WSDL-First 289

    Generating Service Code Using Svcutil 294

    Generating WCF Service Code Using WSCF.blue 297

    Generating ASMX Service Code Using WSCF.classic 302

10.3 Service Façade 304

10.4 Concurrent Contracts 307

10.5 Service Loose Coupling and Service Capability
Granularity. 308

10.6 Service Abstraction. 313

10.7 Validation Abstraction 315

10.8 Exception Shielding 319

10.9 Service Discoverability 321

    In-line Documentation. 322

    REST and Hypermedia 323

    Service Profiles 323

10.10 Metadata Centralization 325

**CHAPTER 11: Service-Orientation
with .NET Part III: Reusability and Agnostic
Service Models. 327**

11.1 Service Reusability and the Separation of Concerns . . . 329

    Functional Decomposition. 330

    Service Encapsulation. 332

    Agnostic Context. 332

    Agnostic Capability. 334

    Utility Abstraction 335

    Entity Abstraction 336

    The Inventory Analysis Cycle 337

    Additional Design Considerations. 339

11.2 Case Study Example: Utility Abstraction
with a .NET Web Service. 339

11.3 Case Study Example: Entity Abstraction
with a .NET REST Service 351

CHAPTER 12: Service-Orientation with .NET Part IV: Service Composition and Orchestration Basics......369

12.1 Service Composition 101 371
Service-Orientation and Service Composition 371
Service Composability (PSD) 373
Capability Composition and Capability Recomposition 374
Capability Composition........375
Capability Recomposition 375
Composition Roles 377
Service Layers........377
Non-Agnostic Context........379
Process Abstraction and Task Services 380

12.2 Orchestration........382
Process Abstraction, Process Centralization, and Orchestrated Task Services........382
Process Centralizationand Tools........384
Process Abstraction and WS-BPEL 385
State Repository and Compensating Service Transaction 385
State Repository with .NET........386
Compensating Service Transaction 387
Other Patterns........388
Microsoft Orchestration Platforms: WF and BizTalk Server 388

CHAPTER 13: Orchestration Patterns with WF........393

13.1 Process Abstraction and Orchestrated Task Services ..397
A Brief History of WF Service Contract Support 397
Publishing WF Workflows as Web Services and Activities 399
Workflows Published as ASMX Services 399
Workflows Published via WCF 3.5 Activities........408
Workflows Published via WCF 4.0 Activities........410
Workflows Published via ExternalDataExchange Services........413
WS-I BasicProfile Support........417

Publishing WF Workflows as REST Services 419

JSON Encoding 421

Send and Receive Activity Configuration 422

Orchestrated Task Services with REST and WF 4.0 423

13.2 Process Centralization 425

Centralized Process Maintenance 425

WS-BPEL Support 426

13.3 State Repository 426

SQL Persistence Service and Scaling Out in WF 3.0 429

SQL Persistence Service and Scaling Out in WF 4 431

13.4 Compensating Service Transaction 434

Creating Compensations 434

Triggering Compensations 435

13.5 Case Study Example 436

**CHAPTER 14: Orchestration Patterns with
BizTalk Server 441**

14.1 Process Abstraction and Orchestrated Task Services . . 443

Orchestrated Task Service Contracts 445

WS-* Support 447

Case Study Example 448

14.2 Process Centralization 450

Centralized Process Maintenance 450

WS-BPEL Support 451

Exporting BizTalk Orchestrations to WS-BPEL 451

Importing WS-BPEL Processes into BizTalk 454

14.3 State Repository 455

14.4 Compensating Service Transaction 456

Case Study Example 459

PART III: INFRASTRUCTURE AND ARCHITECTURE

CHAPTER 15: Enterprise Service Bus with BizTalk Server and Windows Azure. 465

15.1 Microsoft and the ESB. 466

15.2 Integration with BizTalk 467
   Application Integration 101 467
   The BizTalk Hub-Bus Model 469

15.3 The ESB Toolkit 470
   Itineraries 472
      Itineraries Types *474*
      The Itinerary Lifecycle. *475*
   Resolvers. 476
   Adapter Providers 478
      WCF-Custom and REST Services. *479*

15.4 Distributed and Scalable ESB Architecture 480
   Configuring for High-Availability 480
   Techniques for Scaling 481
   Distributed ESBs 482

15.5 Cloud-Enabling the ESB with Windows Azure 483
   Receiving Messages from Azure's AppFabric Service Bus 484
   Sending Messages to Azure's AppFabric Service Bus. 485

15.6 Governance Considerations 487
   SLA Enforcement. 488
   Monitoring 488
   Preparing Project Teams 489

15.7 Mapping the Microsoft Platform to the Enterprise Service Bus Pattern. 490

**CHAPTER 16: Windows Azure Platform
AppFabric Service Bus 493**

16.1 Introducing the Service Bus 494
   Connectivity Fabric 494
   Message Buffers 496
   Service Registry 497

16.2 Service Bus and REST 498
   REST-Based Service Design 498
   REST-Based Service Consumer Design 499
   Message Buffers and REST 499

16.3 Service Bus Connectivity Models 499
   Eventing 500
   Service Remoting 501
   Tunneling 501

16.4 Working with Windows Azure Platform AppFabric
Service Bus 503
   Setting up the AppFabric Service Bus 504
   Defining a REST-Based Service Bus Contract 513
   Creating the Service Bus Message Buffer 514

**CHAPTER 17: SOA Security with .NET
and Windows Azure 517**

17.1 Authentication and Authorization with WCF 518
   Direct and Brokered Authentication 518
     Direct Authentication. *518*
     Brokered Authentication *519*
     Authentication Patterns in WCF *520*
   Role-Based Authorization 520
     Authorization Roles in WCF *521*
     Authorizing Operations with Roles *523*
   Claims-Based Authorization 524
     Claims Processing in WCF *526*
     Implementing Claims-Based Authorization. *527*
     Access Control in Windows Azure *528*
     Designing Custom Claims *529*

Case Study Example. 530

17.2 Windows Identity Foundation (WIF) 533
    Digital Identity 534
        The Identity Metasystem *534*
    Windows Cardspace 536
    Active Directory Federation Services (ADFS) 539
    WIF Programming Model. 540
        WCF Integration *540*
        Programming Windows Cardspace *540*
    Developing a Relying Party. 541
    Developing an Identity Provider 542

17.3 Windows Azure Security 543
    Cloud Computing Security 101. 543
        Cross-Domain Access Control *544*
        Hybrid Cloud Security. *545*
        Inter-Organization Service Composition Security *545*
        External Identity Providers *546*
        Claims-Based Access Control, As-A-Service. *546*
    Windows Azure Platform AppFabric Access Control Overview . 548
        Access Control Step-by-Step *550*
        Access Control and REST. *552*
    Access Control Service Authorization Scenarios 553
        Hybrid Cloud Authorization Model *553*
        Public Cloud Authorization Model. *554*
        Cloud-to-Cloud Authorization Model. *554*

    Case Study Example. 555

**CHAPTER 18: Service-Oriented Presentation
Layers with .NET 557**

    18.1 Windows Presentation Foundation
    and the Prism Library 559
        Shell. 561
        Views. 562
            View Discovery versus View Injection. *563*
        Regions 563

Modules. 565
Shared Services 566

18.2 Design Patterns for Presentation Logic. 567
User Interface Patterns 567
Composite View [CJP] *568*
Command [DP]. *568*
UI Mediator *568*
Separated Presentation *568*
Modularity Patterns 569
Separated Interface [PEA] *570*
   . *Plug-In [PEA]*. *570*
Event Aggregator [PEA] *570*
Inversion of Control [DP]. *570*
Dependency Injection [PEA]. *570*
Service Locator [CJP]. *571*

18.3 A Simple Service-Oriented User Interface 571
Creating the Project. 571
Dynamically Loading Modules 579

CHAPTER 19: Service Performance Optimization. 583

19.1 Overview 584
Optimization Areas 585
Service Implementation Processing 585
Service Framework Processing. 586
Wire Transmission Processing. 586

19.2 Service Performance Optimization Techniques 586
Caching to Avoid Costly Processing. 587
Intermediary *589*
Service Container *589*
Service Proxy *590*
Caching Utility Service *590*
Comparing Caching Techniques *591*
Cache Implementation Technologies 592
Computing Cache Keys 593

Case Study Example. 594

   Method 1. . . . . *597*

   Method 2. . . . . *598*

   Caching REST Responses 599

   Monitoring Cache Efficiency 601

   Reducing Resource Contention 603

   Request Throttling. 604

   Throttling With WCF *605*

Case Study Example. 606

   Request Throttling with BizTalk Server *607*

   Coarse-Grained Service Contracts. 608

Case Study Example. 609

   Selecting Application Containers 610

   Performance Policies 612

Case Study Example. 620

   REST Service Message Sizes 621

   Hardware Encryption. 622

   Transport Encryption. *622*

   Message Encryption. *623*

   Custom Encryption Solution *623*

   High Performance Transport. 625

Case Study Example. 626

   MTOM Encoding 627

Case Study Example. 628

   Performance Considerations for Service Contract Design 630

Case Study Example. 631

   Impact on Service-Orientation Principles 633

19.3 Service Composition Performance
Optimization Techniques. 637

   Transformation Avoidance and Caching. 637

   Asynchronous Interactions 639

   Parallelize Where Possible 641

   Parallel Activity in WF *641*

   Parallel Execution in BizTalk Server *643*

   Replicator Activity in WF. *644*

Consider Co-Hosting When Necessary 645
Compose High Performance Services 648
Impact on Service-Orientation Principles 648

CHAPTER 20: SOA Metrics with BAM 653

20.1 SOA Metric Types 654

20.2 Introducing BizTalk BAM 655
BizTalk and BAM 655
BAM Solution Architecture 656
The BAM Management Utility 659
The Tracking Profile Editor (TPE) 659
Real-Time vs Scheduled Aggregations 660

20.3 Activities and Views 661
Roles-based Views for Service Governance 662
Creating Views 663

20.4 BAM APIs 665
Event Streams 665
DirectEventStream (DES) 665
BufferedEventStream (BES) 665
OrchestrationEventStream (OES) 666
IPipelineContext Interface 666
Abstracted APIs for Service Metrics 666
Metrics for Service Compositions 669
WCF and WF Interceptors 670
Notifications 670
Rapid Prototyping 671

20.5 Managing BAM 672
Database Outages 672
Security 672
Scripting Deployment 673
Reporting 676

Case Study Example 677

PART IV: APPENDICES

APPENDIX A: Case Study Conclusion **685**

APPENDIX B: Industry Standards Reference **687**

APPENDIX C: Service-Orientation Principles Reference **691**

APPENDIX D: SOA Design Patterns Reference **707**

APPENDIX E: The Annotated SOA Manifesto **795**

      The Annotated SOA Manifesto 796

APPENDIX F: Additional Resources **809**

      Consuming Services with WCF 811

            Introduction 811

            Cleaning Up Resources 812

            The Proper Disposal and Closing of an ICommunicationObject 812

            The ICommunicationObject.Close() Method 812

            The ICommunicationObject.Abort() Method 814

            Abort() versus Close() 814

            IDisposable for Cleaning Up Resources 814

            IDisposable and Its Relation to ClientBase and ChannelFactory 815

            Cleaning Up Resources with the Using Block 816

            Cleaning Up Resources with the Try-Catch-Finally-Abort Pattern 817

            Handling Exceptions and Cleaning Up Resources with the Try-Close-Catch-Abort Pattern 818

            Cleaning Up Resources in a Convenient Way 819

How to Handle Connections when Consuming Services
Using WCF 822

Conclusion 823

About the Authors **825**

David Chou 825

John deVadoss 825

Thomas Erl 826

Nitin Gandhi 826

Hanu Kommalapati 827

Brian Loesgen 827

Christoph Schittko 828

Herbjörn Wilhelmsen 828

Mickey Williams 828

About the Contributors **829**

Scott Golightly 829

Darryl Hogan 829

Kris Horrocks 829

Jeff King 830

Scott Seely 830

About the Foreword Contributors **831**

David Chappell 831

S. Somasegar 831

Index **833**

Foreword by S. Somasegar

Within the last decade, service-oriented architecture has moved from infancy to ubiquity, precipitating and, in many ways, enabling the next paradigm of information technology—cloud computing. As the Software + Services model becomes the norm, businesses that embrace SOA will smoothly transition to the cloud, enabling better scaling, availability, and cost efficacy of their services.

Service-oriented architecture is the magic behind many of the Internet-based applications and services that seamlessly integrate information and data from multiple sources into a single experience. The loosely-coupled design of SOA allows developers to take advantage of existing services to build their applications, dynamically adapt to changes in those services, and offer their own services to other application developers. From a developer perspective, it is best to have tools and frameworks that enable you to write ONLY the code that you need to write. SOA allows developers to do just that—focus on building the unique parts of their applications by enabling them to reuse existing services others have already written to solve common problems.

Microsoft has long promoted a real-world approach to SOA that focuses on helping organizations create business value by translating business challenges into opportunities. A real-world approach is typically based on rapid, agile iterations of design, implementation, and assessment, resulting in solutions that are able to better track and align to the changing needs of the organization and its business environment.

To developers, service-orientation offers a technology model with the potential for effectively creating and maintaining 'evolvable' applications: applications that are better able to change and grow with the business. To the CIO, service-orientation offers strategies and tools for nurturing existing IT assets while simultaneously fostering the development of new capabilities. The 'rip and replace' tactic of the past to deal with changing technology and business needs is facing extinction, thanks primarily to the increasing adoption of service-orientation and the pervasive nature of service-oriented architectures. The encapsulation of existing assets behind service-based interfaces provides structured access to legacy systems and applications while facilitating the opportunity for continuous improvement of the underlying business capabilities behind the interface.

However, keep in mind that architecture is a means to an end. The end goal is to create continuing value for your business, and a real-world approach based on proven practices offers a viable map to help get you there. With the emergence of the cloud as an attractive platform for both consumer and business computing, the principles underlying loose-coupling and service-orientation are increasingly relevant beyond the four walls of the data center. Services are more and more being developed and deployed beyond the confines of the firewall.

Microsoft's innovative new platforms and tools, including Windows Azure and SQL Azure, as well as Windows Azure platform AppFabric, Visual Studio 2010, and .NET Framework 4, enable organizations to extend their service-oriented architectures into the cloud, creating a hybrid Software + Services model. The Microsoft platforms and tools provide businesses with the choice to leverage the 'right' technologies, whether on-premises or in the cloud, truly putting the customer in control, and organizations that build on a proven set of service-oriented patterns and practices set themselves up for greater success in a Software + Services world.

This book is the result of mining and collating proven practices from the field. The authors have done an excellent job of explaining the architectural designs and goals behind SOA as well as real-world examples of SOA usage to build elegant IT solutions. It is my hope that this work plays a role in helping you realize loosely coupled, service-oriented solutions, on-premises and in the cloud, using Microsoft platforms and tools.

—*S. Somasegar*
  Senior Vice President, Developer Division, Microsoft

Foreword by David Chappell

What is SOA? In the dozen or so years that the term has been around, service-oriented architecture has meant lots of different things. Some vendors saw it as a way to sell whatever it was they were offering, and so they jumped on the SOA bandwagon with both feet. Other people interpreted SOA in business terms, viewing it as a way to structure how different parts of an organization interact.

Yet from all of this confusion, one clear fact has emerged: The technology of service-orientation has real value. Whether or not it helps vendors sell products or managers organize their business, taking a service-oriented approach to development can make life better for the people who build and maintain applications.

The core reason for this is simple. Since applications rarely live out their lives in isolation, why not design those apps from the start with future connections in mind? Creating software that can expose and consume services marks the end of application silos, and it's fundamental to the value of service-orientation.

Doing this well requires two things. The first is a grasp of how to apply services effectively. Over time, our industry has evolved a set of patterns to help us create and connect applications in a service-oriented style. As with patterns in any other area, those for service-orientation attempt to codify best practices, helping all of us learn from what's gone before rather than reinvent these wheels on our own.

The second thing that's needed is a solid understanding of the technologies used to create service-oriented software. If you're working in the .NET world, there are quite a few things to get your mind around. Windows Communication Foundation provides a unified approach to creating and consuming services, for example, while Windows Workflow Foundation offers a generalized approach to orchestrating them. BizTalk Server takes an explicitly integration-oriented approach to the problem, while the Windows Azure platform brings services to the cloud. And even though the .NET Framework is common to all of these technologies, using them effectively isn't so easy. Each brings its own complexity to the party, and each can be combined with the others in various ways.

Explaining the intersection of these two worlds—service-orientation and .NET technologies—is exactly what this book does. Its team of specialist authors provides a concrete, usable guide to this combination, ranging from the fundamentals of service-orientation to the more rarified air of .NET services in the cloud and beyond. If you're creating service-oriented software on the Microsoft platform—that is, if you're a serious .NET developer—mastering these ideas is a must.

—*David Chappell*
  Chappell & Associates (San Francisco, CA, USA)

Acknowledgments

Special thanks to the following reviewers who generously volunteered their time and expertise (in alphabetical order):

Joshua Anthony, Co-founder and President, Habanero Business Development AB

Jacquelyn Crowhurst, Director of Platform Evangelism

Kevin P. Davis, Ph.D., Software Architect

Danny Garber, US Azure Community Lead, SOA Solution Architect, Microsoft

Kris Horrocks, Senior Technical Product Manager, Microsoft Application Platform, Microsoft

Jan Arend Jansen, Senior IT Architect, Wolters Kluwer

Burley Kawasaki, Director of Product Management, Connected Systems Division, Microsoft

Krishna Kothumbaka, Senior IT Architect

Arman Kurtagic, Consultant, Omegapoint AB

Bob Laskey, General Manager of Platform Evangelism, Microsoft

Thomas Rischbeck, IT Architect, Innovation Process Technology

Ricardo Schlüter, ICT Architect, Parnassia Bavo Group

Scott Seely, Co-founder, Tech in the Middle, and President, Friseton, LLC

Steve Sloan, Product Manager, Microsoft

Alan Smith, Consultant, Know IT Stockholm

Tharun Tharian, Senior Product Manager, Developer Platform & Tools, Microsoft

Jim Webber, ThoughtWorks

Scott Zimmerman, Solutions Architect, Microsoft

Chapter 1

Introduction

1.1 About this Book

1.2 Objectives of this Book

1.3 Who this Book is For

1.4 What this Book Does Not Cover

1.5 Prerequisite Reading

1.6 How this Book is Organized

1.7 How Principles and Patterns are Used in this Book

1.8 Symbols, Figures, and Style Conventions

"It's the transformation of our software, it's the transformation of our strategy and our offerings across the board to fundamentally embrace services."

—Ray Ozzie, Chief Software Architect, Microsoft

1.1 About this Book

Documenting the intersection between the technology capabilities of a vendor product-based platform and the demands and requirements of the service-orientation design paradigm is always an interesting exercise. You find yourself exploring parts of the platform that go well beyond those labeled with the word "service" to discover strengths and weaknesses that have a direct bearing on the potential to realize the very specific goals associated with service-oriented computing.

The body of work provided in this book is the result of a three-year study of Microsoft platform technologies in relation to service-orientation. I was fortunate to work with authors and contributors (most with Microsoft) who collaborated and advanced the study at different intervals, each providing individual expertise and insights.

The use of design principles and patterns in this book proved especially helpful. Because each principle or pattern had been previously well-defined and documented in detail, there was no room for interpretation with its application to or comparison with Microsoft technologies.

One of the greatest revelations of this effort was the variety of options you have when working with Microsoft technologies. I had an initial expectation that we would be documenting very specific combinations of products and technologies for building service-oriented solutions and service-oriented technology architecture implementations. It turns out that there are many choices, each with its own set of pros and cons. This type of diversity is important, as it can help you create and optimize individual services differently and independently, while still remaining within the same overall technology platform.

As you dive into the many topics covered by this book, I encourage you to keep the big picture in mind. Building services as units of service-oriented logic is about shaping software programs in a specific way in support of achieving a specific target state. That target state is the big picture. The ultimate goal is for your services to collectively establish an environment that is naturally responsive to on-going business change.

Finally, another important consideration is that the big picture doesn't always have to be "big." The scope in which you choose to apply service-orientation can vary from a modest segment within the IT enterprise to an entire business domain and beyond. As stated in the SOA Manifesto: "Keep efforts manageable and within meaningful boundaries." The definition of those boundaries is up to you, based on what you can realistically manage.

These factors will further influence how you choose to assemble service-oriented technology environments using Microsoft technologies. Having them in the back of your mind as you study the upcoming chapters will give you a constant context and also some baseline criteria as you consider each technology option in relation to service-orientation and your unique business objectives and requirements.

> **NOTE**
>
> The annotated version of the SOA Manifesto is published in Appendix E.

1.2 Objectives of this Book

Collectively, these chapters were written with the following primary goals in mind:

- to provide coverage of contemporary Microsoft distributed technologies and modern service technologies

- to explain how Microsoft cloud computing technologies and platforms can be leveraged by service-oriented technology architectures

- to document the application of service-orientation principles to the Microsoft technology platform

- to explore the application of SOA design patterns to various .NET and Azure technologies and solutions built with these technologies

- to provide coverage of Microsoft infrastructure extensions and administration tools relevant to service-oriented solution deployment and governance

1.3 Who this Book is For

This book can be used as a tutorial and a reference text and is intended for the following types of readers:

- Developers and architects new to .NET and Windows Azure who will supplement this book with additional tutorials to learn how to design and build service-oriented solutions using Microsoft platform technologies.

- Experienced .NET developers and architects who want to learn how to apply service-orientation principles and SOA design patterns in order to create services and service-oriented solutions.

- Developers and architects who want to learn more about Windows Azure and AppFabric.

- Enterprise architects that want to learn more about how to position and establish enterprise service bus and orchestration platforms within the IT enterprise.

- Developers who want to build solutions using modern Microsoft service technologies.

1.4 What this Book Does Not Cover

This is not a "how-to" book for .NET or SOA. Although the six chapters in Part I contain a great deal of introductory coverage of modern .NET and Windows Azure technologies, the overall purpose of this book is to explore the intersection of Microsoft platform technologies and the application of service-orientation principles and SOA design patterns. This book intends to empower you with the knowledge required to properly utilize Microsoft products and technologies for the creation of services, service compositions, service-oriented solutions, and service-oriented technology architectures.

1.5 Prerequisite Reading

This book assumes you have a basic knowledge of:

- the .NET framework
- fundamental XML concepts
- fundamental service-orientation

If you have not yet worked with XML, you can read some of the brief tutorials published at www.soaspecs.com. If you are new to SOA, you can get a basic understanding of service-oriented computing, service-orientation, and related design patterns by studying the content at the following Web sites:

- www.whatissoa.com

- www.soaprinciples.com

- www.soapatterns.org

- www.soa-manifesto.com

To further ensure that you have a clear understanding of key terms used and referenced in the upcoming chapters, you can also visit the online master glossary for this book series at www.soaglossary.com to look up definitions for terms that may not be fully described in this book.

Even if you are an experienced SOA practitioner, we suggest you take the time to have a look at these online resources. A great deal of ambiguity has surrounded SOA and service-oriented computing and these explanations and definitions will ensure that you fully understand key terms and concepts in relation to this book and the book series as a whole.

Here are some recommendations for additional books that elaborate on key topics covered by this title:

- *SOA Principles of Service Design* – A comprehensive documentation of the service-orientation design paradigm with full descriptions of all of the principles referenced in this book.

- *SOA Design Patterns* – This is the official SOA design patterns catalog containing descriptions and examples for most of the patterns referenced in this book. You can also look up concise descriptions for these patterns at www.soapatterns.org and in Appendix D.

- *Web Service Contract Design & Versioning for SOA* – Any content pertaining to contract-first or WSDL, XML Schema, and WS-Policy development and design, development, and versioning will be aided by the detailed coverage in this title.

- *Service-Oriented Architecture: Concepts, Technology, and Design* – The coverage of service-oriented analysis and design processes in this title supplements the technology-centric focus of this book with methodology-related topics.

The following titles are currently in development as part of the Prentice Hall Service-Oriented Computing Series from Thomas Erl:

- *SOA with Java* – A book dedicated to building services and service-oriented solutions with Java development tools and technologies, with an emphasis on Web services and REST services.

- *SOA Governance* – This book explores a wide range of organizational and technological governance topics, including Web service contract versioning and evolution.

- *SOA with REST* – This book documents the convergence of REST and SOA by establishing how REST services can be realized in support of service-orientation. Salient topics are reinforced with comprehensive case studies using modern REST frameworks in combination with contemporary SOA models, patterns, practices, and concepts.

- *Modern SOA Infrastructure* – The aim of this book is to explore modern infrastructure technologies and practices for mainstream service-oriented architectures and solutions. This book provides in-depth coverage of contemporary infrastructure technology components and further provides new design patterns that extend and build upon previously documented SOA design patterns.

- *Cloud Computing & SOA* – This book is focused on the convergence of SOA and Cloud Computing. It will provide a comprehensive reference for the technologies and practices that are emerging around the adoption of Software as a Service (SaaS), Platform as a Service (PaaS) and Infrastructure as a Service (IaaS) as they pertain private, public and community clouds in support of service-orientation and service-oriented solution design.

For the latest information regarding the release of these new books, visit www.soabooks.com.

1.6 How this Book is Organized

This book begins with Chapters 1 and 2 providing introductory content and case study background information respectively. All subsequent chapters are grouped into the following parts:

- Part I: Fundamentals

- Part II: Services and Service Composition

- Part III: Infrastructure and Architecture
- Part IV: Appendices

Part I: Fundamentals

The first six chapters cover introductory topics related to SOA, service-orientation, and the broad range of past and present Microsoft distributed technologies.

Chapter 3: SOA Fundamentals

This chapter provides an overview of key terms and concepts associated with SOA, service-orientation, and service-oriented computing.

Chapter 4: A Brief History of Legacy .NET Distributed Technologies

This chapter begins with distributed computing basics, and then proceeds to summarize the evolution of Microsoft distributed technologies, including COM, DCOM, COM+ Services, .NET Enterprise Services, .NET Remoting, MSMQ, System.Transactions, and XML Web Services (ASMX), including Web Services Enhancements (WSE).

Chapter 5: WCF Services

This chapter introduces the Windows Communication Foundation (WCF) platform, with an emphasis on service technologies and implementation and hosting options. Areas of focus include service contracts and service consumer design requirements. WCF services are used in examples throughout subsequent chapters.

Chapter 6: WCF Extensions

The exploration of various architectural extensions to WCF provided in this chapter acts as a continuation of Chapter 5. Extensions covered include security, transactions, routing, discovery, management tools, and extensibility options.

Chapter 7: .NET Enterprise Services Technologies

Further architectural and infrastructure building blocks are provided by .NET Enterprise Service Technologies. This chapter provides introductory coverage of SQL Server, Windows Workflow Foundation (WF), Windows Server AppFabric, Application Blocks, and Software Factories.

Chapter 8: Cloud Services with Windows Azure

Following a section that covers basic cloud computing concepts and terminology, this chapter delves into the Windows Azure Platform to cover specific topics, such as Azure roles and storage options, as well as tutorial-style coverage of how Web services and REST services can be created for deployment within Windows Azure.

Part II: Services and Service Composition

When working with service-orientation, a service is a software program with specific characteristics. Many of these characteristics foster the ability of a service to be repeatedly aggregated into different service compositions. This part of the book contains a series of chapters that explore how service-orientation principles and patterns can be applied to build units of service-oriented solution logic (services) in support of strategic service-oriented computing goals, with a special emphasis on support for future composability requirements.

Chapter 9: Service-Orientation with .NET Part I: Service Contracts and Interoperability

The design and standardization of service contracts is a focal point when building service-oriented solutions. This chapter provides numerous examples and coverage of .NET technologies shaped by the application of the relevant design principles, patterns, and practices (including the Standardized Service Contract principle and the Canonical Schema, Data Model Transformation, Canonical Protocol, and Canonical Expression patterns).

Chapter 10: Service-Orientation with .NET Part II: Coupling, Abstraction, and Discoverability

This chapter explores the application of numerous patterns and principles in relation to service coupling, abstraction, and discoverability requirements and concerns. Patterns and principles covered include Service Loose Coupling, Decoupled Contract, Service Façade, Concurrent Contracts, Service Abstraction, Validation Abstraction, Service Discoverability, and Metadata Centralization.

Chapter 11: Service-Orientation with .NET Part III: Reusability and Agnostic Service Models

With an emphasis on fostering the reusability potential of services, this chapter explores the application of the Service Reusability principle from modeling, design, and development perspectives via the application of fundamental service identification and definition patterns, including Functional Decomposition, Service Encapsulation, Agnostic

Context, Agnostic Capability, Utility Abstraction, and Entity Abstraction. The latter sections in the chapter contain detailed case study examples for the development of utility and entity services using Web service and REST service technologies, respectively.

Chapter 12: Service-Orientation with .NET Part IV: Service Composition and Orchestration Basics

This chapter covers fundamental service composition theory and discusses the importance of the Service Composability principle in relation to the Capability Composition, Capability Recomposition, Service Layers, Non-Agnostic Context, and Process Abstraction patterns. The latter half of the chapter acts as a prelude to Chapters 13 and 14 by providing introductory coverage of patterns relevant to Microsoft orchestration platforms, including Process Centralization, State Repository, Compensating Transaction, and the Orchestration compound pattern itself.

Chapter 13: Orchestration Patterns with WF

Using the Orchestration compound pattern (and its core member patterns) as a basis, this chapter explores relevant technologies and features of the Windows Workflow Foundation (WF) platform.

Chapter 14: Orchestration Patterns with BizTalk Server

Similar in structure to Chapter 13, this chapter covers technologies and features of the BizTalk Server product in relation to the Orchestration compound patterns and the core patterns that comprise it.

Part III: Infrastructure and Architecture

The chapters in this part of the book cover specialized topics and extensions that pertain to layers of technology architecture and infrastructure relevant to the development and governance of service-oriented solutions and inventories of services.

Chapter 15: Enterprise Service Bus with BizTalk Server and Windows Azure

The primary focus of this chapter is on how the BizTalk Server product is expanded via the ESB Toolkit and how .NET based enterprise service bus implementations can be further extended into the realm of cloud computing via Windows Azure. (Note that this chapter does not specifically explore the Microsoft technology platform from the Enterprise Service Bus compound pattern perspective, as that is covered separately in the *Modern SOA Infrastructure* book as part of this book series.)

Chapter 16: Windows Azure Platform AppFabric Service Bus

This chapter is dedicated to providing an overview of the Windows Azure Platform AppFabric Service Bus and contains various examples that explore its usage, especially with REST-based services.

Chapter 17: SOA Security with .NET and Windows Azure

Security is a primary concern when building services and service-oriented solutions because if the security of an agnostic service is breached, it can impact several service compositions. This chapter covers basic security patterns (such as Direct Authentication and Brokered Authentication) in relation to .NET technologies and further provides an overview of the Windows Identity Foundation platform. The chapter concludes with a section dedicated to security concerns raised by Windows Azure.

Chapter 18: Service-Oriented Presentation Layers with .NET

There are various ways to abstract, design, and develop presentation logic in support of service-orientation. This chapter describes the Windows Presentation Foundation and Prism Library and explores its usage from a patterns perspective.

Chapter 19: Service Performance Optimization

One of the common myths of service-oriented computing is that performance must always be sacrificed when building reusable and composable services. This chapter provides a number of techniques that demonstrate how, using the many modern technology and infrastructure advances, service performance and reliability can be optimized while continuing to support the application of service-orientation principles.

Chapter 20: SOA Metrics with BAM

This final chapter explains the business activity monitoring features provided by BizTalk Server, and how they can be applied specifically for the collection of metrics relevant to service usage, scalability, and general service governance.

Part IV: Appendices

Appendix A: Case Study Conclusion

This appendix provides a conclusion of the case study storyline, as it pertains to Standard Mold IT enterprise environment.

Appendix B: Industry Standards Reference

A list of referenced industry standards is provided in this appendix.

Appendix C: Service-Orientation Principles Reference

This appendix provides the profile tables (originally from *SOA Principles of Service Design*) for the service-orientation design principles referenced in this book.

Appendix D: SOA Design Patterns Reference

This appendix provides the profile tables (originally from *SOA Design Patterns*) for the SOA design patterns referenced in this book.

Appendix E: The Annotated SOA Manifesto

This appendix provides the annotated version of the SOA Manifesto declaration.

Appendix F: Additional Resources

A list of relevant Web sites and an article for the *SOA Magazine* are provided as supplementary resources.

1.7 How Principles and Patterns are Used in this Book

As part of its exploration of service-orientation in relation to the Microsoft technology platform, this book references and uses established design principles and patterns throughout its chapters.

Sources

The principles of service-orientation were originally documented in the book *SOA Principles of Service Design*. Referenced design patterns originated in the following design patterns publications:

- [CJP] "Core J2EE Patterns" (Sun Microsystems, java.sun.com, 2001-2002)

- [DP] "Design Patterns: Elements of Reusable Object-Oriented Software" by Erich Gamma, Ralph Johnson, Richard Helm, John Vlissides (Addison-Wesley, 1995, ISBN: 0201633612)

- [JG] "Tales from the Smart Client" by John Gossman (blogs.msdn.com, 2005)

- [MPP] Microsoft Patterns & Practices Group

- [PEA] "Patterns of Enterprise Application Architecture" by Martin Fowler (Pearson Education, 2003, ISBN: 0-321-12742-0)

- [SDP] "SOA Design Patterns" by Thomas Erl (Prentice Hall, 2009, ISBN: 978-0-13-613516-6)

- [TAL] "MVP: Model-View-Presenter The Taligent Programming Model for C++ and Java" by Mike Potel (Taligent, 1996)

- [TR] Trygve M. H. Reenskaug

Reference Notation

Note how each of the listed publications is associated with a code in square brackets. This code is repeated every time a pattern name is mentioned within body text or title text (with the exception of chapter and top-level section titles).

Profile tables for all 85 of the original patterns from the *SOA Design Patterns* book are provided in Appendix D. Therefore, instead of a code, the actual page number of the corresponding profile table is provided each time a pattern from this publication is referenced.

Similarly, because the profile tables of the eight service-orientation principles are also provided in Appendix C, referenced design principle names are further supplemented with the corresponding page number. However, in order to maintain a distinction between principles and patterns, the page number for each principle is placed in rounded parentheses instead of square brackets.

For example, the following statement first references a service-orientation design principle, then an SOA design pattern, and finally a pattern from another publication:

"…the Service Loose Coupling (695) principle is supported via the application of Decoupled Contract [735], which is comparable to the Separated Interface [PEA] pattern…"

Note, as also demonstrated in this sample statement, a principle or a pattern can be referenced with or without being qualified. In other words, the statement *"…when the Decoupled Contract [735] pattern is applied…"* has the same meaning as *"…when Decoupled Contract [735] is applied…"*

1.8 Symbols, Figures, and Style Conventions

Symbol Legend

This book contains a series of diagrams that are referred to as *figures*. The primary symbols used throughout all figures are individually described in the symbol legend located on the inside of the front cover.

How Color is Used

The color red is occasionally used to highlight text, especially within code samples. Generally, the highlighted code will be related to the current topic being discussed.

Additional Information

The following sections provide supplementary information and resources for the *Prentice Hall Service-Oriented Computing Series from Thomas Erl.*

Updates, Errata, and Resources (www.soabooks.com)

Information about other series titles and various supporting resources can be found at www.soabooks.com. You are encouraged to visit this site regularly to check for content changes and corrections.

Master Glossary (www.soaglossary.com)

To avoid content overlap and to ensure constant content currency, the books in this series do not contain glossaries. Instead, a dedicated Web site at www.soaglossary.com provides a master glossary for all series titles. This site continues to grow and expand with new glossary definitions as new series titles are developed and released.

Referenced Specifications (www.soaspecs.com)

The chapters throughout this book reference XML and Web services specifications and standards. The www.soaspecs.com Web site provides a central portal to the original specification documents created and maintained by the primary standards organizations.

SOASchool.com™ SOA Certified Professional (SOACP)

This text book is an official part of the SOA Certified Professional curriculum and is used in conjunction with courses and exams for the SOA .NET Developer Certification program. The course materials that are part of this program provide additional content and lab exercises that further explore topics covered in this book. For more information, see www.soaschool.com.

The *SOA Magazine* (www.soamag.com)

The *SOA Magazine* is a regular publication provided by SOA Systems Inc. and Prentice Hall/PearsonPTR and is officially associated with the *Prentice Hall Service-Oriented Computing Series from Thomas Erl*. The *SOA Magazine* is dedicated to publishing specialized SOA articles, case studies, and papers by industry experts and professionals. The common criteria for contributions is that each explore a distinct aspect of service-oriented computing.

Notification Service

If you'd like to be automatically notified of new book releases in this series, new supplementary content for this title, or key changes to the previously listed Web sites, use the notification form at www.soabooks.com.

Chapter 2

Case Study Background

2.1 How Case Studies Are Used

2.2 Case Study Background #1: Standard Mold

2.3 Case Study Background #2: Superior Stamping

2.1 How Case Studies Are Used

Case study examples are an effective means of exploring abstract topics within real world scenarios. The background information provided in this short chapter establishes the basis for an on-going storyline. The chapters in Parts II and III contain occasional *Case Study Example* sections that draw directly from the scenarios described in this chapter. In order to more easily identify these sections, a light gray background is used.

The case studies examine the IT and business environments of two fictional organizations: Standard Mold, a small company with a modest IT enterprise, and Superior Stamping, a large corporation with an enterprise-class IT ecosystem. Though facing different challenges, these organizations have an established business relationship.

2.2 Case Study Background #1: Standard Mold

Standard Mold is a small supplier of molds for automotive parts manufacturers. It is a privately held company that relies heavily on a small base of customers for the majority of their revenue. As such, they must continually find ways to improve their productivity and efficiency. The president of the company feels that they can create new capabilities and a competitive advantage by adopting service-orientation.

History

Boasting a 25-year history, Standard Mold is well established in the industry. It has survived many of the ups and downs of the automotive industry, in part due to its reputation for quality work. Superior Stamping is one of Standard Mold's largest customers.

Technical Infrastructure

The company runs mostly off-the-shelf software and typically adapts business processes to the tools it purchases. The computing infrastructure is managed by a staff of ten working under an IT director. The few silo-based custom applications in the Standard Mold enterprise were developed by outside solution providers. These systems were simply developed as point solutions without much attention given to their strategic usage or eventual integration requirements.

Standard Mold primarily relies on the following applications to operate its business:

- A commercial Accounting System is used for transaction processing as well as CRM functionality. The accounting clerk is responsible for managing customer contact information and accounts payable and receivable data in this system. Information originates from several different sources, including a small outside sales staff.

- A custom client-server job Scheduling and Management System controls resource allocation and project management functionality for current and future projects. This system consists of a traditional desktop client and a database that is hosted on a workstation residing in the IT department. It is used by most personnel in the back office for resource planning and status reporting for customers.

Business Goals and Obstacles

The company in recent years is finding itself under more pressure from emerging competitors. Intense global pressure is forcing Standard Mold to produce its goods faster and at a lower cost. Business process automation is quickly becoming as important as manufacturing automation. The business is now in a position of obligation with respect to adopting modern technology.

A business improvement task force, consisting of management staff and two key long-serving individual contributors, has come to the conclusion that efficiencies can be gained by specifically streamlining the sales process. Outside sales personnel currently track opportunities on paper and produce customer quotes whenever their schedules allow them to return to the office. Customers can wait up to three business days before requested jobs are quoted back to them. In most cases it takes two full weeks to turn a customer request into an active project.

Standard Mold must find a better way to leverage technology in order to remain profitable. As the case study examples begin, they have already started to automate the sales process by refactoring the job scheduling application with services. The expectation is that sales personnel will soon be able to provide cost estimates and generate orders in real time.

Plans are also underway to automate B2B data exchanges. Namely, invoice management and order processing services are being developed. Also, no ties currently exist between the job management and accounting systems. The task force has determined that this is a key efficiency inhibitor because a great deal of manual intervention is required to carry out customer billing. Invoices are mailed to customers even though many of these customers are able and willing to participate in some form of electronic data exchange.

Standard Mold produces a catalog of machine tools that is used by several of its customers. A paper version of the catalog is printed and distributed to the organization's contract customers at great expense to Standard Mold. An electronic version of the paper catalog is available on request. In its present state, the catalog is not very useful from a process automation standpoint, so the company has decided to adopt services and SOA as a means to integrate the catalog into its business processes.

2.3 Case Study Background #2: Superior Stamping

Superior Stamping is a premier supplier of parts to several automobile manufacturers. They are a subsidiary to a large global conglomerate, but they enjoy a good amount of autonomy. The parent company does not dictate technology decisions, but they are increasingly emphasizing that Superior Stamping maintain steady growth.

History

Superior Stamping started as a small local business, but grew through acquisition over the years, as did many of their competitors. These acquisitions provided revenue growth, but differences in business processes were a detriment to efficiency. Many of the companies acquired by Superior Stamping are expected to maintain their own independence, thereby creating a disjointed, bureaucratic culture.

Technical Infrastructure

Superior Stamping operates a suite of applications cobbled together to satisfy business needs that emerged as the business grew. Much of the original IT staff is still in place and they have not been encouraged to develop new skills. The company does use some Windows servers, but they are mostly related to file, print, and directory functions.

Superior Stamping relies heavily on a set of specific applications:

- A Procurement System has been developed and extended over the past several years, but it is now starting to show its age.

- An Order Management System has also been in use for several years. It is functional, but not readily extensible.

It has not been possible to automate the integration points between these systems and external vendors. Data input is a manual process carried out by data entry clerks and transactions initiated by these systems must go through a multi-step process of approvals.

These and other shortcomings are starting to affect the company's ability to close business deals and their revenues are showing signs of decline.

Business Goals and Obstacles

The company has grown significantly over the last several years thanks to contracts they have earned to build parts for several of the most popular cars on the market. However, a recent economic downturn has impacted their fortunes and they are now required to submit to demands to produce the same parts at significantly reduced prices.

The company's growth has stalled and earnings are starting to go down while they have observed competitors continue to grow. Adding to the competitive pressure is the requirement from many customers for a predominantly automated business exchange.

The company is hoping for cost reductions by streamlining common business functions. They have chosen to adopt SOA in support of a plan to position automation solution logic as IT assets and to standardize and reuse this logic over the long term. Every business unit will be expected to embrace services and adapt their priorities and strategies accordingly.

Part I

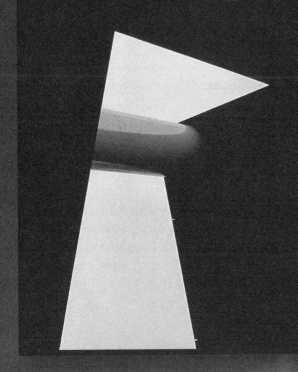

Fundamentals

Chapter 3: SOA Fundamentals

Chapter 4: A Brief History of Legacy .NET Distributed Technologies

Chapter 5: WCF Services

Chapter 6: WCF Extensions

Chapter 7: .NET Enterprise Services Technologies

Chapter 8: Cloud Services with Windows Azure

This initial set of chapters cover basic topics pertaining to .NET and Windows Azure technologies and SOA and service-orientation. Note that unlike chapters in subsequent parts, the coverage of service-orientation principles and SOA design patterns related to .NET and Windows Azure technologies is kept relatively separate from the abstract coverage.

Where appropriate throughout Chapters 4–8 "SOA Principles & Patterns" boxes appear to highlight some of the more significant relationships between principles, patterns, and technologies. "SOA Principles & Patterns" boxes do not appear in subsequent parts of the book. As described later, the chapters in Part II introduce a different type of box that only lists principles and patterns referenced inline within the chapter text.

Chapter 3

SOA Fundamentals

3.1 Basic SOA Terminology

3.2 Service-Oriented Computing Goals

3.3 Further Reading

Before we get into the many topic areas that pertain to .NET and Azure technologies and platforms, we first need to establish some fundamental terms and concepts associated with service-oriented computing, service-oriented architecture, and service-orientation.

If you have already read other books in this series (in particular, *SOA Design Patterns* and *SOA Principles of Service Design*), then you can safely skip this chapter. If you are new to SOA and service-orientation, this chapter will provide only a concise overview.

3.1 Basic SOA Terminology

This section borrows some content from SOAGlossary.com to provide the following term definitions:

- Service-Oriented Computing
- Service-Orientation
- Service-Oriented Architecture (SOA)
- Services
- Service Models
- Service Composition
- Service Inventory
- Service-Oriented Analysis
- Service Candidate
- Service-Oriented Design
- Service Contract
- Service-Related Granularity
- SOA Design Patterns

The following defined terms are throughout subsequent chapters.

Service-Oriented Computing

Service-oriented computing is an umbrella term that represents a new generation distributed computing platform. As such, it encompasses many things, including its own design paradigm and design principles, design pattern catalogs, pattern languages, a distinct architectural model, and related concepts, technologies, and frameworks.

Service-oriented computing builds upon past distributed computing platforms and adds new design layers, governance considerations, and a vast set of preferred implementation technologies, many of which are based on the use of Web services and REST services.

In this book we occasionally reference the strategic goals of service-oriented computing as they tie into the utilization of .NET and Azure technologies.

Service-Orientation

Service-orientation is a design paradigm intended for the creation of solution logic units that are individually shaped so that they can be collectively and repeatedly utilized in support of the realization of the specific strategic goals and benefits associated with SOA and service-oriented computing.

Solution logic designed in accordance with service-orientation can be qualified with "service-oriented," and units of service-oriented solution logic are referred to as "services." As a design paradigm for distributed computing, service-orientation can be compared to object-orientation (or object-oriented design). Service-orientation, in fact, has many roots in object-orientation and has also been influenced by other industry developments.

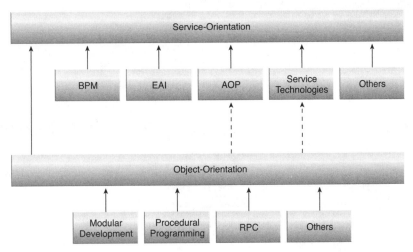

Figure 3.1
Service-orientation is very much an evolutionary design paradigm that owes much of its existence to established design practices and technology platforms.

The service-orientation design paradigm is primarily comprised of eight specific design principles, each of which is explored in relation to .NET service development and, where appropriate, also cloud-based service development with Azure:

- *Standardized Service Contract (693)* – "Services within the same service inventory are in compliance with the same contract design standards."

- *Service Loose Coupling (695)* – "Service contracts impose low consumer coupling requirements and are themselves decoupled from their surrounding environment."

- *Service Abstraction (696)* – "Service contracts only contain essential information and information about services is limited to what is published in service contracts."

- *Service Reusability (697)* – "Services contain and express agnostic logic and can be positioned as reusable enterprise resources."

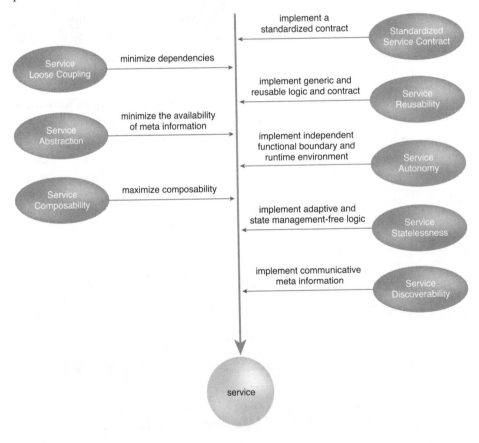

Figure 3.2
The principles on the left have a regulatory influence, whereas the application of the principles on the right primarily results in concrete characteristics being established within the service architecture.

- *Service Autonomy (699)* – "Services exercise a high level of control over their underlying runtime execution environment."

- *Service Statelessness (700)* – "Services minimize resource consumption by deferring the management of state information when necessary."

- *Service Discoverability (702)* – "Services are supplemented with communicative meta data by which they can be effectively discovered and interpreted."

- *Service Composability (704)* – "Services are effective composition participants, regardless of the size and complexity of the composition."

Service-Oriented Architecture (SOA)

Service-oriented architecture is a distributed technology architectural model for service-oriented solutions with distinct characteristics in support of realizing service-orientation and the strategic goals of service-oriented computing.

As a form of technology architecture, an SOA implementation can consist of a combination of technologies, products, APIs, supporting infrastructure extensions, and various other parts. The actual complexion of a deployed service-oriented architecture is unique within each enterprise; however, it is typified by the introduction of new technologies and platforms that specifically support the creation, execution, and evolution of service-oriented solutions. As a result, building a technology architecture around the service-oriented architectural model establishes an environment suitable for solution logic that has been designed in compliance with service-orientation design principles.

NOTE

Historically, the term "service-oriented architecture" (or "SOA") has been used so broadly by the media and within vendor marketing literature that it has almost become synonymous with service-oriented computing itself.

The SOA Manifesto (published at www.soa-manifesto.org) is a formal declaration authored by a diverse working group comprised of industry thought leaders during the 2nd International SOA Symposium in Rotterdam in 2009. This document establishes, at a high level, a clear separation of service-oriented architecture and service-orientation in order to address the ambiguity that had been causing confusion in relation to the meaning of the term "SOA."

An annotated version of the SOA Manifesto is published at www.soa-manifesto.com.

Note that the following service-oriented architecture types exist:

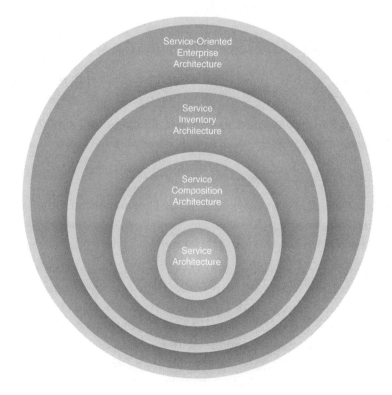

Figure 3.3

The layered SOA model establishes the four common SOA types: service architecture, service composition architecture, service inventory architecture, and service-oriented enterprise architecture. (These different architectural types are explained in detail in the book *SOA Design Patterns*.)

Services

A *service* is a unit of logic to which service-orientation has been applied to a meaningful extent. It is the application of service-orientation design principles that distinguishes a unit of logic as a service compared to units of logic that may exist solely as objects, components, Web services, or REST services.

Subsequent to conceptual service modeling, service-oriented design and development stages implement a service as a physically independent software program with specific design characteristics that support the attainment of the strategic goals associated with service-oriented computing.

Each service is assigned its own distinct functional context and is comprised of a set of capabilities related to this context. Therefore, a service can be considered a container of capabilities associated with a common purpose (or functional context). Capabilities are expressed in the service contract.

It is important to view and position SOA and service-orientation as being neutral to any one technology platform. By doing so, you have the freedom to continually pursue the strategic goals associated with service-oriented computing by leveraging on-going service technology advancements.

Any implementation technology that can be used to create a distributed system may be suitable for the application of service-orientation. Three common service implementation mediums currently exist: components, Web services, and REST services.

Purchase Order

o SubmitOrder
o CheckOrderStatus
o ChangeOrder
o CancelOrder

Figure 3.4

The chorded circle symbol is used to represent a service, primarily from a contract perspective.

Services as Components

A *component* is a software program designed to be part of a distributed system. It provides a technical interface comparable to a traditional application programming interface (API) through which it exposes public capabilities as *methods*, thereby allowing it to be explicitly invoked by other programs.

Components have typically relied on platform-specific development and runtime technologies. For example, components can be built using Java or .NET tools and are then deployed in a runtime environment capable of supporting the corresponding component communications technology requirements, as implemented by the chosen development platform.

Figure 3.5

The symbols used to represent a component. The symbol on the left is a generic component that may or may not have been designed as a service, whereas the symbol on the right is labeled to indicate that it has been designed as a service.

core service logic

service contract

NOTE

Building service-oriented components is one of the topics covered in this book as well as the book *SOA with Java*, another title in the *Prentice Hall Service-Oriented Computing Series from Thomas Erl.*

Services as Web Services

A *Web service* is a body of solution logic that provides a physically decoupled technical contract consisting of a WSDL definition and one or more XML Schema definitions and also possible WS-Policy expressions. The Web service contract exposes public capabilities as *operations*, establishing a technical interface but without any ties to a proprietary communications framework.

Service-orientation can be applied to the design of Web services. The fact that Web services provide an architectural model whereby the service contract is physically decoupled and vendor-neutral is conducive to several of the design goals associated with service-orientation.

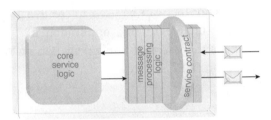

Web service acting as a service provider

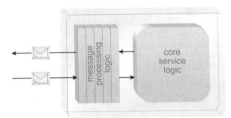

Portions of a Web service acting as a service consumer

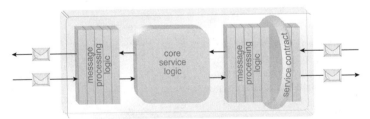

Web service transitioning through service consumer and provider roles

Figure 3.6

Three variations of a single Web service showing the different physical parts of its architecture that come into play, depending on the role it assumes at runtime. Note the cookie-shaped symbol that represents the service contract wedged in between layers of agent-driven message processing logic. This is the same chorded circle symbol shown earlier but from a different perspective.

Services as REST Services

REST services (or RESTful services) are designed in compliance with the REST architectural style. A REST service architecture focuses on the resource as the key element of abstraction, with an emphasis on simplicity, scalability, and usability. REST services can be further shaped by the application of service-orientation principles.

Figure 3.7

A REST service, depicted similar to a Web service, except for the service contract symbol that indicates the service is accessed via a uniform contract.

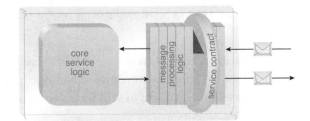

Service Models

A *service model* is a classification used to indicate that a service belongs to one of several predefined types based on the nature of the logic it encapsulates, the reuse potential of this logic, and how the service may relate to domains within its enterprise.

The following three service models are common to most enterprise environments and therefore common to most SOA projects:

- *Task Service* – A service with a non-agnostic functional context that generally corresponds to single-purpose, parent business process logic. A task service will usually encapsulate the composition logic required to compose several other services in order to complete its task.

- *Entity Service* – A reusable service with an agnostic functional context associated with one or more related business entities (such as invoice, customer, claim, etc.). For example, a Purchase Order service has a functional context associated with the processing of purchase order-related data and logic.

- *Utility Service* – Also a reusable service with an agnostic functional context, but this type of service is intentionally not derived from business analysis specifications and models. It encapsulates low-level technology-centric functions, such as notification, logging, and security processing.

Service models play an important role during service-oriented analysis and service-oriented design phases. Although the just listed service models are well established, it is not uncommon for an organization to create its own service models. Often these new classifications tend to be derived from one of the aforementioned fundamental service models.

.NET services based on different service models are discussed in detail in Parts II and III of this book. Be sure not to confuse this term with the terms "delivery models" and "deployment models" used in Windows Azure sections in relation to cloud computing.

Agnostic Logic and Non-Agnostic Logic

The term "agnostic" originates from Greek and means "without knowledge." Therefore, logic that is sufficiently generic so that it is not specific to (has no knowledge of) a particular parent task is classified as *agnostic* logic. Because knowledge specific to single purpose tasks is intentionally omitted, agnostic logic is considered multi-purpose. On the flipside, logic that is specific to (contains knowledge of) a single-purpose task is labeled as *non-agnostic* logic.

Another way of thinking about agnostic and non-agnostic logic is to focus on the extent to which the logic can be repurposed. Because agnostic logic is expected to be multi-purpose, it is subject to the Service Reusability (697) principle with the intention of turning it into highly reusable logic. Once reusable, this logic is truly multi-purpose in that it, as a single software program (or service), can be used to automate multiple business processes.

Non-agnostic logic does not have these types of expectations. It is deliberately designed as a single-purpose software program (or service) and therefore has different characteristics and requirements.

Service Composition

A *service composition* is an aggregate of services collectively composed to automate a particular task or business process. To qualify as a composition, at least two participating services plus one composition initiator need to be present. Otherwise, the service interaction only represents a point-to-point exchange.

Service compositions can be classified into primitive and complex variations. In early service-oriented solutions, simple logic was generally implemented via point-to-point exchanges or primitive compositions. As the surrounding technology matured, complex compositions became more common.

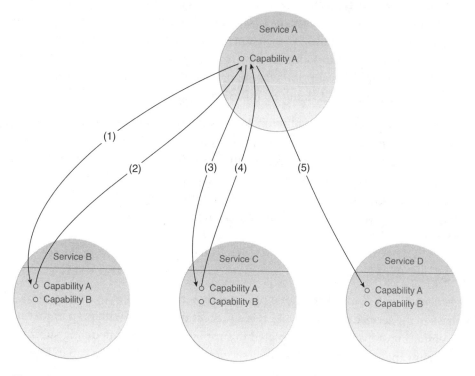

Figure 3.8

A service composition comprised of four services. The arrows indicate a sequence of modeled message exchanges. Note arrow #5 representing a one-way, asynchronous data delivery from Service A to Service D.

Much of the service-orientation design paradigm revolves around preparing services for effective participation in numerous complex compositions—so much so that the Service Composability (704) design principle exists, dedicated solely to ensuring that services are designed in support of repeatable composition.

In this book you will notice some .NET terms used to refer to the equivalent of a service composition. For example, we can generally assume that applications will be comprised of composed services.

Service Inventory

A *service inventory* is an independently standardized and governed collection of complementary services within a boundary that represents an enterprise or a meaningful segment of an enterprise. When an organization has multiple service inventories, this term is further qualified as *domain service inventory*.

Service inventories are typically created through top-down delivery processes that result in the definition of *service inventory blueprints*. The subsequent application of service-orientation design principles and custom design standards throughout a service inventory is of paramount importance so as to establish a high degree of native inter-service interoperability. This supports the repeated creation of effective service compositions in response to new and changing business requirements.

Because this book is focused heavily on low-level programming topics, we only get occasional opportunities to take a step back and look at larger-scale perspectives that involve inventory-level design and architecture considerations. It is a good idea to keep in mind that when we explore areas, such as the application of service-orientation design principles, or conformance to design standards, or even the regulated usage of industry standards, we generally do so within the scope of a given service inventory boundary.

Service-Oriented Analysis

Service-oriented analysis represents one of the early stages in an SOA initiative and the first phase in the service delivery cycle. It is a process that begins with preparatory information gathering steps that are completed in support of a service modeling sub-process that results in the creation of conceptual service candidates, service capability candidates, and service composition candidates.

The service-oriented analysis process is commonly carried out iteratively, once for each business process. Typically, the delivery of a service inventory determines a scope that represents a meaningful domain or the enterprise as a whole. All iterations of a service-oriented analysis then pertain to that scope, with an end-result of a service inventory blueprint.

A key success factor of the service-oriented analysis process is the hands-on collaboration of both business analysts and technology architects. The former group is especially involved in the definition of service candidates within a business-centric functional context because they understand the business processes used as input for the analysis and because service-orientation aims to align business and IT more closely.

Service Candidate

When conceptualizing services during the service modeling sub-process of the service-oriented analysis phase, services are defined on a preliminary basis and still subject to a great deal of change and refinement before they are handed over to the service-oriented design project stage responsible for producing physical service contracts.

The term "service candidate" is used to help distinguish a conceptualized service from an actual implemented service. You'll notice a few references to service candidates in this book, especially in some of the early case study content.

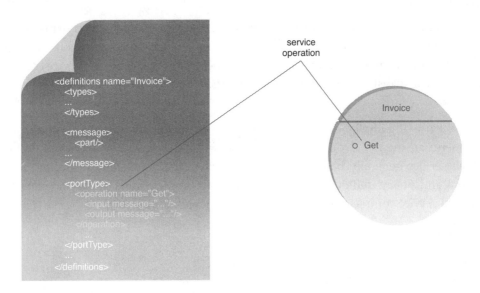

Figure 3.9
The Get operation (right) is first modeled and then forms the basis of the actual operation definition within a WSDL document (left).

Service-Oriented Design

The *service-oriented design* phase represents a service delivery lifecycle stage dedicated to producing service contracts in support of the well-established "contract-first" approach to software development.

The typical starting point for the service-oriented design process is a service candidate that was produced as a result of completing all required iterations of the service-oriented analysis process. Service-oriented design subjects this service candidate to additional considerations that shape it into a technical service contract in alignment with other service contracts being produced for the same service inventory.

There is a different service-oriented design process for each of the three common service models (task, entity, and utility). The variations in process steps primarily accommodate different priorities and the nature of the logic being expressed by the contract.

There are specific issues that come to the forefront when attempting to follow a "contract-first" process using .NET technologies and tools. These are primarily addressed in Part II.

Service Contract

A *service contract* is comprised of one or more published documents that express meta information about a service. The fundamental part of a service contract consists of the documents that express its technical interface. These form the technical service contract, which essentially establishes an API into the functionality offered by the service via its capabilities.

When services are implemented as Web services, the most common service description documents are the WSDL definition, XML schema definition, and WS-Policy definition. A Web service generally has one WSDL definition, which can link to multiple XML Schema and policy definitions. When services are implemented as components, the technical service contract is comprised of a technology-specific API.

Figure 3.10

The standard symbol used to display a service contract (left) and one that is accessed via a uniform contract (right).

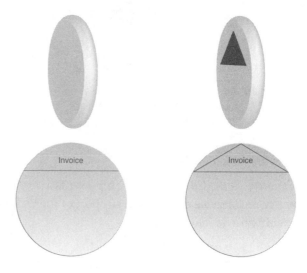

Services implemented as REST services are commonly accessed via a uniform contract, such as the one provided by HTTP. Service contracts are depicted differently depending on whether a uniform contract is involved.

A service contract can be further comprised of human-readable documents, such as a Service Level Agreement (SLA) that describes additional quality-of-service features, behaviors, and limitations. Several SLA-related requirements can also be expressed in machine-readable format as policies.

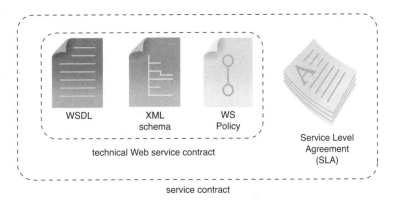

Figure 3.11
The common documents that comprise the technical Web service contract, plus a human-readable SLA.

Within service-orientation, the design of the service contract is of paramount importance—so much so, that the Standardized Service Contract (693) design principle and the aforementioned service-oriented design process are dedicated solely to the standardized creation of service contracts.

NOTE
Service contract design and versioning for Web services is a topic specifically covered in the book *Web Service Contract Design & Versioning for SOA*, as part of this series.

Service-Related Granularity

When designing services, there are different granularity levels that need to be taken into consideration, as follows:

- *Service Granularity* – Represents the functional scope of a service. For example, fine-grained service granularity indicates that there is little logic associated with the service's overall functional context.

- *Capability Granularity* – The functional scope of individual service capabilities (operations) is represented by this granularity level. For example, a GetDetail capability will tend to have a finer measure of granularity than a GetDocument capability.

- *Constraint Granularity* – The level of validation logic detail is measured by constraint granularity. The more coarse constraint granularity is, the less constraints (or smaller the amount of validation logic) a given capability will have.

- *Data Granularity* – This granularity level represents the quantity of data processed. For example, from a Web service contract perspective, this corresponds to input, output, and fault messages. A fine level of data granularity is equivalent to a small amount of data.

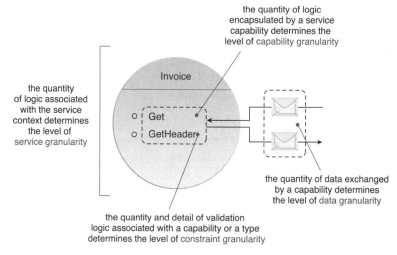

Figure 3.12

The four granularity levels that represent various characteristics of a service and its contract. Note that these granularity types are, for the most part, independent of each other.

Because the level of service granularity determines the functional scope of a service, it is usually determined during analysis and modeling stages that precede service contract design. Once a service's functional scope has been established, the other granularity types come into play and affect both the modeling and physical design of a service contract.

SOA Design Patterns

A design pattern is a proven solution to a common design problem. The SOA design pattern catalog provides a collection of design patterns that provide practices and techniques for solving common problems in support of service-orientation.

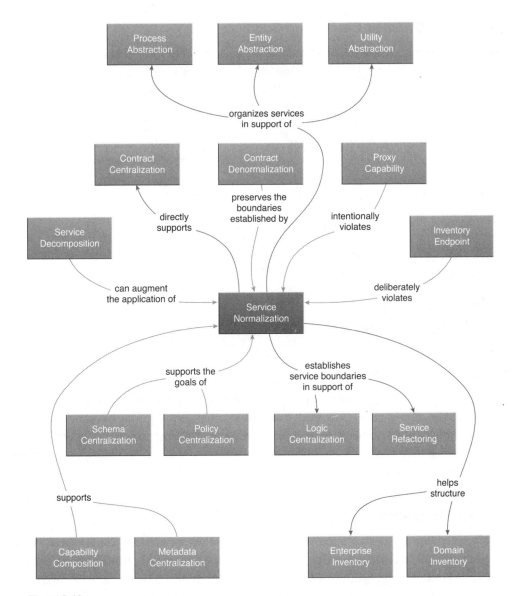

Figure 3.13

SOA design patterns form a design pattern language that allows patterns to be applied in different combinations and in different sequences in order to solve various complex design problems.

3.2 Service-Oriented Computing Goals

This section briefly mentions the overarching goals and benefits associated with service-oriented computing. An understanding of these benefits and goals helps provide a strategic context for many of the suggested techniques and practices in this guide.

Here's the basic list of the goals and benefits of service-oriented computing:

- Increased Intrinsic Interoperability
- Increased Federation
- Increased Vendor Diversification Options
- Increased Business and Technology Domain Alignment
- Increased ROI
- Increased Organizational Agility
- Reduced IT Burden

Let's describe these further.

Increased Intrinsic Interoperability

For services to attain a meaningful level of intrinsic interoperability, their technical contracts must be highly standardized and designed consistently to share common expressions and data models. This fundamental requirement is why project teams often must take control of their service contracts instead of allowing them to be auto-generated and derived from different sources.

Increased Federation

Service-oriented computing aims to achieve a federated service endpoint layer. It is the service contracts that are the endpoints in this layer, and it is only through their consistent and standardized design that federation can be achieved. This, again, is a goal that is supported by the ability of a project team to customize and refine service contracts so that they establish consistent endpoints within a given service inventory boundary.

Increased Vendor Diversification Options

For a service-oriented architecture to allow on-going vendor diversification, individual services must effectively abstract proprietary characteristics of their underlying vendor technology. The contract remains the only part of a service that is published and available to consumers. It must therefore be deliberately designed to express service capabilities without any vendor-specific details. This extent of abstraction allows service owners to extend or replace vendor technology.

Vendor diversification is especially attainable through the use of Web services, REST services, and various supporting industry standards that help establish a non-proprietary communications framework.

Increased Business and Technology Domain Alignment

The service layers that tend to yield the greatest gains for service-oriented environments are those comprised of business-centric services (such as task and entity services). These types of services introduce an opportunity to effectively express various forms of business logic in close alignment with how this logic is modeled and maintained by business analysts.

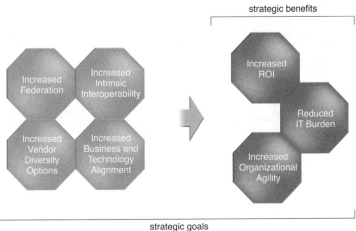

Figure 3.14
The latter three goals listed in the previous bullet list represent target strategic benefits that are achieved when attaining the first four goals.

3.3 Further Reading

- Explanations of the service-oriented computing goals and benefits are available at WhatIsSOA.com and in Chapter 3 of *SOA Principles of Service Design*. While it's recommended to have an understanding of these goals and benefits, it is not a prerequisite for the topics covered in this book.

- For information about SOA types and the distinct characteristics of the service-oriented technology architecture, see Chapter 4 of *SOA Design Patterns*.

- Design principles are referenced throughout this book but represent a separate subject matter that is covered in *SOA Principles of Service Design*. Introductory coverage of service-orientation as a whole is also available at SOAPrinciples.com and all eight principle profile tables are provided in Appendix C of this book.

- For a comparison of service-orientation and object-orientation concepts and principles, see Chapter 14 in *SOA Principles of Service Design*.

- Numerous design patterns are discussed throughout the upcoming chapters. These patterns are part of a greater SOA design patterns catalog that was published in the book *SOA Design Patterns*. Pattern profiles are available online at the SOAPatterns.org community site, and pattern profile tables for design patterns referenced in this book are further provided in Appendix D.

- Definitions for the terms introduced in this chapter can also be found at SOAGlossary.com.

See www.soabooks.com for additional reading resources.

Chapter 4

A Brief History of Legacy .NET Distributed Technologies

4.1 Distributed Computing 101

4.2 .NET Enterprise Services

4.3 .NET Remoting

4.4 Microsoft Messaging Queue (MSMQ)

4.5 `System.Transactions`

4.6 Web Services (ASMX and WSE)

4.7 REST Service Processing with `IHttpHandler`

To make the most of the future, you need to have an understanding of the past. This chapter provides a concise historical recap of Microsoft distributed technologies that paved the evolutionary path to the modern service technologies we work with today. If you are already experienced with these traditional technology sets, you may want to skip ahead to Chapter 5. However, if you are relatively new to the world of .NET and Windows Azure, this chapter will help provide perspective and will further clarify some historical references made in later chapters.

The technologies we're about to cover include:

- COM, DCOM and COM+ Services

- .NET Enterprise Services

- .NET Remoting

- MSMQ

- `System.Transactions`

- XML Web Services (ASMX) and Web Services Enhancements (WSE)

Windows Communication Foundation (WCF) is the primary technology framework covered in this book. WCF unifies and replaces all the legacy distributed technologies covered in this chapter into a single programming model. Chapters 5 and 6 are dedicated to WCF.

4.1 Distributed Computing 101

Before we can jump into coverage of the specific legacy technologies, we first need to briefly establish the primary forms of distributed computing, each of which represents an evolutionary milestone.

Client-Server

Enterprise computing originally began with the classic mainframes and monolithic applications, but eventually there was a shift in logic disbursement that led to the separation of logic across the front (user-facing) end and the back (LAN-facing) end. This was termed client-server architecture, as depicted in Figure 4.1.

Figure 4.1

The client is responsible for validating user input, dispatching calls to the server, and executing business logic. The server encapsulates some of the business logic as part of the database.

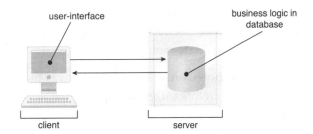

Variations of client-server architecture include having the business logic only on the client (embedded within rich user interfaces) and splitting the business logic between the client and the server.

Benefits of the client-server model included:

- multiple clients can access the same version of the server-side business logic

- back-end data is centralized in a shared database

While advantages over monolithic applications were evident, client-server architectures also introduced some challenges:

- scalability became difficult because the database could become a major bottleneck

- a dedicated, active database connection from each client to the database server was often required, leading to processing overhead that often further inhibited scalability

- depending on the extent of business logic residing with the client, application governance and versioning could become burdensome (depending on how many client workstations needed to be kept in synch)

Although it wasn't perfect, the client-server architectural model is noted as the earliest incarnation of distributed computing and therefore laid an important foundation for what followed.

Distributed Architecture

Distributed architecture, also known as n-tier architecture, evolved in response to the scalability and manageability limitations of client-server architecture. The distributed architectural model essentially moves business logic from the client into components that can also reside on the client, but most often are located on the server.

Server-side components share and manage pools of database connections alleviating concurrent data access from multiple clients by allowing a single database connection that can accommodate multiple users.

A classic distributed architectural model was the 3-tier architecture, where distributed applications were organized into presentation, business, and data tiers, as shown in Figure 4.2.

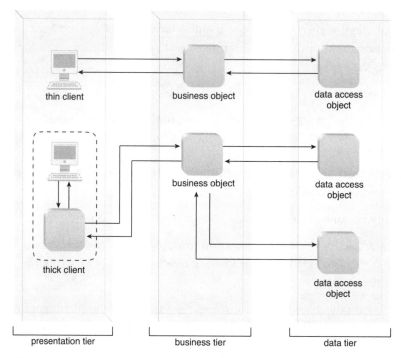

Figure 4.2
A typical 3-tier architecture, separated into the presentation, business, and data tiers.

The middle business tier generally contained the bulk of the business logic. Various infrastructure advances, including clustering, helped improve the scalability of business and data tiers, enabling distributed applications to often facilitate hundreds of simultaneous users. The centralization of business logic on the server-side further helped reduce maintenance and versioning effort. Another benefit to this model was that it made centralized business logic accessible to different types of clients, such as hand-held devices and browsers.

Though considered a major advancement in distributed computing, traditional distributed applications still faced some significant challenges:

- They were often built to automate specific business processes, making them difficult to change when the business process logic changed.

- They were often difficult to integrate with other applications. Because their distributed architecture exposed multiple access points, convoluted enterprise integration architectures could manifest themselves over time.

- They were often difficult to scale to very large user deployments, especially when providing Web access to thousands of potential concurrent users.

- They were often platform-specific, which could result in vendor lock-in situations.

NOTE

One of the origins of distributed computing is RPC (Remote Procedure Calls). In the 1990s, distributed computing moved from procedural programming to object-oriented programming. Remote Method Invocation (RMI) is the object-oriented equivalent of RPC in that it enabled objects on one machine to be accessed by other objects (or applications) running on other machines, by making the remote objects appear local. Several RMI-like protocols are currently in use, including Java Remote Invocation Call (Java RMI), Common Object Request Broker Architecture (CORBA), and Microsoft's own Distributed Component Object Model (DCOM), which later evolved into .NET Remoting. DCOM essentially extended the original COM model by enabling COM components to communicate across networked computers. Traditional distributed technologies from Microsoft are covered in the next section.

Service-Oriented Architecture

As explained previously in Chapter 3, the service-oriented architectural model is a further evolution of traditional distributed architectural models. It is defined via a series of concrete characteristics that allow a given application to be comprised of multiple services that can be repeatedly composed and evolved in response to on-going business change.

SUMMARY OF KEY POINTS

- Distributed communication protocols are used to enable distributed communication architectures. Computing has moved from procedural programming to object-oriented programming and from object-oriented to service-oriented programming. Communication protocols have evolved with the industry to keep pace with these advancements.

- Scalability and performance expectations from a solution have increased over time. Early requirements to scale an application to be used within a small department were easily met by client-server architecture. With the advent of the Internet, solutions were required to scale to thousands of users. N-tier and peer-to-peer distributed architectures evolved to meet these requirements. Service-oriented architecture takes the benefits provided by distributed architectures further by enabling interoperability and several other benefits explained throughout this book.

- Microsoft has provided several technologies to enable developing solutions based on distributed architectures. These technologies include COM, COM+ services, MSMQ, DCOM, .NET Enterprise Services, ASMX (Web services), .NET Remoting, and Web Services Enhancements (WSE). WCF unifies and replaces these technologies into a single unified programming model.

4.2 .NET Enterprise Services

It All Began with COM (and DCOM)

COM helped encapsulate object-oriented systems into binary components. It supported encapsulation by preventing leakage of implementation details, and logic encapsulated in COM components could only be accessed if it had been exposed via a public interface. DCOM extended COM to enable communication across different computers, as shown in Figure 4.3.

DCOM established a secure remote protocol that leverages the security framework provided by the native Windows operating system. For example, it used Access Control Lists (ACL) to secure components that could then be configured using the DCOMCNFG tool.

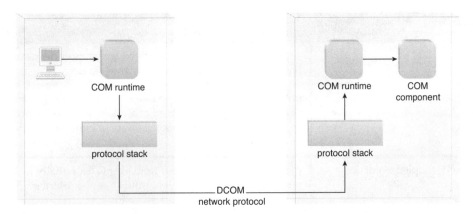

Figure 4.3
DCOM extended COM by allowing COM components to communicate across physical boundaries.

DCOM had several disadvantages, including the use of "keep-alive" pinging (also known as distributed garbage collection), which required that the client periodically ping distributed objects. If the distributed object did not receive a message for a specified duration of time, it was deactivated and eventually destroyed. Distributed garbage collection was error-prone, increased network traffic, and did not scale well beyond local networks. DCOM was therefore not suitable for WANs.

Furthermore, DCOM communicated via live TCP connections over specific ports, which made it complex to configure across multiple computers and firewalls, and even less suitable for communication over the Internet.

COM+ Services

COM+ services extended COM by providing services with increased scalability and throughput that could individually host COM components. The out-of-the-box services provided by COM+ included object pooling, just-in-time activation, constructor string configuration, synchronization, security, queued components, loosely coupled events, . and several others. Table 4.1 provides a list of primary COM+ services.

COM+ Service	Description
transactions	supported distributed transactions across multiple databases, including databases from other vendors
queued components	provided an easy way to invoke and execute components asynchronously and allowed processing to occur regardless of the availability or accessibility of either the sender or the receiver
loosely coupled events	provided support for late-bound events (essentially the plumbing code to implement publish-and-subscribe systems)
just-in-time activation (JITA)	could be configured to handle just-in-time activation necessary for smart client access
synchronization	multithreaded COM+ components could use synchronization locks
security	provided a role-based security model and a supporting programming model
role-based security	provided a mechanism to define roles for applications and the ability to authorize applications (at the component, interface, or method levels) based on those roles
private components	provided a mechanism to mark a component as private (which meant it could be seen and activated only by other components in the same application)
SOAP service	allowed an existing component to be published as a SOAP-based Web service

Table 4.1
A list of available COM+ services.

With the release of Windows XP, a new version of the COM+ services emerged. COM+ version 1.5 enhanced existing COM+ services and introduced additional services, including:

- configurable isolation level (in COM+ 1.0, "SERIALIZABLE" was the only isolation level allowed for transactions)

- applications could be run as Windows services

- memory gates were introduced, which prevented objects from being constructed if the free memory in the system fell below a certain threshold

- COM+ components could be used more than once (typically, helper components or shared components needed to be shared across COM+ applications)

.NET Assemblies

A .NET assembly was a set of files containing classes, metadata, and executable code. An assembly was the smallest versionable, installable unit in .NET. It contained a manifest that stored metadata describing the classes and how these classes related to one another. The runtime read this manifest to obtain information about the contents of the assembly. The manifest could further contain references to other assemblies it depended on. Unlike unmanaged COM+ components, .NET assemblies could be deployed by simply being copied to the target machine.

.NET assemblies could be classified as either private or shared. Private assemblies were used by a single application, whereas shared assemblies could be accessed by multiple applications on the same machine. .NET allowed several versions of the same assembly to be installed, thereby eliminating many problems that existed previously with sharing unmanaged COM+ components between applications. This flexibility helped alleviate the "DLL hell" problem that haunted the COM+ world before .NET was introduced.

Distributed Transaction Coordinator

TRANSACTIONS IN A NUTSHELL

With transactions, a group of related actions occurs as a single, atomic unit. If all actions complete successfully inside a transaction, the transaction is committed and the updated data is written permanently. If any of the actions fail, all actions are rolled back. Distributed transactions are based on the two-phase commit protocol, which consists of a "prepare" phase and a "commit" phase. During the prepare phase, all participants in the transaction must agree to complete the actions successfully. If a participant aborts, all the other participants in the transaction will roll back any changes made up until that point. If the prepare phase is successful across all participants in the transaction, the commit phase is started and data is permanently affected across all systems.

.NET Enterprise Services supported distributed transactions, wherein a given transaction could span multiple databases. As shown in Figure 4.4, the two-phase commit is coordinated by a transaction manager. In Enterprise Services, the Distributed Transaction Coordinator (DTC) plays the role of a transaction manager (based on the X/Open XA industry standard).

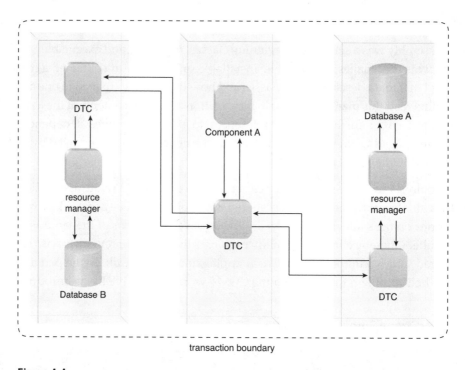

transaction boundary

Figure 4.4

A single distributed transaction that affects multiple databases. The transaction is started by Component A. The connections to databases A and B are established by the DTCs, all three of which coordinate the same transaction. If any one DTC aborts the transaction, it will notify the other participating DTCs to roll back changes. If the prepare phase is successful, the transaction will be committed.

When .NET first arrived, it did not provide its own component technology but relied on COM+ services and built upon the COM+ infrastructure. COM+ services could be accessed from both managed and unmanaged code. The programming model to access COM+ services in .NET was simplified with .NET Enterprise Services.

.NET used classes residing in the `System.EnterpriseServices` namespace to access COM+ services. A .NET component that used COM+ services was called a "serviced" component. To take advantage of COM+ services, a .NET class had to be derived from the base class `ServicedComponent`.

Example 4.1 represents a simple scenario involving a transaction, where the `Greet-Caller` method updates multiple databases with the caller's name and returns a greeting message to the caller.

```
using System;
using System.Collections.Generic;
using System.Text;
using System.EnterpriseServices;
[assembly: ApplicationName("GreetingComponent")]
[assembly: AssemblyKeyFileAttribute("Greeting.snk")]
namespace Greetings{
  [Transaction(TransactionOption.Required)]
  [ObjectPooling(MinPoolSize = 2, MaxPoolSize = 50)]
  [JustInTimeActivation]
  public class Greetings : ServicedComponent
  {
    [AutoComplete]
    public string GreetCaller(string callerName)
    {
      return "Hello " + callerName;
    }
    protected override bool CanBePooled()
    {
      return true;
    }
  }
}
```

Example 4.1

Here's a quick overview of what this code sample accomplishes.

The `Greetings` class is enabled to use transactions using the `Transaction` attribute and `AutoComplete` attribute. When the `AutoComplete` attribute is used, `SetComplete()` or `SetAbort()` are not to be called. If an exception is thrown in a transaction, `SetAbort()` is called automatically and if no exception occurs, `SetComplete()` is called automatically. The `CanBePooled()` method is overridden and set to return `true` to enable object-pooling. Since just-in-time activation is also used, the `Dispose()` function is never called. The object is deactivated, but not destroyed.

.NET Enterprise Services and Service-Orientation

.NET Enterprise Services imposed some limitations when it came to service design. For example, communication was dependent on DCOM and the client proxy was tightly coupled to the server. This made it difficult to fully apply the Standardized Service Contract (693) and Service Loose Coupling (695) principles and further inhibited one of the primary objectives of service-oriented computing, which is to increase options for exploring vendor diversity.

SUMMARY OF KEY POINTS

- COM was a founding development platform that enabled the creation of distributed applications. COM binary components supported the application of object-orientation and .NET Enterprise Services made available services provided by COM+ in .NET.

- DCOM extended COM and COM+ to support communication among objects across process and machine boundaries.

- COM+ services became the next generation of COM by providing services for increased scalability and throughput, such as object pooling and transactions.

- .NET Enterprise Services and COM+ together with DTC supported distributed transactions.

4.3 .NET Remoting

Remoting was introduced primarily to address limitations in COM and DCOM. As with DCOM, it provided a distributed computing mechanism that allowed clients to instantiate components on remote computers. However, it allowed for the client and server components to be configured using an XML configuration file, essentially enabling .NET Remoting to perform remote communication by sending binary messages and XML messages based on SOAP. It was designed expressly for .NET-to-.NET communication requirements.

.NET Remoting Architecture

Similar to other distributed technologies, .NET Remoting uses a proxy object for communication (Figure 4.5). The proxy class impersonates remote objects locally and abstracts out the plumbing required for cross-process communication. In essence, the proxy class intercepts calls and communicates with the remote object on behalf of the client.

Figure 4.5

Multilayered .NET Remoting architecture stack using a proxy object.

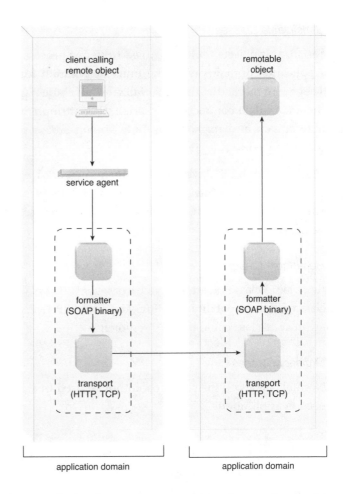

The package object communicates with the formatter component that packages the client request and server response in a suitable format. The formatter serializes the message to SOAP or a binary format.

The formatter then communicates with the transport channel that uses the appropriate transport protocol to transmit the data. This multilayered .NET Remoting architecture is extensible and allows new formatters and channels to be introduced. The channel and formatter for an existing .NET application can be changed in the application configuration file without recompiling the code.

The ability to configure a distributed application using a configuration file was very effective. This practice was carried forward to ASP.NET Web services and later to WCF.

.NET Remoting provided three primary groups of classes:

Serializable Classes

Serializable objects could be copied from one process or application domain to another. Application domains were the units of isolation for the common language runtime. They were marked with the serializable attribute. Serializable classes typically played the role of data contracts. The serializable attribute was used to serialize a class into a byte stream and marshal the byte stream across process boundaries where it was reconstructed.

Most .NET types that were part of the framework were serializable. This included basic data types, such as integers, numbers, and dates, as well as complex structures such as strings and datasets. Custom classes could be made serializable by decorating them with `[serializable]`.

Remotable Classes

Remotable classes were derived from `System.MarshalByRefObject`. It provided the class with the capability to be invoked remotely. Every public property and method in a `Remotable` class could be used remotely.

Ordinary Classes

Normal classes on their own could not be used in a .NET Remoting scenario, but were used in applications.

Hosting .NET Remoting Components

Remotable objects, created by deriving the class from `System.MarshalByRefObject`, had to be hosted in an application domain for it to be accessed remotely. .NET Remoting components could be hosted in several ways, including the following.

Windows Service

A Windows service started automatically when the server started and was simple to maintain. However, it came with several disadvantages. .NET Remoting did not include its own security model, and therefore the plumbing code for authentication, authorization, and confidentiality needed to be custom-developed. Building security required working with channels and formatters, which was not a trivial task. Further, a Windows service did not include high availability and scalability infrastructure. Hosting a .NET component in a Windows service had limited applicability and was primarily used in smaller implementations when security and scalability were not important.

IIS Hosting Under ASP.NET

Remoting server-side objects could be hosted in Internet Information Service (IIS). This approach had several advantages, including inheriting the security, auditing, and scalability infrastructure provided by IIS. Security features supplied by IIS included authentication, authorization, and confidentiality using secure communications. Also, a .NET component hosted in IIS could be configured to use Windows authentication. Forms authentication was not supported, as .NET Remoting could not access cookies.

This design introduced several challenges. The objects had to use the HTTP channel to be hosted in IIS. The IIS worker process could recycle the ASP.NET worker process and, as a result, .NET Remoting could only be used as a single-call object. Other activation modes, including singleton and client-activated objects (explained shortly), were not supported in IIS.

Hosting a .NET Remoting Component in a Console Application

.NET Remoting components could also be hosted in a console application. In this case, the console application had to remain running to accept remote calls. Writing a host based on a console application was simple. However, this approach was typically used for demos and testing. It was completely unsuitable for a production environment, as it did not include security and scalability infrastructure.

.NET COM+ Services

.NET Remoting objects could be hosted in component services (COM+ services) and leveraged various services, such as transactions, just-in-time (JIT), and object pooling. Remoted classes had to inherit from `MarshalByRefObject`, and COM+ components inherited from `ServicedComponent`. `ServicedComponent`, which was derived from `ContextBoundObject`, was further derived from `MarshalByRefObject`. Therefore, service components were remotable objects and it was possible to have COM+ services encapsulate .NET Remoting classes.

In practice this was extremely unintuitive to develop and configure, and was further made difficult by the fact that Microsoft had not provided any real guidance for using COM+ services with .NET Remoting.

.NET Remoting Configurations

.NET Remoting could be used in different ways and configured for different purposes. For example, the primary design choices offered by .NET Remoting included:

- activation types

- message formats

- communication protocols

- object lifetime management

Each of these is explained in the following sections.

Activation Types

Remoting objects could be classified as server-activated objects (SAO) or client-activated objects (CAO). Server-activated objects were objects with lifetimes controlled by the server. They were instantiated when a client invoked a method for the first time. Server-activated objects were also referred to as "well-known" objects because their location was always known. Server-activated objects could be activated as *SingleCall* or *Singleton*.

SingleCall objects were stateless objects automatically created on the server when a client invoked a method (Figure 4.6). These objects were only created for the duration of the method and each call required a new instance of the object to be created. Because SingleCall objects were stateless, they could easily be clustered by hosting them on multiple machines.

Figure 4.6

Each client call creates a remote object instance and the corresponding object is destroyed after the call is completed.

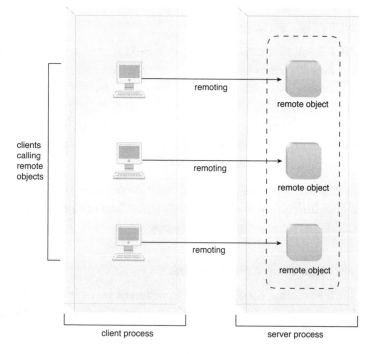

A .NET Remoting object could be configured as a `SingleCall` object in the application configuration file, as shown here:

```
<service>
 <wellknown mode="SingleCall" type="Greet.Greet Service,
  Hello" objectUri="HelloService.soap" />
</service>
```

Example 4.2

With Singleton, a sole instance of the object was created and all clients were served by that instance (Figure 4.7). The Singleton object retained state between every client and it had to be thread-safe as multiple clients could concurrently access object methods.

Figure 4.7
Multiple clients access the same object on the server with singleton activation model.

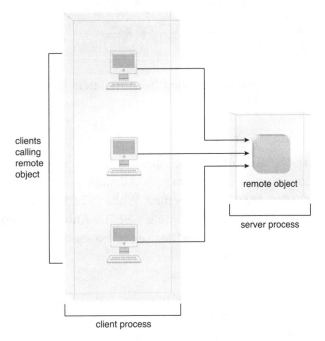

clients calling remote object

remote object

server process

client process

A .NET Remoting object could be configured as a `Singleton` object in the application configuration file, as follows:

```
<service>
  <wellknown mode="Singleton" type="Greet.Greet Service,
  Hello" objectUri="HelloService.soap" />
</service>
```

Example 4.3

With client-activated objects, one instance of the remote object was created on the server for each client at the request of the client. The instance retained state between client operation calls and once activated by a client it could not be used by other clients. The client-activated objects were created on the server when the client called `new` or `Activator.CreateInstance()`. The client controlled the lifetime of the remote object using the lifetime leasing system. Also, client-activated objects did not need a URL and the `wellknown` tag was replaced by the `activated` tag.

A .NET Remoting object could be configured as a client-activated object in the application configuration file, as shown here:

```
<service>
  <activated type="Hello.HelloService, Hello"
  objectUri="HelloService.soap" />
</service>
```

Example 4.4

.NET Remoting provided two formatters (binary and SOAP) and two channels (TCP and HTTP).

Message Formats

The binary formatter serialized data to a proprietary .NET format, whereas the SOAP formatter serialized data to SOAP messages. These SOAP messages were larger and less efficient than the binary data. While .NET Remoting could generate SOAP messages, it did not create corresponding WSDL definitions. Using SOAP as the formatter therefore did not directly enable the use of Web services.

Communication Protocols

The `TcpChannel` option relied on the TCP protocol and was well suited for high performance internal applications. `HttpChannel` used the HTTP protocol and was better for communication via the Internet and broader deployments. A .NET Remoting component could be hosted in IIS 5.0/6.0 only if it used HTTP for transport. Configuring a channel also required a port number over which the data was transmitted.

The formatter is defined in the application configuration file. For example, here we use the binary formatter over HTTP:

```
<channel ref="http" useDefaultCredentials="true" port="0">
  <clientProviders>
    <formatter ref="binary"/>
  </clientProviders>
</channel>
```

Example 4.5

Object Lifetime Management

Singleton and client-activated objects had state, while SingleCall objects were stateless. After a stateful object was created on the server, it had to be released after serving its purpose. Over time, unreleased objects would use up valuable server resources that could end up "choking" the server. In .NET Remoting, distributed garbage collection was addressed using the lifetime leasing system, which was considered an improvement over the keep-alive packets used in DCOM.

With the lifetime leasing system, objects were allowed to live for a fixed length of time. If an object was required for a longer period, another process had to renew its lease. With a Singleton, the object lease was managed by the server. The lease for a client-activated object was managed by the client that created the remote object.

.NET Remoting permitted objects to be marshaled between the client and the server either by value or by reference. With Web services, objects were only passed by value, and then serialized and reconstructed on the client.

.NET Remoting and Service-Orientation

.NET Remoting introduced several innovative features that were eventually incorporated into WCF. However, there were significant limitations when attempting to apply service-orientation to .NET Remoting-based solutions.

For example:

- It was highly proprietary and was therefore not designed to support open interoperability among services. .NET Remoting objects could only be used with other .NET clients and was primarily used as part of closed distributed solutions that did not need to publish contracts or APIs. It essentially was designed to accommodate .NET CLR-to-CLR communication.

- It lacked the ability to share contracts as it does not include a mechanism for interface discovery. Once the .NET Remoting server had been developed, its interface had to be separated in an assembly and provided directly to the service consumer (client), which then had to generate a proxy from this assembly.

- It was not wire-compatible with ASMX and WCF even when configured to use the SOAP formatter and HTTP as a transport. This was because .NET Remoting relied on RPC/Encoded SOAP, whereas WCF and ASMX use the WS-I Basic Profile (which requires DOC/Literal encoding).

- It was not easily ported to WCF. Migrating .NET Remoting code to WCF was, for the most part, a rewrite of the service interface layer.

- It inhibited the application of the Service Autonomy (699) principle. With .NET Remoting, the service consumer was tightly coupled to the service and the assembly with the completed interface had to be shipped to the service consumer so that it could be consumed. This tight coupling resulted in a significant loss of autonomy potential.

- Service-oriented design generally relies on a "contract first" approach in support of the Standardized Service Contract (693) principle. .NET Remoting was more geared toward bottom-up development. Although Singletons and CAOs could not directly be used to design the service contract, they could play a key role in implementing the logic behind the service.

- It has several hosting limitations and did not offer a security model.

SUMMARY OF KEY POINTS

- .NET Remoting was introduced to overcome problems inherent in the COM and DCOM frameworks by providing a configurable communication platform.

- .NET Remoting did away with distributed garbage collection and introduced several new approaches to managing object lifetimes.

- .NET Remoting provided alternative formatters and channels.

- .NET Remoting was most suitable for .NET-to-.NET communication.

4.4 Microsoft Messaging Queue (MSMQ)

MSMQ was introduced as part of Windows NT 4.0. It established intermediary messaging queues that enabled reliability and scalability. An MSMQ implementation was typically comprised of three major components:

- *sending application* – The sending application prepared the message and placed it into the queue.

- *message queues (storage)* – The message was persisted in the message store.

- *receiving application* – The receiving application retrieved the message from the queue and processed it. Alternatively, MSMQ notified an application when a message was received.

As shown in Figure 4.8, the application sending the message and the application receiving the message were not tightly coupled. If the receiving application was offline, all messages were persisted. Once the receiving application was back online, messages were automatically retrieved and processed. This significantly increased the reliability of messaging-based applications.

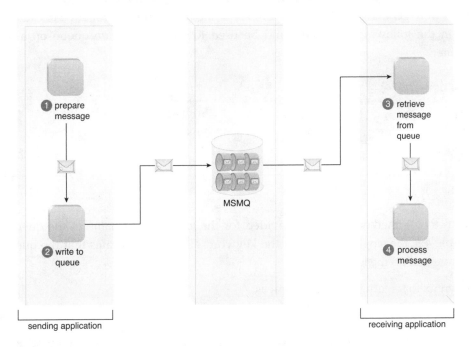

Figure 4.8

Messaging with MSMQ consisted of a sending application, message queue and receiving application.

The Queues

Message storage in MSMQ was simply referred to as the "queues." MSMQ supported two types of queues:

- private (local to a machine)

- public (published in the Active Directory and available across the enterprise)

Applications running on different servers throughout the network could find and use public queues via the Active Directory.

The original MSMQ implementation introduced had a complex programming model and had to be accessed via a COM interface. .NET later simplified MSMQ by introducing the `System.Messaging` namespace, which contained several classes, including `Message` and `MessageQueue`. The `Message` class was used to create and use messages, whereas the `MessageQueue` class contained functionality to work with and manipulate MSMQ queues.

MSMQ was not installed by default and had to be enabled on the server. Queues could be created programmatically or manually using the MMC console. Programmatically, queues were generated by using the `Create()` method in the `MessageQueue` class. The code in the following example could be used to create a private queue on a local machine:

```
string queuePath = @".\private$\NewQueue";
MessageQueue MessageQ;
if (MessageQueue.Exists(queuePath))
  MessageQ = new MessageQueue(queuePath);
else
  MessageQ = MessageQueue.Create(queuePath);
```

Example 4.6

The `Create()` method must be provided for the location and name of the queue. In Example 4.6, the single dot (`.`) and the keyword `Private$` indicates that the queue is being created on the local machine.

The syntax for creating a public queue is:

`MachineName\QueueName`.

Queues could be deleted via the MMC or by invoking the `Delete()` method in the `MessageQueue` class, as shown here:

```
MessageQueue MessageQ;
MessageQ.Delete(".\Private$\NewQueue")
```

Example 4.7

Sending and Receiving Messages

The `Send` method of the `MessageQueue` class was used by the sending application to post a message to a queue, as follows:

```
MessageQueue MessageQ;
Message Message;
MessageQ = new MessageQueue(".\Private$\NewQueue");
Message = new Message("This is a message");
MessageQ.Send(Message);
```

Example 4.8

The `send` method took an object as the first parameter to denote the message body. The argument could be a `Message` object or any other object. If the object was not of type `Message`, it was serialized and stored in the message body.

Serializing objects across process and machine boundaries was not new at the time and had already been supported by .NET Remoting, DCOM, and Web services. MSMQ, however, provided the ability to deliver objects asynchronously and reliably so that they could survive server crashes and reboots. The messages could, in effect, persist indefinitely until they were retrieved and consumed. To transfer objects, MSMQ required a formatter to be specified.

Three formatters were provided:

- `ActiveXMessageFormatter` (used to serialize ActiveX objects)

- `BinaryMessageFormatter` (serialized objects using binary serialization)

- `XMLMessageFormatter` (used XML to serialize messages)

The `MessageQueue` class contained two methods that supported reading a message from a queue:

- `Receive`

- `Peek`

The `Receive` method resulted in removing a message from the queue. (The `Peek` method was similar, but the message was not actually removed.)

Provided here is an example demonstrating the `Receive` method:

```
string queuePath = @".\private$\NewQueue";
MessageQueue MessageQ;
Message message;
MessageQ = new MessageQueue(queuePath);
message = MessageQ.Receive;
```

Example 4.9

The `Receive` method would indefinitely block processing. However, the class contained several overloads, one of which took in the `TimeSpan` argument that allowed an exception to be generated if a message was not returned in a specified time span.

In this example, the `TimeSpan` has been set to 1 second:

```
message = MessageQ.Receive(New TimeSpan(1000));
```

Example 4.10

The `Peek` and `Receive` methods were synchronous in nature and could be invoked asynchronously by using the methods `BeginPeek()` and `EndPeek()` or `BeginReceive()` or `EndReceive()`.

MSMQ and Service-Orientation

As per Asynchronous Queuing [712] and Enterprise Service Bus [741], messaging queues remain an important part of service-oriented infrastructure. Their use supports the application of the Service Loose Coupling (695) principle by establishing a middle tier that physically decouples services from service consumers.

As discussed in Chapter 5, MSMQ went on to become a building block of WCF and therefore continued to remain an important extension in support of service-oriented solution design.

SUMMARY OF KEY POINTS

- MSMQ enabled reliable and scalable application communication and helped loosen coupling between sender and receivers.

- MSMQ supported both private and public queues.

- MSMQ originally supported several aspects of service-orientation and continues to do so as part of WCF.

4.5 System.Transactions

.NET 1.0 and .NET 1.1 equated single resource transactions with ADO.NET and distributed resource transactions with .NET Enterprise Services. .NET 2.0 brought these two models together as the System.Transactions library, which established a simpler and more intuitive programming model with improved performance. (In fact, the System.Transactions library continues to be the framework for transactions in .NET 3.5 and .NET 4.0, as discussed in later chapters.)

Distributed Resource Transactions

A single resource transaction involved a single object and a single database, as shown in Figure 4.9. It was basically implemented in ADO.NET using an explicit programming model.

A distributed resource transaction, on the other hand, may have had two or more objects that interacted with each other, along with two or more database resources (Figure 4.10).

Prior to System.Transactions, the most common means of implementing DTCs was via .NET Enterprise Services (as discussed previously in this chapter). Specifically, the System.EnterpriseServices namespace was used.

transaction
boundary

Figure 4.9

A single resource transaction involves only one object and one database.

Figure 4.10

A distributed resource transaction may involve multiple objects and multiple databases.

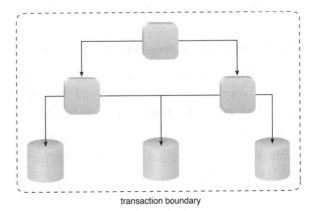

transaction boundary

This had several disadvantages:

- It forced a class to inherit from the `ServicedComponent` class, which then required the assembly to be signed and registered in the GAC. This practice was time-consuming and difficult to maintain, thereby raising the barrier to using transactions.

- It forced the use of distributed DTCs, even when a single object or a single resource was involved. The overhead imposed a noticeable performance cost.

- It required administering the component in COM+ services, which was cumbersome.

- .NET Enterprise Services transactions were tightly coupled to COM+ design considerations, forcing applications to factor in just-in-time activation, object pooling, state-aware programming model, and so on.

`System.Transactions` was introduced to alleviate these problems and to provide a simpler programming interface.

Some of its features included the following:

- It supported both single-resource transactions and distributed resource transactions and was incorporated directly into the CLR.

- The `System.Transactions` namespace supported any resource manager that could speak either OLE transactions or the broadly adopted WS-AtomicTransaction protocol.

- It contained classes that allowed you to write your own transactional application and resource manager and create and participate in a transaction with one or more participants.

- The `System.Transactions` infrastructure supported transactions initiated in SQL Server, ADO.NET, MSMQ, and the MSDTC.

Explicit and Implicit Programming Models

`System.Transactions` included both explicit and implicit programming models. The explicit programming model was implemented using the `Transaction` class and the implicit programming model was based on the `TransactionScope` class.

The `Transaction` class was used to pass the transaction to the `System.Data` class or the database. The `TransactionScope` class was used to scope a code section into a transaction, as shown here:

```
using System;
using System.Transactions;
class Program
{
  static void Main(string[] args)
  {
    using (TransactionScope ts = new TransactionScope())
    {
      ts.Complete();
    }
  }
}
```

Example 4.11

In this example, calling the Complete() method results in the transaction being committed. If an exception was thrown inside the using construct, the TransactionScope would be disposed before the Complete() method was called (resulting in the transaction being rolled back).

Ambient Transactions

System.Transactions further introduced the concept of "ambient" transactions. An ambient transaction was a transaction executed by code. Ambient transactions could be referenced using the Current property of the Transaction class. Transaction.Current flowed around with the code and was referenced as follows:

```
Transaction ambientTransaction = Transaction.Current();
```

Example 4.12

NOTE
In Chapter 5 we'll learn how WCF continues to use System. Transactions via both implicit and explicit programming models.

SUMMARY OF KEY POINTS

- `System.Transactions` provided a platform for implementing distributed resource transactions by separating the application programming from the transaction management.

- Although considered a legacy .NET technology, WCF continues to rely on `System.Transactions` as a foundation for transaction management.

NOTE

The Web services industry standards referenced in the next section and throughout subsequent chapters in this book can be accessed via www.soaspecs.com.

The industry standards collectively supported by ASMX and WSE are:

- SOAP
- WSDL
- WS-Policy
- WS-PolicyAttachments
- WS-Addressing
- WS-Security
- WS-ReliableMessaging
- WS-MetadataExchange

Detailed coverage of the first five industry standards on this list is further provided in the book *Web Service Contract Design & Versioning for SOA*. Concise coverage of all of these industry standards is provided in the book *Service-Oriented Architecture: Concepts, Technology & Design*. Both of these titles are part of this book series.

4.6 Web Services (ASMX and WSE)

With .NET, Web services were originally developed using ASP.NET together with IIS. ASP.NET provided an extensive framework built on top of the CLR for developing both Web services and general Web sites.

XML Web Services (ASMX)

Web services were officially referred to as "XML Web Services" and were further termed with the ASMX acronym because, when developed with ASP.NET, their logic was placed into a file with the .asmx extension.

Specifically, this file contained:

- the ASP.NET @WebService directive

- code to implement the Web service or a reference to a file that implements the Web service logic (also known as the "code-behind" file)

The typical implementation for a Web service was contained in a code-behind file that is actually referenced using the @WebService directive, as follows:

```
<%
  @WebService
  Language="C#"
  CodeBehind="~/App_Code/DemoService.cs"
  Class="DemoService"
%>
```

Example 4.13

The .NET API used to implement a Web service was contained in the System.Web. Services namespace. Classes and attributes from the namespace used to implement the Web service included:

- WebService attribute

- WebMethod attribute

Let's briefly explain each.

The WebService Attribute

This attribute has to be applied to a class in order to designate it as a Web service, as follows:

```
using System;
using System.Web;
using System.Web.Services;
using System.Web.Services.Protocols;
[WebService(Description = "Demo Service",
```

```
              Namespace = "http://www.example.org")]
[WebServiceBinding(ConformsTo = WsiProfiles.BasicProfile1_1)]
interface IDemoService
{
    string Greet();
}
public class DemoService : System.Web.Services.WebService, IDemoSer-
vice
{
[WebMethod]
public string Greet() {
    return "Hello World";
}
}
```

Example 4.14

In this example, the Web service was defined using a .NET interface definition, thereby decoupling the service definition from the service contract (which, incidentally, makes the service easier to manage, reuse, and migrate to WCF).

The `WebService` attribute accepted three parameters, as shown in Table 4.2.

Parameter	Description
Description	a brief description of the Web service to help a human user understand its purpose
Name	the name of the Web service (included in the WSDL file and used by service consumers to target the service)
Namespace	the XML namespace for the Web service

Table 4.2
The parameters for the `WebService` attribute.

The `WebMethod` Attribute

The `WebMethod` attribute was used to tag operations in a class that could be exposed by a Web service. For an operation to be available to the service consumer it had to be a public method and further had to be annotated with a `WebMethod` attribute, as was shown in Example 4.14.

The `WebMethod` attribute contained optional parameters that could be used to customize each operation, as listed in Table 4.3.

Parameter	Description
`BufferResponse`	when `BufferResponse` is set to `true`, ASP.NET buffers the entire response before sending it to the client—a very efficient, default setting
`CacheDuration`	enables caching the results of a Web service operation (ASP.NET will cache results for a unique set of parameters for the specified duration of time)
`Description`	used to describe an operation for a human user to comprehend the Web method
`EnableSession`	used to enable session state for a Web method
`MessageName`	used to uniquely identify overloaded methods using an alias (default value is the name of the method)
`TransactionOption`	enables a Web method to participate in a transaction (disabled by default)

Table 4.3
The parameters for the `WebMethod` attribute.

Web Service Enhancements (WSE)

ASMX primarily supported the creation of Web services based on SOAP and WSDL. It originally did not include support for other WS-* industry standards, most notably WS-Security.

Microsoft subsequently released Web Services Enhancements (WSE) as an extension for the initial ASMX platform. WSE added support for various WS-* standards that introduced new features, such as message-layer security, content-based routing, and support for policies (which corresponded to the WS-Security, WS-Addressing, and WS-Policy standards respectively).

4.7 REST Service Processing with `IHttpHandler`

Prior to the release of .NET 3.5, the .NET framework provided an extent of support for REST service development and message exchanges via the `IHttpHandler` that was part of the IIS pipeline. This runtime event-driven program was able to process incoming HTTP requests via standard HTTP methods. The ASP.NET MVC could be used to provide a moderate amount of control, while handling the basic message dispatching responsibilities.

This mechanism was primarily based on fundamental HTTP communication. It by no means provided a sophisticated REST-friendly infrastructure, but instead simply leveraged the Web-centric nature of REST messaging over HTTP.

SUMMARY OF KEY POINTS

- XML Web services were developed using ASP.NET, a development platform built on top of the CLR and closely associated with IIS.

- WSE was released to extend ASMX by providing support for WS-* standards, such as WS-Security, WS-Policy, and WS-Addressing.

- Limited support for REST service development and messaging was provided by the `IhttpHandler` handler as part of IIS.

> **NOTE**
>
> This concludes our historical tour of legacy distributed technologies. The next chapter will delve into the Windows Communication Foundation (WCF) in order to establish the contemporary platform that has effectively superseded everything covered so far in this chapter.

Chapter 5

WCF Services

5.1 Overview

5.2 Service Contracts with WCF

5.3 Service Implementation with WCF

5.4 Service Hosting with WCF

5.5 Service Consumers with WCF

This chapter provides fundamental coverage of the WCF platform in relation to service contract, service logic, service hosting and service consumer development for Web services and REST services.

5.1 Overview

WCF is the fundamental platform for developing service-oriented solutions with .NET. This chapter introduces WCF and the unified programming model it represents. WCF supersedes and unites all of the legacy distributed technologies covered in Chapter 4.

As shown in Figure 5.1, WCF was one of the major building blocks of the .NET 3.0 framework, which further introduced Windows Workflow Foundation (WF), Windows Presentation Foundation (WPF), and the Windows Cardspace, which was subsequently superseded by the Windows Identity Framework (WIF). WCF was further extended and expanded with the subsequent releases of the .NET 3.5 and .NET 4.0 frameworks.

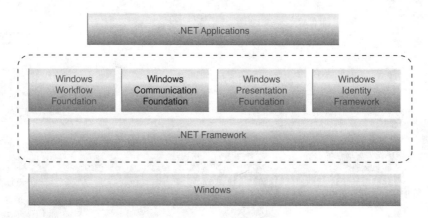

Figure 5.1
WCF is one of several primary building blocks of the .NET framework.

WCF provides features that directly support the application of service-orientation principles. Various extensions and technologies within WCF were designed to increase the potential of realizing SOA-friendly qualities within solutions (such as loose coupling, autonomy, statelessness, composability, discoverability, and reusability) with the ultimate goal of propagating broad interoperability across the IT enterprise.

All of the Web services standards listed in Chapter 4 are supported by WCF. In fact, the WSDL language has established itself as a standard interface definition language (IDL) for WCF services. Metadata can be documented for each service so that corresponding WSDL definitions can be discovered using metadata exchange points.

The release of .NET 3.5 further equipped WCF with a dispatcher system specifically for REST-based services. This REST-aware dispatcher is able to route incoming messages to the appropriate class through transport and protocol channels. Transport channels move data to and from the network, while protocol channels move data between application and transport channels.

As previously mentioned, the WCF platform brings together legacy distributed technologies into a single unified programming model (Figure. 5.2).

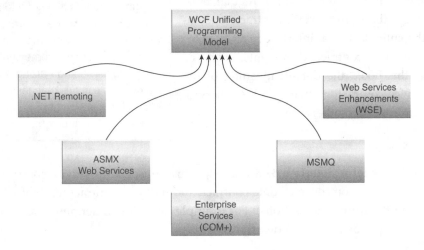

Figure 5.2

The unified programming model established by WCF is encapsulated in the `System.ServiceModel` and `System.ServiceModel.Security` namespaces.

WCF is discussed and explored throughout this book. In this chapter we'll cover some of the basics, including its support for industry standard technologies and protocols and aspects of its platform that relate to security, reliable communications, transactions, and cross-platform interoperability.

Let's begin with an explanation of the WCF communications framework.

5.2 Service Contracts with WCF

WCF Terminology

Before we begin, let's first establish some WCF terms and associate them with common SOA terms and concepts.

WCF Service Contract

Within WCF, the term "service contract" refers to the technical interface exposed by a WCF service and corresponds to the ServiceContract attribute explained shortly. A service contract is comprised of an interface contract and a service endpoint.

As explained in Chapter 3, within regular SOA terminology, the term "service contract" encompasses the entire technical interface in addition to human-readable contract documents, such as SLAs. In this book, the default meaning of the term "service contract" is that of a WCF service contract unless noted otherwise.

Interface Contract

Within WCF, the term "interface contract" refers to a subset of the service contract comprised of the operation contract, data contract, and message contract (each of which is explained in the upcoming sections). For example, in a WSDL definition, an interface contract corresponds to abstract description.

Operation Contract

The operation contract is the definition of a WCF service operation, method, or capability exposed as part of the interface contract.

Data Contract

Service contracts commonly contain data models to define the structure and typing of message data being exchanged. The de facto means of expressing data models is via the XML Schema Definition Language (XML Schema). Within WCF, XML schemas are referred to as data contracts, especially in relation to service contracts and messages.

> **SOA PRINCIPLES & PATTERNS**
>
> A fundamental principle of service-orientation is that services share a formal contract that can express a collection of capabilities in a standardized manner. The Standardized Service Contract (693) principle essentially advocates a "contract first" approach to service development, which requires that we take full control of service contract design and development. Canonical Expression [715] and Canonical Schema [718] fully support this principle by establishing design standards that need to be adhered to by service contracts within a given service inventory boundary. There are some challenges to fully standardizing service contracts in this manner with WCF. These are primarily addressed in Chapter 9.

Message Contract

As previously mentioned, WCF services interact with each other by the exchange of SOAP messages. Within WCF, the SOAP message design and structure is referred to as the message contract. A message contract can be comprised of definitions for one or more SOAP headers and the SOAP body.

Service Endpoint

The wire-level details required for a service consumer to physically connect to and invoke a service are defined in the service endpoint. Within WCF, the service endpoint is comparable to the concrete description part of a WSDL definition. As explained later, a service endpoint is comprised of address, binding, and contract parts.

The following set of sub-sections explore service contract development with WCF in detail.

The `ServiceContract` and `OperationContract` Attributes

A service contract is first created by adding the `ServiceContract` and `OperationContract` attributes to a .NET interface:

```
using System;
using System.ServiceModel;
namespace HelloWorld
{
  [ServiceContract]
  public interface IGreetings
  {
      [OperationContract]
      string Greet1();
  }
}
```

Example 5.1

The `ServiceContract` attribute indicates that the interface is a service contract for a WCF service and the `OperationContract` attribute identifies which methods of the interface define service operations.

After the contract has been defined, it is created in a .NET class by implementing the interface, as follows:

```
class Greetings : IGreetings
{
    public string Greet()
    {
        return "Hello World";
    }
}
```

Example 5.2

The name of the interface is IGreetings and the namespace is HelloWorld. The default name and namespace of the contract can be changed by using the name and namespace parameters of the ServiceContract interface:

```
using System;
using System.ServiceModel;
namespace HelloWorld
{
[ServiceContract
  (Namespace=NewNamespace", Name="NewContract")]
public interface IGreetings
    {
        [OperationContract(Name="GreetRequestor")]
        string Greet();
    }
}
```

Example 5.3

The internal behavior of a service contract can be changed using behavior attributes. For example, a service can save (persist) its data across sessions using the SessionMode parameter:

```
namespace HelloWorld
{
  [ServiceContract(SessionMode=SessionMode.Required)]
  public interface IGreetings
  {
    [OperationContract(Name="GreetRequestor")]
    string Greet();
  }
}
```

Example 5.4

A class that implements a service contract is called a *service-type*. The service-type exchanges data with the service consumer and interaction of the service-type is controlled by the `behavior` attribute (described shortly).

The service contract must be qualified with a service endpoint in the App.Config or Web.Config file hosted with the contract. The service endpoint contains the `address`, `binding` and `contract` attributes to expose the service to the outside world. As shown in Example 5.5, the `address` attribute specifies where the service can be found, the `binding` attribute indicates the service communicates over TCP, and the `contract` attribute links the service endpoint to the WCF service contract.

> **SOA PRINCIPLES & PATTERNS**
>
> The `ServiceContract` attribute and the `OperationContract` attribute can be directly applied to the class. In this scenario, the WCF runtime infers the interface from the class. This practice is not recommended, as it runs contrary to the Standardized Service Contract (693) principle. As advocated by Decoupled Contract [735] and the Service Loose Coupling (695) principle, decoupling the service contract from the service type allows any number of service types to be implemented for a specific service contract, so that one service type can be replaced with another without impacting service consumers that have formed dependencies on the service contract.

```
<endpoint name="EndPoint1"
  address="net.tcp://localhost:1234"
  binding="netTcpBinding"
  contract="IGreetings"
/>
```

Example 5.5

Service endpoints are discussed shortly. First, we need to cover the `DataContract` and `MessageContract` attributes.

Data Models and the `DataContract` Attribute

In WCF, the `DataContract` attribute is used to generate an XML schema from a CLR type. Members of a data type will not be serialized unless the `DataMember` attribute is applied, allowing members of the data type to opt-in. The `DataContract` construct uses `XmlFormatter` to handle serialization and deserialization of the CLR type, thereby abstracting the complexity involved with generating XML schemas. `XmlFormatter` is also used to de-serialize the XML schema into a CLR type allowing it to be easily consumed by service consumers.

WCF comes with two XML serializers, namely `XmlSerializer` and `XmlFormatter`. `XmlFormatter` is the successor to `XmlSerializer` and is the default implementation in WCF. It is used when the `DataContract` and `DataMember` attrib-

SOA PRINCIPLES & PATTERNS
As mentioned earlier, a primary focal point when applying the Standardized Service Contract (693) principle is the standardization of the data model exposed by the contract. In fact, this fundamental practice is the basis of Canonical Schema [718], the pattern that is applied specifically for establishing a consistent and standardized data architecture. The XML Schema Definition Language (XML Schema) has become the de-facto means of defining data models for service contracts that can be shared across platforms. The Validation Abstraction [792] pattern is further commonly applied to ensure that schema content is balanced and optimized in support of the Service Abstraction (696) principle and to avoid negative consumer-to-contract coupling, as per the Service Loose Coupling (695) principle.

utes are used in a CLR data type. Data contracts are passed between the service and its consumer. The class shown in the following example is a CLR type used to return data from the service:

```
public class Account
{
    public string Account_Number;
    public string Account_Name;
    public string Type;
    public string Cash;
    public string Investments;
}
```

Example 5.6

The CLR type can be serialized to an XML schema document by applying the `DataContract` and `DataMember` attributes, as shown here:

```
using System.Runtime.Serialization;
[DataContract(Namespace = "Finance", Name = "AccountContract")]
public class Account
{
    [DataMember(Name = "Account_Number")]
    public string Account_Number;
    [DataMember(Name = "Account_Name")]
    public string Account_Name;
    [DataMember(Name = "Type", Order = 1)]
    public string Type;
    [DataMember(Name = "Cash", Order = 1)]
    public string Cash;
    [DataMember(Name = "Investments", Order = 2)]
    public string Investments;
    [DataMember(Name = "Total", Order = 2)]
    public string Total;
}
```

Example 5.7

The DataContract attribute forces the CLR data type to be serializable in order to be used as a parameter in an operation. One data contract can be a sub-class of another data contract.

XmlFormatter provides less control over how data is serialized to XML. By limiting flexibility, data contracts created using XmlFormatter are optimized for performance and support better versioning. On the other hand, XmlSerializer provides very precise control over how data is represented in XML.

Messaging and the MessageContract Attribute

At its core, WCF uses messages for communication and has a deep commitment to implementing these messages using industry standard protocols, namely SOAP and XML Schema (Figure 5.3).

Messages can be transmitted using industry standard transport protocols, such as HTTP, HTTPS, and TCP, as well as MSMQ and named pipes. Support for sending

Figure 5.3

Messages pass between the service provider and service consumer.

messages over custom transport protocols is also
provided. Both simple and complex message
exchange patterns (MEPs) can be expressed,
including synchronous and asynchronous inter-
changes.

Higher level WCF features that layer on top of
the messaging framework include extensions for
reliability, transactions, queuing, and security features, such as encryption for message confidentiality and digital signing for message integrity.

The `message` class in the `System.ServiceModel`
namespace can be used to access the contents of a
message at the most basic level. By default, these
messages are untyped; they conform to the SOAP
`Envelope` construct and can therefore further
contain both `Body` and `Header` constructs.

> **SOA PRINCIPLES & PATTERNS**
>
> Two fundamental patterns that can
> be realized with the use of SOAP
> messages are Service Messaging
> [780] and Messaging Metadata
> [753], the latter of which directly
> relates to the usage and function of
> SOAP message headers. The mes-
> sage content structure itself is gen-
> erally defined using XML Schema,
> which is often regulated by the
> application of Canonical Schema
> [718] together with the Standard-
> ized Service Contract (693), Service
> Loose Coupling (695), and Service
> Abstraction (696) principles.

Message contracts are a WCF mechanism used to exercise precise control over the processing
of SOAP messages. Whenever a program needs to receive and process message content, it
needs to undergo a complete data transformation in order for the underlying service logic to
accept it and use it.

The WCF API includes message-related classes that allow you to work at a very granular level. These classes include `MessageContract`, `MessageHeader` and `MessageBody`,
all of which are used as attributes to describe the structure of SOAP messages.

In the following code listing, the XML schema produced by the `MsgHeader` data contract
will appear in the SOAP header block. The `MsgBody` data contract will appear in the
SOAP body.

```
 [DataContract]
public class MsgHeader {
  [DataMember]
  public string loginName;
  [DataMember]
  public string password;
}
[DataContract]
public class MsgBody
{
```

```
  [DataMember(Order=1)]
  public string name;
  [DataMember(Order=2)]
  public int phone;
  [DataMember(Order=3)]
  public int email;
}
  [MessageContract]
  public class ContactMessage {
  [MessageHeader]
  public MsgHeader msgHeader;
  [MessageBody]
  public MsgBody msgBody;
}
```

Example 5.8

To use the MessageContract developed in Example 5.8, the parameter of the operation needs to be changed, as shown here:

```
  [ServiceContract]
public interface IContactService
{
  [OperationContract]
  public void InsertContact(ContactMessage contactMessage);
}
```

Example 5.9

Prior to using the message contract, the SOAP message on the wire would exist as follows:

```
<S:Envelope>
  <S:Header>
  </S:Header>
  <S:Body>
  </S:Body>
</S:Envelope>
```

Example 5.10

The InsertContact operation would now create the following SOAP message:

```
<S:Envelope>
  <S:Header>
    <S:loginName>user</S:loginName>
    <S:password>password</S:password>
  </S:Header>
  <S:Body>
    <S:name> ... </S:name>
    <S:phone> ... </S:phone>
    <S:email> ... </S:email>
  </S:Body>
</S:Envelope>
```

Example 5.11

NOTE
.NET version 3.5 SP1 expanded the reach of the data contract serializer by relaxing the need of having `[DataContract]`/`[DataMember]` on types and by supporting an interoperable mechanism for dealing with object references.

Service Endpoints and the `endpoint` Element

The information required for a service consumer to invoke a given service is expressed with the `endpoint` element, which effectively establishes what is called a *service endpoint*.

Specifically, a service endpoint contains the following parts:

- *address* – the location of the service

- *binding* – service invocation requirements (including information about security and reliability policies)

- *contract* – a reference to the service contract that the service endpoint applies to

Service endpoints (Figure 5.4) abstract the underlying service logic and implementation. You are further able to choose which service operations from the service contract to explicitly or implicitly expose.

Figure 5.4

A service consumer communicates with the service using information provided by the endpoint.

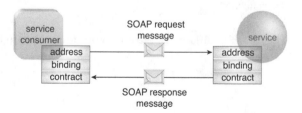

The `endpoint` construct can be configured in the Web.Config file or the App.Config file, as shown here:

```
<system.serviceModel>
  <services>
    <service name="AccountService">
      <endpoint name="EndPoint1"
        address="net.tcp://localhost:1234"
        binding="netTcpBinding"
        contract="IAccount" />
    </service>
  </services>
</system.serviceModel>
```

Example 5.12

A single service can have more than one service endpoint. In the next example, the `IAccount` contract can be accessed on port 1234 using TCP, as well as port 8000 using HTTP:

```
<system.serviceModel>
  <services>
    <service name="AccountService">
      <endpoint name="EndPoint1"
        address="net.tcp://localhost:1234"
        binding="netTcpBinding"
        contract="IAccount" />
      <endpoint name="EndPoint3"
        address="http://localhost:8000"
        binding="basicHttpBinding"
        contract="IAccount" />
    </service>
  </services>
</system.serviceModel>
```

Example 5.13

NOTE

The service endpoint, as expressed via the `endpoint` element, is further represented by the `ServiceEndpoint` class in WCF and is collectively comprised of an `EndpointAddress` class, a `Binding` class, and a `ContractDescription` class corresponding to the endpoint's address, binding, and contract.

Address

Location transparency is achieved using the endpoint address, which specifies where the service can be found, as well as the transport protocol used to communicate with it. The `address` attribute is assigned a Uniform Resource Identifier (URI), as follows:

```
[transport]://[domain or machine]:[optional port]
net.tcp://localhost:1234
```

Example 5.14

URIS IN A NUTSHELL

URIs are short strings used to identify a resource over a network or the Web. For example, "http://www.example.org:322/accounts.svc/secureEndpoint" is a valid URI.

This URI has four parts:

- transport – specifies the transport protocol used to reach the resource (for example, "http", "ftp", "mailto", "urn", "mms", etc.)

- location – the location of the server (for example, "www.example.org")

- port – port where the resource is available (for example, "322")

- path – the exact location of the resource (for example, "/accounts.svc/secureEndpoint")

The sample URI we just introduced can be interpreted as follows: "The resource is located on the server www.example.org and can be reached using the HTTP protocol. It can be accessed on port 322 and the path to it is "/accounts.svc/secureEndpoint."

The endpoint address is represented in WCF by the `EndpointAddress` class, which includes a URI, an identity, and a collection of optional headers (Figure 5.5).

The primary purpose of this class is to represent the URI. It also contains properties that include an identity and a collection of optional headers. These headers are used to provide additional,

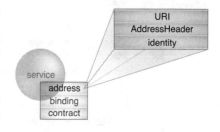

Figure 5.5

The parts of the EndpointAddress class in WCF.

more detailed information. For example, they may indicate which instance of a service should be used to process an incoming message from a particular consumer.

The endpoint address can be specified imperatively in the code or declaratively through configuration. Defining the endpoint address in configuration is preferred, as the address and binding values used for development will (hopefully) be different from the corresponding values used for when the service is deployed in a production environment. Keeping the address and binding in the configuration file allows them to change without requiring recompilation and redeployment of the service.

Bindings

A binding is used to configure wire-level invoca-tion details for a service. Service consumers are required to communicate with a service by com-plying to the binding requirements specified in the service endpoint. A binding is represented by the binding class in WCF; the binding class con-tains a name, namespace, and a collection of bind-ing elements (Figure 5.6).

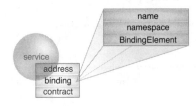

Figure 5.6

Various attributes of the WCF binding class.

The name and namespace uniquely identify the binding within the overall service meta-data. Figure 5.7 lists the various binding elements that can be used to further specific binding requirements.

Figure 5.7

The primary binding elements.

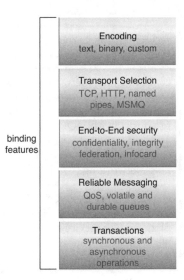

Through its extensibility features, WCF service binding supports binary encoding for performance, MTOM for large payloads, and text and custom encoding. Security, reliable messaging, and transaction-related binding elements are explained in more detail in the upcoming *WCF Security* and *WCF Transactions* sections (in Chapter 6).

WCF provides a set of pre-defined binding that can simplify the creation of service endpoints if you find one that meets your requirements. These "system-provided" bindings are listed in Table 5.1.

Name	Purpose
`BasicHttpBinding`	interoperability with Web services supporting the WS-BasicProfile 1.1 and Basic Security Profile 1.0
`WSHttpBinding`	interoperability with Web services supporting the WS-* protocols over HTTP
`WSDualHttpBinding`	duplex HTTP communication where the receiver of an initial message will not reply directly to the initial sender (but may transmit any number of responses over a period of time via HTTP in conformity with WS-* protocols)
`WSFederationBinding`	HTTP communication where access to the resources of a service can be controlled based on the credentials issued by an explicitly-identified credential provider
`NetTcpBinding`	secure, reliable, high-performance communication between WCF services across a network
`NetNamedPipeBinding`	secure, reliable, high-performance communication between WCF services on the same machine
`NetMsmqBinding`	communication between WCF services via MSMQ
`MsmqIntegrationBinding`	communication between a WCF service and another software program via MSMQ
`NetPeerTcpBinding`	communication between WCF services via Windows Peer-to-Peer Networking
`NetTcpRelayBinding`	enables a service to work with service bus features from the .NET Services offerings in the Windows Azure Services platform (the service bus is a relay service that makes it possible to establish connectivity through clouds across organizational boundaries)

Name	Purpose
BasicHttpRelayBinding	the `BasicHttpBinding` maps to this binding to enable a service to work with service bus features from .NET Services (the relay counterpart establishes a listener in the cloud instead of listening locally)
WebHttpRelayBinding	this binding maps to the `WSHttpBinding` binding to enable a service to work with service bus features from .NET Services (the relay counterpart establishes a listener in the cloud instead of listening locally)
WebHttpBinding	uses the HTTP transport channel with "Web Message Encoding" which enables data formats, such as Text and XML or JSON over HTTP in support of REST service development (as explained in the upcoming *REST Service Classes and Attributes* section)

Table 5.1

A list of the system-provided WCF bindings.

System-provided bindings are optimized for specific scenarios. For example, the `WSHttpBinding` is designed for interoperability with services that implement various WS-* specifications. The `BasicHttpBinding` works well with ASMX 2.0 Web services.

Bindings can be further classified as *interoperable bindings* and *WCF-to-WCF bindings*, whereas the former are suitable for cross-platform data exchange and the latter are intentionally proprietary and require both the service and its consumers to be implemented with .NET using WCF. The primary motivation to use WCF-to-WCF bindings is increased runtime performance optimization.

Interoperable bindings include `BasicHttpBinding`, `WsHttpBinding`, and `WsDualHttpBinding`. WCF-to-WCF bindings include `NetTcpBinding`, `NetNamedPipeBinding`, `NetMsmqBinding`, and `NetPeerTcpBinding`.

Most of the bindings are conceptually similar and leverage previous distributed technologies.

Here are some examples:

- There are two bindings based on HTTP protocol, one with WS-* extensions and the other without. The `BasicHttpBinding` binding (which does not include WS-* extensions) is analogous to ASMX, whereas the `WSHttpBinding` binding (which does include WS-* extensions) is analogous to ASMX with WSE.

- The NetTcpBinding binding is analogous to .NET Remoting.

- WCF includes two MSMQ bindings, MsmqIntegrationBinding and NetMsmqBinding. The NetMsmqBinding does not support SOAP and is analogous to native MSMQ. The MsmqIntegrationBinding binding extends NetMsmqBinding to include SOAP support.

- The NetNamedPipeBinding is analogous to named pipes and is suitable for communication between WCF processes on the same machine.

- Besides bindings that map to existing distributed technologies, there are a couple of bindings that extend beyond more specialized distributed platforms. For example, the wsFederationHttpBinding binding is designed to leverage the Identity Metasystem which is a part of Windows Cardspace.

Contract

Within the service endpoint, the contract is a reference to the service type that is exposed to the outside world. The contract is essentially used to answer the question: "What capabilities does the service provide?" By design, the service endpoint should be decoupled from the service implementation, and the contact parameter links an endpoint to the service implementation.

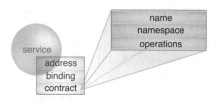

Figure 5.8

The WCF contract class contains a reference to an interface that defines the contract.

A contract is represented by the ContractDescription class in WCF, and contains a reference to an interface that defines the actual contract details (Figure 5.8).

A ContractDescription object is used to describe contracts and their operations. Each operation is based on a message exchange pattern. The name and namespace attributes are used to uniquely identify the contract in the service's metadata.

REST Service Classes and Attributes

WCF supports popular REST content type formats, such as JSON, XML, ATOM, and RSS. .NET 3.5 introduced the System.ServiceModel.Web assembly, which provides several classes and attributes that support the development of REST services. As with regular Web services in WCF, attributes are used to communicate intent to the System.ServiceModel runtime. Specifically, the following classes and attributes are available:

- WebGet

- WebInvoke

- URITemplate

- WebServiceHost

- WebServiceHostFactory

REST attributes build upon and provide information to the aforementioned dispatcher mechanism (Figure 5.9) to enable the routing of messages to the appropriate internal service logic.

Let's take a closer look at the first three attributes from the preceding list (the remaining two are covered in the upcoming *Service Hosting with WCF* section).

The WebGet *Attribute*

As part of the System.ServiceModel.Web assembly, the WebGet attribute is used to implement a service endpoint that is accessed by a consumer using the HTTP GET method.

The best way to understand this attribute is to revisit the WCF service contract. Here is a basic example:

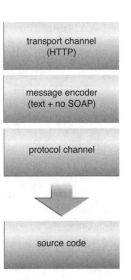

Figure 5.9
REST classes build upon the WCF dispatcher.

```
using System;
using System.ServiceModel;
namespace HelloWorld
{
  [ServiceContract]
  public interface IGreetings
  {
      [OperationContract]
      string Greet(string Name);
  }
}
```

Example 5.15

The ServiceContract attribute establishes the service contract and the OperationContract attribute identifies which methods of the interface are actual operations of the interface contract. After the service contract is defined, it can be implemented as a .NET class, as shown here:

```
class Greetings : IGreetings
{
  public string Greet(string Name)
  {
    return "Hello World";
  }
}
```

...and with the WebGet attribute, the service operation can be converted as follows:

```
using System;
using System.ServiceModel;
using System.ServiceModel.Web;
namespace HelloWorld
{
  [ServiceContract]
  public interface IGreetings
  {
    [OperationContract]
    [WebGet(
      BodyStyle = WebMessageBodyStyle.Bare,
      RequestFormat = WebMessageFormat.Xml,
      ResponseFormat = WebMessageFormat.Xml,
      UriTemplate = "/GreetingService/{Name}")]
    string Greet(string Name);
  }
}
```

Example 5.16

The WebGet attribute basically notifies the WCF runtime that the operation must be mapped to the HTTP Get method.

The WebGet attribute accepts the parameters listed in Table 5.2.

Parameter	Values	Description
BodyStyle	Bare Wrapped WrappedRequest WrappedResponse	indicates to the runtime whether the request and response messages should be wrapped by the WCF infrastructure (when set to Bare no wrapping is provided)
RequestFormat	Json Xml	specifies the de-serialization format for all incoming HTTP requests

Parameter	Values	Description
ResponseFormat	Json Xml	specifies the serialization format for all outgoing HTTP responses (the request and response objects can be formatted differently)
UriTemplate	parameterized relative URI	sets the relative REST-based URI for the operation and maps parameters from the URI to the operation contract

Table 5.2
Parameters for the WebGet attribute.

The WebInvoke *Attribute*

Whereas the WebGet attribute is specifically used to map a service operation to the HTTP GET method, the WebInvoke attribute allows service operations to be mapped to other HTTP methods. Although it defaults to the POST method, it can be changed to PUT and DELETE using the method parameter.

For example, using the WebInvoke attribute, the service operation in this example can be converted, as follows:

```
using System;
using System.ServiceModel;
using System.ServiceModel.Web;
namespace HelloWorld
{
  [ServiceContract]
  public interface IGreetings
  {
    [OperationContract]
    [WebInvoke(
      Method = "POST",
      UriTemplate ="Greet?Name={Name}")]
    string Greet(string Name);
  }
}
```

Example 5.17

The `WebInvoke` attribute includes all the same parameters as the `WebGet` attribute, including `BodyStyle`, `RequestFormat`, `ResponseFormat`, and `UriTemplate` (explained shortly), but also contains the additional `Method` parameter. `Method` is used to specify the HTTP method that corresponds to the mapped operation.

In the next example, we specified POST as the HTTP method. A RESTful service can be consumed directly using the `System.Net.WebClient` class and the service consumer does not require a proxy object:

```
System.Net.WebClient client = new System.Net.WebClient();
client.UploadString
  ("http://localhost:8000/GreetingsService/
    Greet?Name=John", "POST", String.Empty);
```

Example 5.18

WCF `UriTemplate` *Attribute*

Finally, the `UriTemplate` attribute is used to map URI parameters to operation parameters. The `URITemplate` class is a part of the `System.ServiceModel.Web` assembly and it uses placeholders to indicate parameters to be passed to the method. The value of the property tells the runtime how to map incoming requests and query string values to function arguments.

The following set of examples show a `UriTemplate` usage in different scenarios, each of which resolves to a WCF operation:

```
[WebGet(UriTemplate="/catalog/{category}")]
public List<CatalogCategory>
  GetSubcategories(string category){}
```

Example 5.19

If a request comes in as `GET/catalog/drillBits`, the WCF runtime will call:

```
GetSubcategories("drillBits")
```

Example 5.20

Likewise, one could support a query string for the previous, as follows:

```
[WebGet(UriTemplate="/catalog?cat={category}")]

public List<CatalogCategory>
  GetSubcategories(string category){}
```

Example 5.21

When parameters appear as part of a query string, the infrastructure matches the parameters based on their pairings instead of the location in the query. However, path matches are always position-based.

That is, given the following template:

```
[WebGet(UriTemplate="/catalog?cat=
  {category}&sub={subcategory}")]
public List<CatalogItem>
  GetItems(string category, string subcategory){}
```

Example 5.22

…both of these URLs will have the same behavior:

```
GET /catalog?cat=drillBits&sub=carbide
GET /catalog?sub=carbide&cat=drillBits
```

These statements invoke:

```
GetItems("drillBits", "carbide");
```

Example 5.23

…but as a path, we get different behavior:

```
[WebGet(UriTemplate=
  "/catalog/{category}/{subcategory}")]
public List<CatalogItem>
  GetItems(string category, string subcategory){}
```

Example 5.24

Both these URLs will have different behavior:

```
GET /catalog/drillBits/carbide
GET /catalog/carbide/drillBits
```

These statements invoke:

```
GetItems("drillBits", "carbide"); //GET /catalog/drillBits/carbide
GetItems("carbide", "drillBits"); //GET /catalog/carbide/drillBits
```

Example 5.25

Finally, the following code fragment demonstrates the use of the `UriTemplate` class:

```
UriTemplate template = new
UriTemplate("{culture}/library/
{typeInformation}");
Uri baseAddress = new Uri("http://www.example.org/");
Uri formattedUri = template.BindByPosition(
  baseAddress,
  "en-US",
  "Article1.asp");
```

Example 5.26

The output of this code is:

```
http://www.example.org/en-US/Article1.asp
```

Faults and the `FaultContract` Attribute

Any given operation can encounter an unexpected error at any time. Errors can be either logic or infrastructure-related. In .NET, errors are trapped in the `try-catch` block and handled based on the error type. For example:

```
try
{
  ... try something ...
}
catch (Exception e)
{
  ... do something ...
}
```

Example 5.27

Service-orientation stipulates service autonomy. Therefore, a service should not have to depend on the service consumer to handle the error and recover from it. Conversely, the service consumer is decoupled from the service implementation and does not need to understand its implementation details. Local technology-specific error messages may not provide any value to the service consumer and may even represent a security threat when error messages contain private details about the service implementation.

It therefore is not recommended to pass technology-specific errors as SOAP Faults. Error notifications should not be part of the contract between the service and its consumers. If a service fails on an operation call, it should ideally not have an impact on the service consumers.

WCF does not, by default, return unhandled exceptions as SOAP Faults. To return an actual SOAP Fault, the service needs to throw a generic type `FaultException<T>` where `T` is a data contract that defines the fault.

This is also known as a fault contract, which can look like this:

```
[DataContract]
public class ServiceFault
{
  [DataMember]
  public string OperationName;
  [DataMember]
  public string ExceptionMessage;
}
```

Example 5.28

A service defines a fault contract by applying the `FaultContract` attribute, which results in the `ServiceFault` data contract being published with the schema:

```
[ServiceContract]
public interface IGreetings
{
  [OperationContract]
  [FaultContract(typeof(ServiceFault))]
  string Greet();
}
```

Example 5.29

`Greetings` is a service-type implementation for `IGreetings`. When the service traps an error in the `Greet()` method, it creates an instance of the `ServiceFault` class and populates the `OperationName` and `ExceptionMessage` attributes. The fault contract is then marshaled to the service consumer:

```
class Greetings : IGreetings
{
  public string Greet()
  {
    try
    {
      return "Hello World";
    }
    catch (Exception ex)
    {
      ServiceFault fault = new ServiceFault();
      fault.OperationName = "Greet";
      fault.ExceptionMessage = ex.Message;
      throw new FaultException<ServiceFault>(fault);
    }
  }
}
```

Example 5.30

The service consumer will then need to write an appropriate `catch` statement to manage exceptions:

```
try
{
  string response = proxy.Greet();
  Console.WriteLine(response);
}
catch(FaultException<ServiceFault> ex)
{
  Console.WriteLine("Fault:" +
    ex.Detail.OperationName.ToString() +
    " -" + ex.Detail.ExceptionMessage.ToString());
}
```

Example 5.31

MEX Endpoints

In order to consume a service, the service consumer needs to import the service contract and generate a proxy class. However, the service consumer may first need to locate the service metadata in order to do so. To enable this level of service discovery, the service makes its metadata available and accessible via industry standard protocols.

When we use the term "metadata" here, we are referring to the familiar set of service contract-related documents, including:

- WSDL definitions
- XML schemas
- policies and security policies

Metadata exchange (MEX) is a mechanism based on the WS-MetadataExchange specification and designed for the online retrieval of service metadata by service consumers. This is accomplished by having the service expose an *MEX endpoint*. As illustrated in Figure 5.10, the service responds to an MEX request by returning an MEX response message containing the requested metadata.

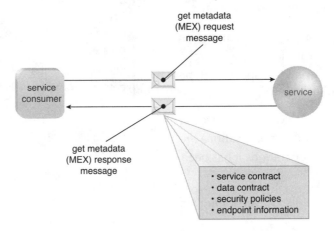

Figure 5.10
A metadata exchange between a service and a service consumer.

A WCF service can expose an MEX endpoint as long as the service registers at least one of TCP, HTTP, or IPC base addresses in the service endpoint. An MEX endpoint has its own address and is explicitly made available by the service owner.

Metadata for a service is published to the service address with "/MEX" appended to it. For example, if the service address is "http://www.example.org:322/acconts.svc," the corresponding MEX address would be "http://www.example.org:322/acconts.svc/mex."

Versioning Considerations

Over its lifetime, a service may need to be augmented for any number of reasons, including in response to changes in hosting infrastructure. Some types of changes can be kept internal to the underlying service logic and implementation, whereas others may impact the actual service contract.

For example:

- the service's address may need to be changed if the service implementation is moved to a new physical location

- the service's binding information may need to change if the service is forced to support a different transport (with perhaps different security settings)

- the published service contract itself will likely be changed if modifications are required to the operations it has been exposing

SOA PRINCIPLES & PATTERNS
As advocated by the Service Abstraction (696) principle, to whatever extent possible, changes to a given service contract should be hidden from service consumers, so that services and service consumers can be versioned and evolved independently, with minimal impact on each other. In some cases it may be necessary to apply Concurrent Contracts [726] so that a given service publishes multiple versions of its data contract.
Other patterns that relate directly to contrct versioning include Compatible Change [723], Version Identification [793], and Terminiation Notification [787].

There are three established versioning strategies:

- Strict Strategy (new change, new contract)

- Flexible Strategy (backwards compatibility)

- Loose Strategy (backwards and forwards compatibility)

Each strategy approaches versioning in a different way, based on requirements and the measure of "impact control" you need to exercise over your service contracts.

NOTE
Descriptions of these versioning strategies, and how they apply to XML Schema, WSDL, and WS-Policy, are covered in detail in Chapters 20, 21, 22, and 23 of the book *Web Service Contract Design & Versioning for SOA*.

Data contracts are one of several attributes of a service that must be versioned for a service.

In support of the Flexible Strategy where the emphasis is on preserving backwards compatibility, backwards compatible changes can be implemented in the service endpoint by not altering the name and namespace of established data contracts and data members. Instead, if new name and namespace values are required, the original values can be preserved using the name and namespace parameters feature, as follows:

```
[DataContract
  (Namespace = "Finance", Name = "AccountContract")]
[DataMember(Name = "Total")]
```

Example 5.32

The data types returned by the data members and the order in which the data members are presented are not modified, and newly added data members appear after existing data members.

It is generally not recommended to use parameters initially. When a second version is required, all new operations can have the order parameter set to 2. The version after that will have the order parameter for all new data members set to 3, and so on. Note that changing any property of existing data members, such as the `IsRequired` property, will result in a non-backwards-compatible change.

> **NOTE**
>
> Previous versions of .NET supported generating CLR code from XML Schema and the generation of XML schemas from CLR types using the XML Schema Definition Tool (XSD.exe). With data contracts, this functionality is incorporated into the CLR and optimized for performance.

SUMMARY OF KEY POINTS

- The WCF service contract represents the technical interface of a WCF service.

- The interface contract expresses the abstract part of a service contract, and is comprised of operation contracts, message contracts, and data contracts.

- The service endpoint expresses the concrete part of a service contract by establishing the wire-level details for invoking the service.

- WCF does not support SOAP faults by default, but they can be programmatically defined.

- An MEX endpoint enables service consumers to dynamically retrieve meta-data about a corresponding service.

- There are different versioning strategies that can be used to evolve service contracts.

- WCF includes support for REST based services using `WebGet`, `WebInvoke` and several other classes in the `System.ServiceModel.Web` assembly.

5.3 Service Implementation with WCF

Behaviors

Behaviors are used to control the internal workings of a service. They are classes that extend or modify a service type and define the runtime aspect of the service. WCF behaviors can be applied to one or more services and are classified accordingly. Behaviors are considered the primary part of WCF extensibility.

> **SOA PRINCIPLES & PATTERNS**
>
> With the Service Abstraction (696) principle, service-orientation emphasizes the need to hide what lies beneath a service, which is why service contracts are positioned to abstract underlying service logic and implementation details. Within this context, WCF behaviors are used to model the "behind-the-scenes" service implementation.

The WCF platform provides a suite of built-in behaviors that address common behavioral customizations. An example is the transaction behavior, which is used to control and auto-complete transaction activities. Other behaviors include concurrency, instancing, throttling, thread-binding, faults, exceptions, metadata customization, instance pooling and JITA, impersonation, authorization, and security.

Behaviors can be applied to a service and operation using the `ServiceBehavior` and `OperationBehavior` attributes. Behaviors can also be used to extend and modify channels and endpoints.

The following example augments the default service implementation by changing its instance management and concurrency mode behaviors:

```
[ServiceContract]
[ServiceBehavior(
  InstanceContextMode = InstanceContextMode.Single,
  ConcurrencyMode = ConcurrencyMode.Multiple)]
public interface IGreetings
{
```

```
[OperationContract]
string Greet();
}
```

Example 5.33

NOTE
Custom behaviors can be defined by implementing the `IServiceBehavior` class.

Instancing

The `InstanceContextMode` parameter is used to control how instances are created, wheras the `ConcurrencyMode` parameter indicates the threading model parameter used by the service. In Example 5.33, the service is a singleton with concurrency set to mutithreaded.

Throttling controls, another example of a configurable service behavior, are used to place usage limits on a service to prevent over-consumption. Throttling controls can place limits on the number of concurrent calls, connections, instances, and pending operations. This form of throttling is carried out on a per service type and affects all instances of the service and all of its endpoints. Unlike the `InstanceContextMode` parameter, which is configured in code, the throttling behavior is configured in the configuration file:

```
<behaviors>
  <behavior
    name="ThrottlingBehavior">
      <throttling maxConcurrentCalls="5"
      maxConnections="10"
      maxInstances="10"
      maxPendingOperations="10" />
  </behavior>
</behaviors>
```

Example 5.34

Instancing is used to control how many instances of a service can run at the same time. WCF includes four instance models, as listed in Table 5.3. Instancing is enabled using service behaviors and the `InstanceContextMode` parameter.

Instance Models	Description
per call	the default behavior of a service (an instance of the service is created per client call requiring that the per call option of an operation be stateless)
per session	one instance of the service is created per session and cannot be shared across sessions
shareable	one instance of the service is created per session and can be shared across sessions
single	only one instance of the service is created for all incoming service calls (an option used primarily to implement single-ton services)

Table 5.3
A list of WCF instance models.

A Sample Implementation

Various concepts were previously covered, including Data Contracts, Message Contracts, Endpoint Address, Faults, Behaviors, Bindings, Metadata Exchange (MEX) and others.

The following example pulls together several of the individual elements, attributes and classes to present a very simple but complete service implementation. The Greeting service has two operations: Greet1 and Greet2. Greet1 accepts a name parameter and returns a string with "Hello" prefixed to the name. Greet2 accepts a data contract comprised of populated First Name and Last Name fields and returns a string with "Hello" appended to the name.

```
using System;
using System.ServiceModel;
using System.Runtime.Serialization;
namespace HelloService
{
  [ServiceContract(Namespace = "HelloService", Name = "IGreet")]
  public interface IGreet
  {
    [OperationContract]
    string Greet1(string name);
    [OperationContract]
    string Greet2(NameContract nameContractValue);
  }
```

```
public class Greet : IGreet
{
  public string Greet1(string name)
  {
    return "Hello: " + name;
  }
  public string Greet2(NameContract nameContractValue)
  {
    return "Hello: " + nameContractValue.FirstName;
  }
}
[DataContract]
public class NameContract
{
  [DataMember]
  public string FirstName {get; set;}
  [DataMember]
  public string LastName {get; set;}
}
}
```

Example 5.35

In order to host the service in IIS, we need to create an ".svc" file and reference the service using the ServiceHost directive as shown here:

```
<%
  @ServiceHost Language=C# Debug="true"
  Service="HelloService.Greet"
  CodeBehind="~/App_Code/Greet.cs"
%>
```

Example 5.36

Finally, we need to configure the service endpoint's address, binding, and contract in the Web.Config file:

```
<configuration
  xmlns="http://schemas.microsoft.com/.NetConfiguration/v2.0">
  <system.serviceModel>
    <services>
      <service name="HelloService.Greet"
        behaviorConfiguration="GreetTypeBehaviors">
        <endpoint
```

```
          address="mex"
          binding="mexHttpBinding"
          contract="HelloService.IGreet" />
    </service>
  </services>
  <behaviors>
    <serviceBehaviors>
      <behavior name="GreetTypeBehaviors" >
        <serviceMetadata httpGetEnabled="true" />
        <serviceDebug includeExceptionDetailInFaults="true"/>
      </behavior>
    </serviceBehaviors>
  </behaviors>
  </system.serviceModel>
</configuration>
```

Example 5.37

The httpGetEnabled=true behavior indicates a WSDL definition is published with the service. includeExceptionDetailInFaults=true configures the service to return unhandled exceptions as faults and includeExceptionDetailInFaults=false will raise the actual exception to the service consumer.

SUMMARY OF KEY POINTS

- Behaviors are the types that modify or extend the service's functionality and control the internal behavior of a service.

- Instancing settings determine the amount of allowed concurrent services instances.

5.4 Service Hosting with WCF

A WCF service is independent of the hosting environment, allowing the most appropriate hosting model to be selected without the need to change anything in the service.

There are several options when it comes to hosting WCF services:

- Internet Information Services (IIS)

- Windows Activation Service (WAS) installed with IIS 7.0

- any managed application process, including console, Windows Forms, Windows Presentation Foundation (WPF)

- any managed Windows service applications

The `ServiceHost` class can be used to host a WCF service when IIS or WAS is not used. The `ServiceHost` instance must be initialized with the base address and one or more endpoints that include binding and contract parameters, as shown in the following example:

```
ServiceHost host =
  new ServiceHost(typeof(IService));
host.AddEndpoint(typeof(IService),Binding, Uri);
host.Open();
```

Example 5.38

The `ServiceHost` constructor is provided with the service type and an array of base addresses. Each base address must have a different transport specified in its URI. The actual address of each endpoint is derived relative to the base address. If there is more than one base address associated with the `ServiceHost` instance, the appropriate one is used based on the transport protocol. The base addresses are typically stored and retrieved from the application's configuration file.

An application domain is a construct of a CLR that is the unit of isolation of an application. The main purpose of the hosting environment is to provide a worker process in an application domain for the `ServiceHost` to run.

The hosting environment is a process and runs as an identity. Therefore, it also provides a default security context to the service being hosted. Some hosting environments are more sophisticated than others and can provide features such as process recycling or application restart on failure.

Design considerations to be mindful of when choosing a hosting environment include:

- availability
- reliability
- manageability
- deployment

All hosting environments in the following list support the application of service-orientation, so choosing the correct environment comes down to addressing the type of transport and security parameters used to expose a service, scalability requirements, and SLA requirements.

- self-hosting

- Managed Windows Service

- IIS 5.1 and IIS 6.0

- Windows Activation Service (WAS)

Note that any service must be hosted within a runtime environment that creates and controls its context and lifetime.

Self-Hosted Services

A *self-hosted* service can be any managed application or application domain. Managed applications include Windows Forms applications, console applications, or Windows services. Similar to other hosting environments, the `ServiceHost<T>` generic class is used to host WCF endpoints within any .NET application. If the host is a Windows Forms or console application, it must be running to provide an application domain to host the communication endpoints.

> **SOA PRINCIPLES & PATTERNS**
>
> A primary service-orientation principle that can greatly impact service hosting considerations is Service Autonomy (699). It advocates that services have as much control over their underlying execution environment as possible in order to guarantee a high level of behavioral predictability. This generally implies that allocated resources are desirable, whereas shared resources are not.

Self-hosted services offer unique advantages, such as using TCP, IPC, or MSMQ for transport, utilizing HTTP with multiple ports (besides port 80), and programmatic access to hosting features. With self-hosting, the service is not limited to HTTP-based addresses as is the case with IIS.

It is a flexible approach, but it has the least amount of server features. It is not a valid option if you need high availability, reliability, and a management view. The most common scenario for self-hosting is a smart client application which, when you fire it up, provides a connection point for other applications. Peer-to-peer applications are a common example of self-hosted services.

The following example shows a service that, when implemented in a Windows Forms application or a Console application, would be classified as self-hosted. In this case the `ServiceHost` class is instantiated by providing the constructor the interface and base addresses (and the binding is inferred from the address which is in the configuration file shown in Example 5.39).

```
Uri[] baseAddresses = new Uri[]
{
  new Uri(ConfigurationManager.AppSettings["tcpBaseAddress"]),
  new Uri(ConfigurationManager.AppSettings["httpBaseAddress"])
};
ServiceHost serviceHost =
  new ServiceHost(typeof(AccountService), baseAddresses);
serviceHost.Open();
```

Example 5.39

The base address collection provided to the `ServiceHost` instance is dynamically configured by reading the settings from the Web.Config file:

```
<appSettings>
  <add key="tcpBaseAddress"
    value="net.tcp://localhost:1234"/>
  <add key="httpBaseAddress"
    value="http://localhost:8000"/>
</appSettings>
```

Example 5.40

The `ServiceHost` class uses endpoint information, such as the address, binding, and contract, to initialize and create a process and its underlying communication stack in the application domain that receives messages:

```
<services>
  <service name ="AccountService">
    <endpoint name="EndPoint1"
      address=""
      binding="netTcpBinding"
      contract="IAccount"/>
    <endpoint name="EndPoint2"
      address=""
      binding="basicHttpBinding"
      contract="IAccount"/>
```

```
    </service>
  </services>
```

Example 5.41

.NET 4.0 simplifies WCF configuration by providing a default configuration and behavior. The default configuration also includes a default endpoint. Therefore, it is possible to consume a WCF service with no supporting configuration file. The binding defaults to basic HTTP (`BasicHttpBinding`), but if a different binding is required, it needs to be changed in the App.Config file. This allows you to rapidly create a Web service similar to .ASMX development.

Note that this technique is not generally recommended when applying service-orientation as it tends to promote RPC-style inter-service relationships.

Managed Windows Services

Enterprise server applications require high availability, reliability, and a management view for on-going maintenance. Windows services provides these features.

Using Windows services to host a service requires hosting the `ServiceHost` instance from the WCF API in `System.ServiceProcess`. A Windows service is created in .NET by inheriting from the `ServiceBase` class, which lives in the `System.ServiceProcess` assembly. When a Windows service starts up, it calls the `OnStart` method and the `ServiceHost` instance is executed. Once the Windows service stops, the `ServiceHost` is closed, thereby tying the lifespan of the WCF service to that of the Windows service:

```
using System.ServiceModel;
using System.ServiceProcess;
public class AccountWindowsService : ServiceBase
{
  ServiceHost serviceHost;
  public override void OnStart( string[] args )
  {
    this.serviceHost = new ServiceHost( typeof( T ) );
    this.serviceHost.AddEndpoint( ... );
    this.serviceHost.Open();
  }
  public override void OnStop()
  {
    this.serviceHost.Close();
  }
}
```

Example 5.42

Hosting in Windows services is useful when the lifetime of the service needs to be controlled by the operating system. It is also beneficial when the service has to run under the identity of a restricted account in the background and can use any transport included in WCF.

IIS Process Boundary

In IIS, an application is the application domain and an application pool is the *process boundary*. IIS includes health monitoring and recycling, allowing it to monitor both the application domain and the application pool and to recycle them if it determines idle behavior (indicating that IIS has choked and is not able to service message requests).

IIS further includes on-demand service activation via HTTP, which means that an IIS application pool is only activated by the IIS infrastructure when it receives an HTTP message. IIS also manages the lifecycle of the host.

Some benefits of hosting a service in IIS include:

- scalability and several clustering features

- process recycling, health monitoring, idle shutdown, message based activation

- security

Hosting a service in IIS 5.0 and 6.0 limits the transport to HTTP and HTTPS. IIS 7.0 includes Windows Activation Services and can host services with other transport protocols.

A service that needs to be hosted in IIS is typically represented by a .svc file, and with ASP.NET it is separated from content using code-behind files. The .svc file uses the `ServiceHost` directive to identify and link to the code-behind file containing the service class, as shown here:

```
<%
  @ServiceHost language="cs"
  Class="GreetingService"
  CodeBehind="~/App_Code/GreetingService.cs"
%>
```

Example 5.43

The .svc file can be hosted in an IIS virtual directory, but in order to make a service public, it must be configured in the Web.Config file:

```
<system.serviceModel>
  <services>
    <service type="GreetingService">
      <endpoint
        address=""
        binding="basicHttpBinding"
        contract="GreetingService" />
    </service>
  </services>
</system.serviceModel>
```

Example 5.44

Typically, the address in the Web.Config file is set to an empty string, as this address is relative to the address of the .svc file in IIS. To host this .svc file in IIS, the .svc extension must be mapped to the ASP.NET process (aspnet_isapi.dll), which can be set in the IIS Application Configuration Window.

Once a service is hosted in IIS, it can be accessed using a Web browser. In this case, the URL to access the service is:

```
http://localhost/GreetingService.svc
```

Windows Activation Services (WAS)

Windows Activation Service (WAS) is a system service introduced with Windows Vista. It is the activation part of IIS 7.0 and can also be installed and configured separately.

IIS 5.0 and IIS 6.0 are appropriate hosting platforms as long as the only transport used is HTTP. WAS is built upon the IIS 6.0 activation model by generalizing the IIS 6.0 process model and extending it to other transports, such as TCP and MSMQ (Figure 5.11).

WAS architecture introduces *listener adapters*—infrastructure components that bridge particular network protocols to the WAS interface. The listener adapter communicates messages to WAS and requests that it activate worker processes. WAS includes listener adapters for all activation scenarios in WCF, including http, net.tcp, net.pipe, and net.msmq.

Since WAS is built on IIS 6, it provides all the features included in IIS, such as process recycling, application pooling and isolation, identity management, health activation monitoring, message based activation, and so on. Similar to hosting a service in IIS, hosting a service in WAS requires a .svc file which is a pointer to a code-behind file containing the service class.

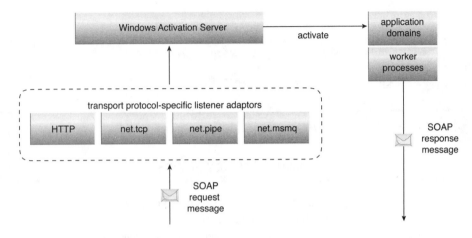

Figure 5.11
The Windows Activation Services (WAS) architecture is built upon the IIS 6.0 activation model.

Hosting REST Services

WCF provides the `WebServiceHost` for REST-based services, which is a REST-aware equivalent of the `ServiceHost` class. `WebServiceHost` ensures that the transport is HTTP and wires up the service endpoints to the REST dispatcher. It also works with `WebServiceHostFactory` and the WCF configuration-less model.

Each .svc file contains two WCF-specific attributes:

- *Service* – indicates which type implements the service behind the endpoint

- *Factory* – determines which `ServiceHostFactory` to use as a host for the service implementation

When the `Factory` attribute is absent, the supporting WCF infrastructure will set the value to `System.ServiceModel.Activation.ServiceHostFactory`. This particular factory depends on the Web.Config file to figure out how to host the service, expose endpoints, and attach any behaviors.

Because a REST service has a well-defined set of behaviors, instead of explicitly stating what the binding and behavior set looks like, you can set the `Factory` attribute to `System.ServiceModel.Activation.WebServiceHostFactory` and skip any configuration altogether. In fact, the following `CatalogService` (found in CatalogService.svc and CatalogService.svc.cs) does just that:

```
<%@
  ServiceHost Language="C#" Debug="true"
  Service="StandardMold.Catalog.CatalogService"
  Factory="System.ServiceModel.
   Activation.WebServiceHostFactory"
%>
```

Example 5.45

SUMMARY OF KEY POINTS

- In order to activate a WCF service, it must be hosted in a runtime environment or a host process. There are a number of host processes that are suitable for hosting services, including self-hosting, Managed Windows Service, IIS, and WAS.

- Each hosting environment has pros and cons with respect to service management, security, and transport types.

- WAS is a part of IIS 7.0, but can also be installed and configured separately. WAS has the broadest support for transport protocols, security, and server features such as process recycling and object pooling.

- `WebServiceHost` is provided specifically in support of REST service hosting.

5.5 Service Consumers with WCF

In order to access a service, a consumer program must import the service contract and other dependencies. WCF services typically expose their contract using an address of the service endpoint or its MEX endpoint.

If the service consumer is implemented within WCF, it uses a proxy class that is a CLR type to access the service contract. The service may have more than one endpoint, in which case the service consumer must have a proxy for each endpoint of the service. The proxy class encapsulates every aspect of the service, including its operations, address, and binding. It also includes methods to manage the lifecycle of the proxy and its connection to the service.

Visual Studio has tools for importing service metadata, generating the proxy class, and integrating the generated proxy class into a Visual Studio solution. This can be done using the Add Service reference feature in the solution explorer. Under the hood, Visual

Studio uses the Service Metadata Tool (svcutil.exe). Besides supporting Visual Studio, this tool provides several options through switches that can be used to generate proxies for different scenarios.

There are three ways a service consumer implemented in WCF can consume a service:

1. Using the Service Metadata Tool

2. Writing the Proxy Class for a Service

3. Using the `ChannelFactory` Class

Let's explore each individually.

Using the Service Metadata Tool

The Service Metadata Tool, which can be accessed from the command prompt, is used to create the client proxy and the client configuration file. To use this tool, the service consumer needs to know where the service is located and how to connect to it. Therefore, the client configuration file must contain the same endpoint information as the service to which it is connecting. The address and binding data can be found in the service provider's endpoint and can be accessed using an MEX endpoint or the actual endpoint address.

The Service Metadata Tool is given the endpoint address and the names of the proxy and configuration files to output. In the following example, the service endpoint is located at "http://localhost:8000/Accounts" and the Service Metadata Tool will generate two files: proxy.cs and App.Config. The proxy.cs file will contain the generated proxy class and App.Config will contain endpoint information to support the proxy class.

```
svcutil http://localhost:8000/Accounts/out:proxy.cs /Config:app.config
```

Example 5.46

The next step is to include the generated files into the development project. The generated class, which represents the contract, can now be accessed by instantiating the proxy class:

```
AccountProxy proxy = new AccountProxy("EndPoint1");
string response = proxy.GetHoldings();
Console.WriteLine(response);
proxy.Close();
```

Example 5.47

In this code fragment, `proxy` is the typed instance of the contract and `EndPoint1` identifies an endpoint in the client application's configuration file.

Writing the Proxy Class for a Service

The proxy class generated by the Service Metadata Tool uses the generic `ClientBase<T>` class, which is defined as:

```
public class ClientBase<T> :IDisposable
{
  protected ClientBase
    (string endpointConfigurationName);
  protected ClientBase(
    Binding binding,
    EndpointAddress
    remoteAddress);
  public void Close();
  public void Dispose();
  protected T InnerProxy{get;}
}
```

Example 5.48

Note that the `ClientBase<T>` class can also be used to create a proxy class by writing code to access a service.

The service consumer needs to instantiate a `ClientBase<T>` object and provide the constructor with either the endpoint defined in the configuration file or the address and binding objects. `InnerProxy` method then returns a typed instance of the contract.

The following example demonstrates the creation of a proxy class for a service:

```
[ServiceContract]
public interface IGreetings
{
  [OperationContract]
  string Greet();
}
```

Example 5.49

A typed proxy for the service contract is created using this code:

```
public partial class GreetingsProxy :
  ClientBase<IGreetings>, IGreetings
{
  public GreetingsProxy(string configurationName) :
    base(configurationName){}
  public string Greet()
  {
    return Channel.Greet();
  }
}
```

Example 5.50

The client instantiating the `GreetingsProxy` must give it the endpoint by either referring to the configuration file or by providing the address and binding objects.

Using the `ChannelFactory` Class

WCF provides channels that allow an operation in a service to be invoked directly without using the Service Metadata Tool. It is mostly suitable in a closed development environment, where the client has direct access to the endpoint information.

The `ChannelFactory<T>` class in `System.ServiceModel` is used to create a proxy at
runtime. The `ChannelFactory<T>` constructor is given either the endpoint name in the
application's configuration file or the endpoint object. `CreateChannel` is a typed
method that returns the `IGreet` proxy. The typed proxy class can be used to access all
operations exposed by the service contract:

```
ChannelFactory factory =
  new ChannelFactory<IGreet>("Endpoint1");
IGreet proxy = factory.CreateChannel();
string greeting = proxy.Greet("Hello World");
Console.WriteLine(greeting);
```

Example 5.51

The configuration file contains the endpoint information used in the `ChannelFactory`
constructor:

```
<system.serviceModel>
<client>
  <endpoint configurationName="Endpoint1"
    address="http://localhost/GreetingsService"
```

```
    binding="basicHttpBinding"
    contract="IGreet" />
  </client>
</system.serviceModel>
```

Example 5.52

Regenerating the proxy class each time a service changes can be inefficient. However, creating a proxy on the fly can result in performance degradation. Considerations such as this need to be taken into account before deciding on the most appropriate approach.

> **NOTE**
>
> See also Appendix F for the "Consuming Services with WCF" article by Herbjörn Wilhelmsen that was originally published in the *SOA Magazine*.

SUMMARY OF KEY POINTS

- To use the capabilities provided by a service, a client needs to generate a proxy class in its native representation. WCF includes a Service Metadata Tool to generate the proxy class and supporting files.

- The proxy class generated using the Service Metadata Tool uses the generic `ClientBase<T>` class. The proxy class can also be derived by creating a proxy class manually and implementing `ClientBase<T>`.

- Service operations can be accessed directly without using the Service Metadata Tool. This approach is mostly suitable in a closed development environment where the client has access to the endpoint information. The proxy is generated at runtime using the `ChannelFactory<T>` generic class.

Chapter 6

WCF Extensions

6.1 WCF Security

6.2 WCF Transactions

6.3 WCF Router

6.4 WCF Discovery

6.5 WCF Extensibility

6.6 WCF Management Tools

6.1 WCF Security

Services and service consumers are often on opposite sides of trust boundaries.

A trust boundary is a physical or virtual boundary within which actual levels of trust can vary. A trust boundary can be an application process, a machine, or even the Internet itself. When SOAP messages flow through a trust boundary, they may need to be transmitted between nodes, through firewalls, across intermediaries, and so on.

Each of these points of contact can introduce message security threats, such as breach of integrity, breach of confidentiality, breach of authentication, and breach of authorization.

BASIC SECURITY TERMS IN A NUTSHELL

Integrity is the ability to detect if a message has been tampered with. Confidentiality is the ability to keep the message unreadable by others except the intended recipient. Authentication is the ability to verify the identity of the sender and authorization is the ability to verify if a user is allowed to do what it is requesting to do.

Basic security terminology is established in *Service-Oriented Architecture: Concepts, Technology, and Design*, as well as *SOA Design Patterns*.

A service may be accessed by a service consumer over the Internet or via a local intranet. Cross-service Internet communication typically relies on the exchange of username and password credentials to identify users. On an intranet, Windows security using Active Directory over TCP is common for authentication. Certificates are also frequently used to identify service consumers in both environments.

WCF bindings support confidentiality, integrity, and authentication. It is important to understand that WCF does not automatically provide protection against threats. Attacks, such as SQL injection and XML parser attacks, will generally require attention to service logic and general infrastructure configuration.

Security controls work consistently across bindings. If a binding changes, security settings will simply be carried forward. WCF supports both transport-layer security and message-layer security.

While most of the security detail is incorporated into the platform and preconfigured, two factors need to be considered when designing WCF services and service compositions:

- security mode
- credential type

The security mode is based on credentials. Credentials provide claims made by a service consumer to the service. Claims are packaged in security tokens that are contained in messages that can travel over process and machine boundaries. WCF authenticates and authorizes these claims.

Supported credential types include:

- Username
- Kerberos
- X509

Let's talk more about security modes and how they process these types of credentials.

Security Modes

Credentials can be transmitted using either the *transport security mode* (transport-layer security) or the *message security mode* (message-layer security), as shown in Table 6.1.

The transport security mode relies on the use of the Secure Sockets Layer (SSL) technology to encrypt the transport. This provides performance benefits and a simplified security architecture. The downside is that it does not support newer and richer types of credentials, such as SAML tokens, and is primarily suitable for point-to-point communication, as opposed to communication that involves intermediaries.

The message security mode enables claims to be secured within the message. It is extensible in support of different credential types (such as SAML) and ensures that protected content cannot be read or tampered with by intermediaries along a given message path. The downside is an increase in runtime processing requirements.

WCF also supports *mixed mode security*, which allows integrity and confidentiality requirements to be addressed by SSL, while authentication and authorization requirements are satisfied within the message.

Security Mode	Description
none	no security is provided at the transport or message layers
transport	transport-layer security is used, meaning HTTPS is employed to secure the integrity and confidentiality of the transport
message	message-layer security is used for integrity, confidentiality, and authentication
mixed mode	a combination of transport security and message security modes can be used

Table 6.1
A list of WCF security modes.

Note that when the transport security mode is chosen, authentication requirements can be addressed using the options listed in Table 6.2.

Options	Description
none	no authentication credentials are required by the service (all service consumers access the service anonymously and are granted complete access)
basic	the service consumer provides username and password credentials to the service in plain text (because the transport has been secured, sending username and password as plain text is not considered a threat)
digest	the service consumer provides username and password credentials to the service (the password is encrypted before it is sent)
windows	the service uses Windows authentication (Kerberos is the default authentication mechanism and the user is authenticated against Active Directory)
certificate	the service consumer provides an X509 certificate to the service

Table 6.2
A list of Windows integrated security options.

Security industry standards provide the preferred means of establishing security architectures in support of inherent interoperability among services. These standards include WS-Trust, WS-SecureConversation, WS-SecurityPolicy, WS-Security and the WS-I Basic Security Profile.

A service does not need to be constrained by a single binding or security setting. The same service can be exposed over multiple bindings. For example, one service may be exposed via the Internet using a simple WS-I Basic Security Profile binding over HTTPS, as well as over TCP for local consumers in the same domain using Windows authentication.

> **SOA PRINCIPLES & PATTERNS**
>
> Service-orientation requires that the concept of interoperability be extended to security wherever possible in order to minimize the impact of security controls and mechanisms on the application of the Service Reusability (697) and Service Composability (704) principles. Patterns that directly support the WCF Security message mode (for message-layer security) include Data Confidentiality [730] and Data Origin Authentication [733], both of which can be applied using WS-Security in conjunction with industry standard technologies, such as XML-Encryption and XML-Signature, respectively.

Authorization

WCF provides several extensibility hooks that allow you to plug in the authorization policy of your choice and check the validity of the claims.

Supported authorization plug-ins include:

- ASP.NET membership and role providers

- Authorization Manager

- custom-developed code

- .NET role-based security infrastructure

For example, using `Thread.CurrentPrincipal` is the standard way to access a service consumer's identity in .NET. If the type of credentials is set to "Windows," then `Thread.CurrentPrincipal` will point to `WindowsPrincipal` and you can determine if the consumer belongs to a valid role by using `WindowsPrincipal.IsInRole`, as follows:

```
IPrincipal user = Thread.CurrentPrincipal;
if (user.IsInRole(@"DomainName\contributors "))
{
```

```
    ... allow users to contribute ...
}
```

Example 6.1

Federated Identity

In WCF, federated identity represents the ability to enable an organization to accept and process identities issued by other organizations. WCF allows different partner organizations to have the same single sign-on experience, even when they use services that are external to their domain. Federation automates the existing trust relationship between partners, which, in turn, tends to reduce potential mistakes, latency, and maintenance costs.

> **SOA PRINCIPLES & PATTERNS**
>
> WCF supports the use of SAML, an industry standard that can be applied to establish a single sign-on mechanism for a given service composition or even an entire service inventory. This also commonly relates to the application of Brokered Authentication [714].

SUMMARY OF KEY POINTS

- WCF supports message confidentiality and integrity and provides a model of authentication using several industry-standard security tokens.

- The security requirements can be satisfied at the transport layer using SSL, or at the message layer where claims are carried in the SOAP message. WCF also supports a mixed-mode security that allows both message security and transport security to be used in conjunction.

- WCF provides extensibility hooks that allow you to plug in an authorization policy based on ASP.NET membership and role providers, Authorization Manager, .NET role-based security infrastructure, or custom developed solutions.

> **NOTE**
>
> Security in relation to WCF, .NET, and Windows Azure is covered in Chapter 17.

6.2 WCF Transactions

Basic concepts regarding transactions were covered in Chapter 4 where we introduced some of the original .NET technologies used to enable and manage cross-service transactions. A de-facto industry standard that governs transactions across Web services is WS-AtomicTransaction, which is an extension of (and provides a set of transaction protocols for) the WS-Coordination standard. WCF implements the WS-AtomicTransaction standard and provides a range of transaction-related features, all of which are encompassed in the `System.Transactions` namespace (also explained in Chapter 4).

> **NOTE**
>
> The WS-Coordination and WS-AtomicTransaction industry standards are described in more detail in the book *Service-Oriented Architecture: Concepts, Technology, and Design*. The original specifications can be accessed via www.soaspecs.com.

A WCF transaction is carried out by two mechanisms:

* transaction manager

* resource manager

The resource manager keeps track of durable or volatile data during the lifespan of a given transaction. The transaction manager works with the resource manager to provide a guarantee of atomicity and isolation. In WCF, transactions can be applied to a service using the `ServiceBehavior` or `OperationBehavior` attributes.

Operation Attributes for Transactions

An operation attribute allows the internal behavior of a transaction to be changed in a manner that is specific to an operation. In the following code sample, the `TransactionFlowOption` attribute allows the `DebitAccount` operation to be invoked inside another transaction. The `TransactionScopeRequired` operation ensures that if the calling process does not include a transaction, a new transaction will be initiated by the `DebitAccount` operation.

> **SOA PRINCIPLES & PATTERNS**
>
> The majority of coverage of WCF Transactions pertains to the application of Atomic Service Transaction [713], which can be applied using the WS-AtomicTransaction and WS-Coordination industry standards. This pattern is appropriate whenever ACID-style transactions with rollback capability are required.

```
[TransactionFlow(TransactionFlowOption.Allowed)]
[OperationBehavior(TransactionScopeRequired = true,
  TransactionAutoComplete = true)]
void DebitAccount(string accountNo, double amount);
```

Example 6.2

Operation attributes used to change the internal behavior of an operation are:

TransactionScopeRequired

Setting the TransactionScopeRequired attribute to "true" specifies that the operation must be a part of a transaction. If one is not available, a new transaction will be created.

TransactionAutoComplete

Setting the TransactionAutoComplete attribute to "true" indicates that the code need not be implicitly told to abort or commit a transaction. If all the operations in a transaction complete successfully, the transaction will automatically commit itself. Setting the property to false requires you to write code to either commit or roll back the transaction.

TransactionFlow

The TransactionFlow attribute is used to verify at design-time if an operation will accept incoming transaction calls. Possible values for this parameter are as shown in Table 6.3.

Parameter Value	Description
Allowed	transactions may flow through to the operation
Mandatory	the transaction context created earlier must flow through
NotAllowed	transactions created earlier will not flow through to the new operation

Table 6.3
Parameter values of the TransactionFlow attribute.

Service Attributes for Transactions

Service attributes allow the internal behavior of a transaction to be changed to better meet your requirements. In Example 6.3, if the session in whose context the transaction executes expires, the transaction will be allowed to complete. The isolation level is set to `ReadCommitted`, implying that transactions can read volatile data but cannot modify it.

```
[ServiceBehavior(InstanceContextMode =
  InstanceContextMode.Single
  ConcurrencyMode = ConcurrencyMode.Multiple,
  TransactionAutoCompleteOnSessionClose = true,
  TransactionIsolationLevel=
    System.Transactions.IsolationLevel.ReadCommitted)]
  class AccountService : IAccount
  {
    . . .
  }
```

Example 6.3

Service attributes that can be used to change the internal behavior of transactions include:

TransactionIsolationLevel

In order to maintain data integrity, a transaction must obtain locks on the data involved with the transaction. Obtaining locks comes at the expense of concurrency, thereby preventing other transactions from accessing the same data, and perhaps associated resources.

When a transaction is created, the isolation level for the transaction must be specified. This value determines the level of access that other transactions will have to volatile data. Transaction isolation level options available to the `TransactionIsolationLevel` parameter are listed in Table 6.4.

Isolation Level	Description
ReadCommitted	permits reading committed (permanent) changes to the data by simultaneous transactions (it also does not permit modifying volatile data)
ReadUncommitted	uses the optimistic concurrency model (permits reading and modifying of volatile data)

continues

Isolation Level	Description
RepeatableRead	permits reading volatile data but does not permit modifying it (but it does permit adding new data)
Serializable	permits reading volatile data, but does not permit either modifying existing data or adding new data (outcome is similar to transactions executed one after the other—serially)
Snapshot	uses the optimistic concurrency model and guarantees that all reads made in a transaction will see a consistent snapshot of the database (the transaction will be committed only if the updates made in the transaction do not conflict with any updates made since that snapshot)

Table 6.4

A list of level options for transaction isolation.

TransactionAutoCompleteOnSessionClose

A transaction runs in the context of a session initiated by invoking the service. This attribute sets the behavior of the transaction if the session (within the context it runs in) closes. Setting the TransactionAutoCompleteOnSessionClose attribute to "true" will allow transactions to complete. By default, this property is set to "false," indicating that transactions executing in the context of the session will be aborted, causing them to be rolled back.

TransactionTimeout

The TransactionTimeout attribute specifies the time by which a transaction must be completed. If the transaction continues beyond the specified timeout interval, it is automatically aborted and rolled back. The transaction timeout property is subject to change and should be set in the configuration file.

```
<behaviors>
  <behavior
    name="ServiceBehaviorAttribute"
    returnUnknownExceptionsAsFaults="true"
    TransactionTimeout="00:00:05"/>
</behaviors>
```

Example 6.4

Durable Services

A service is considered "durable" when it can survive conditions like a server shutdown, host recycling, and other runtime disruptions. This is typically accomplished in a service by persisting the message and the state of the service.

Both BizTalk Server and Windows Workflow (WF) have support for durable and long running services. WF implements a long-running service by providing the developer a *persistence service* that will hydrate and dehydrate workflow instances. This persistence mechanism is extensible and allows you to create your own variation to persist Workflow instances. (WCF implemented a similar mechanism to persist the state of a service in .NET 3.5.)

For example, the following service contract describes a stateful, long running interaction:

```
[ServiceContract]
public interface IDoWork
{
   [OperationContract]
   string DoWork(string text);
}
```

Example 6.5

The interface we just defined can be annotated as a durable service by using `Durable-ServiceBehavior` and `DurableOperationBehavior`, as shown here:

```
[Serializable]
[DurableServiceBehavior]
public class DoWork : IDoWork
{
   private string CurrentText ;
   [DurableOperationBehavior(CanCreateInstance = true)]
   string DoWork(string text);
}
```

Example 6.6

In this example, the DoWork operation sets the instantiation and completion of a service instance. The persistence service must be configured in order to serialize the state of the instance. This is done by using the `wsHttpContextBinding` attribute in the configuration file. .NET 3.5 introduced SQL scripts that allow for the creation of a database that persists the service instance, similar to the process used to persist a workflow instance (as explained in Chapter 7). In this manner the persistence service allows the WCF service instance state to be preserved, even if the host is recycled.

> **SOA PRINCIPLES & PATTERNS**
>
> Compensating Service Transaction [724] is a pattern that is naturally applied with the use of durable services. Long-running transactions that span service activities that may need to be persisted are often unable to afford the resource allocation required by atomic transactions that guarantee rollback functionality. Note that this pattern is commonly applied via the usage of Undo operations and methods within service contracts.

SUMMARY OF KEY POINTS

- WCF unifies legacy Microsoft transaction management systems into a standardized and centralized transaction management system.

- The WCF programming model significantly simplifies working transactions.

- WCF provides granular control over the internal behavior of transactions using service-level and operation-level attributes. These behavior attributes can be used to control several parameters, including isolation level, transaction scope, and others.

6.3 WCF Router

With WCF the service consumer sends a message to the service using a generated proxy. Both the service consumer and service rely on a compatible configuration that is shared between them.

Decoupling services from service consumers has several benefits, including the ability to independently leverage non-functional features, such as message-logging, security logic, fault tolerance, and various forms of routing processing.

Although building a router service was possible with .NET 3.5, version 4.0 of the .NET framework provides the *WCF Router*, an intermediary that can be configured as a service or service agent to receive and forward messages to target services based on various factors.

The WCF Router can be configured as an active or passive intermediary. An active WCF routing service can provide a range of runtime processing, such as security, message encoding, reliable sessions, and protocol compatibility. As a passive intermediary (meaning the router logic can alter policies and protocols, but not message structure or content), it can perform various forms of runtime routing logic, such as content-based routing, rules-based routing, and load-balancing.

> **SOA PRINCIPLES & PATTERNS**
>
> The use of the WCF Router extension as a passive intermediary can be considered an application of Intermediate Routing [748], a pattern that encompasses the utilization of event-driven intermediary processing logic (primarily via Service Agent [770]) to transparently intercept, process, and forward messages at runtime. While this type of processing is nothing new, WCF Router represents its implementation as a native part of WCF.

The `RoutingService` Class

The WCF Router is equipped with a built-in filtering mechanism that allows you to specify the criteria used to dynamically determine message paths. For example, a message may need to be routed based on action, an XPath query, or its actual content.

WCF provides the `System.ServiceModel.RoutingService` class, and as with any other WCF service, the routing service can be hosted in IIS/WAS or it can be self-hosted in a Windows application or a Windows service.

The following example shows the contents of a .svc file with directives for hosting `RoutingService` in IIS:

```
<%
  @ServiceHost
  Service="System.ServiceModel.Routing.RoutingService,
    System.ServiceModel.Routing,
      version=4.0.0.0,
      Culture=neutral,
    PublicKeyToken=31bf3856ad364e35"
%>
```

Example 6.7

This next example shows `RoutingService` in a self-hosted environment:

```
using (ServiceHost serviceHost =
  new ServiceHost(typeof(RoutingService)))
{
  try
  {
    serviceHost.Open();
    Console.WriteLine
      ("Routing service running. Press <Enter> to exit");
    Console.ReadLine();
    serviceHost.Close();
  }
  catch(CommunicationException)
  {
    serviceHost.Abort();
  }
}
```

Example 6.8

Routing Contracts

The RoutingService class supports the routing of messages that are part of synchronous (request-response) data exchanges as well as asynchronous and request-response exchanges over duplex protocols. The router can also multicast these two message exchange types.

The generic routing contracts available in the System.ServiceModel.Routing namespace to configure the router are listed in Table 6.5.

Routing Contract	Supports
IRequestReplyRouter	WCF Sessions: if present Transactions: if present Asynchronous Messages: no Multicast: no
ISimplexDatagramRouter	WCF Sessions: if present Transactions: no Asynchronous Messages: yes Multicast: yes

Routing Contract	Supports
ISimplexSessionRouter	WCF Sessions: required Transactions: no Asynchronous Messages: yes Multicast: yes
IDuplexSessionRouter	WCF Sessions: required Transactions: if present Asynchronous Messages: yes Multicast: yes

Table 6.5
Interface routing contracts used for different routing options.

Each of these routing contracts supports a different set of message exchange patterns and channel properties. Consequently, you may have to set up different routing endpoints for a service contract if your contract's operations are designed with different message exchange or transaction requirements.

> **NOTE**
>
> The RoutingService class supports the numerous SOAP-based WCF bindings (BasicHttpBinding, WSHttpBinding, NetTcpBinding, etc.); however, it does not support the WebHttpBinding for REST services. Routing logic for REST services can be implemented with IIS Modules for Application Request Routing and UrlRewrite.

Routing Configuration

The routing service is configured using a set of rules in the service's configuration file or via the RoutingConfiguration object applied to RoutingExtension in the service host.

Routing rules consist of message filters and routing targets. The routing service applies these filters to incoming messages and if a message matches the filter criteria, it is routed to appropriate target service(s).

Let's take a look at the basic steps required to configure a routing service and its filters:

Step 1: Define Endpoints

One or more endpoints need to be defined for the routing service. The following example shows one such endpoint:

```
<services>
  <service
    behaviorConfiguration="RouterBehavior"
    name="System.ServiceModel.Routing.RoutingService">
    <endpoint address="http://router.example.org/router"
      binding="basicHttpBinding"
      name="RequestResponse"
      contract="System.ServiceModel.Routing.
        IRequestReplyRouter" />

    ... add additional endpoints as necessary ...

  </service>
</services>
```

Example 6.9

Step 2: Configure Service Behavior

The routing service's behavior needs to be defined with the `routing` element in order to link the service to the routing rules in `filterTableName`, as follows:

```
<serviceBehaviors>
  <behavior name="RouterBehavior">
    <routing
      filterTableName="routingRules"
      routeOnHeadersOnly="false" />
  </behavior>
</serviceBehaviors>
```

Example 6.10

Step 3: Enumerate Target Endpoints

Potential routing destinations (the target service endpoints) need to be defined. Note that while the contracts of the destination service endpoints must match, the bindings and binding configurations do not have to be identical. This allows for any required runtime policy adjustments and protocol transformation.

SOA PRINCIPLES & PATTERNS

The ability to dynamically set and augment transport protocols at runtime is comparable to the application of Protocol Bridging [764], a pattern that generally represents runtime protocol transformation at the transport and messaging levels. Classic protocol bridging logic is found in intermediate broker products, such as those that represent Service Broker [771] as part of Enterprise Service Bus [741]. The WCF Router implementation of this logic can be potentially considered a joint application of Protocol Bridging [764] with Intermediate Routing [748], as the bridging-related processing is carried out as a result of routing logic.

The following example shows two identified target service endpoints defined within the `client` element construct:

```
<client>
  <endpoint
    address="http://server1.example.org/Customers.svc"
    binding="basicHttpBinding"
    contract="*"
    name="CustomerService1" />
  <endpoint
    address="http://server2.example.org/Customers.svc"
    binding="basicHttpBinding"
    contract="*"
    name="CustomerService2" />
</client>
```

Example 6.11

Step 4: Define Message Filters

Next, message filter criteria need to be defined for routing services in the service host. In this example, the `prefix` attribute of the `add` element defines the prefix for the custom XML namespace referenced in XPath expressions, which are used to express the filter criteria:

```
<routing>
  <namespaceTable>
    <add prefix="my" namespace=
      "http://services.example.org/names"/>
  </namespaceTable>
  <filters>
    <filter name="CategoryFilter1" filterType="XPath"
      filterData="/s12:Envelope/s12:Header/
        my:MsgCategory = 1" />
    <filter name="CategoryFilter2" filterType="XPath"
      filterData="/s12:Envelope/s12:Header/
        my:MsgCategory = 2" />
  </filters>
</routing>
```

Example 6.12

Table 6.6 lists the filter types available in .NET 4.0, each of which can be used to define different matching behavior.

Filter Type	Matching Criteria
`Action`	matches a specific SOAP action
`XPath`	evaluates an XPath expression against the entire message (header and body)
`EndpointAddress`	matches the endpoint address (hostname matching is optional)
`EndpointAddressPrefix`	matches the endpoint address against a specified prefix (hostname matching is optional)
`EndpointName`	matches against the name of the endpoint receiving the message
`MatchAll`	matches all incoming messages
`Custom`	defines custom filter types based on the `MessageFilter` class
`And`	combines two filters into one new filter

Table 6.6
Filter types to define different matching behaviors.

Step 5: Create a Filter Table

Group the filters applied by a service instance using the `filterTable` element, as shown here:

```
<routing>
  <filters>
    ...
  </filters>
  <filterTables>
    <filterTable name="routingRules">
      <add filterName=" CategoryFilter1"
        endpointName="CustomerService1"/>
      <add filterName=" CategoryFilter2"
        endpointName="CustomerService2"/>
    </filterTable>
  </filterTables>
</routing>
```

Example 6.13

The routing service is now able to match any incoming message against these filters and can then forward each message to target service endpoints with matching criteria.

> **NOTE**
>
> The routing service can change its filter configuration without restarting the service when you pass a new set of `RoutingConfiguration` parameters to `RoutingExtension` in the service host. A new configuration cannot be applied by changing the configuration file.

Fault Tolerance

Service consumers often need to implement logic to deal with fluctuating service availability. This can be undesirable because it can lead to uncontrolled duplication, but more importantly, inconsistent handling of various error types. The involvement of intermediary logic within the routing service provides an opportunity to handle service availability problems transparently to service consumers. For example, the routing service can determine whether to route messages to alternate destinations when a preferred destination service endpoint is not available or too slow to respond.

Alternate destination endpoints can be identified as *backup lists* in the configuration file or programmatically, as follows:

```
<routing>
  <backupLists>
    <backupList name="CustomerServiceBackups">
      <add endpointName="CustomerService2" />
      <add endpointName="CustomerService3" />
    </backupList>
  </backupLists>
</routing>
```

Example 6.14

The next example shows a filter rule that references the backup list defined in Example 6.14:

```
<routing>
  <filterTables>
    <filterTable name="filterTable1">
      <add filterName="CategoryFilter1"
        endpointName="CustomerService1"
```

```
          backupList="CustomerServiceBackups"/>
      </filterTable>
    </filterTables>
</routing>
```

Example 6.15

The routing service transmits messages to a backup location when it receives a SOAP
Fault with a timeout exception or an exception derived from `CommunicationException`.
The service sequences through the backup list until it receives a response message or a
SOAP fault that does not indicate timeout or communication problems.

SUMMARY OF KEY POINTS

- The WCF Router provides intrinsic functionality for various types of runtime
  routing requirements by establishing a routing service that can be configured as an active or passive intermediary.

- The routing service can increase fault tolerance by routing traffic away from
  unavailable services transparently to the service consumer and through the
  use of backup lists.

- Routing rules can be based on message content or target service endpoint
  information.

6.4 WCF Discovery

WS-Discovery is a multicast protocol used to discover services within a network. It provides a standardized means of discovering services at runtime by allowing services to
locate other services using UDP multicast messages or via a discovery proxy.

To find a target service, a service consumer sends a probe message to a multicast group.
Target services that match the probe then send responses directly to the service consumer informing it of their existence. A service consumer can also look for endpoint
address changes if a service's network location changed.

Version 4.0 of the .NET framework introduced the WCF Discovery extension, a mechanism based on the WS-Discovery industry standard. It enables service redundancy,
dynamic load balancing, and even fault tolerance (where if one service fails to respond,
another service that satisfies the criteria can be dynamically located).

Being able to discover services dynamically simplifies the maintenance of service dependencies and increases the overall robustness of a service inventory because an alternative to a failed or unavailable service can quickly be located without explicit reconfiguration steps. Dynamic discovery and announcements can also be necessary in highly dynamic scenarios, such as in a dynamic cloud environment where new service instances go online or offline, depending on current usage patterns.

> **NOTE**
>
> To view the WS-Discovery specification, visit www.soaspecs.com.

Discovery Modes

WCF supports two discovery modes: ad hoc and managed:

- *Ad hoc discovery* allows services to locate other services on their local subnet and announce their availability when they go online or offline. Each service on the network can receive and respond to multicast discovery queries for targeted discovery needs.

- *Managed discovery* introduces a dedicated discovery proxy into the environment. This proxy manages service availability information and responds to discovery queries to reduce the overall network traffic related to discovery announcements and queries and further allows for the discovery of services available outside the local subnet.

All classes related to the WS-Discovery protocol are encapsulated in the `System.ServiceModel.Discovery` library.

A service can respond to probe messages by adding a well-known endpoint and service behavior to manage the endpoint. As it is standard practice in WCF, both can be set programmatically or via configuration files.

The UDP endpoint is a standard WCF endpoint. The next example shows the `endpoint` element adding a discovery endpoint. Specifically, the `kind` attribute (introduced with .NET 4.0) is used to identify the standard endpoints:

```
<services>
  <service name="Example.Services.CustomerService"
    behaviorConfiguration="DiscoveryBehavior">

    ... service application endpoint ...
```

```
    <endpoint
      name="udpDiscoveryEpt"
      kind="udpDiscoveryEndpoint" />
  </service>
</services>
```

Example 6.16

Note that standard endpoints are configured machine-wide in the Machine.Config file. You can override the configuration in the Web.Config file, if necessary.

WCF 4.0 includes a service behavior to manage probe requests received on the discovery endpoint. This behavior is added to the service's configuration, as shown here:

```
<behaviors>
  <serviceBehaviors>
    <behavior name="DiscoveryBehavior">
      <serviceDiscovery />
    </behavior>
  </serviceBehaviors>
</behaviors>
```

Example 6.17

A probe request includes a number of "find" criteria, a service contract, or a service's URL scope. If a service matches all the find criteria, it responds with a `FindMatch` response containing its location, the matching criteria, and available metadata.

The probing service can retrieve the metadata from the response and evaluate it to determine how to handle the discovered service.

Shown here is an endpoint configuration with custom discovery metadata:

```
<endpoint
  address=""
  binding="basicHttpBinding"
  contract="ICustomerService"
  behaviorConfiguration="CustomMetadataBehavior" />
<endpointBehaviors>
  <behavior name="CustomMetadataBehavior">
    <endpointDiscovery enabled="true">
      <extensions>
```

```
        <MyCustomMetadata>Highly Scalable</MyCustomMetadata>
      </extensions>
    </endpointDiscovery>
  </behavior>
</endpointBehaviors>
```

Example 6.18

Locating a Service Ad Hoc

A service consumer can send out WS-Discovery probe messages to locate available services. The probe query can include compatibility criteria, such as a service contract or a service scope. Query parameters are encoded in a `FindCriteria` object.

There are two types of query criteria:

- *contract type names* – searches for services with endpoints that implement the specified contract names

- *scope* – searches for services with endpoints that match the specified scope (scopes are defined in the endpoint's behavior and several matching options for complete or partial matches exist)

The `DiscoveryClient` class provided by WCF manages probes and raises `FindProgressChangedEventArgs` events when `ProbeMatch` responses come in:

```
discoveryClient =
  new DiscoveryClient(new UdpDiscoveryEndpoint());
discoveryClient.FindProgressChanged +=
  new EventHandler<FindProgressChangedEventArgs>
  (OnFindProgressChanged);
discoveryClient.FindCompleted +=
  new EventHandler<FindCompletedEventArgs>
  (OnFindCompleted);
discoveryClient.FindAsync
  (new FindCriteria(typeof(ICustomerService)),
    discoveryClient);
```

Following this, we are submitting an asynchronous discovery query over UDP. `ParseResult` examines the service contract, scope, and metadata to determine if the responding service meets the requirements:

```
private void OnFindProgressChanged(
  object sender, FindProgressChangedEventArgs e)
{
  ParseResult(e.EndpointDiscoveryMetadata);
}
```

Example 6.19

The `DiscoveryClient` class also implements a synchronous `Find()` method that takes a `FindCriteria` parameter that specifies query and query completion criteria, such as the number of responses or the time to wait for responses.

`DiscoveryClient` also exposes a `Resolve()` method to locate a replacement for a service that's been previously available at a known address. Calling `Resolve()` follows the same pattern as `Find()`.

Sending and Receiving Service Announcements

Services can announce their availability when they come online or go offline. These announcements can be received by all services listening for them. You configure a service to transmit announcements by adding `announcementEndpoints` to the `serviceDiscovery` behavior, as shown in Example 6.20. The service then issues announcements to the configured endpoint.

```
<behavior name="DiscoveryBehavior">
  <serviceDiscovery>
    <announcementEndpoints>
      <endpoint name="udpEndpointName"
        kind="udpAnnouncementEndpoint"/>
    </announcementEndpoints>
  </serviceDiscovery>
</behavior>
```

Example 6.20

The standard `udpAnnouncementEndpoint` is preconfigured in WCF. Each announcement includes the service endpoint location and contract, as well as endpoint-specific metadata.

In highly dynamic environments, service consumers may want to track available services instead of probing for availability or relying on the discovery proxy. Probing introduces additional latency and therefore should not occur as part of the logic that resolves service locations. Frequent multicast probing further results in unnecessary network traffic. Instead, a consumer of dynamically available services can listen for announcement broadcasts and maintain its own list of services.

Services interested in receiving local UDP discovery announcements must open up a listener on the `udpAnnouncementEndpoint` endpoint. WCF provides a pre-built `AnnouncementService` class to handle service announcements. This class can raise the `OnOnlineAnnouncement` and `OnOfflineAnnouncement` events to the hosting application.

This example shows a listener configured for announcement services:

```
<services>
    ... application service information ...

  <service name="AnnouncementListener">
    <endpoint kind="udpAnnouncementEndpoint" />
  </service>
</services>
```

Example 6.21

Next, we register events with `AnnouncementService`:

```
AnnouncementService announcementService =
  new AnnouncementService();
announcementService.OnlineAnnouncementReceived +=
  new EventHandler<AnnouncementEventArgs>
    (this.OnOnlineAnnouncement);
announcementService.OfflineAnnouncementReceived +=
  new EventHandler<AnnouncementEventArgs>
    (this.OnOfflineAnnouncement);
```

Example 6.22

The events receive an `EndpointDiscoveryMetadata` object, just like the response to a discovery probe. A `FindCriteria` object determines if the metadata matches endpoint requirements. In the following example, we query an `EndpointDiscoveryMetadata` announcement for compatibility with the `ICustomerService` contract:

```
private void OnlineAnnouncement
  (object sender, AnnouncementEventArgs e)
{
  EndpointDiscoveryMetadata metadata =
    e.EndpointDiscoveryMetadata;
```

```
FindCriteria criteria =
  new FindCriteria(typeof(ICustomerService));
if (criteria.IsMatch(metadata))
{
  ... further examine endpoint metadata ...
  ... store endpoint address for service access ...
}
```

Example 6.23

Discovery Proxies for Managed Discovery

Ad hoc discovery is a suitable approach for static and smaller local service networks, where all services live on the same subnet and multicasting probes or announcements don't add a lot of network chatter.

Larger environments, with services distributed across multiple subnets (or highly dynamic networks), need to consider a *Discovery Proxy* to overcome the limitations of ad hoc probing. A Discovery Proxy can listen to UDP announcements on the standard udpAnnouncementEndpoint for service registration and de-registration, but also expose DiscoveryEndpoint via a WCF SOAP binding.

The implementation requirements for a Discovery Proxy can vary from a simple implementation that keeps an in-memory cache of available services, to implementations that require databases or scale-out solutions, like caching extensions provided by Windows Server AppFabric. WCF provides a DiscoveryProxy base class that can be used for general proxy implementations.

Discovering from a Discovery Proxy

Discovering services registered with a Discovery Proxy follows the steps for ad hoc discovery discussed earlier. Instead of multicasting a UDP message, DiscoveryClient now needs to contact the Discovery Proxy. Details about the discovery contract are encapsulated in the DiscoveryEndpoint class. Its constructor only takes parameters for the communication protocol details, binding, and address.

Here we are configuring a discovery client to query the Discover Proxy:

```
DiscoveryEndpoint proxyEndpoint =
  new DiscoveryEndpoint(
  new NetTcpBinding(),
  new EndpointAddress(proxyAddressText.Text));
this.discoveryClient = new DiscoveryClient(proxyEndpoint);
```

Example 6.24

Implicit Service Discovery

Our coverage of WCF Discovery so far has focused on the explicit discovery of services. However, it is worth noting that WCF Discovery can also perform the same queries behind-the-scenes, when you configure endpoints as `DynamicEndpoint` programmatically or in the configuration file. This allows for highly dynamic, adaptive environments where virtually no location-specific details are maintained as part of code or configuration.

A client endpoint, for example, can be configured to locate a service that matches on scope and contract. In the following example, we configure `DynamicEndpoint` to locate a service with matching contract and metadata:

> **SOA PRINCIPLES & PATTERNS**
>
> The consistent application of the Service Discoverability (702) principle is vital for WCF Discovery features to be succesfully applied across a service inventory, especially in regard to managed discovery. The application of Canonical Expression [715] ties directly to the definition and expression of any published service metadata. And, of course, Metadata Centralization [754] represents the effective incorporation of a service registry as a central discovery mechanism.

```
<client>
  <endpoint kind="dynamicEndpoint"
    binding="basicHttpBinding"
    contract="ICustomerService"
    endpointConfiguration="dynamicEndpointConfiguration"
    name="dynamicCustomerEndpoint" />
</client>
<standardEndpoints>
  <dynamicEndpoint>
    <standardEndpoint name="dynamicEndpointConfiguration">
      <discoveryClientSettings>
        <findCriteria duration="00:00:05" maxResults="1">
          <types>
            <add name="ICustomerService"/>
          </types>
          <extensions>
            <MyCustomMetadata>
              Highly Scalable
            </MyCustomMetadata>
          </extensions>
        </findCriteria>
      </discoveryClientSettings>
    </standardEndpoint>
  </dynamicEndpoint>
</standardEndpoints>
```

Example 6.25

With this configuration, the service consumer can create a proxy object to the server with the following code:

```
ICustomerService svc =
  new ChannelFactory<ICustomerService>
    ("dynamicCustomerEndpoint").CreateChannel();
```

Example 6.26

SUMMARY OF KEY POINTS

- WCF Discovery enables ad hoc and managed discovery and service address resolution together with support for the WS-Discovery industry standard.

- With WCF Discovery, services can announce their availability via UDP broadcasts.

- A Discovery Proxy can provide discoverability across subnets and `DynamicEndpoint` provides a programming model that abstracts the details of the discovery process.

6.5 WCF Extensibility

The WCF platform provides built-in support for a range of distributed communication protocols, including transport and message encoding protocols using *channel bindings*.

Available channel bindings include:

- protocol channel bindings that determine security, reliability and context flow settings

- transport channel bindings that determine the underlying transport protocol (including TCP and HTTP)

- message encoding bindings that determine the encoding at the wire (including text/XML, binary, and MTOM)

Although these default channel bindings will cover common communication scenarios, there may be certain requirements that can only be accommodated via further customization. For this purpose, WCF provides an extensibility model with several extension points.

Before we explore the extensibility model, we first need to establish how WCF can be represented with two fundamental architectural layers.

WCF Layers

As shown in Figure 6.1, WCF is partitioned into two main layers: the service model layer and the channel layer.

The service model layer essentially provides a programming model that enables solutions to use WCF. For example, all the information about user-defined service contracts is found in this layer.

Underneath the service model layer is a shared message layer used as the transport and also known as the channel layer. The channel layer provides several communication channels and is also known as the *channel stack*. Addresses and bindings defined in the service model layer provide the mechanisms used to control the channel stack. Bindings define the transport and addresses define the destinations of messages.

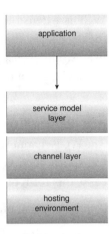

Figure 6.1
WCF includes the service model layer and the channel layer.

Layered Extensibility

Figure 6.2 further expands on the layered view by illustrating how the proxy and dispatcher relate to the service model layer and represent touch points for services. You'll notice that underneath the proxy and dispatcher are the protocol and transport channel stacks. The protocol channels are used to process SOAP messages, add security, and add and remove headers, whereas the transport channels are used to send and receive messages.

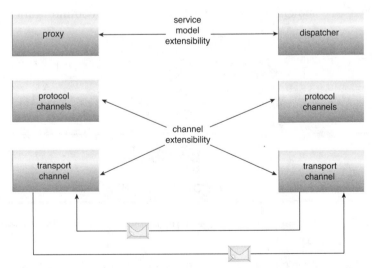

Figure 6.2
WCF can be extended at the service model layer and channel layer.

WCF is extensible at the service model layer and at the channel layer. If you need to make changes that affect service behavior, then you need to ensure that service model extensibility is used. If the requirement affects changes to the message at the wire level, channel layer extensibility is used.

Channel Layer Extensibility

The WCF channel extensibility model can be used to extend channels for non-supported transports such as UDP and SMTP or other custom and proprietary transports. Specifically, this form of extensibility at the channel layer allows for:

- the creation of new transports

- integration with incompatible and proprietary systems

- implementation of custom infrastructure protocols

The ability to create and extend WCF with new transports can be used to simplify integration between incompatible systems. For example, WCF channels can be customized to talk RMI on the wire in order to integrate with a Java application. Channel layer extensibility also allows for the creation of custom infrastructure channels, such as proprietary SOAP-level compression.

In the next example, the address, binding and contract are set and associated with a host. The binding indicates the runtime is going to construct a channel stack optimized for TCP with binary as the message encoding for efficient message transfer. The `host.Open();` statement invokes channels and channel listeners to enable communication.

```
ServiceHost host = new ServiceHost(typeof(MyService));
Uri address = new Uri("net.tcp://temp/service/endpoint");
Binding binding = new NetTcpBinding();
Type contract = typeof(IContract);
host.AddEndpoint(address, binding, contract);
host.Open();
```

Example 6.27

SUMMARY OF KEY POINTS

- WCF has built-in support for a range of protocols, and further allows these protocols to be extended.

- The WCF platform can be split into the service model layer and the channel model layer, both of which can be extended.

6.6 WCF Management Tools

Deployed services need to be tuned for performance, managed, and administered in order to meet SLA requirements. Service custodians are typically responsible for managing services through these post-implementation lifecycles.

Administration

Address and binding information are decoupled from a service and stored in the application configuration file. Setting up and maintaining these settings is typically an administrative task. WCF provides two types of related APIs:

- tools that allow the administrator to examine and manipulate the points and control points exposed by WCF

- instrumentation functions that expose these data points and control points

By default, WCF installs several granular performance counters that capture metrics at the service level, operation level, and service endpoint level. These performance counters are extensible, allowing for the creation of custom variations.

All management tools for Windows, including IBM Tivoli, Microsoft MOM, and HP OpenView, work through Windows Management Instrumentation (WMI). WCF includes a WMI provider. Administrators need to switch on this WMI provider for the service in the configuration file in order to make the service visible in the management tool. The management tool then allows you to examine which services are running and query exposed endpoints.

Troubleshooting

WCF provides tracing support, which can facilitate message tracking and general debugging. Tracing metrics rely on application instrumentation and diagnostics data used for fault monitoring. WCF traces can also be used across all services within a given service composition in order to provide an end-to-end view of message paths.

When tracing is enabled, WCF emits data for operation calls, exceptions, and other significant processing events across all services. WCF tracing is based on the use of `System.Diagnostics` for which we need to define trace listeners in the configuration file. This form of tracing is not enabled by default, and requires that a trace listener be created in the application's configuration file, as shown here:

```
<system.diagnostics>
  <sources>
    <source name="System.IO.Log" switchValue="Verbose">
      <listeners>
        <add name="xmlListener"
          type="System.Diagnostics.XmlWriterTraceListener"
          initializeData= "c:\traceLogs\" />
      </listeners>
    </source>
  </sources>
</system.diagnostics>
```

Example 6.28

In the preceding example, the `XmlWriterTracelListener` is used to emit XML. Since the trace output is an XML file, the location where the XML file must be deposited is specified using the `initializeData` setting. Each source can have any number of listeners associated with it.

The `switchValue` setting controls the trace level, which is the level of detail for messages emitted to the listener. Trace levels available in WCF are listed in Table 6.7.

Trace Level	Level of Detail
off	no data is emitted
critical	only unhandled exceptions that result in stopping the application are logged
error	all exceptions are logged even if the service is up and running
warning	a problem occurred or may occur but the service is up and functioning correctly
information	all important and successful events are logged
verbose	all successful events are logged

Table 6.7
A list of WCF trace levels.

Logging Messages

Messages passed between the services and their consumers are not logged automatically. Message logging must be enabled in the configuration file and, similar to the trace listeners, message logging also requires that a listener be created, as follows:

```
<system.diagnostics>
  <sources>
    <source name="System.ServiceModel.MessageLogging">
      <listeners>
        <add name="LogMessages"
          type="System.Diagnostics.XmlWriterTraceListener"
            initializeData="c:\logs\messages" />
      </listeners>
    </source>
  </sources>
</system.diagnostics>
```

Example 6.29

This listener logs all messages as text to the folder `c:\logs\messages`. The following `messageLogging` setting is used to filter and manage logged messages.

```
<diagnostics>
  <messageLogging
    logEntireMessage="true"
    logMalformedMessages="true"
    logMessagesAtServiceLevel="true"
    logMessagesAtTransportLevel="true"
    maxMessagesToLog="300"
    maxSizeOfMessageToLog="200" />
</diagnostics>
```

Example 6.30

SUMMARY OF KEY POINTS

- WCF includes a WMI provider that can be turned on to enable management tools.

- WCF builds on `System.Diagnostics` to log trace data and introduces listeners for tracing and message logging.

> **NOTE**
>
> The focus of this book is on the design and development of services and service-oriented solutions. This introductory section is further supplemented by the business activity monitoring coverage in Chapter 20. Beyond that, post-implementation governance topics are not covered in depth.

Chapter 7

.NET Enterprise Services Technologies

7.1 SQL Server

7.2 Windows Workflow Foundation (WF)

7.3 Application Blocks and Software Factories

7.4 Windows Server AppFabric

7.5 BizTalk Server

WCF establishes a foundation that provides a service runtime environment with many APIs and extensions. The .NET framework provides several additional building blocks (collectively known as .NET Enterprise Services) that can leverage WCF to further expand the range of features and functionality for creating a service-oriented eco-system.

This chapter focuses on several of these building blocks, namely:

- SQL Server

- Windows Workflow Foundation (WF)

- Application Blocks and Software Factories

- Windows Server AppFabric

- BizTalk Server

These products and technologies are covered as part of the introductory content in this book because they will be referenced in relation to further topics in subsequent chapters.

NOTE
Another .NET Enterprise Services building block is Windows Identity Foundation (WIF), which is covered in Chapter 17.

7.1 SQL Server

SQL Server 2005 and 2008 extend core database functionality to include analysis, reporting, integration, replication, and notification services. SQL Server databases can play a significant role in the design of service-oriented solutions due to the many ways they can support cross-service loose coupling and state management deferral.

Some of the primary SQL Server technologies and features most relevant to service-oriented solution design include:

- Native XML Web Services

- Service Broker

- Query Notification Services

- SQL CLR integration

Additionally, SQL Server's native support for XML directly facilitates the XML-based SOAP messaging framework provided natively by WCF.

Native XML Web Services Support

Web service technologies and industry standards compliance are intrinsic to SQL Server and can be leveraged in many different ways. Provided here is a list of characteristics and features that describe different aspects of Web service support and are directly relevant to service-oriented solution architecture:

- SQL Server can expose Web service contracts based on WSDL, SOAP, and WS-Security.

- SQL Server can receive data via XML and SOAP messages in addition to traditional persistent binary connections.

- SQL Server Web service access is built on top of the Microsoft Windows Server HTTP kernel-mode driver (`Http.sys`).

- SQL Server has the ability to process and transform SOAP messages into native formats used by internal database components, such as stored procedures.

- SQL Server provides a runtime environment to host service endpoints.

- SQL Server provides application pooling and other activation logic.

- The ability to host a service endpoint within SQL Server is supported, thereby leveraging other features, such as transactions, data management, and security.

- SQL Server provides a separate Service Broker, which includes a tightly integrated messaging feature that receives, processes, and sends messages reliably.

- SQL Server databases are event-driven, allowing you to raise events based on changes taking place in the data.

- SQL Query is provided by SQL Server as a means of notification that enables data-dependent caches to be notified when an underlying database has changed.

- SQL CLR integrates the .NET CLR into databases, allowing automation logic to be written in C# or VB.NET and processed directly inside SQL Server (thereby reducing latencies due to remote data access).

- SQL Server allows you to mark a stored procedure or a scalar value function as a Web service and program against it using SOAP-compliant clients. This approach is well-suited for developing entity and utility services.

A Web service hosted in SQL Server maps directly to a stored procedure or a function. In this example we create such a stored procedure:

```
CREATE PROC dbo.GetCustomersProc
AS
  SELECT
    FirstName,LastName
  FROM
    dbo.Customers
```

Example 7.1

SQL Server 2005 introduced the new CREATE ENDPOINT statement to create HTTP and TCP endpoints, which continues to be supported in SQL Server 2008. The next code sample creates an endpoint called Customers that maps to the dbo.GetCustomersProc stored procedure:

```
http://localhost/Customers?wsdl.
CREATE ENDPOINT Customers
  STATE = STARTED
AS HTTP
(
  PATH = '/Customers',
  AUTHENTICATION = (INTEGRATED),
  PORTS = (CLEAR),
  SITE = 'localhost'
)
FOR SOAP
(
  WEBMETHOD 'GetCustomers'
    (NAME='SQLWS.dbo.GetCustomersProc'),
  BATCHES = DISABLED,
  WSDL = DEFAULT,
  DATABASE = 'SQLWS',
  NAMESPACE = 'http://example.org/samples'
)
GO
```

Example 7.2

The CREATE ENDPOINT statement has several possible arguments, as explained in Table 7.1.

Argument	Description
STATE	specifies if the initial state of the endpoint is started or stopped
AS HTTP	the transport protocol to use (TCP or HTTP)
PATH	the URL the service consumer will use to reach the service
AUTHENTICATION	how clients will be authenticated (supported options include BASIC, DIGEST, NTLM, KERBEROS, and INTEGRATED)
PORTS	specifies whether the client will listen on SSL or CLEAR text
SITE	the host name of the computer
FOR SOAP	specifies whether the endpoint uses SOAP messaging
WEBMETHOD	used to map a Web method to an underlying stored procedure or function
WSDL	specifies whether WSDL generation is supported for the endpoint
DATABASE	the database that contains the stored procedure and data
NAMESPACE	the XML namespace for the message

Table 7.1
Arguments supporting the CREATE ENDPOINT statement.

SQL Server endpoints support basic, digest, integrated (NTLM or Kerberos), and regular SQL Server authentication in addition to WS-Security, which allows security tokens to be passed using the username token headers for authentication. SQL Server endpoints are off by default and need to be explicitly enabled using the GRANT CONNECT statement. Channels can be secured with SSL using the PORTS argument listed in Table 7.1.

SQL Server Native Web Services support is tightly integrated with the Windows Server Kernel-mode HTTP listener as shown in Figure 7.1. This precludes the need for IIS to be installed and managed on the server.

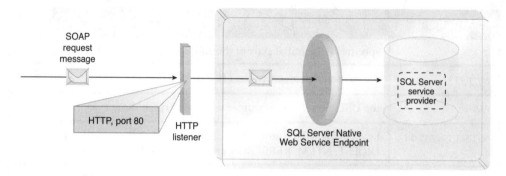

Figure 7.1

The HTTP listener receives the request over port 80 and directs the request to the endpoint defined within SQL Server.

Endpoints created can be listed by querying the catalog view. All endpoints created can be queried using the following SQL statement:

```
SELECT * FROM sys.endpoints;
```

Endpoints that specifically use HTTP for transport can be accessed using the SQL statement:

```
SELECT * FROM sys.http_endpoints;
```

SOAP methods and the associated database objects can be accessed using the following SQL statement:

```
SELECT * FROM sys.endpoint_webmethods;
```

Service Broker (SSB)

SSB is a messaging extension that integrates reliable message processing functionality with SQL Server databases and is primarily useful when service compositions rely on the guaranteed delivery of ordered messages. Messages sent using SSB are durable, which ensures that if message processing logic fails (or the system itself fails), the message survives and is placed back into the receive queue.

> **SOA PRINCIPLES & PATTERNS**
>
> The .NET Service Broker (SSB) should not be confused with the Service Broker [771] compound pattern. As explained shortly, SSB can actually be considered an application of Reliable Messaging [767], whereas Service Broker [771] is primarily concerned with the runtime transformation of messages in order to overcome consumer-service disparity.

Essentially, when messages are sent to service endpoints, services place them in a queue from where they are picked up and processed. Each message is processed by an internal service program (typically a stored procedure), as shown in Figure 7.2.

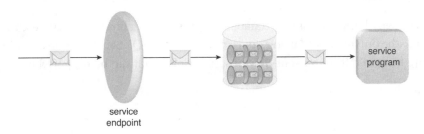

Figure 7.2
The message travels from the service endpoint to the queue and then to the service program.

SSB can be configured so that multiple instances of the service program can be used to process incoming messages. The queue is a database table and therefore leverages all the reliability features in SQL Server, such as recovery in the event of a database failure and guaranteed delivery to the queue using database transactions.

In addition to performing standard request-response message exchanges, SSB also handles correlation and concurrency of messages between the services and consumers. It introduces *dialogs*, which are bidirectional streams of messages between two endpoints. All messages in a dialog are sent in order, and the order is maintained across input threads and machine restarts. Each message includes a conversation handle to identify the dialog.

To avoid any concurrency issues, SSB provides a way of grouping dialogs used for a specific task via *conversation groups*. A conversation group is implemented with a *conversation group identifier* included with all messages in all dialogs contained in the conversation group. When a message is received from any of the dialogs in a conversation group, the group is locked and the lock is held by the receiving transaction. This allows services to be resilient to problems that are caused by simultaneous processing of a single message.

Message types are grouped into contracts and are used to describe all the messages received by a specific dialog. Contracts are grouped together to form a service. A service represents the dialogs required to process messages, and it can be associated with one or more queues.

The result of implementing a service endpoint with SQL Server is that the service logic is much more closely bound to the data. This makes it possible to natively trigger events within the logic as a result of data changes because the service logic is bound to query notifications and events.

When changes happen inside a database, notifications about the change can also be pushed to the outside world using query notifications. SQL Server has an eventing infrastructure built into it with event-driven service logic that can be triggered by:

- data changes

- message arrival

- timer firing (triggers the service logic at the end of an interval to execute and do something)

SSB complements the Native XML Web Services implementation in SQL Server. A service endpoint implemented in SQL Server using Native XML Web Services can be augmented using SSB to make the endpoint implementation reliable and scalable.

The upcoming code examples show the interaction between messages, services, and queues based on the simple scenario depicted in Figure 7.3.

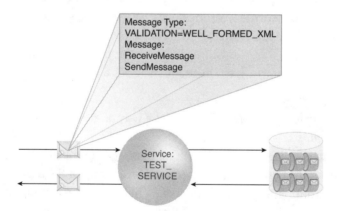

Figure 7.3
Interaction between messages, services, and queues in Service Broker.

In order to work with SSB, it must be enabled using the ALTER DATABASE command:

```
ALTER DATABASE databasename SET ENABLE_BROKER
```

A stored procedure must be created to encapsulate the service logic required to process a message:

```
CREATE PROCEDURE ProcessMessage
AS
BEGIN
  SET NOCOUNT ON;
  -- Process Logic
END
```

Example 7.3

A message is subsequently created with validation type WELL_FORMED_XML (a statement that allows well-formed XML messages to be processed):

```
CREATE MESSAGE TYPE ReceiveMessage
  VALIDATION = WELL_FORMED_XML;
CREATE MESSAGE TYPE SendMessage
  VALIDATION = WELL_FORMED_XML;
```

Example 7.4

Here we create a contract for the message:

```
CREATE CONTRACT [MessageContract]
(
  [SendMessage] SENT BY INITIATOR,
  [ReceiveMessage] SENT BY TARGET
)
```

Example 7.5

Next, a queue is associated with a stored procedure. The queue activates the stored procedure ProcessMessage when a message arrives:

```
CREATE QUEUE REQUEST_QUEUE
  WITH STATUS=ON,
  ACTIVATION
  (
    PROCEDURE_NAME = ProcessMessage,
    MAX_QUEUE_READERS = 3,
    EXECUTE AS SELF
  );
CREATE QUEUE RESPONSE_QUEUE
```

Example 7.6

Each service exists as an endpoint in SSB, so to create a service we need to use the queue MESSAGE_QUEUE and associate it to the message contract MessageContract.

This service will only accept messages that conform to MessageContract:

```
CREATE SERVICE REQUEST_SERVICE
  ON QUEUE [REQUEST_QUEUE]
  (
    [MessageContract]
  );
CREATE SERVICE RESPONSE_SERVICE
  ON QUEUE [RESPONSE_QUEUE]
  (
    [MessageContract]
  );
```

Example 7.7

At this point, all the necessary SSB objects have been created and can be used in queuing solutions. This next example shows how messages can be sent to the REQUEST_QUEUE queue:

```
DECLARE @RequestDialog UNIQUEIDENTIFIER
BEGIN TRANSACTION
BEGIN DIALOG @RequestDialog
  FROM SERVICE RESPONSE_SERVICE
  TO SERVICE 'REQUEST_SERVICE'
  ON CONTRACT MessageContract
  WITH LIFETIME = 1000;
SEND ON CONVERSATION @RequestDialog
  MESSAGE TYPE SendMessage (N'My Request Message');
SEND ON CONVERSATION @RequestDialog
  MESSAGE TYPE SendMessage (N'My Request Message 2');
COMMIT TRANSACTION
```

Example 7.8

The listing starts with creating a unique identifier that will be assigned to the dialog. The BEGIN DIALOG statement is used to open a new dialog with SSB. The FROM SERVICE statement identifies the initiator of the messages, while the TO SERVICE statement identifies the target. The SEND statement sends messages, which are received by the target service and added to the queue.

Query Notification

Query Notification solves the problem of having to poll a database to get updated data. With Query Notification, SQL Server can notify .NET routines when any data manipulation language (DML) operations, such as insert, update, or delete are invoked (which are performed on specified database tables).

SOA PRINCIPLES & PATTERNS
The functionality provided by Query Notification is comparable to messaging exchange mechanisms that result from the application of Event-Driven Messaging [743].

As shown in the following example, the notification cycle starts from .NET 2.0 applications using the `SqlDependency` class in `System.Data.SqlClient` namespace. `SqlDependency` object takes `SQLCommand` object as the parameter. When the data changes, SQL Server raises an event that invokes the `GetNotified` method.

```
SqlConnection conn = new SqlConnection
  (DBConnectionString);
SqlCommand cmd = new SqlCommand
  ("SELECT FirstName,LastName FROM dbo.Customers", conn);
SqlDependency depend = new SqlDependency(cmd);
SqlDependency.Start(DBConnectionString);
depend.OnChange += new OnChangeEventHandler
  (GetNotified);
static void GetNotified(object caller,
  SqlNotificationEventArgs e)
{
  string msg = "Notified Received";
}
```

Example 7.9

XML Support in SQL Server

SQL Server 2005 includes a native data type called XML. The XML data type supports both typed and untyped XML and a table can contain one or more columns of type XML in addition to relational columns. The XML data types can be queried using XQuery, which includes XPath 2.0 for navigating the XML document and a language for modifying XML data. Besides XQuery, T-SQL includes support for transforming data between XML and relational format seamlessly using FOR XML and OPENXML.

XML documents are stored as BLOBs in order to support XML characteristics such as recursive processing. SQL Server includes an XML schema collection to persist schemas in the database. The XML data type can be linked to an XML schema in the collection to enforce schema constraints on XML instances.

Indexes play an important role in optimizing relational tables for searches. SQL Server extends the concept of indexes to XML documents. Very large XML documents can be indexed using a primary XML index on an XML column. The primary XML index provides efficient evaluation of queries on XML data.

SUMMARY OF KEY POINTS

- SQL Server extensions include Native XML Web Services, Service Broker (SSB), and deep support for XML at the database level.

- Native XML Web Services can be used to expose stored procedures and user-defined functions in a database as a Web service, allowing SQL Server to act as a service by creating and hosting endpoints.

- SQL Server Query Notification enables applications to request a notification from SQL Server when the result of a query changes. Query notifications also allow an application to rely on cached data until the data changes.

- SQL Server includes extensive support for processing XML documents including the ability to query, parse, transform, index, and generate XML documents.

7.2 Windows Workflow Foundation (WF)

It is generally possible to describe a business process as a workflow comprised of a discrete series of steps that involves people and software. WF is a Windows platform specifically for workflow technology (Figure 7.4). At its core, WF enables the execution of steps required to complete a business process. It is used to construct workflow-enabled services and service compositions for which it provides the following:

- an extensible programming model

- a workflow engine

- design tools for Visual Studio

- a mechanism to invoke services and to publish workflows as services

WF technology is applicable to document-centric workflows, human workflows, business rules-driven workflows, and other variations. It is used to enable both human and automated workflow steps and to wire up opaque blocks of functionality called activities.

WF Architecture

The major parts of the WF platform (Figure 7.4) include workflow, activities, the WF base activity library, the WF runtime engine, and WF runtime services. Each part is further explained in Figure 7.5 and Table 7.2.

Figure 7.4

Windows Workflow Foundation (WF) as a building block of the .NET framework.

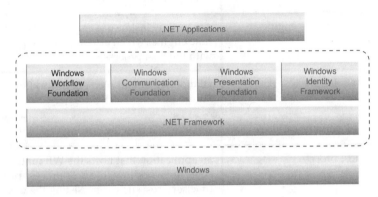

Figure 7.5

The major moving parts of the WF platform.

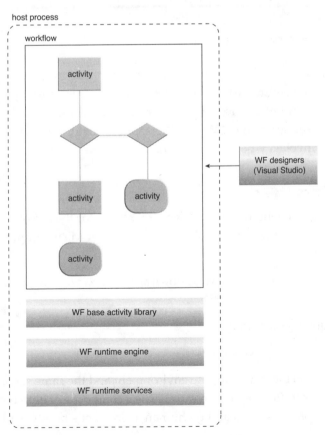

Part	Description
activity	a unit of work or a discrete step in a business process
workflow	a sequence of activities
WF runtime engine	a workflow instance is created and executed by the WF runtime engine (which also manages state and communication with the host process)
WF designers	UI tools used to implement a workflow using shapes (Visual Studio includes a WF designer)
WF runtime services	services that provide hosting flexibility and communication
host process	an application that hosts the WF runtime engine which executes the workflow (the host process provides support for runtime services, such as persisting the workflow's state)

Table 7.2
Descriptions of the major parts of WF.

WF runtime services are connection points for plug-in resource providers. For example, the default persistence behavior provided by the runtime engine can be changed by providing a runtime service. WF further supports compensating transactions for a given runtime service activity. Within the solution logic, WF can define actual *compensators* that are invoked when exceptions occur.

Workflows

A strategic benefit to using WF is that it allows for the use of a common workflow technology to build workflow solutions across other Microsoft products and .NET solution environments.

WF supports both system workflows and human workflows by supporting two built-in workflow types:

- sequential workflows
- state machine workflows

Both rely on the same runtime environment and the same set of standard WF activities. A single workflow definition can also be a composite of both types, containing activities that rely on the system and on human action. Let's briefly explore each workflow type a bit more.

Sequential Workflows

Sequential workflows execute activities in a pre-defined pattern. This workflow type is better suited for system workflows because the execution of activities closely resembles a flowchart with branches, decision logic, loops, and other control structures.

State Machine Workflows

State machine workflows execute activities as external events occur. This type (based on the well-known Finite State Machine) is better suited for workflows involving human intervention. The subsequent activity to be executed depends on the current state and the event it has received. State machine workflows are useful when the sequence of events is not known in advance or when the number of possibilities makes defining all possible paths impractical.

Workflow Designer

An advantage of creating applications using workflows is the ability to define the workflow graphically, which is why WF includes a designer for Visual Studio. By default, the activities appear in the toolbox, letting a developer drag and drop them onto the tool's design surface to create a workflow. The workflow designer is a convenient way to interact with the workflow namespace.

SOA PRINCIPLES & PATTERNS

By using WF, rather than embedding workflow routines into the core logic of individual services, each step in the business process is defined explicitly in a graphic designer and executed by the workflow engine. This corresponds directly to Process Centralization [763] together with additional patterns that co-exist to establish an environment as per the Orchestration [758] compound pattern.

The resulting level of separation can cleanly partition agnostic and non-agnostic logic allowing for the definition of reusable services that are independently maintainable. This is essentially the basis of Functional Decomposition [747], which is commonly further supplemented with the sequential application of Service Encapsulation [775], Agnostic Context [710], Non-Agnostic Context [756], and Agnostic Capability [709]. These foundational service patterns can be applied to form primitive service modeling and design processes that are initiated with well-defined workflow logic and carried out using WF tools, such as Workflow Designer (explained shortly).

Applying these patterns generally leads to the need to further define the functional contexts of services via Service Layers [779], such as those established by the application of the Utility Abstraction [791], Entity Abstraction [742], and Process Abstraction [762]. Agnostic utility and entity services that result from the application of the former two patterns need to be separated within or outside of WF in order to avoid unnecessary performance overhead and synchronization issues due to deployment-level dependencies on the orchestrated task service logic that encapsulates parent workflow routines.

Workflows created with the designer are stored in a file based on XAML, a declarative XML language used to define objects, their properties, relationships, and interactions. Upon execution, the runtime engine takes the XAML workflow and creates workflow instances. While there is only one XAML-based workflow file, there can be multiple workflow instances running at any given time.

The designer allows you to model a Sequential Workflow Console Application or a State Machine Workflow Console Application. After selecting the appropriate model you need to add activities by dragging and dropping them from the toolbar. (Note that the console application contains a sub main method that is used to start the workflow.)

Workflow Persistence (with WF)

Workflows can be dehydrated from memory and can later be re-hydrated and re-activated. WF supports dehydration of the instance state by allowing a workflow instance to be serialized to a data store, such as SQL Server. The workflow instance can be restored to the original execution state at any time by de-serializing the data based on events or messages.

The `SqlWorkflowPersistenceService` class in WF is designed to connect workflows with SQL Server. In order to use this persistence service, we need to create a database in SQL Server with the schema that the persistence service uses. WF comes with SQL scripts to create the database and schema used by the persistence service.

The database and schema scripts are typically placed in the following folder after installing WF:

…\Microsoft.NET\Framework\v3.0\Windows Workflow Foundation\SQL

The scripts provided by WF are `SqlPersistenceService_Schema.sql` and `SqlPersistenceService_Logic.sql`. The former defines the structure of the database and the latter defines the stored procedures.

The following example provides code that creates an instance of `SqlWorkflowPersistenceService` and an instance of the workflow runtime. The workflow runtime is used to generate an instance of Workflow1 by dehydrating it from the persistence database. The runtime starts the instance and the instance ID is stored in the ID property for later use. Finally, the workflow runtime stops and the state is de-serialized back to the database.

```
void Load()
{
  WorkflowRuntime workflowRuntime = new WorkflowRuntime();
  SqlWorkflowPersistenceService sqlPersistenceService =
    new SqlWorkflowPersistenceService(this.connectionString);
  workflowRuntime.AddService(sqlPersistenceService);
  workflowRuntime.StartRuntime();
  WorkflowInstance instance =
    workflowRuntime.CreateWorkflow(typeof
    (WFWorkflow.CalcWorkflow));
  this.id = instance.InstanceId;
  instance.Load();
  instance.Start();
  workflowRuntime.StopRuntime();
}
```

Example 7.10

WF includes a tracking service that allows a developer to save information about a workflow's execution to the database. For example, the start date, time and end date, time of a workflow and its activities can be saved to the database.

> **NOTE**
>
> This section is intentionally titled *Workflow Persistence (with WF)* to distinguish it from the *Workflow Persistence (with AppFabric)* section later in this chapter, where additional features and classes provided by Windows Server AppFabric are covered (some of which further relate to and extend WF).

Communicating with the Host Container

The base WF library includes the `CallExternal-Method` and `HandleExternalEvent` activities used for communication with the host based on the request-response message exchange pattern.

The WF has a built-in `CallExternalMethod` activity, which can raise an event to be consumed by the host. The host application needs to implement an event handler for receiving response arguments from the workflow using a standard

> **SOA PRINCIPLES & PATTERNS**
>
> Persisting workflow logic via a database is a classic application of State Repository [785] as a result of the application of the Service Statelessness (700) principle to the task or controller service that resides within WF runtime environment.

event-or-delegate pattern. The activity can also be used to send data from the workflow to the host. The `HandleExternalEvent` is used by the workflow instance to capture an event raised by the host application.

It is critical for the interface outside the runtime execution context to communicate with the code in the host application process. The barrier is bridged using a service designed in the runtime environment called the `ExternalDataExchangeService`. This service allows you to make calls into a running workflow instance using events, and to call out from a running workflow using method calls. In order to hook up the workflow to the host service, it must contain a class that implements the interface that is intended for communications. This interface will use the `ExternalDataExchange` attribute to signal the workflow designer and runtime that this interface is intended for communication between the host and workflow.

Once all these code artifacts are defined, the `CallExternalMethod` and `HandleExternalEvent` activities can be hooked up to the host service using the WF designer.

Activities

A workflow is a sequence of activities executed by the workflow engine. An activity should be modeled as a real-world action required for completing a parent business process. An activity is a class that encapsulates logic and can potentially be reused across different workflows.

WF includes several activities known as the base activity library. Activities from the base activity library are commonly used with sequential workflows (Table 7.3).

Activity	Description	
IfElse	allows conditions to be specified in the workflow and the runtime engine evaluates each condition and acts upon it based on the result (the IfElse activity can contain other IfElse activities and a default IfElse activity if no other condition is met)	**Looping and Synchronization**
While	accepts a condition and evaluates it at the beginning of every iteration (if the condition is true, the child activity is run repeatedly until the condition becomes false)	
Replicator	executes a child activity a given number of times (similar to the foreach statement in C#)	

Activity	Description	
Sequence	is used to execute a group of activities, one at a time, in a predefined order	**Looping and Synchronization**
Parallel	executes two or more sequences of activities in parallel or in an interleaved manner (all sequence activities must be completed before the workflow moves to the next activity)	
Listen	is used to idle the workflow process and wait for a wake-up call (the Listen activity is typically used when human interaction is required—it serializes the workflow and goes into a passive mode when it is waiting for human intervention and upon receiving an event, it reactivates the workflow and continues with the processing logic)	**Human Intervention**
EventDriven	is implemented by using the EventDriven activity (a Listen activity must contain EventDriven activities and child activities that represent human events)	
HandleExternalEvent	is invoked when an event specified in an interface is raised (the HandleExternalEvent activity is used by WF to communicate with an external service)	
Delay	is used to suspend the execution of the workflow for a specified amount of time	
Code	allows source code to be injected directly into the workflow (it fires the ExecuteCode event that executes the code, plus this activity can call an external assembly)	**Execution**
CallExternalMethod	is used to call a method in a class available to the workflow (the interface and its implementation must be available in the same assembly)	
InvokeWorkflow	invokes another workflow to start executing	

continues

Activity	Description	
`InvokeWebService`	invokes a Web service external to the work-flow application (creates a Web reference to a Web service and allows operations on the service to be invoked)	
`WebServiceInput`	enables a workflow to receive a Web service request	
`WebServiceOutput`	pairs with a `WebServiceInput` activity to respond to a service request (to use this activity, the `WebServiceInput` activity must be configured first)	**Execution**
`TransactionScope`	is used to represent `System.Transactions` in WF (supports all the properties currently supported by `System.Transactions`)	
`Terminate`	is used to terminate the execution of the workflow	

Table 7.3
Base library activities commonly used with sequential workflows.

State machine workflows provide a way of defining workflows that match an organization's business process by using states, events, and transitions to model workflow logic. A state represents a snapshot of the business process. The workflow is always in one state and will transition to a new state when it receives an event. Typically, some action will take place in the outside world for the state in the workflow to be transitioned to a new state. On reaching the final state, the workflow is completed.

The base activity library includes several activities designed to enable state machine workflows (Table 7.4).

A state machine workflow is commonly consumed by one or more UI components that must reflect the current state of the workflow and allow users to only perform legal events. WF includes the `StateMachineWorkflowInstance` class that provides an API to manage and query a state machine workflow. The class includes properties used to fetch the current state name and find legal transitions for the state. It also includes properties that provide a history of all the states the workflow has been through.

Activity	Description
`State`	represents a state in a state machine workflow (when an event arrives, the workflow will transition from one state activity to a new state activity)
`EventDriven`	represents an event handler in a state machine and is placed inside a state activity
`SetState`	is used to model transitions in a state machine workflow (includes the `TargetStateName` property that points to the destination state)
`StateInitialization` `StateFinalization`	used to perform pre- and post-processing in a state and run when the state machine transitions into the state containing the initialization activity (the `StateFinalization` activity runs when the state machine transitions out of a state)

Table 7.4
Base library activities commonly used with state machine workflows.

Workflow Runtime Environment

A workflow instance is created and executed by the workflow runtime engine. The runtime engine relies on several runtime services for persisting the workflow's state, managing transactions, tracking workflow's execution, and other features. Each instance of the runtime engine can support multiple instances of a workflow concurrently. The workflow instance runs in a host process or in an application domain and can be hosted on ASP.NET Web sites, Windows forms, Windows services, Web services, or SharePoint.

The runtime engine is powered by runtime services that provide an execution environment for transactions, persistence, tracking changes, timer, and threading. Runtime services can be augmented by plugging in custom services that allow changing the behavior of the runtime engine to meet the specific needs of the execution environment.

For most workflow implementations, the default implementation of runtime services satisfies the needs of the execution; however, in some cases the behavior may need to be altered. For example, the workflow may require the host application and the runtime engine to communicate differently, which would require building custom services.

The workflow execution starts by creating an instance of the workflow. It proceeds with carrying out activities until it is required to idle the execution, at which point the instance state is persisted to disk.

WF Programming Model

WF classes are encapsulated in three namespaces, as shown in Figure 7.6.

Figure 7.6

Workflow Foundation classes are encapsulated in three namespaces. The `System.Workflow.Runtime` assembly further contains the `WorkflowRuntime` class that is used to create an instance of a workflow.

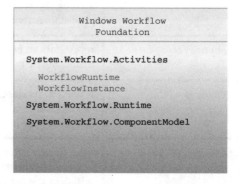

Figure 7.7 illustrates a simple sequential workflow that contains a Calculator activity. To automate this workflow, the host will need to instantiate it and provide it with parameters including the input values and the operation to perform.

Figure 7.7

A simple sequential workflow containing one activity that represents calculation logic.

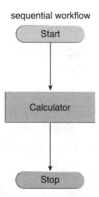

In the following example, we show this workflow hosted in a console application:

```
using System.Workflow.Runtime;
using System.Workflow.Runtime.Hosting;
namespace WFWorkflow
{
  class Program
  {
    static void Main(string[] args)
    {
      using(WorkflowRuntime
```

```
    workflowRuntime = new WorkflowRuntime())
    {
      AutoResetEvent
        waitHandle = new AutoResetEvent(false);
      workflowRuntime.WorkflowCompleted
        += delegate
        (object sender,
          WorkflowCompletedEventArgs e)
          {waitHandle.Set();};
      workflowRuntime.WorkflowTerminated
        += delegate
        (object sender,
          WorkflowTerminatedEventArgs e)
    }
    {
      Console.WriteLine(e.Exception.Message);
      waitHandle.Set();
    };
    WorkflowInstance instance =
      workflowRuntime.CreateWorkflow
      (typeof(WFWorkflow.CalcWorkflow));
    instance.Start();
    waitHandle.WaitOne();
    }
  }
 }
}
```

Example 7.11

In the preceding example, the host process initiates the workflow runtime and then starts the workflow method itself. The workflow runtime is started up by instantiating the workflowRuntime class. Passing in the workflow type to the CreateWorkflow method then creates a workflow instance class. The Start method on the workflow instance kicks off the workflow business process.

There are several events raised by the workflow runtime environment. These include WorkflowCompleted and WorkflowTerminated (the latter of which is called when there is an error). The previous example uses anonymous delegates, as WorkflowTerminatedEventArgs provides information on the exception that was generated. When the WorkflowCompleted event is called, we set the waitHandle value.

Passing Parameters into a Workflow Instance

Parameters are passed to a workflow instance using the `Dictionary` object. The `Creat-Workflow` operation has an overloaded operation that takes not only the workflow type but also a `Dictionary` object that accepts parameters. The code fragment in this next example demonstrates this:

```
Type type = typeof(WFWorkflow.CalcWorkflow);
Dictionary<string, object>
  parameters = new Dictionary<string, object>();
parameters.Add("Value1", 11);
parameters.Add("Value2", 19);
parameters.Add("Operation", "+");
WorkflowInstance instance =
  workflowRuntime.CreateWorkflow(type, parameters);
instance.Start();
```

Example 7.12

Returning Parameters from a Workflow Instance

The `WorkflowCompletedEventArgs` in the `WorkflowCompleted` event returns an output parameter, as shown here:

```
AutoResetEvent waitHandle = new AutoResetEvent(false);
workflowRuntime.WorkflowCompleted
  += delegate
  (object sender,
  WorkflowCompletedEventArgs e)
{
  int total = (int)e.OutputParameters["Result"];
  Console.WriteLine(total);
  waitHandle.Set();
};
```

Example 7.13

Output parameters are collections and data is extracted from collection and cast into an integer. The names of the input parameters passed into the workflow instance automatically map to the names of properties defined inside the workflow class. In this case, the `Result` property maps directly to the `result` parameter returned. The input properties are used to initialize private variables in the workflow instance:

```
public partial class CalcWorkflow :
  SequentialWorkflowActivity
{
  private int value1 = 0;
  private int value2 = 0;
  private int result = 0;
  private String operation;

  public int Value1
  {
    set{value1 = value;}
  }
  public int Value2
  {
    set{value2 = value;}
  }
  public string Operation
  {
    set{operation = value;}
  }
  public int Result
  {
    get{return result;}
  }
  private void Calculator_ExecuteCode
    (object sender, EventArgs e)
  {
    if (operation == "+")
      {result = value1 + value2;}
  }
}
```

Example 7.14

Workflow-Enabled Services

Only a workflow that uses the `WebServiceReceive` activity can be published as a Web service. A simple scenario would be to create a workflow project and add `WebServiceReceive` and `WebServiceResponse` activities to it. In this case, the workflow is activated by calling a method on the Web service and returning a value when the processing is complete. In Visual Studio, a workflow project can be published as a Web service by right-clicking on a workflow project and selecting "Publish as Web service." This action will create an ASP.NET project, with ASMX and Web.Config files.

Versioning Orchestrations

Orchestrations in WF can be versioned in two ways:

1. *Execute the XOML file* – In this case, the service reads the .XOML file and creates a Workflow instance using the CreateWorkflow method. The XOML file does not support versioning; the file can be manually versioned.

2. *Use assembly level versioning* – Each assembly has a version number, and two assemblies that differ by version number are considered by the runtime to be different assemblies. The assembly version can be managed by modifying the assembly.cs file prior to deployment.

Note that because with assembly-level versioning a new version of a workflow is treated as a new assembly version by the runtime, different assembly versions can run concurrently.

WF Extensibility

WF provides various extensibility points that are broad and do not impose semantics on the user. For example, if we are extending the persistence mechanism, WF does not stipulate that we use either the data-store or the serialization techniques.

WF's extensibility model allows almost every aspect of WF to be extended. Some common extensibility requirements include:

- creating custom policies
- creating workflow tracking services
- adding new activities for persistence, tracking, and communication
- creating domain-specific activities

WF has a visual designer used in Visual Studio that can also be extended to create domain-specific designers.

Business Rules

A service-oriented solution is typically modeled so as to factor out task services because these services encapsulate business non-agnostic activities specific to the overarching business process. The WF visual designer can be used to glue together various business activities that involve business rules that are exposed in one of two ways:

1. Conditions can be used with built-in and custom activities to change their execution behavior. There are several built-in rules-based activities that enable conditional logic:

   - `IfElse` (provides decision logic)

   - `While` (provides looping behavior)

   - `Replicator` (analogous to a for-each statement)

   Also supported is the conditioned activity group (CAG) that can provide rules-driven behavior over a collection of activities.

2. PolicyActivity, a rules engine that comes embedded with WF, can be used with a specialized workflow activity class that encapsulates a RuleSet which is stored in a .rules file. At runtime, PolicyActivity retrieves the rules from the .rules file and executes the rules.

> **SOA PRINCIPLES & PATTERNS**
>
> The PolicyActivity engine can be used to apply Rules Centralization [768] so as to centralize business rules logic in the RuleSet, effectively establishing a rules service.

SUMMARY OF KEY POINTS

- WF allows for the modeling and execution of business processes that can include activities with human and system touch points.

- WF architecture consists of activities and workflows. Activities are discrete steps used to define a workflow.

- WF includes a base library, workflow runtime engine, visual designer, runtime services, and a host process for executing workflows.

- WF supports two built-in workflow types: sequential workflow and state machine workflow.

7.3 Application Blocks and Software Factories

.NET provides several resources designed to provide generic processing logic and guidance based on best practices. Application Blocks and Software Factories collectively represent these resources.

Application Blocks

When developing different services, there are utility or infrastructure functions that are commonly required by multiple solutions, regardless of the nature of their business logic.

Some examples of cross-cutting utility logic include:

- exception management

- data access

- logging and instrumentation

- authentication and authorization

SOA PRINCIPLES & PATTERNS

Application Blocks are directly comparable to out-of-the-box utility services that result from the application of Utility Abstraction [791] and Agnostic Context [710]. They are so generic that when Domain Inventory [738] is applied to a given enterprise, they can be utilized within a cross-domain scope, as per Cross-Domain Utility Layer [729].

Normally, we would attempt to build a series of utility services to encapsulate these types of logic so as to make them reusable and recomposable in support of multiple service-oriented solutions.

Over the years, the Patterns and Practices Group at Microsoft has identified common bodies of utility logic and packaged them into a series of reusable components called *Application Blocks*.

NOTE

The "Patterns & Practices Group" at Microsoft was introduced to develop reusable open-source libraries to solve common infrastructure tasks and thereby bootstrap the development process. Several members of this group contributed patterns to the *SOA Design Patterns* book. For more information see http://msdn.microsoft.com/practices/.

Application Blocks are reusable components used to address common challenges in enterprise software development. They encapsulate the best practices and development guidelines and are available as Visual Studio projects with source code. Application Blocks are also available as compiled binaries that can be directly included in development solutions. The benefits provided by Application Blocks echo many of the strategic goals and benefits of service-oriented computing in general:

- modular development and reusability for increased ROI

- standardization of the development platform and the utility service layer

- significant increase in developer productivity and overall responsiveness

- enable project teams to focus more on business logic rather than low-level mechanics

- establish a healthy level of decoupling between the utility logic and business logic

- improve effectiveness of service governance

The available Application Blocks are listed in Table 7.5.

Application Block	Description
Exception Handling	used to implement consistent exception handling policies in logical application tiers
Security Application	performs authentication, authorization, role membership checking, and profile access
Data Access	used to create, test, and maintain the data access layer (arguably the most commonly used block)
Caching Application	provides a flexible and extensible caching mechanism (can be used on the server-side and client-side)
Smart Client Application	used to build modular smart client applications
Configuration Application	used to simplify the ability to read and write configuration information from a variety of data sources
Cryptography Application	simplifies introducing cryptographic functionality in .NET services (abstracts DPAPI, symmetric encryption and hashing, and uses a configuration tool to simplify key management)
Logging and Instrumentation	allows services to be "instrumented" with logging and tracing calls

Table 7.5
A list of available Application Blocks.

> **NOTE**
>
> The collection of all the Application Blocks listed in Table 7.5, with the exception of the Smart Client block, is referred to as the Enterprise Library. It is important to note that the Enterprise Library and the Application Blocks are not a part of the .NET framework. They follow an open source licensing model and are not directly supported by Microsoft.

Software Factories

A Software Factory is a collection of related software artifacts, such as reusable code, components, documentation, code generators, and visual designers. Software Factories increase the quality and predictability of services developed by standardizing solution templates used for developing services. Software Factories can help establish domain-specific services with improved consistency and quality by integrating automation scenarios deeply into Visual Studio using templates and code generation.

Guidance Toolkits

Software Factories are built using the Guidance Automation Extensions (GAX) and the Guidance Automation Toolkit (GAT).

GAX allows architects and developers to automate development tasks within the Visual Studio environment and provides a runtime environment that must be installed to start working with GAT.

GAT extends the Visual Studio environment by allowing you to author integrated user experiences. The toolkit enables the automation of development activities and integrates reusable code into services. Guidance toolkits contain several components that work together to provide automation functionality, as listed in Table 7.6.

Web Services Software Factory

When working with WCF, it is common to run into decision points around when to use a data contract, when to use a message contract, and how to determine the relationship between these contracts. The Web Services Software Factory provides guidance on these issues. It is a part of Microsoft's Software Factory initiative and provides guidance packages that help build solutions based on Web services. The ideas around using data contracts, message contracts, and service contracts are not difficult, but using these technologies in a consistent and uniform way is critically important.

Function	Description
recipes	automate repetitive activities that a developer would usually perform manually to reduce errors and increase consistency
actions	units of work defined by a sequence of recipes
wizards	walks developers through one or more pages gathering values and is associated with a recipe that is used to gather values for the recipe
type converters	validate the value of a field and are used to convert them to the representation used by the recipe
Visual Studio templates	used to create Visual Studio solutions and add projects (templates can be associated with recipes, which in turn are associated with wizards)

Table 7.6
Guidance automation toolkit components.

Specifically, this Software Factory contains guidance packages for:

- ASMX

- WCF

- DataAccess Layer

- WS-Security using ASMX

The scope of the individual guidance packages ranges from the service proxy to the database access layer. The Service Factory includes guidance for designing messages and service entities, mapping message entities to business entities, persisting the business entity into the database, security, and exception management.

The Web Service Software Factory supports wizard-driven development of data contracts, message contracts, and service contracts. Data contracts are reusable artifacts in a project, whereas message contracts are not reusable and are specific to the operation they are being received and sent from. This Service Factory further supports the use of SOAP faults by simplifying the creation of fault contracts and attaching the fault contracts to services.

As shown in Figure 7.8, the Web Service Software Factory organizes solutions into the service layer, business layer, and resource access layer.

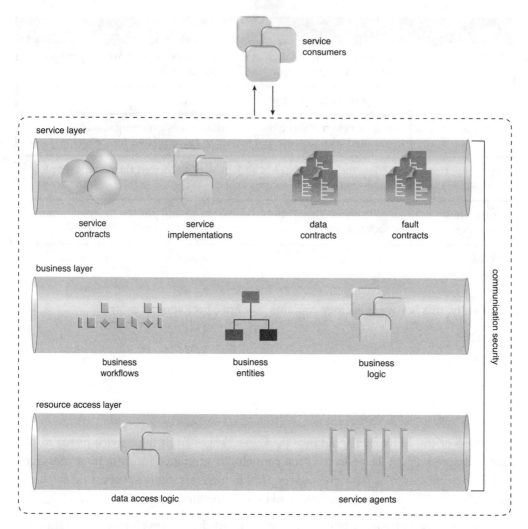

Figure 7.8

The service layer is further decomposed to contain service contract, service implementation, data contract, and fault contract projects. Service Factory provides a "create service implementation" recipe that creates the actual implementation. The business layer contains business-centric artifacts and the resource access layer is primarily used to abstract data access logic.

SUMMARY OF KEY POINTS

- Enterprise Library is a collection of Application Blocks that provide utility-centric logic that can be reused by different services and service-oriented solutions.

- A Software Factory is a collection of related software artifacts provided to help improve the quality and predictability of services being developed.

7.4 Windows Server AppFabric

NOTE

The following section is focused exclusively on Windows Server AppFabric, which should not be confused with *Windows Azure platform AppFabric*, which is explained in Chapter 8.

Windows Server AppFabric provides a runtime and hosting services for WF and WCF services built for version 4.0 of the .NET framework. It is best viewed as an extension to the application server available on Windows Server 2008 (and Windows Server 2008 R2). The purpose of Windows Server AppFabric is to make it easier to build, scale, and manage WCF and WF service compositions that are hosted in IIS/WAS.

Its primary features include:

- configurable hosting environment

- workflow persistence

- in-memory application cache platform

- manageability extensions

- application server event collection

- distributed caching services

Figure 7.9 shows how Windows Server AppFabric builds upon and extends the functionality in Windows Server and the .NET framework.

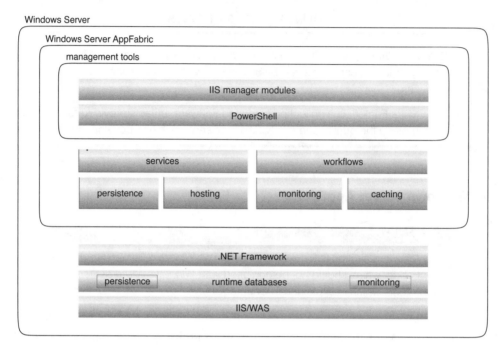

Figure 7.9

Extensions and features provided by Windows Server AppFabric.

Configurable Hosting Environment

Let's begin by explaining how Windows Server AppFabric extends the functionality of the Windows Process Activation Service (WAS). Essentially, it enables services hosted in AppFabric to still have messaging-based activation, application, and worker recycling, while also supporting centralized administration and support for both HTTP and non-HTTP protocols. This allows services to take advantage of specific WCF features, such as unnamed endpoints and default configuration (which reduces the amount of configuration that has to be specified by applying reasonable default values when explicit values are not provided).

Windows Server AppFabric also enables the hierarchical combination of configuration files (which is actually similar to the functionality that has existed in ASP.NET for many years). Values can be defined once at the machine level and changed only when needed by a particular application. This effectively relieves us of the need to continually specify values for endpoints and behaviors. The default values for a service allow you to communicate with your service using a contract derived from the public interface over `basicHttpBinding`.

These default values result in a simpler Web.Config file for WCF services. In Visual Studio 2010, the default template for the `system.serviceModel` part in Web.Config only defines entries for `serviceMetadata` and `serviceDebug`.

Workflow Persistence (with AppFabric)

Workflow persistence represents Windows Server AppFabric's ability to capture and store the state of a workflow to durable storage, independent of any machine or process information. When a workflow is persisted, it provides a well-known point of recovery in the event of machine failure. The workflow logic can be later removed from memory to free resources, when required.

The .NET framework 4.0 includes the `SQLWorkflowInstanceStore` class used to persist workflow state. It also contains the Workflow Management Service (WMS), which provides management tasks for workflow services.

Installing Windows Server AppFabric automatically installs WMS and configures it as a service.

This installation routine also provides the option to:

- create the persistence database
- add an `sqlWorkflowInstanceStore` element to the appropriate configuration file (root, site, application, or service)
- store the connection information in the configuration file

Windows Server AppFabric uses `sqlStoreProvider` to communicate with the database. The following example shows the `connectionStrings` and `sqlWorkflowInstanceStore` elements that can be added to a Web.Config file to take advantage of the workflow persistence extension:

```
<connectionStrings>
  <add name="WorkflowPersistenceStore"
    connectionString="..." />
</connectionStrings>
<system.serviceModel>
  <behaviors>
    <serviceBehaviors>
      <behavior>
        <sqlWorkflowInstanceStore
          connectionStringName="WorkflowPersistenceStore"
          hostLockRenewalPeriod="00:30:00"
```

```
        instanceEncodingOption="None"
        instanceCompletionAction="DeleteAll"
        instanceLockedExceptionAction="NoRetry"/>
      </behavior>
    </serviceBehaviors>
  </behaviors>
</system.serviceModel>
```

Example 7.15

Windows Server AppFabric contains tools that can be used to view and control work-flow instances. For example, a dashboard is provided so that you can display WCF call history, WF instance history, and the number of persisted WF instances. Using these tools, you can also view tracked WF instances and, in some cases, suspend, resume, cancel, or terminate a workflow instance.

In-Memory Application Cache Platform

One method of scaling services to handle larger workloads is to cache non-volatile data close to the services that use the data. Windows Server AppFabric provides a distributed in-memory application cache that establishes a unified data view while automatically synchronizing the data across all of the servers participating in the distributed cache. The primary server is responsible for updating the additional secondary servers.

The in-memory application cache (Figure 7.10) can scale to hundreds of servers and provides automatic load balancing and fail-over to a secondary node if the primary node is unavailable. Policies that govern cache eviction ensure that unneeded data can be removed from the cache after a specified time period, or when the cache is full and the data has not been accessed in a while. This cache runs in a separate cache host process. A named cache is created that can span multiple

> **SOA PRINCIPLES & PATTERNS**
>
> In-memory application caching can be fully leveraged as a primary state deferral mechanism when applying the Service Statelessness (700) principle. AppFabric Caching Services are comparable to the system-provided utility services that generally result from Stateful Services [786] and the synchronization feature is comparable to the application of Service Data Replication [773] in support of state data replication. The configuration control made available by the Windows Server AppFabric caching extensions allow for potential increases in individual service autonomy, as per the Service Autonomy (699) principle.

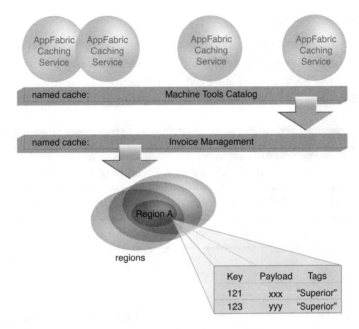

Figure 7.10

The moving parts of the in-memory application cache provided by Windows Server AppFabric.

machines and cache host processes. The service stores name value pairs in the named cache and if you need greater control over the allocation of cache resources, you can create a region.

Each service is responsible for managing its own cache and the items in the cache. The following example shows how to create a cache named "orders" and add an Order object to it:

```
DataCacheFactory fac = new DataCacheFactory();
DataCache orders = fac.GetCache("orderscache");
orders.Put("order1", new Order(...));
```

Example 7.16

The cache host process is created by calling the GetCache method on a DataCacheFactory object. A new order is then added with the key order1.

Manageability Extensions

Due to their distributed nature, service compositions can present special management challenges, especially when they involve services hosted on a large number of different machines. Windows Server AppFabric extends existing management and monitoring tools by providing the set of IIS Manager applets listed in Table 7.7.

Applet	Description
Dashboard	provides a graphical view of WF workflows and WCF services
Endpoints	used to manage endpoints declared in configuration files
Services	used to view and configure WCF and WF services

Table 7.7
IIS Applets provided by Windows Server AppFabric.

Windows Server AppFabric further provides a Windows PowerShell management interface that you can use to script changes to the default configurations and to run scripts across multiple machines. You can further create custom applets and PowerShell cmdlets.

Application Server Event Collector

Another way to monitor actively running services is to collect and analyze event information. WCF or WF services can emit event data that is sent to a high performance Event Tracing for Windows (ETW) session. Windows Server AppFabric includes an Event Collector Service that can collect the events and send them to a monitoring database. Analysis tools can then be used to query the data for monitoring purposes.

SUMMARY OF KEY POINTS

- Windows Server AppFabric adds layers of extensions upon the .NET framework to address service scalability, performance, configuration, and monitoring.

- A primary feature of Windows Server AppFabric is the in-memory, distributed cache that helps reduce the time needed to access in-memory data while also providing redundancy and fault tolerance.

- Windows Server AppFabric uses familiar tools and extensibility models to enable runtime service management and monitoring.

7.5 BizTalk Server

BizTalk Server is a middleware platform that provides native messaging, broker, and orchestration features along with numerous extensions. Its original purpose was to act as a middle-tier hub for integration purposes, but it has evolved into a comprehensive set of technologies that provide various forms of services-based intermediary processing in support of service, service composition, and service inventory architectures that can leverage and build upon orchestration and enterprise service bus-style platforms.

The BizTalk technology architecture is comprised of various parts that all, in some way, relate to the BizTalk Server engine that lies at the core of the BizTalk Server product. The engine drives two primary components: messaging and orchestration (Figure 7.11).

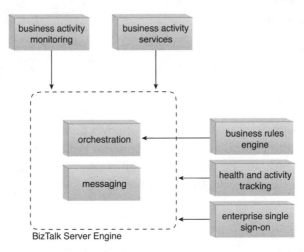

Figure 7.11
Orchestration and messaging are the main components of the BizTalk Server engine.

Messaging is what allows BizTalk Server to enable communication within its boundaries and between BizTalk and external systems and services. It relies heavily on adapters and can support a variety of protocols and data formats.

Orchestration is used for creating and executing business process and composition logic. The orchestration component (also referred to as the *orchestration engine*) is built on top of the messaging component.

The BizTalk Server engine is augmented with several productivity tools, including:

- business rules engine
- health and activity tracking
- enterprise single sign-on
- business activity monitoring
- business activity services

The business rules engine allows you to customize the orchestration component by making it simpler and faster to change business rules.

The health and activity tracking tool lets you monitor and manage the BizTalk engine and any orchestrations it may be running. It is commonly used to track all sent and received messages.

> **SOA PRINCIPLES & PATTERNS**
>
> Several of the features that pertain to and build upon BizTalk Server's messaging framework relate to how the Enterprise Service Bus [741] compound pattern can be applied to the Microsoft technology platform in general. Similarly, BizTalk Server's native orchestration capabilities lay the foundation for how the Orchestration [758] compound pattern can be applied. Chapters 13 and 14 explore the application of the Orchestration [758] pattern in more detail.

Enterprise single sign-on is an extension of Windows Enterprise security that provides the ability to map authentication credentials between Windows and non-Windows systems. It is enabled by a set of processes in BizTalk Server that provide user account and password mapping, caching single sign-on for multiple Windows domains, and password synchronization.

Business activity monitoring (BAM) is comprised of a set of tools and services used to monitor transactions in real time and view key performance indicators of a business process being automated by a given orchestration. BAM is covered in detail in Chapter 20.

Finally, business activity services are used to manage interaction with trading partners and are focused on the utilization of BizTalk for business-to-business (B2B) purposes.

BizTalk Server Architecture

The underlying architecture of BizTalk Server is modular and allows for the distribution of various processing functions to different servers. It supports high fault tolerance and enables scaling out with increasing load. You can dedicate some servers to exclusively process incoming or outgoing messages, while other servers can execute orchestration logic, transform and transmit messages, and manage process state. As shown in Figure 7.12, the MessageBox SQL Server database stores messages and connects the pieces of the overall architecture.

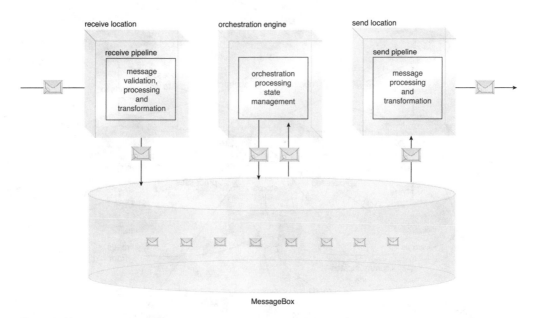

Figure 7.12
The modular BizTalk architecture is underpinned by the SQL Server MessageBox.

BizTalk's architecture recognizes that not all IT enterprises can publish Web service endpoints for their applications. The adapter model in BizTalk Server therefore extends orchestration capabilities beyond the use of Web services. Applications accessed via a number of legacy protocols and enterprise software packages can participate in orchestrations. These adapters can bridge the transport and protocol gaps between proprietary products, such as IBM MQSeries or SAP, and the orchestration engine.

Figure 7.13 provides an illustrative overview of the logical relationships and responsibilities of the primary parts of the BizTalk architecture.

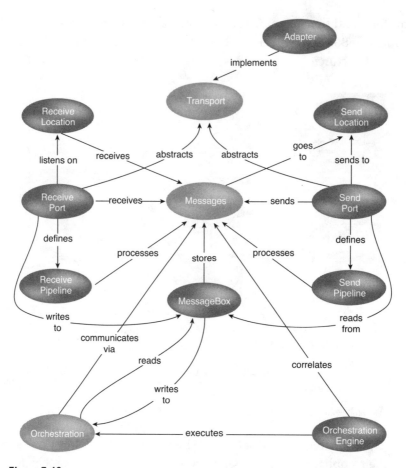

Figure 7.13

A conceptual view of BizTalk architecture with the moving parts within the BizTalk Server architecture. The green-colored oval symbols represent native parts of the BizTalk environment.

Messaging

XML is the fundamental data representation technology that underlies the different layers of BizTalk technology. Messages and service contracts are expressed with XML types and transformation logic is based on the use of XSLT. XPath expressions can be executed as part of workflow decision points and in message assignments.

Pipelines

Figure 7.14 provides some insight into the message processing mechanics of BizTalk Server. Messages are sent to receive adapters, which are available for most communication mechanisms, including files, Web services, and HTTP. The receive pipeline contains a pipeline of components used to convert messages from their native format to XML documents. XML messages are then delivered to the MessageBox hosted in SQL Server.

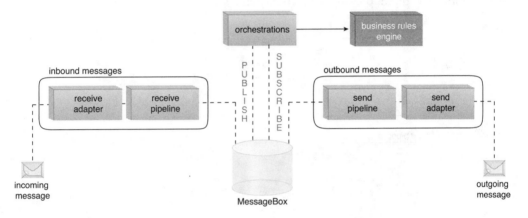

Figure 7.14

BizTalk Server contains several components through which the message passes.

All messages are converted into XML before they can be consumed by the orchestration engine. The business rules engine augments the orchestration module by providing a simpler way to express complex sets of rules in a business process. Each orchestration must subscribe to the type of message it wants to receive. The appropriate XML message is processed by the orchestration engine, which results in a new XML message being created. The processed XML is then sent through the send pipeline, which changes the XML message to the native format required by the destination system. The message is then transmitted to the destination system using the send adapter.

> **NOTE**
>
> BizTalk publish-and-subscribe messaging and legacy adapters are covered separately in upcoming sections.

Pipeline Components

BizTalk Server engine only works with XML documents internally, and pipelines are used to convert a document from its native format to XML. The receive pipeline is responsible for preparing the XML message and publishing it to the MessageBox. A pipeline is a series of components (that exist as .NET assemblies) that are executed in sequence. Each component provides specific processing logic to a message, such as decryption, encryption, parsing, or XML Schema validation, as shown in Figure 7.15.

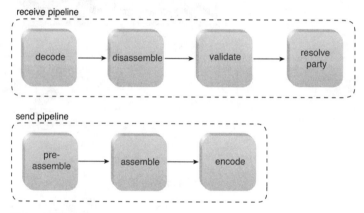

Figure 7.15
The receive and send pipelines in BizTalk Server are each composed of a number of components.

Let's take a closer look at the components from Figure 7.15, each of which represents a separate message processing stage:

1. *decode* – decodes or decrypts the received message

2. *disassemble* – converts a native message into an XML message

3. *validate* – validates the XML using an XML schema

4 *resolve party* – identifies the party associated with the message

5. *pre-assemble* – performs message processing before assembling the message

6. *assemble* – assembles the message from XML to its native format

7. *encode* – encodes or encrypts the message before transmitting it to the send port

The process of converting a message from its native format to an XML message may require a series of transformations that will be performed on a message as it is being sent and received. For example, a comma-delimited flat file may need to be converted to an XML message. The disassemble component is responsible for this transformation.

Ports and Locations

To enable cross-service messaging you need to establish endpoints, ports, and locations. An endpoint is a logical representation of a location (generally expressed as a URL) that provides a physical address for message data received or sent. There are receive and send locations and corresponding ports, as follows:

1. *receive location* – a physical location or an adapter type

2. *receive port* – a logical grouping of receive locations—ports are used to abstract physical endpoints in BizTalk Server

3. *send location* – a logical grouping of send locations

4. *send port* – a physical location or an adapter type—ports are used to abstract physical endpoints in BizTalk Server

It is possible to completely bypass the orchestration engine and have a message sent directly from the receive pipeline to the send pipeline, thereby making BizTalk Server behave like a messaging system. Messages originating from the receive ports are deposited to the MessageBox. They are then delivered to the send ports that subscribe to specific messages, in effect creating a subscription-based mechanism. The send pipeline can subscribe to messages based on the properties set on messages by the receive pipeline.

Adapters

Through the use of adapters the BizTalk platform can be accessed and interacted with by a variety of products, applications, and services. Adapters are essentially responsible for overcoming transport disparity between incompatible systems and services. BizTalk adapters specifically contain internal mapping logic that transforms external protocols into native BizTalk-supported protocols and vice versa.

BizTalk Server includes several built-in adapters, including a Web services adapter, a file adapter, an HTTP adapter, an MSMQ adapter, an SMTP adapter, and even a POP3 adapter. Besides built-in adapters, there is also a substantial third-party adapter marketplace. All adapters are based on a common BizTalk Server adapter framework that provides a set of base classes used to create and run adapter logic.

Let's briefly highlight some adapters relevant to upcoming topics:

1. *Web Services Adapter* – The adapter used for Web service communication allows for the sending and receiving of SOAP messages over HTTP.

2. *WCF Adapter* – Similar to the Web services adapter, the BizTalk Server WCF adapter provides full support for the WS-* stack, including various security, reliable messaging, and transaction processing specifications. The WCF adapter is essentially used to connect WCF services to BizTalk Server.

> **SOA PRINCIPLES & PATTERNS**
>
> Although several runtime transformation-related patterns exist (such as Data Model Transformation [732] and Data Format Transformation [731]), the pattern most synonymous with the use of adapters is Protocol Bridging [764].

3. *SQL Server Service Broker Adapter* – SQL Server Service Broker (SSB) adapter for BizTalk Server allows BizTalk Server to participate in SSB conversations as a target or as an initiator. SSB communication is based on the dialog concept where a dialog is comprised of a reliable stream of messages between two services.

Context Properties

When message processing logic is defined, the details of that logic are generally not part of the message payload data. This is why metadata is required. Message metadata can be associated with and attached to the body content of messages travelling through the BizTalk environment.

There are two practical ways this can be achieved:

1. as an envelope around the message, where the message itself becomes the payload in an envelope that also contains a header section for the metadata

2. as BizTalk context properties

The envelope approach is perfectly valid and quite common. However, it requires that a transformation occur every time a message is received by BizTalk Server in order to insert the message into an envelope. Most likely another transformation prior to message delivery is required to remove the envelope (unless the message is being delivered to a service that understands or requires the actual envelope). This transformation logic can impose processing overhead on every message flowing through the system.

BizTalk context properties are associated with a message for the duration of its lifetime inside the BizTalk Server environment. Context properties are created and added to messages as they are received, or at any point in their lifecycle inside BizTalk. As they are not physically part of the message, context properties are by definition lost when a message leaves the BizTalk boundary (although you can demote values from message context into message content by use of a property schema and XML Assembler pipeline component).

It is important to note that regardless of whether you choose to work with context properties, the downstream logic is the same. The only difference is the source of the message metadata. Additionally, you may opt to host some of the metadata in external stores, such as a registry.

NOTE

The association of metadata to messages is a concept embodied in the fundamental Messaging Metadata [753] pattern. The most common means of applying this pattern has historically been through the use of SOAP messages that contain separate body and header sections (the latter of which contains the metadata). However, the use of BizTalk context properties also represents a legitimate means of realizing this pattern, albeit in a non-industry-standard manner.

Itineraries

The BizTalk architecture allows for the decoupling of services and the use of message metadata to route messages to services. As a result, services can be autonomous, self-contained units that are not aware of each other. Orchestration and service composition logic are two primary means of tying services together for specific purposes. However, there is a third option provided specifically by BizTalk Server and one that is especially worth noting because it can coordinate services while still being part of larger orchestrations.

Itineraries (a form of microflow) are intended for simple, short-running service compositions and message flows. Itineraries include a broker capability that allows you to perform conditional branching from inside an itinerary. This should only be used sparingly and when required, as it is another point in which you can embed business logic.

Itineraries allow you to do something like call a service, transform the response, call a second service, and then a third service. There are no transactional or compensation semantics in an itinerary, as these types of features are beyond their ability and purpose.

It is important to note that there may be circumstances that warrant the use of itineraries and messaging only-type solutions that do not involve orchestrations. For example, simple message flows that do not require complex runtime processing can be based solely on itineraries and thereby avoid the overhead of invoking an orchestration.

> **NOTE**
>
> Chapter 15 discusses itineraries in more depth as part of its coverage of BizTalk Server in relation to the enterprise service bus.

Unified Exception Management

Effective exception management takes on increased importance within complex orchestration logic as debugging failures in a loosely coupled solution can be challenging. By using a well-planned exception management strategy, it is possible to construct solutions that can not only record failures, but also potentially invoke compensation processes or services in response to exception conditions.

Exceptions fall into one of two categories:

- business exceptions

- system exceptions

BizTalk solutions can span multiple technologies, including orchestrations, pipeline components, Web services (internal and external), and custom assemblies. They are therefore often required to cross security and organizational boundaries. A unified exception handling mechanism can provide exception handling capabilities for all of these disparate participants and technologies.

BizTalk Server 2006 first introduced the notion of failed message routing which, for the first time, allowed for the creation of message subscribers that failed during receipt (such as when messages did not conform to an expected XML schema). If we take that approach and apply it to exception management, then we can create a mechanism that will allow processes encountering failures to publish an exception message and handlers that will subscribe to those exception messages.

This loosely coupled approach to exception management offers several benefits:

- By decoupling exception handling from the process itself, we have the opportunity to stratify assemblies so that exception management for a given process becomes a separate assembly that can be versioned and deployed without affecting the currently deployed and running process.

- Multiple handlers can potentially respond to a given type of exception, as may be the case if we want to track metrics for all exceptions that occur within a given boundary.

- A message-oriented exception management system allows for the creation of both generic and targeted handlers.

In a fully functional message-based exception management strategy, you will also have the ability to include, as payload in the exception message, any messages that may have been in-flight at the time the exception condition was encountered. With this information you will have the capacity to potentially reconstruct those messages in an exception handler, thereby allowing for repair and re-submission.

In a repair and resubmit scenario, users can access InfoPath forms on a SharePoint site, perhaps edit data in the form, or approve it, and submit it. This technique is effective in situations where a message can be repaired by changing a value or where a human intervention approval step may be required (as explained earlier).

In order to implement a unified exception management system, you first need to create a schema that defines what an exception message looks like. A well-defined XML schema will include enough information that both generic and targeted handlers will be able to either generically or selectively subscribe to.

This may include such items as:

- *Application* – the application name (for example, Payroll)

- *Process* – a specific process that encountered the exception condition (for example, PrintCheck)

- *Exception Message* – human-meaningful description of the failure (for example, cannot contact printer)

- *Fault Code* – a standardized code used as a filter condition by subscribers (typically, codes are governed and allocated by a centralized group in order to ensure there is no overlap)

- *Severity* – allows you to set varying priority handlers (for example, a handler may listen for critical severity exceptions and invoke a human notification process)

SUMMARY OF KEY POINTS

- BizTalk Server is a middleware platform that establishes services-centric intermediary processing layers with features relevant to both Orchestration [758] and Enterprise Service Bus [741] patterns.

- BizTalk Server includes several adapters, including adapters for Web services, WCF, and SQL Server Service Broker.

- Key features that can be used to build upon the BizTalk architecture include context properties, itineraries, and unified exception management.

Chapter 8

Cloud Services with Windows Azure

8.1 Cloud Computing 101

8.2 Windows Azure Platform Overview

8.3 Windows Azure Roles

8.4 Hello World in Windows Azure

8.5 A Web Service in Windows Azure

8.6 A REST Service in Windows Azure

8.7 Windows Azure Storage

Microsoft's Software-plus-Services strategy represents a view of the world where the growing feature-set of devices and the increasing ubiquity of the Web are combined to deliver more compelling solutions. Software-plus-Services represents an evolutionary step that is based on existing best practices in IT and extends the application potential of core service-orientation design principles.

Microsoft's efforts to embrace the Software-plus-Services vision are framed by three core goals:

- user experiences should span beyond a single device
- solution architectures should be able to intelligently leverage and integrate on-premise IT assets with cloud assets
- tightly coupled systems should give way to federations of cooperating systems and loosely coupled compositions

The Windows Azure platform represents one of the major components of the Software-plus-Services strategy, as Microsoft's cloud computing operating environment, designed from the outset to holistically manage pools of computation, storage and networking; all encapsulated by one or more services.

8.1 Cloud Computing 101

Just like service-oriented computing, cloud computing is a term that represents many diverse perspectives and technologies. In this book, our focus is on cloud computing in relation to SOA and Windows Azure.

Cloud computing enables the delivery of scalable and available capabilities by leveraging dynamic and on-demand infrastructure. By leveraging these modern service technology advances and various pervasive Internet technologies, the "cloud" represents an abstraction of services and resources, such that the underlying complexities of the technical implementations are encapsulated and transparent from users and consumer programs interacting with the cloud.

At the most fundamental level, cloud computing impacts two aspects of how people interact with technologies today:

- how services are consumed

- how services are delivered

Although cloud computing was originally, and still often is, associated with Web-based applications that can be accessed by end-users via various devices, it is also very much about applications and services themselves being consumers of cloud-based services. This fundamental change is a result of the transformation brought about by the adoption of SOA and Web-based industry standards, allowing for service-oriented and Web-based resources to become universally accessible on the Internet as on-demand services.

One example has been an approach whereby programmatic access to popular functions on Web properties is provided by simplifying efforts at integrating public-facing services and resource-based interactions, often via RESTful interfaces. This was also termed "Web-oriented architecture" or "WOA," and was considered a subset of SOA. Architectural views such as this assisted in establishing the Web-as-a-platform concept, and helped shed light on the increasing inter-connected potential of the Web as a massive collection (or cloud) of ready-to-use and always-available capabilities.

This view can fundamentally change the way services are designed and constructed, as we reuse not only someone else's code and data, but also their infrastructure resources, and leverage them as part of our own service implementations. We do not need to understand the inner workings and technical details of these services; Service Abstraction (696), as a principle, is applied to its fullest extent by hiding implementation details behind clouds.

With regards to service delivery, we are focused on the actual design, development, and implementation of cloud-based services. Let's begin by establishing high-level characteristics that a cloud computing environment can include:

- generally accessible

- always available and highly reliable

- elastic and scalable

- abstract and modular resources

SOA PRINCIPLES & PATTERNS

There are several SOA design patterns that are closely related to common cloud computing implementations, such as Decoupled Contract [735], Redundant Implementation [766], State Repository [785], and Stateful Services [786]. In this and subsequent chapters, these and other patterns will be explored as they apply specifically to the Windows Azure cloud platform.

- service-oriented

- self-service management and simplified provisioning

Fundamental topics regarding service delivery pertain to the cloud deployment model used to provide the hosting environment and the service delivery model that represents the functional nature of a given cloud-based service. The next two sections explore these two types of models.

Cloud Deployment Models

There are three primary cloud deployment models. Each can exhibit the previously listed characteristics; their differences lie primarily in the scope and access of published cloud services, as they are made available to service consumers.

Let's briefly discuss these deployment models individually.

Public Cloud

Also known as external cloud or multi-tenant cloud, this model essentially represents a cloud environment that is openly accessible. It generally provides an IT infrastructure in a third-party physical data center that can be utilized to deliver services without having to be concerned with the underlying technical complexities.

Essential characteristics of a public cloud typically include:

- homogeneous infrastructure

- common policies

- shared resources and multi-tenant

- leased or rented infrastructure; operational expenditure cost model

- economies of scale and elastic scalability

Note that public clouds can host individual services or collections of services, allow for the deployment of service compositions, and even entire service inventories.

Private Cloud

Also referred to as internal cloud or on-premise cloud, a private cloud intentionally limits access to its resources to service consumers that belong to the same organization that owns the cloud. In other words, the infrastructure that is managed and operated for one organization only, primarily to maintain a consistent level of control over security, privacy, and governance.

Essential characteristics of a private cloud typically include:

- heterogeneous infrastructure

- customized and tailored policies

- dedicated resources

- in-house infrastructure (capital expenditure cost model)

- end-to-end control

Community Cloud

This deployment model typically refers to special-purpose cloud computing environments shared and managed by a number of related organizations participating in a common domain or vertical market.

Other Deployment Models

There are variations of the previously discussed deployment models that are also worth noting. The *hybrid cloud*, for example, refers to a model comprised of both private and public cloud environments. The *dedicated cloud* (also known as the hosted cloud or virtual private cloud) represents cloud computing environments hosted and managed off-premise or in public cloud environments, but dedicated resources are provisioned solely for an organization's private use.

The Intercloud (Cloud of Clouds)

The intercloud is not as much a deployment model as it is a concept based on the aggregation of deployed clouds (Figure 8.1). Just like the Internet, which is a network of networks; intercloud refers to an inter-connected global cloud of clouds. Also like the World Wide Web, intercloud represents a massive collection of services that organizations can explore and consume.

From a services consumption perspective, we can look at the intercloud as an on-demand SOA environment where useful services managed by other organizations can be leveraged and composed. In other words, services that are outside of an organization's own boundaries and operated and managed by others can become a part of the aggregate portfolio of services of those same organizations.

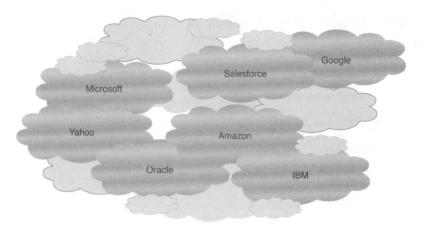

Figure 8.1
Examples of how vendors establish a commercial intercloud.

Deployment Models and Windows Azure

Windows Azure exists in a public cloud. Windows Azure itself is not made available as a packaged software product for organizations to deploy into their own IT enterprises. However, Windows Azure-related features and extensions exist in Microsoft's on-premise software products, and are collectively part of Microsoft's private cloud strategy. It is important to understand that even though the software infrastructure that runs Microsoft's public cloud and private clouds are different, layers that matter to end-user organizations, such as management, security, integration, data, and application are increasingly consistent across private and public cloud environments.

Service Delivery Models

Many different types of services can be delivered in the various cloud deployment environments. Essentially, any IT resource or function can eventually be made available as a service. Although cloud-based ecosystems allow for a wide range of service delivery models, three have become most prominent:

Infrastructure-as-a-Service (IaaS)

This service delivery model represents a modern form of utility computing and outsourced managed hosting. IaaS environments manage and provision fundamental computing resources (networking, storage, virtualized servers, etc.). This allows consumers to deploy and manage assets on leased or rented server instances, while the service providers own and govern the underlying infrastructure.

Platform-as-a-Service (PaaS)

The PaaS model refers to an environment that provisions application platform resources to enable direct deployment of application-level assets (code, data, configurations, policies, etc.). This type of service generally operates at a higher abstraction level so that users manage and control the assets they deploy into these environments. With this arrangement, service providers maintain and govern the application environments, server instances, as well as the underlying infrastructure.

Software-as-a-Service (SaaS)

Hosted software applications or multi-tenant application services that end-users consume directly correspond to the SaaS delivery model. Consumers typically only have control over how they use the cloud-based service, while service providers maintain and govern the software, data, and underlying infrastructure.

Other Delivery Models

Cloud computing is not limited to the aforementioned delivery models. Security, governance, business process management, integration, complex event processing, information and data repository processing, collaborative processes—all can be exposed as services and consumed and utilized to create other services.

> **NOTE**
>
> Cloud deployment models and service delivery models are covered in more detail in the upcoming book *SOA & Cloud Computing* as part of the *Prentice Hall Service-Oriented Computing Series from Thomas Erl*. This book will also introduce several new design patterns related to cloud-based service, composition, and platform design.

IaaS vs. PaaS

In the context of SOA and developing cloud-based services with Windows Azure, we will focus primarily on IaaS and PaaS delivery models in this chapter. Figure 8.2 illustrates a helpful comparison that contrasts some primary differences. Basically, IaaS represents a separate environment to host the same assets that were traditionally hosted on-premise, whereas PaaS represents environments that can be leveraged to build and host next-generation service-oriented solutions.

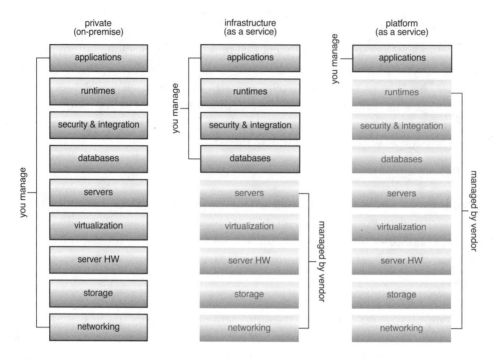

Figure 8.2
Common differentiations between delivery models.

We interact with PaaS at a higher abstraction level than with IaaS. This means we manage less of the infrastructure and assume simplified administration responsibilities. But at the same time, we have less control over this type of environment.

IaaS provides a similar infrastructure to traditional on-premise environments, but we may need to assume the responsibility to re-architect an application in order to effectively leverage platform service clouds. In the end, PaaS will generally achieve a higher level of scalability and reliability for hosted services.

IN PLAIN ENGLISH

An on-premise infrastructure is like having your own car. You have complete control over when and where you want to drive it, but you are also responsible for its operation and maintenance. IaaS is like using a car rental service. You still have control over when and where you want to go, but you don't need to be concerned with the vehicle's maintenance. PaaS is more comparable to public transportation. It is easier to use as you don't need to know how to operate it and it costs less. However, you don't have control over its operation, schedule, or routes.

SUMMARY OF KEY POINTS

- Cloud computing enables the delivery of scalable and available capabilities by leveraging dynamic and on-demand infrastructure.

- There are three common types of cloud deployment models: public cloud, private cloud, and community cloud.

- There are three common types of service delivery models: IaaS, PaaS, and SaaS.

8.2 Windows Azure Platform Overview

The Windows Azure platform is an Internet-scale cloud computing services platform hosted in Microsoft data centers. Windows tools provide functionality to build solutions that include a cloud services operating system and a set of developer services. The key parts of the Windows Azure platform are:

- Windows Azure (application container)

- Microsoft SQL Azure

- Windows Azure platform AppFabric

The Windows Azure platform is part of the Microsoft cloud, which consists of multiple categories of services:

- *cloud-based applications* – These are services that are always available and highly scalable. They run in the Microsoft cloud that consumers can directly utilize. Examples include Bing, Windows Live Hotmail, Office Live, etc.

- *software services* – These services are hosted instances of Microsoft's enterprise server products that consumers can use directly. Examples include Exchange Online, Share-Point Online, Office Communications Online, etc.

> **SOA PRINCIPLES & PATTERNS**
>
> The infrastructure and service architectures that underlie many of these native services (as well as cloud-based services in general) are based on direct combined application of Stateful Services [786] and Redundant Implementation [766]. This is made possible by leveraging several of the built-in extensions and mechanisms provided by the Windows Azure platform (as explained in this chapter and Chapter 16).

- *platform services* – This is where the Windows Azure platform itself is positioned. It serves as an application platform public cloud that developers can use to deploy next-generation, Internet-scale, and always available solutions.

- *infrastructure services* – There is a limited set of elements of the Windows Azure platform that can support cloud-based infrastructure resources.

Figure 8.3 illustrates the service categories related to the Windows Azure platform. Given that Windows Azure is itself a platform, let's explore it as an implementation of the PaaS delivery model.

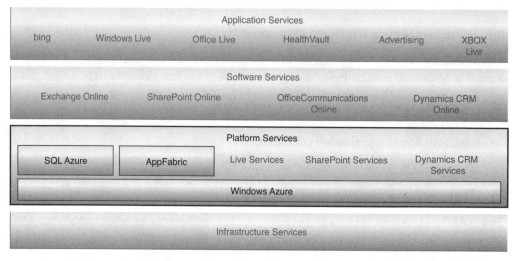

Figure 8.3

A high-level representation of categories of services available in the Windows Azure cloud.

The Windows Azure platform was built from the ground up using Microsoft technologies, such as the Windows Server Hyper-V-based system virtualization layer. However, the Windows Azure platform is not intended to be just another off-premise Windows Server hosting environment. It has a cloud fabric layer, called the *Windows Azure Fabric Controller*, built on top of its underlying infrastructure.

The Windows Azure Fabric Controller pools an array of virtualized Windows Server instances into a logical entity and automatically manages the following:

- resources

- load balancing

- fault-tolerance

- geo-replication

- application lifecycle

These are managed without requiring the hosted applications to explicitly deal with the details. The fabric layer provides a parallel management system that abstracts the complexities in the infrastructure and presents a cloud environment that is inherently elastic. As a form of PaaS, it also supports the access points for user and application interactions with the Windows Azure platform.

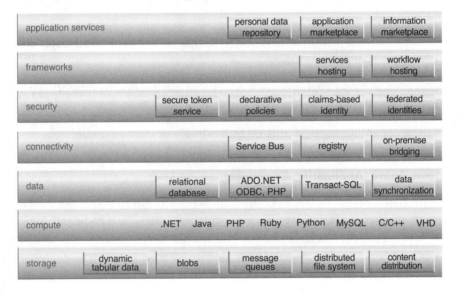

Figure 8.4

An overview of common Windows Azure platform capabilities.

The Windows Azure platform essentially provides a set of cloud-based services that are symmetric with existing mainstream on-site enterprise application platforms (Figure 8.4).

For example:

- *storage services* – a scalable distributed data storage system that supports many types of storage models, including hash map or table-like structured data, large binary files, asynchronous messaging queues, traditional file systems, and content distribution networks

- *compute services* – application containers that support existing mainstream development technologies and frameworks, including .NET, Java, PHP, Python, Ruby on Rails, and native code.

- *data services* – highly reliable and scalable relational database services that also support integration and data synchronization capabilities with existing on-premise relational databases

- *connectivity services* – these are provided via a cloud-based service bus that can be used as a message intermediary to broker connections with other cloud-based services and services behind firewalls within on-premise enterprise environments

- *security services* – policy-driven access control services that are federation-aware and can seamlessly integrate with existing on-premise identity management systems

- *framework services* – components and tools that support specific aspects and requirements of solution frameworks

- *application services* – higher-level services that can be used to support application development, such as application and data marketplaces

All of these capabilities can be utilized individually or in combination.

Windows Azure (Application Container)

Windows Azure serves as the development, service hosting, and service management environment. It provides the application container into which code and logic, such as Visual Studio projects, can be deployed. The application environment is similar to existing Windows Server environments. In fact, most .NET projects can be deployed directly without significant changes.

A Windows Azure instance represents a unit of deployment, and is mapped to specific virtual machines with a range of variable sizes. Physical provisioning of the Windows Azure instances is handled by the cloud fabric. We are required only to specify, by policy, how many instances we want the cloud fabric to deploy for a given service.

We have the ability to manually start and shut down instances, and grow or shrink the deployment pool; however, the cloud fabric also provides automated management of the health and lifecycles of instances. For example, in the event of an instance failure, the cloud fabric would automatically shut down the instance and attempt to bring it back up on another node.

Windows Azure also provides a set of storage services that consumers can use to store and manage persistent and transient data. Storage services support geo-location and offer high durability of data by triple-replicating everything within a cluster and across data centers. Furthermore, they can manage scalability requirements by automatically partitioning and load balancing services across servers.

Also supported by Windows Azure is a VHD-based deployment model as an option to enable some IaaS requirements. This is primarily geared for services that require closer integration with the Windows Server OS. This option provides more control over the service hosting environment and can better support legacy applications.

SQL Azure

SQL Azure is a cloud-based relational database service built on SQL Server technologies that exposes a fault-tolerant, scalable, and multi-tenant database service. SQL Azure does not exist as hosted instances of SQL Server. It also uses a cloud fabric layer to abstract and encapsulate the underlying technologies required for provisioning, server administration, patching, health monitoring, and lifecycle management. We are only required to deal with logical administration tasks, such as schema creation and maintenance, query optimization, and security management.

A SQL Azure database instance is actually implemented as three replicas on top of a shared SQL Server infrastructure managed by the cloud fabric. This cloud fabric delivers high availability, reliability, and scalability with automated and transparent replication

---

SOA PRINCIPLES & PATTERNS

Services deployed within Windows Azure containers and made available via Windows Azure instances establish service architectures that, on the surface, resemble typical Web service or REST service implementations. However, the nature of the back-end processing is highly extensible and scalable and can be further subject to various forms of Service Refactoring [783] over time to accommodate changing usage requirements. This highlights the need for Windows Azure hosted services to maintain the freedom to be independently governed and evolved. This, in turn, places a greater emphasis on the balanced design of the service contract and its proper separation as part of the overall service architecture.

Specifically, it elevates the importance of the Standardized Service Contract (693), Service Loose Coupling (695), and Service Abstraction (696) principles that, through collective application, shape and position service contracts to maximize abstraction and cross-service standardization, while minimizing negative forms of consumer and implementation coupling. Decoupled Contract [735] forms an expected foundation for Windows Azure-hosted service contracts, and there will generally be the need for more specialized contract-centric patterns, such as Validation Abstraction [792], Canonical Schema [718], and Schema Centralization [769].

and failover. It further supports load-balancing of consumer requests and the synchronization of concurrent, incremental changes across the replicas. The cloud fabric also handles concurrency conflict resolutions when performing bi-directional data synchronization between replicas by using built-in policies (such as *last-writer-wins*) or custom policies.

Because SQL Azure is built on SQL Server, it provides a familiar relational data model and is highly symmetric to on-premise SQL Server implementations. It supports most features available in the regular SQL Server database engine and can also be used with tools like SQL Server 2008 Management Studio, SQLCMD, and BCP, and SQL Server Integration Services for data migration.

> **SOA PRINCIPLES & PATTERNS**
>
> In addition to reliability and scalability improvements, SQL Azure's replication mechanism can be used to apply Service Data Replication [773] in support of the Service Autonomy (699) principle. This is significant, as individual service autonomy within cloud environments can often fluctuate due to the heavy emphasis on shared resources across pools of cloud-based services.

Windows Azure Platform AppFabric

In Chapter 7, as part of our coverage of .NET Enterprise Services, we introduced Windows Server AppFabric. This represents the version of AppFabric that is local to the Windows Server environment. *Windows Azure platform AppFabric* (with the word "platform" intentionally not capitalized), is the cloud-based version of AppFabric that runs on Windows Azure.

Windows Azure platform AppFabric helps connect services within or across clouds and enterprises. It provides a Service Bus for connectivity across networks and organizational boundaries, and an Access Control service for federated authorization as a service.

The Service Bus acts as a centralized message broker in the cloud to relay messages between services and service consumers. It has the ability to connect to on-premise services through firewalls, NATs, and over any network topology.

Its features include:

- connectivity using standard protocols and standard WCF bindings

- multiple communication models (such as publish-and-subscribe, one-way messaging, unicast and multicast datagram distribution, full-duplex bi-directional connection-oriented sessions, peer-to-peer sessions, and end-to-end NAT traversal)

- service endpoints that are published and discovered via Internet-accessible URLs

- global hierarchical namespaces that are DNS and transport-independent

- built-in intrusion detection and protection against denial-of-service attacks

Access Control acts as a centralized cloud-based security gateway that regulates access to cloud-based services and Service Bus communications, while integrating with standards-based identity providers (including enterprise directories such as Active Directory and online identity systems like Windows Live ID). Access Control and other Windows Azure-related security topics are covered in Chapter 17.

> **SOA PRINCIPLES & PATTERNS**
>
> The Windows Azure Service Bus complies to the familiar Enterprise Service Bus [741] compound pattern, and focuses on realizing this pattern across network, security, and organizational domains.
>
> Service Bus also provides a service registry to provide registration and discovery of service metadata, which allows for the application of Metadata Centralization [754] and emphasizes the need to apply the Service Discoverability (702) principle.

Unlike Windows Azure and SQL Azure, which are based on Windows Server and SQL Server, Access Control Service is not based on an existing server product. It uses technology included in Windows Identity Foundation and is considered a purely cloud-based service built specifically for the Windows Azure platform environment.

SUMMARY OF KEY POINTS

- The Windows Azure platform is primarily a PaaS deployed in a public cloud managed by Microsoft.

- Windows Azure platform provides a distinct set of capabilities suitable for building scalable and reliable cloud-based services.

- The overall Windows Azure platform further encompasses SQL Azure and Windows Azure platform AppFabric.

8.3 Windows Azure Roles

A cloud service in Windows Azure will typically have multiple concurrent instances. Each instance may be running all or a part of the service's codebase. As a developer, you control the number and type of roles that you want running your service.

Web Roles and Worker Roles

Windows Azure roles are comparable to standard Visual Studio projects, where each instance represents a separate project. These roles represent different types of applications that are natively supported by Windows Azure. There are two types of roles that you can use to host services with Windows Azure:

- Web roles

- worker roles

Web roles provide support for HTTP and HTTPS through public endpoints and are hosted in IIS. They are most comparable to regular ASP.NET projects, except for differences in their configuration files and the assemblies they reference.

Worker roles can also expose external, publicly facing TCP/IP endpoints on ports other than 80 (HTTP) and 443 (HTTPS); however, worker roles do not run in IIS. Worker roles are applications comparable to Windows services and are suitable for background processing.

Virtual Machines

Underneath the Windows Azure platform, in an area that you and your service logic have no control over, each role is given its own virtual machine or VM. Each VM is created when you deploy your service or service-oriented solution to the cloud. All of these VMs are managed by a modified hypervisor and hosted in one of Microsoft's global data centers.

Each VM can vary in size, which pertains to the number of CPU cores and memory. This is something that you control. So far, four pre-defined VM sizes are provided:

- small – 1.7ghz single core, 2GB memory

- medium – 2x 1.7ghz cores, 4GB memory

- large – 4x 1.7ghz cores, 8GB memory

- extra large – 8x 1.7ghz cores, 16GB memory

Notice how each subsequent VM on this list is twice as big as the previous one. This simplifies VM allocation, creation, and management by the hypervisor.

Windows Azure abstracts away the management and maintenance tasks that come along with traditional on-premise service implementations. When you deploy your service into Windows Azure and the service's roles are spun up, copies of those roles are replicated automatically to handle failover (for example, if a VM were to crash because of hard drive failure). When a failure occurs, Windows Azure automatically replaces that "unreliable" role with one of the "shadow" roles that it originally created for your service.

This type of failover is nothing new. On-premise service implementations have been leveraging it for some time using clustering and disaster recovery solutions. However, a common problem with these failover mechanisms is that they are often server-focused. This means that the entire server is failed over, not just a given service or service composition.

When you have multiple services hosted on a Web server that crashes, each hosted service experiences downtime between the current server crashing and the time it takes to bring up the backup server. Although this may not affect larger organizations with sophisticated infrastructure too much, it can impact smaller IT enterprises that may not have the capital to invest in setting up the proper type of failover infrastructure.

Also, suppose you discover in hindsight after performing the failover that it was some background worker process that caused the crash. This probably means that unless you can address it quick enough, your failover server is under the same threat of crashing.

Windows Azure addresses this issue by focusing on application and hosting roles. Each service or solution can have a Web frontend that runs in a Web role. Even though each role has its own "active" virtual machine (assuming we are working with single instances), Windows Azure creates copies of each role that are physically located on one or more servers. These servers may or may not be running in the same data center. These shadow VMs remain idle until they are needed.

Should the background process code crash the worker role and subsequently put the underlying virtual machine out of commission, Windows Azure detects this and automatically brings in one of the shadow worker roles. The faulty role is essentially discarded. If the worker role breaks again, then Windows Azure replaces it once more. All of this is happening without any downtime to the solution's Web role front end, or to any other services that may be running in the cloud.

Input Endpoints

Web roles used to be the only roles that could receive Internet traffic, but now worker roles can listen to any port specified in the service definition file. Internet traffic is received through the use of *input endpoints*. Input endpoints and their listening ports are declared in the service definition (*.csdef) file.

Keep in mind that when you specify the port for your worker role to listen on, Windows Azure isn't actually going to assign that port to the worker. In reality, the load balancer will open two ports—one for the Internet and the other for your worker role. Suppose you wanted to create an FTP worker role and in your service definition file you specify port 21. This tells the fabric load balancer to open port 21 on the Internet side, open pseudo-random port 33476 on the LAN side, and begin routing FTP traffic to the FTP worker role.

In order to find out which port to initialize for the randomly assigned internal port, use the `RoleEnvironment.CurrentRoleInstance.InstanceEndpoints["FtpIn"].IPEndpoint` object.

Inter-Role Communication

Inter-Role Communication (IRC) allows multiple roles to talk to each other by exposing internal endpoints. With an internal endpoint, you specify a name instead of a port number. The Windows Azure application fabric will assign a port for you automatically and will also manage the name-to-port mapping.

Here is an example of how you would specify an internal endpoint for IRC:

```
<ServiceDefinition xmlns=
  "http://schemas.microsoft.com/ServiceHosting/2008/10/
  ServiceDefinition" name="HelloWorld">
  <WorkerRole name="WorkerRole1">
    <Endpoints>
      <InternalEndpoint name="NotifyWorker" protocol="tcp" />
    </Endpoints>
  </WorkerRole>
</ServiceDefinition>
```

Example 8.1

In this example, `NotifyWorker` is the name of the internal endpoint of a worker role named `WorkerRole1`. Next, you need to define the internal endpoint, as follows:

```
RoleInstanceEndpoint internalEndPoint =
RoleEnvironment.CurrentRoleInstance.
  InstanceEndpoints["NotificationService"];
this.serviceHost.AddServiceEndpoint(
  typeof(INameOfYourContract),
  binding,
```

```
String.Format("net.tcp://{0}/NotifyWorker",
    internalEndPoint.IPEndpoint));
WorkerRole.factory = new ChannelFactory<IClientNotification>(binding);
```

Example 8.2

You only need to specify the IP endpoint of the other worker role instances in order to communicate with them. For example, you could get a list of these endpoints with the following routine:

```
var current = RoleEnvironment.CurrentRoleInstance;
var endPoints = current.Role.Instances
  .Where(instance => instance != current)
  .Select(instance => instance.InstanceEndpoints["NotifyWorker"]);
```

Example 8.3

IRC only works for roles in a single application deployment. Therefore, if you have multiple applications deployed and would like to enable some type of cross-application role communication, IRC won't work. You will need to use queues instead.

SUMMARY OF KEY POINTS

- Windows Azure roles represent different types of supported applications or services.

- There are two types of roles: Web roles and worker roles.

- Each role is assigned its own VM.

8.4 Hello World in Windows Azure

The following section demonstrates the creation of a simple "Hello World" service in a Windows Azure hosted application.

NOTE

If you are carrying out the upcoming steps with Visual Studio 2008, you will need to be in an elevated mode (such as Administrator). A convenient way of determining whether the mode setting is correct is to press the F5 key in order to enter debug mode. If you receive an error stating *"the development fabric must be run elevated,"* then you will need to restart Visual Studio as an administrator.

> Also, ensure the following on your SQL Express setup:
>
> - SQL Server Express Edition 2008 must be running under the '.\SQL-EXPRESS' instance
>
> - your Windows account must have a login in .\SQLEXPRESS
>
> - your login account is a member of the sysadmin role
>
> If SQL Express isn't configured properly, you will get a permissions error.

1. Create a Cloud Service Project

First you need to open the New Project window to create a new cloud service project using VB.NET or C# (Figure 8.5).

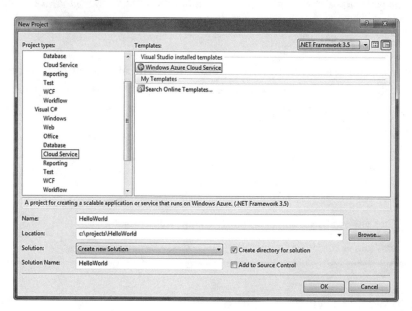

Figure 8.5
The New Project window.

2. Choose an ASP.NET Web Role

After you click OK on the New Project window, the New Cloud Service Project wizard will start. You will then see a window (Figure 8.6) that will allow you to choose the type of role that you would like as part of your service deployment.

For the Hello World project, you will only need the ASP.NET Web Role type. Once you select this role, you can choose the role name.

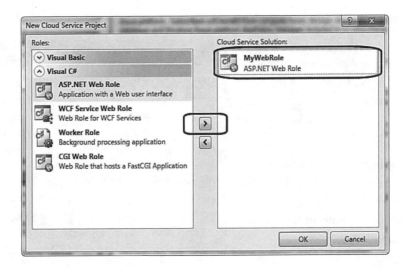

Figure 8.6
The New Cloud Service Project window.

3. Create the Solution

After clicking OK, the wizard will generate the solution, which you can then view using the Solution Explorer window (Figure 8.7).

Figure 8.7
The HelloWorld solution structure displayed in the Solution Explorer window.

4. Instantiate the Service

Now you can open the Default.aspx file using the Solution Explorer window, put "Hello, Cloud!" in the Body element and press F5 to run. You should see something like what is shown in Figure 8.8.

This example was executed locally on IIS. If we were to deploy this service into the Windows Azure cloud, it would still be running in IIS because it is hosted in a Web role.

> **SOA PRINCIPLES & PATTERNS**
>
> Mainstream SOA design patterns and service-orientation principles can be applied to Windows Azure-hosted services very similarly to how they are applied to internal enterprise-hosted services. Furthermore, Windows Azure-hosted services support different service implementation mediums (such as Web services and REST services) and allow for the same service to be accessed via multiple protocols. This supports the creative application of specialized patterns, such as Concurrent Contracts [726] and Dual Protocols [739].

Figure 8.8
The HelloWorld service in action.

SUMMARY OF KEY POINTS

- The development environment for Windows Azure is fully integrated into Visual Studio, which provides a simulated runtime for Windows Azure for local desktop-based development and unit testing.

- Creating and deploying cloud-based services with Windows Azure is simplified using available wizards and development UIs.

8.5 A Web Service in Windows Azure

In this section example, we take a closer look at a Web service that is deployed to Windows Azure in order to better understand the code-level impacts of moving a service to a cloud.

Let's assume we moved a service contact interface definition and a data contract into a custom C# project. We choose ServiceClient to test our service and ServiceDemo contains the Windows Azure application configuration and definition files.

We further opt to host this project in a Web role, which means that there is a little bit of bootstrapping that needs to be done. The WebRole class inherits from the RoleEntry-Point class, which contains methods that are used by Windows Azure to start or stop the role. You can optionally override those methods to manage the initialization or shutdown process of your role. Worker roles must extend RoleEntryPoint, but it is optional for Web roles. The Visual Studio tools will automatically extend this class for you, as you can see from the WebRole.cs code:

```csharp
using System.Linq;
using Microsoft.WindowsAzure.Diagnostics;
using Microsoft.WindowsAzure.ServiceRuntime;
using System.Diagnostics;
namespace ServiceDemo_WebRole
{
  public class WebRole : RoleEntryPoint
  {
    public override bool OnStart()
    {
      DiagnosticMonitor.Start("DiagnosticsConnectionString");
      RoleEnvironment.Changing += RoleEnvironmentChanging;
      Trace.TraceInformation("WebRole starting...");
      return base.OnStart();
    }
    private void RoleEnvironmentChanging(object sender,
      RoleEnvironmentChangingEventArgs e)
    {
      if (e.Changes.Any(change => change is
        RoleEnvironmentConfigurationSettingChange))
      {
        e.Cancel = true;
      }
    }
  }
}
```

Example 8.4

Our cloud service project includes two configuration files: ServiceDefinition.csdef and ServiceConfiguration.cscfg. These files are packaged together with the cloud service when it is deployed to Windows Azure.

The ServiceDefinition.csdef file contains the metadata needed by the Windows Azure environment to understand the requirements of the service, including the roles it contains. It also establishes configuration settings that will be applied to all specified service roles:

```
<ServiceDefinition name="ServiceDemo" xmlns=
  "http://schemas.microsoft.com/ServiceHosting/2008/10/
  ServiceDefinition">
  <WebRole name="ServiceDemo_WebRole">
    <InputEndpoints>
      <InputEndpoint name=
        "HttpIn" protocol="http" port="80" />
    </InputEndpoints>
    <ConfigurationSettings>
      <Setting name="DiagnosticsConnectionString" />
    </ConfigurationSettings>
  </WebRole>
</ServiceDefinition>
```

Example 8.5

The ServiceConfiguration.cscfg file sets values for the configuration settings defined in the service definition file and specifies the number of instances to run for each role. Here is the ServiceConfiguration.cscfg for the ServiceDemo service project:

```
<ServiceConfiguration serviceName="ServiceDemo"
  xmlns="http://schemas.microsoft.com/
  ServiceHosting/2008/10/ServiceConfiguration">
  <Role name="ServiceDemo_WebRole">
    <Instances count="2" />
    <ConfigurationSettings>
      <Setting name="DiagnosticsConnectionString"
        value="UseDevelopmentStorage=true" />
    </ConfigurationSettings>
  </Role>
</ServiceConfiguration>
```

Example 8.6

The `Instances` element tells the Windows Azure runtime fabric how many instances to spin up for the ServiceDemo_WebRole role. By default, Visual Studio tools set this to "1", but this is generally not a good idea. If you only have one role running and it crashes, it could take a while before Windows Azure spins up another one. However, if you had multiple roles and one goes down, the application wouldn't experience a work stop while a new instance is being generated. This is why it is a good practice to have at least two role instances per role.

In the `ConfigurationSettings` section, there is a statement worth singling out:

```
<Setting name="DiagnosticsConnectionString"
  value="UseDevelopmentStorage=true" />
```

Example 8.7

There is a set of logging and diagnostic APIs that you can use to instrument your code and provide better traceability. With these APIs, you can not only detect and troubleshoot problems, but you can also gain insight into the overall performance of an application.

This line of code passes in the configuration setting name that is equal to the connection string for the storage account that the Diagnostic Monitor needs to use to store the diagnostic data. By default, the setting name is `DiagnosticsConnectionString`, but you can name it whatever you like as long as the name matches up with the service definition and service configuration files.

In the WebRole.cs, you will see the following statement:

```
DiagnosticMonitor.Start("DiagnosticsConnectionString");
```

Example 8.8

This line of code starts up the Diagnostic Monitor when the role starts. By default, the connection string is set to use development storage, such as the SQL table that was created when the SDK was installed. Before you deploy the service to the Windows Azure cloud, you will need to update this setting with the storage account name and account key information.

For example:

```
<ConfigurationSettings>
  <Setting name="DiagnosticsConnectionString"
    value="DefaultEndpointsProtocol=https;AccountName=
    [ACCOUNT NAME};AccountKey=[ACCOUNT KEY]" />
</ConfigurationSettings>
```

Example 8.9

If we take a look at the Web role's Web.Config file, we'll also see that the project wizard automatically created the following:

```
<system.diagnostics>
  <trace>
    <listeners>
      <addtype="Microsoft.WindowsAzure.Diagnostics.
        DiagnosticMonitorTraceListener,
        Microsoft.WindowsAzure.Diagnostics, Version=1.0.0.0,
        Culture=neutral, PublicKeyToken=31bf3856ad364e35"
        name="AzureDiagnostics">
        <filter type=""/>
      </add>
    </listeners>
  </trace>
</system.diagnostics>
```

Example 8.10

This creates a tracing listener for the diagnostic monitor, which means that we continue to use the System.Diagnostics.Trace class for instrumentation. The diagnostic monitor will just hook into those calls and push them into storage.

The following examples show the IOrderService interface contract and the Order data contract, followed by the final output:

```
namespace Contract
{
  [ServiceContract]
  public interface IOrderService
  {
    [OperationContract]
    int CreateOrder(Order o);
    [OperationContract]
    void UpdateOrder(string id, Order o);
    [OperationContract]
```

```
    Order GetOrderByOrderId(string id);
    [OperationContract]
    List<Order> GetOrdersByCustomer(string custName);
    [OperationContract]
    List<Order> GetOrders();
    [OperationContract]
    void DeleteOrder(string id);
  }
}
```

Example 8.11

```
namespace Contract
{
[DataContract(Namespace=
  "http://example.cloudapp.net/servicedemo/1.0")]
  public class Order
  {
    [DataMember]
    public int OrderId { get; set; }
    [DataMember]
    public string OrderItem { get; set; }
    [DataMember]
    public string CustomerName { get; set; }
  }
}
```

Example 8.12

```
namespace ServiceDemo_WebRole
{
  [ServiceBehavior(InstanceContextMode =
    InstanceContextMode.Single,
    AddressFilterMode =
    AddressFilterMode.Any)]
  public class OrderService : Contract.IOrderService
  {
    int id = 0;
    List<Order> Orders = new List<Order>();
    #region IOrderService Members
    int IOrderService.CreateOrder(Order o)
    {
      o.OrderId = ++id;
      Orders.Add(o);
      return o.OrderId;
```

```
    }
    void IOrderService.UpdateOrder(string id, Order o)
    {
      var first = Orders.First(order =>
        order.OrderId ==
        Convert.ToInt64(id));
      first = o;
    }
    List<Order> IOrderService.GetOrders()
    {
      return Orders;
    }
    void IOrderService.DeleteOrder(string orderId)
    {
      Orders.RemoveAll(order =>
        order.OrderId.Equals
        (Convert.ToInt64(orderId)));
    }
    Order IOrderService.GetOrderByOrderId(string orderId)
    {
      return Orders.First(o =>
        o.OrderId.Equals(Convert.ToInt64(orderId)));
    }
    public List<Order> GetOrdersByCustomer(string custName)
    {
      return (string.IsNullOrEmpty(custName)) ?
        Orders : Orders.FindAll(o =>
        o.CustomerName.Equals(custName));
    }
    #endregion
  }
}
```

Example 8.13

Note that the `InstanceContextMode` setting is set to to single because we want to use the same service object instance across the communication session established between the service and its consumer. In a real world scenario, you would choose a more robust solution like SQL Azure or Windows Azure table storage (covered later in this chapter).

Let's briefly walk through the steps required to actually deploy the service to Windows Azure.

1. Create a Host Service and Storage Service

When you create a storage service, you have to create a globally unique storage account name, not to be confused with the overarching Windows Azure account that is mapped to your Windows LiveID. For our example, we chose juggercloud as the account name and received three storage endpoints. Two access keys are also generated.

Before we deploy our Web service, however, we will update the Web role service configuration *.cscfg file with the account name and account key information, as follows:

```
<ServiceConfiguration serviceName="StandardMoldHost"
  xmlns="http://schemas.microsoft.com/
  ServiceHosting/2008/10/ServiceConfiguration">
  <Role name="ServiceDemo_WebRole">
    <Instances count="2" />
      <ConfigurationSettings>
       <Setting name="DiagnosticsConnectionString"
         value="DefaultEndpointsProtocol=https;
         AccountName=standardmold;AccountKey=01g820j...==" />
      </ConfigurationSettings>
   </Role>
</ServiceConfiguration>
```

Example 8.14

2. Create and Deploy a Service Package

We deploy the service by uploading a package through the Windows Azure portal. When using the Windows Azure UI, we can navigate to the host service to determine whether we are deploying to staging or production.

There's really no difference in hardware resource configuration between these two settings. In fact, the separation between the two environments is managed through the network load balancer's routing tables.

Once we click "Deploy," the package and configuration file will be uploaded.

NOTE
We could have also pulled these bits from a Windows Azure storage account. For example, we could create a custom MSBuild task leveraged within a Team Foundation Server Team Build definition file. Instead of dropping the package to a normal file drop, this would upload it into blob storage using the REST API, or perhaps even leverage Windows Azure Drive.

3. Promote the Service to Production

Let's imagine the previous step initially deployed the service to staging so that we could test it before moving it into the production enviroment. The Windows Azure UI allows you to invoke the service by clicking "Run," resulting in a page similar to Figure 8.9.

```
OrderService Service

You have created a service.

To test this service, you will need to create a client and use it to call the service. You can do this using the svcutil.exe tool from the co

svcutil.exe http://rd00155d317ed4:20000/OrderService.svc?wsdl

This will generate a configuration file and a code file that contains the client class. Add the two files to your client application and use t

C#

class Test
{
    static void Main()
    {
        OrderServiceClient client = new OrderServiceClient();

        // Use the 'client' variable to call operations on the service.

        // Always close the client.
        client.Close();
    }
}

Visual Basic

Class Test
    Shared Sub Main()
        Dim client As OrderServiceClient = New OrderServiceClient()
        ' Use the 'client' variable to call operations on the service.

        ' Always close the client.
        client.Close()
    End Sub
End Class
```

Figure 8.9

After verifying that the Web service is performing as desired, it can be deployed to production (Figure 8.10).

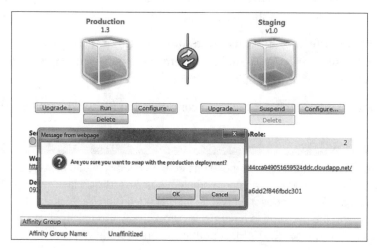

Figure 8.10

8.6 A REST Service in Windows Azure

In order to explore how REST services are created and exist within Windows Azure, this section takes the Web service from the previous section and makes it RESTful. But, before we dive into the implementation details of this change, let's first take a step back and think about REST-specific design considerations.

REST Service Addressing

A common design practice with REST services is to make the addressing (the manner in which target resources are addressed) as intuitive as possible. The social bookmarking site Delicious is a great example of this.

With Delicious, every bookmark has one or more tags (think of tags as categories). Tags essentially replace folders within Web browsers with categories. In relation to our discussion, you can also group tags into a bundle, which basically creates "tag clouds." Access to tagged bookmarks is provided via REST services. Table 8.1 shows a set of sample URLs that can be used to get back a list of bookmarks for Azure, SOA, and Azure+SOA, respectively.

URL	Description
http://delicious.com/tag/azure	returns a list of bookmarks that have been tagged with Azure
http://delicious.com/tag/soa	returns a list of bookmarks that have been tagged with SOA
http://delicious.com/tag/soa+azure	returns a list of bookmarks that have been tagged with SOA and Azure

Table 8.1
Sample URLs used to retrieve different values from REST services at delicious.com.

What's important about this example is that we are able to search, create and update a large network of data via REST without writing code. The HTTP GET method and the appropriate URLs are all we need.

Returning to our Order service, we first need to define an appropriate resource addressing structure for the order data, as shown in Table 8.2.

Action	IOrderService Operation Name	URI Address Template	HTTP Method
get a list of all orders	GetOrders	./orders	GET
get an order given the order ID	GetOrderByOrderId	./order/{id}	GET
get a list of orders for a given customer	GetOrdersByCustomer	./orders/{custName}	GET
create an order	CreateOrder	./orders	POST
update an order	UpdateOrder	./order/{id}	PUT
delete an order	DeleteOrder	./order/{id}	DELETE

Table 8.2
The resource addressing structure for the Order service.

Creating a Windows Azure REST Service

We now need to carry out a series of steps to make this a REST service:

1. Add a reference to System.ServiceModel.Web in the Contract project.

2. Add HTTP attributes to the methods defined in the IOrderService interface.

3. Update the WCF behavior.

4. Update the OrderService.svc file by adding a Web factory reference.

The System.ServiceModel.Web namespace contains classes that make up the Web HTTP programming model.

For our purposes, we need to focus on the following:

- WebGetAttribute (maps to an HTTP GET)

- WebInvokeAttribute (maps to HTTP POST, PUT, and DELETE)

- WebMessageFormat (defines the format of the response message)

For the GET method, we use the WebGet attribute. We then use the UriTemplate attribute to define the addressing structure from Table 8.2. This is a manual process, which means that it's easy to make mistakes. It is therefore important to lay out the URI structure prior to working with the code.

We also need to specify the {token} parameters. For example, if we were calling the GetOrderByOrderId operation of the Web service via SOAP, we would just pass in the order ID argument by calling the Web method. But with REST, everything is through HTTP methods and URIs. The service consumer doesn't call GetOrderByOrderId directly, but rather does the HTTP GET method on http://server/OrderService.svc/order/2, where "2" is the order ID value.

Next, we need to determine the response message format by setting ResponseFormat to return XML messages.

Here's what IOrderService looks like now:

```
[ServiceContract]
public interface IOrderService
{
  [WebInvoke(Method="POST",
    UriTemplate="orders",
    ResponseFormat=WebMessageFormat.Xml)]
  [OperationContract]
  int CreateOrder(Order o);
  [WebInvoke(Method="PUT",
    UriTemplate="order/{id}",
    ResponseFormat=WebMessageFormat.Xml)]
  [OperationContract]
  void UpdateOrder(string id, Order o);
  [WebGet(UriTemplate="order/{id}",
    ResponseFormat=WebMessageFormat.Xml)]
  [OperationContract]
  Order GetOrderByOrderId(string id);
  [WebGet(UriTemplate="orders/{custName}",
    ResponseFormat=WebMessageFormat.Xml)]
  [OperationContract]
  List<Order> GetOrdersByCustomer(string custName);
  [WebGet(UriTemplate="orders",
    ResponseFormat=WebMessageFormat.Xml)]
  [OperationContract]
  List<Order> GetOrders();
  [WebInvoke(Method="DELETE",
    UriTemplate="order/{id}",
    ResponseFormat=WebMessageFormat.Xml)]
  [OperationContract]
  void DeleteOrder(string id);
}
```

Example 8.15

We now need to update the WCF behavior in the Web.Config file by changing the endpoint binding to `WebHttpBinding` and the endpoint behavior to a Web behavior, as shown here:

```
<services>
  <servicebehaviorConfiguration=
    "ServiceDemo_WebRole.ServiceDemoBehavior"
    name="ServiceDemo_WebRole.OrderService">
    <endpoint address="" binding="WebHttpBinding"
      contract="Contract.IOrderService"
      behaviorConfiguration="Web">
    </endpoint>
  </service>
</services>
<behaviors>
  <endpointBehaviors>
    <behavior name="Web" />
  </endpointBehaviors>
  <serviceBehaviors>
    <behavior name=
      "ServiceDemo_WebRole.ServiceDemoBehavior">
  </serviceBehaviors>
</behaviors>
```

Example 8.16

Finally, we have to update the OrderService.svc file to include `WebServiceHostFactory`, as shown here:

```
<%@
  ServiceHost Language="C#" Debug="true"
  Service="ServiceDemo_WebRole.OrderService"
  CodeBehind="OrderService.svc.cs"
  Factory="System.ServiceModel.
    Activation.WebServiceHostFactory"
%>
```

Example 8.17

`WebServiceHostFactory` provides instances of `WebServiceHost` in managed
hosting environments, where the host
instance is created dynamically in
response to incoming messages. This is
necessary because the service is being
hosted using a Web role in IIS.

SOA PRINCIPLES & PATTERNS
Cloud-based REST service architecture relates to several SOA design patterns relevant to REST service design. These are covered separately in the book *SOA with REST* as part of the *Prentice Hall Service-Oriented Computing Series with Thomas Erl*.

Finally, to deploy the REST version of
the Order service to Windows Azure, we can follow the same steps described in the previous *A Web Service in Windows Azure* section.

SUMMARY OF KEY POINTS

- Programming models and deployment processes for Web services are very similar and consistent between cloud-based services in Windows Azure and on-premise services in Windows Server.

- Most significant differences with cloud-based services in Windows Azure are managed via service configurations.

- Development and deployment of REST-based services in Windows Azure are also consistent with the on-premise platform.

8.7 Windows Azure Storage

Windows Azure provides the following set of storage services (collectively referred to as Windows Azure Storage), each of which is suitable for different types of data access requirements:

- *Tables* provide structured storage, as they do in regular databases. Essentially, each table consists of a set of data entities that each contain a set of properties.

- *Queues* provide reliable storage and delivery of messages. They are often used between roles to communicate with each other.

- *Blobs* are used to store large binary objects (files). They provide a simple interface for storing named files along with metadata and include support for CDN (Content Delivery Network).

- *Windows Azure Drives* provide durable NTFS volumes for Windows Azure applications.

Windows Azure Storage supplies a managed API and a REST API, both of which essentially provide the same level of functionality. The managed API is provided through the Microsoft.WindowsAzure.StorageClient namespace. To interact with the storage services, you can also use familiar programming interfaces, such as ADO.NET Data Services (available in the .NET framework version 3.5 SP1).

Note that access to storage is regulated via Windows Azure Storage accounts that use 256-bit secret keys. Also, there are some storage size limitations. For example, each storage account will have a maximum 100 terabytes of total storage capacity.

Tables

Windows Azure Tables (WATs) are similar to relational tables insofar as they both are used to store structured data. However, it's important to understand that WAT storage is not a relational database management system for the cloud (that's what SQL Azure is for). In other words, there is no support for common database features, such as joins, aggregates, stored procedures, or indexes.

WATs were built primarily to realize scalability, availability, and durability of data. Individual tables can be scaled to billions of entities (rows) with data totaling into the order of terabytes. Part of the scaling algorithm is that as application traffic and usage grows, WATs will automatically scale out to potentially tens, to hundreds, to thousands of servers. With regards to availability, each WAT is replicated at least three times.

Entities and Properties

Windows Azure Storage introduces some specific terminology and relationships for WATs:

- You create a *storage account*, each of which can have multiple *tables*.

- Data stored within a table is organized into *entities*. A database row is comparable to an entity.

- Each entity contains a set of *properties*. A database column is comparable to a property.

- A table is comprised of a set of entities, each of which is comprised of a set of properties.

Each entity contains two key properties that together form the unique ID of the entity in that table. The first key is the *PartitionKey*, which allows you to group entities together.

This tells the Windows Azure Storage system to not split this group up when scaling out the table.

In other words, partition keys are used to group table entities into partitions that provide a unit of scale that Windows Azure Storage uses to properly load balance data. Partition keys also allow you to control the physical locality of the entity data. Everything within a partition will live on a single server.

The second key is the *RowKey*, which provides uniqueness within a partition in that the PartitionKey together with the RowKey uniquely identify a given entity (as well as the sort order). You can think of these two keys as a clustered index for a table.

The third required attribute is the *Timestamp*, which is a read-only attribute used to control optimistic concurrency. That is, if you try to update a row that another program has already updated, your update attempt will fail because of the timestamp mismatch.

Data Access

When interacting with entities and properties, you are provided the full range of regular data access functions (get, insert, update, delete), in addition to special features, such as the partial update (merge), the entire update (replace), and the entity group transaction.

Entity group transactions allow you to atomically perform multiple insert, update, and delete commands over a set of entities in the same partition as part of a single transaction.

Queues

As with traditional messaging queues, the Windows Azure queues provide a reliable intermediary mechanism for delivering messages. For example, a common scenario is to set up a queue as the communication proxy between an application's Web role (of which there may be one or two instances) and its worker roles (of which there can be many instances). For this scenario you would likely set up at least two queues. The first would allow the Web role to submit messages for the worker roles to process. The worker roles would poll the queue for new messages until one is received. The second queue would then be for the worker roles to communicate back to the Web role. This architecture allows the Web role to delegate and spread out resource-intensive work to the worker roles.

Just like with tables, queues are scoped by the storage account that you create. An account can have many queues, each of which can contain an unlimited amount of messages. Also, dequeued counts are tracked, allowing you to determine how often a given message has been dequeued by a worker process.

Queues offer a range of data access functions, including the ability to create, delete, list, and get/set queued metadata. Additionally, you can add (enqueue) and retrieve (dequeue) sets of messages, and delete and "peek" at messages individually.

Blobs

Each storage account can have containers that can be used to store blobs. There is no limit to the number of containers that you can have as long as they will fit into your storage account limit.

Containers have the ability to set public or private access policies. The private access level will only allow access to consumers that have been given permission. Public access allows any consumer to interact with the container's blobs using a URL. You can also have container metadata, which, like blob metadata, is stored in name-value pairs.

You have two choices for the type of blob that you can use: block and page. Both types have characteristics that make them applicable to specific requirements.

Block Blobs

A block blob is primarily geared towards streaming media files. Each blob is organized into a sequential list of "blocks" that can be created and uploaded out of order and in parallel for increased performance. Once uploaded, each block is in an uncommitted state, meaning that you cannot access the blob until its blocks are committed. To commit the blocks as well as define the correct block order, you use the `PutBlobList` command.

Each block is immutable and is further defined by a block ID. After you have successfully uploaded a block, that block (identified by its block ID) cannot be changed. That also means that if you have updated a block on-premise, then you will need to re-upload or copy the entire block with the same block ID.

Blobs can be accessed via an available REST API that provides standard data access operations, as well as special functions, such as *CopyBlob* that allows you to copy an existing blob to a new blob name.

Page Blobs

Page blobs are suitable for random I/O operations. With this kind of blob, you must first pre-allocate space (up to 1TB), wherein the blob is divided into 512-byte "pages." To access or update a page, you must address it using a byte offset. Another key difference is that changes to page blobs are immediate.

You can expand the blob size at any point by increasing its maximum size setting. You are also allowed to shrink the blob by truncating pages. You can update a page in one of two ways: *PutPage* or *ClearPage*. With PutPage, you specify the payload and the range of pages, whereas ClearPage basically zeroes out a page range up to the entire blob. There are several other commands that can be used to work with page blobs.

Windows Azure Drive

Windows Azure Drive is a storage service that provides a durable NTFS volume for Windows Azure applications. An application needs to mount the volume prior to using it and, when done, the application then unmounts the same volume. Throughout this period, the volume data is kept intact, even if the application should crash.

A Windows Azure Drive volume is actually a page blob. Specifically, it exists as a page blob that has been formatted as an NTFS single volume virtual hard drive (VHD). As such, these drives can be up to 1TB in size.

SUMMARY OF KEY POINTS

- Windows Azure Storage provides a set of services for distributed cloud-based data storage.

- The four types of storage services provided are tables, queues, blobs, and Windows Azure Drive.

- Windows Azure Storage services are available via both .NET managed APIs and REST-based APIs.

Part II

Services and Service Composition

Chapter 9: Service-Orientation with .NET Part I: Service Contracts
            and Interoperability

Chapter 10: Service-Orientation with .NET Part II: Coupling, Abstraction,
            and Discoverability

Chapter 11: Service-Orientation with .NET Part III: Reusability and
            Agnostic Service Models

Chapter 12: Service-Orientation with .NET Part IV: Service Composition
            and Orchestration Basics

Chapter 13: Orchestration Patterns with WF

Chapter 14: Orchestration Patterns with BizTalk Server

The six chapters in this part of the book are focused exclusively on the application of service-orientation design principles and SOA design patterns to services and service compositions built using .NET technologies. Unlike the chapters in Part I, principles and patterns are now regularly referenced inline as various topics are covered. Therefore, an understanding of the covered .NET technologies as well as any referenced design principles and patterns is required in order to fully work through these chapters.

Note that each chapter in Part II begins with an "SOA Principles & Patterns Referenced in This Chapter" box that, as the title states, contains a list of the design principles and patterns referenced within a given chapter. The intention of this list is to give you advance notice of topic areas that you may want to read up on prior to proceeding.

Chapter 9

Service-Orientation with .NET Part I: Service Contracts and Interoperability

9.1 Standardized Service Contract

9.2 Canonical Schema

9.3 Data Model Transformation

9.4 Canonical Protocol

9.5 Canonical Expression

WCF (together with the .NET framework extensions and Windows Azure) establishes a broad, almost all-encompassing platform for service development, deployment, and hosting. When building entire service inventories upon such a platform, we need to consider that one of the primary goals of service-oriented computing in general is that of Increased Vendor Diversification Options.

This strategic goal aims to establish service-oriented technology architecture in such a manner that best-of-breed technologies can be leveraged on the back-end, while preserving a federated service endpoint layer on the consumer-side, which is related to another primary goal called Increased Federation.

An important aspect of the Increased Vendor Diversification Options goal is the "Options" part. This goal does not advocate that you diversify your IT enterprise. Doing so unnecessarily can lead to increased governance burden and increased cost of ownership. For example, if WCF, .NET, and Windows Azure continue to empower you to maximize business requirements fulfillment, the collective environment they establish can be highly effective for broad SOA adoption. By leveraging common platform class libraries, system services, repositories, and other mechanisms, we are, in effect, repeatedly applying the Canonical Resources [717] pattern and reaping its ownership benefits on a potentially grand scale.

The goal of Increased Vendor Diversification Options simply states that you should always retain the *option* of being able to bring in technologies and products from other vendors. That way, when justified, you can diversify in order to increase your business requirement fulfillment potential. In other words, avoid vendor lock-in so that, over time, you are not inhibited by a specific vendor's product roadmap (which may end up straying from the direction in which you need to evolve your business automation solutions).

To realize this goal we need to go back to the aforementioned goal of Increased Federation, a goal that is directly tied to the application of the Federated Endpoint Layer [745] pattern. By establishing a layer of standardized service contracts (endpoints) federated within a given service inventory boundary, we create an inter-service communications framework that is completely abstracted from the technologies, platforms and products that comprise individual, back-end, service architecture implementations.

It is this form of clean, far-reaching abstraction that gives us the freedom to diversify without having to rip-and-replace an entire ecosystem. Instead, we can continue to leverage existing vendor platforms as they remain useful and beneficial, and then refactor individual service architectures independently to augment and grow our inventory of services in tandem with on-going business change.

The success factors behind both the Increased Vendor Diversification Options and Increased Federation strategic goals can be mapped to the appropriate design, development, and architectural positioning of service contracts. These factors are critical to the realization of the Increased Intrinsic Interoperability goal that is core to the overall objective and long-term target state advocated by service-orientation.

The attainment of an intrinsic level of interoperability within each service is a broad topic with numerous sub-topics, many of which are addressed by various chapters in this book. This chapter kicks things off by exploring the application of .NET technologies with key principles and patterns that pertain to service contract development and the creation of federated service endpoints.

9.1 Standardized Service Contract

This principle advocates the standardization of service contracts that exist within a given service inventory boundary (Figure 9.1). Within this context, standardization can refer to the usage of industry standards (such as WSDL and XML Schema), but primarily the focus is on custom design standards that are pre-defined and regulated (such as canonical data models).

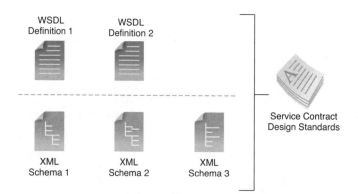

Figure 9.1

The application of the Standardized Service Contract (693) principle relies heavily on the use of design standards that regulate contract design across services within a given service inventory.

Contract-First

To ensure that contracts are consistently standardized requires that we seize programmatic control over how contracts are created, which is the basis of the *contract-first* approach that is predominantly used when applying this principle.

There are various ways of going about contract-first development with .NET. The primary consideration is in determining in what sequence to define the various parts of a service contract.

For example, here is a common three-step process:

1. Create or Reuse Data Contract

A WCF data contract most commonly exists as an XML schema that defines the data structure and data types (as part of the overall data model) for a given set of data that is exchanged by a service capability.

Following patterns, such as Canonical Schema [718] and Schema Centralization [769], this step may involve creating a new data contract to be used by one or more services or it may involve reusing an already existing (and standardized) data contract. The latter circumstance may be due to a data contract that was previously customized or there may be a requirement to use a data contract that exists as an industry standard XML Schema (such as HR-XML or LegalML).

NOTE
Schema Centralization [769] and reusable schemas are discussed shortly in the *Canonical Schema* section.

2. Create Message Contract

The body content of a given message transmitted or received by a service capability is primarily predefined by the data contract. The message contract encompasses the data contract and further defines metadata in the message header, as per Messaging Metadata [753]. Message contracts within WCF are primarily built using the SOAP `Body` and `Header` constructs. Part of this step may also involve predefining fault contracts for exception conditions.

SERVICE MODELING & SERVICE CANDIDATES

Prior to applying any contract-first development approach, it is generally assumed that some extent of service modeling has already been completed. The service modeling process is part of the service-oriented analysis stage within a service's overall delivery cycle. Service modeling produces conceptual services called *service candidates* that form the basis of service contracts. Often significant up-front analysis is carried out in order to define several service candidates for a specific service inventory before physically building any one service contract. This effectively creates a service inventory blueprint that allows the basic parts of service contracts to be well-defined and further refined through iteration, prior to entering the design and development phases.

3. Create Interface Contract

The interface contract is commonly equated to the abstract description of a WSDL document wherein operation contracts are defined. When working with REST services, the interface contract can be considered the subset of HTTP methods that are supported as part of the overall uniform contract for a given service.

The interface contract and its operations or methods express the externally invokable functionality offered by a service. An interface contract pulls together the data and message contracts and associates them with appropriate operations or methods.

NOTE
For detailed coverage of carrying out contract-first processes with .NET technologies, see the *Decoupled Contract* section in Chapter 10.

Standardized Service Contract (693) and Patterns

Beyond carrying out a contract-first approach to service design, there are many more facets to applying the Standardized Service Contract (693) principle. Several of these additional aspects will come up in the subsequent sections exploring SOA design patterns related to service interoperability.

SUMMARY OF KEY POINTS

- The application of the Standardized Service Contract (693) principle commonly involves following a contract-first approach to service-oriented design.

- The Standardized Service Contract (693) principle is closely associated with several patterns, including Canonical Schema [718], Schema Centralization [769], Canonical Protocol [716], and Canonical Expression [715], all of which support its application in different ways.

9.2 Canonical Schema

The XML Schema Definition Language is a highly successful industry standard that has received broad cross-platform support within, and well beyond, the SOA industry. With this language you can use industry standard markup syntax to not only express the structure and validation rules of business documents, but you can also use a series of built-in data types to represent the actual data. This allows you to define complete data models in a manner that is independent of any proprietary database or data representation technology.

Canonical Schema [718] establishes standardized XML Schema definitions (Figure 9.2), which makes this a pattern that can be applied in direct support of Standardized Service Contract (693).

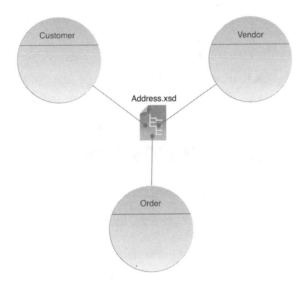

Figure 9.2
By sharing a canonical schema definition, different services increase their respective compatibility and interoperability.

Schema Centralization [769], a related pattern that mandates that schema definitions be shared among service contracts, can be applied together with Canonical Schema [718] to help create a flexible and streamlined data architecture that acts as a foundation layer for a set of federated service contracts (Figure 9.3). The abstraction achieved by such a data architecture allows you to build underlying services using .NET, Java, or any other back-end implementation platform that supports XML Schema processing.

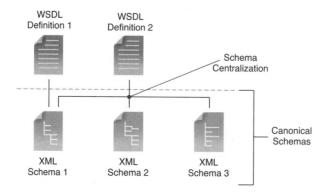

Figure 9.3

When canonical schemas are centralized, they are essentially reused by different service contracts, resulting in increased normalization across the service data and endpoint architecture.

Creating Schemas with Visual Studio

To build canonical XML schemas that we will eventually want to centralize, we need to master the XML Schema Definition Language and customize these schemas using an editor, such as the one provided by Visual Studio.

> **NOTE**
>
> This book does not provide tutorial coverage of the XML Schema Definition Language. If you are new to XML Schema, refer to Chapters 6, 12, and 13 of the book *Web Service Contract Design & Versioning for SOA*.

Let's now put together some simple schemas. Figure 9.4 shows a preview of the person schema displayed in the Visual Studio 2010 Schema View. We can also refer to the person schema as the person *type*, because it essentially establishes a complex type for the person entity.

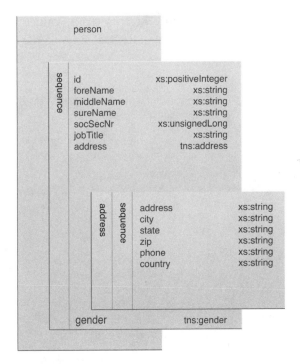

Figure 9.4
XML Schema types defined.

We'll begin with putting together the gender type first:

```
<xs:schema xmlns:xs=http://www.w3.org/2001/XMLSchema
  targetNamespace="http://schemas.example.org/
    enterprise/models/v1"
  xmlns="http://schemas.example.org/
    enterprise/models/v1"
  xmlns:mstns="http://schemas.example.org/
    enterprise/models/v1"
  version="1.0.1"
  elementFormDefault="qualified">
  <xs:simpleType name="gender">
    <xs:restriction base="xs:string">
      <xs:enumeration value="male" />
      </xs:enumeration value="female" />
    </xs:restriction>
  </xs:simpleType>
</xs:schema>
```

Example 9.1

The validation logic in this schema only accepts string values that are "male" and "female." The gender type is saved as a separate XML schema file called gender.xsd.

Next, let's create the address type:

```
<xs:schema xmlns:xs="http://www.w3.org/2001/XMLSchema"
  targetNamespace="http://schemas.example.org/
    enterprise/models/v1"
  xmlns="http://schemas.example.org/
    enterprise/models/v1"
  xmlns:mstns="http://schemas.example.org/
    enterprise/models/v1"
  version="1.0.1"
  elementFormDefault="qualified">
  <xs:complexType name="address">
    <xs:sequence>
      <xs:element name="address" type="xs:string" />
      <xs:element name="city" type="xs:string" />
      <xs:element name="state" type="xs:string" />
      <xs:element name="zip" type="xs:string" />
      <xs:element name="phone" type="xs:string" />
      <xs:element name="country" type="xs:string" />
    </xs:sequence>
  </xs:complexType>
</xs:schema>
```

Example 9.2

The address type accepts strings for all of its child elements. This type is also saved in a separate schema file (called address.xsd).

Finally, here's the content for the person type, which is stored in the person.xsd file:

```
<xs:schema xmlns:xs=
  "http://www.w3.org/2001/XMLSchema"
  xmlns:tns="http://schemas.example.org/
    enterprise/models/v1"
  targetNamespace="http://schemas.example.org/
    enterprise/models/v1"
  xmlns:mstns="http://schemas.example.org/
  enterprise/models/v1"
  version="1.1.20"
```

```
  elementFormDefault="qualified">
  <xs:include schemaLocation="Gender.xsd"/>
  <xs:include schemaLocation="Address.xsd"/>
  <xs:complexType name="person">
    <xs:sequence>
      <xs:element name="ID" type="xs:positiveInteger" />
      <xs:element name="foreName"
        type="xs:string" minOccurs="1"/>
      <xs:element name="middleName" type="xs:string" />
      <xs:element name="surName"
        type="xs:string" minOccurs="1"/>
      <xs:element name="socSecNr" type="xs:unsignedLong"
        minOccurs="1" maxOccurs="1"/>
      <xs:element name="jobTitle"
        type="xs:string" minOccurs="0" maxOccurs="1" />
      <xs:element name="address" type="tns:address" />
      <xs:element name="gender" type="tns:gender" />
    </xs:sequence>
  </xs:complexType>
  <xs:element name="person" type="tns:person" />
</xs:schema>
```

Example 9.3

Note how the types of elements address and gender refer to the types created in the address.xsd and gender.xsd respectively. Two statements are necessary in order to make the address element refer to the type defined in the address.xsd file. The first refers to the previously created schema:

```
<xs:include schemaLocation="address.xsd"/>
```

The second specifies that the element address should be of this type:

```
<xs:element name="address" type="tns:address"/>
```

Also note that there is an element in the person XML schema that has the type of person. This makes it possible to send the person type as a message. The gender and address types do not have such an element because we are not planning to use them on their own to define individual messages.

At this point our catalog of XML schemas looks like this:

Figure 9.5

The catalog of XML schemas.

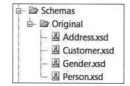

Generating .NET Types

The types we have created can be used "as is" for message definitions in BizTalk, but to use them for WCF (or ASMX) services, we need to generate .NET types using a utility program called svcutil that is shipped with Visual Studio. To generate these types, use the following statement at the Visual Studio command prompt:

```
svcutil  /dcOnly  /l:cs  person.xsd  address.xsd  gender.xsd
```

Apart from referring to the previously created XML schema files, we are also using these two switches:

- /dcOnly – instructs svcutil to create data contracts for us

- /l:cs – instructs svcutil that the language (l) of the generated code should be C# (cs)

The code that scvutil generates based upon our types looks like this:

```
namespace schemas.example.org.enterprise.models.v1
{
  using System.Runtime.Serialization;
  [System.Diagnostics.DebuggerStepThroughAttribute()]
  [System.CodeDom.Compiler.GeneratedCodeAttribute
    ("System.Runtime.Serialization", "4.0.0.0")]
  [System.Runtime.Serialization.DataContractAttribute
    (Name = "person", Namespace =
    "http://schemas.example.org/enterprise/models/v1")]
  public partial class person : object,
    System.Runtime.Serialization.IExtensibleDataObject
  {
    private System.Runtime.Serialization.
      ExtensionDataObject extensionDataField;
    private long idField;
    private string foreNameField;
```

```
private string middleNameField;
private string surNameField;
private ulong socSecNrField;
private string jobTitleField;
private schemas.example.org.enterprise.models.v1.
  address addressField;
private schemas.example.org.enterprise.models.v1.
  gender genderField;
public System.Runtime.Serialization.
  ExtensionDataObject ExtensionData
{
  get
  {
    return this.extensionDataField;
   }
   set
   {
     this.extensionDataField = value;
   }
}
  [System.Runtime.Serialization.
    DataMemberAttribute(IsRequired = true)]
  public long id
  {
    get
  {
    return this.idField;
  }
    set
  {
    this.idField = value;
  }
}
[System.Runtime.Serialization.
  DataMemberAttribute(IsRequired = true,
  EmitDefaultValue = false, Order = 1)]
public string foreName
{
  get
{
  return this.foreNameField;
}
  set
{
  this.foreNameField = value;
```

```
    }
  }
  [System.Runtime.Serialization.
    DataMemberAttribute(IsRequired = true,
    EmitDefaultValue = false, Order = 2)]
  public string middleName
  {
    get
  {
    return this.middleNameField;
  }
    set
  {
    this.middleNameField = value;
  }
}
[System.Runtime.Serialization.DataMemberAttribute
  (IsRequired = true, EmitDefaultValue = false, Order = 3)]
  public string surName
  {
    get
  {
    return this.surNameField;
  }
    set
  {
    this.surNameField = value;
  }
}
[System.Runtime.Serialization.DataMemberAttribute
  (IsRequired = true, Order = 4)]
  public ulong socSecNr
  {
    get
  {
    return this.socSecNrField;
  }
  set
  {
    this.socSecNrField = value;
  }
}
[System.Runtime.Serialization.DataMemberAttribute
  (EmitDefaultValue = false, Order = 5)]
  public string jobTitle
```

```
  {
    get
  {
    return this.jobTitleField;
  }
    set
  {
    this.jobTitleField = value;
  }
}
[System.Runtime.Serialization.DataMemberAttribute
  (IsRequired = true, EmitDefaultValue = false, Order = 6)]
  public schemas.example.org.enterprise.models.v1.address address
  {
    get
  {
    return this.addressField;
  }
    set
  {
    this.addressField = value;
  }
}
[System.Runtime.Serialization.DataMemberAttribute
  (IsRequired = true, Order = 7)]
  public schemas.example.org.enterprise.models.v1.gender gender
  {
    get
  {
    return this.genderField;
  }
    set
  {
    this.genderField = value;
  }
  }
}
[System.Diagnostics.DebuggerStepThroughAttribute()]
[System.CodeDom.Compiler.GeneratedCodeAttribute
  ("System.Runtime.Serialization", "4.0.0.0")]
    [System.Runtime.Serialization.DataContractAttribute
  (Name = "address", Namespace = "http://schemas.example.org/
    enterprise/models/v1")]
    public partial class address : object,
      System.Runtime.Serialization.IExtensibleDataObject
```

```
  {
    private System.Runtime.Serialization.
      ExtensionDataObject extensionDataField;
    private string addressMemberField;
    private string cityField;
    private string stateField;
    private string zipField;
    private string phoneField;
    private string countryField;
    public System.Runtime.Serialization.
      ExtensionDataObject ExtensionData
    {
      get
    {
      return this.extensionDataField;
    }
      set
    {
      this.extensionDataField = value;
    }
  }
  [System.Runtime.Serialization.DataMemberAttribute
    (Name = "address", IsRequired = true,
     EmitDefaultValue = false)]
  public string addressMember
  {
    get
  {
    return this.addressMemberField;
  }
    set
  {
    this.addressMemberField = value;
  }
}
[System.Runtime.Serialization.DataMemberAttribute
  (IsRequired = true, EmitDefaultValue = false)]
  public string city
  {
    get
  {
    return this.cityField;
  }
    set
  {
```

```
      this.cityField = value;
  }
}
[System.Runtime.Serialization.DataMemberAttribute
  (IsRequired = true, EmitDefaultValue = false)]
  public string state
  {
    get
    {
    return this.stateField;
  }
    set
    {
    this.stateField = value;
  }
}
[System.Runtime.Serialization.DataMemberAttribute
  (IsRequired = true, EmitDefaultValue = false)]
  public string zip
  {
    get
    {
    return this.zipField;
  }
    set
    {
    this.zipField = value;
  }
}
[System.Runtime.Serialization.DataMemberAttribute
  (IsRequired = true, EmitDefaultValue = false, Order = 4)]
  public string phone
  {
    get
    {
    return this.phoneField;
  }
    set
    {
    this.phoneField = value;
  }
}
[System.Runtime.Serialization.DataMemberAttribute
  (IsRequired = true, EmitDefaultValue = false, Order = 5)]
  public string country
```

```
  {
    get
  {
    return this.countryField;
  }
    set
  {
    this.countryField = value;
  }
 }
}
[System.CodeDom.Compiler.GeneratedCodeAttribute
  ("System.Runtime.Serialization", "4.0.0.0")]
[System.Runtime.Serialization.DataContractAttribute
  (Name = "gender", Namespace = "http://schemas.
  example.org/enterprise/models/v1")]
  public enum gender : int
  {
    [System.Runtime.Serialization.
      EnumMemberAttribute()]
    male = 0,
    [System.Runtime.Serialization.
      EnumMemberAttribute()]
    female = 1,
  }
}
```

Example 9.4

NOTE

As an alternative to the svcutil utility, you can also use the xsd.exe
utility, which will create .NET types that are serialized using the
`XMLSerializer` rather than the `DataContractSerializer`.

Using the `DataContract` Library

You can also create these types by using code directly with .NET, instead of working with XML schema markup code. This next example shows how to create the three types in .NET using the `DataContract` and `DataMember` attributes.

```csharp
[DataContract(Name = "person", Namespace =
"http://schemas.example.org/enterprise/models/v1")]
public class Person : object,
System.Runtime.Serialization.IExtensibleDataObject
{
  [DataMember(IsRequired = true)]
  public int Id
  {
    get;
    set;
  }
  [DataMember(IsRequired=true,
    EmitDefaultValue=false, Order = 1)]
  public string ForeName
  {
    get;
    set;
  }
  [DataMember(IsRequired = true,
    EmitDefaultValue=false, Order = 2)]
  public string MiddleName
  {
    get;
    set;
  }
  [DataMember(IsRequired = true,
    EmitDefaultValue=false, Order = 3)]
  public string SurName
  {
    get;
    set;
  }
  [DataMember(IsRequired = true,
    EmitDefaultValue=false, Order = 4)]
  public ulong SocSecNr
  {
    get;
    set;
  }
  [DataMember(Order = 5)]
  public string JobTitle
  {
    get;
    set;
  }
  [DataMember(Order = 6)]
```

```
public Address Address
{
  get;
  set;
}
[DataMember(Order = 7)]
public Gender Gender
{
  get;
  set;
}
private System.Runtime.Serialization.
  ExtensionDataObject extensionDataField;
public System.Runtime.Serialization.
  ExtensionDataObject ExtensionData
{
  get
  {
  return this.extensionDataField;
  }
  set
  {
  this.extensionDataField = value;
  }
}
}
```

Example 9.5

The address and gender types are created as separate classes that use `DataContract` and `DataMember` attributes. The `DataContract` attribute is used to let .NET know that this is a data contract and that it should be serialized using `DataContractSerializer`. This serializer will only serialize fields that are annotated with the `DataMember` attribute.

Apart from signaling to the `DataContractSerializer` that a particular element should be serialized, the `DataMember` attribute accepts named arguments.

Specifically, the named arguments used in Example 9.5 are:

- `Order` – affects the order in which the fields of the type are serialized

- `IsRequired` – instructs consumers and services whether or not a field is required

- `EmitDefailtValue` – when set to false, the default value (for example, 0 for an int) will not be serialized

The `DataMember` attribute has several other arguments that can come in handy. For example, should you require a different name in the .NET code and the serialized message, the `Name` attribute lets you change the name of the serialized value.

Figure 9.6 shows the resulting library created so far.

Figure 9.6

The Service Library defined so far, including Address, Gender, and Person class definitions.

SUMMARY OF KEY POINTS

- Canonical Schema [718] establishes the requirement for schemas used by services within a service inventory to be standardized.

- Visual Studio provides an editor that allows for the definition of XML schemas.

- With .NET, XML Schema types can be created with the XML Schema markup language or through the use of the DataContract library.

9.3 Data Model Transformation

One goal of the Standardized Service Contract (693) principle is to avoid having to transform data at runtime. This means that the more successfully and broadly we are able to apply this principle, the less need we will have for patterns like Data Model Transformation [732]. However, even when seeking service contract standardization, there are situations where this pattern is necessary.

For example:

- When an IT enterprise has multiple domain service inventories, each collection of services can be subject to different design standards. In this case, when required to enable cross-inventory communication (or when creating a service composition comprised of services from multiple service inventories), any disparity in message data models will need to be overcome by applying Data Model Transformation [732].

- When data needs to be shared between different organizations (or organizational entities), Data Model Transformation [732] will generally be required unless Canonical Schema [718] has been successfully applied via the use of custom or industry-standard message schemas.

- When services encapsulate legacy systems and resources, they will inevitably need to transform data between legacy data models and the standardized data model defined in the service contracts. In this case, Data Model Transformation [732] is carried out within the service architecture.

- When services within a service inventory are not all successfully standardized (meaning the Standardized Service Contract (693) principle was not applied to its full extent), Data Model Transformation [732] will be required to enable the necessary interoperability.

Data Model Transformation [732] is generally carried out by creating mapping logic between disparate schemas or data types (Figure 9.7). This type of logic can often become complex and is sometimes even impossible to develop when the disparity between data models is too large.

Figure 9.7

Service A sends a message to Service B. The message sent by Service A contains address data that was defined by a schema that is different than the schema Service B uses in its service contract for this same information. Therefore, transformation logic is processed by a service agent in order to transform the message at runtime into data that complies with Service B's schema.

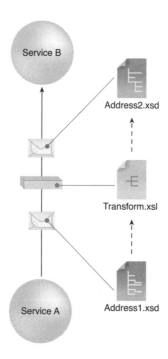

For example, you may encounter mandatory fields in one model that don't exist in the other. In such a case, transforming in one direction may work, but transforming in the opposite direction may not. The following example demonstrates by showing how we may not be able to determine which value(s) belong in the `middleNames` element:

Data Model #1

```
<person1>
  <foreNames>Max</foreNames>
  <middleNames>Carl</middleNames>
  <surNames>von Sydow</surNames>
</person1>
```

Data Model #2

```
<person2>
  <name>Max Carl von Sydow</name>
</person2>
```

Example 9.6
Transforming from Data Model #1 to Data Model #2 works, but the opposite transformation is more difficult.

Besides the potential complexity of mapping logic, there are other well-known impacts of applying this pattern. The additional logic will introduce development and governance effort, and can further affect the performance of services and service compositions (sometimes significantly so, especially with more complex mapping logic).

The following sections briefly show three ways to apply Data Model Transformation [732] using .NET technologies.

Object-to-Object

A message sent by a service consumer to a service can be serialized from XML into an object, translated into another object, and then serialized into XML again. This may be a suitable approach when you must use all or most of the data in the message, either for passing the information onto another service or for some other purpose.

The first step in this process is to understand the mapping requirements. Let's take, for example, a scenario where we need to transform data defined by a person type into a customer type (Figure 9.8). The logic behind this transformation could be as follows:

- map the `person.id` field to the `customer.id` field

- map the `person.foreName` field to the `customer.firstName` field

- map the `person.surName` field to the `customer.lastName` field

- map the `person.address.phone` field to the `customer.phone` field

- map the `person.gender` field to the `customer.gender` field

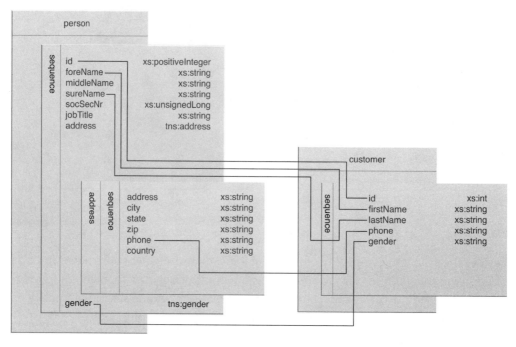

Figure 9.8
Mapping fields from the person type to the customer type.

After generating proxy clients for the different services with the "Add service reference" feature of Visual Studio, we also have .NET code that represents a person and a customer. The translation could then be programmed using a static extension method as shown here:

```
public static Customer TransformPersonToCustomer
  (this Person person)
{
  Customer customer = new Customer();
  customer.id = person.Id;
  customer.firstName = person.ForeName;
  customer.lastName = person.SurName;
  customer.phone = person.Address.PhoneNr;
```

```
    customer.gender = IntToEnum<customergenderType>((int)
      person.gender);
    return customer;
}
public static T IntToEnum<T>(int value)
{
    return (T)Enum.ToObject(typeof(T), value);
}
```

Example 9.7

This code was written knowing that person and customer use the same integer representations of male and female. The next example shows how this translation logic is applied on the message retrieved from the first service before sending it to the second. (Note that since this logic was written as an extension method it can be called as if it was a method of the person class.)

```
PersonServiceClient personService = new PersonServiceClient();
var aPerson = personService.GetPerson(2);
var customerFromPerson =
  getPersonData.TransformPersonToCustomer();
CustomerServiceClient customerService = new
  CustomerServiceClient();
customerService.UpdateCustomer(customerFromPerson);
```

Example 9.8

LINQ-to-XML

Sometimes you may want to transform a type but you only need to transform a subset of the overall type. In those cases, deserializing a large document and building a large object graph can be wasteful and can make code more sensitive to future changes in data structures.

To handle this situation you can use LINQ-to-XML on the raw message that is returned from a service, as follows:

```
Message messageOut = channel.Request(messageIn);
XmlReader readResponse = messageOut.GetReaderAtBodyContents();
XmlDocument doc = new XmlDocument();
doc.Load(readResponse);
var xDoc = XDocument.Parse(doc.OuterXml);
XNamespace xmlns2 = xDoc.Root.Attribute("xmlns").Value;
```

```
var transformed = from d in xDoc.Descendants
  (xmlns2 + "personElement")

select new Customer
{
  firstName = d.Element(xmlns2 + "foreName").Value,
  lastName = d.Element(xmlns2 + "surName").Value,
  id = Convert.ToInt32(d.Element(xmlns2 + "id").Value),
  gender = (Customer.genderType)
    Enum.Parse(typeof(Customer.genderType),
    d.Element(xmlns2 + "gender").Value),
    phone = d.Element(xmlns2 + "address").
    Element(xmlns2 + "phonenr").Value,
};
```

Example 9.9

In this example, the response content from the message issued by the service is received;
along with the namespace, the incoming XML structure is transformed into an object.
Note that this code would continue to work even if the namespace of the response
changes. The only change that can break this code is if one of the elements that are
explicitly asked for is removed or has its name altered. An additional benefit of this
approach is that we can process data types that are not otherwise easily handled in WCF,
such as the xsd:choice construct.

XSLT Transformation

An option that is useful for avoiding deserialization is XSLT. By defining mapping logic
with the XSLT language, we only take the data that we are interested in into our objects
and leave the rest. XSLT can be used by different parts of the .NET platform and is a commonly supported industry standard, meaning that it may also be used with some legacy
systems.

Here's a sample XSLT transformation:

```
<xsl:stylesheet version="1.0"
  xmlns:xsl="http://www.w3.org/1999/XSL/Transform"
  xmlns:b="http://schemas.example.org/enterprise/models/v1"
  xmlns:a="http://schemas.example.org/enterprise/models/v2">
  <xsl:template match="/">
    <a:customerElement>
      <a:id>
```

```
          <xsl:value-of select="b:personElement/b:id"/>
      </a:id>
      <a:firstName>
          <xsl:value-of select="b:personElement/b:foreName"/>
      </a:firstName>
      <a:lastName>
          <xsl:value-of select="b:personElement/b:surName"/>
      </a:lastName>
      <a:phone>
          <xsl:value-ofselect=
          "b:personElement/b:address/b:phonenr"/>
      </a:phone>
      <a:gender>
          <xsl:value-of select="b:personElement/b:gender"/>
      </a:gender>
    </a:customerElement>
  </xsl:template>
</xsl:stylesheet>
```

Example 9.10

The semantics of this transformation logic are quite straight forward in that the markup shows how to find the values for an element.

Using WCF, you could apply this XSLT transformation as follows:

```
Message messageOut = channel.Request(messageIn);
XmlReader readResponse = messageOut.GetReaderAtBodyContents();
XslCompiledTransform xslt = new XslCompiledTransform();
xslt.Load("XMLMessages/TransformationPersonToCustomer.xslt");
using (MemoryStream ms = new MemoryStream())
{
  XmlWriterSettings ws = new XmlWriterSettings();
  ws.Encoding = Encoding.UTF8;
  using (XmlWriter xmlWriter = XmlWriter.Create(ms, ws))
  {
    xslt.Transform(readResponse, xmlWriter);
  }
  xmlWriter
}
```

Example 9.11

SUMMARY OF KEY POINTS

- Although Data Model Transformation [732] is a pattern we try to avoid when applying Standardized Service Contract (693) and Canonical Schema [718], it is still commonly applied within service-oriented architectures.

- With .NET, three common ways of applying Data Model Transformation [732] are object-to-object, LINQ-to-XML, and XSLT.

9.4 Canonical Protocol

In heterogeneous environments it is common for systems to have difficulties communicating directly. Some may be using the TCP as a transport protocol, while others may only be capable of using HTTP over TCP, or even SOAP (over HTTP and TCP). Even when two legacy systems use the same protocol, they might be using different versions, which can result in the same communication-level incompatibility.

A technique for overcoming these problems is via Protocol Bridging [764]. In essence, this pattern involves placing an intermediary in between two pieces of software that converts between the incompatible protocols, thereby enabling them to exchange data. As with Data Model Transformation [732], applying this pattern will lead to increased development effort and increased performance overhead.

The Standardized Service Contract (693) principle further helps establish the standardized interoperability on the protocol level with the help of the Canonical Protocol [716] pattern, which requires that communication protocol (including protocol versions) be regulated among services within the same service inventory boundary.

Of course, this leads to the question of which protocol to choose. The choice of protocol will be dependent on the choice of service implementation medium. Currently there are three common service implementation options:

- components

- Web services

- REST services

The following sections explore the differences of each in relation to building services with WCF.

Web Service

A Web service uses a WSDL definition and one or more XML schemas to specify its interfaces. Its protocol is usually based on the use of SOAP over HTTP. Figure 9.9 shows a Web service implemented in WCF with the IUserBankService interface and Figure 9.10 illustrates the DataContract for representing the User class.

Figure 9.9

This Web service has methods (operations) for creating, getting, updating and modifying a user.

Figure 9.10

The User class and associated properties.

As shown in the following example, the interface is created and annotated with the ServiceContract and OperationContract attributes.

```
[ServiceContract]
  public interface IUserBankService
  {
    [OperationContract]
    void CreateUser(Core.Models.User user);
```

```
    [OperationContract]
    Core.Models.User GetUser(Guid userId);
    [OperationContract]
    void ModifyUser(Core.Models.User modifiedUser);
    [OperationContract]
    void DeleteUser(Guid userId);
}
```

Example 9.12

The `ServiceContract` attribute indicates that it's a WCF service and the `Opera-tionContract` attribute indicates that the method that is annotated with this attribute needs to be exposed by the service. Note that these attributes are used irrespective of the kind of service we're creating with WCF.

The interface is then implemented in a class, as shown here:

```
public class UserBankService:IUserBankService
{
  public void CreateUser(Core.Models.User user)
  {
    throw new NotImplementedException();
  }
  public Core.Models.User GetUser(Guid userId)
  {
    throw new NotImplementedException();
  }
  public void ModifyUser(Core.Models.User modifiedUser)
  {
    throw new NotImplementedException();
  }
  public void DeleteUser(Guid userId)
  {
    throw new NotImplementedException();
  }
}
```

Example 9.13

As you can see, no attributes are used on the class as they were already used on the interface. To make the service actually do something, we would need to populate the method definitions with code.

Note that we could have decorated the class and the methods in the class with the WCF attributes. By instead decorating the interface, we have applied the Decoupled Contract [735] pattern by separating the service definition from its implementation.

Second, there is nothing in our code so far that specifies that this should be a Web service. To make it into a Web service, we can add a configuration. This next example shows the relevant part of the configuration that implements this service as an actual Web service:

```
...
<system.serviceModel>
  <services>
    <service name="Core.Services.UserBankService">
      <endpoint address="..." binding="basicHttpBinding"
        contract="Core.Services.IUserBankService">
        ...
      </endpoint>
    </service>
  </services>
  ...
</system.serviceModel>
...
```

Example 9.14

`basicHttpBinding` is what makes this service into a Web service, as it instructs WCF to use a WS-BasicProfile Web service communication mechanism with HTTP as transport and messages encoded as text/XML.

REST Service

When designing a service as a REST service we can still use WCF and the resulting code is actually quite similar to that of a Web service implementation. Figure 9.11 shows an interface that corresponds to the previous Web service example.

As with the Web service interface definition, the REST service interface is annotated with WCF attributes:

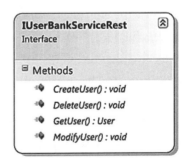

Figure 9.11

The interface definition for the REST service is identical to the previous definition for the Web service, except for the name.

```
[ServiceContract]
public interface IUserBankServiceRest
{
  [OperationContract]
  [WebInvoke(Method = "POST", BodyStyle =
    WebMessageBodyStyle.Bare,
    ResponseFormat = WebMessageFormat.Xml)]
  void CreateUser(Core.Models.User user);
  [OperationContract]
  [WebGet(UriTemplate="users/{userId}")]
  Core.Models.User GetUser(string userId);
  [OperationContract]
  [WebInvoke(Method = "PUT")]
  void ModifyUser(Core.Models.User modifiedUser);
  [OperationContract]
  [WebInvoke(Method = "DELETE")]
  void DeleteUser(Guid userId);
}
```

Example 9.15

The `ServiceContract` and `OperationContract` attributes are still there, but we also added `WebInvoke` and `WebGet` attributes. These attributes (originally introduced in .NET framework 3.5) are specific for a REST service implementation and specify operation behaviors.

The `WebInvoke` attribute makes it possible for methods to invoke using the HTTP protocol. This attribute takes some arguments, and the most significant of these is the method argument. The valid values of the method argument correspond to the POST, PUT, and DELETE HTTP methods. The HTTP protocol offers additional methods, but these are the only ones supported by the `WebInvoke` attribute. (The `WebGet` attribute also allows you to specify that a method should be possible to invoke using HTTP GET.)

After creating the interface we again need a class that implements it. Just as with a Web service, we can use all the attributes directly on the class.

Component

Components differ from Web service and REST service implementation options in that they are more technology and platform specific, especially in relation to transport protocols. A component is implemented in a certain language and uses certain frameworks. Therefore, in order to use a component you need to have access to the component technology locally.

Another differentiator is that the service is not called remotely. Rather, you instantiate a component locally and use its API, which is why components are said to be more tightly coupled than Web services and REST services.

In the following example we can use the same class as we used earlier when we implemented a Web service. Instead of calling it remotely as a Web service we use it as follows:

```
UserBankService serviceAPI = new UserBankService();
  serviceAPI.CreateUser(new Core.Models.User()
  {
    UserId = Guid.NewGuid(),
    Address = "MyAdress",
    FirstName = "John",
    LastName = "Smith",
    PhoneNumber = "0332133333",
    SocSecNumber = "730X29"
    }
);
```

Example 9.16

Another WCF Option: Named Pipes

When you develop services in WCF you can also consider the use of named pipes as the transport protocol. This option is similar to using a WCF library as a component because you cannot choose the technology platform for the consumer freely.

The benefit, compared to the component option, is that a service exposed through named pipes runs as an independent process. However, a service exposed using named pipes can only be accessed when the service consumer is installed on the same machine.

Access can be enabled by changing the binding of the service to `NetNamedPipeBinding`.

Dual Protocols with WCF

Although limiting service interaction within a service inventory to one transport protocol is desirable, it can sometimes introduce limitations that make some service requirements hard to fulfill. There may be circumstances that warrant the use of a secondary protocol to complement the primary protocol, as per Dual Protocols [739]. This pattern is commonly applied when the primary protocol introduces performance issues or when a new protocol is introduced as the primary protocol and a period of transition is allowed for the migration of services from the now demoted protocol (the secondary protocol) to the new primary protocol.

WCF enables the application of Dual Protocols [739] by allowing additional endpoints to be added to services via configuration with little or no change to existing code. Configuring a new endpoint is a matter of adding a new address and binding—the `ServiceContract` part can be reused.

SUMMARY OF KEY POINTS

- Canonical Protocol [716] is concerned with establishing baseline interoperability on the transport and messaging protocol layers.

- Different service implementation mediums will generally require different applications of this pattern.

- The Dual Protocols [739] pattern allows for primary and secondary protocols to be standardized within a service inventory.

9.5 Canonical Expression

When a service is created and included in a service inventory, it is important that future service consumers (or rather those humans that develop the software that consume services) will be able to understand the capabilities that the service exposes. To make this easier to understand we utilize naming conventions, as per Canonical Expression [715]. These conventions should be applied to both the name of the service as well as its individual service capabilities.

Service Naming Conventions

The name of a service should generally communicate its functional context. The goal of Canonical Expression [715] is to realize this clarity but also to ensure that all services within a given service inventory are named consistently.

For example, you may want to avoid having an Order service and a PurchaseStatistics service in the same inventory (assuming that Order and Purchase refers to the same thing). To resolve this type of situation, the services could be renamed with "Order" or "Purchase," but not both. As shown in Figure 9.12, this means that the service should be named Purchase or PurchaseStatistics – or – Order or OrderStatistics.

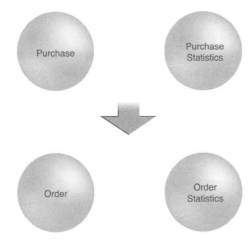

Figure 9.12
Service naming conventions limit the naming options
of services.

Service Capability Naming Conventions

Naming service capabilities depends on the type of implementation medium used for
the service.

With Web service operations, naming preferences are similar to the naming conventions
of methods used with components.

For example, each operation or method name should:

- describe its purpose (preferably using a verb+noun format)
- be as long as necessary
- describe the return value (if there is one)

For Web service operation and component method naming, it is usually required to standardize certain types of wording to ensure consistency. For example, here are some
words that could be used interchangeably:

- estimate ⇔ forecast
- forward ⇔ relay
- cease ⇔ finish

For example, we want to avoid having a GetOrderStatus operation alongside a RetrieveStatisticsPerOrderMode operation because "Get" and "Retrieve" can be considered comparable verbs. With naming standards we can ensure that the capabilities will be consistent (like GetOrderStatus and GetStatisticsPerOrderStatus).

For REST services, the focus is on the naming of resources. In order to support consumer requirements, it may be necessary to expose several resources with overlapping naming data. In this case, naming becomes especially important as you wouldn't want consumer designers to misunderstand which resource their program needs to access.

Because REST services rely on the use of Uniform Contract (generally via HTTP methods), the method does not define the naming of the actual capability. The design effort is instead shifted to determining which resources to expose as well as the structure of input and output messages.

SUMMARY OF KEY POINTS

- Canonical Expression [715] aims to establish content consistency across service contract definitions within a service inventory.

- Most commonly, this pattern is applied via naming conventions for services and service capabilities.

Chapter 10

Service-Orientation with .NET Part II: Coupling, Abstraction, and Discoverability

10.1 Service Loose Coupling

10.2 Decoupled Contract

10.3 Service Façade

10.4 Concurrent Contracts

10.5 Service Loose Coupling and Service Capability Granularity

10.6 Service Abstraction

10.7 Validation Abstraction

10.8 Exception Shielding

10.9 Service Discoverability

10.10 Metadata Centralization

SOA PRINCIPLES & PATTERNS REFERENCED IN THIS CHAPTER

- Compatible Change [723]
- Concurrent Contracts [726]
- Contract Centralization [727]
- Contract Denormalization [728]
- Decoupled Contract [735]
- Dual Protocols [739]
- Exception Shielding [744]
- Metadata Centralization [754]
- Service Abstraction (696)
- Service Discoverability (702)
- Service Façade [776]
- Service Loose Coupling (695)
- Validation Abstraction [792]

Each of the referenced service-orientation principles was briefly introduced in Chapter 3. The respective principle and pattern profile tables are available in Appendices C and D.

The goal of Increased Intrinsic Interoperability ties directly into both the Increased Organizational Agility and Increased ROI strategic benefits, in that it lays the foundation for repeated service composition. Services that are naturally compatible, interoperable, and designed with the inherent flexibility to participate in aggregated solutions, establish an environment in which new or augmented business processes can be automated in less time and with less expense and effort.

Several principles and patterns are geared toward shaping service architectures in support of achieving this level of flexibility. This is why one of the distinguishing characteristics of the service-oriented technology architectural model is, in fact, composition-centricity.

This chapter highlights several notable principles and patterns that contribute to this characteristic, and explores their application with .NET technologies. Additional principles and patterns that further support intrinsic interoperability and composition-centricity are covered throughout subsequent chapters.

10.1 Service Loose Coupling

The goal of the Service Loose Coupling (695) principle is to allow services to develop and evolve with minimal impact on each other, a consideration that is key to achieving the Increased Organizational Agility goal of service-oriented computing.

This principle is primarily concerned with design-time dependencies, with a particular focus on the technical service contract. Coupling considerations apply, regardless of service implementation medium.

When applying the Service Loose Coupling (695) principle to a service architecture, we need to understand the different kinds of coupling (good and bad) that can exist.

- *logic-to-contract coupling* – This refers to the coupling of the internal service logic to the service contract. It is generally considered a positive form of coupling that preserves the service contract's independence from the underlying service implementation.

- *contract-to-logic coupling* – The opposite of logic-to-contract coupling is contract-to-logic coupling. When the service contract is dependent on the underlying service logic, it results in an architecture contrary to the goals of the Service Loose Coupling (695) principle because changes to the logic can impact the service contract and, consequently, service consumers that have formed dependencies on the service contract.

- *contract-to-technology coupling* – Similar to contract-to-logic coupling, this negative coupling type results from forcing service consumers to bind to a platform-specific technology protocol in order to invoke a service. For example, expecting consumers to send a serialized `DataSet` object to a WCF service or returning such an object to the consumer will introduce this kind of coupling.

- *contract-to-implementation coupling* – This type of negative coupling results from directly expressing characteristics of the underlying service implementation (the physical data models of databases or APIs of legacy software, for example) within the service contract.

- *contract-to-functional coupling* – This negative coupling type can sneak into a service when generic logic is designed with a particular business process or pre-built consumer in mind. As a result, the service contract can become dependent on the underlying functionality.

- *consumer-to-implementation coupling* – This form of negative coupling occurs when the Contract Centralization [727] pattern is not consistently applied. Allowing consumer programs to bypass a published technical contract in order to directly access underlying resources was also a common side-effect of point-to-point integration architectures.

- *consumer-to-contract coupling* – A positive coupling type that results from service consumers having limited access to the service contract. Consumer-to-contract coupling is the desired result of Contract Centralization [727].

Note how all described coupling types revolve around how the service contract is defined and architecturally positioned (Figure 10.1).

> **NOTE**
>
> For complete descriptions of these coupling types, visit
> www.soaglossary.com or see Chapter 7 in *SOA Principles of Service Design.*

Service Loose Coupling (695) and Patterns

The exploration of the Service Loose Coupling (695) principle is a large subject area that is further covered in upcoming chapters (and covered in detail in other books). The next set of sections highlight a set of patterns associated with this principle.

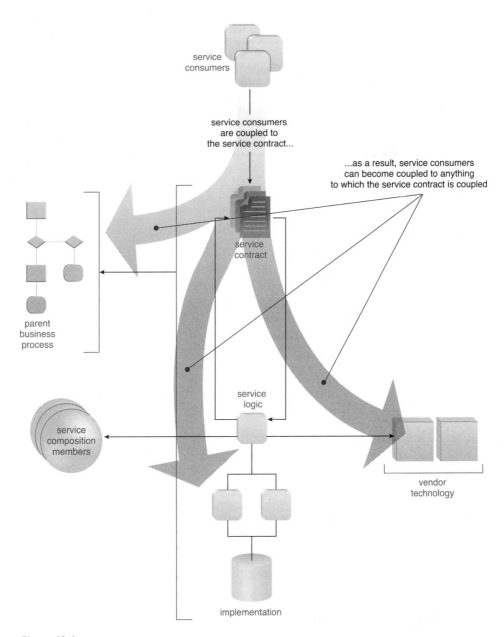

Figure 10.1

This diagram (originally from the *SOA Principles of Service Design* book) illustrates how consumer-to-contract coupling alone can be insufficient when the service contract is negatively coupled to other parts of the service implementation

SUMMARY OF KEY POINTS

- The Service Loose Coupling (695) principle advocates reducing dependencies between service consumers and the service contract, as well as between the service contract and the underlying service implementation.

- There are various forms of positive and negative coupling types that are taken into consideration when applying this principle.

10.2 Decoupled Contract

Ultimately, the combination of logic-to-contract and consumer-to-contract is considered to establish the healthiest foundation for achieving balanced loose coupling within and between services. The most effective way of realizing this is by establishing a service contract that is physically independent of both service consumers and its underlying implementation (Figure 10.2). This is the goal of the Decoupled Contract [735] pattern.

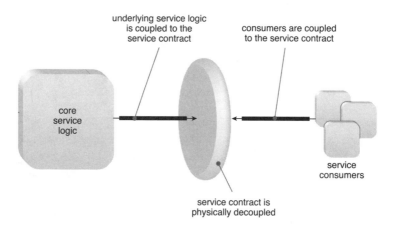

Figure 10.2
A decoupled service contract is physically separated from other parts of the technology architecture.

By positioning the service contract as a standalone artifact, we force the service implementation to adhere to the contract and we allow for the Contract Centralization [727] pattern to be applied in such a way that service consumers cannot become dependent on the service implementation.

When building services with .NET, there are several ways of accomplishing this, as explored in these next sections.

WSDL-First

For services built as Web services, the contract-first approach described in Chapter 9 effectively becomes the WSDL-first approach, which entails physically creating the service WSDL and XML Schema definitions.

The upcoming code snippets and examples will build upon the library of schemas that we constructed in Chapter 9. Based on the data types we will create message types that are essentially XML schemas tailored for use in specific messages. Thereafter, we will create a WSDL definition that imports these schemas.

Our service will have three operations:

- GetPerson
- GetAllPersons
- UpdatePerson

These operations will use the person type that we created in Chapter 9. We need to import that type into a new XML schema, as follows:

```
<xs:import namespace=
  "http://schemas.example.org/enterprise/models/v1"
  schemaLocation="Personperson.xsd"/>
```

Example 10.1

We also need to create a namespace that matches the namespace of the imported XML schema:

```
xmlns:persondata="http://schemas.example.org/
  enterprise/models/v1"
```

Lastly, when we want to use the person type in an element we declare its type like this:

```
type="persondata:person"
```

The completed message schema that we place in the PersonServiceMessages.xsd file looks like this:

```
<xs:schema elementFormDefault="qualified"
  xmlns:xs="http://www.w3.org/2001/XMLSchema"
  xmlns:persondata=
  "http://schemas.example.org/enterprise/models/v1"
```

```xml
 xmlns:tns=
 "http://schemas.example.org/enterprise/service/v1"
 targetNamespace=
 "http://schemas.example.org/enterprise/service/v1">
<xs:importnamespace=
 "http://schemas.example.org/enterprise/models/v1"
 schemaLocation="Person.xsd"/>
 <xs:element name="GetPerson">
   <xs:complexType>
     <xs:sequence>
       <xs:element name="personId"
         type="xs:positiveInteger" minOccurs="0"  />
     </xs:sequence>
   </xs:complexType>
 </xs:element>
 <xs:element name="GetPersonResponse">
   <xs:complexType>
     <xs:sequence>
       <xs:element name="person"
       type="persondata:person"
       minOccurs="0"  nillable="true"/>
     </xs:sequence>
   </xs:complexType>
 </xs:element>
 <xs:element name="GetAllPersons">
   <xs:complexType>
     <xs:sequence/>
   </xs:complexType>
 </xs:element>
 <xs:element name="GetAllPersonsResponse">
   <xs:complexType>
     <xs:sequence>
       <xs:element name="person"
       type="persondata:personList"
       minOccurs="0"  nillable="true"/>
     </xs:sequence>
   </xs:complexType>
 </xs:element>
 <xs:element name="UpdatePerson">
   <xs:complexType>
     <xs:sequence>
       <xs:element name="updatablePerson"
       type="persondata:person"
       minOccurs="0"  nillable="true" />
     </xs:sequence>
   </xs:complexType>
```

```
    </xs:element>
    <xs:element name="UpdatePersonResponse">
      <xs:complexType>
        <xs:sequence>
          <xs:element name="success" type="xs:boolean" />
        </xs:sequence>
      </xs:complexType>
    </xs:element>
</xs:schema>
```

Example 10.2

After creating the message types, they are imported into the WSDL definition. Using the `import` statement we showed earlier, the WSDL definition is structured as follows:

```
<definitions xmlns:tns=
  "http://schemas.example.org/enterprise/service/v1"
  xmlns:soap12="http://schemas.xmlsoap.org/wsdl/soap12/"
  xmlns:soap="http://schemas.xmlsoap.org/wsdl/soap/"
  xmlns:personMessages=
  "http://schemas.example.org/enterprise/service/v1"
  xmlns:xsd="http://www.w3.org/2001/XMLSchema"
  name="PersonService"
  targetNamespace=
  "http://schemas.example.org/enterprise/service/v1"
  xmlns="http://schemas.xmlsoap.org/wsdl/">
<wsdl:documentation
  xmlns:wsdl="http://schemas.xmlsoap.org/wsdl/"/>
<types>
  <xsd:schema>
    <xsd:import schemaLocation="PersonServiceMessages.xsd" />
  </xsd:schema>
</types>
<message name="getPersonIn">
  <wsdl:documentation xmlns:wsdl=
    "http://schemas.xmlsoap.org/wsdl/" />
  <part name="parameters"
    element="personMessages:GetPerson" />
</message>
<message name="getPersonOut">
  <wsdl:documentation xmlns:wsdl=
    "http://schemas.xmlsoap.org/wsdl/" />
  <part name="parameters"
    element="personMessages:GetPersonResponse" />
</message>
```

```
<message name="getAllPersonsIn">
  <wsdl:documentation  xmlns:wsdl=
    "http://schemas.xmlsoap.org/wsdl/" />
  <part name="parameters"
    element="personMessages:GetAllPersons" />
</message>
<message name="getAllPersonsOut">
  <wsdl:documentation xmlns:wsdl=
    "http://schemas.xmlsoap.org/wsdl/" />
  <part name="parameters"
    element="personMessages:GetAllPersonsResponse" />
</message>
<message name="updatePersonIn">
  <wsdl:documentation xmlns:wsdl=
    "http://schemas.xmlsoap.org/wsdl/" />
  <part name="parameters"
    element="personMessages:UpdatePerson" />
</message>
<message name="updatePersonOut">
  <wsdl:documentation xmlns:wsdl=
    "http://schemas.xmlsoap.org/wsdl/" />
  <part name="parameters" element=
    "personMessages:UpdatePersonResponse" />
</message>
  <portType name="PersonServiceInterface">
  <wsdl:documentation xmlns:wsdl=
    "http://schemas.xmlsoap.org/wsdl/" />
    <operation name="GetPerson">
      <wsdl:documentation xmlns:wsdl=
        "http://schemas.xmlsoap.org/wsdl/" />
      <input message="tns:getPersonIn" />
      <output message="tns:getPersonOut" />
    </operation>
    <operation name="GetAllPersons">
      <wsdl:documentation xmlns:wsdl=
        "http://schemas.xmlsoap.org/wsdl/" />
      <input message="tns:getAllPersonsIn" />
      <output message="tns:getAllPersonsOut" />
    </operation>
    <operation name="UpdatePerson">
      <wsdl:documentation xmlns:wsdl=
        "http://schemas.xmlsoap.org/wsdl/" />
      <input message="tns:updatePersonIn" />
      <output message="tns:updatePersonOut" />
    </operation>
```

```
  </portType>
  <binding name=
    "BasicHttpBinding_PersonServiceInterface
    "type="tns:PersonServiceInterface">
  <soap:binding transport=
    "http://schemas.xmlsoap.org/soap/http" />
    <operation name="GetPerson">
      <soap:operation soapAction=
        "http://schemas.example.org/enterprise/service/v1:
        getPersonIn" style="document" />
      <input>
        <soap:body use="literal" />
      </input>
      <output>
        <soap:body use="literal" />
      </output>
    </operation>
    <operation name="GetAllPersons">
      <soap:operation soapAction=
        "http://schemas.example.org/enterprise/service/v1:
        getAllPersonsIn" style="document" />
      <input>
        <soap:body use="literal" />
      </input>
      <output>
        <soap:body use="literal" />
      </output>
    </operation>
    <operation name="UpdatePerson">
      <soap:operation soapAction=
        "http://schemas.example.org/enterprise/service/v1:
        updatePersonIn" style="document" />
      <input>
        <soap:body use="literal" />
      </input>
      <output>
        <soap:body use="literal" />
      </output>
    </operation>
  </binding>
</definitions>
```

Example 10.3

To summarize, the WSDL definition we created includes:

- an import of the message schemas

- definitions of messages (for example, "getPersonIn") that refer to the imported message schemas

- the service interface that specifies operations and refers to the declared messages

- the binding that specifies SOAP operations for the previously specified operations

> **NOTE**
>
> The book *Web Service Contract Design & Versioning for SOA* is dedicated to the markup languages required to design and version service contracts for Web services and also includes coverage of WS-Addressing and WS-Policy.

Now that we have a Web service contract and associated data model designed via the WSDL-first approach, we need to make it part of our development environment so that we can build the corresponding implementation logic.

There are several tools that can be used for this purpose. The three tools we highlight in the upcoming sections are:

- svcutil

- WSCF.blue

- WSCF.classic

Be sure to study the pros and cons of each tool before choosing which to make part of a standard service-oriented design process for Web services.

Generating Service Code Using Svcutil

The svcutil utility can be used to generate code based on an existing WSDL definition. To launch this utility, we need to type the following statement in the Visual Studio command prompt:

```
svcutil -serializer:datacontractserializer  -namespace:*,
schemas.woodgroove.com.enterprise
PersonService.wsdl AddressType.xsd
GenderType.xsd Person.xsd Pers
onServiceMessages.xsd /l:cs
```

Example 10.4

An abbreviated version of the code that is subsequently generated is shown here:

```
[System.CodeDom.Compiler.GeneratedCodeAttribute
("System.ServiceModel", "4.0.0.0")]
[System.ServiceModel.ServiceContractAttribute
(Namespace="http://schemas.example.org/enterprise/service/v1",
ConfigurationName="schemas.example.org.enterprise.
PersonServiceInterface")]

public interface PersonServiceInterface
{
[System.ServiceModel.OperationContractAttribute
(Action="http://schemas.example.org/enterprise/service/v1:getPer-
sonIn", ReplyAction="*")]
[return: System.ServiceModel.MessageParameterAttribute(Name="person")]
schemas.example.org.enterprise.person GetPerson(long personId);
[System.ServiceModel.OperationContractAttribute(Action="http://schemas
.example.org/enterprise/service/v1:getAllPersonsIn", ReplyAction="*")]
[return:System.ServiceModel.MessageParameterAttribute
(Name="person")]
schemas.example.org.enterprise.personList GetAllPersons();
[System.ServiceModel.OperationContractAttribute(Action="http://schemas
.example.org/enterprise/service/v1:updatePersonIn", ReplyAction="*")]
[return:System.ServiceModel.MessageParameterAttribute
(Name="success")]
bool UpdatePerson(schemas.example.org.enterprise.person
updatablePerson);
}
[System.Diagnostics.DebuggerStepThroughAttribute()]
[System.CodeDom.Compiler.GeneratedCodeAttribute("System.Runtime.
Serialization", "4.0.0.0")]
[System.Runtime.Serialization.DataContractAttribute
(Name="person", Namespace="http://schemas.example.org/enterprise/
models/v1")]

public partial class person : object,
System.Runtime.Serialization.IExtensibleDataObject…
[System.Diagnostics.DebuggerStepThroughAttribute()]
[System.CodeDom.Compiler.GeneratedCodeAttribute("System.Runtime.
Serialization", "4.0.0.0")]
[System.Runtime.Serialization.DataContractAttribute(Name="addressType"
,Namespace="http://schemas.example.org/enterprise/models/v1")]

public partial class addressType : object, System.Runtime.
Serialization.IextensibleDataObject...
[System.CodeDom.Compiler.GeneratedCodeAttribute("System.Runtime.
Serialization", "4.0.0.0")]
```

```
[System.Runtime.Serialization.DataContractAttribute(Name="gender-
Type",Namespace="http://schemas.example.org/enterprise/models/v1")]

public enum genderType : int...
[System.Diagnostics.DebuggerStepThroughAttribute()]
[System.CodeDom.Compiler.GeneratedCodeAttribute("System.Runtime.
Serialization", "4.0.0.0")]
[System.Runtime.Serialization.CollectionDataContractAttribute
(Name="personList",
Namespace="http://schemas.example.org/enterprise/models/v1",
ItemName="person")]

public class personList :
System.Collections.Generic.List<schemas.example.org.enterprise.
person>...
[System.CodeDom.Compiler.GeneratedCodeAttribute("System.ServiceModel",
"4.0.0.0")]

public interface PersonServiceInterfaceChannel :
schemas.example.org.enterprise.PersonServiceInterface, System.
ServiceModel.IclientChannel...
[System.Diagnostics.DebuggerStepThroughAttribute()]
[System.CodeDom.Compiler.GeneratedCodeAttribute("System.ServiceModel",
"4.0.0.0")]

public partial class PersonServiceInterfaceClient : System.
ServiceModel.ClientBase<schemas.example.org.enterprise.
PersonServiceInterface>, schemas.example.org.enterprise.
PersonServiceInterface
```

Example 10.5

What we have here consists of an interface for the actual service and classes for message types. This is convenient as it establishes a structure compliant with the service contract (as per logic-to-contract coupling). That the service is generated as an interface makes sense as you would not want to change the generated code in order to implement your service. This further allows you to start writing code to implement the service without having to worry about the code being overwritten if regenerating the service code should become necessary.

The commonly used WCF attributes we should all be familiar with by now are ServiceContract, OperationContract, DataContract, and DataMember.

When your service is ready to be deployed, WCF will allow you to point consumers to the previously created WSDL file rather than an automatically generated WSDL file from WCF (the files will look different). To do this simply add this XML statement to the service configuration file:

```
<serviceMetadata httpGetEnabled="true"
  externalMetadataLocation="\path\personservice.wsdl"/>
```

Generating WCF Service Code Using WSCF.blue

WSCF.blue is a third party Visual Studio add-in that was created in support of contract-first development. This tool allows you to create WSDL files and generate WCF code from the WSDL markup code. WSCF.blue is a wizard-driven tool and we will therefore be briefly stepping through its screens in this section.

You begin by right-clicking on the PersonServiceMessages.xsd file and choosing the "Create WSDL Interface Description" option (Figure 10.3).

Figure 10.3

This command starts a multi-step wizard that guides you through the creation of a WSDL file and also helps you generate service code.

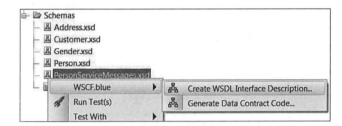

The next set of wizard dialogs are labeled according to steps, as follows:

- *Step 1* – The first step lets you specify basic settings, like service name, namespace and documentation (Figure 10.4).

- *Step 2* – You can add message schemas (other than the ones that are in the file that we right-clicked), as shown in Figure 10.5. Note that in our particular example we do not need to do carry out this step.

- *Step 3* – You can specify Web service operations, which can also be automatically inferred by the tool (Figure 10.6).

- *Step 4* – You can determine the message parameters for the individual operations (Figure 10.7).

- *Step 5* – Here you are presented with a checkbox that allows you to directly move on to a code generation dialog (Figure 10.8).

The final dialog will be pre-loaded with the newly created WSDL file and will allow you to choose from generating a client-proxy or a service-stub. For our example, we will be proceeding with the service-stub.

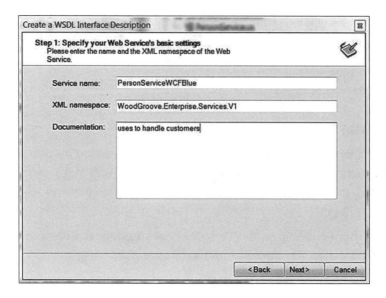

Figure 10.4
The Create a WSDSC Interface Description dialog, Step 1.

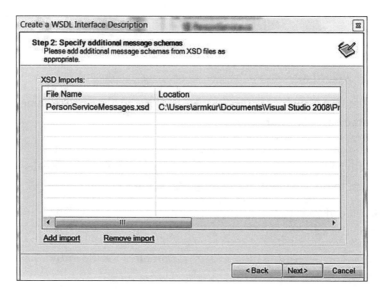

Figure 10.5
The Create a WSDSC Interface Description dialog, Step 2.

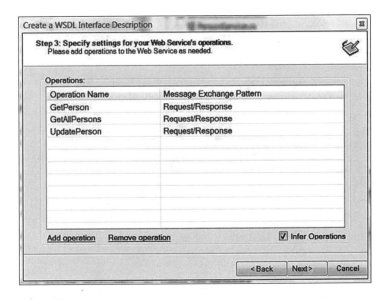

Figure 10.6
The Create a WSDSC Interface Description dialog, Step 3.

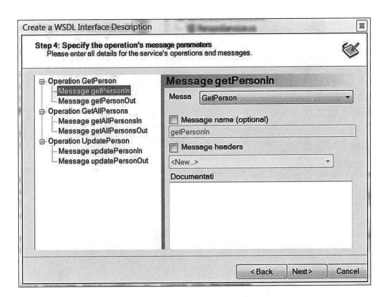

Figure 10.7
The Create a WSDSC Interface Description dialog, Step 4.

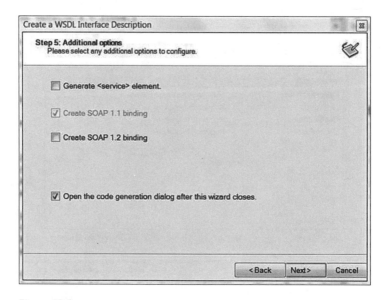

Figure 10.8

The Create a WSDSC Interface Description dialog, Step 5.

Figure 10.9

The Code Generation dialog.

The generated code looks familiar, with the exception that the data classes are not serialized using the `DataContractSerializer` but rather the `XmlSerializer`. This is deliberate as `XmlSerializer` supports a wider range of schema constructs.

```
[System.CodeDom.Compiler.GeneratedCodeAttribute
("System.ServiceModel", "3.0.0.0")]  [System.ServiceModel.
ServiceContractAttribute(Namespace="schemas.example.org.enterprise.
service.v1", ConfigurationName="IPersonServiceWCFBlue")]
  public interface IPersonServiceWCFBlue
  {
// CODEGEN: Generating message contract since the wrapper namespace
(http://schemas.example.org/enterprise/service/v1) of message
GetPersonRequest does not match the default value
(schemas.example.org.enterprise.service.v1) [System.ServiceModel.
OperationContractAttribute(Action="schemas.example.org.enterprise.
service.v1:getPersonIn", ReplyAction="*")] [System.ServiceModel.
XmlSerializerFormatAttribute(SupportFaults=true)]

GetPersonResponse GetPerson(GetPersonRequest request);
// CODEGEN: Generating message contract since the wrapper namespace
(http://schemas.example.org/enterprise/service/v1) of message
GetAllPersonsRequest does not match the default value (schemas.
example.org.enterprise.service.v1) [System.ServiceModel.
OperationContractAttribute(Action="schemas.example.org.enterprise.
service.v1:getAllPersonsIn", ReplyAction="*")]
[System.ServiceModel.XmlSerializerFormatAttribute(SupportFaults=true)]

GetAllPersonsResponse GetAllPersons(GetAllPersonsRequest request);
// CODEGEN: Generating message contract since the wrapper namespace
(http://schemas.example.org/enterprise/service/v1) of message
UpdatePersonRequest does not match the default value (schemas.
example.org.enterprise.service.v1) [System.ServiceModel.
OperationContractAttribute(Action="schemas.example.org.enterprise.
service.v1:updatePersonIn", ReplyAction="*")]
[System.ServiceModel.XmlSerializerFormatAttribute(SupportFaults=true)]
UpdatePersonResponse UpdatePerson(UpdatePersonRequest request);
}
```

Example 10.6

Generating ASMX Service Code Using WSCF.classic

The WSCF.blue tool has a predecessor called WSCF.classic. This version of the tool is very similar to the current version, but with one big difference: the WSCF.classic tool instead generates ASMX service code. The code generation dialog looks similar to the one in the WSCF.blue but the options are different as shown in Figure 10.10.

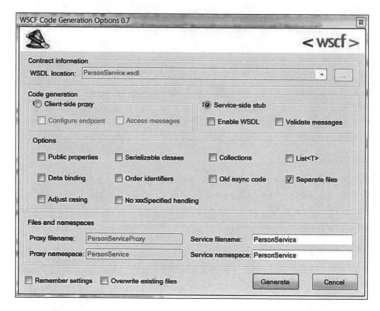

Figure 10.10
WSCF.classic options.

The generated code is annotated with the familiar `WebMethod` attribute of ASMX:

```
Version=0.7.6319.1
#endregion
namespace PersonServiceWCFBlue
{
  using System.Diagnostics;
  using System.Web.Services;
  using System.ComponentModel;
  using System.Web.Services.Protocols;
  using System;
  using System.Xml.Serialization;
  using System.Web;
/// <remarks/> [System.CodeDom.Compiler.GeneratedCodeAttribute
("System.Web.Services", "2.0.50727.4016")] [System.Web.Services.
```

```
WebServiceAttribute(Namespace="schemas.example.org.enterprise.
service.v1")] [System.Web.Services.WebServiceBindingAttribute(Name=
"BasicHttpBinding_PersonServiceWCFBlueInterface",
Namespace="schemas.example.org.enterprise.service.v1")]
public partial class BasicHttpBinding_PersonServiceWCFBlueInterface :
System.Web.Services.WebService, IBasicHttpBinding_PersonServiceWCF-
BlueInterface
{public BasicHttpBinding_PersonServiceWCFBlueInterface()
{
}
/// <remarks/>
[System.Web.Services.WebMethodAttribute()] [System.Web.Services.
Protocols.SoapDocumentMethodAttribute("schemas.example.org.
enterprise.service.v1:getPersonIn",
RequestNamespace="http://schemas.example.org/enterprise/service/v1",
ResponseNamespace="http://schemas.example.org/enterprise/service/v1",
Use=System.Web.Services.Description.SoapBindingUse.Literal,
ParameterStyle=System.Web.Services.Protocols.SoapParameterStyle.
Wrapped, Binding="BasicHttpBinding_PersonServiceWCFBlueInterface")]
[return: System.Xml.Serialization.XmlElementAttribute("person",
IsNullable=true)]
public virtual person GetPerson([System.Xml.Serialization.
XmlElementAttribute(DataType="positiveInteger", ElementName=
"personId")] string personId)
{throw new System.NotImplementedException();}
/// <remarks/>
[System.Web.Services.WebMethodAttribute()]
[System.Web.Services.Protocols.SoapDocumentMethodAttribute("schemas.
example.org.enterprise.service.v1:getAllPersonsIn",
RequestNamespace="http://schemas.example.org/enterprise/service/v1",
ResponseNamespace="http://schemas.example.org/enterprise/service/v1",
Use=System.Web.Services.Description.SoapBindingUse.Literal,
ParameterStyle=System.Web.Services.Protocols.SoapParameterStyle.
Wrapped, Binding="BasicHttpBinding_PersonServiceWCFBlueInterface")]
[return: System.Xml.Serialization.XmlArrayAttribute("person",
IsNullable=true)]
[return:
System.Xml.Serialization.XmlArrayItemAttribute(Namespace="http://
schemas.example.org/enterprise/models/v1", IsNullable=false)]
public virtual person[] GetAllPersons()
{throw new System.NotImplementedException();}
/// <remarks/>
[System.Web.Services.WebMethodAttribute()]
[System.Web.Services.Protocols.SoapDocumentMethodAttribute("schemas.
example.org.enterprise.service.v1:updatePersonIn",
RequestNamespace="http://schemas.example.org/enterprise/service/v1",
```

```
ResponseNamespace="http://schemas.example.org/enterprise/service/v1",
Use=System.Web.Services.Description.SoapBindingUse.Literal,
ParameterStyle=System.Web.Services.Protocols.SoapParameterStyle.
Wrapped, Binding="BasicHttpBinding_PersonServiceWCFBlueInterface")]
[return: System.Xml.Serialization.XmlElementAttribute("success")]
public virtual bool UpdatePerson([System.Xml.Serialization.
XmlElementAttribute(IsNullable=true, ElementName="updatablePerson")]
person updatablePerson)
{throw new System.NotImplementedException();}
}}
```

Example 10.7

NOTE

This section has been focused solely on Web service contract design in
support of Decoupled Contract [735]. REST services are not addressed
as they naturally realize Decoupled Contract [735] by requiring the application of Uniform Contract.

SUMMARY OF KEY POINTS

- Decoupled Contract [735] is a fundamental and critical pattern when applying the Service Loose Coupling (695) principle.

- When working with Web services and .NET, this pattern can be applied via
  a WSDL-first approach and one of several tools used to generate code from
  the resulting WSDL and XML Schema definitions.

10.3 Service Façade

When pursuing logic-to-contract coupling, additional coupling flexibility can be built
into the service architecture by further establishing layers of implementation logic. Service Façade [776] advocates the positioning of façade components between the service
contract and the core service logic (Figure 10.11), as well as between the core service logic
and the underlying service implementation resources (in particular legacy resources).

The former positioning protects the core service logic from changes to the contract or
impacts that may result from the application of Concurrent Contracts [726] (as explained
in the next section).

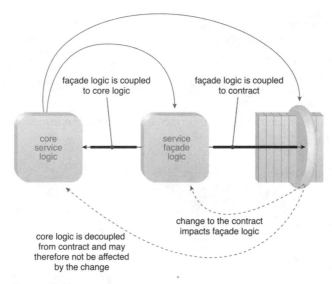

Figure 10.11

A service façade component used to establish an internal layer of abstraction.

The latter positioning of the façade logic allows for core business logic to be captured in one layer and logic proprietary to specific parts of the implementation (such as databases or legacy APIs) to reside in a different layer. When those underlying legacy resources need to be changed or replaced in the future, the impact to the service architecture is further shielded.

Typically a Service Façade [776] can contain code that:

- chooses which methods or functions to call in the core implementation

- compensates for changes in logic and/or data model so that logic-to-contract coupling is retained

- allows the core business logic to remain physically separate and stable if the service contract itself should need to change

The following series of examples shows how you could build a façade that removes address information from a person.

Consider first the service interface:

```
[ServiceContract]
interface IPersonService
{
```

```
  [OperationContract]
  person GetPerson(int personId);
}
```

Example 10.8

The following class implements the interface and returns the information that another
.NET class produces:

```
class PersonService : IPersonService
{
  public person GetPerson(int personId)
  {
    return ServiceImplementation.GetPersonById(personId);
  }
}
```

Example 10.9

Another class can also implement the interface, but notice that this class doesn't just
return the information that ServiceImplementation creates:

```
class SimplePersonService : IPersonService
{
  public person GetPerson(int personId)
  {
    var person = ServiceImplementation.
      GetPersonById(personId);
    person.address = null;
    return person;
  }
}
```

Example 10.10

The class that really implements most of the underlying façade functionality is
ServiceImplementation, as follows:

```
class ServiceImplementation
{
  public static person GetPersonById(int personId)
  {
```

```
    return new person { id = personId };
  }
}
```

Example 10.11

Note how in the preceding example, the two different façade components implement WCF code (since they implement the interface that is annotated with WCF attributes), but the core service logic is not WCF code. This allows the core implementation to exist unaware of WCF.

SUMMARY OF KEY POINTS

- Service Façade [776] introduces one or more layers of logic within service architectures to help further loosen coupling internally.

- Façade components can shield coarse service logic from changes to the service contract and service implementation.

10.4 Concurrent Contracts

As previously mentioned, Service Façade [776] can support the use of multiple technical contracts, as per Concurrent Contracts [726]. Valid reasons for creating multiple contracts include:

- different consumers with different levels of trust (some consumers will be unaware of some of the capabilities that a service exposes)

- reduction of service contract governance burden (not all consumers are affected by individual contract changes)

- application of Dual Protocols [739] (because some consumers cannot comply with the primary protocol)

Another common reason for having multiple contracts is versioning. When a new version of a service contract is developed and put into production, it is often difficult to get all consumers to switch over at the same time. In fact, some consumers may not switch at all. A technique for accommodating these situations is the application of Concurrent Contracts [726] in support of allowing a service to be accessed via different versions of the same contract.

Figure 10.12 illustrates how this pattern is commonly applied together with Service Façade [776] in order to establish a contract-specific layer of logic in support of the Service Loose Coupling (695) principle.

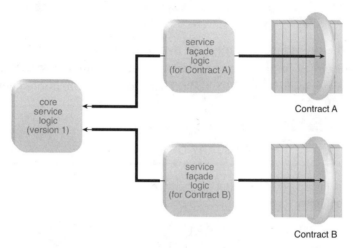

Figure 10.12

Façade logic is placed in between two service contracts and the core service logic to allow for core service logic to remain decoupled from the contracts and from logic specific to the contracts.

SUMMARY OF KEY POINTS

- Concurrent Contracts [726] enables a service to have more than one service contract in order to accommodate different service consumers or versioning requirements.

- This pattern is commonly applied together with Service Façade [776].

10.5 Service Loose Coupling and Service Capability Granularity

It is worth noting that when designing service contracts in support of service-orientation, there is a tendency to pay close attention to granularity. In Chapter 3 we introduced the four types of granularity that relate to service contract design. Here, we single out capability granularity in order to highlight one of the most important changes from how technical interfaces have been traditionally designed.

Each service capability encapsulates an independent set of functionality. Sometimes this functionality will impose specific requirements that pre-determine the capability's granularity. Other times, we will be able to set the granularity based on other factors. A general trend with service contracts is to provide coarse-grained service capabilities that accomplish more with less cross-service interaction. To understand why this is important to service-orientation, let's begin by looking at a traditional fine-grained component interface:

```
public class LineItem
{
  public int ItemSeqNo;
  ...
}
public class customer
{
  public string CompanyName;
  public string CompanyAddress;
  ...
}
public class OrderStatus
{
  public bool OK;
  public int OrderNumber;
  ...
}

/*the order manager*/
public interface IOrderManager
{
  OrderStatus CreateOrder();
  OrderStatus AddLineItem(int orderNumber, LineItem item);
  OrderStatus AddCustomerInfo(int orderNumber, customer customer);
  OrderStatus SubmitOrder(int orderNumber);
}
public class OrderManager : IOrderManager
{
  public OrderStatus CreateOrder()
  { throw new NotImplementedException(); }
  public OrderStatus AddLineItem(int orderNumber, LineItem item)
  { throw new NotImplementedException(); }
  public OrderStatus AddCustomerInfo(int orderNumber, customer
customer)
  { throw new NotImplementedException(); }
  public OrderStatus SubmitOrder(int orderNumber)
```

```
    { throw new NotImplementedException(); }
  }

/*client application that uses OrderManager*/
public class OrderApplication
{
  public void SubmitOrder()
  {
    OrderStatus status;
    LineItem item;
    customer customer;
    IOrderManager orderManager = new OrderManager();
    //create order
    status = orderManager.CreateOrder();
    if (!status.OK)
      { throw new Exception("Cannot create order!"); }
    item = new LineItem { ItemSeqNo = 1138 };
    status = orderManager.AddLineItem(status.OrderNumber, item);
    if (!status.OK) { throw new Exception("Cannot add item 1138!"); }
    item = new LineItem{ItemSeqNo=327};
    status = orderManager.AddLineItem(status.OrderNumber, item);
    if (!status.OK) { throw new Exception("Cannot add item 327!"); }
    customer = new customer { CompanyName = "Cutit supreme customer"
};
    status = orderManager.AddCustomerInfo(status.OrderNumber, cus-
tomer);
    if (!status.OK) { throw new Exception("Cannot add customer
info!"); }
    status = orderManager.SubmitOrder(status.OrderNumber);
    if (!status.OK) { throw new Exception("Cannot submit order!"); }
    return;
  }
}
```

Example 10.12

An example of fine-grained, object-oriented style technical interface.

The methods in the preceding example can be unsuitable for service capabilities for two primary reasons:

- *consumer-to-logic coupling* – For example, changing the order of the capabilities should be performed by verifying that the items of an order are in stock before creating the order.

- *chatty interface* – The consumer will have to call multiple capabilities (CreateOrder, AddLineItem, AddCustomerInfo and SubmitOrder) and will also have to call the same capability several times (AddLineItem) to carry out a single task. If the service is implemented as a Web service or a REST service, this would add considerable network overhead.

The code style in the following example demonstrates how this interface would be designed with coarse-grained service capabilities. Note that this code belongs inside applications and components and is not suitable for consumer-to-service calls.

```
[DataContract]
public class Order
{
  [DataMember]
  public customer customer;
  [DataMember]
  public LineItem[] LineItems;
  ...
}
[DataContract]
public class LineItem
{
  [DataMember]
  public int ItemSeqNo;
  ...
}
[DataContract]
public class customer
{
  public string CompanyName;
  public string CompanyAddress;
  ...
}
[DataContract]
public class OrderStatus
{
  [DataMember]
  public bool Success;
  [DataMember]
  public int OrderNumber;
  ...
}

[ServiceContract]
```

```
public interface IOrderManager
{
  [OperationContract]
  OrderStatus SubmitOrder(Order order);
}

class OrderManager : IOrderManager
{
  public OrderStatus SubmitOrder(Order order)
  {
    ...
    OrderStatus status = new OrderStatus();
    status.Success = true;
    status.OrderNumber = 94;
    return status;
  }
}

/*ServiceConsumer uses a generated
proxy class to call the Web service*/
class ServiceConsumer
{
  public boolSubmitOrderToService()
  {
    Order order = new Order();
    List<LineItem> items = new List<LineItem>();
    LineItem item = new LineItem();
    item.ItemSeqNo=1138;
    items.Add(item);
    item = new LineItem();
    item.ItemSeqNo = 327;
    items.Add(item);
    order.LineItems = items.ToArray();
    customer customer = new customer();
    customer.CompanyName = "Cutit supreme customer";
    order.customer = customer;
    IOrderManager orderManagerProxy = new OrderManager();
    OrderStatus orderStatus =
      orderManagerProxy.SubmitOrder(order);
    return orderStatus.Success;
  }
}
```

Example 10.13

An example of a coarse-grained service contract.

In this example, the service is called only once (via the SubmitOrder operation), minimizing network overhead. However, the code inside the SubmitOrder operation might still look a lot like the code from Example 10.12.

Note that coarse-grained capabilities also have a potential downside. Because they tend to perform more processing at the same time, there is the risk that they end up carrying out more logic than a given service consumer may actually require. When warranted, a service contract can accommodate different service consumers by providing both fine and coarse-grained variations of the same service capabilities. This is the basis of the Contract Denormalization [728] pattern.

SUMMARY OF KEY POINTS

- Although it is not a requirement, it can be beneficial to design service contracts with more coarsely grained service capabilities.

- For situations where both fine and coarse grained variations of a service capability are required, the Contract Denormalization [728] pattern can be applied.

10.6 Service Abstraction

The Service Abstraction (696) principle in essence advocates regulated information sharing when it comes to information about a service's behavior, architecture, and implementation. The objective of this principle is to turn services into black boxes so that their implementations can be modified or evolved independently from service consumers that may already be using the service's capabilities.

When applying this principle, we classify the common types of information available about a service into four categories referred to as meta abstraction types (Figure 10.13):

1. functional information

2. technology information

3. programmatic information

4. quality-of-service information

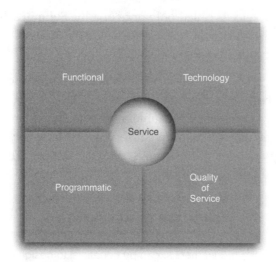

Figure 10.13
The four meta abstraction types used when working with
Service Abstraction (696).

Of these four types of meta information, usually technology and quality-of-service details make their way into actual published contracts. It is generally considered unnecessary for service consumer designers to need access to the rest of the information. Steps are therefore taken to intentionally hide or limit access to this information so as to avoid consumer-to-implementation coupling and the temptation for service consumers to further optimize their programs in relation to how the service architecture currently exists.

Service Abstraction (696) is also applied at a more detailed level to the actual service contract itself, as explained in the upcoming Validation Abstraction [792] pattern description.

SUMMARY OF KEY POINTS

- Service Abstraction (696) is concerned with turning services into black boxes by reducing the amount of unnecessary information published about a service and introducing access control to regulate information hiding.

- When applying this principle, it is helpful to categorize the types of information that can be made available about a service into functional, technology, programmatic, and quality-of-service information.

10.7 Validation Abstraction

Regardless of whether you are building services as Web services or REST services, you can define message schemas with data types and validation logic that establish specific constraints and a specific level of validation granularity.

Strongly typed service contracts and data models have the benefit of sparing services from having to process messages that do not comply to certain types of baseline data standards. On the other hand, there can be long-term consequences to publishing this type of granular validation logic in public service contracts used by service consumers. Namely, if the logic needs to change (due to changes in overarching business requirements or otherwise), then there may be the need to introduce new versions of the service contract and assume the governance responsibilities that come along with that circumstance.

The Service Abstraction (696) principle asks us to consider how much detail we absolutely need to publish in service contracts and encourages us to trim away any unnecessary constraints in support of optimizing the service contract for increased longevity and reduced governance burden (Figure 10.14).

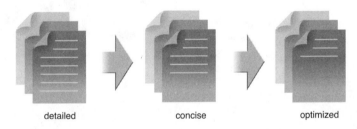

detailed   concise   optimized

Figure 10.14

Optimizing the service contract will reduce the overall quantity of contract content.

The flipside of this approach is that the validation logic may need to be deferred to an intermediary or inside the service logic itself.

The primary objective of Validation Abstraction [792] is to further protect services and their consumers from the impacts of change. When you have reason to believe that some parts of a message structure may be volatile, there is good reason to consider not hard coding those parts into a message schema.

For example, let's say that you have a type called `ApplicationClassType` containing an enumeration of different classes that an application pertains to:

```
<xsd:simpleType name="ApplicationClassType">
  <xsd:restriction base="xsd:string">
    <xsd:enumeration value="CDA"/>
    <xsd:enumeration value="TRU"/>
    <xsd:enumeration value="CMI"/>
    <xsd:enumeration value="TER"/>
    <xsd:enumeration value="LBR"/>
    <xsd:enumeration value="LBA"/>
    <xsd:enumeration value="MAG"/>
    <xsd:enumeration value="IST"/>
  </xsd:restriction>
</xsd:simpleType>
```

Example 10.14

If you need to add an enumeration value to this list, you will need to create a new version of the schema, as follows:

```
<xsd:simpleType name="ApplicationClassType">
  <xsd:restriction base="xsd:string">
    <xsd:enumeration value="CDA"/>
    <xsd:enumeration value="TRU"/>
    <xsd:enumeration value="CMI"/>
    <xsd:enumeration value="TER"/>
    <xsd:enumeration value="LBR"/>
    <xsd:enumeration value="LBA"/>
    <xsd:enumeration value="MAG"/>
    <xsd:enumeration value="IST"/>
    <xsd:enumeration value="GER"/>
  </xsd:restriction>
</xsd:simpleType>
```

Example 10.15

This is considered a backwards-compatible change (as per Compatible Change [723]), meaning you may not need to force consumers to be updated after the change is made. However, if a consumer wants to use the new value ("GER") it may need to update in order to be made aware of its existence. A non-backwards-compatible change, such as if MAG were no longer a valid ApplicationClassType, will require that existing consumers be updated.

A means of loosening this constraint when applying Validation Abstraction [792] could be to specify the ApplicationClassType as follows:

```
<xsd:simpleType name="ApplicationClassType">
  <xsd:restriction base="xsd:string">
    <xsd:length value="3"/>
  </xsd:restriction>
</xsd:simpleType>
```

Example 10.16

This way, when you add GER to the list of accepted values you will not need to change the structure of any messages. The downside of this approach is that you have to solve two things, namely validating the `ApplicationClassType` field *inside* the service logic and informing service consumers of when the range of acceptable values changes.

One way of informing consumers without having to rely on human communication is to expose a separate service capability that returns the most current list of values for the `ApplicationClassType`. This list can then be retrieved and cached inside consumers to avoid repeated communication overhead.

The validation of the field can be performed by creating a class that produces a list of `ApplicationClass` values and then creating an extension method that takes a string and checks if it is part of the list of values:

```
public static class Validators
{
  private static List<string> listOfApplicationClass;
  static Validators()
  {
    listOfApplicationClass = GetListOfApplicationClass();
  }
  private static List<string> GetListOfApplicationClass()
  {
    var list = new List<string>();
    list.Add("CDA");
    list.Add("TRU");
    list.Add("CMI");
    list.Add("TER");
    list.Add("LBR");
    list.Add("LBA");
    list.Add("MAG");
    list.Add("IST");
    list.Add("GER");
    return list;
  }
}
```

```
static List<string> ListOfApplicationClass
{
  get { return listOfApplicationClass; }
}
static bool ApplicationClassIsValid
  (this string applicationClass)
{
  return ListOfApplicationClass.Contains(applicationClass);
}
}
```

Example 10.17

Inside your service implementation you could then validate the incoming string for the application class as shown here:

```
if (!applicationClass.ApplicationClassIsValid())
{
  ... return error message to consumer ...
}
```

Example 10.18

If the validation code inside your service implementation finds that the `Application-ClassType` field is not valid, an exception is raised, responding to the consumer with an error message (and the consumer would need to be prepared to handle this kind of error).

As demonstrated here, applying Validation Abstraction [792] can actually result in extra development effort and more complex service and consumer logic. This can be justified when the long-term savings in governance effort and expense are considered worthwhile.

SUMMARY OF KEY POINTS

- The optimization of service contract content is the goal of Validation Abstraction [792].

- This pattern supports the application of Service Abstraction (696), with an emphasis on service contract design.

- The application of Validation Abstraction [792] tends to decrease (make coarser) the validation granularity of service contracts.

10.8 Exception Shielding

What is often overlooked as a source of potentially harmful information about the internal implementation of a service are exceptions or error messages. Services are sometimes designed to return detailed data about the nature of a given exception, thereby inadvertently disclosing information about their underlying architecture that can be abused by malicious consumer programs.

Exception Shielding [744] prescribes that exception information be *sanitized* prior to being sent to consumers. The sanitization of exception data is usually based on a process whereby some or all parts of the actual exception information are removed or replaced with data considered safe.

NOTE

The Exception Shielding [744] pattern is considered a security pattern. It is covered here as it demonstrates a specialized application of the Service Abstraction (696) principle. Other security topics are covered in Chapter 17.

In WCF there is a configuration setting that will make WCF replace all exceptions with a generic SOAP fault message, thereby not revealing anything unwanted to service consumers.

Here's the statement that needs to be configured:

```
<serviceDebug includeExceptionDetailInFaults="False" />
```

Example 10.19

Another alternative is to remove this configuration line altogether as the default behavior of WCF is to not include exception details in fault messages. This will still return a SOAP fault, but it will not be useful to consumers.

Here is how this type of fault message will look:

```
<s:Fault xmlns:s="http://schemas.xmlsoap.org/soap/envelope/">
  <faultcode xmlns:a="http://schemas.microsoft.com/
    net/2005/12/windowscommunicationfoundation/dispatcher">
    a:InternalServiceFault
  </faultcode>
  <faultstring xml:lang="en-US">
```

```
        The server was unable to process the request due
        to an internal error. For more information about
        the error, either turn on
        IncludeExceptionDetailInFaults (either from
        ServiceBehaviorAttribute or from the
        &lt;serviceDebug&gt;configuration behavior)
        on the server in order to send the
        exception information back to the client,
        or turn on tracing as per the Microsoft .NET
        Framework SDK documentation and inspect the
        server trace logs.
    </faultstring>
</s:Fault>
```

Example 10.20

You may actually want to provide more information in faults and even return different faults in different situations (for example when encountering a "Quota" error when a consumer has used the service more than the service's SLA allows or a "Temporarily Unavailable" error when some of the service's essential resources are offline).

Note also that the original exception produced by the service logic may contain information that is important for systems maintenance or customer support and therefore may need to be logged. For these types of situations, the sanitized fault message content can still include a unique ID that can be sent to the customer in order to allow for the correlation of the exception with the logged details.

In WCF, this type of behavior is built-in, in that all logs created within an activity (a service call) will have the same `ActivityId`. You can make sure that this `ActivityId` is propagated to composed services so that all logs in a service composition can be found using the same `ActivityId`.

To propagate the `ActivityId` to other WCF services and clients, you will need to add some configuration details because even when the propagateActivity attribute value is set to "true," you may find that the `ActivityId` is still not propagated.

This is because you still need to configure a listener, as shown here:

```
<system.diagnostics>
  <sources>
    <source name="System.ServiceModel"
      propagateActivity="true">
      <listeners>
```

```
        <add name="defaultListener"
          type="System.Diagnostics.DefaultTraceListener" />
      </listeners>
    </source>
  </sources>
</system.diagnostics>
```

Example 10.21

These configuration settings need to be made on both ends of a message exchange (service and consumer). WCF passes the ActivityId around in a message header that is also added to fault messages.

SUMMARY OF KEY POINTS

- Exception Shielding [744] sanitizes error messages generated by the service so that messages created in response to exceptions only contain safe information.

- Exception Shielding [744] is a security-related pattern that further supports the goals of Service Abstraction (696).

10.9 Service Discoverability

Service discoverability is primarily about answering one question: Is the functionality that we need already available or do we need to create or purchase it? In order to answer this question properly we need to know a number of things, including:

- where to search for existing functionality

- the purpose, capabilities, and functional boundary of any known service

- sufficient information about service availability and service-level guarantees

For this information (Figure 10.15) to be available and understandable to a range of project team members, we need to take the time to ensure that it is sufficiently discoverable and interpretable. This is what the Service Discoverability (702) principle is concerned with.

Figure 10.15

When revisiting the meta abstraction types established by the Service Abstraction (696) principle, the application of Service Discoverability (702) is focused on the functional and quality-of-service types.

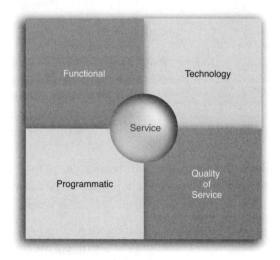

In-line Documentation

Service Discoverability (702) is not just about documenting the service, its capabilities, and messages, it is about ensuring that whatever documentation is produced has a high level of communications quality.

Another aspect to consider is how to organize the documentation and to where it should be published. Inline annotations can be added to XML schemas and WSDL definitions using the `xsd:annotation` and `wsdl:documentation` elements, respectively:

```
<xsd:annotation>
  <xsd:documentation>
    this data model is...
  </xsd:documentation>
</xsd:annotation>

<wsdl:documentation>
  this service is...
</wsdl:documentation>
```

Example 10.22

If you choose to write you contracts in code using WCF, there is no built-in mechanism for doing this. The extensibility features of .NET and WCF make it possible to create custom `Documentation` and `Annotation` attributes that can export documentation from your .NET code into generated XML Schema and WSDL definition files.

> **NOTE**
>
> If the documentation is placed within XML Schema and WSDL definitions, it is possible to generate slightly more human readable documents based upon those files using third-party tools (such as XSDdoc and WSDLdoc) that output the documentation in HTML format.

REST and Hypermedia

Documenting the resources and related capabilities for REST services is something that you can consider doing with WADL or even WSDL 2.0. However, it is generally expected that REST services be effectively discovered via human-readable links.

HATEOAS (Hypermedia as the Engine of Application State) can be used to establish links used by the service in order to guide service consumers through the process of making multiple related service invocations. The service adds links to its response messages to identify a number of suitable subsequent actions. Service consumers can then traverse these links and dynamically choose what to do next.

Service Profiles

Throughout its lifespan, information about a service will generally be recorded in a service profile document (Figure 10.16). Although the service profile is owned by the service custodian and, due to requirements raised by Service Abstraction (696), is not typically published in its entirety, there can be opportunities to make portions of the service profile available as part of the service SLA or any other form of publicly accessible information.

SUMMARY OF KEY POINTS

- Service Discoverability (702) is concerned with ensuring the communications quality of information published about a service in order to improve the discoverability and interpretability of this information.

- The communications quality of service information can be improved by adding inline annotations to service contract documents, creating intuitive hypermedia links for REST services, and using service profiles as a source of service metadata.

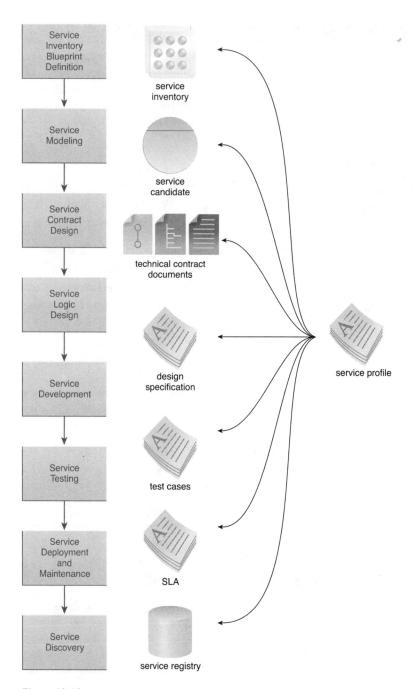

Figure 10.16

All of the information published for discoverability and interpretability purposes is usually also found within the service profile, in addition to many more details that are kept private by the service custodian.

10.10 Metadata Centralization

The Service Discoverability (702) principle prepares services for eventual discovery, but this principle itself does not require the existence of a service registry. Centralizing service metadata into a registry for discovery purposes is the result of applying Metadata Centralization [754], a pattern that introduces the need for a standardized service discovery process (Figure 10.17).

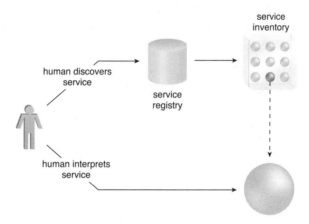

Figure 10.17

The traditional design-time discovery process, whereby a human searches and explores service metadata recorded in a central registry. The extent to which Service Discoverability (702) is applied consistently to services within a service inventory will determine how effectively Metadata Centralization [754] can be realized.

UDDI is an integral standard within the Web services stack. It defines an interoperable and standards-based approach for publishing and discovering services in a service-oriented environment regardless of the platform. By providing a layer of indirection between the service consumer and the service, UDDI simplifies managing changes such as version updates, security policy changes, and service termination.

The UDDI initiative included public and private registries. The public registry (UBR) was discontinued and UDDI has moved toward supporting the internal Web services infrastructure of businesses. The UDDI 3.0 specification extends its support for internal Web services by introducing federated control in operational environments.

Windows 2003 includes a UDDI service registry as a core feature. Microsoft's UDDI implementation is primarily geared towards enabling developer reuse and dynamic configuration at runtime. Windows 2003 Enterprise UDDI Services are tightly integrated with Visual Studio.NET and the Microsoft Office Web Services Toolkit. The implementation also integrates with Active Directory for authentication and authorization.

In addition to accessing the contents of the UDDI repository using an API, the service registry contents can be posted on the Web for searching, publishing, and coordination.

SUMMARY OF KEY POINTS

- Metadata Centralization [754] advocates the use of a central service registry (within a given service inventory) as a means of enabling service discovery.

- .NET provides integrated support for the UDDI industry standard for creating a service registry and programmatic access via Visual Studio.

Chapter 11

Service-Orientation with .NET Part III: Reusability and Agnostic Service Models

11.1 Service Reusability and the Separation of Concerns

11.2 Case Study Example: Utility Abstraction with a .NET Web Service

11.3 Case Study Example: Entity Abstraction with a .NET REST Service

SOA PRINCIPLES & PATTERNS REFERENCED IN THIS CHAPTER

- Agnostic Capability [709]
- Agnostic Context [710]
- Domain Inventory [738]
- Entity Abstraction [742]
- Functional Decomposition [747]
- Non-Agnostic Context [756]
- Service Encapsulation [775]
- Service Reusability (697)
- Utility Abstraction [791]

The previous two chapters have focused primarily on service architecture characteristics that help attain standardization and federation across service inventory boundaries in support of fostering intrinsic interoperability. To fully leverage the inherent flexibility we build into service architectures and the natural compatibility we establish among services, we need to turn our attention to how the core service logic itself is defined individually and in relation to other services within the same domain.

In this chapter we explore the application of the Service Reusability (697) principle in relation to a series of service identification, service definition, and service abstraction patterns that help reveal how agnostic logic is shaped, refined, and further classified in support of maximizing reuse potential.

11.1 Service Reusability and the Separation of Concerns

The SOA design patterns catalog establishes a set of foundational service patterns responsible for identifying and defining the scope of functional service contexts and boundaries, as well as service capabilities. As shown in Figure 11.1, the majority of these patterns pertain and lead to the definition of agnostic logic suitable for reuse and therefore subject to the Service Reusability (697) principle.

As explained in the upcoming sections, the combined application of these patterns essentially carries out the separation of concerns in support of the service-orientation paradigm.

NOTE
The following five sections contain abbreviated content and diagrams borrowed from Chapter 11 of *SOA Design Patterns*. The purpose of this content is to establish these foundational patterns and their proposed application sequence in relation to subsequent content and topics in this book. If you are already familiar with service identification and definition patterns, feel free to skip ahead to the two *Case Study Example* sections in this chapter.

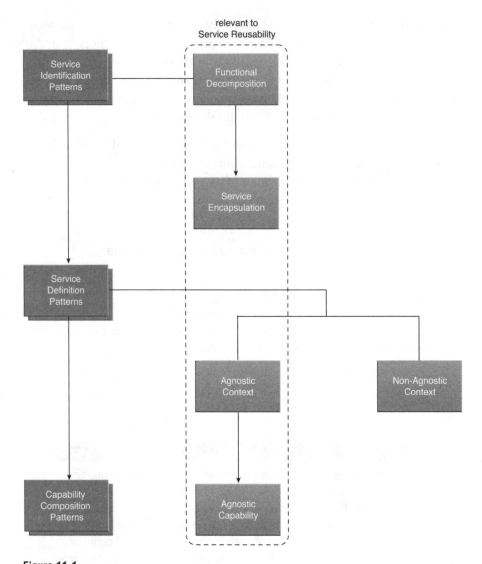

Figure 11.1

These foundational service patterns can be combined to establish a primitive service modeling process that results in the definition of service candidates and service capability candidates.

Functional Decomposition [747]

The separation of concerns theory is based on an established software engineering principle that promotes the decomposition of a larger problem into smaller problems (called concerns) for which corresponding units of solution logic can be built.

The rationale is that a larger problem (the execution of a business process, for example) can be more easily and effectively solved when separated into smaller parts. Each unit of solution logic that is built exists as a separate body of logic responsible for solving one or more of the identified, smaller concerns (Figure 11.2). This design approach forms the basis for distributed computing and is essentially embodied by the Functional Decomposition [747] pattern.

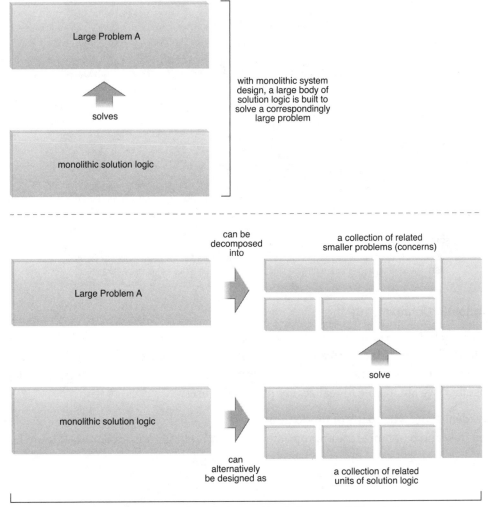

Figure 11.2

On its own, Functional Decomposition [747] results in the decomposition of the larger problem into smaller problems. The actual definition of solution logic units occurs through the application of subsequent patterns.

Service Encapsulation [775]

When assessing the individual units of solution logic that are required to solve a larger problem (carry out a business process), we may realize that only a subset of the logic is suitable for encapsulation within services. This identification of service logic is accomplished via the application of the Service Encapsulation [775] pattern (Figure 11.3).

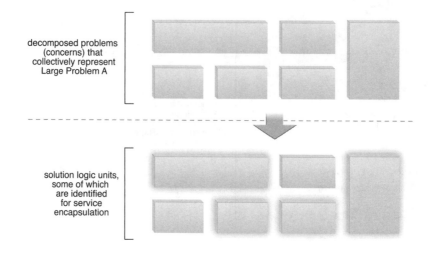

decomposed problems (concerns) that collectively represent Large Problem A

solution logic units, some of which are identified for service encapsulation

Figure 11.3

Some of the decomposed solution logic is identified as being not suitable for service encapsulation. The highlighted blocks represent logic to which this pattern was successfully applied.

Agnostic Context [710]

After the initial decomposition of solution logic we will typically end up with a series of solution logic units that correspond to specific concerns. Some of this logic may be capable of solving other concerns, but by grouping single-purpose and multi-purpose logic together, we are unable to realize any potential reuse.

By identifying what parts of this logic are not specific to known concerns, we are able to separate and reorganize the appropriate logic into a set of agnostic contexts (Figure 11.4).

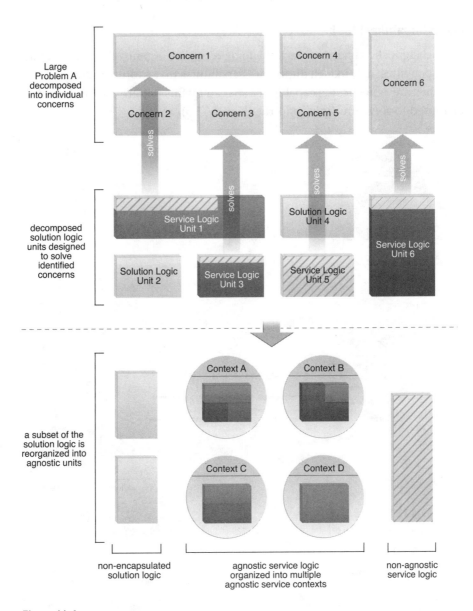

Figure 11.4

Decomposed units of solution logic will naturally be designed to solve concerns specific to a single, larger problem. Units 1, 3, and 6 represent logic that contains multi-purpose functionality trapped within a single-purpose (single concern) context. The application of this pattern results in a subset of the solution logic being further decomposed and then distributed into services with specific agnostic contexts.

Agnostic Capability [709]

Within each agnostic service context, the logic is further organized into a set of agnostic service capabilities. It is, in fact, the service capabilities that address individual concerns. Because they are agnostic, the capabilities shaped by this pattern are multi-purpose and can be reused to solve multiple concerns (Figure 11.5).

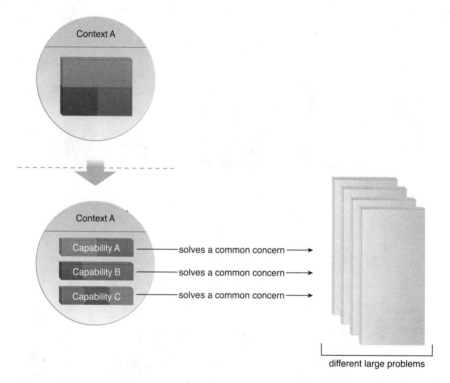

Figure 11.5

A set of agnostic service capabilities is defined, each capable of solving a common concern.

Utility Abstraction [791]

The application of the Utility Abstraction [791] pattern results in the separation of common cross-cutting functionality that is neither specific to a business process nor a business entity. This establishes a specialized agnostic functional context limited to utility logic. The resulting type of service is referred to as a utility service and the repeated application of this pattern within a service inventory results in the creation of a logical utility layer (Figure 11.6).

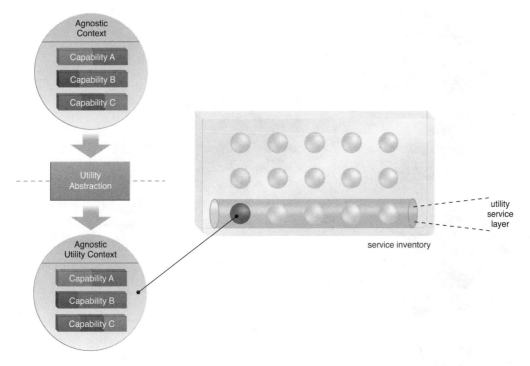

Figure 11.6
The application of Utility Abstraction [791] restricts the agnostic context of the service to utility logic.

Entity Abstraction [742]

Every organization has business entities that represent key artifacts relevant to how operational activities are carried out. The application of Entity Abstraction [742] shapes the functional context of a service so that it is limited to logic that pertains to one or more related business entities. As with Utility Abstraction [791], the repeated application of this pattern establishes its own logical service layer (Figure 11.7).

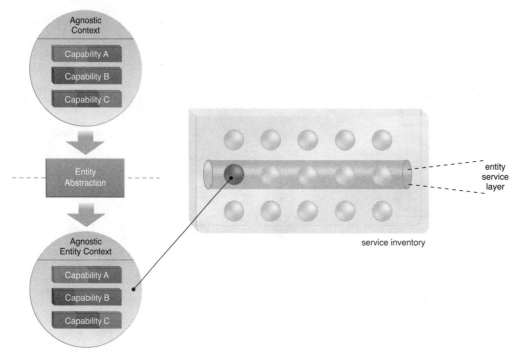

Figure 11.7

The application of Entity Abstraction [742] restricts the agnostic context of the service to entity logic.

The Inventory Analysis Cycle

When viewing the preceding set of patterns, one can see there are steps within a service-oriented analysis process. It is important to realize that this process (and its steps) is preferably carried out iteratively, as part of a cycle that identifies, defines, and also *refines* agnostic service contexts and agnostic capabilities.

This is commonly accomplished by decomposing a set of business processes that belong to a given domain within the IT enterprise. This domain represents the boundary of a planned service inventory. By iterating through a separate analysis and functional decomposition of each business process, agnostic service candidates and their capabilities can be continually refined until they reach a state where their reuse potential has been fully determined before they are physically designed and developed. This takes the guesswork out of applying the Service Reusability (697) principle in that the reuse of each service is pre-determined based on the current state of the business. Future business change is naturally accommodated by leveraging the inherent characteristics and flexibility established by this and other principles.

Each of these service candidates is added to a collection that eventually results in a blueprint of the service inventory, as illustrated in Figure 11.8. The depicted analysis cycle is one of several ways to incorporate service-oriented analysis within an SOA methodology. A key consideration here is that the extent to which the cycle needs to be iterated is directly related to the scope of the planned service inventory. When applying Domain Inventory [738] within an IT enterprise, multiple service inventories can co-exist and can be independently planned and defined with different approaches, each iterating through their own cycles within manageable boundaries.

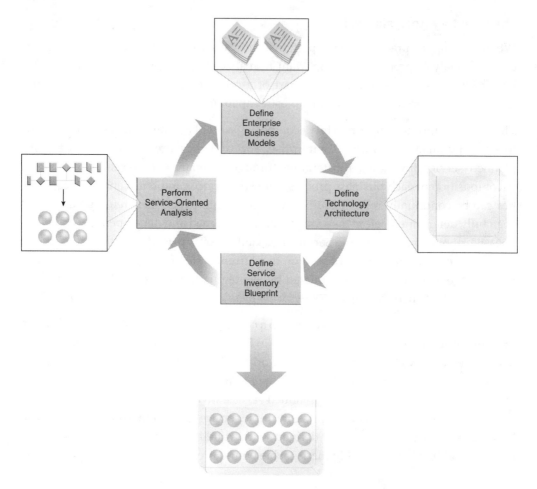

Figure 11.8

The cycle begins with the definition of business models (such as entity relationship models and business process definitions) and takes practical considerations into account via a step dedicated to the on-going definition of the required technology architecture that corresponds to the scope of the planned service inventory. As service candidates are produced or
refined through repeated iterations of the service-oriented analysis (and service modeling) phase, required business models are defined or updated, the technology architecture is accordingly augmented, and the service inventory blueprint is
gradually populated.

Additional Design Considerations

While we've been primarily focused on the identification, definition, and classification of reusable service logic, it's important to acknowledge that the Service Reusability (697) principle encompasses several more considerations that shape the service logic and its support architecture, including:

- robustness of reusable service logic

- sufficiently generic and flexible service contracts and functionality

- testing and quality assurance to ensure sufficient "real world" reusability

These types of characteristics, many of which are shaped by design techniques borrowed from the commercial software product development industry, help prepare service logic for a broad range of reuse scenarios.

SUMMARY OF KEY POINTS

- Service Reusability (697) is concerned with the identification of reusable logic as well as ensuring that the service architecture itself is capable of real world reuse.

- Several foundational service identification and definition patterns can be applied during iterations of the service-oriented analysis phase in order to identify, define, separate, and refine agnostic logic suitable for reuse.

11.2 CASE STUDY EXAMPLE: UTILITY ABSTRACTION WITH A .NET WEB SERVICE

Standard Mold is interested in creating a Notification service. They have a number of different systems that already notify people about IT system failures and outages, but this legacy architecture requires that their SMS sending software support four different SMS vendors, and has therefore become complex and expensive to maintain (Figure 11.9).

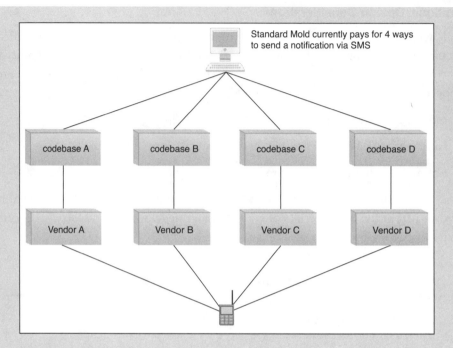

Figure 11.9
The current status of Standard Mold's SMS-sending software.

Furthermore, they want to expand the use of their notifications, as follows:

- they would like managers to be notified when inventory is running low

- customers may need to be notified when specific types of new inventory arrive at the warehouse

- the billing department may want to be able to notify customers as soon as payments are considered overdue

The team of architects responsible for designing these new notification functions is still interested in issuing notifications with SMS. Even though it is more costly and restrictive than issuing e-mail notification messages, business analysts have determined that SMS notifications are more likely to be received and read sooner.

The design of the service begins with the application of the Standardized Service Contract (693) principle by following a contract-first approach. Architects design a

NotificationMessage, a NotificationStatus type and a WSDL definition with a Notify-BySms operation and then proceed to use the WCF.blue tool to generate implementation code from the WSDL definition.

A single SMS vendor was chosen for use by the new service. This vendor provides a proprietary .NET API that the service will need to access. A sample code fragment used to interact with this API is shown here:

```
TransmitterClientProxy proxy = new TransmitterClientProxy();
int smsid =
proxy.SendShortTextMessage
(
  12309723, //customer id
  "T0pSecre7", //password
  1, //priority
  "You recieved this SMS from Standard Mold",
    //message of SMS
  7002348234781, //receiver
  null, //delay hours
  true, //delivery report wanted
  "https://standardmold.com/delivery_report/{messageId}
    /{state}" // delivery report address
);
```

Example 11.1

Some of the parameters for this API are populated using configuration and message-specific parts of the SMS message. The actual text message and the receiving phone number is populated using the incoming request message.

The Notification service's NotifyBySms operation and related NotifyBySmsRequest message are designed independently of this API. As a result, contract-to-logic coupling is avoided, allowing Standard Mold architects to change SMS vendors in the future, if required.

The Notification service needs to be able to perform its processing in an asynchronous fashion. Therefore, architects determine that it would be sufficient for the service to issue one-way notification messages without the need for any acknowledgement of receipt by service consumers.

Specifically, the NotifyBySms operation is designed to works as follows:

1. When the notification request reaches the Notification service, it saves some information about the notification, gives it a NotificationId value, and puts the request in a queue.

2. The Notification service sends a response to the service consumer containing the newly generated NotificationId. As a result, the consumer is able to use this ID value when it wants to poll for the status of the message.

3. A transaction wraps this functionality in order to ensure the integrity of the database and the queue insertions. On the other side of the queue a Windows service is positioned to listen, send the SMS, and update the database accordingly. A transaction is also used here to ensure these steps are carried out together.

The technologies chosen for this service architecture are:

- .NET

- WCF

- SQL Server

- MSMQ

The service interface (called the Notification_receiver) is implemented using WCF. A transaction scope is defined to keep the SQL Server database (Notification_db) and MSMQ queue (Notification_queue) processing together.

To make interacting with MSMQ easier, they wrap the queue in a WCF interface. Notification_sender is the Windows service on the other end of the queue that uses a transaction scope to read a message from MSMQ, send a message using the API (not part of the transaction), and save the status of the message in the database. This architecture is illustrated in Figure 11.10.

This design allows the different parts of the service to be scaled independently, depending on future needs and requirements. The sender can be scaled out if necessary without touching the receiver, and the receiver part can be scaled out without touching the sender.

The GetNotificationStatus operation was created in order to allow consumers to find out more about the status of the notification (whether or not the SMS was sent or even opened).

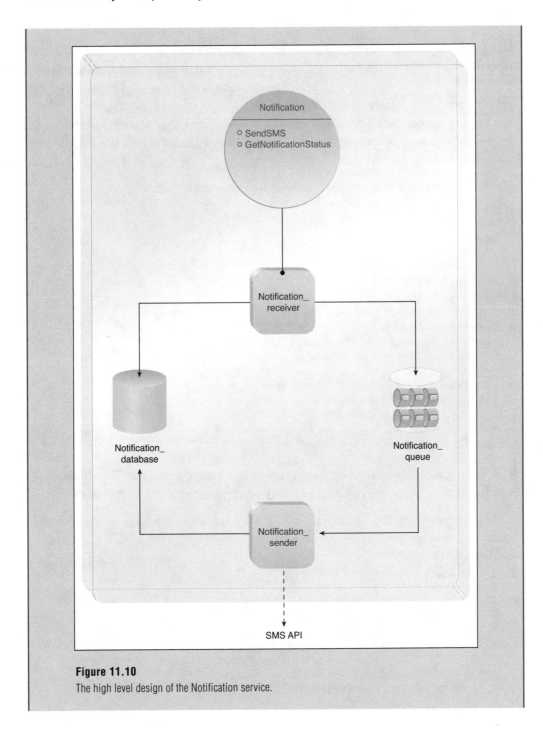

Figure 11.10
The high level design of the Notification service.

Using the previously created NotificationId, service consumers can get the same kind of information as the NotifyBySms operation returns (the status of the notification). However, when calling the GetNotificationStatus operation, the consumer does get a return value signifying that the SMS was sent or opened, in case the recipient has already opened the SMS using a cell phone. This functionality was made possible by the SMS vendor and allows for a delivery report address to be added to the call using their proprietary API.

The WCF interface of the service (receiver) looks like this:

```
[ServiceContract
  (Name = "Notification",
   Namespace = "http://schemas.standardmold.com/
     enterprise/services/v1")
]

public interface INotificationReceiver
{
  [OperationContract]
  NotificationResponse NotifyBySms
    (NotificationMessage message);
  [OperationContract]
    NotificationResponse GetNotificationStatus
    (Guid NotificationId);
}
```

Example 11.2

The implementation of the GetNotificationStatus method is relatively straightforward. It basically gets the status of a specific NotificationId from the database.

The NotifyBySms method is also simple, in that it extracts the MessageId from the incoming message headers. The data type of the MessageId is UniqueId. From this field, a GUID is extracted and passed along with the notification message to the ProcessMessage method:

```
public NotificationResponse NotifyBySms
  (NotificationMessage message)
{
  UniqueId messageId = OperationContext.Current.
  IncomingMessageHeaders.MessageId;
    Guid messageGuid = Guid.Empty;
  if (messageId.TryGetGuid(out messageGuid))
```

```
   {
     return this.ProcessMessage(message, messageGuid);
   }
   else
   {
     return new NotificationResponse
     {
       MessageStatus = Status.Failed
     };
   }
}
```

Example 11.3

The ProcessMessage method first uses the `DataAccess` class to check if the notification was processed before. If not, it attempts to save the message to the database and put it in the queue. This is done inside a transaction scope, so either both or neither of these operations succeed. In case of a failure, the status of the notification in the response message is set to "failed."

As previously mentioned, the notification may have been processed before a response is constructed using the current status of this notification that was returned from the database. In this case, the status can be saved (if the notification was not yet sent), or it can be set to another status value, such as "sent" (if the notification was sent to the consumer).

The following example shows how the message is saved to the database (with status "saved") and placed in the queue. Possible responses include the communication of success with the `NotificationId` value or a response of failure in case of an exception condition.

```
private NotificationResponse ProcessMessage
    (NotificationMessage message, Guid messageGuid)
{
  NotificationResponse response = null;
  Guid notificationId = Guid.Empty;
  var notificationData =
    DataAccess.GetNotificationData(messageGuid);
  if (notificationData.NotificationNotProcessed)
  {
    try
    {
```

```
      using (var scope = new TransactionScope())
      {
        notificationId = DataAccess.SaveMessage
          (message, messageGuid);
            MsMqAction.SendToMsmq(message, notificationId);
            scope.Complete();
      }
      response = new NotificationResponse
      {
        MessageStatus = Status.Saved,
        NotificationId = notificationId
      };
      }
      catch
      {
      response = new NotificationResponse
      {
        MessageStatus = Status.Failed
      };
    }
  }
  else
  {
    response = new NotificationResponse
    {
      MessageStatus = notificationData.MessageStatus,
      NotificationId = notificationData.NotificationId
    };
  }
  return response;
}
```

Example 11.4

The DataAccess class checks the messageGuid. If it was set by the client (that is, the messageGuid is not Guid.Empty), it attempts to find it in the database using LINQ to SQL. If it was found in the database, the NotificationId and NotificationStatus properties are set in a NotificationData object:

```
public NotificationData GetNotificationData(Guid messageGuid)
{
  using (NotifyDBDataContext db = new NotifyDBDataContext())
  {
    var notificationEntry =
```

```
      (from notification in db.NotificationDataEntries
        where notification.MessageId == messageGuid
        select notification).SingleOrDefault();
   if (notificationEntry != null)
   {
     return new NotificationData
     {
       NotificationId =
         notificationEntry.NotificationId,
       NotificationStatus =
         notificationEntry.NotificationStatus
     };
   }
 }
 return new NotificationData();
}
```

Example 11.5

The NotificationData class is also important in this example as it helps the ProcessMessage method determine if it should go on to process this notification, or simply return status information about it. If the notification was already processed, the NotificationData instance that the GetNotificationData method returns will contain values for NotificationId and NotificationStatus.

```
public class NotificationData
{
  public Guid NotificationId { get; set; }
  public Status NotificationStatus { get; set; }
  /// <summary>
  /// if NotificationId was not set this
  /// notification was not processed
  /// </summary>
  public bool NotificationNotProcessed
  {
    get
    {
      return NotificationId.Equals(Guid.Empty);
    }
  }
}
```

Example 11.6

The SendToMsmq method is responsible for putting the notification inside the MSMQ queue by creating an MSMQ message and then using WCF to put the message into the queue:

```
public void SendToMsmq
  (NotificationMessage message, Guid notificationId)
{
  IdentifiedNotification notification =
    new IdentifiedNotification
    {
    NotificationId = notificationId,
    NotificationMessage = message
  };
  var msmqMessage = new MsmqMessage
    <IdentifiedNotification>(notification);
  msmqMessage.Priority = MessagePriority.Highest;
  var client = new MsmqNotificationClient
    ("NotificationEndpoint");
  client.PutNotification(msmqMessage);
  client.Close();
}
```

Example 11.7

Standard Mold architects build a WCF program that communicates with MSMQ queue by creating an interface and a client implementation along with some simple configuration:

```
[ServiceContract]
public interface IMsmqNotificationQueue
{
  [OperationContract(IsOneWay = true, Action = "*")]
  void PutNotification(MsmqMessage
    <IdentifiedNotification> msg);
}
public partial class MsmqNotificationClient :
  ClientBase<IMsmqNotificationQueue>, IMsmqNotificationQueue
{
  public MsmqNotificationClient() { }
  public MsmqNotificationClient(string configurationName)
    : base(configurationName) { }
  public MsmqNotificationClient
    (Binding binding, EndpointAddress address)
    : base(binding, address) { }
```

```
public void PutNotification
  (MsmqMessage<IdentifiedNotification> message)
{
  base.Channel.PutNotification(message);
}
}
```

Example 11.8

The significant configuration is as follows:

```
<client>
  <endpoint
    address="msmq.formatname:
      DIRECT=OS:.\private$\NotificationSMS"
    binding="msmqIntegrationBinding"
    contract="MsMqIntegration.IMsmqNotificationQueue"
    bindingConfiguration="NotificationEndpointBinding"
    name="NotificationEndpoint"
  />
</client>
```

Example 11.9

Developers choose to use the msmqIntegrationBinding because netMsmqBinding would make it more complicated to deserialize messages from the queue when implementing the sender.

The sender is implemented as a Windows service using the MSMQ API. It sets up a listener for the queue in the OnStar method.

```
protected override void OnStart(string[] args)
{
  string queueName = ConfigurationManager.
    AppSettings["queueName"];
  if (!MessageQueue.Exists(queueName))
    MessageQueue.Create(queueName, true);
    MessageQueue queue = new MessageQueue(queueName);
    queue.ReceiveCompleted +=
    new ReceiveCompletedEventHandler
      (MessageReceiveCompleted);
    queue.BeginReceive();
}
```

Example 11.10

Finally, the MessageReceive method sends the SMS using the legacy API (currently the API provided by the SMS vendor). It also removes the message from the queue and updates the notification status in the database.

```
static void MessageReceiveCompleted(object sender,
  ReceiveCompletedEventArgs asyncResult)
{
  var queue = (MessageQueue)sender;
  using (var scope = new TransactionScope())
  {
    var message = queue.EndReceive(asyncResult.AsyncResult);
    message.Formatter =
      new XmlMessageFormatter(new Type[]
      {typeof(IdentifiedNotification)});
    var identifiedNotification =
      (IdentifiedNotification)message.Body;
    SmsSender.Send(identifiedNotification.
      NotificationMessage);
    DataAccess.UpdateStatus(identifiedNotification.
      NotificationId, Status.Sent);
    scope.Complete();
  }
  queue.BeginReceive();
}
```

Example 11.11

The Notification service is ready for deployment. In support of applying the Service Discoverability (702) principle, the Standard Mold team decides to publish supporting documentation alongside the service contract and SLA. This content is intended for project teams building service consumers and provides guidelines on how to effectively use the Notification service, along with sample code that demonstrates how to call the service using a WCF service consumer:

```
NotificationResponse response = null;
System.Xml.UniqueId messageId = new
System.Xml.UniqueId(Guid.NewGuid());
WcfClient.Using(new NotificationClient(), client =>
{
  using (new OperationContextScope(client.InnerChannel))
  {
    OperationContext.Current.
      OutgoingMessageHeaders.MessageId = messageId;
    response = client.NotifyBySms(new NotificationMessage
```

```
   {
     Recipient = "+13263827",
     Message = "Please note that something happened"
   });
 }
});
```

Example 11.12

11.3 CASE STUDY EXAMPLE:
ENTITY ABSTRACTION WITH A .NET REST SERVICE

Over the course of several years Standard Mold has collected various types of customer-related data. They started out with a simple data model, but different departments added data based on other pre-defined and ad-hoc models, some of which were specific to departmental systems. The resulting disparity led to redundant data and even different terminology used by different departments to refer to the same types of data.

To resolve these problems, several information modeling workshops were arranged and attended by departmental business experts. After some debate and effort, an agreement was reached as to a standard taxonomy used to describe the common business entities and attributes. The resulting entity relationship model is shown in Figure 11.11.

Standard Mold architects identify the need for a Customer entity service that can be positioned to provide centralized processing of customer-related data and functions. During a service modeling effort, SOA analysts define a Customer service based on the previously defined entity relationship model.

Architects choose to build the Customer service as a REST service to make the service functionality available to consumer programs that do not support SOAP and necessary WS-* standards, and to leverage HTTP caches for performance reasons.

Figure 11.12 illustrates the planned interaction between the Customer REST service and service consumers.

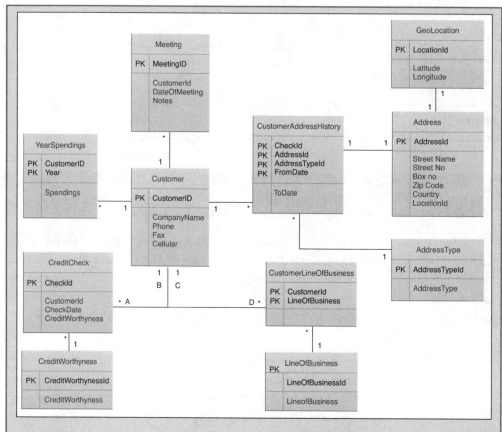

Figure 11.11
The Standard Mold entity relationship model.

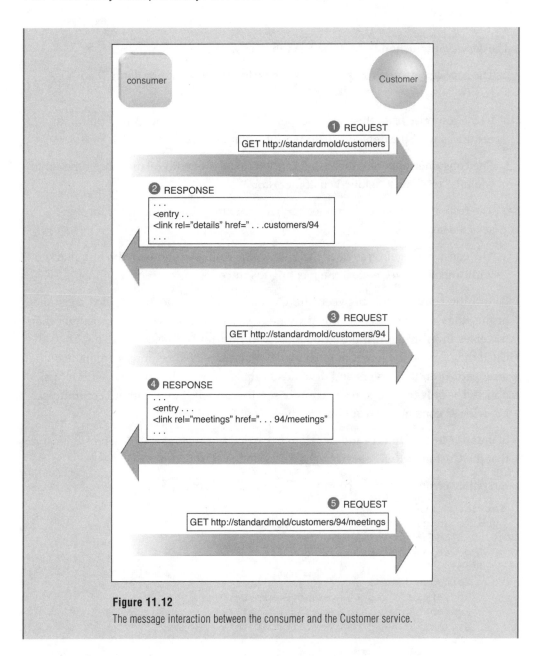

Figure 11.12
The message interaction between the consumer and the Customer service.

The service interaction is described as follows:

1. The service consumer requests a list of customers using a pre-defined address (URI).

2. In the response from the Customer service, links are embedded that point at resources with the detailed customer information.

3. The consumer traverses these links and uses the link with relationship type set to "details" to request detailed customer data.

4. The response from the Customer service contains a link to meetings for the selected customer.

5. The consumer again traverses the links in the response and uses the link marked with "meetings" to request the meeting resource for the current customer.

Before the conversation between the Customer service and the service consumer begins, the Customer service only provides a service entry point. The consumer then traverses links in the response documents to find related resources. This gives the Customer service the freedom to change both how related resources are named and arranged. Even the servers and domains of the uri:s can be changed without prior notice. The only thing that the Customer service cannot change without communicating with its consumers in advance is the URI of the entry point.

Standard Mold architects and developers carried out several specific steps to ensure that the Customer REST service behaves as depicted in Figure 11.11.

First, they created a service contract using WCF attributes:

```
[ServiceContract]
  public interface ICustomerServiceRest
  {
    [OperationContract]
    [WebInvoke(
      Method = "PUT",
      BodyStyle = WebMessageBodyStyle.Bare,
      ResponseFormat = WebMessageFormat.Xml,
      UriTemplate = "/customers/create"
    )]
    void CreateCustomer(Customer customer);
    [OperationContract]
    [WebInvoke(
      Method = "POST",
```

```
      BodyStyle = WebMessageBodyStyle.Bare,
      ResponseFormat = WebMessageFormat.Xml,
      UriTemplate = "/customers/{customerId}"
    )]
    void UpdateCustomer(string customerId, Customer customer);
    [OperationContract]
    [WebInvoke(
      Method = "DELETE",
      UriTemplate = "/customers/{customerId}"
    )]
    void DeleteCustomer(string customerId);
    [OperationContract]
    [WebGet(UriTemplate = "/customers/{customerId}")]
    Atom10FeedFormatter GetCustomerDetails(string customerId);
    [OperationContract]
    [WebGet(UriTemplate = "/customers")]
    System.ServiceModel.Syndication.
      Atom10FeedFormatter GetCustomers();
    [OperationContract]
    [WebGet(UriTemplate = "/customers/{customerId}/meetings")]
    Atom10FeedFormatter GetCustomerMeetings(string customerId);
  }
```

Example 11.13

The GetCustomers method acts as the entry point to the service and is called using the "customers" relative URI and the GET verb:

```
public Atom10FeedFormatter GetCustomers()
{
  List<Models.Customer> customers = DB.GetCustomers();
  if (customers != null)
  {
    Uri uri = OperationContext.Current.
      IncomingMessageHeaders.To;
    Atom10FeedFormatter formatter = null;
    SyndicationFeed feed = new SyndicationFeed();
    feed.LastUpdatedTime = DateTime.Now;
    feed.Id = WebOperationContext.Current.IncomingRequest.
      UriTemplateMatch.RequestUri.ToString();
    feed.Title = new TextSyndicationContent("Customers");
    feed.AddSelfLink(uri);
    List<SyndicationItem>
      items = new List<SyndicationItem>();
    foreach (var customer in customers)
```

```
{
    SyndicationItem item = new SyndicationItem();
    item.Title = new TextSyndicationContent
      (customer.CompanyName);
    item.Content = SyndicationContent.
      CreateXmlContent(customer);
    SyndicationLink detailsLink =
      new SyndicationLink
    (
      new Uri
      (
        OperationContext.Current.
        IncomingMessageHeaders.To.AbsoluteUri
        + "/" + customer.CustomerId
      )
    );
    detailsLink.RelationshipType = "details";
    detailsLink.Title = "Details";
    item.Links.Add(detailsLink);
    items.Add(item);
  }
  feed.Items = items;
  formatter = new Atom10FeedFormatter(feed);
  WebOperationContext.Current.
  OutgoingResponse.ContentType
    = Microsoft.ServiceModel.Web.ContentTypes.Atom;
  return formatter;      }
  WebOperationContext.Current.
    OutgoingResponse.SetStatusAsNotFound();
  return null;
}
```

Example 11.14

The DB.GetCustomers method fetches a list of customer records from the database. In this list, only two of the customer fields (CompanyName and CustomerId) are populated. This is a performance optimization technique used by Standard Mold developers, because if all details of the Customer entity are returned in a list, it would likely introduce unnecessary runtime processing and bandwidth consumption.

After retrieving the customer list, the Atom Publishing Protocol is used to represent the resource. This protocol was chosen because it allows for the embedding of links in resource descriptions in a standardized fashion so that they can be easily found by service consumers.

A details link is added to the customer list that consumers can use to obtain detailed information about a given customer. The XML output from the GetCustomers method looks like this:

```
<feed xmlns="http://www.w3.org/2005/Atom">
  <title type="text">Customers</title>
  <id>http://standardmold/customerservice/customers</id>
  <updated>2010-01-10T17:34:20+01:00</updated>
  <link rel="self" type="application/atom+xml" href=
    "http://standardmold/customerservice/customers"/>
  <entry>
    <id>uuid:445cf20f-4eb0-4772-bad5-a44b51c48145;id=91</id>
    <title type="text">WoodGroove Ltd</title>
    <updated>2010-01-10T16:34:20Z</updated>
    <link rel="details" title="Details" href=
      "http://standardmold/customerservice/customers/91"/>
    <content type="text/xml">
      <Customer xmlns=
        "http://schemas.datacontract.org/2004/07/
        EntityService.Models"xmlns:i=
        "http://www.w3.org/2001/XMLSchema-instance">
        <CompanyName>WoodGroove Ltd</CompanyName>
        <CustomerId>91</CustomerId>
      </Customer>
    </content>
  </entry>
  <entry>
    <id>uuid:445cf20f-4eb0-4772-bad5-a44b51c48145;id=92</id>
    <title type="text">Microsoft </title>
    <updated>2010-01-10T16:34:20Z</updated>
    <link rel="details" title="Details" href=
      "http://standardmold/customerservice/customers/92"/>
    <content type="text/xml">
      <Customer xmlns="http://schemas.datacontract.org
        /2004/07/EntityService.Models" xmlns:i=
        "http://www.w3.org/2001/XMLSchema-instance">
        <CompanyName>Microsoft</CompanyName>
        <CustomerId>92</CustomerId>
      </Customer>
    </content>
  </entry>
  <entry>
    <id>uuid:445cf20f-4eb0-4772-bad5-a44b51c48145;id=93</id>
    <title type="text">First Office</title>
```

```xml
      <updated>2010-01-10T16:34:20Z</updated>
      <link rel="details" title="Details" href=
        "http://standardmold/customerservice/customers/93"/>
      <content type="text/xml">
        <Customer xmlns="http://schemas.datacontract.org
          /2004/07/EntityService.Models" xmlns:i=
          "http://www.w3.org/2001/XMLSchema-instance">
          <CompanyName>First Office</CompanyName>
          <CustomerId>93</CustomerId>
        </Customer>
      </content>
    </entry>
    <entry>
      <id>uuid:445cf20f-4eb0-4772-bad5-a44b51c48145;id=94</id>
      <title type="text">Bosna</title>
      <updated>2010-01-10T16:34:20Z</updated>
      <link rel="details" title="Details" href=
        "http://standardmold/customerservice/customers/94"/>
      <content type="text/xml">
        <Customer xmlns="http://schemas.datacontract.org
          /2004/07/EntityService.Models" xmlns:i=
          "http://www.w3.org/2001/XMLSchema-instance">
          <CompanyName>Bosna</CompanyName>
          <CustomerId>94</CustomerId>
        </Customer>
      </content>
    </entry>
</feed>
```

Example 11.15

Sample service consumer code is developed to test the traversing of the XML to find the details link.

First the GetDetailsLink method is created:

```csharp
private static Uri GetDetailsLink(Uri entryPoint, string customerId)
{
  using (AtomPubClient atomHttpClient = new AtomPubClient())
  {
    SyndicationFeed feeds = atomHttpClient.GetFeed(entryPoint);
    foreach (SyndicationItem customerFeedItem in feeds.Items)
    {
      foreach (SyndicationLink customerItemLink
        in customerFeedItem.Links)
      {
```

```
    if
    (
      customerItemLink.RelationshipType.
        Equals("details") &&
      customerItemLink.Uri.ToString().
        EndsWith(customerId)
    )
    {
      return customerItemLink.Uri;
    }
   }
  }
 }
return null;
}
```

Example 11.16

A test run of the service consumer retrieves the details link for customer 94 by calling the method with the following parameters:

```
Uri customerDetailsLink
  = GetDetailsLink(new
Uri("http://standardmold/customerservice/customers"),
  "94");
```

Example 11.17

When the service consumer uses this link to request customer details, the GetCus-tomerDetails method of the Customer service is executed. The implementation of this method is similar to the GetCustomers method in that it uses the Atom protocol and adds links to the customer details data.

```
public Atom10FeedFormatter GetCustomerDetails(string customerId)
{
  Customer customer = DB.GetCustomerById
    (Int32.Parse(customerId));
  if (customer != null)
  {
    List<SyndicationItem> items = new
      List<SyndicationItem>();
    SyndicationItem item = new SyndicationItem();
    item.Title = new TextSyndicationContent
      (customer.CompanyName);
```

```
   item.Content = SyndicationContent.
     CreateXmlContent(customer);
   SyndicationLink editLink = new SyndicationLink
   (
     WebOperationContext.Current.
     IncomingRequest.UriTemplateMatch.RequestUri
   );
   editLink.RelationshipType = "edit";
   editLink.Title = "Edit";
   item.Links.Add(editLink);
   SyndicationLink meetingLink = new SyndicationLink
   (
     new Uri
     (
       WebOperationContext.Current.IncomingRequest.
       UriTemplateMatch.RequestUri.ToString() + "/meetings"
     )
   );
   meetingLink.RelationshipType = "meetings";
   item.Links.Add(meetingLink);
   items.Add(item);
   SyndicationFeed feed = new SyndicationFeed
   {
     Id = WebOperationContext.Current.IncomingRequest.
     UriTemplateMatch.RequestUri.ToString(),
       Title = new TextSyndicationContent
       (customer.CompanyName)
   };
   feed.AddSelfLink
     (WebOperationContext.Current.
     IncomingRequest.GetRequestUri());
   feed.Items = items;
   Atom10FeedFormatter formatter = new
     Atom10FeedFormatter(feed);
     WebOperationContext.Current.
     OutgoingResponse.ContentType
     = Microsoft.ServiceModel.Web.ContentTypes.Atom;
   return formatter;
 }
 WebOperationContext.Current.
   OutgoingResponse.SetStatusAsNotFound();
 return null;
}
```

Example 11.18

This time, several links are added to the only entry in the feed. This entry contains detailed customer information and the link to related meetings.

Here is the XML output from this method:

```
<feed xmlns="http://www.w3.org/2005/Atom">
  <title type="text">Bosna</title>
  <id>http://standardmold/customerservice/customers/94</id>
  <updated>2010-01-10T16:36:46Z</updated>
  <link rel="self" type="application/atom+xml"
    href="http://standardmold/customerservice/
    customers/94"/>
  <entry>
    <id>uuid:445cf20f-4eb0-4772-bad5-a44b51c48145;id=94</id>
    <title type="text">Bosna Jedina</title>
    <updated>2010-01-10T16:36:46Z</updated>
    <link rel="edit" title="Edit"
      href="http://standardmold/customerservice/
      customers/94"/>
    <link rel="meetings"
      href="http://standardmold/customerservice/
      customers/94/meetings"/>
    <content type="text/xml">
      <Customer xmlns="http://schemas.datacontract.org/
        2004/07/EntityService.Models"
        xmlns:i="http://www.w3.org/
        2001/XMLSchema-instance">
        <Cellular>+387(0)63912910</Cellular>
        <CompanyName>Bosna</CompanyName>
        <CustomerId>94</CustomerId>
        <Fax>+387(0)63912911</Fax>
        <Phone>+387(0)79900900</Phone>
        <TimeStamp>AAAAAAAAD6I=</TimeStamp>
      </Customer>
    </content>
  </entry>
</feed>
```

Example 11.19

The following method is created to get a meetings link from a customer details response:

```
private static Uri GetMeetingsLink(Uri customerDetailsUri)
{
```

```
using (AtomPubClient atomHttpClient = new AtomPubClient())
{
  SyndicationFeed feeds = atomHttpClient.GetFeed
    (customerDetailsUri);
  foreach (SyndicationItem customerFeedItem in feeds.Items)
  {
    foreach (SyndicationLink customerItemLink
      in customerFeedItem.Links)
    {
      if (customerItemLink.RelationshipType.Equals("meetings"))
      {
          return customerItemLink.Uri;
      }
    }
  }
}
return null;
}
```

Example 11.20

To obtain this link, the consumers use the URI returned by the GetDetailsLink method:

```
Uri meetingsUri = GetMeetingsLink(customerDetailsLink);
```

The URI points at the meetings resource for company 94, and the consumer is able to get the desired list of meetings.

The XML output by this method is as follows:

```
<feed xml:base="http://standardmold/customerservice/
  customers/94/meetings" xmlns="http://www.w3.org/2005/Atom">
  <title type="text">Customers Metting, CustomerId=94</title>
  <id>http://standardmold/customerservice/
    customers/94/meetings</id>
  <updated>2010-01-10T17:38:13+01:00</updated>
  <entry>
    <id>uuid:445cf20f-4eb0-4772-bad5-a44b51c48145;id=7</id>
    <title type="text">Meeting Id:1</title>
    <updated>2010-01-10T16:38:13Z</updated>
    <content type="text/xml">
      <Meeting xmlns="http://schemas.datacontract.org/
        2004/07/EntityService.Models"
        xmlns:i="http://www.w3.org/2001/
```

```
XMLSchema-instance">
<customerId>94</customerId>
<dateofmeeting>2010-10-10T00:00:00</dateofmeeting>
<meetingId>1</meetingId>
<notes>
```

Example 11.21

It's our experience that taking personal notes at meetings somehow breeds respect and approval from superiors, and managers enjoy having a simple list of bullet points and action items at-hand. The long and short—if you have to suffer through the meeting anyways, make it a habit to provide a valuable account to meeting organizers... you will be rewarded with respect and trust.

```
            </notes>
        </Meeting>
      </content>
    </entry>
    <entry>
      <id>uuid:445cf20f-4eb0-4772-bad5-a44b51c48145;id=8</id>
      <title type="text">Meeting Id:2</title>
      <updated>2010-01-10T16:38:13Z</updated>
      <content type="text/xml">
        <Meeting xmlns="http://schemas.datacontract.org/
          2004/07/EntityService.Models"
          xmlns:i="http://www.w3.org/2001/
          XMLSchema-instance">
          <customerId>94</customerId>
          <dateofmeeting>2010-11-11T00:00:00</dateofmeeting>
          <meetingId>2</meetingId>
          <notes>
             We started on time with 3 members and the other team members
arrived shortly thereafter
          </notes>
        </Meeting>
      </content>
    </entry>
</feed>
```

Example 11.22

A method that can obtain this XML from the Customer service and return a list of Meeting objects looks like this:

```
private static List<Meeting> GetCustomerMeetingList(Uri meetingsUri)
{
  var customerMeetings = new List<Meeting>();
  using (AtomPubClient atomHttpClient = new AtomPubClient())
  {
    if (meetingsUri != null)
    {
      SyndicationFeed customerMeetingsFeed =
        atomHttpClient.GetFeed(meetingsUri);
      foreach (var item in customerMeetingsFeed.Items)
      {
        var customerMeetingXmlContent = item.Content
          as XmlSyndicationContent;
        if (customerMeetingXmlContent != null)
        {
          var customerMeeting =
            customerMeetingXmlContent.
            ReadContent<Meeting>();
          customerMeetings.Add(customerMeeting);
        }
      }
    }
  }
  return customerMeetings;
}
```

Example 11.23

To actually get the list of meetings, the service consumer calls the method using the meeting list URI that was returned from the GetMeetingsList:

```
List<Meeting>meetingList=GetCustomerMeetingList(meetingsUri);
```

With a preliminary version of the service architecture completed, Standard Mold architects decide to make further improvements by ensuring that customer data is not inadvertently overwritten in the database. A timestamp column is added and updated via a SQL server stored procedure that updates customer information only if the timestamp in the database remains unchanged:

```
CREATE PROCEDURE [dbo].[UpdateCustomer]
 @id as uniqueidentifier,
 @cName as nvarchar(50),
 @phone as  nvarchar(50),
 @fax as nvarchar(50),
```

```
 @cell as nvarchar(50),
 @updateTag as timestamp
AS
BEGIN
 BEGIN TRY
   SET NOCOUNT ON;
   --do not update if [TimeStamp] has been changed
   UPDATE dbo.Customer WITH (ROWLOCK)
   SET
     [CompanyName] = @cName,
     [Phone] = @phone,
     [Fax] = @fax,
     [Cellular] = @cell
   WHERE [CustomerId]  = @id
   AND [TimeStamp] = @updateTag
   END TRY

   BEGIN CATCH
   SELECT ERROR_NUMBER(), ERROR_LINE(),ERROR_MESSAGE()
   END CATCH
END
```

Example 11.24

With a simple check in the data access code, it is possible to find out how many rows are affected. If the result is 0 rows, then something went wrong. Most likely the customer was changed by another request before the current request could make the update.

The code that allows this to be discovered can be found inside the UpdateCustomer method. It uses the Enterprise Library Data Access Block in order to make the database access logic more compact than it would be had it been written using ADO.NET directly:

```
public bool UpdateCustomer(Customer customer)
{
  using
  (
    var dbCommand =
      Database.GetStoredProcCommand
      (StoredProcedures.UPDATECUSTOMER)
  )
  {
    Database.AddInParameter
```

```
  (
    dbCommand, "@id", DbType.Guid, customer.CustomerId
  );
  Database.AddInParameter
  (
    dbCommand, "@cName", DbType.String,
      customer.CompanyName
  );
  Database.AddInParameter
  (
    dbCommand, "@phone", DbType.String,
      customer.Phone
  );
  Database.AddInParameter
  (
    dbCommand, "@fax", DbType.String,
      customer.Fax
  );
  Database.AddInParameter
  (
    dbCommand, "@cell", DbType.String,
      customer.Cellular
  );
  Database.AddInParameter
  (
  dbCommand, "@updateTag", DbType.Binary,
    customer.TimeStamp
  );
  int rowsAffected =
    Database.ExecuteNonQuery(dbCommand);
  return rowsAffected == 1;
  }
}
```

Example 11.25

If the UpdateCustomer method returns "false," the update was not successful. This should normally be communicated back to the service consumer, as follows:

```
public void UpdateCustomer
  (EntityService.Models.Customer customer)
{
  try
  {
    bool updated = DB.UpdateCustomer(customer);
```

```
    if (updated)
      WebOperationContext.Current.
        OutgoingResponse.StatusCode
        = System.Net.HttpStatusCode.OK;
    else
      WebOperationContext.Current.
        OutgoingResponse.StatusCode
        = System.Net.HttpStatusCode.Conflict;
  }
  catch
  {
    ... exception handling code ...
    WebOperationContext.Current.OutgoingResponse.StatusCode
      = System.Net.HttpStatusCode.InternalServerError;
  }
}
```

Example 11.26

The consumer of the Customer service will get an HTTP response with the following status if the optimistic lock failed:

```
409 Conflict
```

This is exactly what is expected of a REST service in this situation. Standard Mold developers, however, choose to add more information to the response so that service consumers can understand the nature of the conflict.

If an unexpected exception occurs, the service consumer will instead receive the following status, which communicates that there is a problem in the service:

```
500 Internal server error
```

If everything proceeds as expected the consumer will get the response code:

```
200 OK
```

Chapter 12

Service-Orientation with .NET Part IV: Service Composition and Orchestration Basics

12.1 Service Composition 101

12.2 Orchestration

SOA PRINCIPLES & PATTERNS REFERENCED IN THIS CHAPTER

- Agnostic Context [710]

- Atomic Service Transaction [713]

- Capability Composition [721]

- Capability Recomposition [722]

- Compensating Service Transaction [724]

- Data Model Transformation [732]

- Domain Inventory [738]

- Enterprise Service Bus [741]

- Entity Abstraction [742]

- Logic Centralization [751]

- Non-Agnostic Context [756]

- Orchestration [758]

- Process Abstraction [762]

- Process Centralization [763]

- Rules Centralization [768]

- Service Composability (704)

- Service Layers [779]

- Service Normalization [781]

- State Repository [785]

- Three-Layer Inventory [788]

- Utility Abstraction [791]

This brief chapter highlights common service composition considerations as they pertain to .NET services and technologies. Many of the actual topic areas related to these considerations are covered in subsequent chapters.

The last section concludes with an introduction to service orchestration. This content acts as a preamble to Chapters 13 and 14 that explore orchestration with Microsoft technologies in more detail and from a patterns perspective.

12.1 Service Composition 101

One of the fundamental characteristics that distinguish service-oriented technology architecture from other forms of distributed architecture is composition-centricity, meaning that there is a baseline requirement to inherently support both the composition and *re-composition* of the moving parts that comprise a given solution.

In this section, we cover some fundamental aspects of composition in relation to service-orientation by briefly describing relevant principles and patterns.

Service-Orientation and Service Composition

A baseline requirement for achieving the strategic goals of service-oriented computing is that services must be inherently composable. As a means of realizing these goals, the service-orientation design paradigm is therefore naturally focused on enabling flexible composition.

This dynamic is illustrated in Figure 12.1, where we can see how the collective application of service-orientation principles share software programs into services that are essentially "composition-ready," meaning that they are interoperable, compatible, and composable with other services as part of the same service inventory. The scope of this service inventory can vary, as long as it is meaningfully cross-silo (as per Domain Inventory [738]).

The key aspect of what is being shown in Figure 12.1 is not that services can be aggregated after delivery. All distributed systems are comprised of aggregated software programs. What is fundamentally distinct about how service-orientation positions services is that they are repeatedly composable, allowing for subsequent recomposition.

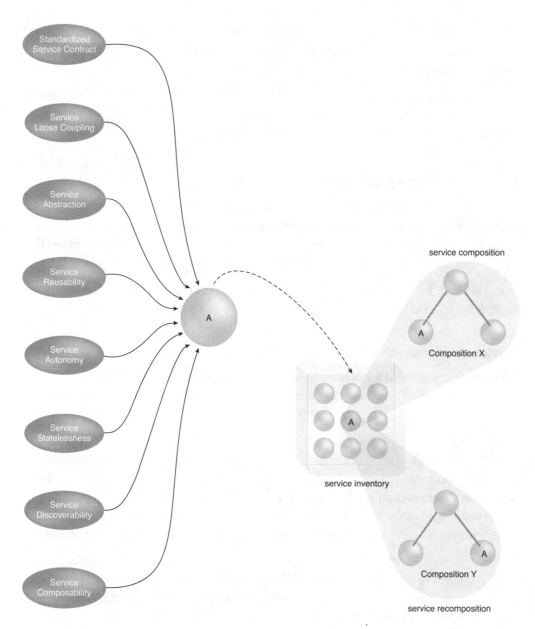

Figure 12.1

Service A is a software program shaped into a unit of service-oriented logic by the application of service-orientation design principles. Service A is delivered within a service inventory that contains a collection of services to which service-orientation principles were also designed. The result is that Service A can participate initially in Composition X and, more importantly, can be pulled into additional service compositions, as required.

This is what lies at the core of realizing organizational agility as a primary goal of adopting service-oriented computing. By having a set of services (again, within the scope determined by the service inventory only) naturally interoperable and designed for participation in complex service compositions, we are able to fulfill new business requirements and automate new business processes by augmenting existing service compositions or creating new service compositions with reduced effort and expense. This target state is what leads to the Reduced IT Burden goal of service-oriented computing (as explained in Chapter 3).

Service Composability (704)

Among the eight service-orientation design principles, there is one that is specifically relevant to service composition design. The Service Composability (704) principle is solely dedicated to shaping a service into an effective composition participant. All other principles support Service Composability (704) in achieving this objective (Figure 12.2). In fact, as a regulatory principle, Service Composability (704) is applied primarily by ensuring that the design goals of the other seven principles are realized to a sufficient extent.

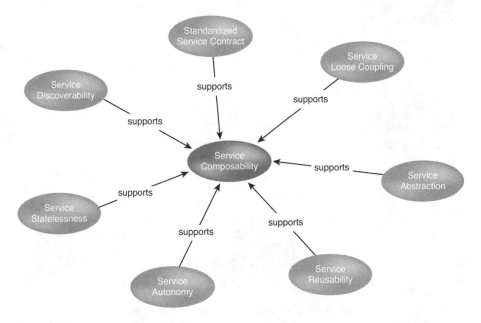

Figure 12.2

A common objective of all service-orientation design principles is that they shape services in support of increasing composability potential.

Capability Composition [721] and Capability Recomposition [722]

As discussed in Chapter 11, fundamental service identification and definition patterns can be assembled into an application sequence that forms a primitive service modeling process. However, those patterns result only in the separation of logic into individual functional contexts and capabilities.

The application of these fundamental patterns needs to be followed by patterns that reassemble the separated logic into aggregates. This is the purpose of Capability Composition [721] and Capability Recomposition [722] (Figure 12.3).

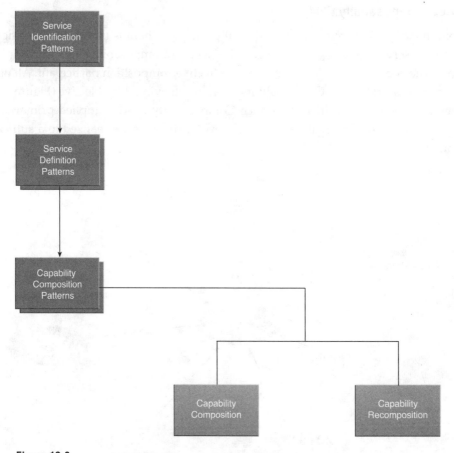

Figure 12.3

Capability Composition [721] is one of two patterns applied subsequent to the application of service identification and definition patterns. The relevance of the Capability Recomposition [722] pattern is explained in the following section.

Capability Composition [721]

Capability Composition [721] represents a pattern that is applied to assemble the decomposed service logic together into a specific service composition capable of solving a specific larger problem (Figure 12.4).

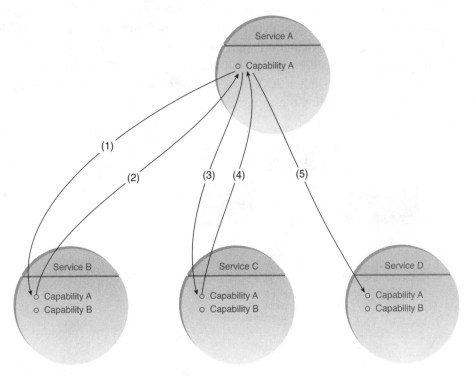

Figure 12.4

Although generally referred to as service composition, services that compose each other actually do so via their individual service capabilities, hence the name of this pattern.

The importance of this pattern, beyond forming the basis for the basic aggregation of service functionality, is that it reinforces fundamental patterns, such as Logic Centralization [751] and Service Normalization [781]. It does so by preserving the functional boundaries established by service contexts in that it requires a service that needs access to logic outside of its context to access this logic via the composition of another service.

Capability Recomposition [722]

As previously mentioned, the recomposition of services is a fundamental and distinctive goal of service-oriented computing. This pattern specifically addresses the repeated involvement of a service via the repeated composition of a service capability. The patterns relationship diagram shown in Figure 12.4 highlights how service identification and definition patterns, together with Capability Composition [721], essentially lead up to opportunities to apply Capability Recomposition [722].

A very important consideration here is that the application of Capability Recomposition [722] has a different purpose and different requirements than Capability Composition [721]. As covered earlier, service-orientation design principles are geared specifically toward enabling the application of Capability Recomposition [722]. And, as further shown in Figure 12.5, most other SOA design patterns solve their respective design problems in support of enabling the application of this pattern.

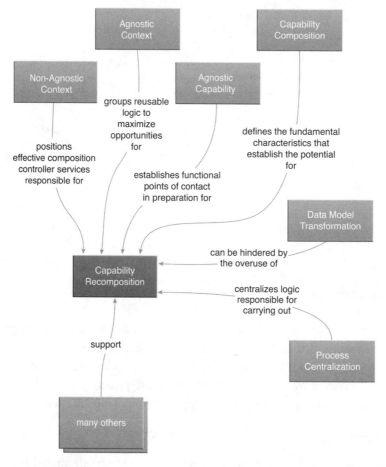

Figure 12.5

Because of how core the repeated composability of services is to service-orientation and SOA, Capability Recomposition [722] has many relationships with other SOA design patterns.

Composition Roles

With the potential for Capability Recomposition [722] to be applied frequently, a given service can find itself participating in different ways within a given service composition. Therefore, in order to better identify and describe the interaction between services within a service composition architecture, a set of runtime roles exist:

- *composition controller* – The service with a capability that is executing the parent composition logic required to compose capabilities within other services.

- *composition member* – A service that participates in a service composition by being composed by another service.

- *composition initiator* – The program that initiates a service composition by invoking the composition controller. This program may or may not exist as a service.

- *composition sub-controller* – A variation of the composition controller role that is assumed by a service carrying out nested composition logic (within a capability that is composing one or more other service capabilities while itself also being composed).

Services assume composition roles within the context of different service compositions, depending on the logic executed by service capabilities. In other words, a service's capabilities will automatically enlist the service in one or more composition roles.

> **NOTE**
>
> For more descriptive information about composition roles, see Chapter 13 in *SOA Principles of Service Design* and the composition role definitions published at www.soaglossary.com.

Service Layers [779]

In Chapter 11 we explored the definition and overall creation of services based on the entity and utility service models that correspond to the Entity Abstraction [742] and Utility Abstraction [791] patterns respectively. These service models represent the two most common agnostic functional contexts for services (in other words, they represent the two popular means of further applying the Agnostic Context [710] pattern).

When we abstract common types of logic into collections of services based on the same underlying service model, we end up establishing service layers. These logical layers are the result of the application of the Service Layers [779] pattern, which provides us with an opportunity to organize and classify all services within a given service inventory.

Service Layers [779] requires that at least two layers exist, and these layers are generally based on a fundamental separation of agnostic and non-agnostic service logic. Therefore, we typically end up with a task service layer, followed by a service layer based on one or more agnostic service models, as shown in Figure 12.6.

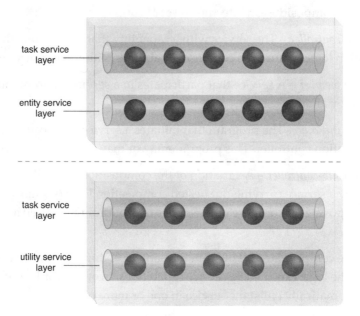

task service
layer

entity service
layer

task service
layer

utility service
layer

Figure 12.6

At minimum, Service Layers [779] requires that two logical layers of services be established within a service inventory.

The Three-Layer Inventory [788] compound pattern essentially indicates that the most common application of Service Layers [779] is via the combined application of Entity Abstraction [742], Utility Abstraction [791], and Process Abstraction [762]. This establishes a logical layered architecture that tends to encompass the natural hierarchy formed by most service compositions (Figure 12.7).

NOTE
The top layer shown in Figure 12.7 is defined via the application of the Process Abstraction [762] pattern, which is explained shortly, following the *Non-Agnostic Context [756]* section.

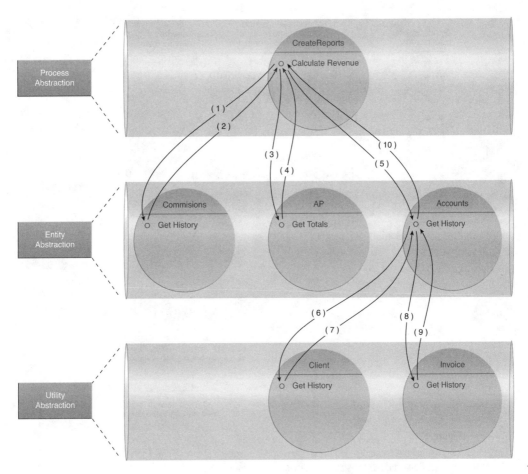

Figure 12.7

A composition of services that forms a hierarchy that spans the three service layers represented by the Three-Layer Inventory [788] pattern.

Non-Agnostic Context [756]

The fundamental service identification and definition patterns that were covered in Chapter 11 focused on the separation of multi-purpose or agnostic service logic. When decomposing business process logic as part of a service-oriented analysis, what remains after multi-purpose logic is separated logic that is specific to the business process. Because this logic is considered single-purpose in nature, it is classified as non-agnostic. The encapsulation of non-agnostic logic within a service is the basis of the Non-Agnostic Context [756] pattern (Figure 12.8).

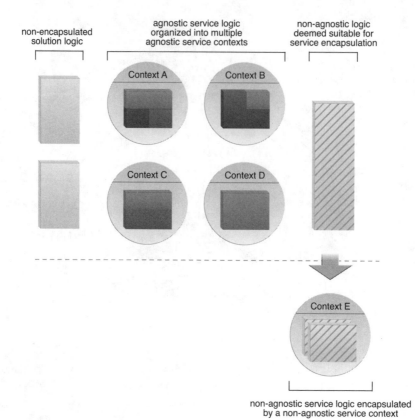

Figure 12.8

By revisiting the decomposition process covered in Chapter 11, we can now apply Non-Agnostic Context [756] to establish a service context for the separated non-agnostic logic.

Process Abstraction [762] and Task Services

The types of agnostic services covered in the preceding chapter are generally (but not always) dependent on the existence of abstracted, non-agnostic business process logic that is encapsulated in task services (Figure 12.9).

This is the result of the combined application of Non-Agnostic Context [756] and Process Abstraction [762].

> **NOTE**
>
> The runtime role that is most commonly associated with the task service model is the composition controller because the functional scope of these services is typically focused on a parent business process. A variation of the task service model, called the orchestrated task service, is discussed in the upcoming *Orchestration* section.

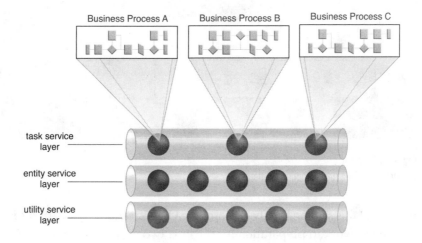

Figure 12.9
Each task service represents a part of a parent service layer and is responsible for encapsulating logic specific to parent business process logic.

SUMMARY OF KEY POINTS

- The effective and repeatable composition of services lies at the heart of service-orientation, and is essential to the attainment of several strategic goals.

- Key patterns that relate directly to enabling service composition in support of the Service Composability (704) principle include Capability Composition [721], Capability Recomposition [722], Non-Agnostic Context [756], and Process Abstraction [762].

12.2 Orchestration

Orchestration builds upon service composition by aiming to establish a physical environment capable of centrally executing and governing multiple automated business processes. The Orchestration [758] compound pattern represents such an environment via the co-existent application of a set of specific patterns (Figure 12.10).

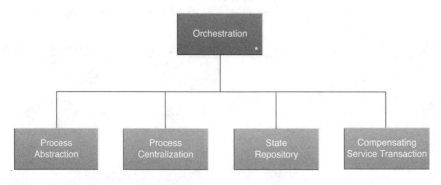

Figure 12.10
The Orchestration [758] compound pattern.

The remainder of this section briefly explores the Orchestration [758] patterns in relation to the .NET framework in preparation for the next two chapters that cover the WF and BizTalk Server orchestration environments in detail.

Process Abstraction [762], Process Centralization [763], and Orchestrated Task Services

The Process Abstraction [762] pattern is fundamental to orchestration because an orchestration platform is designed specifically to house and execute parent business process logic. Process Centralization [763] is equally fundamental because an orchestration platform enables the centralized hosting, execution, and governance of the same parent business process logic.

The application of Process Abstraction [762] alone results in the creation of task services, as explained earlier in the *Service Composition 101* section. However, it is the combined application of Process Abstraction [762] and Process Centralization [763] that defines the orchestrated task service model. This is because orchestrated task services are distinguished from regular task services by the fact that they are hosted within an orchestration platform.

In other words, although they logically still abstract the same non-agnostic service logic into a separate layer (Figure 12.11), they are different in how they are physically implemented and administered.

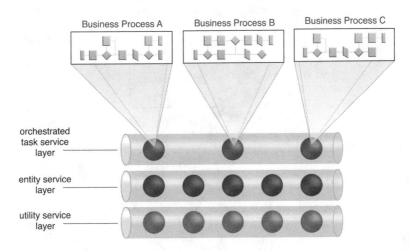

Figure 12.11

Orchestrated task services appear identical to task services when viewed from a logical service layers perspective.

Orchestrated task services are built within and upon the specific features and architectural components that comprise an orchestration environment. This changes the baseline complexion of the task service architecture to such an extent that a separate service model classification is warranted.

As with any type of service, what qualifies a body of orchestration logic as a service is the existence of a service contract. Within the .NET framework, a body of orchestration logic is commonly referred to as just an *orchestration*, regardless of whether it exists as an orchestrated task service. Figure 12.12 shows how the common elements of .NET orchestration platforms relate to each other, including how they relate specifically to orchestrations.

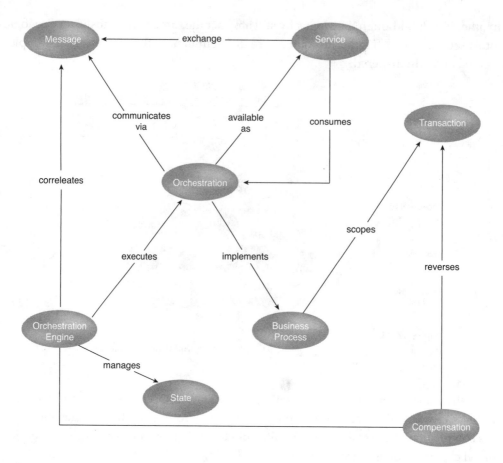

Figure 12.12

A conceptual view of architectural elements common to .NET orchestrations.

Process Centralization [763] and Tools

.NET orchestration environments provide graphical tools to simplify the process of defining and maintaining complex orchestration logic. Windows Workflow Foundation, for example, allows you to dynamically load orchestration code, whereas BizTalk Server provides management and monitoring tools to gather intelligence about running process instances and, if necessary, managing updates to orchestration assemblies. Both platforms provide process designers, such as the one shown in Figure 12.13.

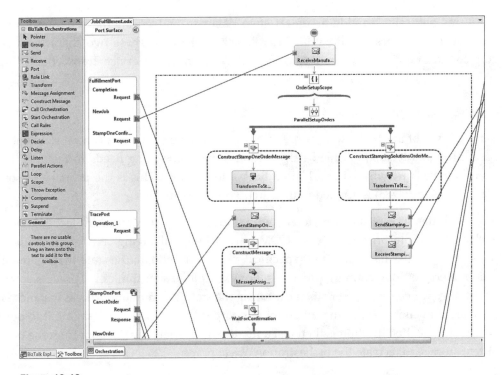

Figure 12.13

The BizTalk Orchestration Designer displaying a process flow that can be further modified using a toolbox of orchestration activities.

Process Abstraction [762] and WS-BPEL

Orchestration platforms are commonly associated with the use of WS-BPEL as a means of expressing parent business process logic in an executable syntax. The WS-BPEL industry standard has a colorful history that has been well documented in other books in this series. Both Chapters 13 and 14 will cover the extent to which WS-BPEL is supported by .NET orchestration platforms.

State Repository [785] and Compensating Service Transaction [724]

Whereas regular task services tend to encapsulate parent business process logic that can be executed within reasonable timeframes as part of single, runtime service activities, orchestrations offer the ability to create and manage long-running service activities.

The execution time of a given orchestration can span from a few seconds to hours or even days, especially if it involves human interaction. This is why orchestration platforms naturally provide a central state database and an alternative transaction mechanism that does not allow for the rollback of changes. These two characteristics correspond to the State Repository [785] and Compensating Service Transaction [724] patterns respectively.

State Repository [785] with .NET

During times of inactivity, long-running processes can be stored in a central state database through a technique called dehydration. When processing needs to resume, the process logic is rehydrated and loaded back into memory. This is the primary reason State Repository [785] is applied within orchestration platforms.

Managing this type of state previously with traditional .NET component technologies, such as .NET Enterprise Services or COM+, was often challenging. .NET orchestration tools, on the other hand, are built specifically to accommodate the state management requirements of long-running processes. For example, if you think of a process as an object of type `orchestration`, then capturing the state of a running process instance is equivalent to taking a snapshot of all the properties of that object and saving it to persistent storage. Rehydration is then just a matter of deserializing the data from the persistent storage to recreate the orchestration object graph.

Figure 12.14 shows how only active process instances reside in the orchestration engine. Idle process instances, such as those waiting to receive messages, are dehydrated and stored in persistent storage (usually SQL Server).

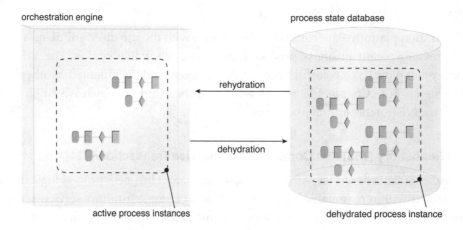

Figure 12.14
The orchestration engine dehydrates idle process instances to a database to conserve server resources.

Compensating Service Transaction [724]

The parent business process logic encapsulated by an orchestrated task service can be extended with routines designed to respond to various exceptions that may occur at runtime in relation to an overarching transaction. These routines are commonly employed as an alternative to ACID-style transactions when it makes sense not to preserve the state of the process prior to the transaction. As a result, a rollback of all changes that occurred prior to the exception is not required. The Compensating Service Transaction [724] pattern allows for a failed transaction to be handled via this pre-defined exception logic, referred to as compensation logic (as shown in Figure 12.15).

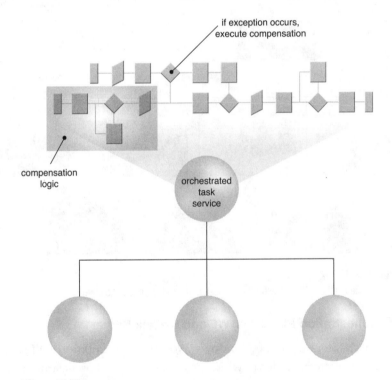

Figure 12.15

Compensation logic is pre-defined as part of the overall business process logic encapsulated by the orchestrated task service controlling a transaction as part of a service composition.

Both WF and BizTalk Server provide different features for defining compensations. Because compensation logic is part of the overall workflow or process definition, the same tools are generally used.

Other Patterns

The extended patterns hierarchy for the Orchestration [758] compound pattern includes the additional Atomic Service Transaction [713], Data Model Transformation [732], and Rules Centralization [768] patterns (Figure 12.16). When applied in conjunction with the core patterns, these optional patterns provide further features and capabilities that can enhance and extend orchestration platforms. Both WF and BizTalk Server provide support for these patterns (as shown in the upcoming Table 12.1), but their coverage specifically in relation to orchestration is beyond the scope of Chapters 13 and 14.

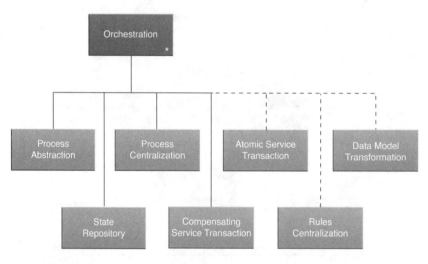

Figure 12.16

The extended patterns hierarchy for the Orchestration [758] compound pattern.

Microsoft Orchestration Platforms: WF and BizTalk Server

The next two chapters examine Windows Workflow Foundation (WF) and BizTalk Server, two .NET platforms, each of which provides a range of orchestration capabilities. These chapters specifically approach this exploration from a patterns perspective by focusing on the patterns associated with the Orchestration compound pattern.

Table 12.1 highlights the differences in the respective platforms in how they provide support for the attainment of the feature-sets associated with the patterns.

Orchestration Patterns	WF	BizTalk Server
Process Abstraction [762]	2	1
Process Centralization [763] (tools)	2	1
State Repository [785]	2	1
Compensating Service Transaction [724]	2	1
Rules Centralization [768]	2	1
Atomic Service Transaction [713]	2	1
Data Model Transformation [732]	2	1

Table 12.1

Support for patterns mapped to different parts of the Microsoft technology platform. (1 = Native and configuration-only support, 2 = Can be created, 3 = Not applicable or not supported.) Note that with both WF and BizTalk Server, State Repository [785] is applied with the use of SQL Server.

NOTE
This same type of patterns-centric assessment matrix is used in Chapter 15 in relation to the parts of the .NET framework that support the patterns associated with the Enterprise Service Bus [741] compound pattern.

Each platform has distinct strengths and weaknesses with regard to feature-set, flexibility, cost, and the effort necessary to build, run, and maintain orchestrated solutions. Table 12.2 provides further insight into some key areas of comparison, many of which will be covered in more detail in Chapters 13 and 14.

Characteristic	WF	BizTalk Server
APIs	.NET, WF object model	XML, .NET orchestration library, BizTalk object model
architecture foundation	.NET	XML and .NET
autonomy	orchestrations are autonomous or embedded in other applications	orchestrations are fully autonomous

continues

Characteristic	WF	BizTalk Server
composability	composition of Web services and custom WF activities, and orchestrations are composable as services or directly	composition of Web services and legacy applications, and orchestrations are composable as services or directly
cost	free of charge as part of the .NET framework	licensed by processor
discovery	services are discoverable via published WSDL definitions or inside the developer tool	services are discoverable via published WSDL definitions
extensibility	high extensibility for customized execution, state persistence and support for other protocols and transports via custom activities	extensibility to support additional transports, protocols, and message processing
formal contracts	light support for service contracts in the form of .NET interfaces	strong support for XML Schema and WSDL-based contracts
industry standards	support for SOAP, WSDL. WS-*	strong support for XML, SOAP, WSDL, and WS-* with WCF integration and limited support for WS-BPEL
messaging	general support for asynchronous messaging, resource management, and XML-based message exchanges	
reusability	reusable via Web services and directly inside the orchestration engine (other forms of reuse possible with custom development)	reusable via Web services, queue endpoints, file drop, and directly inside the orchestration engine
rules engine	rules based on facts in .NET objects	complex rules based on facts in XML documents, .NET objects, and database records
scalability	medium scalability through custom extensions for persistence and activity scheduling	high scalability through clustering and distributable functionality

Characteristic	WF	BizTalk Server
state management	process state is stored in memory, SQL Server, or custom data store	process state is stored in SQL Server
tools	re-hostable orchestration design, Web service publishing	orchestration design, data mapping, Web service publishing, runtime monitoring and deployment

Table 12.2

A comparison of orchestration-related characteristics provided by WF and BizTalk Server platforms.

SUMMARY OF KEY POINTS

- Orchestrated task services encapsulate the same type of non-agnostic, parent business process logic as task services, but they are distinguished via their implementation as part of an orchestration platform.

- The Orchestration [758] compound pattern is comprised of a set of patterns that collectively define the core requirements of an orchestration platform.

- Microsoft provides two alternative orchestration platforms: Windows Workflow Foundation and BizTalk Server. These are explored individually in Chapters 13 and 14.

Chapter 13

Orchestration Patterns with WF

13.1 Process Abstraction and Orchestrated Task Services

13.2 Process Centralization

13.3 State Repository

13.4 Compensating Service Transaction

13.5 Case Study Example

SOA PRINCIPLES & PATTERNS REFERENCED IN THIS CHAPTER

- Atomic Service Transaction [713]
- Canonical Schema [718]
- Compensating Service Transaction [724]
- Decoupled Contract [735]
- Dual Protocols [739]
- Metadata Centralization [754]
- Orchestration [758]
- Process Centralization [763]
- Service Statelessness (700)
- Standardized Service Contract (693)
- State Repository [785]

Even though Microsoft does not officially position WF as an orchestration platform, it possesses many of the characteristics associated with the patterns that comprise the Orchestration [758] compound pattern (Figure 13.1).

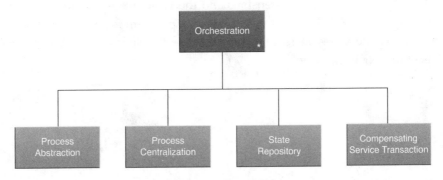

Figure 13.1

The Orchestration [758] compound pattern hierarchy.

WF's terminology can obscure its nature of an orchestration engine. Microsoft intends to address a broader spectrum of business logic processing with WF, including support for business processes that involve interactions with humans. Therefore, WF refers to automated business processes as *workflows* and not orchestrations.

Microsoft ships WF with .NET 3.0—initially, WF supported basic Web service functionality. .NET 3.5 delivered improvements to simplify exposing workflows as message-based WCF services. .NET 4.0 continues the evolution by integrating WF with Windows Server AppFabric and by extending the options for message correlation.

Version 4.0 still lacks some of the enterprise-class features provided by dedicated workflow and orchestration products, since it is only intended as a platform for workflow and orchestration products. WF provides all the necessary extension interfaces to add features common in other products, such as clustering and monitoring, but leaves the implementation of these features to full-blown products like BizTalk server. Going forward, Microsoft is going to integrate orchestration capabilities into Windows Azure AppFabric to provide a highly scalable orchestration platform in the cloud.

Many shortcomings can also be overcome by implementing the missing features by yourself. The Windows SDK ships with some basic management and monitoring tools, but they are not as full-featured as the ones you would find in orchestration and management products. They merely illustrate what is possible and serve as a starting point for your own implementations.

WF still allows you to build service-oriented applications that fully adhere to the principles of SOA. Together with other components of the .NET Framework, such as ASP.NET Web services (ASMX), the Web Services Enhancements (WSE), or WCF, the AppFabric Application Server Extensions and the Windows Activation Service (WAS) that's included in IIS7, WF can provide a low-cost platform for basic service orchestration. Figure 13.2 illustrates the relationships between the elements of WF and other components of the .NET Framework.

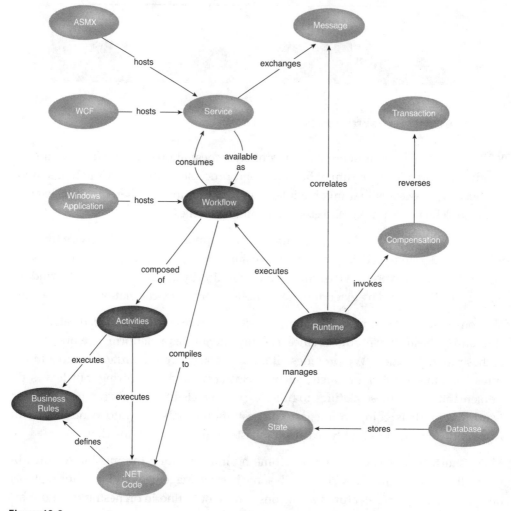

Figure 13.2

Logical relationships between the elements of WF (dark ovals) and elements of the .NET framework (light ovals).

> **NOTE**
>
> If you are new to WF, be sure to read through the introductory coverage in Chapter 7.

13.1 Process Abstraction and Orchestrated Task Services

An orchestrated task service encapsulates a body of business process (workflow) logic and makes it accessible via a published service contract. This section explores the many ways of applying Decoupled Contract [735] with WF as a means of establishing orchestrations as standalone and independently invokable services. We further explore the various industry standards supported by WF, each of which provides different implementation options for the creation of orchestrated task services.

WF relies on the industry standards support provided by WCF and ASMX to position orchestrations as services. The WCF programming model abstracts transports and policies into Send and Receive message exchanges and WF translates this model into corresponding Send and Receive messaging activities. With ASMX, activities can be published and interacted with via WS-I BasicProfile compliant workflows.

A Brief History of WF Service Contract Support

Support for creating technical service contracts improved as WF evolved from version 3.0 to 4.0. With WF 3.0, there was no actual notion of formal contracts. Workflow containers essentially passed opaque `Dictionary` types to workflow instances in order to move data from the consumer-side to the workflows being positioned as services.

The options for defining formal service contracts for workflows published as a Web service with WF 3.0 were:

- Define the contract explicitly as a .NET interface and publish the workflow as an ASMX Web service with the "Publish as Web service" feature in Visual Studio. This approach worked for contracts with simple message exchange patterns and limited scalability requirements.

- Define the contract as an interface following the requirements for WF's `External-DataExchange` services, and publish the workflow manually. This provided broader support for message exchange patterns and communication protocols, but could require custom development of the service container in order to meet scalability and fault tolerance requirements.

- Define the contract explicitly as a .NET interface with WCF contract attributes and implement all communication with the workflow via the `Receive` and `Send` activities introduced with .NET 3.5. Like the workflow-first option, this approach took advantage of the benefits of WCF, but provided greater flexibility for custom service contract design.

Despite these options, under the covers, WF 3.0 workflows were hosted as in-process services that did not support strongly typed interfaces. It was with version 3.5 of WF Workflow Services that support for formal contracts was introduced. The contract could be defined implicitly with the interface definition dialog introduced in Visual Studio, thereby creating a "workflow-first" approach. Visual Studio 2008 added an Interface designer to define a WCF interface inside the workflow designer and bind the interface to the new `Send` and `Receive` activities.

WF 4.0 introduced support for actual contract-first style development with regular WCF service contracts through the use of WCF messaging activities. As a result, workflows themselves can be strongly-typed. Parameters are declared as workflow input or output, either in the Workflow Designer (Figure 13.3) or in code using the `InParameter<T>`, `OutParameter<T>`, and `InOutParameter<T>` types.

These parameters can be defined as message types declared in the form of WCF contracts in order to allow for the reuse of contract definitions for in-process services.

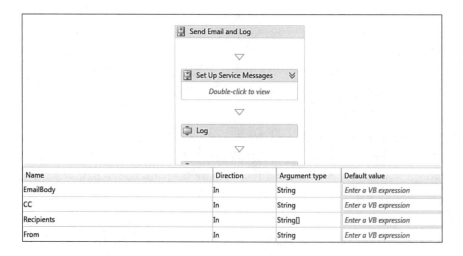

Name	Direction	Argument type	Default value
EmailBody	In	String	Enter a VB expression
CC	In	String	Enter a VB expression
Recipients	In	String[]	Enter a VB expression
From	In	String	Enter a VB expression

Figure 13.3

The Workflow Designer in Visual Studio 2010 provides a UI for the definition of workflow parameters.

Publishing WF Workflows as Web Services and Activities

Because of the diverse options available to apply Decoupled Contract [735] with WF in support of creating orchestrated task services, and because of the importance of choosing the correct option based on your requirements (and the version of WF you are using), we will take the time to explore the details of the following approaches:

- Workflows Published as ASMX Services

- Workflows Published via WCF 3.5 Activities

- Workflows Published via WCF 4.0 Activities

- Workflows Published via `ExternalDataExchange` Services

Note that the option you choose can have a significant impact on the application of the Standardized Service Contract (693) principle. In an environment where multiple implementations of WF co-exist, there may be the need to consider Dual Protocols [739] as a means of support for disparate WF service contracts within the same service inventory.

Workflows Published as ASMX Services

Visual Studio offers the "Publish as Web Service" option to expose a body of workflow logic as an ASMX Web service. It requires the definition of a .NET interface that serves as the formal contract for the service. Each interface method maps to either a one-way operation (for methods of type void) or a request-response operation (for methods with a non-void return type).

> **NOTE**
>
> WF does not require decorating the interface with any special attributes (such as `WebMethod`) to publish a workflow as a Web service.

The following interface translates to a request-response operation because the method has a non-void return type:

```
public interface ICustomerService
{
  CustomerInfoResponse GetCustomerInfo(
    CustomerInfoRequest request);
}
[Serializable]
```

```
[XmlRoot(Namespace=
  "http://example.org/Service/Customer")]
public class CustomerInfoRequest
{
  ...
}
[Serializable]
[XmlRoot(Namespace =
  "http://example.org/Service/Customer")]
public class CustomerInfoResponse
{
  ...
}
```

Example 13.1

In the preceding example, `WebServiceInputActivity`, `WebServiceOutputActivity` and `WebServiceFaultActivity` bind a workflow to this interface. Each `WebServiceIn-putActivity` corresponds to a method in the interface contract as illustrated in Figure 13.4.

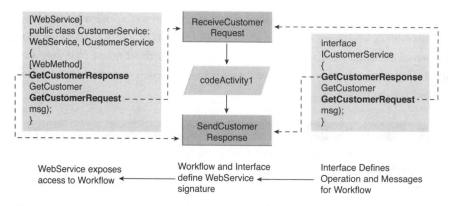

Figure 13.4

Service contracts are defined as .NET interfaces. Each interface method maps to a `WebServiceInput` and possibly a `WebServiceOutput` activity.

The activity's `InterfaceType` and `MethodName` properties shown in Figure 13.4 link the activity to the method on the interface. Any method parameters defined by the interface are added to the activity as properties (Figure 13.5). You can bind them to dependency properties on the workflow to make them available to all other activities.

The `WebServiceOutputActivity` and the `WebServiceFaultActivity` handle responses for request-response message exchanges. Figure 13.5 shows the WF implementation of the interface in Figure 13.6.

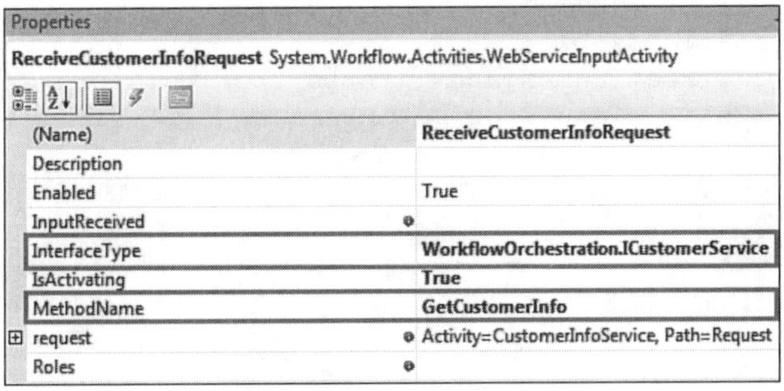

Figure 13.5

The `InterfaceType` and `MethodName` properties configure the service operation for a `WebServiceInputActivity`.

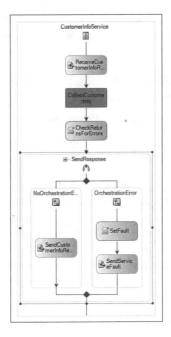

Figure 13.6

`WebServiceInput` and `WebServiceOutput` bind a workflow to a formal .NET interface contract and allow publishing the workflow as an ASMX service.

The `WebServiceInput` activity is configured to handle the `GetCustomerInfo` method and stores the received message in a workflow property. In the example from Figure 13.6, all logic to collect the customer information is factored into a custom activity. If this custom activity succeeds, then the `WebServiceOutput` activity sends the response message. Otherwise the `WebServiceFault` sends an appropriate SOAP fault to the caller.

WF also supports publishing workflows with asynchronous interfaces, such as this one where the `SubmitOrder` operation does not return anything:

```
public interface IOrderService
{
  void SubmitOrder(OrderDataMessage msg);
}

[Serializable]
[XmlRoot(Namespace = "http://example.org/Service/Order")]
public class OrderDataMessage
{
  ...
}
```

Example 13.2

Once again, the `WebServiceInput` activity provides a strongly-typed Web service interface. Figure 13.7 shows how you can provide a typed service wrapper for an asynchronous service operation.

After you define the .NET interface and the workflows are developed, you can publish the entire workflow project to an ASMX Web service by selecting "Publish as Web Service" from the context menu in the Solution Explorer or from the Workflow menu (Figure 13.8).

There are some limitations to keep in mind with regard to reusability when deciding between the different options to expose a workflow as a service.

First, the initial release of WF does not provide tools or activities to support formal contracts that express policies beyond the WS-I BasicProfile. With the "Publish as Web Service" feature, workflows are completely decoupled from their external interface and independent of any particular service host. The contract definition does not include any details about message encoding or service policies.

Second, the formal contract definition for the "Publish as Web service" feature lacks control over the XML-related aspects of the service contract,

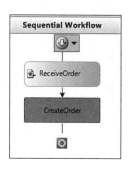

Figure 13.7

Asynchronous service operations bind only to a `Web-ServiceInput` activity.

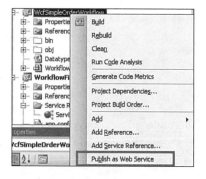

Figure 13.8

The project context menu in the Visual Studio solution explorer includes an option to publish a workflow project as an ASMX Web service.

such as the XML namespace of the service, its XML encoding, etc. The generated Web service honors any XML serialization attributes from `System.Xml.Serialization` on message classes and data classes, but it ignores any attributes you may have put on the interface definition that drives the generation of the `WebService`-derived class and methods exposed via the `WebMethod` attribute.

Take the service definition in the following code fragment:

```
[System.Web.Services.WebService( Namespace =
"http://example.org/QuoteService" )]
public interface SimpleOrderService
{
  [System.Web.Services.Protocols.SoapDocumentMethod
    (RequestNamespace="http://example.org/Quotes" )]
  ns0.QuoteResponse CreateQuote(ns0.QuoteRequest param1);
  ns0.ApproveResponse ApproveOrder
    (ns0.ApproveRequest quoteData);
  ns0.RejectResponse RejectOrder(ns0.RejectRequest quoteData);
}
[System.Xml.Serialization.XmlRoot(
Namespace="http://example.org/Quotes" )]
public class QuoteRequest
{
    public Product quoteData;
    public Customer customerData;
}
```

Example 13.3

The service interface and the `QuoteRequest` class are both decorated with attributes to control the XML namespaces of the service and the request data type in the serialized SOAP messages. The generated service, however, does not include the namespace definition for the service. Only the namespace on the `CreateQuote` element is present:

```
<soap:Envelope xmlns:xsi=
  "http://www.w3.org/2001/XMLSchema-instance"
  xmlns:xsd="http://www.w3.org/2001/XMLSchema"
  xmlns:soap="http://schemas.xmlsoap.org/soap/envelope/">
  <soap:Body>
    <CreateQuote xmlns="http://tempuri.org/">
      <param1 xmlns="http://example.org/Quotes2">
        <quoteData />
        <customerData />
      </param1>
```

```
    </CreateQuote>
  </soap:Body>
</soap:Envelope>
```

Example 13.4

Because the ability to define namespaces and service types is important to the application of Canonical Schema [718], let's cover a work-around whereby we side-step the "Publish as Web Service" option by building the Web service manually.

Start with a Web service class that follows the requirements of WorkflowWebHosting-Module to expose a workflow as an ASMX Web service such as the one shown here:

```
[WebServiceBinding(ConformsTo =
  WsiProfiles.BasicProfile1_1, EmitConformanceClaims = true)]
public class OrderService_WebService :
  System.Workflow.Activities.WorkflowWebService
{
  public OrderService_WebService() :
    base(typeof(OrderService))
    {
    }
  [WebMethodAttribute(Description = "SubmitOrder",
    EnableSession = false)]
  [SoapDocumentMethod(
    RequestNamespace="http://example.org/service",
    ResponseNamespace="http://example.org/service" )]
  public virtual void SubmitOrder(
    WorkflowWebService.OrderDataMessage msg)
  {
    this.Invoke(typeof(WorkflowWebService.IOrderService),
      "SubmitOrder", true, new object[] {msg});
  }
}
```

Example 13.5

The service class derives from System.Workflow.Activities.WorkflowWebService and each WebMethod marshals the request to the workflow via the Invoke method provided by that base class (similar to what the auto-generated service class would do).

By implementing your own service call, you can add attributes from the System.Web.Services.Protocols namespace to shape the XML of the request and response messages. For example, in the preceding code fragment, we added a `SoapDoc-umentMethod` attribute to the XML namespace `http://example.org/service` instead of the auto-generated namespace for the service's request and response messages.

Next, you need an .asmx file for ASP.NET to expose the Web service. If you compile the `WorkflowWebService` class into a separate assembly, the ASMX file would look like this:

```
<%@WebService Class=
"WorkflowOrchestration.OrderService_WebService"%>
```

The "Publish as Web Service" option configures the `WorkflowWebHostingModule` in the Web service's `App.Config` file for you. If you choose to bypass this feature and publish the workflow yourself, you have to complete the following steps:

1. Compile the workflow and the `WorkflowWebService` derived class into a .NET assembly.

2. Create an `.asmx` file to define an endpoint for the `WorkflowWebService` derived class

3. Add the `WorkflowRuntime` section definition for the ASP.NET runtime to parse the WF-specific settings.

4. Configure the `ManualWorkflowSchedulerService` and the `DefaultWorkflow-CommitWorkBatchService` services for proper execution of the workflow in the ASP.NET environment.

5. Add references to the WF assemblies to allow dynamic compilation of the `.asmx` file.

6. Configure the `WorkflowWebHostingModule,` which controls the life cycle of the `WorkflowHost` in the ASP.NET application.

The following example shows the content you need to add to the configuration file:

```
<configuration>
  <configSections>
    <section name="WorkflowRuntime" type=
    "System.Workflow.Runtime.Configuration.
    WorkflowRuntimeSection,System.Workflow.Runtime,
    Version=3.0.00000.0, Culture=neutral,
    PublicKeyToken=31bf3856ad364e35" />
  </configSections>
  <WorkflowRuntime Name="WorkflowServiceContainer">
```

```
    <Services>
      <add type="System.Workflow.Runtime.
      Hosting.ManualWorkflowSchedulerService,
      System.Workflow.Runtime,Version=3.0.0.0,
      Culture=neutral,PublicKeyToken=31bf3856ad364e35"/>
        <add type="System.Workflow.Runtime.
        Hosting.DefaultWorkflowCommitWorkBatchService,
        System.Workflow.Runtime,Version=3.0.0.0,
        Culture=neutral,PublicKeyToken=31bf3856ad364e35"/>
    </Services>
</WorkflowRuntime>
<system.web>
  <compilation debug="false">
    <assemblies>
      <add assembly="System.Design,Version=2.0.0.0,
      Culture=neutral,PublicKeyToken=B03F5F7F11D50A3A"/>
      <add assembly="System.Drawing.Design,Version=2.0.0.0,
      Culture=neutral,PublicKeyToken=B03F5F7F11D50A3A"/>
      <add assembly="System.Transactions,Version=2.0.0.0,
      Culture=neutral,PublicKeyToken=B77A5C561934E089"/>
      <add assembly="System.Workflow.Activities,
      Version=3.0.0.0, Culture=neutral,
      PublicKeyToken=31BF3856AD364E35"/>
      <add assembly="System.Workflow.ComponentModel,
      Version=3.0.0.0, Culture=neutral,
      PublicKeyToken=31BF3856AD364E35"/>
      <add assembly="System.Workflow.Runtime,
      Version=3.0.0.0, Culture=neutral,
      PublicKeyToken=31BF3856AD364E35"/>
      <add assembly="Microsoft.Build.Tasks,Version=2.0.0.0,
      Culture=neutral, PublicKeyToken=B03F5F7F11D50A3A"/>
      <add assembly="System.Messaging,Version=2.0.0.0,
      Culture=neutral, PublicKeyToken=B03F5F7F11D50A3A"/>
      <add assembly="System.Runtime.Remoting,
      Version=2.0.0.0, Culture=neutral,
      PublicKeyToken=B77A5C561934E089"/>
      <add assembly="System.DirectoryServices,
      Version=2.0.0.0, Culture=neutral,
      PublicKeyToken=B03F5F7F11D50A3A"/>
      <add assembly="System.Windows.Forms,
      Version=2.0.0.0, Culture=neutral,
      PublicKeyToken=B77A5C561934E089"/>
      <add assembly="Microsoft.Build.Utilities,
      Version=2.0.0.0, Culture=neutral,
      PublicKeyToken=B03F5F7F11D50A3A"/>
      <add assembly="Microsoft.Build.Framework,
```

```
          Version=2.0.0.0, Culture=neutral,
          PublicKeyToken=B03F5F7F11D50A3A"/>
       </assemblies>
     </compilation>
     ...
     <httpModules>
       <add type="System.Workflow.Runtime.
         Hosting.WorkflowWebHostingModule,
         System.Workflow.Runtime,Version=3.0.0.0,
         Culture=neutral, PublicKeyToken=31bf3856ad364e35"
         name="WorkflowHost"/>
     </httpModules>
   </system.web>
</configuration>
```

Example 13.6

WF does not provide a solution for identifying the target workflow instance for a received message based on the message content. The `WorkflowWebHostingModule` implements a message correlation solution, but it relies on HTTP Cookies rather than message content, which requires cookie-enabled service consumers (and is an approach discouraged in the WS-I Basic Profile).

A further limitation to keep in mind when selecting ASMX as the hosting environment for WF orchestrations is associated with threading. The ASMX workflow hosting module does not handle overlapping response-request operations because of the way the `WorkflowWebHostingModule` handles threading. That means you can't receive messages for an instance while a request-response operation is pending.

The `WorkflowWebHostingModule` executes the workflow on the ASP.NET thread that handles the Web request—that thread is blocked until the workflow sends the response to the initial request. If the Web server receives another request for that same workflow instance before the outstanding request is sent, the service responds with a SOAP fault.

Unfortunately, you cannot change this behavior without writing your own replacement of the `WorkflowWebHostingModule` because this module controls the `WorkflowHost` and manages the `WorkflowHost`'s life cycle. You can still choose different persistence in the Web service's `Web.Config` file, but the `WorkflowWebHostingModule` hardwires the threading and the scheduling services when you rely on Visual Studio to publish a workflow as an ASMX service. With that limitation in mind, it can be more desirable to design each interaction with the workflow using asynchronous operations.

Workflows Published via WCF 3.5 Activities

Visual Studio 2008 and the .NET Framework 3.5 added the `Send` and `Receive` activities for messaging-style communication via WCF to WF (Figure 13.9).

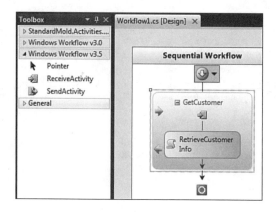

Figure 13.9

The `SendActivity` and `ReceiveActivity` composite activities used to communicate via WCF endpoints.

The `Receive` activity is similar to the `WebServiceInput` activity for ASMX services, but it can receive messages from any kind of WCF endpoint. The `Send` activity corresponds to the `WebServiceInvoke` activity for calling WS-I BasicProfile services, but the `Send` activity supports both asynchronous and request-response messaging patterns.

The formal service contract definitions for these activities are based on WCF contracts, and therefore support all transports and polices supported by WCF. This means they can handle synchronous and asynchronous message exchange patterns even over WCF's duplex channels.

You can quickly bind a workflow to an existing WCF contract, as shown in the following example where we bind the `ICustomerService` interface to the `Send` and `Receive` activities with the `Choose` Operation dialog (Figure 13.10):

```
[ServiceContract]
public interface ICustomerService
{
  [OperationContract]
  CustomerInfoResponse GetCustomerInfo(
    CustomerInfoRequest request);
  [OperationContract(IsOneWay=true)]
  void SubmitOrder(OrderDataMessage msg);
```

```
}
[Serializable]
[DataContract(Namespace=
  "http://example.org/Service/Customer")]
public class CustomerInfoRequest
{
  ...
}
[Serializable]
[DataContract(Namespace =
  "http://example.org/Service/Customer")]
public class CustomerInfoResponse
{
  ...
}
[Serializable]
[DataContract(Namespace = "http://example.org/Service/Order")]
public class OrderDataMessage
{
  ...
}
```

Example 13.7

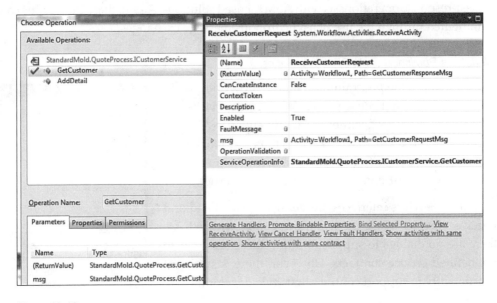

Figure 13.10

Editing the `ReceiveActivity`'s `ServiceOperationInfo` property opens the Choose Operation dialog to bind the activity to an interface method.

You can also define a new WCF service contract with the `Choose` Operation dialog if you don't already have one before you build the workflow. Visual Studio will create the necessary metadata to expose the workflow as a service.

With Workflow Services hosting, you expose your workflow like any other WCF service. You can host the service in a custom container or using WAS and allow access to the workflow through a .svc file.

> **NOTE**
>
> Contracts created in the `Choose` Operation dialog do not explicitly show up in code. They are defined implicitly by setting the `ServiceOpera-tionInfo` on the `Receive` activity. You can still refer to them in `end-point` configurations in the service's application configuration file.

The options for routing incoming messages to the appropriate workflow instance with WCF are more flexible than with ASMX services. In addition to a cookie-based solution, the WF runtime in .NET 3.5 can also perform routing based on special correlation tokens in SOAP headers.

The threading model for WCF-based services has similar limitations for overlapping request-response operations as with ASMX-based solutions. Again, these limitations can be mitigated through the use of asynchronous message exchanges.

Workflows Published via WCF 4.0 Activities

WF 4.0 changes the programming model for workflows in that workflows, and consequently Workflow Services, are exclusively developed either declaratively in XAML or imperatively in a .NET language, such as C#. Workflows are strongly typed with interfaces defined via `InParameter`, `OutParameter` and `InOutParameter` properties.

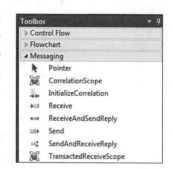

Workflow Services interfaces are defined by the Send and Receive activities inside the workflow. Unlike with WF 3.5, there are no dialogs to support binding these activities to pre-defined service contracts. However, there is sufficient functionality to support contract-first style development.

Figure 13.11

The Toolbox window showing `Send` and `Receive` activities.

The WF 4.0 `Send` and `Receive` activities can reference contract type definitions for their message types (Figure 13.11).

For example, a pair of `Send` and `Receive` activities could implement the request-response operation `GetCustomerData` in the `ICustomerService`:

```
[ServiceContract(Namespace =
  "http://example.org/contracts/CustomerService")]
interface ICustomerService
{
  [OperationContract]
  GetCustomerResponse
  GetCustomerData(GetCustomerRequest msg);
}
[DataContract(Namespace=
  "http://example.org/operations/customer" )]
public class GetCustomerResponse
{
  [DataMember]
  public Customer CustomerData;
  ...
}
[DataContract(Namespace =
  "http://example.org/operations/customer")]
public class GetCustomerRequest
{
  [DataMember]
  public string customerId;
  ...
}
```

Example 13.8

Implementing this contract with the Workflow Designer requires that you set some properties manually to bind to the contract instead of relying on a dialog-driven process. You need to first configure the `Receive` property of the `ReceiveRequest` activity for the `GetCustomerRequest` message.

Then you can configure the activity according to the message style in the contract. If the service expects to receive just the `GetResponseRequest` message without a wrapping XML element, you select the Message option in the Content Definition dialog (Figure 13.12).

Figure 13.12

Message types define service operation messages.

The inferred contract for the service interface ignores the operation name and expects the raw message inside the SOAP body as shown here:

```
<s:Body>
  <GetCustomerRequest xmlns=
    "http://example.org/operations/customer">
    <customerId>20</customerId>
  </GetCustomerRequest>
</s:Body>
```

Example 13.9

For fine-grained control over the message shape, including SOAP headers and element protection, messages can be defined as Message Contracts with the `MessageContract` attribute, just like message types outside of Workflow Services. Selecting the `XmlSerializer` option for message serialization allows for even more control over the message formatting (Figure 13.13).

Figure 13.13

WCF messaging activities expose properties for configuring serialization formats.

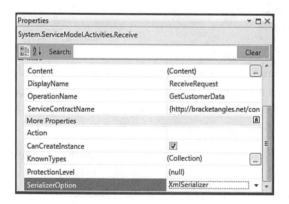

The `Receive` activity can also be configured for a SOAP message containing an element to represent the operation name if the service naming should reflect an RPC-style operation. Instead of selecting the Message option in the Content Definition dialog, you can choose the Parameters option and define a parameter of the message type (Figure 13.14).

Figure 13.14

Service parameters must map to workflow variables or parameters.

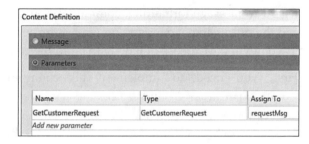

The resulting service interface expects the additional `GetCustomerData` element:

```
<s:Body>
  <GetCustomerData xmlns="http://tempuri.org/">
    <GetCustomerRequest xmlns:d4p1=
    "http://example.org/operations/customer" xmlns:i=
    "http://www.w3.org/2001/XMLSchema-instance">
      <d4p1:customerId i:nil="true" />
    </GetCustomerRequest>
  </GetCustomerData>
</s:Body>
```

Example 13.10

To qualify the operation name element with an XML namespace, you set the `Service-ContractName` property of the `Receive` activity, as shown in Figure 13.15.

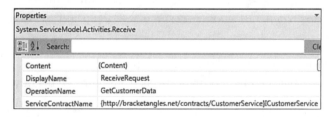

Figure 13.15

WCF messaging activities' `ServiceContractName` property configures the message's XML namespace.

Workflows Published via *ExternalDataExchange* Services

You have the option of building the workflow independently of any communication framework and creating a hosting environment that handles all inbound and outbound communication for you. This approach provides the greatest amount of flexibility with regard to message formatting, communication protocol support, message correlation, and the processing of overlapping request-response operations. However, that flexibility comes at the expense of having to build the communication layer yourself.

First, you need to implement all communications of the workflow with `HandleExternalEvent` and `CallExternalMethod` operations instead of using the communication activities `WebServiceInput`, `WebServiceOutput` and `WebServiceInvoke`. This approach does not work with WF 4.0 because `HandleExternalEvent` and `CallExternalMethod` were removed from the framework. A similar solution can be developed with WF 4.0 bookmarks, but having to program complete custom hosting extensions should be considered a last resort.

You can also choose to build custom activities that work with services provided by your custom hosting environment for sending and receiving messages. The `HandleExternalEvent` and `CallExternalMethod` activities can interact with the custom hosting environment through a communication service. The communication service can post events from the workflow container to the workflow runtime engine and handle method invocations from the workflow. This is an in-process service attached to the `WorkflowHost` to optimize performance and avoid passing security contexts between processes. You can add these services to the `WorkflowHost` object that manages all the workflows.

The upcoming example adds two services to the runtime:

- `ExternalDataExchangeService` (required for communication between the workflow and its host via `HandleExternalEventActivity` and `CallExternalMethod-Activity`)

- `taskService` (a custom service that works together with `ExternalDataExchangeService` to handle method invocations from within workflows)

```
using (WorkflowRuntime workflowRuntime =
  new WorkflowRuntime())
{
  ExternalDataExchangeService dataExchangeService =
    new ExternalDataExchangeService();
  workflowRuntime.AddService(dataExchangeService);
  dataExchangeService.AddService(taskService);
  workflowRuntime.StartRuntime();
}
```

Example 13.11

The workflow runtime automatically calls these services when necessary and the workflow runtime calls the Data Exchange service when it needs to communicate with the workflow host (Figure 13.16).

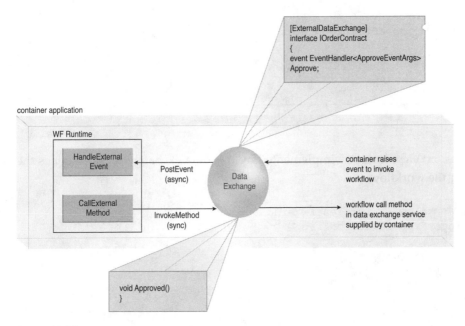

Figure 13.16

A .NET interface defines the inbound and outbound contract for a workflow. `HandleExternalEvent` and `CallExternalMethod` activities handle inbound and outbound communication.

The workflow container passes messages to the workflow by raising an event for the workflow to handle. The contract interface defines the event signature. Behind the scenes, `ExternalDataExchangeService` creates an appropriate event handler and attaches it to the custom event service.

This next example shows that passing data to a workflow is no different than raising any other event in a .NET program:

```
dataExSvc.RaiseApproveOrderEvent(wfId, quoteData);
class OrderDataExchangeService : IOrderContract
{
  public event EventHandler<ApproveOrderEventArgs>
    ApproveOrderEvent;
  public void RaiseApproveOrderEvent(Guid wfId,
    ApproveRequest order, ApproveResponse resp,
```

```
      ManualResetEvent waiter)
  {
    if(ApproveOrderEvent != null)
    {
      ApproveOrderEvent(null,
        new ApproveOrderEventArgs(wfId, order));
    }
  }
  ...
}
```

Example 13.12

The `IOrderContract` interface implemented by this data exchange service defines the contract for the workflow:

```
[System.Workflow.Activities.ExternalDataExchange]
public interface IOrderContract
{
    event EventHandler<CreateQuoteEventArgs>
      CreateQuoteEvent;
    event EventHandler<ApproveOrderEventArgs>
      ApproveOrderEvent;
    event EventHandler<RejectOrderEventArgs>
      RejectOrderEvent;
    void QuoteCreated(QuoteResponse response,
      ManualResetEvent completionEvent);
    void OrderApproved(ApproveResponse response,
      ManualResetEvent completionEvent);
    void OrderRejected(RejectResponse response,
      ManualResetEvent completionEvent);
}
```

Example 13.13

The code highlighted with red represents incoming messages posted to the workflow, whereas the bold code represents outgoing messages originating from the workflow. Note that all incoming interfaces are defined as events with all event argument classes deriving from `ExternalDataEventArgs`. All outgoing interfaces are just straight-forward method definitions.

Since you control how the workflow is published, support for formal contracts depends on how you choose to implement the communication layer.

417

> **NOTE**
>
> When taking into account the Service Discoverability (702) principle and the Metadata Centralization [754] pattern, it is worth noting that because service interfaces for workflows are based on either ASMX or WCF technology, WF orchestrations expose the discovery interfaces provided by these technologies. For example, retrieving the WSDL documents via a URL ending in `?wsdl`.
>
> WCF-based services also support retrieving service metadata, such as WSDL definitions and policy documents, via WS-MetadataExchange. However, you do have to explicitly enable metadata retrieval in WCF.
>
> Visual Studio can present WF orchestrations and services packaged as custom activities in the Toolbox pane to increase developer awareness of the common services approved for broad consumption.
>
> Note also that WF, in combination with WCF 4.0, allows for registration via the WS-Discovery industry standard.

WS-I BasicProfile Support

Publishing workflows as ASMX services enables the use of basic Web services through the `WebServiceInput`, `WebServiceOutput`, and `InvokeWebService` activities. The former two handle requests and responses for a workflow published as an orchestrated task service and the latter allows workflows to interact with Web services. This feature is available in all WF versions, but its limited support for contemporary WS standards makes WCF a commonly preferred option.

Note that when you develop ASMX services without WF, ASMX can emit errors for a non WS-I compliant service interface. With WF services published through WF's "Publish as Web service" feature, you may not see these compliance warnings from the compiler when you publish because the `WebService` class is compiled behind the scenes. You need to separately check your message type definitions for compliant namespace definitions and other incompatibilities caught by the compiler.

> **NOTE**
>
> If you follow a contract-first design approach, you can pay special attention to designing your service contract for WS-I BasicProfile compliance. Tools such as WSCF, WSCF.blue for WCF or the Web service Software Factory can be used to help verify WS-I BasicProfile compliance as part of a contract-first design process.

In WF 3.5 and WF 4.0, WCF support for industry standard transports, protocols and policies transfers to WF Workflow Services. All communication aspects for Web services published into IIS can be configured in the Web.Config file. The `basicHttpBinding` configures a message exchange over SOAP and HTTP. This follows the rules of the WS-I BasicProfile, in both service and consumer endpoint configurations.

Exposing a WCF3.5 Workflow Service in WAS or IIS required a .svc to bind the workflow to an endpoint. The .svc file either referenced a CodeBehind service definition or a workflow in a compiled assembly.

Here is a .svc file example for a compiled workflow:

```
<%@
  ServiceHost Factory="System.ServiceModel.Activation.
  WorkflowServiceHostFactory" Service=
  "StandardMold.QuoteProcess.CustomerService"
%>
```

Example 13.14

The `WorkflowServiceHostFactory` loads the configuration matching the service type from the `system.serviceModel` section in the Web.Config file.

WF 4.0 no longer requires a .svc file, but requires the file extension .xamlx on the workflow definition file for WAS or IIS to host the Workflow Service.

The following configuration snippet applies the `basicHttpBinding` to the service endpoint matching the service type in the .svc file:

```
<system.serviceModel>
  <services>
    <service name="StandardMold.Services.CustomerService"
      behaviorConfiguration=" StandardMold.Services.
      CustomerServiceBehavior">
      <endpoint address="..."
        binding="basicHttpBinding" contract=
        "StandardMold.QuoteProcess.ICustomerService">
      </endpoint>
    </service>
  </services>
  <behaviors>
    ...
  </behaviors>
</system.serviceModel>
```

Example 13.15

Further compliance configuration options, such as securing the message transmission over HTTPS or with user credentials, are available in the behaviorConfiguration section. Hosting Workflow Services in a custom container is supported as well, but hosting in IIS is generally preferred due to the native support for enterprise-scale monitoring, process, and management.

NOTE

Using WF with WCF adds further support for many other WS-* industry standards. For example, applying the wsHttpBinding to an endpoint configures the message exchange for WS-Security over HTTP and simply requires a change to the endpoint's binding in the Web.Config file, as shown here:

```
<endpoint address="..." binding="basicHttpBinding"
```

wsHttpBinding offers a number of behavior settings for security, reliable messaging, and transactions.

Publishing WF Workflows as REST Services

It was possible to build REST consumer programs into WF 3.0 workflows via Code Activities or custom activities, but you had to deal with the primitives in the System.Net namespace to form HTTP requests and parse the responses.

Publishing REST services in WF 3.0 was challenging because ASMX only supported SOAP services. It was possible to write HttpHandlers to accept REST requests, parse URLs, deserialize HTTP bodies and then invoke workflows based on the use of ExternalDataExchange; however, that approach required a fair amount of low level development.

WCF in .NET 3.5 added the "Web Programming Model" to bring the SOA programming model to REST endpoints. The webHttpBinding abstracted REST endpoints in the same way basicHttpBinding allowed access to SOAP endpoints. Attributes like WebGet and WebInvoke could annotate service contracts to shape URLs for REST requests to send request parameters embedded in the URL instead of having to send SOAP bodies.

You were able to combine .NET 3.5 Workflow Services with the Web Programming Model for publishing or consuming REST services with WF. WCF represents REST contracts very similar to SOAP contracts (as an interface with annotations):

```
[ServiceContract(SessionMode = SessionMode.NotAllowed)]
public interface IRESTCustomer
{
  [OperationContract]
  [WebInvoke(Method = "POST",
    UriTemplate = "customers/{cid}")]
    Customer GetCustomer(string cid);
}
```

Example 13.16

In addition to the already familiar *Contract attributes, the contract in the preceding example includes the REST-specific attribute WebInvoke, which binds an interface to a URL and an HTTP method. The base URL is supplied by the binding and parameters are either passed as part of the URL or as URL parameters. This example defines the Get-Customer operation as a POST request to <baseurl>/customers/<cid> (for example http://services.example.org/CustomerService/customers/1234), based on the UriTemplate in the attribute.

The WCF Send and Receive messaging activities can consume the REST service contract just like a SOAP contract. You select an operation from the ServiceContract using the ServiceOperationInfo property dialog for the activities (Figure 13.17).

Figure 13.17
WCF messaging activities can consume REST contracts defined as WCF interfaces.

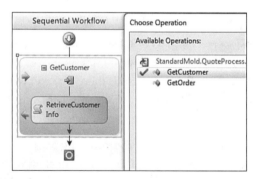

Services hosted in IIS require a .svc file to load the workflow through the WorkflowServiceHostFactory since workflows don't explicitly implement the service contract by deriving from the contract interface. The WorkflowServiceHost infers the contract from the Receive activities.

The .svc file for the previous example could look like this:

```
<%@
  ServiceHost Factory="System.ServiceModel.
    Activation.WorkflowServiceHostFactory"
    Service="WF35Services.RESTCustomerService"
%>
```

Example 13.17

Note the `Factory` attribute pointing to the `WorkflowServiceHostFactory` and the `Service` attribute identifying the workflow type implementing the service.

Self-hosted services are loaded into a `WorkflowServiceHost` through the API and don't require the .svc file. Configuring an endpoint for REST communication requires the `webHttpBinding` and the `webHttp` endpoint behavior:

```
<system.serviceModel>
  <services>
    <service name="WF35Services.RESTCustomerService">
      <endpoint address="" binding="webHttpBinding"
        contract="StandardMold.QuoteProcess.IRESTTest2"
        behaviorConfiguration="REST">
      </endpoint>
    </service>
  </services>
  <behaviors>
    ...
    <endpointBehaviors>
      <behavior name="REST">
        <webHttp/>
      </behavior>
    </endpointBehaviors>
  </behaviors>
</system.serviceModel>
```

Example 13.18

JSON Encoding

WCF expects XML messages, even with the REST binding. You can configure the contract for JSON encoding by adding the `enableWebScript` behavior.

```
<endpointBehaviors>
  <behavior name="REST">
    <webHttp/>
```

```
    <enableWebScript/>
  </behavior>
</endpointBehaviors>
```

Example 13.19

Unfortunately, this behavior conflicts with the `UriTemplate` property. As a work-around, you can set the `ResponseFormat` property to `WebMessageFormat.JSON`.

```
[OperationContract]
[WebInvoke(Method = "GET",
  UriTemplate = "customers/{cid}",
  ResponseFormat=WebMessageFormat.Json)]
Customer GetCustomer(string tid, string msg);
```

Example 13.20

Send and Receive Activity Configuration

Configuring the Send activity to retrieve data from REST services follows the same steps as configuring the Receive activity. The only difference is the configuration of the endpoint. The Send activity exposes a `ChannelToken` property that can reference the client endpoint configuration in the .config file.

Figure 13.18

The `ChannelToken` property binds a Send activity to an endpoint configuration in the configuration file.

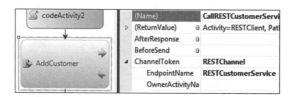

`ChannelToken` requires a unique name and the name of an endpoint configuration. If you're sharing a channel, for example, a proxy to the server for context or performance reasons, then you can also set the `OwnerActivityName` property.

The configuration in Figure 13.18 references a `RESTCustomerService` endpoint that can be configured in detail in the .config file:

```
<system.serviceModel>
  <client>
    <endpoint address="http://localhost:8000/Customers"
      binding="webHttpBinding"contract=
```

```
     "StandardMold.QuoteProcess.ICustomerCollection"
     behaviorConfiguration="rest"name="RESTCustomerService"/>
  </client>
  <behaviors>
    <endpointBehaviors>
      <behavior name="rest">
        <webHttp />
      </behavior>
    </endpointBehaviors>
  </behaviors>
</system.serviceModel>
```

Example 13.21

NOTE

It's technically possible to build long-running REST services with WF and WCF. However, because REST explicitly prohibits operations that rely on multiple HTTP requests, the limitations around message correlation with WF and WCF don't impact the implementation of a RESTful orchestrated task service. An incoming request is always to be serviced by a new instance of a workflow.

Orchestrated Task Services with REST and WF 4.0

WF 4.0 infers `ServiceContracts` instead of linking operation contracts directly to Send and Receive activities. This approach works for SOAP messaging and RPC style services, but it takes away the extension points for the REST `WebInvoke` and `WebGet` attributes. With WF 4.0, REST services are consumed by building custom activities invoking WCF directly.

The following example shows a simple activity calling a REST service.

```
public sealed class GetRESTCustomer : CodeActivity
{
  public InArgument<string> Cid { get; set; }
  public OutArgument<Customer> CustomerResponse { get; set; }
  protected override void Execute(CodeActivityContext context)
  {
  using (WebChannelFactory<IRESTCustomer> cf = new
    WebChannelFactory<IRESTCustomer>
    ("RESTCustomerService"))
```

```
  {
    IRESTCustomer channel = cf.CreateChannel();
    context.SetValue<Customer>
      (CustomerResponse, channel.GetCustomer
      (context.GetValue<string>(Tid)));
  }
 }
}
```

Example 13.22

The definition for `IRESTCustomer` can contain `WebGet` or `WebInvoke` attributes that define the request shape and encoding. The `WebChannelFactory` references an endpoint configuration stored in the App.Config file to externalize behavior details. This simple class includes everything required to invoke a REST service from a WF 4.0 workflow (Figure 13.19).

REST relies on state messaging and prohibits operations that require receiving multiple messages to execute. Thus, a REST service operation can receive a service request, create a new workflow instance, and pass the received parameters to the new instance. WF 4.0 doesn't have a Receive activity, but you can easily implement the workflow instantiation logic in code and implement the necessary service logic in a workflow.

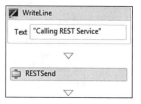

Figure 13.19

Custom code activities can consume REST services in WF 4.0 workflows.

This next example illustrates the bootstrapping of workflow instances in code. Production quality implementations would likely include parameter validation, error handling, security checks, and other functionality. In cases where the WorkflowInvoker's functionality is too limited, the WorkflowApplication provides a more capable alternative.

```
public string GetCustomerData(string cid)
{
  WF4UtilityActivities.RESTservice svc = new
    WF4UtilityActivities.RESTservice();
    svc.Cid = cid;
  IDictionary<string, object> result =
    WorkflowInvoker.Invoke(svc);
    return (string)result["Result"];
}
```

Example 13.23

WF 4.0 exposes input arguments as properties on the workflow class. Custom activities could also return a strongly typed value. XAML-based workflows return a dictionary of named return parameters.

Note also that the implementation of the REST operation includes no REST-specific code. This implementation can therefore be exposed as a REST service or a SOAP endpoint for different service consumers.

SUMMARY OF KEY POINTS

- WF workflows can be encapsulated within and exposed via orchestrated task services with published service contracts. However, different approaches and implementation mediums exist.

- WF relies on .NET Web service frameworks like ASMX and WCF to provide support for industry standards. The combination of WF and WCF, in particular, supports a broad array of open, contemporary Web services standards.

13.2 Process Centralization

The physical centralization of process logic is the basis of the Process Centralization [763] pattern and is fundamental to orchestration platforms in general. Highlighted in this brief section is the tool support provided by WF for centrally maintaining workflowlogic, as well as a statement regarding lack of support for WS-BPEL, an industry standard commonly associated with this pattern.

Centralized Process Maintenance

An advantage of creating applications using workflows is the ability to define the workflow graphically, which is why WF includes a designer for Visual Studio. By default, the activities appear in the toolbox, letting a developer drag and drop them onto the tool's design surface to create a workflow. The workflow designer is a convenient way to interact with the workflow namespace.

Workflows created with the designer are stored in a file based on XAML, a declarative XML language used to define objects, their properties, relationships, and interactions. Upon execution, the runtime engine takes the XAML workflow and creates workflow instances. While there is only one XAML-based workflow file, there can be multiple workflow instances running at any given time.

The designer allows you to model a Sequential Workflow Console Application or a State Machine Workflow Console Application. After selecting the appropriate model, you need to add activities by dragging and dropping them from the toolbar.

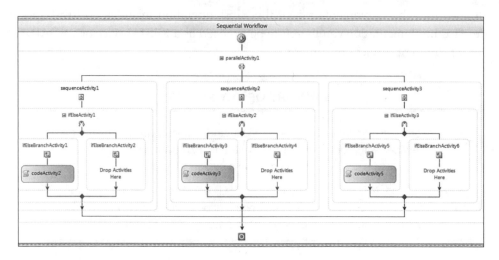

Figure 13.20
An example of sequential workflows being visually depicted by the designer tool.

WS-BPEL Support

The WS-BPEL standard for the definition of an orchestration language emerged about the same time as the majority of the WS-* standards, but it targeted platform-independent business process definitions instead of cross-platform interoperability.

WS-BPEL is not WF's native orchestration language because it does not support all the workflow constructs and styles WF provides. For example, WS-BPEL does not support state-machine type workflows (WF 3.0), flowchart workflows (WF 4.0), nor does it define the integration of a rules engine.

However, with WF 4.0's fully declarative programming model, WF has natively become more comparable to the WS-BPEL language and further supports translation from XAML into WS-BPEL.

13.3 State Repository

Orchestrations are the central place where the flow of business processes are controlled. You could say that the properties of an orchestration and the current point of execution are the state of a process instance. Therefore, it makes sense architecturally to manage process state in the orchestration layer because it promotes the application of the Service Statelessness (700) principle.

The WF runtime (Figure 13.21) implements State Repository [785] through its persistence services. These in-memory services save workflow instances to persistent storage and unload them from memory when possible in order to free up server resources and improve scalability.

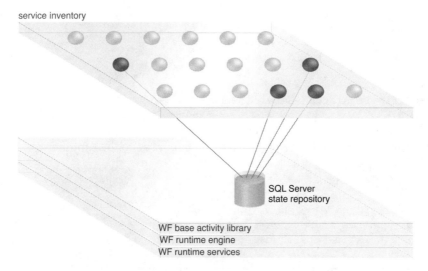

Figure 13.21

The WF runtime positioned within the WF layers that host a SQL Server state repository shared by services also hosted within the overall orchestration environment.

The workflow runtime engine can persist workflows into a database when the workflow goes idle (Figure 13.22); for example, when it's waiting for another message or a response from another Web service. The persistence operations are executed by a persistence service that plugs into an extensibility interface in the runtime engine.

WF3.0 included several persistence services to customize state management and tailor it to different needs. For long running processes and higher scalability requirements, you would likely configure workflows to store state in a SQL Server database with `SqlWorkflowPersistenceService`.

You would add the tables and stored procedures required by the `SqlWorkflowPersistence` service by running the necessary SQL scripts. Next, you would attach a persistence service to the workflow runtime either in code or in the application's configuration file.

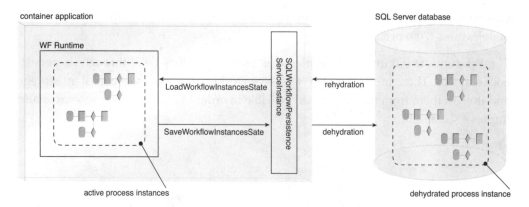

Figure 13.22

The `SqlWorkflowPersistenceService` manages workflow persistence with a SQL Server database as the data store.

This example adds an `SqlWorkflowPersistenceService` to the runtime:

```
using (WorkflowRuntime workflowRuntime =
  new WorkflowRuntime())
{
  workflowRuntime.AddService(
    new SqlWorkflowPersitanceService(true));
}
```

Example 13.24

WF 4.0 expands the persistence functionality and evolves the API. The API abstraction is now called an `InstanceStore`, with a SQL Server-based `InstanceStore` implementation being part of the .NET framework.

`InstanceStores` are architected to be more scalable and flexible than WF 3.0 persistence solutions. Some of the benefits of `InstanceStores` are explicit management of instance ownership, explicit management of instance persistence, and a schema allowing for indexed queries of persisted instances. A Workflow Management Service manages time outs and cleans out abandoned instances.

SQL Persistence Service and Scaling Out in WF 3.0

The built-in support for state management is suitable for intra-solution workflows or smaller scale multi-user applications. These types of systems typically only receive events from a host application, but not from multiple sources. Small-scale multi user applications, such as individual Web services, mostly run on a single server and any given workflow instance will usually need to only interact with one service consumer at a time. Neither application type relies on distributing workflows across multiple computers, which is why WF is a suitable candidate for building these types of orchestrations. Larger solutions often require running workflow on multiple servers for robustness and scalability reasons. Therefore, they need a state management mechanism that works across multiple machines.

The persistence service interface defines instance-locking parameters designed to support these types of distributed scenarios, where multiple distributed workflow engines can execute the same workflow instance. Instance locking is very important, because without it, two servers can process two different messages for the same persisted workflow. Both servers would load the workflow into memory and execute it and it would be impossible to tell which of these two instances is valid.

The `SqlWorkflowPersistenceService` that ships with the .NET framework for storing workflows in a SQL Server database supports locking by writing the ID of the runtime engine where the instance is currently executing into the database.

A scale-out feature can be architected by sharing a persistence database between multiple workflow servers. Workflows are not bound to a server, so each server can receive messages for any persisted workflow and load and execute them because all servers access the same persistence store. The database can be clustered or mirrored for mission critical solutions to avoid a single point of failure in the overall service inventory architecture. Figure 13.23 shows this type of scale out architecture for distributing load across multiple servers.

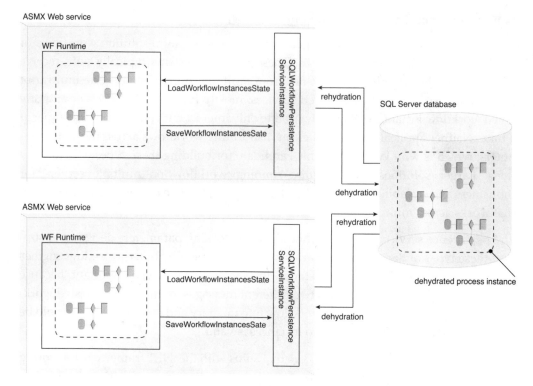

Figure 13.23

`SqlWorkflowPersistenceService` can enable a scale-out solution for workflow-based Web services.

Let's look at the parameter list for the constructor of the `SqlWorkflowPersistenceSer-`
`vice` a little more closely. There are several constructor overloads that can be used to
customize the behavior of the `SqlWorkflowPersistanceService`. One in particular
provides all the parameters necessary to handle distributed deployments:

```
string connectionString = "Data Source=localhost;
  Initial Catalog=SqlPersistenceService;
  Integrated Security=True;
  Pooling=False";
bool unloadOnIdle = true;
TimeSpan ownershipDuration = TimeSpan.MaxValue;
TimeSpan loadingInterval = new TimeSpan(0, 2, 0);
SqlWorkflowPersistenceService persistenceService =
  new SqlWorkflowPersistenceService(
    connectionString, unloadOnIdle,
    ownershipDuration, loadingInterval);
```

Example 13.25

The most important parameter in a scale out scenario is `UnloadOnIdle`. You must set it to "true" for the runtime engine to persist the workflow when it's waiting to receive messages.

The `SqlWorkflowPersistenceService` locks an orchestration instance while it's actively running. If the service receives another message for a currently running instance, the attempt to load the locked instance fails and the WF runtime throws a `WorkflowOwnershipException`.

You can configure the persistence service to retry delivering the message when an instance is locked by setting the service's EnableRetries property to "true." The persistence service then retries to load the locked instance and deliver the message. However, if the workflow isn't in a state to process the message it will throw an exception. Thus, retrying only works if the workflow is in the right state to process the message after it becomes available.

A Web server thread is also locking while the persistence service is retrying to post the message. Therefore, carefully consider whether this setting is the right approach. A decoupled, store-forward approach, for example, could provide a more scalable and robust approach because it avoids tying up server threads. However, to custom build the store-forward and retry logic instead of using built-in functionality would be necessary to fulfill this approach.

SQL Persistence Service and Scaling Out in WF 4

WF 4.0 `InstanceStores` are designed for distributed scale-out scenarios. `InstanceStores` and the Workflow Management Service not only manage instance locking by different hosts, but also process management and abandoned instances.

`InstanceStore` is associated with a workflow host (`WorkflowApplication` or `WorkflowServiceHost`) by assigning an `InstanceStore` object to the `InstanceStore` property, as shown here:

```
using System.Activities.DurableInstancing;
WorkflowServiceHost host = new WorkflowServiceHost(...);
host.DurableInstancingOptions.InstanceStore =
new SqlWorkflowInstanceStore(...);
```

– or –

```
using System.Activities.DurableInstancing;
WorkflowApplication app = new WorkflowApplication(...);
app.InstanceStore = new SqlWorkflowInstanceStore(...);
```

Example 13.26

When hosting a workflow in IIS/WAS, where the `WorkflowServiceHost` is not directly accessible, the `InstanceStore` can also be configured as a `serviceBehavior` in the service's Web.Config file.

```
<serviceBehaviors>
  <behavior>
    ...
    <sqlWorkflowInstanceStore
      connectionString="Data Source=.\SQLEXPRESS;Initial
      Catalog=WorkflowInstanceStore;Integrated
      Security=True;Async=true"instanceEncodingOption="None"
      instanceCompletionAction="DeleteAll"
      instanceLockedExceptionAction="AggressiveRetry"
      hostLockRenewalPeriod="00:00:30">
    </sqlWorkflowInstanceStore>
  </behavior>
</serviceBehaviors>
```

Example 13.27

The configuration options of the SQL `InstanceStore` are similar to the persistence service in WF 3.0, but offer additional customization on storage format, clean-up and retry behavior. The `instanceEncodingOption` controls the storage format. If the option is set to gzip, instances can be stored in gzip format to save space in the database.

The `instanceCompletionAction`, `instanceLockedExceptionAction`, and `hostLock-RenewalPeriod` help with `InstanceStore` maintenance. The `instanceCompletionAction` selects between deleting instances when a workflow completes or, keeping them around—for example, to archive later. The `instanceLockedExceptionAction` specifies what happens when the service tries to load a workflow instance that is currently owned by another host.

Hosts lock instances while they are loaded and release the lock if an instance is unloaded during idle periods. In load-balanced set-ups, multiple hosts may receive requests for a specific workflow instance, but an instance may still be loaded in a different host. If the `instanceLockedExceptionAction` property is set to `SimpleRetry` or `Aggres-siveRetry`, the host will retry to load a locked instance instead of returning a fault to the caller. The two options differ in the algorithm to determine the time interval between retry attempts.

The `hostLockRenewalPeriod` is a safeguard against crashed host processes. A simple boolean flag to indicate a lock does not allow a fail-over scenario when a new host loads instances in a crashed host. With the renewal based locking in WF 4.0, hosts have to actively renew their locks. Instances can be loaded into other hosts or garbage collected by the Workflow Management Service if locks don't get renewed before the lock expires.

The `SqlWorkflowInstanceStore` class exposes properties to set these options in code. Hosting Workflow Services, with the AppFabric extensions installed, allows managing these options through the IIS management UI as shown in Figure 13.24.

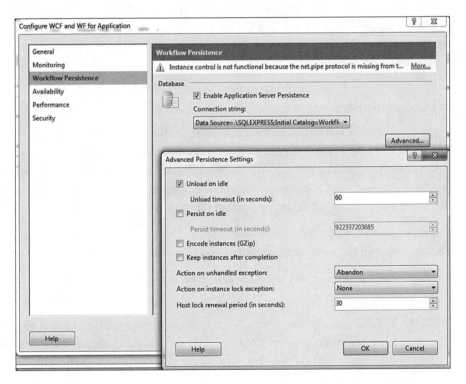

Figure 13.24
`InstanceStore` configuration is available in the AppFabric configuration dialog of the IIS Manager tool.

SUMMARY OF KEY POINTS

- WF can manage a state repository for long running processes. WF 4.0 in particular offers a mature mechanism for managing a central state repository.

- There are different approaches to leveraging SQL persistence services, depending on the version of WF being used.

13.4 Compensating Service Transaction

With WF, compensation logic can be defined via the graphic design by dragging-and-dropping activities, just as you would define regular workflow logic. WF compensations not only support common transaction semantics, they can be also used to clean up the programming model. All code necessary to run compensations is grouped in compensation handlers (similar to `catch()` blocks in C#). The main difference with compensation handlers is that they run when an error occurs after a block of operations has already executed and completed successfully.

Creating Compensations

Other than transactable resources in the context of ACID transactions, compensatable resources must provide explicit access to the compensation logic. WF 3.0 supports the application of Compensating Service Transaction [724] for one or more workflow activities through the `CompensatableSequence` and the `CompensatableTransactionScope` activities. Each has an associated compensation handler that runs when:

- the compensatable scope completed successfully (for example, without throwing an exception), but the orchestration failed with an unhandled exception

- the compensatable scope completed successfully, but a `Compensate` activity triggered the compensation

By default, the WF 3.0 process designer does not show compensation blocks to avoid any distraction from the main process flow. You can switch the designer view from the process flow to the compensation flow by clicking on the compensation handler icon.

WF 4.0 introduces some changes to give you more granular control over the execution of compensation logic. The `CompensatableActivity` allows compensation of the embedded activities when certain conditions are met. The activity's compensation handler runs when:

- the compensatable scope completed successfully (for example, without throwing an exception), but an unhandled exception occurred afterwards and the executing WorkflowApplication's `OnUnhandledException` handler returned `UnhandledExceptionAction.Cancel`

- the compensatable scope completed successfully, but a `Compensate` activity explicitly triggered the compensation (this is true unless the `CompensatableActivity` has been confirmed with the Confirm activity)

The Confirm activity in WF 4.0 can prevent a completed `CompensatableActivity` from running the compensation logic even when compensation is triggered explicitly. This lets workflows mark certain tasks as irreversible, even if a Compensate activity triggers compensation at higher levels.

Triggering Compensations

Note also that you need to trigger compensations explicitly when exceptions are handled in any part of the workflow. Error handlers (such as Fault Handlers in WF 3.0 and Catch activities in WF 4.0) need to invoke the compensation handlers with the Compensate activity.

In WF 3.0, the Compensate activity can only be placed inside a Fault handler or a CompensationHandler. In WF 4.0, you can place Compensate activities in the regular flow of a workflow, but the activity expects a valid CompensationToken. These tokens are only set once a CompensatableActivity completes successfully. Calling Compensate, without a valid token, results in an exception.

Compensate also raises an exception if you invoke it for a `CompensatableActivity` that has been explicitly confirmed with a Confirm activity. Therefore, it's important to wrap Compensate activities in a TryCatch activity.

NOTE

WF also supports Atomic Service Transaction [713] via two-phase ACID transactions inside workflows. A `TransactionScope` or a `CompensatableTransactionScope` can define the scope of a .NET transaction, as provided by the `System.Transactions.Transaction` namespace.

SUMMARY OF KEY POINTS

- WF provides extensive support for Compensating Service Transaction [724].

- Compensation logic needs to be triggered explicitly.

13.5 CASE STUDY EXAMPLE

Most of Standard Mold's repeat customers receive invoices after their order is shipped, but with the increasing automation of processes, the company would also like to offer automated credit card payment.

Standard Mold adds a simple Order Fulfillment service to process payment either through its Invoice service or via the third party Credit Card service. The Order Fulfillment service is implemented as a WF workflow to coordinate shipping, inventory, and payment services (Figure 13.25).

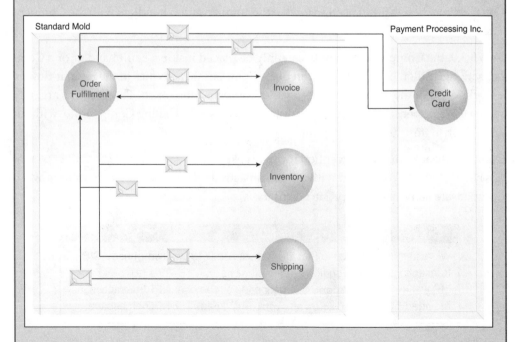

Figure 13.25
The Order Fulfillment service orchestrates internal and external services.

The Order Fulfillment Service orchestrates several local services and a remote service. Figure 13.26 shows how the orchestration first processes orders, and then reduces the inventory to make sure everything is in stock before processing payment and scheduling shipping. Sometimes it may be necessary to undo an operation. The application may call for compensation because the third party Credit Card service denied a customer's credit card, or because a system failure occurs.

Figure 13.26

The Order Fulfillment orchestration handles payments, inventory, and shipping.

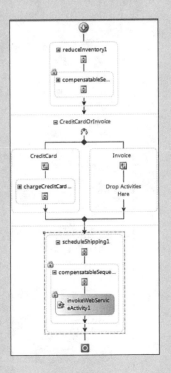

In either case, the orchestration needs to undo the inventory step and add the ordered items back to the inventory. Atomic Service Transaction [713] was not an option because it would limit the scalability of the Order Fulfillment service. Instead, Compensating Service Transaction [724] is applied. The orchestration embeds the interaction with the Inventory service inside a `CompensatableSequence` and invokes a service operation that restocks the ordered items in the compensation handler.

If an exception occurs after the `CompensatableSequence` and the `reduceInventory1` activity completes successfully, the WF runtime automatically invokes the compensation handlers for all completed `Compensatable*` activities.

To enforce the proper compensation behavior for the Credit Card service in all orchestrations, architects wrap the `InvokeWebService` call in a custom activity that consists of a `CompensatableSequence`, calling the Web service and a compensation handler (so that customers are not billed for items that were not delivered).

The compensation logic credits the amount of the charge back to the credit card. With the compensation handler in place within the custom activity, compensation always happens when required. Figure 13.27 shows the main flow of the `ChargeCreditCardActivity` that calls the third party service inside a `CompensatableSequence` activity.

Figure 13.27

The main flow of the `ChargeCreditCard` activity calls the third party credit card service.

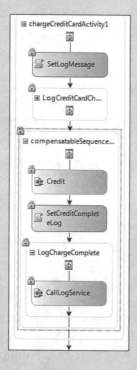

Figure 13.28 shows the `ChargeCreditCard` activity switched to the compensation handler. The activity makes another service call to reverse the charge made to the account and logs the compensation activity.

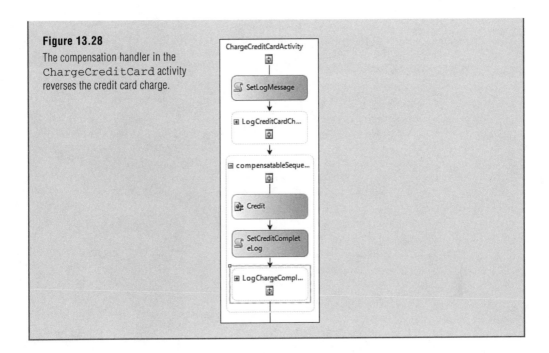

Figure 13.28

The compensation handler in the
`ChargeCreditCard` activity
reverses the credit card charge.

Chapter 14

Orchestration Patterns with BizTalk Server

14.1 Process Abstraction and Orchestrated Task Services

14.2 Process Centralization

14.3 State Repository

14.4 Compensating Service Transaction

SOA PRINCIPLES & PATTERNS REFERENCED IN THIS CHAPTER

- Atomic Service Transaction [713]
- Canonical Schema [718]
- Compensating Service Transaction [724]
- Data Model Transformation [732]
- Event-Driven Messaging [743]
- Functional Decomposition [747]
- Orchestration [758]
- Partial State Deferral [759]
- Process Centralization [763]
- Schema Centralization [769]
- Standardized Service Contract (693)
- State Messaging [784]
- State Repository [785]
- Stateful Services [786]
- Validation Abstraction [792]

With BizTalk Server you can use an orchestration to act as a coordinator for any invoked services, and maintain state information for the overall process. Orchestrations contain the constructs required for transactional semantics as well as compensation, and use the BizTalk host to provide other services such as persistence, failover and tracking.

Unlike WF, which can exist as a server-side or client-side orchestration engine, BizTalk Server is a standalone server product. This chapter specifically explores BizTalk from a patterns perspective in relation to the Orchestration [758] compound pattern (Figure 14.1). It is worth noting that there are several additional features provided by BizTalk that are relevant to the overall topic of orchestration (such as the business rules engine and message correlation) that are not covered in this chapter.

> **NOTE**
>
> This chapter assumes you are familiar with BizTalk Server and the topics covered in Chapter 7. Chapter 15 continues coverage with further topics pertaining to BizTalk features relevant to the enterprise service bus.

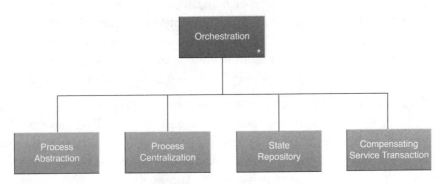

Figure 14.1
The Orchestration [758] compound pattern hierarchy.

14.1 Process Abstraction and Orchestrated Task Services

The encapsulation of BizTalk-defined orchestrations within orchestrated task services is straight forward when compared to WF. BizTalk orchestrations can be constructed for either synchronous or asynchronous invocation. From an orchestration design and implementation perspective, the specifics of how the process will be invoked at runtime are not relevant at design-time, as we are only concerned with the calling message which is done through logical ports.

These logical ports are bound after deployment to physical ports, such as Web services, and it is that binding that will establish the link between the logical design and the physical transport layer. In addition, it is possible to bind more than one physical receive location to a single physical receive port, which enables service invocation in more than one way.

There are several methods by which a BizTalk-hosted orchestration can be invoked:

- bind it through the BizTalk administration tool

- expose the orchestration as a service

- direct-bound messaging through the MessageBox

- start the orchestration via an asynchronous operation (invoking the orchestration from another already-running orchestration)

- call the orchestration using a synchronous operation (invoking the orchestration from another already-running orchestration)

Calling one orchestration from another orchestration will put additional load on the BizTalk infrastructure because additional subscriptions are created in the background. This may or may not be a problem depending on factors such as what the other processes are doing, the current processing volume, and so on. Calling the orchestration via a service means that you are further adding to the overhead of the service call.

Direct-bound messaging through the MessageBox is an approach whereby you use the administrative tooling to bind an orchestration to a receive port. Even though it feels like you are hard wiring them together, behind the scenes, you are just creating a subscription link. The publish-and-subscribe mechanism works by creating and filling these subscriptions. When a new message arrives in the MessageBox, a message agent looks for subscribers and sends the message to any endpoints that have subscriptions. Subscriptions may have been set up in several ways, including:

- binding an orchestration to a receive port

- having a correlated receive waiting for a message

- creating a send port with a filter condition that matches something about the message (type, receive point, value of a routable property, etc.)

Direct binding through the MessageBox allows you to implement loosely coupled solutions in BizTalk by leveraging the underlying publish-and-subscribe mechanism. If a service needs to send a message to another service, rather than doing it directly, it publishes a message to the MessageBox with a metadata key or message property. An appropriate subscriber will then pick up that message based on the common metadata.

Conceptually, this is a state machine. A message with a certain state is published, and any process that is listening for that state picks up the message. This can also be considered an application of the Event-Driven Messaging [743] pattern, where the publication of a message is considered an event, and when a subscriber picks it up, that subscriber is effectively the event handler.

This architectural approach promotes the decomposition of processes into stateless subprocesses, thereby reinforcing the Functional Decomposition [747] pattern and several other patterns that apply to service-orientation when carrying out the separation of concerns.

Orchestrated Task Service Contracts

BizTalk Server supports the creation of orchestrated task service contracts. The part of the contract most emphasized within BizTalk orchestrations is the data model. For example, when defining Web services, we are primarily concerned with XML schemas, instead of XML schemas plus WSDL definitions.

The reasoning behind this is to support a broader range of transport protocols beyond SOAP and HTTP, and allow for the application of the Canonical Schema [718] pattern on a consistent basis as part of the design and development of orchestrations.

Canonical Schema [718] ensures that common schemas are standardized. In BizTalk Server, standardized XML schemas can be positioned to dictate how messages are processed because it requires that XML schemas be developed prior to being mapped and consumed by the orchestration engine. BizTalk provides a built-in schema editor that can be used to design and maintain standardized schema definitions.

Orchestration participants can be required to apply Canonical Schema [718] together with Schema Centralization [769] in order to share standardized schemas with services pulled into the automation of a given business process. In compliance with Schema Centralization [769], XML messages obtained from the receive pipeline or services must conform to the same XML schemas used in the business process design.

You can simply add an existing XML schema definition file to your BizTalk project and bind XML Schema types to incoming and outgoing ports to designate them as the messages that flow through the orchestration.

> **NOTE**
>
> In cases where Canonical Schema [718] is not applied to its full extent (or when enabling communication across domain service inventory boundaries) you can then further define any necessary XML transformations with the schema mapping tool. This then results in the application of Data Model Transformation [732].

Let's briefly cover how you can incorporate Web service contracts with XML schemas using BizTalk and Visual Studio tools.

You can import WSDL contracts through the Add Web Reference feature of Visual Studio. In this case, you can choose to keep the service endpoint location from the WSDL definition, or you can substitute a URL and other service binding information.

If you choose to deploy your BizTalk orchestration as a Web service (effectively creating an orchestrated task service), the BizTalk deployment tools rely on a separate Web services publishing tool to create the Web service in code. You can either select the Web Service Publishing Wizard from the Tools menu in Visual Studio or you can run it directly from the BizTalk Server group in the Start menu.

The wizard publishes an ASMX service that receives messages and passes them on to the BizTalk orchestration engine. The operations from the published port are converted into operations on the published service. The operation name remains as the name of the method decorated with the `WebMethod` or `OperationContract` attributes. The schema type of the port from the orchestration turns into the method's parameter. Visual Studio can also retrieve the ASMX service's WSDL contract and generate the proxy classes to consume the service.

BizTalk further provides the ability to validate incoming and outgoing messages against XML schemas before they are processed by the orchestration. This goes beyond the capabilities of ASMX or WCF and allows for the application of Validation Abstraction [792] so that targeted validation logic can be applied to optimize runtime processing.

The WCF `DataContractSerializer` has some basic message validation capabilities via attributes that are attached to service operations. However, none of them enforce schema constructs as particles, nor do they enforce element cardinality or additional element content or specialized schema constructs, such as `xsd:choice`. These limitations will inhibit the extent to which you can apply Canonical Schema [718], as you may not be able to use all of the features you want from the XML Schema Definition Language.

If your orchestrated services process messages that contain this type of content, the `XML-ReceivePipeline` for the `ReceiveLocation` allows you to specify which schemas to use for validation. Validating outgoing messages requires a custom Message Inspector, which can be built with Visual Studio.

NOTE

Detailed guidance about XML schema validation is available at:
msdn.microsoft.com/en-us/library/cc949095.aspx

WS-* Support

Although BizTalk Server represents a significantly scoped and, at times, all encompassing platform, there are opportunities to leverage its support for open industry standards in order to gain a measure of platform independence.

The entire BizTalk architecture embraces XML at its core. You can publish orchestrations as ASMX Web services using the BizTalk Web service Publishing Tool. It is up to you to ensure compliance of resulting service contracts to the design standards you are applying to all services within a given service inventory (as per the requirements of the Standardized Service Contract (693) principle) and any further standards you may be working with (such as WS-I BasicProfile, for example).

Having an orchestration published as a Web service allows you to leverage other Web service industry standards supported by BizTalk, including:

- MTOM
- WS-Policy
- WS-Policy Attachments
- WS-Metadata Exchange
- SOAP (including Message Security Username Token Profile 1.0, X.509 Token Profile 1.0, and Kerberos Token Profile 1.1)
- WS-Addressing
- WS-SecureConversation
- WS-Trust
- WS-ReliableMessaging

- WS-AtomicTransaction

- WS-Coordination

Support for several of these industry standards resulted from the integration of WCF with BizTalk Server 2006. The WCF Adapter for BizTalk 2006 R2 allowed orchestrations to send or receive messages via all standard or custom WCF bindings.

SUMMARY OF KEY POINTS

- BizTalk provides support for the creation and standardization of orchestrated task service contracts.

- BizTalk supports WSDL, XML Schema, and a number of additional WS-* industry standards.

CASE STUDY EXAMPLE

A project team with Superior Stamping has chosen to expose the Order Fulfillment orchestration as an ASMX Web service. The orchestration receives three different message types grouped into the `OrderFulfillmentPort`, as shown in Figure 14.2.

Figure 14.2
The port definition for the Order Fulfillment orchestration defines three asynchronous operations.

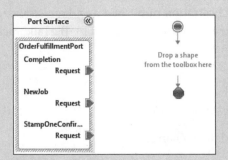

The BizTalk Web services Publishing Wizard is used to create a Web service with three service operations from the port definition. Figure 14.3 shows the summary page for the ASMX service.

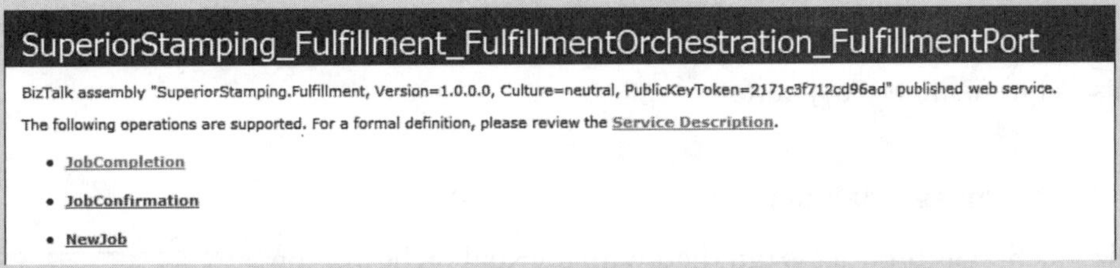

```
SuperiorStamping_Fulfillment_FulfillmentOrchestration_FulfillmentPort

BizTalk assembly "SuperiorStamping.Fulfillment, Version=1.0.0.0, Culture=neutral, PublicKeyToken=2171c3f712cd96ad" published web service.
The following operations are supported. For a formal definition, please review the Service Description.

  • JobCompletion

  • JobConfirmation

  • NewJob
```

Figure 14.3
The ASMX infrastructure provides a Web service summary page for the port from Figure 14.3.

The created Web service embeds the request type from each of the three one-way operations in another XML element with the name of the operation. For example, an XML document for the request of the JobCompletion operation, as defined by the BizTalk message schema, may be created as follows:

```
<Completion xmlns=
  "http://SuperiorStamping.Fulfillment.JobCompletion">
  <OrderId xmlns="...">
    o-1234
  </OrderId>
  <CompletedAt xmlns="...">
    2011-10-16
  </CompletedAt>
</Completion>
```

Example 14.1

Publishing the port as a Web service adds a JobCompletion element around the message, as shown here:

```
<soap:Body>
  <JobCompletion xmlns=
    "http:// SuperiorStamping.Fulfillment/Service">
    <Completion xmlns=
      "http://SuperiorStamping.Fulfillment.JobCompletion">
      <OrderId xmlns="...">
        o-1234
      </OrderId>
      <CompletedAt xmlns="...">
        2011-10-16
      </CompletedAt>
    </Completion>
  </JobCompletion>
</soap:Body>
```

Example 14.2

14.2 Process Centralization

This section highlights centralized process logic definition and governance, as per the Process Centralization [763] pattern.

Centralized Process Maintenance

The BizTalk Server product is bundled with a visual orchestration designer tool that can be used to model business process logic as executable orchestrations. The tool includes several shapes (Figure 14.4) that represent business process steps. From within each shape, .NET assemblies can be invoked. The internal orchestration logic can be exported to (or imported from) WS-BPEL-compliant markup code.

As described in Chapter 13, WF can be used to enable workflow logic that incorporates human involvement. Orchestration capabilities in BizTalk Server, however, are focused only on system-to-system communication via automated business processes. The ability to integrate people into the business process is not supported natively by BizTalk Server.

One way to still incorporate human interaction into BizTalk-controlled business process logic is by using InfoPath and SharePoint technologies. InfoPath forms are XML documents that have two additional XML processing instructions:

- an indication that it is an InfoPath form

- the name of the InfoPath template to use for rendering the XML document

Figure 14.4

The BizTalk toolbox contains shapes to build orchestrations.

SharePoint form libraries can store InfoPath forms. By using the SharePoint adapter, BizTalk can write messages out to a SharePoint site as InfoPath forms that human users can then interact with. The forms can be constructed so that they have a submit process that re-enters an appropriately designed running business process, or perhaps triggers a new business process.

Typically, this submit process will entail writing the document back to a SharePoint library with a given state (for example, a state column at the SharePoint level with a value of "approved") and then having a BizTalk poll (a SharePoint view) set to filter by that state.

By adopting this approach we can actually decouple the act of human intervention from the processing logic within the BizTalk orchestration. This makes human intervention an asynchronous operation that can occur even if the BizTalk environment is not available or is set to only retrieve intervened messages on a scheduled basis.

WS-BPEL Support

Since the 2004 version, BizTalk Server has supported WS-BPEL 1.1 via the import and export of WS-BPEL process definitions. However, there are some limitations, as explained in the following two sections.

Exporting BizTalk Orchestrations to WS-BPEL

Configuring an orchestration for export is a matter of setting the Exportable property to "True," setting the orchestration's Module property to "Exportable," and by further specifying some XML namespaces (Figure 14.5).

Figure 14.5

The Module Exportable and Orchestration Exportable properties must be set to True and XML Namespaces must be defined for Module and Orchestration to configure an orchestration to enable WS-BPEL export.

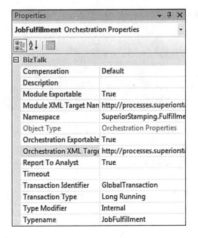

With these configurations in place, BizTalk will emit compiler errors as shown in Figure 14.6 to enforce WS-BPEL compliance when the orchestration project is built.

While configuring WS-BPEL compliance is relatively straightforward, developing actual WS-BPEL orchestrations can be challenging because some of the core functions and primary tools in BizTalk simply do not support the WS-BPEL language.

	Description	File	Line	Column	Project	
⊗ 11	'transform' statement is not permitted under BPEL4WS compliance	JobFulfillment.odx	654	44		
⊗ 12	'transform' statement is not permitted under BPEL4WS compliance	JobFulfillment.odx	663	44		
⊗ 13	'transform' statement is not permitted under BPEL4WS compliance	JobFulfillment.odx	687	44		
⊗ 14	operator 'new' is not permitted under BPEL4WS compliance	JobFulfillment.odx	702	20		
⊗ 15	'xpath(Message_4.NewJobResult, "string(//*[local-name()='JobId']/text())")': xpath(...) construct must occur standalone in an expression under BPEL4WS compliance	JobFulfillment.odx	704	23		
⊗ 16	'System.Diagnostics.Debug.WriteLine': a reference to a member of a .NET type is not permitted under BPEL4WS compliance	JobFulfillment.odx	718	60		

Figure 14.6

The BizTalk compiler reports non-WS-BPEL-compliant constructs as errors.

For example, you must code message assignments and data transformations by hand with XPath expressions instead of creating data transformation rules with the graphical data mapping tool. A single transformation, such as the map in Figure 14.7, will require an XPath-based assignment in an Expression shape.

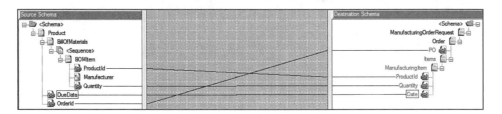

Figure 14.7

The BizTalk data mapper provides a graphical environment to develop message transformations from the source schema on the left into the target schema on the right.

The assignment from the OrderId element on the left to the PO element on the right would read as follows:

```
xpath( StampOneNewOrderMessage.ManufacturingOrderRequest,
/*[local-name()='ManufacturingOrderRequest' and namespace-
uri()='http://StampOne.Fulfillment.ServiceContracts/2006/10']/*
[local-name()='Order' and namespace-uri()='http://StampOne.
Fulfillment.ServiceContracts/2006/10']/*[local-name()='PO' and
namespace-uri()='http://StampOne.Fulfillment.DataTypes/2006/10']" ) =
xpath( JobMessage, /*[local-name()='Product' and namespace-
uri()='http://SuperiorStamping.Fulfillment/ServiceTypes/2006/10']/*
[local-name()='OrderId' and namespace-uri()='http://
SuperiorStamping.Fulfillment/ServiceTypes/2006/10']/text() );
```

Example 14.3

Note that the XPath expression in Example 14.3 only represents one of the mappings in the map from Figure 14.6. Moreover, it is just a direct assignment without any transformation or combination of values. You can improve the readability of the assignments by promoting message elements to properties, but even that can get out of hand when dealing with schemas that have several data items. It can get more complex when using looping. For example, because the XPath language has no way to express loops or iterations, you need to code them as part of your process flow. This reduces readability and maintainability of the orchestration.

A better, more maintainable approach is to provide a simple transformation service or intermediary processing layer that performs Data Model Transformation [732]. The former approach will build an agnostic utility service that can front-end BizTalk transformations to take advantage of its powerful data mapping capabilities. Or, it can be based on XSLT if the service needs to produce output that's not always XML-based. Figure 14.8 and Figure 14.9 show the difference in the architecture with and without a transformation service.

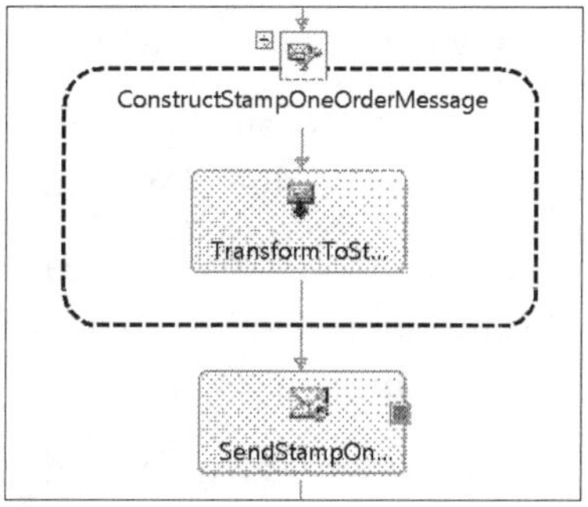

Figure 14.8

The Transformation shape does not export to BPEL.

Figure 14.9

Service calls to a transformation are WS-BPEL-compliant, but add complexity compared to Figure 14.8.

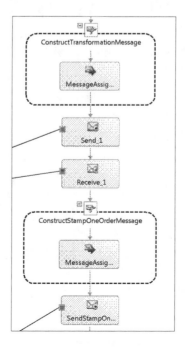

The approach of placing all non-WS-BPEL-compliant features behind Web service interfaces supports service orientation principles and allows for truly portable processes while still taking advantage of the BizTalk toolset. Still, there are significant tradeoffs to consider when evaluating WS-BPEL compliance:

- execution times are longer if the orchestration has to call external services, such as a transformation service, instead of performing the operations in-process

- BPEL compliance adds complexity to orchestrations, thereby increasing development, test, and maintenance efforts

- externalized, autonomous services may provide a greater level of agility because they can be altered without requiring changes to the orchestration

- each autonomous service increases complexity of the architecture (Each service introduces another point of failure, requires monitoring, maintenance, and possibly dedicated servers.)

- each service call adds load to the network infrastructure

Importing WS-BPEL Processes into BizTalk

Importing is slightly easier because you are not required to make architectural decisions when you import a BPEL compliant orchestration.

To import a WS-BPEL process definition, you need to convert the WS-BPEL code by creating a new BizTalk project of type *BizTalk Server BPEL Import Project* in the New Project dialog (Figure 14.10).

BizTalk will walk you through a wizard that allows you to identify the process to import the WSDL definition for the process itself and the WSDL and XML Schema definitions for the orchestrated processes.

SUMMARY OF KEY POINTS

- BizTalk Server provides visual tools for the centralized maintenance of executable process definition logic.

- BizTalk Server provides import and export support for the WS-BPEL industry standard.

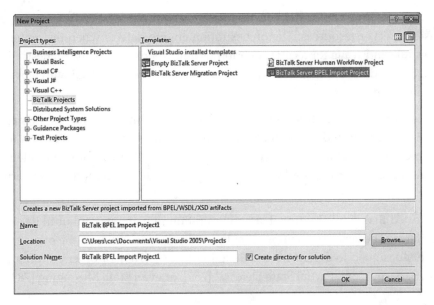

Figure 14.10
BizTalk defines a special project type to import orchestrations in WS-BPEL format.

14.3 State Repository

Microsoft's BizTalk Server manages orchestration state in much the same way as WF, except that state management is not extensible or configurable. BizTalk Server always stores the state of an orchestration in a SQL Server database to ensure durable and scalable storage (Figure 14.11). This results in a natural application of State Repository [785], a pattern that is used for a range of state deferral options.

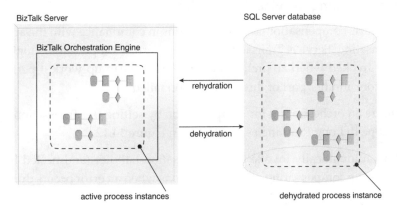

Figure 14.11
The state management mechanism provided by BizTalk Server behaves the same way as its WF counterpart, but appears simpler because the mechanics are abstracted by the BizTalk platform.

The BizTalk runtime engine dehydrates idle orchestration instances whenever possible to conserve server resources. The orchestration engine detects when the orchestration becomes idle and waits for a certain period of time, then persists the orchestration into the SQL Server database and frees up any server resources associated with that instance of the fulfillment process.

BizTalk rehydrates an orchestration when it receives a message for the orchestration instance giving it an indication that it's time to resume processing. For this to work, BizTalk needs to be able to identify data in a message that can uniquely identify the orchestration instance to rehydrate. For this purpose, it is common to use correlation types.

It is expected that, while hydrated, an orchestration remains stateful until its execution is completed. The services composed by the orchestration logic, on the other hand, are preferably designed to defer state via State Repository [785], or other patterns, such as Stateful Services [786], Partial State Deferral [759], or even State Messaging [784].

SUMMARY OF KEY POINTS

- The State Repository [785] pattern is inherently applied within the BizTalk Server platform and is implemented as a SQL Server database.

- BizTalk Server supports different state management and deferral architectures and patterns.

14.4 Compensating Service Transaction

BizTalk supports compensation-style transactions in compliance with the application of the Compensating Service Transaction [724] pattern. Compensation logic generally needs to be invoked when an orchestration needs to clean up work it performed successfully before another part of the orchestration failed.

You configure an orchestration for compensation by setting the Transaction Type property of a Scope to Long Running as illustrated in Figure 14.12.

BizTalk will automatically invoke the compensation handler (and nested handlers) as needed to invoke compensating service operations when an error occurs during the execution of the scope.

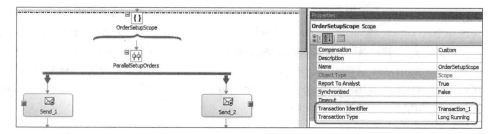

Figure 14.12

A scope's Transaction Type property can be set to compensation-based transactions and ACID transactions.

Just like a catch block behaves as an exception handler in a C# routine, the compensation handler is simply extra logic that is explicitly invoked under certain conditions.

Figure 14.13 shows how each scope can define a separate compensation handler.

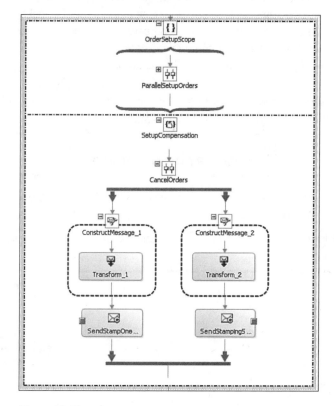

Figure 14.13

The compensation handler on the bottom of a scope executes when the orchestration code inside the scope throws an exception.

The compensation algorithm displayed in Figure 14.13 creates two messages to cancel orders in two other services. Note that when applying Compensating Service Transaction [724], there is no rollback of changes. The most common approach is to equip service contracts with compensating capabilities that correspond to the original capabilities that were executed up until that point (for example, a CreateOrder operation may have a corresponding CancelOrder operation).

NOTE

BizTalk Server also supports the application of Atomic Service Transaction [713] with a two-phase commit protocol. This allows for the ACID transactions to occur within orchestrations and within the scope of broader compensation transactions, if necessary.

For longer-running orchestrations, it is more common to manage exceptions using Compensating Service Transaction [724] because the use of Atomic Service Transaction [713] requires that resources be locked and the original (pre-transaction) state be preserved in order to enable subsequent rollback of changes to the original state.

Prior to the integration of WCF, BizTalk server did not support the WS-AtomicTransaction industry standard. Therefore, BizTalk 2006 and earlier versions could only coordinate transactions across resources where appropriate resource managers are available.

SUMMARY OF KEY POINTS

- BizTalk Server natively provides compensation handles that support the creation of compensating logic.

- BizTalk further supports atomic transactions that can be encompassed by compensations.

CASE STUDY EXAMPLE

Superior Stamping's Order Fulfillment orchestration includes workflow logic in which orders are scheduled with the help of services from two partner organizations: StampOne and Stamping Solutions.

Prior to the actual scheduling of an order, an Allocation service determines which partner should manufacture the parts and build the corresponding bill of materials document. The bill of materials is then passed to the orchestration, which filters it and then dispatches manufacturing jobs accordingly.

The orchestration logic for this process is relatively simple as long as StampOne and Stamping Solutions can manufacture the required quantity of parts by the requested due date. However, should one of these partner organizations be unable to fulfill its commitment, the job needs to be canceled and the entire order needs to be tagged for manual scheduling instead.

Superior Stamping architects determine that the application of Atomic Service Transaction [713] will tightly couple the orchestration and the two services to an extent that is not acceptable due to the critical nature of this process. Instead, they decide to apply Compensating Service Transaction [724] via a solution based on the compensation capabilities of BizTalk.

As shown in Figure 14.14 and Figure 14.15, the two parallel scheduling requests are embedded in a Scope shape with the Transaction Type set to Long Running. The scope also includes a compensation block used to compensate for the failed activities in the scope.

Figure 14.15 shows how the orchestration waits for a response from both services before it exits the Scope. Next, it checks the two responses to see if the jobs were scheduled successfully.

The orchestration throws an exception if the response from either service indicates that it is not able to fulfill the order. BizTalk automatically runs the compensation block displayed in Figure 14.15 because there was no exception handler to catch the exception in the orchestration. The logic inside the compensation block consists of two regular service calls that cancel the order.

Note that the two partner services had to be designed in advance to carry out the compensation logic. Each of the services was given a separate Cancel operation that was invoked in the compensation block.

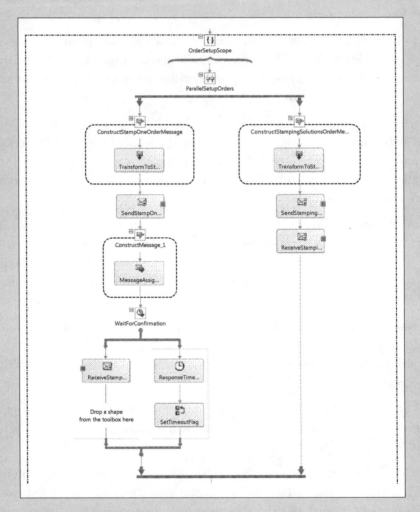

Figure 14.14
The Order Fulfillment orchestration tries to schedule jobs in two services.

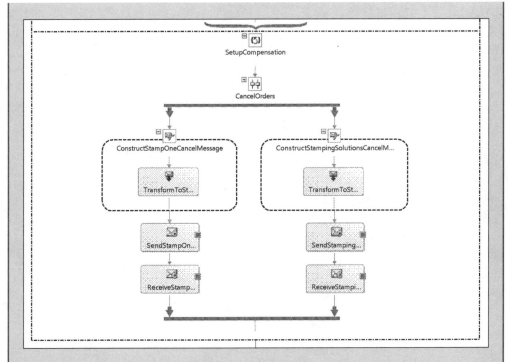

Figure 14.15

The compensation block (technically part of the same orchestration), which provides logic that can reverse and compensate for a failed execution of the primary orchestrated business process.

Part III

Infrastructure and Architecture

Chapter 15: Enterprise Service Bus with BizTalk Server and
        Windows Azure

Chapter 16: Windows Azure Platform AppFabric Service Bus

Chapter 17: SOA Security with .NET and Windows Azure

Chapter 18: Service-Oriented Presentation Layers with .NET

Chapter 19: Service Performance Optimization

Chapter 20: SOA Metrics with BAM

The final set of chapters explore a range of specialized topics that extend and build upon the coverage so far of Microsoft technologies in relation to service-oriented architecture, service-orientation. Unlike the chapters in Parts I and II, these chapters do not use any special style elements to incorporate or highlight design principles or patterns. Service-orientation design principles and SOA design patterns are simply referenced in-line as part of the general body text, wherever appropriate.

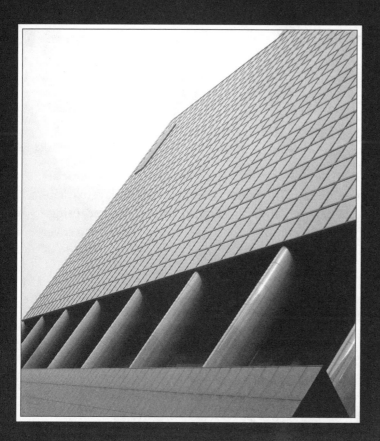

Chapter 15

Enterprise Service Bus with BizTalk Server and Windows Azure

15.1 Microsoft and the ESB

15.2 Integration with BizTalk

15.3 The ESB Toolkit

15.4 Distributed and Scalable ESB Architecture

15.5 Cloud-Enabling the ESB with Windows Azure

15.6 Governance Considerations

15.7 Mapping the Microsoft Platform to the Enterprise Service Bus Pattern

The enterprise service bus (ESB) has become a fundamental part of an enterprise-scale service-oriented solution design. The intermediary processing layers established by contemporary ESB technologies can be positioned to support and bridge communication among on-premise and cloud-based services. In this chapter we cover the Microsoft ESB Toolkit, along with relevant parts of BizTalk Server and Windows Azure.

NOTE

This chapter explores BizTalk Server features and technologies in relation to common characteristics and capabilities of enterprise service bus platforms. If you are not familiar with BizTalk Server, be sure to read the *BizTalk Server* section in Chapter 7 before proceeding. You may also want to look through the orchestration-related coverage of BizTalk Server in Chapter 14.

Note also that the ESB is a primary topic of the book *Modern SOA Infrastructure* as part of the *Prentice Hall Service-Oriented Computing Series from Thomas Erl.* This title covers various architecture and infrastructure topics, including topics that pertain to an ESB reference model and the Enterprise Service Bus [741] compound pattern. Microsoft infrastructure technologies are explored alongside infrastructure platforms from other vendors.

15.1 Microsoft and the ESB

The Enterprise Service Bus concept really took hold in the early 2000s, growing out of the integration middleware space, merging in service-orientation principles along with the increasing popularity of Web services and the emergence and maturation of WS-* specifications.

The term was often a cause for confusion, as different vendors claimed to be offering different types of "ESB products." What actually constituted an enterprise service bus was eventually clarified with the publication of the Enterprise Service Bus [741] pattern in late 2008.

Within the Microsoft community, an ESB was generally not viewed as being a product. Even before the publication of the official Enterprise Service Bus [741] pattern,

Microsoft's view was that the middle tier represented by what was being referred to as enterprise service bus was a form of architectural pattern. From Microsoft's perspective, it offered a certain set of features that could be mapped to the Microsoft technology stack, including WCF and BizTalk Server.

To help clarify this position, Microsoft released the first version of ESB Guidance in late 2006. This publication provided a set of prebuilt components and architectural guidance that explained how to build an ESB with the Microsoft platform. This has since evolved, providing richer functionality with each release, and is now known as the ESB Toolkit.

15.2 Integration with BizTalk

To fully appreciate the purpose and importance of the ESB, we need to understand a bit of the history that led to its creation.

Application Integration 101

In the beginning, we had standalone systems called *silo-based* applications. They created isolated silos of information to address specific, single-purpose automation requirements. They were designed to be self-contained with no need to interact with other applications (Figure 15.1).

Integration at this stage in the evolution meant redundant data entry or some form of file dumping to get information out of one system and into another. The barriers between applications were quite substantial.

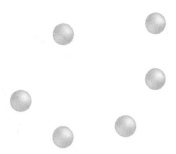

Figure 15.1
Isolated applications without integration.

Next, applications became more tightly bound by means of point-to-point integration channels. Now data could flow more readily between applications, but it turned out that this sort of integration leads to long-term problems, the most notable being the inherent brittleness of the resulting architecture. If either side of a point-to-point integration channel changed its contract, the other would also need to be modified or the integration would cease to function.

Point-to-point integration became increasingly difficult to manage as its proliferation resulted in increasingly large and convoluted enterprise environments (Figure 15.2). In many cases, IT resources would be devoting significant effort and resources to preserving the existing integration architectures, rather than solving new and emerging business requirements. Changes to the integration architectures were inherently difficult and time consuming to accommodate and as the number of connections to a single point increased, versioning that point meant updating an increasing number of integration clients. Versioning and the ultimate decommissioning of integrated applications often led to the need to "rip-and-replace" segments of an enterprise.

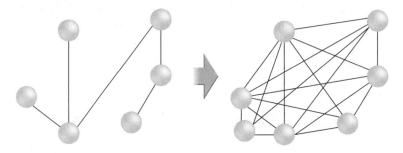

Figure 15.2
Single point-to-point integration leading to complex point-to-point integration over time.

NOTE

It is important to note that silo-based applications and integrated architectures can just as easily be implemented in cloud computing environments (such as Windows Azure) as they can in traditional on-premise environments. Fortunately, the application of service-orientation principles provides us with the opportunity to avoid the mistakes of the past.

Following the point-to-point integration phase, came the advent of messaging-based middleware, event-driven message exchange patterns, and the notion of the hub-and-spoke model. With the resulting integration architecture, a client application sends a message to a central hub that is published to one or more spokes, or message recipients (Figure 15.3).

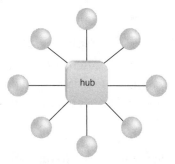

Figure 15.3
The hub and spoke integration model.

The relationship between the publisher and recipients can be defined by configuration, or by using a publish-and-subscribe messaging framework. Following this approach, an application would publish a message that is received by appropriate subscribers.

The two applications involved are naturally loosely coupled because they do not communicate directly with each other, but rather both communicate only with the central hub. Should a third participating application be introduced, it could also subscribe and receive messages and process them without affecting the relationship of the other two applications.

The BizTalk Hub-Bus Model

When BizTalk Server 2004 was released, it took the publish-and-subscribe model a step further into a hybrid model called *hub-bus* that combined the hub-and-spoke model with bus topologies. In a hub-bus model, functionality can be distributed across multiple machines, with multiple hubs sharing a centralized bus (Figure 15.4). As a result, there is no single point of failure. Configuration can be centralized, as are capabilities such as capturing operational and business metrics.

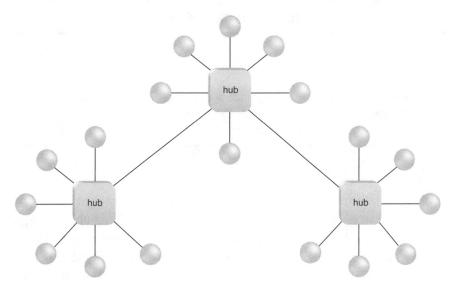

Figure 15.4
The BizTalk hub-bus integration model.

Conceptually, you can think of a BizTalk host as a hub, and all the machines running an instance of that host form a logical hub. The bus encompasses the BizTalk MessageBox (messaging data store) and Management Database (configuration data store), as well as the centralized operational and management capabilities and tools.

From a functionality stratification perspective, a receiving hub combines potentially numerous host instances across multiple machines to provide receiving functionality. After a message is received and stored in the MessageBox, a processing hub picks it up and acts on it. This is an instance of the processing host instance running on a given machine or collection of machines.

This architecture is intended to be scalable in that you can adjust the processing power of a hub by adding more machines and host instances. The MessageBox configuration database and business activity monitoring (BAM) tracking infrastructure use SQL Server databases that can be clustered and made fault tolerant.

However, this architecture did have limitations. For example, it was not possible to geo-distribute the hubs, as they shared a common backend database that introduced network latency. In addition, there was no notion of runtime resolution of artifacts.

SUMMARY OF KEY POINTS

- The repeated creation of silo-based applications led to the creation of point-to-point integration architectures.

- The hub-and-spoke form of integration architecture was introduced by EAI middleware, including BizTalk Server. BizTalk Server further supported a hub-bus variation of this architecture.

15.3 The ESB Toolkit

The ESB Toolkit goes back to 2005 when there was a realization that BizTalk consultants were implementing solutions using similar techniques. The first release of the toolkit grew out of a project to package up this commonality and make it available to the practitioner community. Since that time there has been a steady evolution. The code that is part of the toolkit is treated as product-grade source code, which means it undergoes formal development and testing processes within Microsoft.

The ESB Toolkit now exists as a set of pre-written components, services, and architectural guidance and best practices that extends the capabilities of BizTalk Server by providing the functionality needed to implement the Enterprise Service Bus [741] pattern.

We will shortly look at some of the specific parts of the ESB Toolkit, but first, let's describe the set of core services it natively provides:

- *Resolver service* – This service allows external consumer programs to leverage the resolution mechanism. The Resolver service can be used to abstract service registry access and make it broadly available in a heterogeneous environment.

- *On-ramp service* – This service provides a means for Web service consumers to send messages to the ESB. Web service SOAP headers become message context properties as the message passes through a context setting component in a receive pipeline.

- *Transformation service* – This service allows non-BizTalk applications to access and leverage the BizTalk transformation engine. Specifically, it allows access to all Web service consumers, including those not running on the Microsoft platform.

- *Exception Management service* – By publishing the fault schema using the default BizTalk schema publishing mechanism, this service enables consumers to submit messages so that non-BizTalk (or non-.NET applications) can participate in the ESB exception management scheme (as explained in Chapter 14).

- *BizTalk Operations service* – This service returns information about the current state of BizTalk artifacts.

These core services are available as orchestrations and helper classes, and are also exposed as Web services.

It is important to note that the ESB Toolkit does not in any way change the way that BizTalk works. A lot of the parts of a BizTalk implementation rely on configuration settings. These configuration settings are typically set at development or post-deployment phases. The ESB Toolkit adds the runtime resolution capabilities required for custom, dynamic processing. For example, many global context properties are created for you when a message is constructed or received. The ESB Toolkit uses context properties to house the metadata it needs to operate on a message as it goes through its lifecycle within the ESB.

Just as BizTalk builds on the functionality of the .NET framework and WCF, the ESB Toolkit introduces building blocks layered upon BizTalk Server itself (Figure 15.5).

Working our way through the layers in Figure 15.5 from the top down, the upcoming sections cover these parts of the ESB Toolkit.

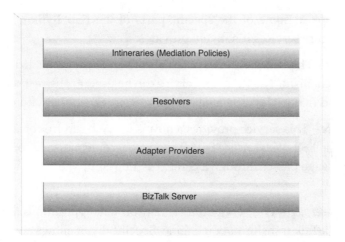

Figure 15.5

The itineraries describe a message flow, the itinerary components make it happen. The resolvers process dynamic runtime lookups and adapter providers are the bridge between .NET and BizTalk adapters, allowing you to take settings that were dynamically determined and apply them with the BizTalk adapters.

Itineraries

The lifecycle of a message inside the BizTalk ESB environment is controlled by *itineraries*. At the simplest level, an itinerary can be thought of as the series of processing steps that are applied to a message.

For example:

1. Receive message.

2. Apply map to message.

3. Send message.

Itineraries can be considered a form of microflow, meaning that they can be used as a lightweight form of service composition. The notion of an itinerary (when classified as a microflow) is not to contain a great deal of business, compensation, and complex branching logic. For that, we have established service composition and orchestration technologies. The goal and appropriate use of an itinerary is to represent a simple series of steps that do not necessarily constitute an entire business process.

The metadata envelope (`Microsoft.Practices.ESB.Itinerary.Schemas.System_ Properties`) contains properties that are related to flow control of messages through the use of itineraries, as shown in Table 15.1.

Property	Description
ServiceName	the name of the service to be invoked (this will typically form part of a message subscription)
ServiceState	current message state generally used as part of a message subscription (examples include "pending," "in process," and "complete")
CurrentServicePosition	an index indicating which step is currently being processed
IsRequestResponse	used to indicate whether a response should be returned
ServiceType	the execution context (for example, it may determine whether a given step should be executed as part of pipeline processing or by an orchestration)
ItineraryHeader	contains the entire itinerary content
ItineraryName	name of the itinerary
ItineraryVersion	version of the itinerary
ItineraryGuid	unique identifier for the itinerary

Table 15.1
Property settings for itineraries.

The ServiceName and ServiceState will typically be used to define a subscription. For example, a subscription may be based on logic such as: "Send me all messages that are of type Order that have a ServiceName of OrderProcess and a ServiceState of pending."

Message publishers (either the service sending messages to the bus, or the proxy that receives the message and puts it on the bus, or the receive pipeline through which the message flows) will set these properties, and then filters on subscribers will use it to determine if a message should be picked up. With this technique, publishers and subscribers are completely autonomous. If you would like to introduce a new subscriber to an existing message flow, it can be deployed and start processing the messages without any need to modify (or even notify) the publishing service.

An itinerary can be comprised of a set of services that need to be invoked in order to process a message. These services can be activated in one of two execution contexts: in the messaging layer or in an orchestration. In either case, when the service completes its logic, it is expected to have advanced the itinerary to the next step. This means the current step is effectively removed to make the next step the current step. It is essentially a stack, with a linear flow of states.

This may seem like a sequential flow, but it doesn't need to be. For example, nothing would prevent multiple agents from listening for the same subscription properties, which would result in a parallel branch in the message flow.

In addition, the starting itinerary may not be the same itinerary that stays with a message throughout the message's lifecycle. One agent may perform an operation on a message and may completely replace its existing itinerary with a new itinerary. This can occur, for example, if an error condition is encountered.

Within the ESB Toolkit, a message's entire itinerary is serialized and stored in the `ItineraryHeader` context property of that message. In order for BizTalk's routing engine to have visibility and to be able to fulfill subscriptions, parts of the current itinerary step are de-normalized and kept in context properties.

Itineraries Types

There are three ways that itineraries can be specified:

- *server-side* – Itineraries can be stored in and retrieved from a centralized repository. There are several ways in which this can be done.

- *client-side hybrid* – In this scenario, the client makes some calls into the ESB infrastructure (for example, resolving an endpoint address) and then constructs an itinerary. The itinerary is then stored in SOAP headers and the message is sent in to the on-ramp.

- *client-side* – Here, the client constructs the itinerary that is stored in SOAP headers. The message is then sent in to the on-ramp.

It should be noted that the client-side and client-side hybrid options are generally less desirable as they put a lot of responsibility on the service consumer to specify what will happen to the message as it is being processed. While in some situations this may be acceptable, it can result in a fairly brittle messaging framework that further introduces responsibilities pertaining to updates and versioning.

The server-side option provides a single source of truth for itineraries (the repository), and relieves service consumers of any responsibility around message processing. They simply send in their messages. In addition, this approach can be used with any transport, as there is no specific reliance on SOAP headers.

The Itinerary Lifecycle

As shown in Figure 15.6, an itinerary is initially created using a visual design surface inside Visual Studio (although itineraries exist as XML, meaning they can also be created in code). The itinerary is then exported either as XML (possibly for migration to other environments) or to the itinerary repository (most likely SQL Server).

At runtime, a message is received at an ESB on-ramp and an itinerary is selected. The itinerary is then applied to the message, meaning the details of the itinerary are added to the message context properties. The message then continues on into the ESB for further processing.

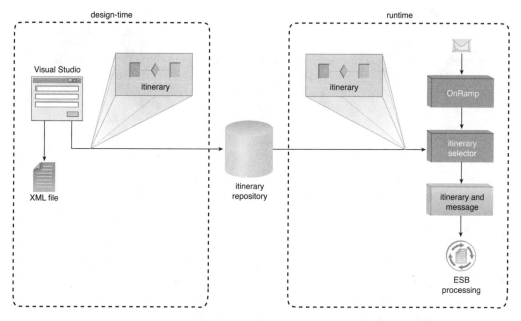

Figure 15.6

An example scenario showing an itinerary, from design-time creation to runtime utilization.

For the actual selection, we use an itinerary selector pipeline (a pipeline that includes an itinerary selector pipeline component that is included with the ESB Toolkit) in the receive location. We then look up the itinerary in the itinerary repository. In the properties of that component, we need to specify a resolver string.

Typically we would do so by using one of the following resolver strings:

- STATIC:// – We hard code the value to be looked up using this static resolver string that specifies which itinerary to use. This puts in a static reference in the itinerary allowing the flow to be changed by updating the itinerary without the need to change the receive location properties.

- `BRI://` – We use this resolver string to query the business rules engine. This allows us to change which itinerary is selected by changing a business rule without changes to code.

Note that resolvers are explained in the next section. The message receipt flow is as shown in Figure 15.7.

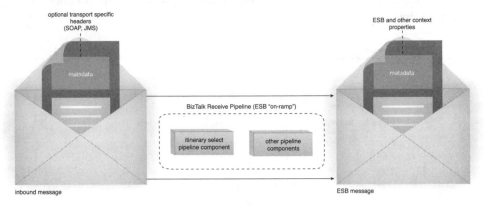

Figure 15.7

Messages exchanged via the itinerary pipeline and the use of resolvers.

Resolvers

Some parts of an ESB infrastructure require the dynamic runtime resolution of values, namely those parts that involve dynamic message routing and transformation. This type of functionality has been abstracted into a series of pre-built components called *resolvers* that are invoked at pre-defined points in a message's lifecycle.

It is the responsibility of the resolver to determine a set of values needed for a runtime query and to then execute this query against an appropriate metadata store. A common example is the UDDI resolver, which is used to query a UDDI registry and return an endpoint location. However, resolvers are not just about endpoints. They can be used to resolve other artifacts, such as maps or itineraries.

Resolvers included with the ESB Toolkit for endpoint resolution include UDDI 2.0, UDDI 3.0, WS-MEX, Static, BRE, and XPath. Resolvers provided for artifact resolution include Static, Static (for itineraries), SQL Server, Composite, BRE (for maps), and BRE (for itineraries).

Resolvers represent one of several extensibility points within the ESB Toolkit. Should you require, for example, endpoint resolution to occur against a custom registry, you can create and register a new resolver.

Resolution can occur as part of the execution of an itinerary or the components can also be invoked programmatically.

Typically, resolution will occur at one of two points:

- when a message is received, if it has some properties that we know will lead to a resolution requirement (for example, the message is routed, but the endpoint address is not yet defined)

- at the last possible moment (just in time or JIT resolution), before a specified operation is performed (for example, if a message is about to be transformed but we don't yet know the map type)

It is possible that resolution can fail when a message is first received. This may occur because a process has not yet run that would provide that information. A resolution failure at this stage is non-fatal because the operation that requires the information is not about to be performed. In addition, as is the case with long-running processes, the location of an endpoint could change from the time the process starts to the time we invoke the service. By using JIT resolution, we are not affected by changes in endpoint location during process execution.

However, if the JIT resolution of an endpoint fails, it is a fatal error because the operation in question would be the next thing that needs to occur and the failure means that we are missing a piece of information required to proceed.

In this scenario, items that require resolution are:

- endpoint addresses

- endpoint configuration information

- map types

Resolution can be performed by querying a variety of sources, for example:

- UDDI

- BizTalk Rules Engine

- XPath into the message itself

- hard coded resolution logic specified through post-deployment configuration (not in code)

- a custom assembly that implements the `IResolver` interface

The last option allows you to effectively extend the resolution mechanism by creating custom assemblies that perform custom actions, such as invoking a Web service or querying a database to perform the resolution.

The resolution mechanism itself is exposed as a Web service although, for performance reasons, the internal ESB components make direct calls to it. Exposure via a Web service contract allows other parties to call directly into the resolution mechanism, if required.

Adapter Providers

The itinerary components provided by the ESB Toolkit exist as .NET components. When resolution is performed by a resolver, a .NET Dictionary object is returned. However, when we go to set adapter properties that will be required for messaging, we need to work with BizTalk adapters, which cannot accept Dictionary objects. *Adapter providers* form a bridge, taking the appropriate values from the Dictionary object and setting the corresponding adapter properties.

The adapter providers provided by the ESB Toolkit include: WCF-BasicHttp, WCF-WsHttp, WCF-Custom, FTP, File, SMTP, and MQSeries. It is worth noting that there are actually fewer adapter providers than there are adapters. This does not mean that the other adapters cannot participate in ESB-based messaging exchanges; it simply means that to use adapters without adapter providers will require a hybrid solution (such as using a static send port subscribing to a specific `ServiceName/ServiceState` combination).

You do not invoke adapter providers explicitly; they are invoked as part of the resolution process. If the resolver connection string contains an `EndPointConfiguration` attribute, it will be populated by the resolution component with a dictionary of name/value pairs. When the resolution process ends (if this attribute is present and populated) the adapter manager will instantiate the appropriate adapter provider. The adapter provider will then iterate through the Dictionary object, setting appropriate properties in the message context that will ultimately be used by the dynamic off-ramp when the message is transmitted.

WCF-Custom and REST Services

Communication with REST services raises specific considerations, for which several architectural options exist. For example:

- From the receiving side, you can expose a REST service that uses the PUT method to submit data to the service. The service would then act as a relay by submitting data into BizTalk as a message. You could do so by interacting with the helper components or core services provided by the ESB Toolkit and directly submitting the message using the direct submit approach, or by invoking a WCF on-ramp service.

- From the sending side (invoking the REST service), you have several options. You can programmatically call a REST service from a helper class and invoke it from an expression shape in an orchestration, but this circumvents the publish-and-subscribe mechanism, and means any changes you make need to be code-level changes.

The WCF-Custom adapter provider opens the door to working with adapters that are part of the BizTalk Adapter Pack, as well as with any other WCF bindings that may be available. Specifically, this adapter provider can be helpful for enabling communication with REST services. You can use the WCF-Custom adapter provider in conjunction with the WebHttpBinding to enable communication directly with REST services. Note that when following this approach with the GET method, you will need to implement a custom behavior.

SUMMARY OF KEY POINTS

- The ESB Toolkit provides a series of pre-built components and services that act as building blocks for extending the native BizTalk Server platform into a fully functional enterprise service bus.

- While the ESB Toolkit builds upon the BizTalk Server platform, it does not change any existing BizTalk capabilities.

- Key layers of building blocks established by the ESB Toolkit include itineraries, resolvers, and adapter providers.

15.4 Distributed and Scalable ESB Architecture

So far in this chapter we have covered ESB capabilities that are built on top of BizTalk Server. To better understand how we can expand this type of architecture, we need to look further under the hood where we can see that, to a large extent, the BizTalk platform is built upon SQL Server, with much of it implemented as a series of stored procedures.

Configuring for High-Availability

From a scalability standpoint, this can be beneficial because it enables us to leverage SQL Server's high-availability SQL clusters. Specifically, the minimal configuration for us to establish a high-availability BizTalk infrastructure would consist of:

- two BizTalk servers (Enterprise Edition)
- one SQL Server cluster (preferably with a fast SAN as a storage subsystem)

This would result in an architecture similar to what is illustrated in Figure 15.8.

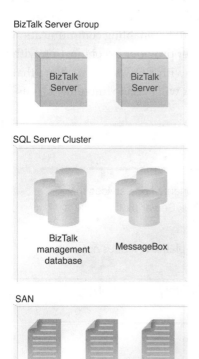

Figure 15.8

A simple high-availability BizTalk infrastructure.

Techniques for Scaling

The Enterprise edition of BizTalk Server is self-clustering, in as much as it shares configuration information that is stored in a common management database. New servers join a group, and start participating in the workload. As a best practice, all servers have the identical configuration, with the same items deployed to the local GACs. Processing can be partitioned by controlling host instance and having only certain host instances running on certain machines.

In the BizTalk administrative tool, a host is a definition of a service. Many of the features of BizTalk message processing, such as throttling and threading, are defined at the host level. A host instance is a Windows Service process that is an instance of the host type running on one or more servers. Multiple instances of a host are used to add processing power (horizontal scaling) and ensure high availability. Only one instance of a specific host is allowed on a BizTalk Server. Note that host instances can be defined on many or all of the BizTalk Servers and enabled or disabled as appropriate to loading conditions.

This partitioning means that you can (for example) have certain machines that are dedicated to receiving messages, others that only send, and still others that only run transformation services. This approach allows you to scale specific partitions as needs evolve and requirements change.

The Systems Center Operations Manager Management Pack for BizTalk Server provides further visibility into the health and activities occurring on the server. Using Operations Manager, it is possible to script compensations to events. For example, if you have two BizTalk Servers running a receiving host instance, and you suddenly receive a surge of messages that stress the servers, you can script a compensating action that starts that host instance on other machines. Most small and medium enterprises will never need to go to this extreme; however, it's reassuring to know that you have the ability to construct adaptive networks that will respond to changing needs and that you can enable services dynamically on an as-required basis.

An example of a high-availability and scalable architecture is shown in Figure 15.9. By studying this diagram we can identify multiple receive hosts behind a load balance that distributes HTTP traffic. Because BizTalk nodes are self-clustering in groups, the load balancer does not affect the nodes. It is strictly there for the Web service.

NOTE
This aforementioned scenario becomes more interesting when incorporating the Windows Azure Service Bus, as explored later in this chapter.

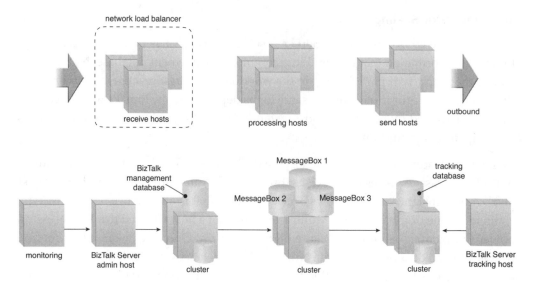

Figure 15.9
High-Availability Infrastructure Diagram (scaled-out sample)

Should there be load pressure over time, more machines can be added to the various BizTalk groups, either dynamically or in advance, to accommodate anticipated usage surges and increased workloads. For example, more processing hosts can be added to accommodate complex processing.

To complete a high-availability BizTalk infrastructure, disaster recovery can be implemented through a combination of the BizTalk backup jobs and log shipping. "Complete" high-availability needs highly-available installations to be mirrored in separate (and geographically separated) data centers, with log shipping being performed through a high-speed connection. You can have high-availability in a given data center, but should there be a catastrophic event that disables the data center, you would need to fail over to the other data center.

Distributed ESBs

No discussion of ESBs would be complete without touching on the topic of distributed (or federated) ESBs. The notion here is that although you already have distributed services within an ESB, you may have additional ESBs within your enterprise, perhaps each in a separate domain service inventory or several within the same service inventory.

Regardless of the stratification reason, the existence of distributed ESB implementations will result in a need to flow messages across ESB boundaries. The ESB Toolkit provides building blocks that can be helpful to enable this type of inter-ESB messaging framework.

If they are in direct communication, then an off-ramp on one ESB would send a message to an on-ramp of another ESB. In other cases, you may opt to relay through an intermediary, where a message is sent from one ESB to the Windows Azure platform Service Bus and from there it is relayed to another ESB.

NOTE

Also worth noting is that there are various strategies you could consider around using SQL Server's replication features to replicate the itinerary repository. You can also explore using UDDI 3.0's syndication capabilities to federate distributed UDDI directories.

SUMMARY OF KEY POINTS

- There are various options to build high-availability environments by using SQL Server clusters and BizTalk Sever groups.

- The Systems Center Operations Manager Management Pack for BizTalk Server provides tools that allow for the monitoring of the health and activities that occurr on BizTalk Servers.

15.5 Cloud-Enabling the ESB with Windows Azure

There are inevitably times when you will need to cross organizational boundaries in order to get trading partners, customers or suppliers integrated into your business processes. Traditionally, in a BizTalk environment, this would mean that you would have Web services hosted in IIS or in the BizTalk process on the BizTalk Servers. You then would reverse-proxy those services to make them available outside the firewall. You will also likely have a load balancer in play for either volume or high-availability purposes.

You would further need to define a security strategy. Crossing a security boundary like this is never easy and commonly introduced moving parts and some degree of risk.

By extending the ESB on-ramp to the Windows Azure platform, we can address several of these concerns. As explained in Chapters 8, 16, and 17, Windows Azure provides the Windows Azure platform Service Bus and the Windows Azure platform Access Control Service. These are both services we can use to extend the BizTalk on-ramp to Windows Azure.

Receiving Messages from Azure's AppFabric Service Bus

The previously described WCF-Custom adapter allows you to select any bindings that are available on a given machine. When you install the Windows Azure platform App-Fabric SDK, you get several new WCF relay bindings that allow you to communicate with the Service Bus. Instead of directly opening our infrastructure to the outside world, we will instead use that relay feature. External partners can publish their messages to the Service Bus, and we will receive them because we are the subscriber.

From an implementation perspective, it is trivial to receive messages from the Service Bus. You just create a new BizTalk receive location, choose one of the relay bindings, set the security credentials, and enable the receive location. Once you are done that, you have created an endpoint in the Service Bus (with an identifying namespace), and the Windows Azure Service Bus will send messages matching that endpoint to you. Figure 15.10 shows what this receive location looks like.

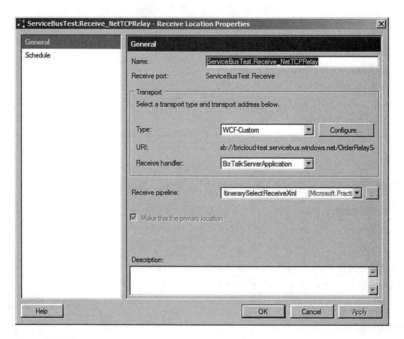

Figure 15.10
Notice the WCF-Custom adapter, as well as the URI, which indicates the Service Bus endpoint address.

The receive pipeline being used here (`ItineraryReceiveXml`), is one of the standard pipelines included with the ESB Toolkit. This means we could potentially implement something like passing a received message into the business rules engine; having a business rules engine evaluation determines which itinerary to use, retrieves that itinerary from the repository and stamps it on the message. This is identical to the sort of sequence we may go through if we were picking up a message from a SharePoint document list or from a flat file. The only difference is we made a couple of minor configuration changes to the WCF-Custom adapter settings and now we have extended our on-ramp to the cloud.

We have a secured pipe up to the Service Bus because we are the ones that initiated and secured the connection (using standard WCF message and transport security options). In addition, anyone publishing messages intended for the service endpoint will need to be authorized by the Windows Azure platform Access Control Service before they can do so. This secures the link from the external organization to the cloud.

Sending Messages to Azure's AppFabric Service Bus

In addition to extending the ESB on-ramp to the cloud, we can take advantage of the Windows Azure platform Service Bus by sending messages to it from our on-premise ESB. Using the WCF-Custom adapter provider and the Windows Azure platform, App-Fabric SDK gives us the necessary relay bindings and we simply need to set the appropriate adapter provider properties.

From a BizTalk perspective, we can use the WCF-Custom adapter with either a static or dynamic send port. From an ESB perspective, though, the preferred approach would be to use an itinerary that uses a dynamic off-ramp (send port) to send the message. This itinerary would specify the processing steps to receive a message, resolve the destination and adapter properties, and then relay the message on (Figure 15.11).

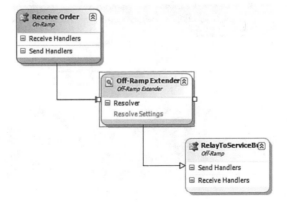

Figure 15.11

A visual representation of a three-step itinerary.

The properties of the Resolve Settings resolver are shown in Figure 15.12. To keep things simple, this example uses a static resolver (which means that the statically defined settings will be dynamically applied when the itinerary is executed).

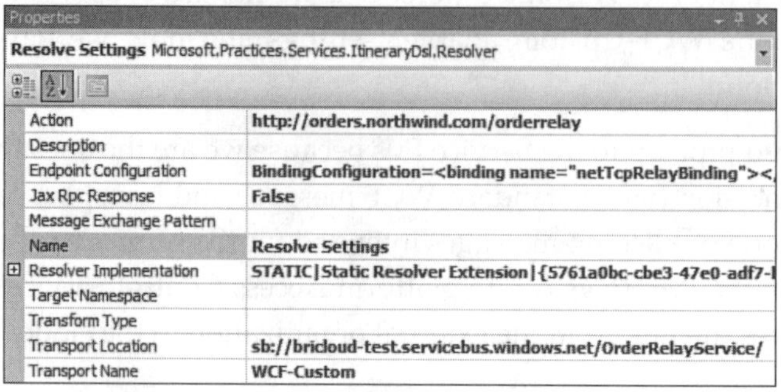

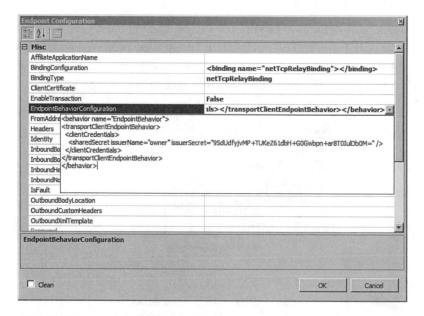

Figure 15.12
Sample Resolve Settings property values.

In order for this to function properly, it is crucial that the Action, Endpoint Configuration and Transport Location properties be set correctly. The Endpoint Configuration properties are now set as shown in Figure 15.13.

Figure 15.13
The Endpoint Configuration settings. This example uses the `netTcpRelayBinding` (one of the bindings you get from installing the Azure AppFabric SDK). There are additional options available to accommodate other messaging patterns, such as multi-case and request-and-response.

SUMMARY OF KEY POINTS

- A BizTalk Server ESB implementation can be extended to the Windows Azure platform.

- The ESB on-ramp can be configured to receive messages from the Windows Azure platform Service Bus.

- No special adapters are required to send messages to the Windows Azure platform Service Bus. This can be accomplished using the WCF-Custom adapter and the WCF-Custom adapter provider included with the ESB Toolkit.

15.6 Governance Considerations

ESB governance is a multi-faceted issue, and can become complex depending on the runtime management requirements and the necessary involvement on an organizational level.

What provisioning ESB-hosted services entail will vary by enterprise, but typical requirements are:

- advertising service availability (service registry or repository)

- implementing monitoring of messages based on type or services

- creation of custom on-ramps

- definition of security policies

The ESB Toolkit does not add a governance layer onto BizTalk or the .NET framework. It does, however, have hooks into some third-party governance solution providers in order to integrate their governance capabilities into a BizTalk-based ESB. In addition, service virtualization solutions, such as the Managed Services Engine (available on Codeplex) can be used as containers for on and off-ramps, allowing policy-driven enforcement of SLAs or tracking at the container level.

When creating a governance plan for your ESB implementation, there are some key considerations to take into account.

SLA Enforcement

Service level agreement (SLA) enforcement means confirming that an agreed upon service level (such as response time or availability) is being met. If you are going to monitor service metrics, there are two common models used:

- observation model

- container model

In a Microsoft context, the observation model could mean instrumenting the service using BizTalk's BAM capabilities (as explained in Chapter 20). Essentially, tracking of events (for example, service start) can be monitored and subsequently reported on. This model can easily be applied over various transport protocols, although it will only capture data you need to provide the logic to respond to conditions outside of the SLAs.

Using the container model is similar, but takes a slightly different approach. The proxy is invoked at the consumer-side of a Web service call. It registers metrics, but can also perform other functions, such as usage metering and service virtualization.

Monitoring

Monitoring of an ESB breaks down into three distinct areas:

- infrastructure monitoring (machine health)

- ESB component monitoring (ESB health)

- custom application and service monitoring (solution/service health)

The first is the server health type of monitoring that is provided by tools such as Microsoft System Center Operations Manager and IBM's Tivoli. This is the lowest level of monitoring in that it provides confirmation that the server is running and specific services are operational through to CPU and memory utilization. In a well planned environment, these tools can give you the ability to not only monitor changing server conditions, but to also react to them and re-assign resources as required.

The next level is concerned with the monitoring of ESB core services and components. At this level, you can leverage BizTalk's BAM capabilities to track service metrics (see Chapter 20). Metrics gathered can include historical trend data, allowing server administrators to spot service latency degradations and other trends that may not be readily apparent from a tabular listing. Furthermore, if you are using BAM scheduled aggregations, the data will be collected in SQL Server Analysis Services OLAP cubes, which allow for new views into service metrics to be created long after the metrics data has been collected. Both the ESB Toolkit and the Managed Services Engine utilize BizTalk BAM for this type of monitoring. In the case of the ESB Toolkit, tracking activity for part of an itinerary is as simple as enabling tracking on that step, and then reporting on it.

Lastly, other applications and services created in an enterprise, but outside of the realm of the ESB core services, can also take advantage of the metrics tracking infrastructure provided by BizTalk BAM.

Preparing Project Teams

Moving to an ESB topology marks a fundamental change for most enterprises, as it can involve deploying a completely new infrastructure along with new development and administration requirements. In order to ensure a smooth transition, it is essential that care and consideration be paid to the soft aspects. Specifically, any transition plan should include:

- training and consulting
- developer tools and SDKs

Training can take many forms. Formal training is generally encouraged given the range of technologies and architectural complexities that can be part of BizTalk Server and ESB Toolkit implementations. Also, you can help reduce common risks by planning and carrying out the initial steps of a transition with the guidance of experienced consultants.

Appropriate developer tools and SDKs can help technology architects and developers work hands-on with BizTalk components and services prior to entering actual project delivery stages. It can further help highlight where additional, non-Microsoft tools and technologies can be incorporated to ensure that the ultimate ESB architecture is in support of an overall vendor-neutral service-oriented architectural model.

Finally, ensuring that any plans, architectures, and infrastructure deployments for a specific ESB implementation are in alignment and encompassed and appropriately positioned with an overarching SOA governance plan is essential to ensuring that the eventual ESB implementation will not unintentionally establish a silo of its own.

SUMMARY OF KEY POINTS

- SLA enforcement and monitoring are key considerations for establishing effective runtime governance of ESBs.

- Attention must be paid to the "soft" aspects of rolling out an ESB, including appropriate training, as well as ensuring that all constituents understand the business value.

15.7 Mapping the Microsoft Platform to the Enterprise Service Bus Pattern

As defined in Chapter 22 of *SOA Design Patterns*: "An Enterprise Service Bus represents an environment designed to foster sophisticated inter-connectivity between services. It establishes an intermediate layer of processing that can help overcome common problems associated with reliability, scalability, and communications disparity."

The ESB is represented as a compound pattern comprised of a series of core and optional patterns that co-exist to establish an environment with a specific feature-set. Figure 15.14 shows the pattern hierarchy that comprises Enterprise Service Bus [741].

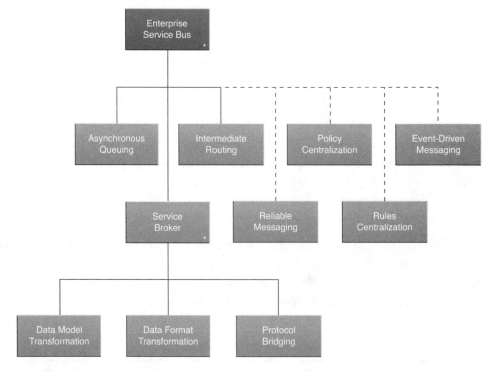

Figure 15.14

The Enterprise Service Bus [741] compound pattern. The patterns connected with dashed lines represent optional extensions to the core model.

One of the most common questions that arise when exploring Enterprise Service Bus [741] patterns in relation to Microsoft platform technologies is whether BizTalk Server itself is a fully functional ESB.

The answer to this depends on the definition of "fully-functional." As shown in Table 15.2, when we take a look at the individual feature-sets represented by the patterns that make up Enterprise Service Bus [741], we can identify several dynamic runtime capabilities that can be provided by Microsoft platform technologies beyond BizTalk Server.

Enterprise Service Bus [741] Pattern	BizTalk Server + ESB Toolkit	Windows Azure Platform	Windows Azure Platform Service Bus	.NET 4.0
Asynchronous Queuing	1	1	3	1 (if using MSMQ) or 2 (if other)
Intermediate Routing	1	2	1	1
Reliable Messaging	1	2	2	1 (WS-Reliable Messaging or MSMQ)
Policy Centralization	1	2	3	2
Event-Driven Messaging	1	2	1	2
Rules Centralization	1	2	3	2
Data Model Transformation	1	2	3	2
Data Format Transformation	1	3	3	2
Protocol Bridging	1	2	3	1 (bridging between WCF bindings)

Table 15.2

Support for patterns mapped to different parts of the Microsoft technology platform. (1 = Native and configuration-only support, 2 = Can be created, 3 = Not applicable or not supported.)

What BizTalk Server and the ESB Toolkit establishes is a series of building blocks that, when combined with other parts of the Microsoft technology stack (and some diligent design effort), can result in a middle-tier technology architecture representative of a full-featured ESB.

> **NOTE**
>
> Coverage of the individual technology architecture and infrastructure components that relate to the individual Enterprise Service Bus [741] patterns is provided in the book *Modern SOA Infrastructure*, as part of the *Prentice Hall Service-Oriented Computing Series from Thomas Erl*.
>
> This book further establishes an ESB reference architecture and explores this reference architecture and the patterns within the context of multiple vendor platforms.

Chapter 16

Windows Azure Platform AppFabric Service Bus

16.1 Introducing the Service Bus

16.2 Service Bus and REST

16.3 Service Bus Connectivity Models

16.4 Working with Windows Azure Platform AppFabric Service Bus

AppFabric is an independent layer of technology built on top of the Windows Azure platform that provides inherent scalability and availability for cloud-based services. These features are enabled via two AppFabric services, Access Control and Service Bus. The Access Control service is described in detail in Chapter 17 as part of the coverage of SOA security topics. In this chapter we focus solely on the AppFabric Service Bus.

16.1 Introducing the Service Bus

As the name suggests, the Service Bus establishes a platform-agnostic messaging infrastructure. It essentially provides a foundation of connectivity fabric that supports a variety of inter-service messaging frameworks and patterns.

Connectivity Fabric

The Service Bus acts as a rendezvous destination on the Internet where services and their consumers can both meet and interact. As shown in Figure 16.1, a service first connects to the Service Bus through an outbound port (or by projecting itself onto the Service Bus), and then establishes a bi-directional socket connection (via TCP or HTTP). This connection session is published on the Service Bus, thereby making it a discoverable service endpoint at a particular rendezvous address.

A service consumer does the same by establishing a connection through an outbound port to interact with the service behind the rendezvous address. Once these network connections are established, the Service Bus can act as an intermediary and relay messages between the service and the consumer program. The service consumer is unaware of the service's actual location; it only needs to know about the rendezvous address that was published and made discoverable on the Service Bus.

The Service Bus also provides a hybrid connectivity mode, which enables a direct, peer-to-peer connection between the services and consumers. In this case, the Service Bus acts as a match-maker by using a mutual port prediction algorithm based on probing information from any services and consumer programs currently connected to the Service Bus service.

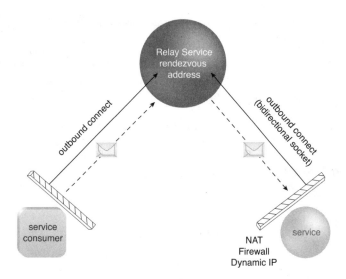

Figure 16.1

The Service Bus acting as a relay service.

If a direct connection is possible, the Service Bus provides the logistics to both the services and consumers, which then attempt to establish the connections and bypass the Service Bus for cross-service interactions. Once these programs are communicating directly, the Service Bus is no longer involved. Direct connections can benefit from improved performance and throughput, and are facilitated transparently (Figure 16.2).

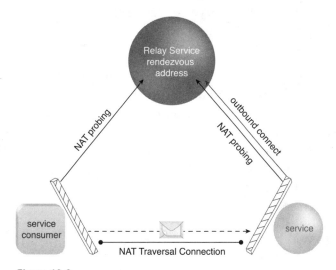

Figure 16.2

The Service Bus enabling direct connectivity.

With the outbound-rendezvous relayed connectivity model, services don't need to be concerned with responding to inbound connections and making specific changes to an on-premise environment as long as the Service Bus is accessible from the service. This connectivity model can also be found in other architectures, such as instant messaging services, voice-over-IP systems, and peer-to-peer file sharing services.

Direct connectivity can be used to support many inter-service messaging patterns for interactions, including:

- bi-directional messaging
- request-response
- one-way unicast
- multicast messaging
- publish-subscribe
- asynchronous messaging
- buffered delivery

Message Buffers

The relayed and hybrid connectivity models leverage WCF relay binding. If either the consumer or the service is not using WCF then all communication will need to be routed through the Service Bus itself. In this case, the Service Bus offers message buffers that provide persistent, asynchronous messaging and support open interoperability with any program capable of making REST calls over HTTP(S).

Service Bus message buffers provide a data structure with first-in, first-out (FIFO) semantics. Messages are held in a buffer until the intended message subscriber pulls them down. The message buffer allows a service (acting as the service producer) to periodically connect to the Service Bus and asynchronously poll for incoming messages through simple HTTP(S) requests (as opposed to persistent TCP connections). Similarly, a service consumer can asynchronously publish messages via HTTP(S) to the rendezvous address within the Service Bus namespace, and then return to poll for any expected response messages.

The subscribing service controls the message buffer's lifetime and when a message buffer expires, it essentially disappears. When a subscribing service creates a new message buffer, it uses a message buffer policy to specify how long the buffer can live after the last time it is polled for messages. This time can span from 1 to 10 minutes. Every time the service polls the buffer, the timer is reset, but once it counts down to 0, the Service Bus essentially deletes the buffer and everything in it (regardless of whether there are active message publishers still pushing messages to the buffer).

Its limited lifespan is a characteristic that distinguishes a message buffer from a message queue. Another distinction pertains to durability. If a non-empty queue node were to crash, any messages within it will still be available after the node is brought back up. Service Bus message buffers have no such guarantees. If a node goes down, all message data is lost, although the buffer's metadata will remain. When the message buffer is brought back online it will be empty.

It can be helpful to view a message buffer as a short-term cache between endpoints or even between a cloud-based projection of an application's (receiver's) TCP buffer.

Message buffers have specific usage quotas, as listed in Table 16.1.

Quota Name	Quota Value
number of simultaneous connections (senders) open per service namespace	100
number of simultaneous listeners per service namespace	25
number of operations per second (does not apply to NetTcp bindings)	10000
number of message buffers per solution namespace	1000
maximum message (in a message buffer) size	64KB
total capacity of a single message buffer	3MB

Table 16.1
Usage quotas for message buffers.

Service Registry

The Service Bus provides a service registry for publishing and discovering service endpoint references using a structured naming system. It exposes a namespace's endpoints through a linked tree of Atom feeds. Service consumers can browse the registry by issuing HTTP GET requests to base addresses. The service endpoints published in the service registry use a global forest of hierarchical namespaces that are DNS and transport independent.

The Service Bus names are projected onto URIs in the following format:

```
<serviceNamespace>.servicebus.windows.net/<name>/<name>/...
```

At its core, the Service Bus namespace is a federated, hierarchical service registry with a structure dictated and owned by "the project." The difference between the Service Bus namespace and a "classic" service registry system (such as DNS or UDDI or LDAP) is that services or messaging primitives are generally not only referenced by the registry. Instead, they are projected straight into the registry so that your consumers can interact with the registry (and those services or messaging primitives projected into the registry) using similar or identical programming interfaces and within the scope of a unified namespace.

In other words, this naming system provides a logical abstraction over the physical details of services projecting service endpoints onto the Service Bus. For example, a given solution's namespace can have names that represent services implemented by multiple project teams using any platform and deployed in separate locations (on-premise or cloud-based).

16.2 Service Bus and REST

The Service Bus is designed to support REST interactions between services and consumers and provides several REST-based APIs for establishing and managing the configurations and relationships implemented in the Service Bus.

REST-Based Service Design

Creating a REST-based service to be projected on Service Bus does not require any special steps beyond what is normally used to make a service REST-accessible.

For services built using the AppFabric SDK, only a few WCF-specific changes are required, none of which are AppFabric-related. Specifically, this entails the addition of a series of attributes to the contract definition to map to commands in REST-specific protocols. Subsequently, we need to use WebHttpRelayBinding from the AppFabric SDK.

Services built with access to the AppFabric SDK can publish their service endpoints on the Service Bus. However, services built without access to the AppFabric SDK will need to accomplish this by working with message buffers.

REST-Based Service Consumer Design

Similar to building services, creating REST-based service consumers that access the Service Bus does not require any special steps other than implementing the basic AppFabric Service Bus programming model (which requires defining and creating a service contract, using a binding and security credentials to connect to the Service Bus, and so on). For this purpose we also need to use the `WebHttpRelayBinding` WCF binding.

As with services, service consumers built without access to the AppFabric SDK will need to interact directly with the Service Bus by working with message buffers (via REST-based APIs).

Message Buffers and REST

Message buffers use the HTTP protocol to expose various operations, such as:

- creating a message buffer

- sending a message to a message buffer

- retrieving a message from a message buffer

- expiring and deleting a message buffer

Message buffers' usage of the protocol relies on Access Control's HTTP authorization model to help enforce access control with the buffer. This means that the Simple Web Token (SWT) mechanism is used to retrieve tokens with HTTP, and then embed the tokens in HTTP request headers. These tokens include claims that are used to determine whether an operation should be allowed.

16.3 Service Bus Connectivity Models

The Service Bus supports the following set of diverse connectivity scenarios that are refactored into three distinct models (also referred to as patterns):

- Eventing

- Service Remoting

- Tunneling

These models can be used to support commonly used service-oriented messaging and interaction patterns between participants, regardless of location (on-premise, public cloud, client devices, etc.).

Eventing

The Eventing model is based on asynchronous, publish-and-subscribe communication over non-persistent connections using sessionless unicast (to one receiver) or multicast (to multiple receivers) datagrams (Figure 16.3).

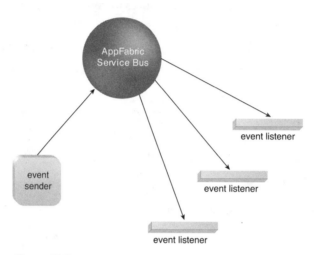

Figure 16.3
The Eventing connectivity model where the Service Bus has several active listeners.

The model can be used for:

- *cloud monitoring* – Events from a cloud-based service can be broadcast over the Internet directly to listeners.

- *monitoring SaaS* – The Service Bus can be an event collection point where notifications from multiple sources, regardless of location, can be aggregated into a single stream for cloud-based monitoring tools.

- *event-driven services composition* – The Service Bus can be used to syndicate and propagate events among participants which can be distributed systems residing at different locations on the Internet.

Service Remoting

The Service Remoting model is generally based on RPC-style or request-response communication as part of one-to-one data exchanges. It typically relies on synchronous communication over persistent connections (which can be shared and reused), but can also support synchronous-over-asynchronous scenarios over non-persistent connections (Figure 16.4).

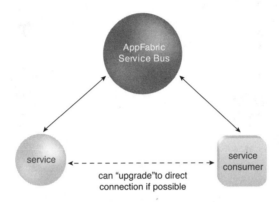

Figure 16.4

The Service Remoting connectivity model, where service and consumer can interact directly.

The model can be used for:

- *service messaging* – Fundamental consumer-to-service data exchange based on the request-and-response message pattern.

- *peer-to-peer applications* – For Internet-enabled device integration, without the need for specialized local networking capabilities for discovery and access control.

- *ad-hoc application groups* – A number of components can rendezvous on the Service Bus and share data and processes for collaboration and/or integration purposes. This effectively forms a dedicated virtual private communications environment for the group.

Tunneling

The Tunneling model is based on two-way communication that can support full-duplex exchanges. As with the Service Remoting model, it is typically used for one-to-one interactions and relies on raw binary streams over dedicated, persistent connections (Figure 16.5).

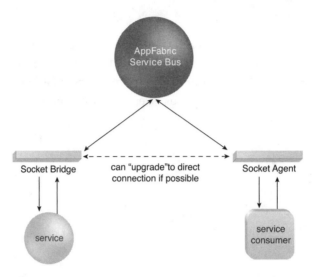

Figure 16.5

The Tunneling connectivity model, as it relies on the usage of socket bridges.

The model can be used for:

- *port forwarding* – This facilitates specialized protocol dependent communication between the service and consumer by embedding and tunneling binary streams as part of service message payloads.

- *reverse Web proxy* – Here the Service Bus is allowed to become the public service endpoint for Web servers running behind FW/NAT environments and not needing to make changes to the physical networking environment.

- *ad-hoc logical network partitioning* – A number of agents and bridges can rendezvous on the Service Bus to effectively create a temporal virtual network environment that allows many-to-many communication among participants attached to the rendezvous address.

SUMMARY OF KEY POINTS

- Windows Azure platform AppFabric Service Bus establishes messaging infrastructure that provides an Internet-based rendezvous destination for services and consumers.

- The Service Bus establishes a service registry for publishing and discovering service endpoint references using a structured naming system.

- The Service Bus supports a diverse set of connectivity models for common service-oriented messaging and interaction requirements.

16.4 Working with Windows Azure Platform AppFabric Service Bus

This next section steps through the creation process of a Service Bus. To begin, you will need to create an AppFabric account that essentially gives you a piece of the AppFabric environment on which you can manage your project, service namespaces, and security settings.

Next, you will need to create a new project and service namespace on the AppFabric portal. Using the AppFabric portal, you can organize groups of service namespaces through projects. For example, you might choose to have a project for service namespaces related to development, a project related to QA, and a project related to production. This type of structure enables you to support a project throughout its lifecycle in parallel without having to worry about sharing the same resources concurrently.

Note that each service namespace must be globally unique so that it can be distinctly identified by the service. When you create a service namespace, you can pick which global region you would like your project to run in. In general, you should pick the region that is physically the closest to your user base.

If you select a namespace, you will see its details, like in Figure 16.6. After confirming the namespace, you will need to install the latest version of the AppFabric SDK.

NOTE
To create this type of account, visit the Windows Azure platform AppFabric portal via: go.microsoft.com
The AppFabric SDK can be downloaded from: www.microsoft.com/ windowsazure/developers/appfabric

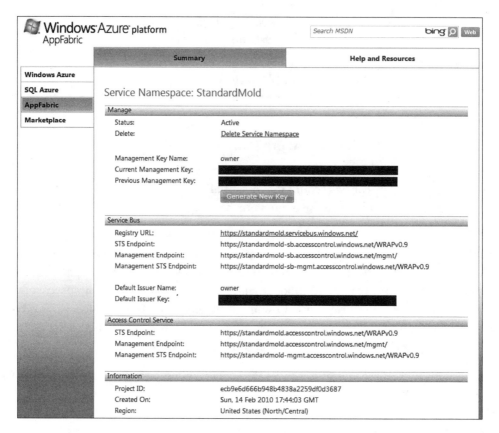

Figure 16.6
An example of a service namespace.

Setting up the AppFabric Service Bus

The Service Bus was optimized for .NET developers using WCF, both in terms of performance and usability. A central component of the Service Bus is the scalable, available, and load balanced messaging fabric relay service that supports a variety of messaging mediums, including SOAP (versions 1.1 and 1.2), REST, and various WS-* standards.

There are some basic tasks that we need to perform to get our service up and running with the Service Bus:

1. Create a service namespace (which we've already done).

2. Define the AppFabric Service Bus contract.

3. Implement the contract.

4. Configure the service by specifying endpoint information and other behavior details.

5. Build and run the service.

6. Build and run the consumer.

Since we've already completed Step 1, we are ready to start building our services and exposing them via the AppFabric Service Bus. That is, we can continue with Steps 2 through 6.

Let's revisit the Order Service we built previously. If you recall, we took a simple WCF service and showed how we could run that service on the Windows Azure platform. Then we made the Order service a REST service on Windows Azure. We are now going to take the Order service off of Windows Azure and host it on-premise. Then we are going to expose it to the Service Bus.

We will begin by defining the contract, for which we are going to also use a custom WCF channel, as follows:

```
using System.Runtime.Serialization;
using System.ServiceModel;
using System.ServiceModel.Web;
using System.Text;
namespace Contract
{
  [ServiceContract(Name="IOrderService", Namespace=
    "http://standardmold.servicebus.windows.net/Order/1.0/")]
  public interface IOrderService
  {
    [OperationContract]
    int CreateOrder(Order o);
    [OperationContract]
    void UpdateOrder(string id, Order o);
    [OperationContract]
    Order GetOrderByOrderId(string id);
    [OperationContract]
    List<Order> GetOrdersByCustomer(string custName);
    [OperationContract]
    List<Order> GetOrders();
    [OperationContract]
    void DeleteOrder(string id);
  }
```

```
  public interface IOrderServiceChannel :
  IOrderService, IClientChannel {}
}
```

Example 16.1

Next, we implement our Service Bus contract:

```
using System;
using System.Collections.Generic;
using System.Linq;
using System.Runtime.Serialization;
using System.ServiceModel;
using System.Text;
using Contract;
namespace OrderService
{
  [ServiceBehavior(Name = "OrderService",
    Namespace =
      "http://standardmold.servicebus.windows.net/Order/1.0/",
    InstanceContextMode = InstanceContextMode.Single,
    AddressFilterMode = AddressFilterMode.Any)]
  public class OrderService : Contract.IOrderService
  {
    int id = 0;
    List<Order> Orders = new List<Order>();
    #region IOrderService Members
    int IOrderService.CreateOrder(Order o)
    {
      o.OrderId = ++id;
      Orders.Add(o);
      return o.OrderId;
    }
          void IOrderService.UpdateOrder(string id, Order o)
    {
      var first = Orders.First(order =>
        order.OrderId == Convert.ToInt64(id));
      first = o;
    }
    List<Order> IOrderService.GetOrders()
    {
      if (Orders.Count == 0)
      {
        Order o = new Order();
        o.OrderId = ++id;
        o.CustomerName = "Bart";
```

```
        o.OrderItem = "Playdough";
        Orders.Add(o);
      }
      return Orders;
    }
    void IOrderService.DeleteOrder(string orderId)
    {
      Orders.RemoveAll(order =>
        order.OrderId.Equals(Convert.ToInt64(orderId)));
    }
    Order IOrderService.GetOrderByOrderId(string orderId)
    {
      return Orders.First(o =>
        o.OrderId.Equals(Convert.ToInt64(orderId)));
    }
    public List<Order> GetOrdersByCustomer(string custName)
    {
      return (string.IsNullOrEmpty(custName))? Orders :
        Orders.FindAll(o => o.CustomerName.Equals(custName));
    }
    #endregion
  }
}
```

Example 16.2

We are going to use a console application to host the
service. We will need to reference the `System.`
`ServiceModel` and `Microsoft.ServiceBus`
assemblies for this purpose (Figure 16.7).

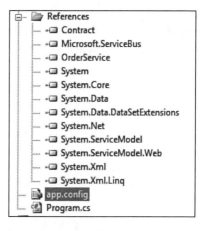

Figure 16.7

A view of references in solution explorer in
Visual Studio.

Now we need to configure the service to make it ready for the Service Bus. You can choose to configure the service programmatically or in an application configuration file:

```
<system.serviceModel>
  <services>
    <service>
      <endpoint address=
        "sb://StandardMold.ServiceBus.windows.net/OrderService"
        binding="basicHttpRelayBinding"
        contract="Contract.IOrderService">
      </endpoint>
    </service>
  </services>
</system.serviceModel>
```

Example 16.3

The binding specifies the protocol used for consumer communication; it does not control the protocol used to connect the service to Service Bus. Rather the `ServiceBusEnvironment.SystemConnectivity` singleton class controls those connectivity settings.

Notice that the address URI begins with `sb://` because it allows us to abstract away the actual underlying protocol. In other words, if we wanted to turn our service into a RESTful service through the Service Bus, we only need to change the binding type from `basicHttpRelayBinding` to `webHttpRelayBinding`.

We also need to set security and authentication. The Service Bus uses two types of security: authentication and end-to-end security. Authentication refers to the steps that our service must perform with the Service Bus before the Service Bus will register the service. It also refers to the authentication steps that a consumer may need to take before the Service Bus grants it access to the service.

Service Bus authentication leverages AppFabric Access Control, which you can programmatically access through a set of APIs that ship with the SDK. Access Control allows you to authenticate via either a shared secret, a SAML token, or a Simple Web Token (SWT).

NOTE
Windows Azure Access Control is covered in detail in Chapter 17.

End-to-end security refers to message and transport-layer security. It follows the same programming model that exists in WCF. Every WCF Service Bus binding has the following four property settings:

- *Mode* – This property defines the security across the entire connection, which ultimately determines the type of security that protects the connection between the service and consumer. You can set this property to None, Message, Transport, or `TransportWithMessageCredential`. The default is Transport, which means that the transport-specific security settings are enabled. If you choose any setting that includes Message or Transport, you will need to set additional properties. In general, Mode follows the standard WCF security programming model.

- *Message* – This property defines security on a per-message basis. If you set end-to-end message security to `EndToEndSecurityMode.Message` or `EndToEndSecurity-` `Mode.TransportWithMessageCredential`, you will need to set additional properties on your binding that control message security. Ultimately, the Message property consists of defining the type of credentials used, as well as the algorithm used to secure the credentials. As with Mode, the message security setting follows the WCF programming model.

- *Transport* – This property is a wrapper for security properties unique for a given transport. For example, the `RelayedOnewayTransportSecurity` class contains the ProtectionLevel setting on the NetEvent and NetOneWay bindings. In contrast, the `HttpRelayTransportSecurity` type sets proxy credentials for BasicHttp and WS2007 bindings. As with the previous properties, Transport security generally follows the WCF security model.

- *RelayClientAuthenticationType* – This is the main security property that is unique to the AppFabric Service Bus because it controls whether service consumers are required to present a security token issued by Access Control when sending messages. As mentioned previously, services are always required to authenticate with Access Control and present an authorization token to the AppFabric Service Bus. However, the Service Bus leaves it to the service itself to decide if a consumer is required to authenticate itself.

To enable consumer-side authentication, you must set the `RelayClientAuthentica-` `tionType` property to `RelayAccessToken` (the default setting). Setting `RelayClientAu-` `thenticationType` to None waives the requirement of a token and therefore you can opt out of authentication on the consumer (sender) in the Service Bus leg of the communication if you are providing your own authentication or if you do not need authentication. The default value is `RelayClientAuthenticationType.RelayAccessToken`.

In this example, we are going to configure the application binding authentication (`RelayClientAuthenticationType`) to `RelayAccessToken`. We will also set the end-point behavior to `sharedSecretClientCredentials`. Using a shared secret means that a consumer will use a predefined secret that it shares with the service. In this case, we are going to use the issuer name/secret combination that the Service Bus automatically generates for us when we create our service namespace.

Here is what our updated configuration file looks like:

```xml
<system.serviceModel>
<bindings>
  <basicHttpRelayBinding>
    <binding name="default">
      <security relayClientAuthenticationType=
        "RelayAccessToken" />
    </binding>
  </basicHttpRelayBinding>
</bindings>
<services>
  <service name="OrderService.OrderService">
    <endpoint
      name="RelayEndpoint" address=
        "sb://StandardMold.ServiceBus.windows.net/OrderService"
      binding="basicHttpRelayBinding"
      bindingConfiguration="default"
      behaviorConfiguration="sharedSecretClientCredentials"
      contract="Contract.IOrderService">
    </endpoint>
  </service>
</services>
<behaviors>
  <endpointBehaviors>
    <behavior name="sharedSecretClientCredentials">
      <transportClientEndpointBehavior
        credentialType="SharedSecret">
        <clientCredentials>
          <sharedSecret issuerName="owner" issuerSecret="
          ...secret..." />
        </clientCredentials>
      </transportClientEndpointBehavior>
    </behavior>
  </endpointBehaviors>
</behaviors>
</system.serviceModel>
```

Example 16.4

Now we are ready to move to Step 5 and create and configure the service host. This process will be similar to how you would normally set up an in-process WCF service host, but there are some additional requirements.

First, we need to set the protocol that our service will use to establish a connection session with the Service Bus. We use the `ServiceBusEnvironment.SystemConnectivity` class and set it to `AutoDetect.ServiceBusEnvironment.SystemConnectivity.Mode = ConnectivityMode.AutoDetect;`.

`SystemConnectivity` returns a singleton instance of type `ConnectivitySettings` which holds the connectivity settings for TCP and HTTP-based endpoints. Setting this to `AutoDetect` instructs our service to first try connecting to the Service Bus using TCP, and if unable to do so, fall back on HTTP. This enables a most efficient connection between the service and the Service Bus. If, however, TCP will never be available for the service, we could save some time by setting the mode to HTTP instead.

If we wanted, we could set the mode to TCP, thus forcing a TCP connection-only scenario. However, it doesn't necessarily buy us anything since TCP is attempted first when using the `AutoDetect` mode.

We can now set up a WCF service host and open a connection:

```
using System;
using System.Collections.Generic;
using System.Linq;
using System.Text;
using System.ServiceModel;
using Microsoft.ServiceBus;
using OrderService;
using System.ServiceModel.Description;
using Microsoft.ServiceBus.Description;
namespace Host
{
  class Program
  {
    static void Main(string[] args)
    {
      ServiceBusEnvironment.SystemConnectivity.Mode =
        ConnectivityMode.AutoDetect;
      ServiceHost h = new ServiceHost
        (typeof(OrderService.OrderService));
      ServiceRegistrySettings serviceRegistrySettings = new
        ServiceRegistrySettings(DiscoveryType.Public);
      serviceRegistrySettings.DisplayName = "OrderService";
```

```
        foreach (ServiceEndpoint se in h.Description.Endpoints)
        {
            se.Behaviors.Add(serviceRegistrySettings);
        }
        h.Open();
        Console.WriteLine("Service address: {0}",
            h.Description.Endpoints[0].Address);
        Console.WriteLine("Press [Enter] to exit:");
        Console.ReadLine();
        h.Close();
    }
  }
}
```

Example 16.5

When we build and run the service, we will see a console window open with the service's listening address (Figure 16.8).

Figure 16.8
A view of the WCF service host with the listening address on the Service Bus.

We can also publish the service into the service registry and make it publicly available with the following code:

```
ServiceRegistrySettings serviceRegistrySettings = new ServiceRegistry-
Settings(DiscoveryType.Public);
serviceRegistrySettings.DisplayName = "OrderService";
foreach (ServiceEndpoint se in h.Description.Endpoints)
{
    se.Behaviors.Add(serviceRegistrySettings);
}
```

Example 16.6

If we set the binding's `clientRelayAuthenticationType` to None, we can simply open up a Web browser and go to http://standardmold.servicebus.windows.net/. We will see our service displayed (Figure 16.9) and if we had other service endpoints, we could do this with them as well.

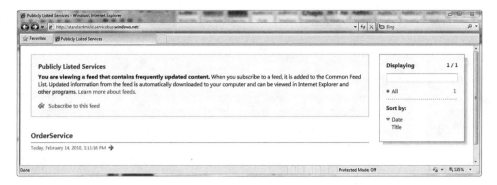

Figure 16.9
The same service end point as viewed directly in the browser.

Defining a REST-Based Service Bus Contract

Enabling REST on our service requires that we use the `WebGet` and `WebInvoke` class attributes on the service contract interface, as follows:

```
[ServiceContract(Name="IOrderService", Namespace=
  "http://standardmold.servicebus.windows.net/Order/1.0/")]
public interface IOrderService
{
  [WebInvoke(Method = "POST"
    , UriTemplate = "orders"
    , ResponseFormat = WebMessageFormat.Xml)]
  [OperationContract]
  int CreateOrder(Order o);
  [WebInvoke(Method = "PUT"
    , UriTemplate = "order/{id}"
    , ResponseFormat = WebMessageFormat.Xml)]
  [OperationContract]
  void UpdateOrder(string id, Order o);
  [WebGet(UriTemplate = "order/{id}"
    , ResponseFormat = WebMessageFormat.Xml)]
  [OperationContract]
  Order GetOrderByOrderId(string id);
  [WebGet(UriTemplate = "orders/{custName}"
    , ResponseFormat = WebMessageFormat.Xml)]
  [OperationContract]
  List<Order> GetOrdersByCustomer(string custName);
  [WebGet(UriTemplate = "orders"
    , ResponseFormat = WebMessageFormat.Xml)]
  [OperationContract]
  List<Order> GetOrders();
```

```
[WebInvoke(Method = "DELETE"
  , UriTemplate = "order/{id}"
  , ResponseFormat = WebMessageFormat.Xml)]
[OperationContract]
void DeleteOrder(string id);
}
```

Example 16.7

Next, we need to change the binding to `webHttpRelayBinding` and set the binding security mode to None. Then, we change our service host application to host our now RESTful service endpoint by using `WebServiceHost` instead of `ServiceHost`.

```
WebServiceHost h = new WebServiceHost(typeof
  (OrderService.OrderService));
```

Example 16.8

To test, we can either create a client application or just use another tool that is capable of creating HTTP REST requests, like Fiddler.

Creating the Service Bus Message Buffer

As described at the beginning of this chapter, message buffers are small, temporary caches of messages that can be held for a short time before they are retrieved. They are particularly useful in Web programming model scenarios when AppFabric Service Bus bindings are not available.

The message buffer protocol relies on the AppFabric Access Control authorization model to help it enforce access control to the message buffer. Specifically, it uses the SWT mechanism, which you receive from Access Control. The message buffer protocol establishes a URI tree structure that helps convey the logical relationship between different types of resources. Table 16.2 provides a summary of message buffer resources and the associated verbs for each resource.

URI	Resource	Operations
/{path}/{buffer}	message buffer	PUT (creates or updates message buffer)
		GET (gets message buffer policy)
		DELETE (deletes the message buffer along with its policy and associated data)

URI	Resource	Operations
`/{path}/{buffer}/messages`	message buffer store	POST (creates message and returns message URI)
`/{path}/{buffer}/messages/head`	first unlocked message	POST (gets the first unlocked message and locks it and returns message content, message URI, lock duration, lock URI, and lock ID) DELETE (retrieves the first locked message and deletes it from the buffer and then returns message content)
`/{path}/{buffer}/messages/{messageid}`	message	DELETE (deletes message and supports delete with lock ID)
`/{path}/{buffer}/messages/{messageid}/{lockid}`	message lock	DELETE (unlocks message)

Table 16.2

Message buffer resources and the associated verbs.

In order to create a message buffer, you will also need to create a message buffer policy, as shown here:

```
string messageBufferLocation =
string.Format("http://{0}.servicebus.windows.net/{1}",
  serviceNamespace, bufferName);
WebClient client = new WebClient();
client.BaseAddress = string.Format("https://{0}-
  sb.accesscontrol.windows.net/", serviceNamespace);
NameValueCollection values = new NameValueCollection();
values.Add("wrap_name", "owner");
values.Add("wrap_password", ownerKey);
values.Add("wrap_scope", messageBufferLocation);
byte[] responseBytes = client.UploadValues
  ("WRAPv0.9", "POST", values);
string response = Encoding.UTF8.GetString(responseBytes);
string token = Uri.UnescapeDataString
  (response.Split('&').Single(value =>
  value.StartsWith("wrap_access_token=",
StringComparison.OrdinalIgnoreCase)).Split('=')[1]);
```

```
string authHeaderValue = string.Format("WRAP
access_token=\"{0}\"", token);
string policy =
  @"<entry xmlns=""http://www.w3.org/2005/Atom"">" +
  @"<content type=""text/xml"">" +
  @"<MessageBufferPolicy
    xmlns=""http://schemas.microsoft.com/
    netservices/2009/05/servicebus/connect""/>" +
  @"<Authorization>RequiredToSend</Authorization>" +
  @"<Discoverability>Managers</Discoverability>" +
  @"<TransportProtection>AllPaths</TransportProtection>" +
  @"<ExpiresAfter>PTnHnMnS</ExpiresAfter>" +
  @"<MaxMessageCount>nnn</MaxMessageCount>" +
  @"<OverflowPolicy>
    [OverflowPolicy enum value]
    </OverflowPolicy>" +
  @"</content>" +
  @"</entry>";
client.BaseAddress = string.Format
  ("https://{0}.servicebus.windows.net/{1}/",
   serviceNamespace, bufferName);
client.Headers[HttpRequestHeader.ContentType] =
  "application/atom+xml;type=entry;charset=utf-8";
client.Headers[HttpRequestHeader.Authorization] =
authHeaderValue;
client.UploadData(String.Empty, "PUT",
  Encoding.UTF8.GetBytes(policy));
Console.WriteLine("Message buffer was created at '{0}'.",
messageBufferLocation);
```

Example 16.9

SUMMARY OF KEY POINTS

- Setting up the Service Bus is a multi-step process that requires the creation of a service namespace, the definition of the service contract, and service endpoint configuration.

- Creating a REST-based Service Bus contract requires the use of the `WebGet` and `WebInvoke` class attributes.

- We can interact with Service Bus message buffers using HTTP methods.

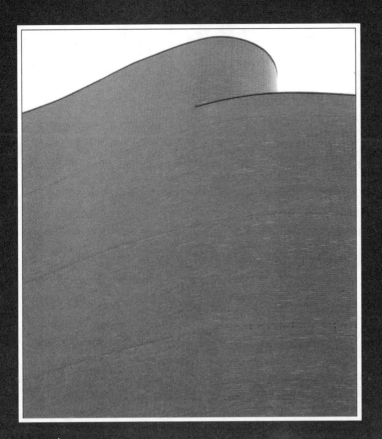

Chapter 17

SOA Security with .NET
and Windows Azure

17.1 Authentication and Authorization with WCF

17.2 Windows Identity Foundation (WIF)

17.3 Windows Azure Security

This chapter is comprised of three relatively independent sections, each of which explores security controls and technologies in relation to a different platform. We begin with further coverage of WCF security mechanisms and continue with an overview of the Windows Identity Foundation (WIF). The chapter concludes with a section dedicated to Windows Azure security, which includes a primer on cloud computing security basics and detailed coverage of Windows Azure Access Control.

17.1 Authentication and Authorization with WCF

This section is a continuation of the *WCF Security* section from Chapter 6. It provides a brief exploration of common security patterns and mechanisms for WCF specific to authentication and authorization. Claims-based authorization in particular will be further discussed later in this chapter in relation to Windows Azure security.

Direct and Brokered Authentication

When aggregating services into compositions, new requirements emerge for authentication. In the past, monolithic systems were able to take into account certain assumptions about the security context from which an application was accessed. Most times, the application owned the user credentials and could simply validate a client's claim by checking the supplied credentials against a database or LDAP store.

Service-oriented solutions can no longer rely on such assumptions. Accessing one service may result in the invocation of multiple services, plus it can be common for a service consumer to require access to multiple different services in order to complete a single task. These new dynamics have introduced new security models for authentication.

Direct Authentication

Direct Authentication [736] is a pattern based upon a trust relationship that exists between the service and service consumer. This trust relationship allows the service to accept a claim of identity directly from the service consumer and validate this claim based on information already owned by the service.

The most common example of first party authentication is the exchange credentials in the form of a user ID and password. The credentials are validated against a security store either owned by or directly accessible within the service implementation (Figure 17.1).

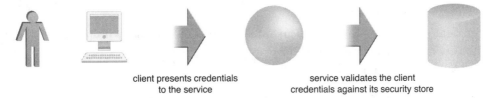

client presents credentials   service validates the client
to the service   credentials against its security store

Figure 17.1

The human end-user, in this case, supplies the credentials to the desktop application acting as the service consumer. These credentials are validated against a data store under the control of the service.

This approach is reminiscent of traditional authentication mechanisms used in point-to-point data exchange, and is therefore common with single service-consumer message exchanges.

Brokered Authentication

Brokered Authentication [714] is typically used in situations where a trust relationship does not exist between a service and a potential service consumer. Instead, separate trust relationships are established between the service and an authentication broker, and between the service consumer and the authentication broker. In other words, the service consumer is responsible for establishing an identity with the authentication broker and this same authentication broker forms a trust relationship with the service (Figure 17.2).

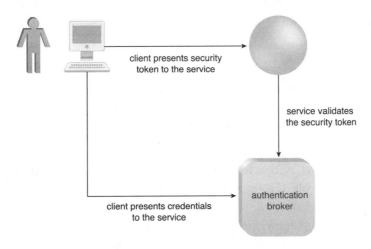

Figure 17.2

When the service consumer is ready to access the service, it presents its credentials to the authentication broker. The authentication broker returns to the consumer a security token that represents a claim of identity. This security token most likely contains some proof of a relationship between the broker and the consumer that the service uses to validate the trust relationship (between the broker and consumer).

Authentication Patterns in WCF

When determining how to establish an authentication mechanism within WCF, decision factors are largely dependent upon the use cases for a given service. Considerations that can affect this decision include:

- the type and location of the existing credential store used within the service inventory

- the trust boundaries associated with the service

- the constraints applied to authorization (explained in the next section)

These decisions should be driven more by business needs rather than technical merits.

The patterns described so far are explained with scenarios that are primarily concerned with uniquely identifying service consumers to the service. However, with service-oriented solutions, authentication often refers to the *mutual* authentication of the consumer and service when taken in the context of the WCF. Mutual authentication allows the service to positively identify the consumer trying to access it and it also enables positive identification of the service by the service consumer.

This is specifically relevant to WCF services that are Internet-facing. Without the ability to verify the authenticity of a service, an attacker could spoof the service and hijack messages. Such an attack could potentially expose sensitive data contained in messages intended for the genuine service.

Role-Based Authorization

Authorization is the practice of managing access to protected resources based on the rights of an individual consumer or a class of consumers. Authorization assumes that authentication (the practice of validating a consumer's identity) has already occurred.

Role-Based Authorization [MPP] is a pattern based on the association of one or more roles with a user or consumer. Access to resources is made available to consumers associated with an appropriate role. It is important to understand that a role does not correlate directly to a group of consumers. A role is simply a specific tag that is assigned to a consumer or group of consumers when the service is deployed.

Role membership can be assigned explicitly (as with Windows security groups) or implicitly according to a set of characteristics possessed by role members. The role itself is a service-specific entity that usually defines a set of permissions.

Users and groups are typically stored in a user directory. The directory can be specific to the purpose, as with Active Directory, or it can be as generic as a SQL Server database.

The service itself defines roles specific to its needs. At runtime it binds the roles to individual service consumers, users, or groups of users/consumers and determines resource access based on these roles. Table 17.1 demonstrates how a resource access request might be resolved to a specific user.

Resource	Role	Role Members
Payroll Data	Managers	Executives
		Managers
	HR Administrators	Ted
		Mary

Table 17.1

The Payroll Data resource is restricted to two roles: Managers and HR Administrators. The Managers group is bound to the Executives and Managers security groups. The HR Administrators role is explicitly bound to two individual users who perform that role.

Authorization Roles in WCF

The .NET Framework provides a built-in mechanism for authorizing access to resources using roles. An authenticated user is represented to the service by a security principal that is attached to the requesting thread. The security principal contains the caller's identity and the roles associated with that user. As a result, the security principal provides the necessary information for the service to perform authorization checks.

The security principal is any type that implements the IPrincipal interface. IPrincipal contains two members: Identity and IsInRole(). Identity is a read-only property that returns the IIdentity instance associated with the security principal, while IsInRole() validates the principal's membership in a given role:

```
public interface IPrincipal
{
  bool IsInRole(string role);
  IIdentity Identity
  {
    get;
  }
}
```

Example 17.1

The IIdentity interface represents the identity of the security principal and contains the user's name and the associated authentication type. Once a user is authenticated, IIdentity is created with the user's name and one of a number of pre-defined authentication types.

.NET provides WindowsIdentity, FormsIdentity, PassportIdentity, X509Identity and GenericIdentity as built-in types. The security principal that contains the identity can be a WindowsPrincipal, GenericPrincipal or a RoleProviderPrincipal, depending upon how the authorization policy of the service is specified.

```
public interface IIdentity
{
  string AuthenticationType
  {
    get;
  }
  bool IsAuthenticated
  {
    get;
  }
  string Name
  {
    get;
  }
}
```

Example 17.2

The security principal is associated with the execution when a service request is invoked. The IPrincipal type is determined by the authorization policy of the service while the IIdentity is appropriate for the security credential received by the service.

The following example illustrates a Windows Authentication binding for a service.

```
<bindings>
  <wsHttpBinding>
    <binding name="WindowsAuthBinding">
      <security mode="Message">
        <message clientCredentialType="Windows" />
      </security>
    </binding>
  </wsHttpBinding>
</bindings>
```

Example 17.3

When the security token is received from the consumer, it is authenticated against the Windows domain, which is the default for the Windows credential type. Once authenticated, IIdentity and IPrincipal are created and attached to the executing thread. Authorization takes place according to the value set by the PrincipalPermissionMode attribute. The default authorization mode is Windows Groups, which relies on the Windows domain as the source of authorization information.

User/consumer credentials can take the form of a username and password, which may not necessarily belong to the Windows domain. In this case, it is possible to specify a custom authentication mode and authorization mode by explicitly providing values for the PrincipalPermissionMode and userNamePasswordValidationMode. In the next example, the service is configured to accept a username/password combination to be authenticated against an ASP.NET role provider (authorization is also performed against the provider).

```
<serviceBehaviors>
  <behavior name="externalServiceBehavior">
    <serviceAuthorization
      PrincipalPermissionMode="UseAspNetRoles" />
      <serviceCredentials>
        <userNameAuthentication
          userNamePasswordValidationMode=
          "MembershipProvider" />
      </serviceCredentials>
  </behavior>
</serviceBehaviors>
```

Example 17.4

In this example, PrincipalPermissionMode is set to UseASPNetRoles. This setting enforces the use of an ASP.NET role provider to enable authorization for the service. Therefore, authorization is performed against the role provider when a service request is made. The resultant security principal would be a RoleProviderPrincipal containing a GenericIdentity to hold the client credentials.

Authorizing Operations with Roles

Activities can be authorized using either declarative or explicit means once the security principal is created. A PrincipalPermission demand should be used in order to ensure consistency across multiple types of security principals due to the existence of underlying differences in the way credentials are validated.

An imperative authorization can be performed by explicitly creating and initializing a `PrincipalPermission` object and calling its `Demand` method:

```
public bool RaiseSalary(double amount)
{
  PrincipalPermission permission =
    new PrincipalPermission(null, "HRAdmins");
  Permission.Demand();
}
```

Example 17.5

Likewise, a declarative demand can be used to decorate an operation enforcing a security check at runtime.

```
[PrincipalPermission
  (SecurityAction.Demand, Role="HRAdmins")]
public bool RaiseSalary(double amount)
{
  ... raise the salary ...
}
```

Example 17.6

In either example, the `PrincipalPermission` is used to validate the identity of the consumer and its right to perform the requested operation.

Claims-Based Authorization

It is generally agreed by many that roles are sufficient for simple cases where the services do not need to provide fine-grained access control over resource and operations. Claims-Based Authorization [MPP] goes a step beyond the use of roles to govern resource access. Many times roles do not provide enough precision to enable the control that you might need for a given service. Claims, however, are able to represent many characteristics needed for different security scenarios, including identity, roles, rights, and other attributes of the consumer that might be of interest to the service.

IN PLAIN ENGLISH

A claim can be literally anything that describes aspects of a subject, be it an actual person or an abstract resource. A claim is endorsed by an authority; which means one observer can decide if the fact the claim represents should be considered true according to the authority's trustworthiness.

For example, the passports we use as a form of identification when traveling outside of our resident countries can be considered as a form of claims-based identity. The passport document represents a token (typically issued and signed by authoritative government agencies), which contains information (or specifically, claims) such as ID number, name, birth date, and other aspects that are associated with an individual.

The passport allows us to enter other countries (security domains) because of an existing trust relationship. The process of supplying credentials to prove or verify our identity only needs to be done once with the passport-issuing agency (as with a Security Token Service). We no longer need to re-authenticate again once we have a valid passport; we just need to present it as a form of trusted token.

A claim represents a right with respect to a particular value. The right can be considered an action, such as read and write, or it can posses a value that can be viewed as some system resource, such as a database, a file, or an operation. Claims are governed by claim type, which is a value representing a category of claims. For example, a service consumer could present a claim of type file with a read right over a value of "resume.doc." This translates to a read permission to the file "resume.doc."

Claims are generic enough to enable rights to be exercised over many different types of objects. For example, an internal consumer of a service might possess a Windows credential as proof of identity, whereas an external consumer accessing the same service may not have a Windows credential that can be validated by the service. The service may therefore require X.509 certificates for these consumers. In either case, the consumers can assert their identities using claims.

As originally explained in Chapter 6, WCF generates claims from security tokens. Security tokens are abstractions of credentials validated by the security policy of the service that populates the security headers of an incoming message. Once the security token is validated, the claims are extracted and placed in the security context of the current operation. The resultant set of claims is known as a *claim set*. A claim set is a collection of claims provided by a common issuer and exists for each set of credentials being authenticated.

The authorization manager allows claim sets to be added to the security context of a request. Claim sets can be created from the security token passed to the service in the message. The goal of the claims created in this manner is to provide a unified mechanism for evaluating the information found in many disparate types of security tokens. The framework extracts the evidence found in these security tokens and represents it as a claim set.

Claim sets can also be added to context administratively. This feature allows additional claims to be added to the security context allowing the local security policy to be represented in the claim set.

The service authorization manager makes the final decision to grant or deny the calling consumer program access to the service's resources. The role of the service authorization manager is to determine the access requirements of the resource in question and inspect the evidence presented by the consumer to determine whether it meets those requirements. The decision is made to grant or deny access based on this evaluation.

Claims Processing in WCF

Claims are a first class citizen of WCF and are represented by the `Claim` type. A claim represents an assertion by a consumer that it has a right to the requested resource. That resource might be possession of an identity or permission, such as read access to a database. Claims can be constructed at runtime by creating an instance of the `Claim` class and setting its `Type`, `Resource` and `Right` properties, as follows:

```
Claim emailClaim = new Claim
  (ClaimTypes.Email,
    "bob@example.org",
    Rights.PossessProperty);
```

Example 17.7

As mentioned previously, a claim set represents a collection of claims issued by the same source. A claim set extracted from a CardSpace token would be placed in the security context with the CardSpace provider identified as the issuer. The Issuer member of `ClaimSet` is another `ClaimSet` that represents the issuer of the consumer program's claims.

`ClaimSet` is an abstract class, meaning you cannot explicitly create an instance of `ClaimSet`. Instead, you must use the `DefaultClaimSet` type or create a new type derived from `ClaimSet` and create an instance of that instead. It is important to note that once the claim set is created, it cannot be changed.

The WCF service model processes the security tokens provided in the message and creates claim sets based on the type of token being processed. The generated claims are placed in the security context and become accessible at runtime through the `AuthorizationContext`.

`AuthorizationContext` contains a quantity of `ClaimSet` equal to the number of security tokens in the request and the number of authorization policies associated with the service.

Accessing claims from the authorization context is quite straightforward as shown here:

```
AuthorizationContext context =
  ServiceSecurityContext.Current.AuthorizationContext;
foreach(ClaimSet claims in context.ClaimSets)
{
  WindowsClaimSet windowsClaims;
  if(claims.GetType() == typeof(WindowsClaimSet))
  {
    windowsClaims = (WindowsClaimSet)claims;
    if(windowsClaims.ContainsClaim(new Claim
      (ClaimTypes.Email,
      "bob@example.org",
      Rights.PossessProperty)) == false)
    throw new Exception("It's not who we want it to be!");
  }
}
```

Example 17.8

Implementing Claims-Based Authorization

The value of a claims-based model is its ability to represent consumer assertions in a consistent manner, regardless of the source of the assertion. Most services need to support consumers regardless of domain or platform affiliation. Authorizing resource access can prove exceptionally difficult without a means to normalize consumer credentials and security demands. Rather than restrict the service to a limited use model (such as roles), we can design a claims-based system that enables us to build a flexible authorization mechanism that is not bound to a specific credential type or collection of roles.

In this way the service can meet the authorization requirements of the consumer designers without affecting business requirements tied to consumer identities (Figure 17.3).

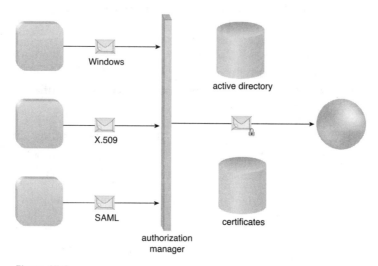

Figure 17.3

The claims-based WCF service model normalizes claims of different types in order to evaluate them in an identical manner.

Access Control in Windows Azure

With Windows Azure services, authorization implementations and integrations can be externalized from the service logic and managed as a set of declarative rules through the use of Access Control. Windows Azure Access Control supports claims-based authorizations in federated identity scenarios, enabling single sign-on across separate security domains.

For example, organizations that leverage Active Directory Federation Services (explained shortly in the *Windows Identity Foundation (WIF)* section) can enable users/consumers to authenticate and sign on to external cloud-based services using the organization's identities.

Access Control features include:

- claims transformation engine using declarative rules and policies

- security token service (STS)

- support for multiple credentials, including Windows Live IDs, SAML tokens, and X.509 certificates

- setup Issuer trust with a simple Web interface or programmatically through APIs

- support for Active Directory and other identity infrastructures

Designing Custom Claims

As is the case with any architectural approach to security, the first step is to determine which resources need to be protected and the requirements necessary to access those resources. The result of this activity becomes the basis of custom claims designed for the service.

Often times, a resource-centric security model is the most straightforward approach to take. The goal of service security is to protect the resources under the care of the service implementation. Resources can be data (such as a business entity) or a physical resource (such as a report). Consumer rights can be established by defining a specific set of actions that can be performed on those resources.

SERVICE PROTECTION PATTERNS

Agnostic services can provide attractive targets for attackers, as each represents a potential single point of failure for multiple service compositions. Attackers can send malformed messages to such services to disrupt their stability or manipulate them to expose sensitive implementation details that further reveal weaknesses or leak private data. The following established design patterns therefore exist to equip the internal service architecture with preventive logic:

- Message Screening [752]
- Exception Shielding [744]

Furthermore, the Service Perimeter Guard [782] pattern provides an opportunity to centralize and reuse common security logic in order to establish an intermediary service as an access point on behalf of other services. Descriptions of these and other referenced security patterns are provided in Appendix D.

SUMMARY OF KEY POINTS

- Both Direction Authentication [736] and Brokered Authentication [714] are natively supported by WCF.

- WCF supports Role-Based Authorization [MPP], which allows for the granular definition of authorization roles to service resources.

- WCF supports Claims-Based Authorization [MPP], which provides increased precision for controlling authorization to service resources.

CASE STUDY EXAMPLE

Standard Mold architects now turn their attention to designing a security architecture for their Order service. It has been agreed to introduce a claims-based authorization mechanism. They proceed with a normalization of client credentials for both internal and external service consumers. The ultimate goal is to create a security model that is identical for all consumers, regardless of origin while providing authorization that is loosely coupled to security requirements of the order business process.

To establish this solution, the Standard Mold architects design a custom claims structure for the Order service. The business entities to be protected by the service are identified as Customers, Orders, and Shipping Notices. Internal consumers might have the ability to create customers and shipping notices, but it would be undesirable for them to create orders. External consumers are most likely customers and would have the rights to create orders, but only to edit customer information for themselves and view shipping notices. Table 17.2 shows how claims are mapped to rights in this custom claims structure.

Resource	User	Rights
Customer	External User	Read and Update Restricted to own records
	Internal User	Create, Read, Update, Delete all customers Must possess Admin rights
Order	External User	Create, Read, Update Restricted to own records
	Internal User	Read, Update, Delete Must possess Admin rights
Shipping Notice	External User	Read Restricted to own records
	Internal User	Create, Read, Update

Table 17.2
A hierarchy of claim types, as they are mapped to users and their respective rights.

The three resources, Customer, Order, and Shipping Notice, map directly to resources in the claims-based model. The rights, Create, Read, Update, and Delete, become claim types.

A secondary restriction on rights granted to external consumers is that they can only manage records related to their own organization (in this case, Superior Stamping). These consumers can present an identity claim with the identity being the customer number assigned to Superior Stamping. Standard Mold can then evaluate both the permission claim type and the identity claim type to determine whether the consumer has permission to access the resource in question. The claims assigned to an external consumer might appear as in Table 17.3.

Claim Type	Resource
ClaimType.Read	Customers
ClaimType.Update	Customers
ClaimType.Create	Orders
ClaimType.Read	Orders
ClaimType.Update	Orders
ClaimType.Delete	Orders
ClaimType.Organization	Customer number

Table 17.3
Claim types assigned to consumer resources.

The following example shows the code used to define the custom claim types and resources:

```
public static class ClaimTypes
{
  public const string Create =
    "http://schemas.example.org/identity/claim/create";
  public const string Read =
    "http://schemas.example.org/identity/claim/read";
  public const string Update =
    "http://schemas.example.org/identity/claim/update";
```

```
  public const string Delete =
    "http://schemas.example.org/identity/claim/delete";
  public const string Organization =
    "http://schemas.example.org/identity/claim/organization";
}

public static class Resources
{
  public const string Customers =
    "http://schemas.example.org/identity/resources/customers";
  public const string Orders =
    "http://schemas.example.org/identity/resources/orders";
}
```

Example 17.9

Creating a claim to assert the consumer's organization association requires the creation of a new claim of type organization with the customer ID as the resource:

```
Claim c = new Claim
  (ClaimTypes.Organization,
   "2022-10582",
   Rights.PossessProperty);
```

Example 17.10

At runtime the set of claims required to access the Standard Mold customer record via the Order service is as follows:

```
public string GetCustomerRecord(string customerID)
{
  AuthorizationContext context =
    ServiceSecurityContext.Current.
    AuthorizationContext;
  foreach(ClaimSet claims in context.ClaimSets)
  {
    X509CertificateClaimSet userClaims;
    if(claims.GetType() == typeof(X509CertificateClaimSet))
    {
      userClaims = (X509CertificateClaimSet)claims;
      if(userClaims.ContainsClaim(new
        Claim(ClaimTypes.Organization, customerID,
        Rights.PossessProperty)) == false)
      throw new SecurityException("Invalid organization");
```

```
    if(userClaims.ContainsClaim(new Claim
      (ClaimTypes.Read, Resources.Customers,
      Rights.PossessProperty)) == false)
    throw new SecurityException ("Access denied");
  }
 }
 return customer;
}
```

Example 17.11

17.2 Windows Identity Foundation (WIF)

Security over the Internet is an on-going concern that, when not addressed adequately, can be directly responsible for the failure of service-oriented solutions, especially those that enable business-to-consumer or business-to-business interaction.

Because the Internet was not designed with a security layer, there are various security technologies and techniques available. When poorly implemented, they can result in phishing scams and identity theft. The IT industry at large is trying to solve this problem by creating a layer of abstraction or indirection across the entire Internet so as to enable an identity that anyone can use. The abstraction is being developed using industry-standard protocols and is commonly referred to as the Identity Metasystem (explained separately in an upcoming section).

On the Windows platform, the Identity Metasystem is implemented in the Windows Identity Foundation or WIF. It is a framework for establishing claims-based identity in services and service compositions. WIF can be used in any services based on the .NET Framework version 3.5 SP1 or higher. Active Directory Federation Services (ADFS) 2.0 (previously known as "Geneva" Server), Windows CardSpace 2.0, and Windows Identity Foundation (previously known as "Geneva" Framework) form the core of Microsoft's claims based Identity Metasystem.

WIF is another major building block of the .NET framework (Figure 17.4) and is available on Windows 7, Windows Vista, Windows 2003, and Windows XP.

In order to understand WIF, the best place to start is digital identity.

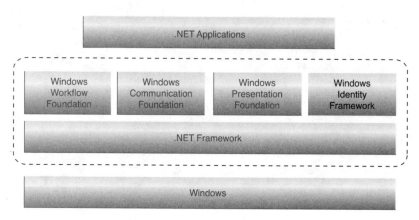

Figure 17.4
Windows Identity Framework was introduced with .NET 3.0.

Digital Identity

Digital identity is a set of claims in a security token that express properties about a subject or user. It identifies a person or a thing in the digital environment where identities are managed differently by different organizations. For example, an individual may have a Yahoo e-mail account, login access to Amazon, and login access to eBay. He or she may also have a network login account at an organization, in which case the identity is stored in Active Directory.

A claim is a statement describing a characteristic of a digital identity. Each digital identity is expressed as a set of claims. All claims describing an identity are put together as a string or an XML document referred to as a security token. A simple security token can contain only one claim, such as username, while a more complex security token will contain many claims, including first name, last name, e-mail address, roles, etc.

Security tokens can be contained within application-level messages and passed around with these messages. Therefore, a service consumer can attach a security token to a message and send it to a service, which then decides if it wants to process the message based on the assertions made by the provided claims.

The Identity Metasystem

There is no consistent way of dealing with digital identities and it is impractical to assume that digital identities will be implemented in a standard way across all organizations and Web sites. In order to interoperate across different secured solutions, the industry proposed an identity layer that resides above the existing security systems and provides secure, industry standardized interoperability. This identity layer is known as the Identity Metasystem.

A consortium of vendors, including Microsoft, developed the Identity Metasystem using XML and Web services standards, including:

- WS-Security

- WS-Trust

- WS-MetadataExchange

- WS-SecurityPolicy

For a service consumer to send to a service a message that includes a security token, the service consumer must know the claims the service requires. The service can publish a policy describing the claims required. Based on this policy, the service consumer will attach a security token to messages it sends to the service. Such a policy supports Service Discoverability (702) by allowing the service consumer to know ahead of time all the claims required to publish messages and to better understand the service's requirements.

However, not all service consumers may have the mechanism to construct security tokens based on claims required by a service. The Identity Metasystem introduces the concept of the Security Token Service (STS) to address this issue. The STS is used to create security tokens and translate security tokens from one type to another. The service consumer can now communicate with an STS to acquire the appropriate security token it requires to interact with the service (Figure 17.5).

Figure 17.5
The service consumer gets the security policy from the service (1); then acquires the security token from the STS (2), and finally passes the token to the service (3).

An STS implementation is security token format agnostic. It provides claims translation and can transform any incoming security token to the desired format using extensibility features, thereby acting as a universal translator of security tokens. For example, an STS can take a custom username and password security token and return an X509 certificate, it can take an X509 certificate and provide an SAML token, and so on. An Identity Metasystem based on an STS-enabled claims-based architecture allows you to connect disparate systems with different security implementations.

At the core of the Identity Metasystem is the WS-Security standard that enables several different types of security tokens. The ability to encode various security tokens in WS-Security forms the basis of the STS. The Identity Metasystem can also leverage WS-MetadataExchange and WS-SecurityPolicy within the WS-* architecture stack for the discovery and definition of policies. Figure 17.6 shows how various WS-* technologies can be used to enable an Identity Metasystem.

Figure 17.6

In this scenario, WS-Security is used to transmit security tokens, and the ability to interchange security tokens is provided by WS-Trust.

> **NOTE**
>
> The Laws of Identity influenced the underlying architecture of the Identity Metasystem. These laws are published at www.identityblog.com.

Windows Cardspace

Windows Cardspace is a part of WIF that acts as an identity selector. A large underpinning of the Windows Cardspace mechanisms is mutual authentication. Up to this point, only the consumer of a security token has been required to provide authentication. This is one of the main reasons phishing has been on the rise. The Identity Metasystem provides a means for the consumer to also authenticate the relying party to determine whether it wishes to release identity information.

Windows Cardspace includes a UI component that enables end-users to participate in the Identity Metasystem and allows developers to build claims-based systems. Each digital identity is displayed as an information card (or InfoCard). The UI builds upon the WS-* enabled Identity Metasystem by allowing users to select a security token that they can use for single-click logins into a variety of systems.

With Windows Cardspace, a user can have a digital card for each of their digital identities. When a digital card is selected, the underlying STS will generate the appropriate security token for the target system. This allows the identity aspect to be abstracted out. When an identity is selected using digital cards, the underlying system synthesizes the appropriate security token. For example, if the target identity system requires Kerberos tokens, the underlying STS will convert the selected digital identity card to a security token based on the Kerberos format. Therefore, Windows Cardspace can be used to log in to an identity system using just one click.

The main components are:

- *identity provider* – The identity provider includes an STS, SSL certificates, and other features. It accepts user credentials, authenticates users, and creates username tokens. An identity provider also acts as an issuer of InfoCards. It can provide one or more token types. It is based on WS-Trust and supports WS-SecurityPolicy to exchange policy information.

- *relying party* – A relying party is a Web site or a Web service that requires identity information. Amazon.com, eBay, or Web services exposed by a corporation are examples of relying parties. A relying party uses WS-MetadataExchange to exchange policy information. The policy itself is based on WS-SecurityPolicy. Other terms used to describe a relying party are "claims aware application" or "claims-based application."

- *client or subject* – The client or subject can be a browser or a smart client application that releases the identity to the relying party. The client controls and consents the release of identity. A client can therefore have several cards and each card can have several claims. When a user logs into the UI of a service-driven solution, the user can provide it the appropriate card for the context.

In the traditional model, the identity provider and the relying party are in the same domain. With the federated identity model proposed by the Identity Metasystem, the relying party can consume a token issued by an identity provider in a different domain and all these systems are completely decoupled.

Figure 17.7 shows the interaction between these roles. When the client tries to connect to a relying party, it expresses requirements that must be met to proceed. These requirements can include specifying an issuer of the security token and various claims that the security token must contain. When the claim requirement comes in from the relying party, only the InfoCards that satisfy these claims light up in the Windows Cardspace user interface.

Windows Cardspace reads metadata from the InfoCard selected by the subject and contacts the identity provider (the STS) for a security token. The data presented to the identity provider includes metadata from the InfoCard and the list of claims from the relying party. The identity provider sends the appropriate security token to the subject, which in turn provides the security token to the relying party. This mechanism decouples the identity provider from the relying party and, unless explicitly specified, the relying party does not need to know who the identity provider is. The relying party makes authorization decisions based on the claims provided to it in the security token.

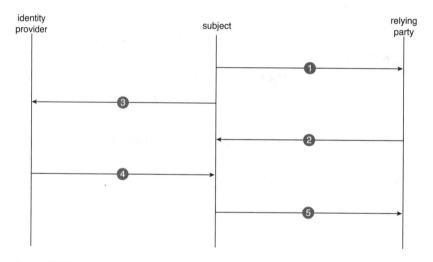

Figure 17.7

The subject contacts the relying party (1), which replies with a token type requirement (2). The subject then contacts the STS to request the token (3). The STS returns the token (4) and the subject provides the token to the relying party (5). Involved in this interaction scenario are the WS-Trust, WS-SecurityPolicy, and WS-MetadataExchange industry standards.

An InfoCard can be either self-issued or issued by an identity provider also known as a card provider. A self-issued card obviously has a lower level of trust with relying parties accepting it.

An InfoCard is a simple file (with a .crd extension) that contains metadata, such as card name, issuer name, images, expiry date, logo images, STS location, and security token types supported. The STS location is a key data attribute that links the card to an identity provider that can be used to generate the appropriate security token. Data stored on the card is minimal; any sensitive information, such as credit card number or social security number, is stored securely in the STS by an identity provider. A digital card is signed by and contains a certificate from the identity provider. Windows Cardspace is security token-agnostic, meaning that it simply acts as a conduit that allows security tokens to flow through it.

A user's computer may contain rogue software that may steal InfoCards files. Windows Cardspace is designed to be secure and mitigate this and similar threats. Identity-related sensitive data is generally stored remotely with an identity provider in a highly secure environment away from the client's computer. The cards only contain metadata used to render the card information visually. In itself, an InfoCard does not contain any data that the relying party requires. In order to acquire a security token, the subject needs to authenticate itself with the identity provider using a PIN or password.

InfoCards can be accessed using WCF, any platform that is WS-* aware, or even via a Web browser. The InfoCard service is a layer above the collection of cards that exposes an API used by IE and WCF. For example, WCF uses an API encapsulated in `System.IdentityModel.Selectors` to access InfoCards on a client machine.

Active Directory Federation Services (ADFS)

An STS is the plumbing that builds, signs, and issues security tokens according to interoperable protocols. ADFS (also displayed with a space as "AD FS") 2.0 is an implementation of an STS. ADFS is built upon WIF and provides seamless access between on-premise software and loud services.

Active Directory and Kerberos provide a single sign-on experience within a Windows domain in an organization. Once a user signs into Windows, file servers, the mail server, database servers, and other resources in the Windows environment can be seamlessly accessed. Under the hood, the Kerberos subsystems on the local computer and the Active Directory authenticate and authorize the request to each resource.

ADFS extends the current Active Directory across platform and organization boundaries. It allows identity information to flow across these boundaries independent of the platforms, solution environments, or security models. With ADFS, a person can log on once and his or her digital identity can be projected across authorization boundaries. These authorization boundaries can separate a different organization or a different platform within the same organization. With ADFS, each organization can maintain its own repository; ADFS then allows different organizations to federate identities across identity stores by providing an individual with a single sign-on experience.

ADFS implements the claims-based security model described earlier and uses WS-Trust, WS-Security, WS-SecurityPolicy, and other WS-* specifications. It uses HTTP as the transport for all communications.

WIF Programming Model

Claims-based identity simplifies authentication, authorization and customization of applications and services. WIF provides a claims-based programming model that includes the following:

- integration with the .NET identity API

- unified API for ASP.NET and WCF

- unified programming model for on-premises and cloud

- configuration-driven (allowing changes to be made at runtime without development effort or recompilation)

- UI tooling for automatic application configuration (including WS-Trust and WS-Federation)

- classes that allow for custom STS development (not recommended when already using ADFS)

- Visual Studio 2010 integration (including tools for establishing and maintaining trust, templates for claims-aware Web sites and services, and ASP.NET controls)

WCF Integration

WIF introduces several new built-in bindings that are designed to leverage ADFS 2.0. The following bindings simplify the process for obtaining and using tokens when ADFS is the identity provider:

- `UserNameWSTrustBinding`

- `CertificateWSTrustBinding`

- `WindowsWSTrustBinding`

- `KerberosWSTrustBinding`

- `IssuedTokenWSTrustBinding`

Programming Windows Cardspace

To further enhance security, Windows Cardspace does *not* include an API to enumerate, edit, delete, or create InfoCards. It also does not support the importing or exporting of InfoCards. The primary programming model for Windows Cardspace is WCF, which requires that services be constructed using `System.ServiceModel`. The service is then enabled to use Windows Cardspace by changing security settings in the application configuration file. This also makes it simple to switch between security bindings, such as X509 certificates, UserName, Kerberos, and InfoCard.

WCF supports all the WS-* standards used by Windows Cardspace, including WS-MetadataExchange, WS-Security, WS-SecurityPolicy, WS-Trust, as well as the Identity Metasystem itself.

WCF supports developing an identity provider and relying party by conforming to requirements listed in the following sections. WCF includes a special binding to indicate that a service uses Cardspace for authentication. If the service consumer specifies this binding, Windows Cardspace will be automatically invoked when a security token is required, and the card selection screen will appear allowing the user to select a digital identity. Behind the scenes, Windows Cardspace will contact the identity provider, acquire a security token, and send the acquired security token to the relying party.

Developing a Relying Party

Provided in this section is a three-step process for building a relying party service with WCF:

1. *Set Up a Certificate*

   The public key from the certificate made available is used to encrypt the security token. The certificate is also used by the Windows Cardspace container on the subject's machine.

2. *Ensure that the Relying Party Accepts Security Tokens from Identity Providers*

   Specify the security token the relying party accepts using WS-SecurityPolicy—in WCF this is done by modifying the configuration file. The following example shows the various attributes used to enable Windows Cardspace to use `wsFederationBinding`:

```
<wsFederationBinding>
  <binding configurationName="FedBinding">
    <security mode="Message">
      <message issuedTokenType=
        "urn:oasis:names:tc:SAML:1.0:assertion">
        <requiredClaimTypes>
          <add claimType=
            "http://schemas.example.org/.../EmailAddress"/>
```

```
        <add claimType=
           "http://schemas.example.org/.../FirstName"/>
      </requiredClaimTypes>
      <tokenRequestParameters>
        <xmlElement>

          ...

        </xmlElement>
      </tokenRequestParameters>
      <issuer address=
         "http://schemas.example.org/.../issuer#self"/>
      </message>
    </security>
  </binding>
</wsFederationBinding>
```

Example 17.12

The example shows that the security token type is defined as SAML. The `requiredClaimTypes` attribute is used to specify the claim types or statements required by the relying party. In such a case we specify that the security token must include `EmailAddress` and `ZipCode`. The `issuer` attribute is used to establish valid issuers of the security token. If the attribute is omitted, it indicates that all identity providers are valid. In this example, only self-issued cards are permitted.

3. *Implement Authorization Logic*

   When a security token arrives, the relying party should have the ability to process the claims and make authorization decisions.

Developing an Identity Provider

With WCF you can also build an identity provider. Provided here are two primary steps:

1. *Create InfoCards*

   The identity provider must be able to create InfoCards in the .crd file format and the card must be signed and delivered to the user. The .crd file includes the issuer name, policy, image, security tokens supported, and the STS server location.

2. *Implement STS Specification*

   The identity provider must implement the STS, as defined by the WS-Trust standard. The core functions a reliable STS must be capable of performing include:

- accepting a request for a security token from the card issued by the user or subject

- authenticating the request

- creating security tokens

- sending security tokens to users

Windows Cardspace includes a local implementation of STS. If the relying party specified the identity provider as self, then Windows Cardspace will use the local implementation of STS.

SUMMARY OF KEY POINTS

- A digital identity is a set of claims that describes a subject. The Identity Metasystem is based on industry standards and establishes the STS, which is used to create and translate tokens from one type to another. WIF is an implementation of the Identity Metasystem.

- The main components of WIF are the identity provider, the relying party, and the subject. The identity provider includes the STS implementation and is used to create and translate security tokens; it is based on WS-Trust. The relying party depends on the security token provided to it and contains the authorization logic. The subject queries the identity provider for a security token and provides it to the relying party.

17.3 Windows Azure Security

Windows Azure and Windows Azure platform AppFabric provide security mechanisms designed to accommodate security concerns specific to accessing and managing cloud-based services. This section begins with a brief cloud computing security tutorial and then delves into the framework and technology behind Access Control.

Cloud Computing Security 101

Cloud-based services and service-oriented solutions deployed on cloud platforms can typically leverage and be designed with existing security frameworks. However, the fact that some or all parts of a given service composition reside in an environment external to the controlled IT enterprise raises several additional security considerations.

Some of the most common distinct security considerations for cloud-based services and service compositions include the following:

- *data privacy* – Your data is being hosted in someone else's data center.

- *shared and virtualized resources* – The service's physical infrastructure, to varying degrees between cloud platforms, may be shared among multiple tenants.

- *multi-tenancy* – The service hosting processes and the exchanged data are executed and managed in shared environments.

- *heterogeneity* – The service may be implemented in a cloud hosting platform that uses highly generic policies and lowest-denominator frameworks, on top of a heterogeneous infrastructure.

- *Internet transit* – Distributed communications are mostly transmitted over public Internet protocols and transports.

- *lack of control* – Cloud platforms abstract infrastructure complexity, which can include hiding the control and administrative mechanisms necessary to meet specific security requirements.

- *lack of standards* – Cloud platforms are mostly specialized implementations. Standards-based data exchange is often supported, but management, governance, and security controls are often abstracted into the implementation and not standardized.

When these types of security issues surface they need to be addressed early on to ensure that services and data remain functional and protected, especially within hybrid architectures that require regular communication within a service composition comprised of services that reside inside and outside of enterprise boundaries.

Cross-Domain Access Control

Cloud computing adds to the service-oriented technology architectural model the dimension of managing access control over services deployed across highly distributed environments. This can be a hybrid cloud model for one organization having assets in both internal and external environments, but it can encompass multi-enterprise collaboration scenarios across different security domains.

Cross-domain access control is about authorization, not authentication. This means that even when spanning domain boundaries, we can reuse existing user authentication and identity management systems, and then extend them to accommodate cloud-based services access requirements.

Hybrid Cloud Security

Hybrid clouds represent the most relevant model when trying to extend an on-premise or internal service-oriented solution to a cloud platform. In general, this points to scenarios where an organization has assets deployed in both on-premise and external cloud environments. The challenge is, now that there are assets deployed outside of the organization's own network environment and security domain, how can we provide secured, single sign-on access to those cloud-based services?

The key is in understanding how we can leverage already centralized security and identity infrastructure without replicating it in another environment and without having distributed services access it over the public Internet.

Traditional practices generally advocate replicating and caching identity directories in different environments across which we want to enable cross-domain interoperability. Such is the case especially when a single IT enterprise has two or more established domain service inventories. However, when exploring this approach with cloud-based services, it can be error-prone, complex and expensive to implement. It would further have to deal with policy distribution, systems management, and auditing. As a result, it may be more practical and effective to try and establish a VPN connection with the cloud provider. But even that option can raise a whole other set of issues.

Ideally, an external cloud environment in a hybrid cloud model would represent a separate security domain. Considerations for access control for cloud-based services would then center on approaches to bridge the separate security domains.

Inter-Organization Service Composition Security

Facilitating service compositions across organizational boundaries is nothing new. It has been a consistent focus area in various past service-oriented architecture implementations, as well as B2B integration architectures and multi-enterprise collaboration frameworks. However, similar to cloud computing, managing access control over automated systems and processes has been challenging.

For example, most implementations today use highly specialized connections (such as FTP, EDI networks, VPNs, dedicated circuits, Web services endpoints exposed in the network perimeter, etc.). These point-to-point models can be brittle in that they suffer from the classic "one-off" syndrome that has plagued silo-based application development and integration architectures. These problems are further compounded when we create individual single-purpose channels for individual partner organizations (or even individual applications with larger partner organizations) and then need to further assume the responsibility of managing identities and their lifecycles.

Different options exist for addressing these issues, including the use of generic or system accounts shared between services and/or individual users. However, ultimately, the considerations in this area also boil down to bridging separate security domains.

External Identity Providers

Online digital identity providers, such as cloud-based authentication services (Windows Live ID, Google Account, Yahoo ID, OpenID, etc.) can be used with various consumer-facing architectures. These implementations evolved from organizations providing their own consumer identity management systems for other organizations to use as a service.

Externalizing consumer-centric membership and identity management systems enables organizations to reuse already provided systems instead of investing in and running their own. It further helps consumers to reduce the number of digital identities they have to manage. However, external identity providers also represent separate security domains, and the same considerations will need to be applied when implementing access control to services intended for these identities to access.

NOTE

The remainder of this section explores Windows Azure security in relation to claims-based authorization. Claims and claims-based authorization were introduced earlier in this chapter in the *Claims-Based Authorization* section.

Claims-Based Access Control, As-A-Service

Claims-based identity is the foundational component in an Identity Metasystem architecture. It helps identity management systems across distinct and autonomous security domains to seamlessly interoperate and provide standards-based, secured access to data and services.

The high-level conceptual components include:

- *claims* – a fact about an entity (the subject) stated by another entity (the authority)

- *trust* – one entity is said to trust another if it considers the claims issued by the other entity to be true

- *tokens* – an XML construct signed by an authority containing claims and (possibly) credentials

- *Security Token Services (STS)* – a Web service that issues security tokens as described by WS-Trust

This model works because it enables a trust relationship between two separate security domains to scale and effectively interoperate in a loosely coupled manner without having to invest in one-off or specialized integration approaches between individual identity systems and management policies. Services don't need to implement their own identity management systems or tightly-coupled integrations with an existing identity infrastructure. They can externalize those aspects and reuse the Identity Metasystem to support single sign-on requirements across multiple security domains.

Claims-based authorization can be used by any form of distributed application regardless of where it is deployed (on-premise, cloud, hybrid, or otherwise). Its flexibility to support virtually all types of generic access control scenarios, plus its support for industry standards-based interoperability, means it can also be used for cloud computing and bridging multiple security domains (such as with hybrid clouds). In fact, claims-based identities can be implemented for cloud-based services the same way they are implemented for on-premise systems. However, there are a few unique aspects that need to be taken into account.

Any solution intended to accommodate the Internet and cloud computing needs to be scalable. In this case, claims-based authorization across multiple security domains traditionally leverages identity federation approaches. However, most identity federation implementations require direct trust relationships with the STS, and applying that same model here means each organization still needs to establish direct trust relationships with each of the security domains it wishes to bridge.

This approach is technically feasible and can still be implemented according to specific requirements. However, given the brittle nature of the resulting security architecture, it would be increasingly more difficult to scale as the organization moves towards more complex service composition models that will likely need to interact with more and more security domains outside the organization's security boundaries.

The appropriate solution is to establish claims-based access control as a (cloud-based) service. Conceptually, this represents a rendezvous destination for trust relationships from separate security domains where it can provide brokered indirect trust and claims mapping and transformation processing. This approach allows an organization to establish one trust relationship with the access control service and then enable it to reuse and extend that one relationship, brokered by the access control service, with any number of distinct security domains that also trust the access control service.

IN PLAIN ENGLISH

Similar to the passport analogy we used in the *Claims-Based Authorization* section earlier in this chapter, airport on-boarding systems represent a form of this access control service. For example, boarding passes represent the primary type of security token that allows us to pass through the layers of airport security gates in order to board a flight (which represents the service we're trying to access). In this case, our passports alone do not grant us this access. However, the passport is used for verification (and claims mapping and transformation processing) for the retrieval of the boarding pass.

The boarding pass is a primary, yet single-purpose, form of token trusted by the airport security systems to access a specific flight. However, our passports can be reused at virtually any airport in the world.

Windows Azure Platform AppFabric Access Control Overview

AppFabric Access Control represents the Windows Azure implementation of the "claims-based access control, as-a-service" concept previously discussed. It is a cloud-based security and access control management service that leverages federated, claims-based identities and a declarative rules model in order to abstract the complexities of cross-domain authorization and interoperability (Figure 17.8). Access Control provides the default security layer for Service Bus, but it can also be used to protect any service implementation (on-premise or cloud-based).

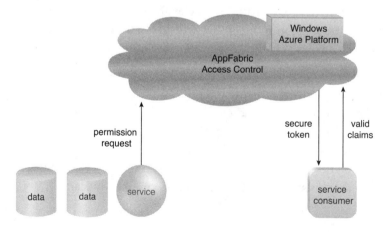

Figure 17.8

Access Control as the security layer to the Windows Azure platform.

The Identity Metasystem model, as discussed earlier in this chapter, is the foundational architecture implemented by Access Control. Access Control exists as the cloud-based service that manages the trust relationships, credentials, identities, roles, and privileges, and also acts as an STS that issues claims and handles claims transformations to enable the use of claims-based identity in enforcing secured access to services.

Unlike traditional claims-based service authorizations, Access Control has a Secure Token Service already integrated into the Service Bus and can be leveraged seamlessly to support cloud-based service authorizations using federated identities without requiring service consumers to implement any part of it.

When a service consumer attempts to connect to a service endpoint on a Service Bus that is protected by the Access Control service, the consumer logic will need to authenticate itself with the Service Bus. The authentication request comes in the form of a security token that is issued by Access Control in order to authenticate the client and subsequently authorize access to the resource (the service).

This same mechanism is enforced on the service end as well, when a service implementation attempts to attach to and listen on a rendezvous address on Service Bus. Specifically, services need to obtain a token issued by Access Control, which contains a claim stating the listen privilege on the requested service. Service consumers, on the other hand, need to obtain a token that contains the send claim. Consumer programs can obtain these tokens from Access Control by supplying credentials that have been granted permissions to access the targeted service endpoints.

Access Control supports several different types of credentials, including:

- shared secrets (simple ID and password, X.509 certificates)
- Simple Web Tokens (SWT)
- SAML tokens

The programming model supported by the WCF-based AppFabric SDK abstracts the complexities in working with various identity frameworks and interacting with the corresponding service implementations. The WCF relay bindings transparently handle the credentials exchange, token acquisition, and token submission for establishing access to service endpoints.

There are three basic components of Access Control:

- the AppFabric management portal
- the management service
- the token-exchange endpoint

You can use the portal to manage the Access Control namespace and the entities within it. The management Web service provides a REST API that can also be used to interact with Access Control.

NOTE
Access Control supports an industry standard protocol called Open Authentication Web Resource Access Protocol, or OAuth WRAP. To learn more about this standard, visit www.soaspecs.com.

Access Control Step-by-Step

Let's now look at the mechanics of Access Control by stepping through the interaction of a service and a service consumer that communicate and exchange claims via Access Control components. Figure 17.9 illustrates the scenario that is further described in the following step-by-step descriptions.

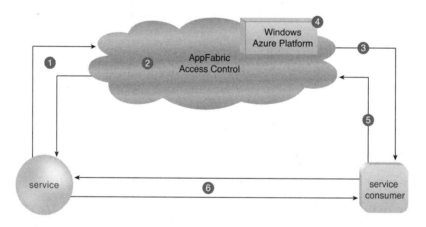

Figure 17.9
Interaction between a service and service consumer via AppFabric Access Control.

The numbers in the following list correspond to the step numbers in Figure 17.9:

1. The listening service and Access Control need to establish a trust relationship with each other by exchanging a 32-byte symmetric key that is refreshed periodically. Then, the service and Access Control negotiate how each will encrypt the claim tokens. To accomplish this, they exchange certificates that contain their public keys. The service sends its public key certificate to Access Control so that it can decrypt the claim tokens from the service. Similarly, Access Control sends its certificate to

the service so that the service may operate on any encrypted tokens it receives from Access Control or directly from requesting consumers. This key exchange is the primary mechanism that the service uses to ensure the integrity of the tokens it receives. This key can be rotated as deemed necessary by the service's security requirements.

2. Next, access control rules are defined for a service consumer. When you create an Access Control account, you are essentially given a piece of the Access Control service. This piece is called a *service namespace*. These rules will control the types of claims that you want Access Control to accept on your behalf (such as the input claims), as well as the claims that you want Access Control to send to the listening service (such as the output claims).

3. At this point, we have configured Access Control and performed the necessary bootstrapping before processing consumer requests. Now, when a service consumer requests the service's public URI that is hosted by the AppFabric Service Bus, it will be authenticated against Access Control (specifically, it will be authenticated against the Access Control service namespace). The consumer request includes an access token that contains a set of claims. These claims live in the Authorization header of the HTTP(S) request message.

NOTE

Access Control provides three mechanisms for requesting an access token:

- The service consumer can send a request in plaintext over an HTTPS/SSL channel. This method doesn't require any message encryption or crypto exchange, making it a relatively simple option.

- A token that has been signed by an approved delegate is provided using an HMAC SHA 256-bit signature. The approved delegate is most likely going to be an already approved STS. The Windows LiveID (WLID) STS provider is a common, well-established example. In this case, a consumer would have already authenticated itself with the WLID STS and received an encrypted token. It then uses this token when requesting an access token with Access Control, which it then sends to Access Control.

- Another option is to request access tokens by leveraging ADFS (specifically, an issued SAML bearer token). With this approach, the service consumer has authenticated itself using its Active Directory domain credentials and, in turn, receives the bearer token from ADFS. The consumer can then use that bearer token in the request.

4. This is where the authorization process begins. The token request input claims are validated against a set of rules whereby the output of these rules either grant or deny the requesting consumer access to the target resource (the service). If request is granted, Access Control returns a Simple Web Token back to the consumer and signs it with an HMAC key that it shares with the service.

5. Now that the service consumer has successfully authenticated its identity and Access Control has returned an SWT with the right set of output claims, the consumer can use that token when communicating with the protected service.

6. The service runs its own validation rules that drive how it behaves with the service consumer.

Note that it is common to prefer an asymmetric key exchange model over the use of a shared key. Since Access Control shares the signing key with the protected service (because the service may want to validate the tokens that it receives from the consumer), there is nothing preventing the service from creating and signing tokens in the same fashion. This means that we (from a consumer perspective) could not tell the difference between a token signed by Access Control and another signed by the protected service. Preventing such scenarios is also known as non-repudiation, which states that a signature should tell us the origin of the data.

As long as we understand this and plan accordingly, it should be possible to continue using shared keys. For example, we don't want to share keys between protected resources. Suppose an attacker compromises one of our services and obtains the signature used to sign tokens. If the compromised service shared its key with another service, then the attacker could start attacking that other service. By giving each resource its own unique signature, we can minimize the damage from potential security breaches.

Access Control and REST

Access Control can be used to protect REST-based service endpoints and support interactions between REST services and REST service consumers. It also provides REST-based APIs for establishing and managing the configurations and relationships implemented in Access Control.

The interaction model for REST-based services is exactly the same as for services built with the AppFabric SDK. The service consumer first uses the OAuth WRAP protocol to request Access Control for access tokens (or claims) to a targeted REST service endpoint. Access Control then verifies the credentials contained in the WRAP request against the pre-configured rules and identity mappings. If the presented information has access privileges, then a set of claims are generated by Access Control, packaged into a token, and returned to the consumer program. The tokens are generated using the SWT format and signed with HMAC SHA 256 encryption.

The service consumer then just needs to include the token in the HTTP Authorization header and send it along with the request message to the targeted REST service end-point. The token may be reused by the consumer until it expires. The REST service implementation can then verify the token by successfully decrypting the contained claims (which may have been transformed by Access Control based on the configured claims transformation and mapping rules), and use that information for processing.

Access Control exposes these token-exchange endpoints for REST service consumers as follows:

- *plaintext* – no cryptography required

- *signed token* – uses a symmetric key and enables simple delegation via the SWT token format

- *SAML bearer token* – enables federated identities with identity providers (such as ADFS v2)

Access Control Service Authorization Scenarios

Access Control supports a diverse set of distributed service authorization scenarios, which can be represented by three high-level authorization models. These models can be used to support commonly used service composition and interaction patterns, regardless of the actual location of participating services.

Hybrid Cloud Authorization Model

This model generally includes services across on-premise (internal) and public (external) cloud environments and a single identity provider; however, claims mapping and transformation processing is typically not required.

This model is commonly used for the following scenarios:

- *enterprise single sign-on* – Access Control can leverage identity federation (such as ADFS v2) to enable an organization to reuse its own identities to access cloud-based services.

- *extranet access* – Access Control can be used to grant access to external consumers in other identity domains to gain access to on-premise services (and in some cases reverse-mapping claims into directory identities to grant access to legacy systems that are not claims-aware).

- *dedicated, single-tenant SaaS* – Similar to enterprise single sign-on, except the cloud-based services are managed by an external organization and considered part of an enterprise's internal environment.

Public Cloud Authorization Model

This model represents the use of public cloud-based services together with multiple identity providers. In this case, claims mapping and transformation processing is typically required.

This model is commonly used for the following scenarios:

- *consumer service* – Access Control can support identity federation with online digital identity providers (such as Windows Live ID), so that the cloud-based service does not have to implement its own identity management system.

- *multi-tenant SaaS* – Similar to consumer service, Access Control can support a cloud-based service to provision access to multiple customer organizations using their own identity management systems via federation.

Cloud-to-Cloud Authorization Model

With this model, services reside in private clouds although cloud-to-cloud interaction with public cloud scenarios may also be supported. Multiple identity providers are involved and claims mapping and transformation processing is also required.

This model is commonly used for the following scenarios:

- *multi-enterprise integration* – Access Control can be used to bridge different security domains in separate organizations and transform claims to the format recognized by the relying party.

- *B2B integration* – Essentially the same scenario as multi-enterprise integration, except security domain trust levels can vary.

SUMMARY OF KEY POINTS

- Claims-based identity is a foundational part of cloud-based security.

- Windows Azure platform AppFabric Access Control is a cloud-based security and access control management service that leverages federated, claims-based identities, declarative rules model, and abstracts the complexities in cross-domain authorization and interoperability.

- Access Control can be used to protect Web service and REST-based service endpoints, and support interactions between service consumers and services as part of complex service compositions.

CASE STUDY EXAMPLE

Standard Mold architects need to provide secure access to its cloud-based services for its internal employees, but they would like employees to use their enterprise identities to perform a single sign-on when accessing these services. This is considered preferable to having to create a new set of external identities that will need to be managed and governed.

They decide to use AppFabric Access Control as a means of regulating access to cloud-based services deployed in the Windows Azure platform. They establish an identity federation relationship with Windows Azure and use internal security groups and user roles that are mapped to pre-defined cloud-based service roles. This results in a security architecture that provides them with fine-grained service authorization based on the employees' existing enterprise identities.

Soon they discover that Superior Stamping will become a pilot user of the new Standard Mold cloud-based Catalog service. Superior Stamping will integrate the catalog into their procurement systems and subsequently automate the process of machine tool ordering. It is expected that this partnership will result in efficiency gains and cost reductions for both companies.

To provide secure access to the Catalog service, Standard Mold architects position the Access Control service to protect the Catalog service endpoint. They further define specific roles and privileges that are mapped to individual service operations.

Superior Stamping, on the other hand, is using ADFS and claims-based authorization to provide its employees with a single sign-on mechanism to remotely access the Catalog service.

By using Access Control, both Superior Stamping and Standard Mold are able to communicate securely without having to invest in specialized security integration implementations with each other's infrastructure. Neither company needs to know anything about the other's identity management implementation. They only need to establish Internet connectivity and a trust relationship with Access Control via standards-based service endpoints and the mapping of Superior Stamping's user roles to Standard Mold's service roles.

Chapter 18

Service-Oriented Presentation Layers with .NET

18.1 Windows Presentation Foundation and the Prism Library

18.2 Design Patterns for Presentation Logic

18.3 A Simple Service-Oriented User Interface

The advent of service-orientation and the subsequent mainstream adoption of SOA have fundamentally changed the way we think about applications, about data, business processes, and the presentation layer.

Prior to SOA, there was often a one-to-one mapping of the client application to the server application. One usually built a client application as an interface, as a channel, or as an access mechanism for associated server-side application logic. The primary, if not the sole, reason the client application existed was to enable the end-user to connect with and use the functionality that resided on the server-side.

Today, SOA influences every facet of IT, whether it is business architecture, information architecture, application architecture, or technology architecture; and service-orientation is the pervasive metaphor for architecting and developing applications. As a result, the presentation layer is no longer just a client-side interface or channel. Presentation layer functionality has evolved to serve as the end-user experience; to explore, to mash-up, and to consume services.

This shift in mindset brings with it additional challenges and responsibilities for architects and developers involved in creating presentation layer logic and UIs. In particular, we need to start by re-evaluating and pinpointing the weaknesses of traditional presentation models.

> **NOTE**
>
> As a thought experiment, review the presentation layer of your most commonly used applications (line of business or otherwise), and ask yourself how many of them are tightly-coupled to a single back-end server or service and how many of them serve as a composite or a mash-up of one or more back-end services and applications.

Here are some examples:

- Designing and developing applications in the traditional monolithic, tightly-coupled style can lead to systems that are difficult and inefficient to maintain. It is cumbersome to add and change capabilities (or substitute existing capabilities) to such a system without breaking other parts of the system. By focusing on Service

Loose Coupling, a service-oriented presentation layer is based on an inherently modular architecture that allows individual modules (capabilities) to evolve independently of the rest of the system logic. It also enables constituent modules to be independently developed, tested and updated with less impact.

- Monolithic systems can constrain presentation layer logic by forcing client applications to become and remain static without any meaningful ability to evolve in response to new functions or business requirements. Service-orientation aims to establish an integrated user experience capable of composing and harmonizing one or more capabilities contributed from disparate back-end services and resources.

- Reuse of business logic was usually not a primary concern with monolithic system design. Due to the loosely coupled nature of front-end services that reside in a service-oriented presentation layer and the emphasis on applying Service Reusability (697) wherever feasible, shared services that perform presentation-side processing are now possible. These services can be reused across standard business automation systems but can also be designed to participate in mashups for ad-hoc composition.

- Monolithic systems were generally delivered by a single project team with a predictable structure and delivery approach. The modular and loosely coupled nature of service-oriented systems and applications further facilitates the ever-increasing distributed nature of project teams, as it is becoming more common for developers, testers, user experience designers, and graphic artists to be distributed geographically or to be involved with a given service's lifecycle during different (pre- and post-deployment) stages.

Essentially, the level of abstraction that services and service layers naturally gain through consistent application of service-orientation principles and specific SOA design patterns can fully carry over to the presentation side. This results in a healthy separation that still enables runtime composition of front and back-end-centric services while enabling individual services to be independently evolved and governed.

18.1 Windows Presentation Foundation and the Prism Library

Windows Presentation Foundation (WPF) was introduced with the .NET framework 3.0 and is comprised of a series of classes and tools that leverage modern advances in graphics and UI technology in support of establishing a framework for highly composable presentation layer design. This framework is specifically based on a partitioning of UI appearance and behavior, essentially allowing a separation of concerns to be applied to logic related to user experience.

Silverlight is a Microsoft development platform (and also the name of a popular browser plug-in) specific to the creation of Web-based, interactive user-interfaces.

NOTE

WPF provides support for the Extensible Application Markup Language (XAML) industry standard. To view the XAML specification, visit www.soaspecs.com. Also, to learn more about Silverlight, visit the official Microsoft Silverlight site at www.silverlight.net.

The Prism Library (also known as the *Composite Application Library for WPF and Silverlight*) was developed by Microsoft in support of building service compositions with WPF and Silverlight. Prism can be considered a manifestation of the Service Composability (704) principle and the Functional Decomposition [747] pattern, as they apply to presentation layer logic. (It further relies on additional UI-centric design patterns, as explained shortly.)

Prism enables the development of client applications that are intrinsically loosely coupled, with a clear separation of user interface artifacts (such as views and toolbars), business logic artifacts (such as service agents and entities), and shared services.

User interface composition is achieved by providing for a common user experience that composes one or more user experience capabilities contributed from various back-end services and resources. This results in the appearance of a seamless, harmonized user experience for the end-user, irrespective of the number and diversity of moving parts on the back-end.

There are five primary parts to the Prism Library:

- shell
- views
- regions
- modules
- shared services

Let's take a look at each separately.

Shell

The *shell* is the top-level or primary window of a body of client-side logic. The shell may be composed of multiple windows, but usually it is just a single main window that contains multiple views (explained shortly), as shown in Figure 18.1. A system itself may have more than one shell or top-level window, and each top-level window acts as the shell for the content that it composes and contains.

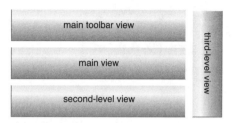

Figure 18.1

The structure of a shell with multiple views.

Specifically, the shell defines:

- the overall appearance of the client UI

- various top-level UI elements (such as the main menu and toolbar)

- styles and borders that are present and visible in the shell layout

- styles, templates, and themes that are applied to the views that are plugged into the shell

The following code shows an implementation of a very simple shell:

```
public partial class SimpleShell : Window, IShellView
{
  public SimpleShell()
  {
    InitializeComponent();
  }
  public void ShowView()
  {
    this.Show();
  }
}
```

Example 18.1

...and the IShellView interface is defined as follows :

```
public interface IShellView
{
   void ShowView();
}
```

Example 18.2

In this simple example, the implementation of `ShowView` calls `Show` on the shell class, which displays the main window. `ShowView` is called as part of the initialization of the client application.

Views

Views are constituent units for UI composition. User controls, data templates, and custom controls are examples of Prism views. Each view basically represents a portion of the user interface. Collectively, the views are composed and rendered in the shell's windows. The part of the UI captured by a view is naturally decoupled from the rest of the client application logic. You can think of a view as a module for UI rendering purposes.

The easiest and most common way to define a view is to define a user control. The following markup shows an example WPF user control:

```
<UserControl
   x:Class="WpfApplication1.SimpleView"
   xmlns="http://schemas.microsoft.com/
      winfx/2006/xaml/presentation"
   xmlns:x="http://schemas.microsoft.com/winfx/2006/xaml"
      Height="25" Width="100">
   <Label>
      A Simple View
   </Label>
</UserControl>
```

Example 18.3

Sometimes a view that is being used by multiple services can become complicated. In this case, it may make sense to break up the view into several child views and have the parent view construct itself using these child views. It may do this statically at design-time, or it may support the adding of child views at runtime. A view that is not fully defined in a single view class is referred to as a *composite view*.

View Discovery versus View Injection

Views can be created and displayed automatically through the view discovery approach (as demonstrated later in this chapter), and also programmatically, through an approach called *view injection*.

With the view discovery approach, a relationship is created in the RegionViewRegistry between a region's name and the type of a view. When a region is created, the region is designed to walk through all of the ViewTypes associated with the region and automatically instantiate and load them. With view discovery, we do not have fine-grained control over when the regions' corresponding views are loaded and displayed.

When following the view injection approach, the application programmatically obtains a reference to a region and injects or adds a view to it. Typically, this is done when a module initializes and also as the result of a user action. With view injection, we have more control over when views are loaded and displayed; we also have the ability to remove views from the region.

Service compositions necessitate the communication and the sharing of context and other associated information across the views. Prism provides multiple techniques for communicating between views, and the region manager enables RegionContext as one of these approaches. RegionContext is particularly useful when there is a need to share context between a parent view and child views that are hosted in a region.

Regions

In composite applications, multiple views may be displayed at runtime in specific locations within the application's user interface. To achieve this, you need to define the locations where the views will appear and how the views will be created and displayed in those locations.

You can determine where views will appear by defining a layout with named locations, known as *regions*. Regions act as placeholders within which one or more views are displayed at runtime. You can locate and add content to regions in the layout without exact knowledge of how or where the region is visually displayed. This allows the layout to change without affecting the modules that add the content to the layout (as shown in Figure 18.2).

Figure 18.2

Illustrating regions used to decouple views from the shell.

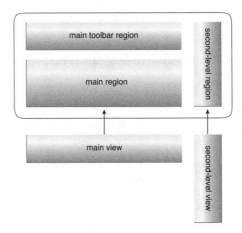

Essentially, regions are used to decouple the view from the location in the shell where the view will be displayed. This allows the layout and the appearance of the application to evolve independently of the views. More specifically, a region is defined by assigning a region name to a WPF or Silverlight control. At runtime, views are added to the named region control, which then displays the view (or views) according to the layout strategy that they implement. For example, a tab control region will lay out its child views in a tabbed arrangement.

The following example demonstrates the use of regions in a shell:

```
<ItemsControl x:Name="MainToolbar"
  Regions:RegionManager.RegionName=
    "MainToolBarRegion" ...>

  ...
  <Controls:AnimatedTabControl
    Regions:RegionManager.RegionName=
      "PrimaryRegion" .../>

    ...
  <Controls:StockDataControl
    Regions:RegionManager.RegionName=
      "StockDataRegion">

    ...
</ItemsControl>
```

Example 18.4

Note that regions can be accessed by their region name and support the addition or removal of views. Views can be created and displayed in regions either programmatically or automatically.

Modules

Up until now we have described the addition of content to the regions in an abstract manner. The actionable part that you use to actually specify the views that will appear in a region is the *module*.

Modules are the logical units of the client application that enable:

- loose coupling

- extensibility and dynamic discovery

- composition

Modules are commonly used to represent service agents or proxies for back-end services. This further enables the invocation of various line-of-business applications and legacy systems and resources. Modules may also be used to represent utility services (such as authentication and logging).

There are different ways of creating and packaging modules, but the most common means is to create a single assembly per module. This assembly contains all of the views, services, and other classes needed by the module. It also must contain a class that derives from IModule, as follows:

```
public interface IModule
{
  void Initialize();
}
```

Example 18.5

Modules go through three lifecycle phases:

1. *Define / Discover Modules*

   In the first phase, information about the modules is added to a catalog or registry. Modules may be defined in regular code or with XAML and they can also be defined by reading in module information from a configuration file. Modules can further be discovered and defined by loading in all annotated modules (assemblies) in a designated directory.

2. *Load Modules*

   Next, modules are loaded from disk into memory in order for initialization purposes. If the assembly is not present on disk, it might have to be retrieved first; for example, by downloading assemblies from the Web using Silverlight XAP files.

3. *Initialize Modules*

Finally, the module is initialized. An instance of the module is created and its `Initialize()` method is invoked. Initialization is the phase where views are registered with regions and where the module is integrated with the application. Integration may involve a number of activities, including them being integrated with the application's navigation structure (such as responding to a user click on a menu item to display a certain view and subscribing to application-specific events).

Shared Services

Prism promotes extensibility by allowing you to add or replace capabilities, as well as *shared services*. Shared services establish the intrinsic loose coupling across and between modules and the shell, which are enabled by the use of dependency injection containers (Figure 18.3).

A dependency injection container (also referred to as a DI container) serves to reduce the coupling between objects via the instantiation of instances of classes and the management of their lifetime. It accomplishes this using external metadata or configuration information.

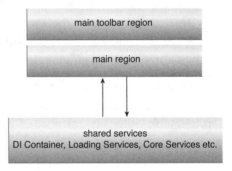

Figure 18.3
Shared services being used by modules.

During the creation of an object, the container injects any dependencies that the object has requested into it. For example, modules often get the container injected so they can register their views and services with that container. In addition to the container, Prism provides a number of shared services, such as those for managing module lifecycles (as per the three phases described in the previous *Modules* section) and managing regions.

SUMMARY OF KEY POINTS

- The Prism library is designed to support the creation of UI-centric service compositions using WPF and/or Silverlight technologies.

- Via the use of views, regions, modules, and shared services Prism allows for the abstraction of recurring, common capabilities that can be made available for reuse.

18.2 Design Patterns for Presentation Logic

Prism uses proven design patterns to increase developer productivity and to promote an architecture that supports modularity and "evolvability," the use of shared services and the minimization of cross-team dependencies.

In this section we will briefly examine a few of the key patterns (Figure 18.4) that are relevant to developing front-end logic for service compositions. Note that these patterns can be applied regardless of whether you are actually using the Prism library.

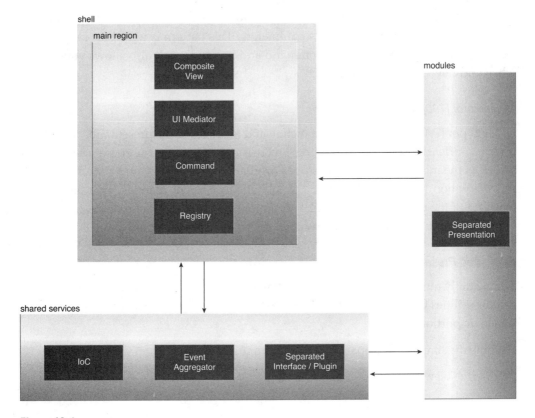

Figure 18.4

Key design patterns for client-centric service composition logic.

User Interface Patterns

The ability to combine individual views into a composite view is the underpinning of applying the Service Composability (704) principle to the development of service-oriented presentation layers. The following design patterns are directly related to enabling the composite user experience.

Composite View [CJP]

The original Composite [DP] pattern enables a client object to treat both single components and collections of components identically. Composite View [CJP] is a variant of Composite [DP] that composes views into tree structures to represent part-whole hierarchies. This enables clients to treat both individual views and compositions of views in a uniform manner. This pattern is core to enabling a composite user experience.

Command [DP]

Command [DP] advocates that objects be used to represent actions, so that a command object encapsulates an action and its parameters. This pattern is useful for establishing a decoupling of the invoker of the command and its handlers. It also allows you to vary when and how an action is fulfilled.

UI Mediator [790]

UI Mediator [790] enables timely interaction and feedback to the presentation layer from a service-oriented solution, providing a consistent, interactive user experience. This serves as the initial recipient of messages originating from the presentation layer, with this mediation logic responding in a timely and consistent manner regardless of the behavior of the underling solution. UI Mediator [790] is a very common design pattern when designing the presentation layer for service-oriented solutions.

Separated Presentation

This actually represents a set of related patterns that promote the clean separation of the responsibilities for the visual user interface of the underlying logic, as well as presentation logic portions.

Patterns that implement separate presentation include:

- Model-View-Controller [TR]

- Model-View-Presenter [TAL]

- Model-View-View-Model [JG] (also known as Presentation Model)

The original Model-View-Presenter pattern was refined into the Supervising [PEA] and Passive View [PEA] patterns. Almost all of these patterns separate out the user interface from the business logic and the presentation logic. Variations between the patterns exist because of the specific ways in which these three capabilities interact with each other. Two of the patterns commonly used with WPF and Silverlight are Presentation Model [POS] and Supervising Presenter [PEA]. Let's briefly examine why.

Presentation Model [PEA] extracts out the user interface controls and visual state (and behavior that is specific to the user interface) into the view class. It does this while also pulling out the presentation layer behavior and state into the presentation model class. The view acts as an observer of the presentation model, and the presentation model acts as an observer of the model (Figure 18.5).

Figure 18.5

A basic representation of the Presentation Model [POS] pattern.

By appropriately designing the presentation model, developers can leverage the powerful data-binding capabilities provided by WPF and Silverlight. With this level of data binding, client-side application data automatically reflects when the underlying data changes.

The Supervising Presenter [PEA] pattern extracts into the view class the user interface controls, visual state, and behavior that are specific to the user interface. This is data bound directly to a model class that serves as the conduit for the application's domain data. The presentation behavior and state to manage the interaction between the view and the model are extracted into the presenter class (Figure 18.6).

Figure 18.6

An abstract representation of Supervising Presenter [PEA].

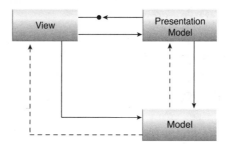

To facilitate the application of this pattern, the model must be designed to support data binding. By appropriately designing this model, you can leverage the data-binding capabilities provided by WPF and Silverlight.

Modularity Patterns

The next set of design patterns are core to enabling the dynamic discovery and composition of modules.

Separated Interface [PEA]

As per its name, Separated Interface [PEA] is used to separate the interface of an object from its implementation, usually by placing the interface definition in a separate package. This pattern is useful for attaining loose coupling by eliminating the need for a client that has a dependency on an interface to be aware of the details of the concrete implementation.

Plug-In [PEA]

The Plug-In [PEA] pattern enables the concrete implementation of a class to be determined at runtime. This removes the need for recompilation, either due to the specific implementation that is used, or because of changes in the implementation.

Event Aggregator [PEA]

This next pattern channels events from multiple objects through a single object to simplify registration for event subscribers. Event Aggregator [MPP] is useful when there are many potential event sources (modules in a service composition) promoting the decoupling of publishers and subscribers so that they can evolve independently.

Inversion of Control [DP]

The Inversion of Control [DP] pattern is used to enable extensibility in a class or library. In this section we are primarily interested in the following two patterns that are derived from Inversion of Control [DP].

Dependency Injection [PEA]

Dependency injection (described earlier in this chapter as a feature of WPF) is a variation of Inversion of Control [DP] that is used with the Prism library. It promotes the decoupling of classes from their dependencies so that these dependencies may be replaced or updated with minimal changes to the classes themselves. During a class's construction phase, it provides any dependent classes to the class.

Because of this, the concrete implementation of the dependencies can be changed more easily as the system evolves. This better supports testability and evolvability of a system over time. It further enables classes to depend on and use other classes whose concrete implementation may not be available or known at design-time. Furthermore, it decouples classes from being responsible from managing the lifetime of their dependencies.

There are specific advantages to using a dependency injection container, because the container:

- injects module dependencies into the module when it is loaded
- is used for registering and resolving presenters and views
- creates presenters and presentation models and injects the view
- injects the composition services (such as the region manager and the event aggregator)

Service Locator [CJP]

Service Locator [CJP] is another variation of Inversion of Control [DP] that allows classes to locate specific services they are interested in without needing to know who implements the service. Frequently, this is used as an alternative to dependency injection, but there are times when a class will need the service location instead of dependency injection (such as when it needs to resolve multiple implementers of a service).

SUMMARY OF KEY POINTS

- The Prism library incorporates a series of proven design patterns.
- Relevant design patterns relate to user interface design and overall presentation layer modularity.

18.3 A Simple Service-Oriented User Interface

To demonstrate some of the concepts, parts, and patterns discussed in this chapter, the following sections step through a simplified process for building a basic user interface as a client application.

Creating the Project

There are essentially five steps to creating a service-oriented client application using WPF or Silverlight with Prism:

1. Create a solution with a shell project.

2. Set up the bootstrapper.

3. Create or reuse user interface modules.

4. Create or reuse the view for the user interface modules.

5. Manage the mapping of views and regions.

Let's start with the creation of a Silverlight application called Composite.Silverlight, using Visual Studio. Figure 18.7 shows the initial screen.

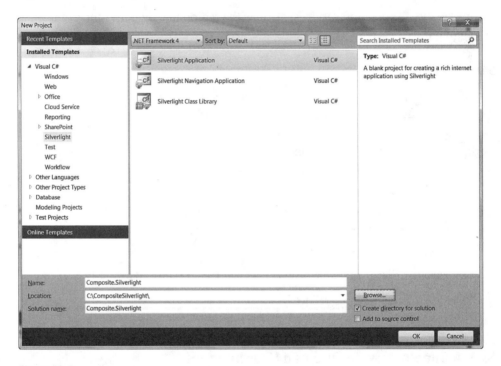

Figure 18.7
Creating the Shell project.

On the *New Silverlight Application* dialog box, make sure the "Host the Silverlight application in a new Web site" option is selected. Visual Studio will create the Composite. Silverlight project and the Composite.Silverlight.Web ASP.NET Web application project. The first project will be the shell project and the second will be a Web project that will host the Silverlight application.

Using Windows Explorer, create a folder named Library.Silverlight inside the solution's folder, and then copy the following assemblies into it:

- `Microsoft.Practices.Composite.dll`

- `Microsoft.Practices.Composite.Presentation.dll`

- `Microsoft.Practices.Composite.UnityExtensions.dll`

- `Microsoft.Practices.Unity.dll`

- `Microsoft.Practices.ServiceLocation.dll`

Now that we have the solution created, we can set up the shell control:

In Solution Explorer, rename the file MainPage.xaml to Shell.xaml. Open the code-behind file MainPage.xaml.cs and rename the Page class to Shell using the Visual Studio refactoring tools.

Let's jump ahead and add an ItemsControl control to the Shell control and associate it with a region called `MainRegion`. In a little while, we will revisit this and dynamically add a view to this region.

In the Shell.xaml file, add the following namespace definition to the root `UserControl` element.

```
xmlns:Regions="clrnamespace:Microsoft.
  Practices.Composite.Presentation.Regions;
  assembly=Microsoft.Practices.Composite.Presentation"
```

Example 18.6

You need this namespace to use an attached property for regions that are defined in Prism.

Next, replace the Grid control in the Shell user control with an `ItemsControl` control named `MainRegion`, as shown here.

```
<ItemsControl Name="MainRegion" />
```

Example 18.7

In the `ItemsControl` control definition, set the attached property `Regions:RegionManager.RegionName` to `MainRegion`, as shown in the following example:

```
<ItemsControl Name="MainRegion"
  Regions:RegionManager.
  RegionName="MainRegion"
/>
```

Example 18.8

This attached property indicates that a region named `MainRegion` is associated to the control.

Now, that we have the Shell project, we need to set up the *bootstrapper*, which is responsible for the initialization of the application. We first need to add a new class file named Bootstrapper.cs to the Composite.Silverlight project.

Add the following `using` statements at the top of the file:

```
using Microsoft.Practices.Composite.Modularity;
using Microsoft.Practices.Composite.UnityExtensions;
```

Example 18.9

Next we have to update the bootstrapper class's signature to inherit from the `Unity-Bootstrapper` class:

```
class Bootstrapper : UnityBootstrapper
{
}
```

Example 18.10

We need to override the `CreateShell` method in the `Bootstrapper` class. In this method, we are creating an instance of the Shell window, displaying it to the user, and then returning it:

```
protected override DependencyObject CreateShell()
{
  Shell shell = Container.Resolve<Shell>();
  Application.Current.RootVisual = shell;
  return shell;
}
```

Example 18.11

Now we need to override the `GetModuleCatalog` method. In this template method, you would typically create an instance of a module catalog, populate it with modules, and return it:

```
protected override IModuleCatalog GetModuleCatalog()
{
  ModuleCatalog catalog = new ModuleCatalog();
  return catalog;
}
```

Example 18.12

Next, we have to open the file App.xaml.cs, and replace the `Application_Startup` event handler with the following code to initialize the bootstrapper when the application starts:

```
private void Application_Startup
  (object sender, StartupEventArgs e)
{
  Bootstrapper bootstrapper = new Bootstrapper();
  bootstrapper.Run();
}
```

Example 18.13

After building and running the application, we should see an empty window, which indicates that we have a functioning, bootstrapped shell. The next step is to create and configure the loading of a user interface module.

To create a new module, we need to add a new Silverlight class library project to the solution, set the project's name to FirstModule, and add references in the module to the following Composite Application Library assemblies:

```
Microsoft.Practices.Composite.dll
Microsoft.Practices.Composite.Presentation.dll
```

Example 18.14

In the `Initialize` method of the module `initializer` class, we have to implement logic to initialize the module. For example, we can register views and services or add views to regions.

We rename the Class1.cs file to FirstModule.cs and open the file FirstModule.cs and add the following `using` statement at the top (we will use it to refer to `Modularity` elements provided by Prism):

```
using Microsoft.Practices.Composite.Modularity;
```
Example 18.15

We change the class signature to implement the `IModule` interface, as shown here:

```
public class FirstModule : IModule
{
}
```
Example 18.16

In the FirstModule class, we add an empty definition of the `Initialize` method:

```
public void Initialize()
{
}
```
Example 18.17

Next, we add a Views folder to the FirstModule project. In this folder, we will store the view implementations. For service interfaces, proxies and agents, it is good practice to create separate sub-folders.

At this point, we have a solution based on Prism with a single module. However, the module is not being loaded into the application yet. Modules go through a three-step process during the application lifecycle:

1. Modules are registered into a module catalog that contains metadata that can be consumed by the module manager service.

2. The module manager service manages the locating and the subsequent initialization of the modules.

3. The module manager instantiates the module `initializer` class of each module and invokes their `Initialize` method.

To populate the module catalog with the FirstModule module metadata, we first add a reference to the module project from the Shell. We open the Bootstrapper.cs file and update the GetModuleCatalog method to register the FirstModule module with the module catalog instance as follows:

```
protected override IModuleCatalog GetModuleCatalog()
{
  ModuleCatalog catalog = new ModuleCatalog()
    .AddModule(typeof(FirstModule.FirstModule));
  return catalog;
}
```

Example 18.18

The next step is for us to create (or reuse) a view for this module. Views are usually user controls, and the addition of a view is accomplished by adding a user control to the module. For this, we need to add a Static FirstModule text block to the view. To do this, we can replace the existing code in the file FirstModuleView.xaml with the following code:

```
<UserControl x:Class="FirstModule.Views.FirstModuleView"
  xmlns="http://schemas.microsoft.com/winfx/
    2006/xaml/presentation"
  xmlns:x="http://schemas.microsoft.com/winfx/2006/xaml">
  <Grid x:Name="LayoutRoot" Background="White">
    <TextBlock Text="Static FirstModule"
      Foreground="Green"
      HorizontalAlignment="Center"
      VerticalAlignment="Center"
      FontFamily="Calibri"
      FontSize="24"
      FontWeight="Bold">
    </TextBlock>
  </Grid>
</UserControl>
```

Example 18.19

Now that we have a view for the module, the final step is to associate a region with the view and to manage this relationship. We first open the FirstModule.cs file and then add the following using statement to the top:

```
using Microsoft.Practices.Composite.Regions;
```

Example 18.20

We create a private read-only instance variable to hold a reference to the region manager by pasting the following code inside the class body:

```
private readonly IRegionManager regionManager;
```

Example 18.21

We then modify the FirstModule class's constructor to obtain a `regionManager` instance through constructor dependency injection and store it in the `regionManager` instance variable. To do this, the constructor has to take a parameter of type `Microsoft.Practices.Composite.Regions.IRegionManager`. We can paste the following code inside the class body to implement the constructor:

```
public FirstModule(IRegionManager regionManager)
{
  this.regionManager = regionManager;
}
```

Example 18.22

In the `Initialize` method, we invoke the `RegisterViewWithRegion` method on the regionManager instance. This method registers a region name with its associated view type in the region of view registry (the registry is responsible for registering and retrieving these mappings).

The `RegisterViewWithRegion` method has two overloads. When we want to register a view directly, we would use the first overload that requires two parameters (the region name and the type of the view), as shown here:

```
public void Initialize()
{
  regionManager.RegisterViewWithRegion
    ("MainRegion", typeof(Views.FirstModuleView));
}
```

Example 18.23

At this point, we have a simple, but functioning, client application that loads and displays a user interface module (Figure 18.8).

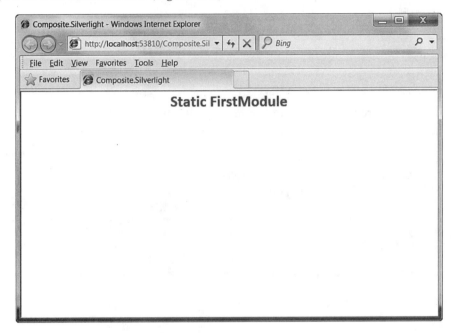

Figure 18.8
The output of a static user interface module.

Now, let's extend this application to demonstrate dynamically loading and composing user interface modules.

Dynamically Loading Modules

In order to enable the dynamic loading of UI modules, we need to add a second module (appropriately called SecondModule) to the solution by using the previously described steps. As per these steps, we will be adding a view for this module called the Second-ModuleView.

We now modify the SecondModuleView user control by adding a `Dynamic Second Module` text block to the view. To do this, we replace the code in the file SecondModule-View.xaml with the following:

```
<TextBlock Text="Dynamic Second Module"
  Foreground="Green"
  HorizontalAlignment="Center"
```

```
  VerticalAlignment="Center"
  FontFamily="Calibri" FontSize="24"
  FontWeight="Bold">
</TextBlock>
```

Example 18.24

As we have done earlier for the FirstModule, we modify the `Initialize()` method in SecondModule to register the `SecondModuleView` with the MainRegion:

```
public void Initialize()
{
  regionManager.RegisterViewWithRegion
    ("MainRegion", typeof(Views.SecondModuleView));
}
```

Example 18.25

In the bootstrapper, we add metadata for the `SecondModule` as follows:

```
catalog.AddModule
  (
    typeof
      (SecondModule.SecondModule),
      InitializationMode.OnDemand
  )
```

Example 18.26

We are informing the catalog that the SecondModule will be loaded on-demand, as our scenario here is to illustrate the dynamic loading and composition of the views.

Next, we add some logic to the FirstModule view to demonstrate the loading and composition of SecondModuleView. We start by adding a button to FirstModule.xaml, as follows:

```
<Button
  Padding="5"
  VerticalAlignment="Center"
  Width="95"
  Click="LoadModule_ButtonClick"
```

```
   Content="Load Module">
</Button>
```

Example 18.27

In the code-behind file (FirstModule.xaml.cs) we add a reference to `Microsoft.Practices.Composite.Modularity` and then a private variable to store the module manager reference:

```
private readonly IModuleManager moduleManager;
```

Example 18.28

We then add a constructor for the `FirstModuleView` to initialize this reference:

```
public FirstModuleView(IModuleManager moduleManager)
  : this()
{
  this.moduleManager = moduleManager;
}
```

Example 18.29

Lastly, we will add a `LoadModule_ButtonClick` handler in the FirstModule.xaml.cs code-behind file:

```
private void LoadModule_ButtonClick
  (object sender, RoutedEventArgs e)
{
  this.moduleManager.LoadModule("SecondModule");
}
```

Example 18.30

At this point, if we compile and execute the solution, we will find that the first module is initialized and loaded statically. Subsequently, if we push the Load Module button, we will see that the second module is loaded dynamically.

Figure 18.9
We now have a simple, but functional, service-oriented user interface comprised of both static and dynamically loading and composed user interface modules.

SUMMARY OF KEY POINTS

The steps required to create a basic service-oriented application with WPF or Silverlight and Prism include setting up a bootstrapper, creating user interface modules and views, and managing the mappings of views and regions.

Chapter 19

Service Performance Optimization

19.1 Overview

19.2 Service Performance Optimization Techniques

19.3 Service Composition Performance Optimization Techniques

The IT industry has historically often traded high levels of performance for high levels of abstraction. Assembler gave way to C, which gave way to Java and .NET because easy-to-maintain code was substituted for acceptable, but not optimal, runtime performance. SOA is no different in this respect. Several service-orientation principles, such as Service Abstraction (696) and Service Loose Coupling (695), seem to demand this type of trade-off.

While some traditional optimization techniques may not be suitable for applications being shaped by service-orientation design principles and patterns, there are newer, more effective techniques that have emerged. These techniques, combined with the modern technology advances offered by .NET, WCF, and Windows Azure, can address service-oriented performance concerns head-on.

19.1 Overview

While performance is only one aspect of service architecture, it is something that can be planned for up front, as part of service-oriented design processes. This is important because guessing where in your service composition architecture performance should, or could, be improved is not a recommended practice.

To know where your efforts should be focused, you need to make sure that you know what is expected of your service.

For example:

- How fast must the service respond?

- How much traffic is the service expected to handle?

- What kind of hardware does the service need to run on?

- How many servers can be used to host service deployments?

If your testing finds that your services do not perform as expected, you must start asking why. This chapter provides several techniques for answering these questions as well as design strategies for overcoming performance challenges with services and service compositions. Before we can explore these techniques and strategies, we need to establish an understanding of what areas of technology architecture they can be applied to.

Optimization Areas

Performance *within* a service is about the average time it takes to process service capabilities. This primarily relates to the scope of a service architecture. Performance *outside* the service architecture (or performance between services) is about the average time required for services to communicate with each other. This relates both to the service composition architecture, as well as the surrounding service inventory architecture.

For the purpose of this chapter, we'll group these performance optimization areas as follows:

- service implementation processing
- service framework processing
- wire transmission processing

Figure 19.1 illustrates these categories and breaks them down further.

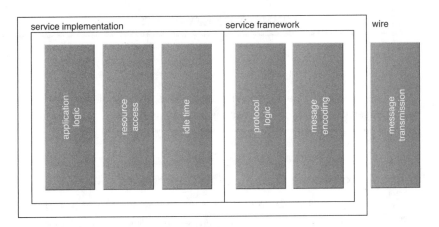

Figure 19.1
Common factors that can contribute to the performance of a service include the implementation logic, the surrounding framework, and the actual wire-level message transmission.

Service Implementation Processing

Executing service logic and accessing resources (such as files, databases) takes time and consumes processing cycles. You can influence the performance of your service architecture not only by efficient implementation of the logic, but also by minimizing access to slower resources and eliminating idle time.

Service Framework Processing

Services frameworks, such as ASMX, WCF, and Windows Azure, can perform significant amounts of processing on behalf of services, depending on factors such as message encoding, communication protocols, transport technology, and policies. Choice of framework and choice of what parts of a framework to incorporate into a service and service composition architectures all end up affecting performance.

Wire Transmission Processing

Depending on message transmissions for inter-service communication, wire transmission processing can introduce various performance challenges, some of which will be out of your control when deploying a service architecture within a greater service inventory architecture. As we will explore later in this chapter, optimizing the design of the service contract can prove effective in reducing messaging-based performance impacts.

SUMMARY OF KEY POINTS

- Traditional performance optimization techniques may not be suitable for service-oriented solution design.

- There are three performance optimization areas: service implementation processing, service framework processing, and wire transmission processing.

19.2 Service Performance Optimization Techniques

Tuning service runtime performance will improve the utilization of individual services as well as the performance of service compositions that aggregate these services. Even though it is important to optimize every service architecture, agnostic services in particular, need to be carefully tuned to maximize their potential for reuse and recomposition.

Because the logic within a service is comprised of the collective logic of service capabilities, we need to begin by focusing on performance optimization on the service capability level.

In this section we will explore several approaches for reducing the duration of service capability processing. The upcoming techniques specifically focus on avoiding redundant processing, minimizing idle time, minimizing concurrent access to shared resources, and optimizing the data transfer between service capabilities and service consumers.

Caching to Avoid Costly Processing

Let's first look at the elimination of unnecessary processing inside a service capability.

Specifically what we'll be focusing on is:

- avoidance of repeating calculations if the result doesn't change
- avoidance of costly database access if the data doesn't change
- developing a better performing implementation of capability logic
- delegating costly capability logic to specialized hardware solutions
- avoidance of costly XML transformations by designing service contracts with canonical schemas

A common means of reducing the quantity of processing is to avoid duplication of redundant capabilities through caching. Instead of executing the same capability twice, you simply store the results of the capability the first time and return the stored results the next time they are requested. Figure 19.2 shows a flow chart that illustrates a simple caching solution.

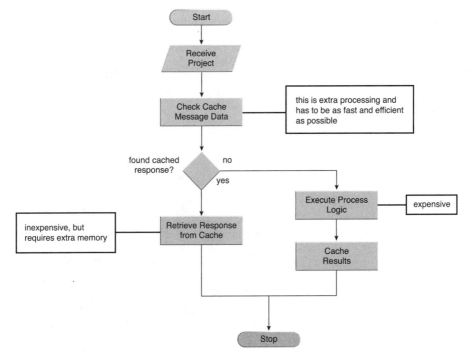

Figure 19.2

Caching the results of expensive business process activities can significantly improve performance.

For example, it doesn't make sense to retrieve data from a database more than once if the data is known to not change (or at least known not to change frequently). Reading data from a database requires communication between the service logic and the database. In many cases it even requires communication over a network connection.

There is a lot of overhead just in setting up this type of communication and then there's the effort of assembling the results of the query in the database. You can avoid all of this processing by avoiding database calls after the initial retrieval of the results. If the results change over time, you can still improve average performance by re-reading every 100 requests (or however often).

Caching can also be effective for expensive computations, data transformations or service invocations as long as:

- results for a given input do not change or at least do not change frequently

- delays in visibility of different results are acceptable

- the number of computation results or database queries is limited

- the same results are requested frequently

- a local cache can be accessed faster than a remotely located database

- computation of the cache key is not more expensive than computing the output

- increased memory requirements due to large caches do not increase paging to disk (which slows down the overall throughput)

If your service capability meets this criteria, you can remove several blocks from the performance model and replace them with *cache access*, as shown in Figure 19.3.

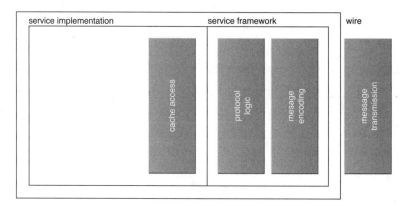

Figure 19.3
The business logic, resource access, and message transformation blocks are removed.

To build a caching solution you can:

- explicitly implement caching in the code of the service

- intercept incoming messages before the capability logic is invoked

- centralize the caching logic into a utility caching service

Each solution has its own strengths and weaknesses. For example, explicitly implementing caching logic inside of a service capability allows you to custom-tailor this logic to that particular capability. In this case you can be selective about the cache expiration and refresh algorithms or which parameters make up the cache key. This approach can also be quite labor intensive.

Intercepting messages, on the other hand, can be an efficient solution because messages for more than one service capability can be intercepted, potentially without changing the service implementation at all.

You can intercept messages in several different places:

Intermediary

An intermediary between the service and the consumer can transparently intercept messages, inspect them to compute a cache key for the parameters, and then only forward messages to the destination service if no response for the request parameters is present in the cache (Figure 19.4). This approach relies on the application of Service Agent [770].

Figure 19.4
Passive intermediaries can cache responses without requiring modifications to the service or the consumer.

Service Container

This is a variation of the previous technique, but here the cache lives inside the same container as the service to avoid introducing a scalability bottleneck with the intermediary (Figure 19.5). Service frameworks, such as ASMX and WCF, allow for the interception of messages with an HTTP Module or a custom channel.

Figure 19.5

Message interception inside the service container enables
caching to occur outside the service implementation without
involving an intermediary.

Service Proxy

With WCF we can build consumer-side custom channels that can make the caching logic
transparent to service consumers and services. Figure 19.6 illustrates how the cache acts
as a service proxy on the consumer side before sending the request to the service. Note
that with this approach you will only realize significant performance benefits if the same
consumer frequently requests the same data.

Figure 19.6

Message interception by a service proxy inside the service
consumer introduces caching logic that avoids unnecessary
network communication.

Caching Utility Service

An autonomous utility service (Figure 19.7) can be used to provide reusable caching
logic, as per the Stateful Services [786] pattern. For this technique to work, the performance savings of the caching logic need to outweigh the performance impact introduced
by the extra utility service invocation and communication. This approach can be justified if autonomy and vendor neutrality are high design priorities.

Figure 19.7
A utility service is explicitly invoked to handle caching.

Comparing Caching Techniques

Each option has its own trade-offs between potential performance increases and additional overhead. Table 19.1 provides a summary.

	intermediary	service container	service proxy	utility service
potential savings	medium: service invocation	medium: service invocation	high: service invocation network access	low: service invocation
extra overhead	high: computing cache key additional network hop for cache miss	medium: computing cache key additional memory consumption on service	low: computing cache key additional memory consumption on service	medium: computing cache key additional memory consumption on service
efficiency	high: cache shared between all consumers	high: cache shared between all consumers	low: client specific	high: cache shared between all consumers
change impact	none: intermediaries can be implemented without affecting existing services	low: server-side configuration file, not service implementation	high: client-side configuration file, not service implementation	high: service implementation

Table 19.1
The pros and cons of different service caching architectures.

Cache Implementation Technologies

When you decide on a caching architecture, keep in mind that server-side message interception can still impact performance because your service will need to compute a cache key and if it ends up with an oversized cache, the cache itself can actually decrease performance (especially if multiple services run on a shared server).

The higher memory requirements of a service that caches data can lead to increased paging activity on the server as a whole. Modern 64 bit servers equipped with terabytes of memory can reduce the amount of paging activity and thus avoid any associated performance reduction. Hardware-assisted virtualization further enables you to partition hardware resources and isolate services running on the same physical hardware from each other.

You can also leverage existing libraries such as the `System.Web.Caching` namespace for Web applications. Solutions like `System.Runtime.Caching` on .NET 4.0 or the Caching Application Block from the Enterprise Library are available for all .NET-based services. These libraries include some more specialized caching features, such as item expiration and cache scavenging. REST services hosted within WCF can leverage ASP.NET caching profiles for output caching and controlling caching headers.

Furthermore, a distributed caching extension is provided with Windows Server App-Fabric that offers a distributed, in-memory cache for high performance requirements associated with large-scale service processing. This extension in particular addresses the following problems of distributed and partitioned caching:

- storing cached data in memory across multiple servers to avoid costly database queries

- synchronizing cache content across multiple caching nodes for low latency and high scale and high availability

- caching partitions for fast look ups and load balancing across multiple caching servers

- local in-memory caching of cache subsets within services to reduce look up times beyond savings realized by optimizations on the caching tier

You also have several options for implementing the message interceptor. ASMX and WCF both offer extensibility points to intercept message processing *before* the service implementation is invoked. WCF even offers the same extensibility on the service consumer side. Table 19.2 lists the technology options for these caching architectures.

	interception	caching
intermediary	ASMX WCF	caching application block `System.Web.Caching` *.NET 4:* `System.Runtime.Caching` AppFabric
service container	ASMX: HTTP Module WCF: Custom Channel	caching application block `System.Web.Caching` *.NET 4:* `System.Runtime.Caching` AppFabric
service proxy	ASMX: Custom Proxy Class WCF: Custom Channel	caching application block AppFabric *REST:* `System.Net.WebClient` *REST:* `System.Net.HttpWebRequest` *.NET 4:* `System.Runtime.Caching`
utility service	none	caching application block `System.Web.Caching` *.NET 4:* `System.Runtime.Caching` AppFabric

Table 19.2

Technology choices for implementing caching architectures.

Computing Cache Keys

Let's take a closer look at the moving parts that comprise a typical caching solution. First, we need to compute the cache key from the request message to check if we already have a matching response in the cache. Computing a generic key before the message has been deserialized is straightforward when:

- the document format does not vary (for example, there is no optional content)

- the messages are XML element-centric and don't contain data in XML attributes or mixed mode content

- the code is already working with XML documents (for example, as with `XmlDocument`, `XmlNode` or `XPathNavigator` objects)

- the message design only passes reference data (not fully populated business documents)

- the services expose RESTful endpoints where URL parameters or partial URLs contain all reference data

In these situations, you can implement a simple, generic cache key algorithm. For example, you can load the request into an `XmlDocument` object and get the request data by examining the `InnerText` property of the document's root node. The danger here is that you could wind up with a very long and comprehensive cache key if your request message contains many data elements.

Computing a message type-specific cache key requires much more coding work and you may have to embed code for each message type. For server-side caching with ASMX Web services, for example, you would add an HTTP Module to the request processing pipeline for the service call. Inside the custom module, you can then inspect data items in the XML message content that uniquely identifies a service request and possibly bypasses the service call.

For client-side caching with ASMX, on the other hand, there is no transparent approach for adding caching logic. Custom proxy classes would have to perform all the caching-related processing. Depending on requirements and the number of service consumers, it might be easier to implement caching logic in the service consumer's code or switch to WCF for adding caching logic transparently.

For WCF-based services, you would define a custom binding with a custom caching channel as part of the channel stack for either the service or the consumer. A custom channel allows access to perform capabilities on the `Message` object. Oftentimes that's more convenient than programming against the raw XML message.

CASE STUDY EXAMPLE

Standard Mold realized that it could improve the performance of its mobile sales force application if it reduced the number of calls across the network. Some of the logic in the application communicated with services across the network each time a process executed. The application made calls to the service even for data items that changed infrequently, such as product descriptions or historical order information.

To improve the responsiveness of the application, Standard Mold decided to add caching to reduce the number of calls across the network. The least intrusive solution was to replace the ASMX-based Web service proxy class in the application with a WCF-based proxy class, and then configure a custom binding that included a caching channel. This approach required only minor modifications to the application code, such as changing the proxy classes and then recompiling the application. All other changes were isolated to the configuration file.

A portion of the configuration file with the custom binding is shown here:

```
<configuration>
  <system.serviceModel>
    <bindings>
      <customBinding>
        <binding name="cachingBasicHttpBinding">
          <caching />
          <textMessageEncoding />
          <httpTransport />
        </binding>
      </customBinding>
    </bindings>
    <client>
      <endpoint
        binding="customBinding"
        bindingConfiguration="cachingBasicHttpBinding"
        contract=" StandardMold.IProductService"
        name="ProductService">
      </endpoint>
    </client>
    <extensions>
      <bindingElementExtensions>
        <add
          name="caching"
          type="SalesApp.CachingElement, SalesApp,
          Version=1.0.0.0, Culture=neutral,
          PublicKeyToken=null" />
      </bindingElementExtensions>
    </extensions>
  <system.serviceModel>
</configuration>
```

Example 19.1

The custom binding added a caching channel based on the Caching Application Block from the Enterprise Library. This gave Standard Mold's developers a starting point because it provided features for cache dependencies, item expiration, item refresh and instrumentation.

An important piece of the caching channel implementation is the `Request` method defined in the WCF's `IRequestChannel` interface. This method examines key data items in the outgoing message and checks a local cache before calling the remote service. The channel returns data from the cache if the application previously asked for the same data and the data is still valid, rather than putting the message on the wire.

```
public Message Request(Message message, TimeSpan timeout)
{
  Message msg = null;
  if (message.Headers.Action == "http://example.org/
    IProductService/GetProductInformation")
  {
    MessageBuffer buffer = message.CreateBufferedCopy(2000);
    Message tempMsg = buffer.CreateMessage();
    XmlDictionaryReader dictread =
      tempMsg.GetReaderAtBodyContents();
    dictread.ReadToFollowing("productId",
      "http://example.org/");
    string productId = dictread.ReadString();
    if (cache.TryGetValue(productId, out msg))
    {
      msg.Headers.RelatesTo = message.Headers.MessageId;
    }
    else
    {
      message = buffer.CreateMessage();
      msg = innerChannel.Request(message, timeout);
      buffer = msg.CreateBufferedCopy(int.MaxValue);
      cache.Add(productId, buffer.CreateMessage());
      msg = buffer.CreateMessage();
    }
  }
  else
  {
    msg = innerChannel.Request(message, timeout);
  }
  return msg;
}
```

Example 19.2

Superior Stamping was looking to improve performance across its service inventory, and identified caching as one of the solutions that could be added to existing services in a transparent manner. Performance of the Product service, for example, would greatly improve through response caching because the company added new products only a few times a year. Superior Stamping architects chose to implement caching in a custom WCF channel.

A scalable and robust implementation of a service binding is more complex than a client-side solution, but at the heart of the solution they apply two methods:

Method 1

With this approach they inspect incoming messages and determine if the response is already present in the cache, as follows:

```
bool CheckResponseCache
  (ref RequestContext requestContext)
{
  if (requestContext == null)
  {
    return true;
  }
  Message originalMessage = requestContext.RequestMessage;
  MessageBuffer buffer =
    originalMessage.CreateBufferedCopy(int.MaxValue);
  requestContext = new CachingRequestContext(this,
    requestContext, buffer.CreateMessage());
  Message responseMessage =
    CheckCache(buffer.CreateMessage());
  if (null != responseMessage)
  {
    requestContext.Reply(responseMessage);
    requestContext.Close();
    requestContext = null;
  }
  else
  {
    needCache = true;
  }
  return requestContext != null;
}
```

Example 19.3

Method 2

The second method intercepts outgoing messages and caches the response if necessary:

```
void OnSend(ref Message msg)
{
  if (needCache == true)
  {
    MessageBuffer buffer =
      msg.CreateBufferedCopy(int.MaxValue);
    Message tempMsg = buffer.CreateMessage();
    XmlDictionaryReader dictread =
      tempMsg.GetReaderAtBodyContents();
    dictread.ReadToFollowing
      ("Id", "http://schemas.datacontract.org/
        StandardMold.ProductService");
    string productId = dictread.ReadString();
    cache.Add(productId, buffer,
      CacheItemPriority.Normal, null,
      new SlidingTime(TimeSpan.FromMinutes(5)));
    msg = buffer.CreateMessage();
  }
}
```

Example 19.4

Finally, the custom channel is added to a `customBinding` in the service's configuration file as shown here:

```
<configuration>
  <system.serviceModel>
    <services>
      <service
        name="StandardMold.ProductService.ProductServiceImpl">
        <endpoint
          binding="customBinding"
          bindingConfiguration="cachingBasicHttpBinding"
          contract=
          "StandardMold.ProductService.IProductService" />
      </service>
    </services>
    <bindings>
      <customBinding>
        <binding name="cachingBasicHttpBinding">
          <caching />
          <textMessageEncoding />
```

```
            <httpTransport />
          </binding>
        </customBinding>
      </bindings>
      <extensions>
        <bindingElementExtensions>
          <add
            name="caching"
            type="CatalogService.CachingElement, CatalogService,
              Version=1.0.0.0, Culture=neutral,
              PublicKeyToken=null" />
        </bindingElementExtensions>
      </extensions>
    </system.serviceModel>
</configuration>
```

Example 19.5

Caching REST Responses

The HTTP protocol defines content caching behavior on the server, on intermediaries, and on the client. This native form of content caching was originally responsible for driving wide-spread support in Web frameworks, like ASP.NET.

With .NET 4.0, WCF adds support for ASP.NET caching profiles. These profiles control the caching behavior on the server as well as sending HTTP headers to control caching on intermediaries and the client.

You configure a WCF REST service for ASP.NET caching with a combination of attributes and configuration file settings. You can begin by attributing the service contract with the AspNetCacheProfile attribute. The attribute is only valid for GET requests, which support how REST uses GET as the preferred verb for read capabilities.

```
[ServiceContract]
public interface ICatalogService
{
  [CapabilityContract]
  [WebGet( UriTemplate="/param/{itemId}")]
  [AspNetCacheProfile("CacheFor20SecondsServer")]
  string GetCatalogItem(string itemId);
  ...
}
```

Example 19.6

The attribute references a named profile stored in the service's configuration file. The service implementation class also needs an attribute to connect the service into the ASP.NET processing pipeline.

```
[AspNetCompatibilityRequirements(
  RequirementsMode =
  AspNetCompatibilityRequirementsMode.Required)]
public class CatalogService : ICatalogService
{
  ...
}
```

Example 19.7

The configuration file further needs to set up the service host for ASP.NET caching, by adding the `aspNetCompatibilityEnabled` attribute:

```
<system.serviceModel>
  <serviceHostingEnvironment
    aspNetCompatibilityEnabled="true" />
  <services>
    <service name="Service">
      <endpoint address="" binding=
      "webHttpBinding" contract="IService" />
    </service>
  </services>
  <bindings>
    <webHttpBinding />
  </bindings>
  ...
</system.serviceModel>
```

Example 19.8

Note that this configuration is at the host level and therefore enables ASP.NET for all services under this host. This could change behavior and performance for other services that don't require capabilities of ASP.NET. You should evaluate carefully if RESTful services and SOAP-based services should run in the same hosting environment.

The caching profile is also stored in the configuration file:

```
<system.web>
  <caching>
    <outputCacheSettings>
```

```
    <outputCacheProfiles>
      <add name="CacheFor20SecondsServer" duration="20"
        enabled="true" location="Server"
        varyByParam="itemId" />
    </outputCacheProfiles>
   </outputCacheSettings>
 </caching>
</system.web>
```

Example 19.9

The profile's `location` attribute indicates where the response can be cached. The preceding example configures server-side caching only, but other values are available to allow clients to cache responses as well. Client-side caching offers higher scalability and better performance because it doesn't increase the service's memory footprint and avoids unnecessary network calls.

If your architecture allows for response caching, caching should be enabled along the transmission chain because not all consumers may be built to support HTTP caching headers. WCF consumers, for example, ignore the caching attributes and repeat network calls even when HTTP Cache-Control headers indicate client-side caching is allowed.

If you consume cacheable data, you may invoke services with the `System.Net.WebClient` or `System.Net.HttpWebRequest` classes to optimize for performance.

Monitoring Cache Efficiency

After you have created a suitable caching architecture, it's important that you monitor the cache for efficiency. `System.Web.Caching` and the Caching Application Block both include numerous performance counters to monitor efficiency metrics, such as the cache hit ratio, the number of cache misses, etc.

The cache hit ratio measures the number of times a cached response was returned divided by the total number of requests. If you notice that your cache hit ratio is low, or your number of misses is growing, then your cache criteria could not match the data requested by consumers or the cached items expired too quickly.

Your caching is probably adding more overhead than it is improving performance of your service. Figure 19.8 and Figure 19.9 show the performance counters available for `System.Web.Caching` and the Caching Application Block.

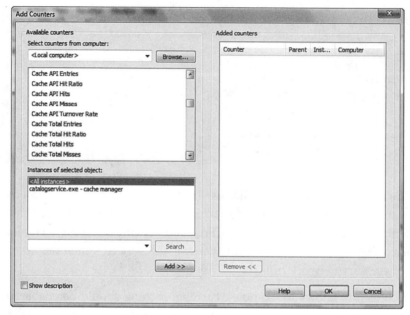

Figure 19.8

The `cache` class in `System.Web.Caching` exposes numerous performance counters to track the efficiency of the cache.

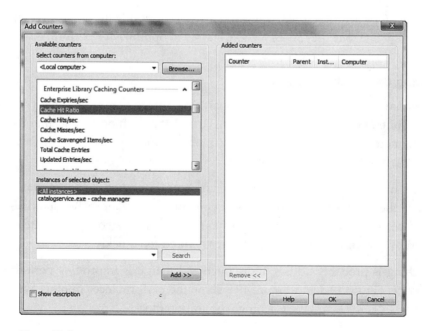

Figure 19.9

The Caching Counters in the Enterprise Library help monitor cache efficiency.

Reducing Resource Contention

By decreasing resource contention we can further improve performance by minimizing the time a service capability spends waiting for access to shared resources.

Shared resources in this context can be:

- CPU time

- memory

- files

- service container threads

- single-threaded code sections

- database connections

- databases (locks, rows, tables)

Several of these may exist as shared resources that can be accessed concurrently, whereas others may be limited to one executing thread.

It's important to understand that even resources that can be accessed concurrently, such as system memory, are not isolated from other programs. Physical memory allocated on behalf of one Web service on a server impacts all other processes on that server because it's not available to other processes. Therefore, allocating large portions of available system memory to one service can actually reduce performance for all other services on that server.

The memory required by the other services may only be available as virtual memory, which means increased paging activity will reduce performance. Each time a service tries to access a page that is not currently loaded, the operating system has to load the page from disk. That is a slow capability compared to accessing a page that's already available in memory (because disks are orders of magnitude slower than memory).

Execution of the service stalls until a page that's currently in memory is written to disk to make room for the requested page, which is then loaded into memory. What disk access essentially does is turn a fast, memory based capability into a slow, disk-based capability that can degrade performance.

You can monitor performance counters built into the Windows operating system and the .NET framework to determine if paging is impacting performance and if you can improve performance by reducing paging.

A high number of Page Faults indicates high contention for available system memory. If requested pages are frequently not available and have to be loaded from disk, you may also want to keep an eye on performance counters like:

- *Memory\\Committed Bytes* to ensure that it doesn't exceed the amount of physical memory in your server (if you cannot tolerate performance degradation due to paging).

- *Memory\\Private Bytes* to check that processes do not impact performance of other processes by allocating all memory for them.

You can best avoid the performance degradation caused by paging by reducing contention for system memory. This way, you reduce contention either by supplying large amounts of physical memory or by reducing concurrent access to the available memory. Likewise, eliminating contention for other system resources improves performance as well.

Request Throttling

Exclusive access to resources reduces contention and thus improves performance. Sometimes you can relieve contention just by adding more resources, more system memory or more CPUs. Other times, adding more resources is not an option, perhaps due to hardware restrictions or a limited number of available database connections. In that case you can avoid concurrency by throttling the number of requests sent to the service. This reduces contention to the number of concurrent service requests, which reduces CPU context switches, and concurrent access to shared resources.

Effective throttling shrinks the idle time component in the performance model as shown in Figure 19.10.

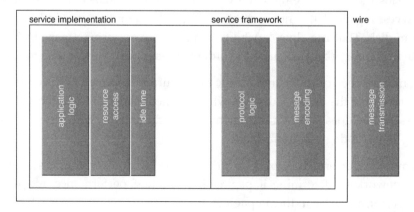

Figure 19.10
Request throttling reduces idle time in a service capability.

Remember though, that throttling is typically scoped to a single service. Throttling can reduce contention within a service, but multiple services sharing a server can still compete for these resources and cause contention and slow downs. You could introduce an intermediary service to throttle access to multiple services, but an intermediate service often introduces performance issues instead of fixing them.

Throttling With WCF

WCF allows for the throttling of messages by adding a throttling behavior to the channel. You can configure the throttling behavior in the service or client configuration file as follows:

```
<configuration>
<system.serviceModel>
    <services>
      <service
        name="..."
        behaviorConfiguration="Throttled" >
        ...
      </service>
    </services>
    ...
    <behaviors>
      <serviceBehaviors>
        <behavior  name="Throttled">
          <serviceThrottling
            maxConcurrentCalls="8"
            maxConcurrentSessions="8"
            maxConcurrentInstances="8" />
          ...
        </behavior>
      </serviceBehaviors>
    </behaviors>
  </system.serviceModel>
</configuration>
```

Example 19.10

This configuration limits concurrent processing to eight and improves performance in scenarios where contention for limited resources causes a problem. Processing more than eight requests simultaneously in a server with less than eight processors would cause costly context switches. Throttling the message processing reduces the amount of concurrency and thus the time lost due to switching context between the processing threads.

With the Windows Server AppFabric Application Server Extensions installed, you can also configure throttling parameters from the IIS Management tool (Figure 19.11).

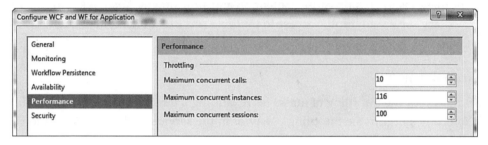

Figure 19.11
IIS Manager with AppFabric extensions can configure service throttling.

Note that as with everything else in WCF, you can configure the concurrency thresholds programmatically. However, placing these values in the configuration file allows for more flexibility to adjust the numbers as necessary without having to recompile code.

CASE STUDY EXAMPLE

Superior Stamping developed an algorithm to optimize the scheduling of manufacturing jobs for yield improvement and better machine utilization. Their ongoing SOA initiative provided a great opportunity to make this algorithm accessible to the scheduling processes across the various business units inside the company.

The algorithm was processing-intensive and optimized to operate on memory resident data. It was not designed for high levels of concurrency, but now that the service has been published for access to the entire enterprise, it was very likely that multiple instances of the algorithm would have to run concurrently on a single server.

The servers are modern multi-CPU, multi-core machines, but initial performance tests quickly confirmed that the execution time of the algorithm went up considerably when the number of requests exceeded the number of processor cores. The effects of context switches and paging on performance were clearly visible.

Rather than re-architecting the optimization algorithm for concurrency (which could have resulted in several months of delay and sub-optimal performance), project architects chose to throttle the number of concurrent executions to correlate to the number of processor cores on the server, as shown here:

```
ServiceHost host =
  new ServiceHost(typeof(OptimizationService));
```

```
int processorCount = System.Environment.ProcessorCount;
ServiceThrottlingBehavior throttle =
  new ServiceThrottlingBehavior();
throttle.MaxConcurrentCalls = processorCount;
throttle.MaxConcurrentInstances = processorCount;
throttle.MaxConcurrentSessions = processorCount;
host.Description.Behaviors.Add(throttle);
host.Open();
```

Example 19.11

Limiting the number of concurrent instances to the number of processors helps reduce costly context switches while the optimization algorithm is running and therefore ensures the shortest possible execution times.

Request Throttling with BizTalk Server

BizTalk Server provides more sophisticated throttling features than WCF. The BizTalk messaging engine continuously monitors several performance counters for each BizTalk host. Under several load conditions, BizTalk throttles message processing when certain performance counters exceed configured thresholds. The engine slows down processing of incoming and outgoing messages to reduce contention for resources, such as memory or server connections. You can configure the thresholds for each BizTalk host from the Administration Console, as shown in Figure 19.12.

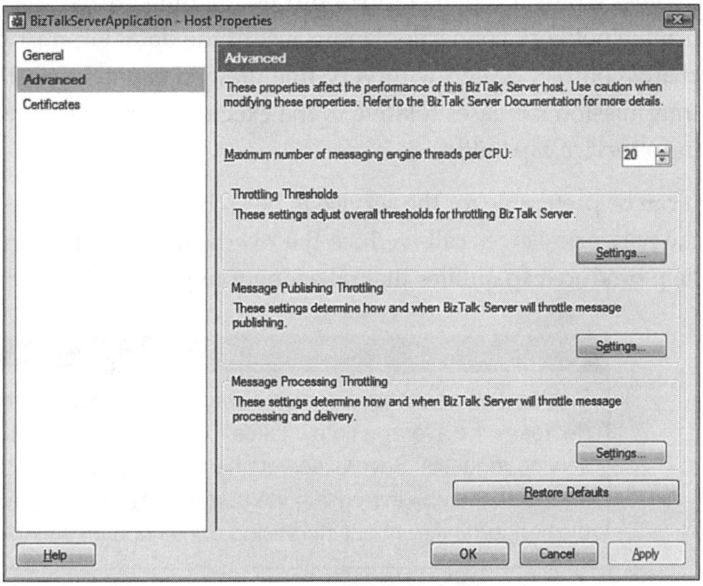

Figure 19.12

BizTalk allows for throttling threshold adjustment.

Throttling offers a relatively simple means of reducing resource contention. But just like with other performance tuning steps, it's important to understand what it can and cannot do. Throttling in WCF happens for a single service, but other services running on the same server could still compete for the equivalent resources. Throttling in BizTalk occurs at the host level. Other BizTalk hosts or services not hosted in BizTalk could compete for the same physical resources on the server.

You can only control contention in a meaningful way when fully applying the Service Autonomy (699) principle to create truly autonomous service implementations that have their own set of dedicated resources, either physically or through hardware-based virtualization. This level of autonomy allows you to commit your servers to hard Service Level Agreement (SLA) requirements.

Coarse-Grained Service Contracts

The capability granularity and constraint granularity of a service contract can greatly impact performance of the service architecture. A service consumer communicating over a network connection can experience significant latency between request and response when exchanging large messages over poor network connections. Network latency is often beyond your control, especially when you consume third party services over a public network. Nevertheless you can architect your services to minimize the performance impact of remote service interactions.

The key consideration to keep in mind is to "make it worth the trip across the network." In other words, keep the ratio of processing time greater than the time it takes to establish the network connection and transmit the data. Figure 19.13 shows the model for a chatty contract design with very fine grained capabilities. The impact of the message transmission increases relative to the execution time the consumer observes for invoking a service capability.

It can be preferable for the service to be architected to reduce the number of calls across the network. Fewer calls reduce the overhead of managing network connections and help produce capabilities that take longer to process than the message transmission.

> **NOTE**
>
> Scaling out is another common approach to reduce contention and decrease the average time it takes for a service to handle concurrent service requests. Several servers handle requests sent to a single service endpoint, thereby increasing the number of messages a service can handle concurrently without increasing contention on a single server.

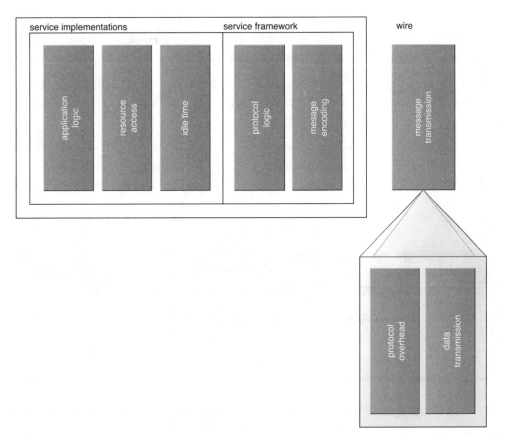

Figure 19.13

The transmission of a message across the wire can result in substantial piece processing.

CASE STUDY EXAMPLE

Standard Mold built an Order Processor service for a set of internal service consumers. Most consumers were located on the company's network and the latency was acceptable for the employees creating new orders. The desktop application for the mobile sales workers required some contract optimizations to reduce chattiness and hide the network latency.

When Standard Mold got ready to open up the service to external business consumer programs, they realized that the Order Processor service contract was inadequate.

The Order Processor service required several round trips to set up and complete a single order. Each trip added overhead that increased the time it took to set up an order.

In addition to the performance implications, each service capability also had to include code to check if the capability was valid (for example, if the order was created or if the user could still add items to the order).

Standard Mold architects layered the Order Manager service on top of the Order Processor Service. The Order Manager service exposed one single, consolidated capability SubmitOrder that avoided unnecessary network trips and also avoided any out of sequence calls from the external consumers. Table 19.3 illustrates the two service contracts.

OrderManager (for external consumers)	OrderProcessor (for internal consumers)
SubmitOrder	ValidateOrder
	CreateOrder
	FillLineItems
	FillCustomerDetails

Table 19.3
The external service contract for submitting orders is very coarse grained. The internal contract is finer grained.

Selecting Application Containers

The choice of a service's hosting model can greatly impact its performance because of the differences in the processing that occur for incoming and outgoing messages. Usually you see a trade-off between robustness and a rich feature set on one hand and high performance on the other. Many features require additional layers of processing between the service endpoint and the service implementation. Each layer adds time and decreases performance.

Let's take a look at four specific hosting models:

- BizTalk Server
- WAS + IIS + AppFabric Application Server Extensions

- self-hosted services

- in-process hosted services

BizTalk Server offers numerous features to increase reliability, availability, and scalability. Unfortunately, many of these features require a fair amount of additional processing and thus, decrease performance because each extra processing step adds to the duration of the execution of a service capability. Figure 19.14 shows the processing steps of a standard BizTalk request.

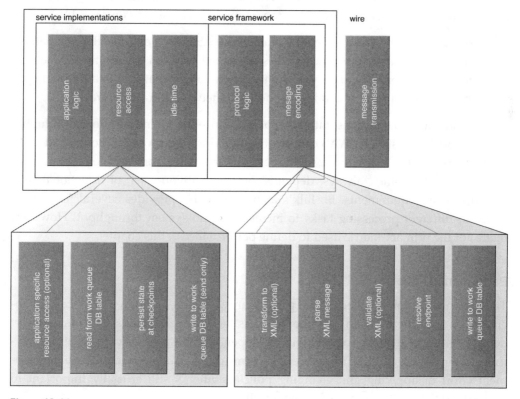

Figure 19.14

BizTalk Server's scalability, robustness and fault tolerance features add overhead to the performance model.

Notice not only the sheer number of steps that occur, but also that state is saved to a database between these steps. Database read and write functions are typically several orders of magnitude slower than in-process memory access. For simple service capabilities, the duration may increase significantly when you host a service inside BizTalk

Server. The additional overhead may be negligible for long-running transactions where the execution time of a process depends on humans or other systems and thus, may not cause a noticeable performance impact.

WAS and IIS perform far less processing steps than BizTalk Server. ASMX services, for example, perform authentication, authorization and, in some cases, parse HTTP cookies to get the service's session state identifier. Those steps may include database lookups or validating user credentials against an Active Directory server, but the message is never stored to a database between those steps. Web services hosted in BizTalk Server perform all the steps for ASMX service plus the steps shown previously in Figure 19.14.

Request processing in WAS can be even leaner than ASMX, when ASP.NET compatibility is disabled and all policy processing is delegated to WCF. If runtime service performance is a high priority, then you can further reduce the latency to a minimum by investing in very fast servers and high-bandwidth network infrastructure.

Properly architected solutions with high performance WCF bindings hosted in highly scalable containers such as WAS can drastically reduce the processing overhead compared to BizTalk Server and thus provide better performance. Your decision for one hosting model or another always depends on your unique set of functional and non-functional requirements. BizTalk's architecture also provides several features to scale out different processing tasks to increase overall system throughput. However, that's not the primary metric used to define performance in this chapter.

Performance Policies

The previous section touched on the performance impacts of different service containers due to the differences in how they process messages. The actual processing effort doesn't just depend on the container; it also depends on the policies you apply to a service endpoint. WCF and BizTalk Server platforms do a great job to reduce the development effort of applying and changing policies, but it's still crucially important to understand the performance differences of different policies.

WCF abstracts policies into bindings that you can apply to a service endpoint, which somewhat obscures the processing steps for these policies. Figure 19.15 illustrates the high-level stages of processing in a binding.

Let's compare the `BasicHttpBinding` and `WsHttpBinding`, as shown in Figure 19.16 and Figure 19.17.

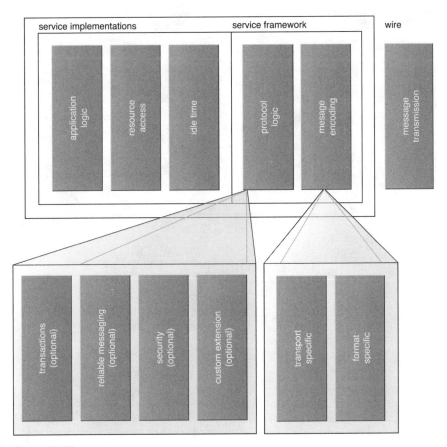

Figure 19.15
WCF Bindings can apply policies for transactions, reliable messaging, security, as well as custom policies.

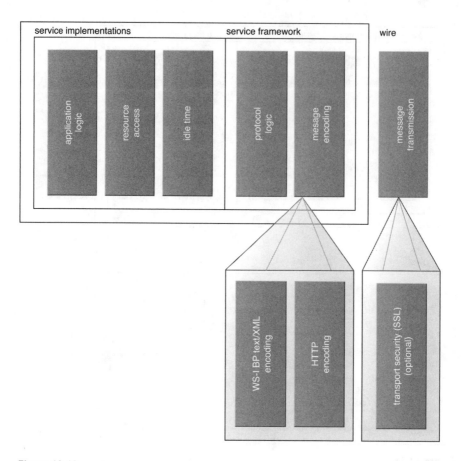

Figure 19.16
The policies included in BasicHttpBinding do not add significant processing.

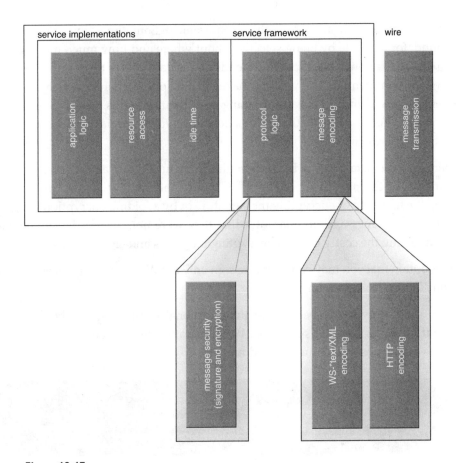

Figure 19.17

The default security policies in WsHttpBinding add a considerable amount of extra message processing.

Both bindings communicate via SOAP and XML over HTTP and both rely on DataContractSerializer to serialize message objects into XML messages. However, their performance is very different.

WsHttpBinding is configured for secure message transmission by default, so that messages are signed, encrypted, and the signature is further encrypted as well. This approach achieves high security, but it also introduces burden with respect to performance. WCF allows you to turn off message security for the WsHttpBinding, which makes performance between the BasicHttpBinding and WsHttpBinding comparable again.

Security isn't necessarily an all or nothing requirement. Sometimes you can find a middle ground, for example by being selective about where and how much message security you'd like to apply. This decision depends on the data you're transmitting. If data is sensitive and confidential, then you may have no other option than signing and encrypting the messages. Your only means of tuning performance in this case is the encryption algorithm you apply and whether you choose to involve special devices to perform encryption in hardware.

In other cases, the data may not be confidential, but you still care about possible attacks. You can reduce the processing overhead of the default setting in WsHttpBinding by avoiding the final step of encrypting the signature or by avoiding encryption altogether. You can still sign messages to guarantee that they were not tampered with; however, you are avoiding the costly steps of encrypting messages and signatures.

Another option that you may consider is to sign only the WS-Addressing headers to protect your service from spoofing.

Security is not only costly because of the additional computing overhead, but also because it increases message size. Table 19.4 illustrates the differences in message size between various unsecured and secured messages.

No security	WS-Addressing (signed headers)	WS-Addressing (signed headers) + Body Signature	WS-Addressing (signed headers) + Body Signature + Body Encryption
`<s:Envelope xmlns:s="http://www.w3.org/2003/05/soap-envelope" xmlns:a="http://www.w3.org/2005/08/addressing"> <s:Header> <a:Action s:mustUnderstand="1">http://www.example.org/SellFast/2007/1/15/ICatalogManager/GetCatalogsResponse</a:Action> <a:RelatesTo>urn:uuid:e0fb4f21-26a4-4764-a49b-a0c314fbba7c</a:RelatesTo> </s:Header> <s:Body> <GetCatalogsResponse xmlns="http://www.example.org/SellFast/2007/1/15"> <GetCatalogsResult xmlns:i="http://www.w3.org/2001/XMLSchema-instance"> <Catalog> <CatalogItems> <CatalogItem>`	`<s:Envelope xmlns:s="http://www.w3.org/2003/05/soap-envelope" xmlns:a="http://www.w3.org/2005/08/addressing" xmlns:u="http://docs.oasis- <s:Envelope xmlns:s="http://www.w3.org/2003/05/soap-envelope" xmlns:a="http://www.w3.org/2005/08/addressing" xmlns:u="http://docs.oasis-open.org/wss/2004/01/oasis-200401-wss-wssecurity-utility-1.0.xsd "> <s:Header> <a:Action s:mustUnderstand="1" u:Id="_3">http://www.example.org/SellFast/2007/1/15/ICatalogManager/GetCatalogsResponse</a:Action> <a:RelatesTo u:Id="_4">urn:uuid:a9118ca3-292b-49ab-9935-4ec3b3742479</a:RelatesTo> <o:Security s:mustUnderstand="1" xmlns:o="http://docs.oasis-open.org/wss/2004/01/oasis-200401-wss-wssecurity-secext-1.0.xsd "> <u:Timestamp u:Id="uuid-`	`open.org/wss/2004/01/oasis-200401-wss-wssecurity-utility-1.0.xsd"> <s:Header> <a:Action s:mustUnderstand="1" u:Id="_4">http://www.example.org/SellFast/2007/1/15/ICatalogManager/GetCatalogsResponse</a:Action> <a:RelatesTo u:Id="_5">urn:uuid:86574c7f-1335-4b0f-8e08-d5016c20a393</a:RelatesTo> <o:Security s:mustUnderstand="1" xmlns:o="http://docs.oasis-open.org/wss/2004/01/oasis-200401-wss-wssecurity-secext-1.0.xsd"> <u:Timestamp u:Id="uuid-5fc77b63-4035-4882-b742-d331b9d4dd72-1"> <u:Created>2007-02-24T18:36:49.656Z</u:Created> <u:Expires>2007-02-24T18:41:49.656Z</u:Expires> </u:Timestamp> <c:DerivedKeyToken u:Id="_0" xmlns:c="http://schemas.xml-soap.org/ws/2005/02/sc"> <o:SecurityTokenReference>`	`<s:Envelope xmlns:s="http://www.w3.org/2003/05/soap-envelope" xmlns:a="http://www.w3.org/2005/08/addressing" xmlns:u="http://docs.oasis-open.org/wss/2004/01/oasis-200401-wss-wssecurity-utility-1.0.xsd"> <s:Header> <a:Action s:mustUnderstand="1" u:Id="_5">http://www.example.org/SellFast/2007/1/15/ICatalogManager/GetCatalogsResponse</a:Action> <a:RelatesTo u:Id="_6">urn:uuid:21219c3c-04d1-4dc7-9621-1fc8979e91dc</a:RelatesTo> <o:Security s:mustUnderstand="1" xmlns:o="http://docs.oasis-open.org/wss/2004/01/oasis-200401-wss-wssecurity-secext-1.0.xsd"> <u:Timestamp u:Id="uuid-0d58f98f-10be-4992-a912-7cfd9f0f86be-1"> <u:Created>2007-02-24T21:29:53.450Z</u:Created> <u:Expires>2007-02-24T21:34:53.450Z</u:Expires> </u:Timestamp> <c:DerivedKeyToken u:Id="_0" xmlns:c="http://schemas.xmlsoap.org/ws/2005/02/sc"> <o:SecurityTokenReference> <o:KeyIdentifier`

No security	WS-Addressing (signed headers)	WS-Addressing (signed headers) + Body Signature	WS-Addressing (signed headers) + Body Signature + Body Encryption

No security

```
        <Descrip-
tion>This is a cool
item</Description>
        <DisplayUn-
til>2007-03-
01T00:00:00-06:00</Di
splayUntil>
        <ProductIm-
age
i:nil="true"></Pro-
ductImage>
        <Product-
Name>The COOL
gadget</Product-
Name>

<VendorSku>sk12345<
/VendorSku>
        </Catalog-
Item>
    </CatalogItems>
        <CatalogNUm-
ber>123</Cata-
logNUmber>
        <ValidUn-
til>2007-03-
01T00:00:00-06:00</Va
lidUntil>
        <VendorNum-
ber>456</Vendor-
Number>
    </Catalog>
    </GetCatalogsRe-
sult>
  </GetCatalogsRe-
sponse>
  </s:Body>
</s:Envelope>
```

WS-Addressing (signed headers)

```
bffedeb2-22c8-426b-8860-
e39d06d2d8bf-1">
        <u:Created>2007-02-
24T21:12:01.758Z</u:Created>
        <u:Expires>2007-02-
24T21:17:01.758Z</u:Expires>
        </u:Timestamp>
    <c:DerivedKeyToken u:Id="_0"
xmlns:c="http://schemas.xmlsoap.o
rg/ws/2005/02/sc">
        <o:SecurityTokenReference>
        </o:KeyIdentifier
ValueType="http://docs.oasis-
open.org/wss/oasis-wss-soap-mes-
sage-security-1.1#EncryptedKeySHA
1"
EncodingType="http://docs.oasis-
open.org/wss/2004/01/oasis-
200401-wss-soap-message-security-1.
0#Base64Binary">02vMtCqaSvmo-
Qcknffldci3IH3g=</o:KeyIdentifier>
    </o:SecurityTokenReference>
        <c:Offset>0</c:Offset>
        <c:Length>24</c:Length>
        <c:Nonce>
        <!—Removed—>
        </c:Nonce>
    </c:DerivedKeyToken>
    <k:SignatureConfirmation
u:Id="_1"
Value="mvclW6gFQQGq9p6GgusD-
Fatt+2I="
xmlns:k="http://docs.oasis-
open.org/wss/oasis-wss-wssecurity-
secext-1.1.xsd"></k:SignatureConfir
mation>
        <Signature
xmlns="http://www.w3.org/2000/0
9/xmldsig#">
        <SignedInfo>
        <CanonicalizationMethod
Algorithm="http://www.w3.org/20
01/10/xml-exc-c14n#"></Canonical-
izationMethod>
        <SignatureMethod
Algorithm="http://www.w3.org/20
00/09/xmldsig#hmac-sha1"></Sig-
natureMethod>
        <Reference URI="#_3">
        <Transforms>
        <Transform
Algorithm="http://www.w3.org/20
01/10/xml-exc-c14n#"></Trans-
form>
        </Transforms>
        <DigestMethod
Algorithm="http://www.w3.org/20
00/09/xmldsig#sha1"></Digest-
Method>

<DigestValue>9xvz9vKuAyziE5bKB
V6qQ1QSfhQ=</DigestValue>
        </Reference>
        <Reference URI="#_4">
        <Transforms>
        <Transform
Algorithm="http://www.w3.org/20
01/10/xml-exc-c14n#"></Trans-
form>
        </Transforms>
        <DigestMethod
Algorithm="http://www.w3.org/20
00/09/xmldsig#sha1"></Digest-
Method>
```

WS-Addressing (signed headers) + Body Signature

```
        <o:KeyIdentifier
ValueType="http://docs.oasis-
open.org/wss/oasis-wss-soap-mes-
sage-security-1.1#EncryptedKeySH
A1"
EncodingType="http://docs.oasis-
open.org/wss/2004/01/oasis-
200401-wss-soap-message-security-
1.0#Base64Binary">bs2ghg-
pVKUCxf21mJRrvshafIfQ=</o:Key
Identifier>
    </o:SecurityTokenReference>
        <c:Offset>0</c:Offset>
        <c:Length>24</c:Length>
        <c:Nonce>
        Removed
        </c:Nonce>
    </c:DerivedKeyToken>
    <k:SignatureConfirmation
u:Id="_1"
Value="dAdN2nqsI3mHUgC7X/k
pK1RJAaQ="
xmlns:k="http://docs.oasis-
open.org/wss/oasis-wss-wssecu-
rity-secext-1.1.xsd"></k:Signature
Confirmation>
        <Signature
xmlns="http://www.w3.org/2000
/09/xmldsig#">
        <SignedInfo>
        <CanonicalizationMethod
Algorithm="http://www.w3.org/2
001/10/xml-exc-c14n#"></Canoni-
calizationMethod>
        <SignatureMethod Algo-
rithm="http://www.w3.org/2000/
09/xmldsig#hmac-sha1"></Signa-
tureMethod>
        <Reference URI="#_3">
        <Transforms>
        <Transform
Algorithm="http://www.w3.org/2
001/10/xml-exc-c14n#"></Trans-
form>
        </Transforms>
        <DigestMethod
Algorithm="http://www.w3.org/2
000/09/xmldsig#sha1"></Digest-
Method>
        <DigestValue>Vyn-
dyUkeBMD4TEsWXcb6nRrF8fs=</
DigestValue>
        </Reference>
        <Reference URI="#_4">
        <Transforms>
        <Transform
Algorithm="http://www.w3.org/2
001/10/xml-exc-c14n#"></Trans-
form>
        </Transforms>
        <DigestMethod
Algorithm="http://www.w3.org/2
000/09/xmldsig#sha1"></Digest-
Method>
        <DigestValue>9KzrQGfaX-
PUD8kxX7R86zTgJy58=</Digest-
Value>
        </Reference>
        <Reference URI="#_5">
        <Transforms>
        <Transform
Algorithm="http://www.w3.org/2
001/10/xml-exc-c14n#"></Trans-
form>
        </Transforms>
```

WS-Addressing (signed headers) + Body Signature + Body Encryption

```
ValueType="http://docs.oasis-
open.org/wss/oasis-wss-soap-message-security-
1.1#EncryptedKeySHA1"
EncodingType="http://docs.oasis-
open.org/wss/2004/01/oasis-200401-wss-soap-
message-security-1.0#Base64Binary">UO/4hH55R
Q8DzckGNdRx7ZsjRdo=</o:KeyIdentifier>
    </o:SecurityTokenReference>
        <c:Offset>0</c:Offset>
        <c:Length>24</c:Length>
        <c:Nonce>
        <!--Removed-->
        </c:Nonce>
    </c:DerivedKeyToken>
    <c:DerivedKeyToken u:Id="_2"
xmlns:c="http://schemas.xmlsoap.org/ws/2005/
02/sc">
        <o:SecurityTokenReference>
        <o:KeyIdentifier
ValueType="http://docs.oasis-
open.org/wss/oasis-wss-soap-message-security-
1.1#EncryptedKeySHA1"
EncodingType="http://docs.oasis-
open.org/wss/2004/01/oasis-200401-wss-soap-
message-security-1.0#Base64Binary">UO/4hH55R
Q8DzckGNdRx7ZsjRdo=</o:KeyIdentifier>
    </o:SecurityTokenReference>
        <c:Nonce>
        <!--Removed-->
        </c:Nonce>
    </c:DerivedKeyToken>
    <e:ReferenceList
xmlns:e="http://www.w3.org/2001/04/xmlenc#"
>
        <e:DataReference
URI="#_4"></e:DataReference>
        <e:DataReference
URI="#_7"></e:DataReference>
        <e:DataReference
URI="#_8"></e:DataReference>
        </e:ReferenceList>
        <e:EncryptedData Id="_8"
Type="http://www.w3.org/2001/04/xmlenc#Ele-
ment"
xmlns:e="http://www.w3.org/2001/04/xmlenc#"
>
        <e:EncryptionMethod
Algorithm="http://www.w3.org/2001/04/xmlen
c#aes256-cbc"></e:EncryptionMethod>
        <KeyInfo
xmlns="http://www.w3.org/2000/09/xmldsig#"
>
        <o:SecurityTokenReference>
        <o:Reference URI="#_2"></o:Refer-
ence>
    </o:SecurityTokenReference>
        </KeyInfo>
        <e:CipherData>
        <e:CipherValue>gI3QfFtu+Ynqjwf-
fiuO7wVxDmi8HCaFtPPQcLewUrBvPxpjEkg-
tyMjcOem3RZZHDvxJouBV86T6iYmbCYOC8eAj
25QAfYLGgdubZBx/aV67wcImSTDzh6+IouksB8f
VwBzLgAVKwCkCXjFNZi5usAatdGWbbR6ytNy
6gOLc+DGK5kXsdb7Pz5Cp8DMAI+d8lAuAah2r4
mfFOCCKt9DPL7dONlD4KTDGtVmBn9TYyAzA
puB3Fl02Y8Y/PGY0uOsEqmw0Y6IHsJs3bCB0FEk
EaxE19qUmthAooYLbArarPqtbT8MUMx5ndcZqk
Z6RSk9CKmHSNG8bg/129fxD33+WRosxxZayH-
LiJR2VyOmUzRnrA=</e:CipherValue>
        </e:CipherData>
        </e:EncryptedData>
        <e:EncryptedData Id="_7"
Type="http://www.w3.org/2001/04/xmlenc#Ele-
ment"
xmlns:e="http://www.w3.org/2001/04/xmlenc#"
```

continues

No security	WS-Addressing (signed headers)	WS-Addressing (signed headers) + Body Signature	WS-Addressing (signed headers) + Body Signature + Body Encryption

Column 2 — WS-Addressing (signed headers):

```
<DigestValue>6lnWGsZ/+hjghR9ma
2JG7ahRd7U=</DigestValue>
      </Reference>
      <Reference URI="#uuid-
bffedeb2-22c8-426b-8860-
e39d06d2d8bf-1">
      <Transforms>
      <Transform
Algorithm="http://www.w3.org/20
01/10/xml-exc-c14n#"></Trans-
form>
      </Transforms>
      <DigestMethod
Algorithm="http://www.w3.org/20
00/09/xmldsig#sha1"></Digest-
Method>

<DigestValue>c9AmGxs+Ql92pON-
tYJ1dKLbaDX8=</DigestValue>
      </Reference>
      <Reference URI="#_1">
      <Transforms>
      <Transform
Algorithm="http://www.w3.org/20
01/10/xml-exc-c14n#"></Trans-
form>
      </Transforms>
      <DigestMethod
Algorithm="http://www.w3.org/20
00/09/xmldsig#sha1"></Digest-
Method>

<DigestValue>EvzI3dC7yCq6AR+tr
CxxdC61Dek=</DigestValue>
      </Reference>
      </SignedInfo>

<SignatureValue>eaHp0ZhBY7/vZZ
milR8NuotRA5k=</Signa-
tureValue>
      <KeyInfo>
      <o:SecurityTokenReference>
      <o:Reference
URI="#_0"></o:Reference>
      </o:SecurityTokenReference>
      </KeyInfo>
      </Signature>
      </o:Security>
   </s:Header>
   <s:Body>
      <GetCatalogsResponse
xmlns="http://www.example.org/S
ellFast/2007/1/15">
      <GetCatalogsResult
xmlns:i="http://www.w3.org/2001/
XMLSchema-instance">
      <Catalog>
      <CatalogItems>
      <CatalogItem>
      <Description>This is a cool
item</Description>
      <DisplayUntil>2007-03-
01T00:00:00-06:00</DisplayUntil>
      <ProductImage
i:nil="true"></ProductImage>
      <ProductName>The COOL
gadget</ProductName>
      <VendorSku>sk12345</Ven-
dorSku>
      </CatalogItem>
      </CatalogItems>
      <CatalogNUmber>123</Cata-
logNUmber>
      <ValidUntil>2007-03-
01T00:00:00-06:00</ValidUntil>
```

Column 3 — WS-Addressing (signed headers) + Body Signature:

```
      <DigestMethod
Algorithm="http://www.w3.org/2
000/09/xmldsig#sha1"></Digest-
Method>

<DigestValue>NJtUpX9PI3u0g/GN
O3MZ28EUKbU=</DigestValue>
      </Reference>
      <Reference URI="#uuid-
5fc77b63-4035-4882-b742-
d331b9d4dd72-1">
      <Transforms>
      <Transform
Algorithm="http://www.w3.org/2
001/10/xml-exc-c14n#"></Trans-
form>
      </Transforms>
      <DigestMethod
Algorithm="http://www.w3.org/2
000/09/xmldsig#sha1"></Digest-
Method>

<DigestValue>BU7e2Dp07z0gZYiR
Vp4yaaMJs5k=</DigestValue>
      </Reference>
      <Reference URI="#_1">
      <Transforms>
      <Transform
Algorithm="http://www.w3.org/2
001/10/xml-exc-c14n#"></Trans-
form>
      </Transforms>
      <DigestMethod
Algorithm="http://www.w3.org/2
000/09/xmldsig#sha1"></Digest-
Method>
      <DigestValue>TblnDyJS-
nyV+0Tl+Sjow088bBQc=</Digest-
Value>
      </Reference>
      </SignedInfo>

<SignatureValue>j1XipZX+6iJm8Ba
lFz/IGj5UNEs=</SignatureValue>
      <KeyInfo>
      <o:SecurityTokenReference>
      <o:Reference
URI="#_0"></o:Reference>
      </o:SecurityTokenReference>
      </KeyInfo>
      </Signature>
      </o:Security>
   </s:Header>
   <s:Body u:Id="_3">
      <GetCatalogsResponse
xmlns="http://www.example.org/
SellFast/2007/1/15">
      <GetCatalogsResult
xmlns:i="http://www.w3.org/2001
/XMLSchema-instance">
      <Catalog>
      <CatalogItems>
      <CatalogItem>
      <Description>This is a cool
item</Description>
      <DisplayUntil>2007-03-
01T00:00:00-06:00</DisplayUntil>
      <ProductImage
i:nil="true"></ProductImage>
      <ProductName>The COOL
gadget</ProductName>

<VendorSku>sk12345</Ven-
dorSku>
      </CatalogItem>
```

Column 4 — WS-Addressing (signed headers) + Body Signature + Body Encryption:

```
>
      <e:EncryptionMethod
Algorithm="http://www.w3.org/2001/04/x
mlenc#aes256-cbc"></e:EncryptionMethod>
      <KeyInfo
xmlns="http://www.w3.org/2000/09/xmld-
sig#">
      <o:SecurityTokenReference>
      <o:Reference
URI="#_2"></o:Reference>
      </o:SecurityTokenReference>
      </KeyInfo>
      <e:CipherData>

<e:CipherValue>phXTEdlcuA4IU9O/+EB86J
PhHkt1iplvC3uNYGGFdM1EQiVmpxFblp3d
pKhXTQBkt2gO3I0Ijoq0VWn6gqNNY3k/8gB
mLOPpumE7XRAZfAZLAyfYZYaTP3ORG-
phwgeRTMAlc5H7KfmVJva9x4TAoDqNSvN
1b9wrFYASikC8waqyINPnx1CDRg6WxrqAfg
mSzABS30RToC3j6MDIxitK4+nLRoj5QfEhkB
n2mW/lhRhex1kLaejqP2yJHTMlHFQfCtydF-
teUkrDwO3JzjSrRHeBx5b4K9HX/VSWA1GA
S0UAnW2+JemhagqEtHdyUoIuFao+0oungt9
nXoaSMTjtxw4+2uTCvHAqUuelMuqR-
RXliNdUkOw4vx53GQinqQed/flYijhh8yP5m
ZLORO6K8Xg9qZTynhh0+28oPaYEgBuUo4d
UdDpznG3LeoXNk3OG66ethz82vFNkoo/B2s
AUwdiDcWZt2TfPRzWVaQnbKstwfMS-
dgzQRwW/qr8IQ5z2PWOuIMiimrwtXR6N
mij9Mh58WPMirrggFC/JTVlWrQPeWjI-
ASM0CjBk/hQjBDFQoQFjuqKUVmL3pEtg81
5I+dQkgewFME2fToAqW+0ogES0U8n0Zx8Z
qd3toRFEgcqZHjWhMw+7+ZFAlku8xflxnf0
WglmAk3lDa2wYVqQjq+GEvD+N63EjFuwP
2HAdxYoosENC4Ris0IsGCXN4o1Jz41XsCEs-
FZcxajDvzJ7EY4kzDIKzGJPxRqVj53FMnzfNt
cs+C5pmMfYsjERru5rQbz1WpQK7T/HOtJX-
dRpIa6zdexP1Q8E3QK+n0MwouhyQU5Loof
/LnSuinE8FL0Xa/iP6wn7qFhY0BM0TbIDxP2
zfFSP8isllGpzVDBpoqQBypVKr8AsCCE-
bxsCGWhdRqyHUs6QJpNLez0CiQsQo-
qyv1OgSnjiVtD4SSlWcJGHoLnubtb+GTPX0
N3Xlcv5lvWxwuW3Bc/15mSgxz8rZXu-
vCZ81Pgv7a0QrbnWgbRcCnOTCWhR1iCzl
mhnf69Cy7YxOzZJRqohIZau7IWx9NyZ6rNd
HgfLOESZfpicwpJNGSfhRIAPbetbKssT//Q
Z5Ae8tWP/AqoWnpp2g0A/ep/QziKi43jR0Z
AkNcZ1kSNws8iVz7EyP7l0bRBxjJix9FWuvh9
95I6fMSC3XVX27uHC5EV/4RUQb6YP1j74H
6UV2/WiXGYgsxZS/AlsVxDLLtqMQBqS9pc
jno9zHZyxOELJwxbqtfzLRUNy9LBx-
DOaRKgCKr4MUVPSk3IZtxEz+PrgS4XuyO4
0lj5DMbL8gJeiUHghpaqvkSzKnA40WNAvkr
D/3rd5dlnJKRrv+0xaf3VQhWvTib7WoO/Jh
CYGxbqal3iP7G2HY7UpJrnA/1dv55ejZR-
wEc+EsvFnfhGgx0jem0Kdcb+Fvq4mnLZK-
mMRKAQHtU+0JMIK1U1Rlb5+Ii0xWbgSPh
YOXuTrfUiQ1M2+S3Pw/xzLYkHRpOt-
DLkeRU/gZvucWJ6RNWdq/BHQ1Rsdli9K2
82oiCbc7dEMMycJt0Psr23Knjm8Cz+1p7XBBI
zNndXCIK0NQti+ExmGzuUXekARJERjg4mo
qVVv/wcTx8F4QBB/B/aNnUi2Iwe0Kykw1T
HJ0mUodLE5m/rB6Ooj1nIstQPaKTcp+8fu+5
5P1QUfdkbB4fjGbj1eXHjlH3rb5A7uZD-
dumV6lLVpkRCj3Hbj1ouHq9xEGwJuTbA40B
86OIIO5fFCqKxCAyYQMR3Xop-
cYFeDnzoXYsAh9FI61fGA1ZAgfcqRgLje+G4
9NA/1Jd1ccfJaHh4oY7IPuK3nLPfKaZh-
BQAUg9Nmd7/mFpGWWteJpta9O8YSO0Nr
5V3r0Ku9v2BsD+M2P5J1zT3wxg+mSpQU+
Do1za+tlxB5ZEghhFMjGYQ8mIVWKWb/SSc
l7cAbaE/v01BA1YUzQufL2OEFktC8a9eUbi0
1JXKzijN3JVsoiRNI/ss1mDphEHnLle-
dOwgW+kJiiai1kRBrPsPJVXTeuqImlIlhQdYj-
```

No security	WS-Addressing (signed headers)	WS-Addressing (signed headers) + Body Signature	WS-Addressing (signed headers) + Body Signature + Body Encryption
	<VendorNumber>456</Vendor- Number> </Catalog> </GetCatalogsResult> </GetCatalogsResponse> </s:Body> </s:Envelope>	</CatalogItems> <CatalogNUmber>123</Cata- logNUmber> <ValidUntil>2007-03- 01T00:00:00-06:00</ValidUntil> <VendorNumber>456</Ven- dorNumber> </Catalog> </GetCatalogsResult> </GetCatalogsResponse> </s:Envelope>	cIQA4ZQWEd9HO6lJG2ht2wshDgvLrWb59SX7d9Poa- SOThf89ZoBEeB6AYRVbqdZ3PxDAKtSmxda61FAOBPU u9j+m1TUiyXY8Z8ORlGRm1qQw5pX4qgnLRg/Xc5XXo kU5c5hE+X1HgjhzQq/WEcPCWHtv3toPCx5J+HWqP- NEPEB3M3fyb6pNAhRn7RyfP/1avmSZNay2lkHUrx- Erde3xhR+3ZyVyE69ZxHLEdCtaGSbF7jJ6CloNGZPh35l auOwmsr7uATr4hztL1vDGGzbJilxXZIzQtIHfgxi3Cl8CY 9jYUi075l12gO5Rrxz5/60wCusCOm1waMo2Ic</e:Ciph erValue> </e:CipherData> </e:EncryptedData> </o:Security> </s:Header> <s:Body u:Id="_3"> <e:EncryptedData Id="_4" Type="http://www.w3.org/2001/04/xmlenc#Content" xmlns:e="http://www.w3.org/2001/04/xmlenc#"> <e:EncryptionMethod Algorithm="http://www.w3.org/2001/04/xmlenc#aes2 56-cbc"></e:EncryptionMethod> <KeyInfo xmlns="http://www.w3.org/2000/09/xmldsig#"> <o:SecurityTokenReference xmlns:o="http://docs.oasis- open.org/wss/2004/01/oasis-200401-wss-wssecurity- secext-1.0.xsd"> <o:Reference URI="#_2"></o:Reference> </o:SecurityTokenReference> </KeyInfo> <e:CipherData> <e:CipherValue>7FZCnwfw52KfxmskwX8MZWt/Vq10 onQzPQORwILfHC1gdMub1E9fH6nyh+0F9mxsvBH3D TTg4QDU5gATE9nz5NdUfcrRppzrwlvpK4VaV5/mC0T pXKT0XbKd+9WJiQl6CtNzS1Pq3pNXoziPGJ9EykVkGd pqBSuy+OJcylGWBIQ+GOeBwVfB47k4oibXXWe6LDeE- oWn5/ClbdHurdoB9OE1cypoSohmQ8yUvE8kDgXV4+F vhT+X+oyHVfofwJK8h1EwMx4dicw6m7YNLfk1cK8Wl gbm1OwrqmRh2XeiM68N30MUj/md4qLlAEl2VtMJqQS QR4XrPxl/iuK4j5TeznoaZdeAMZa+Qvq88OYwJ6LjHM hofoovSFhf7MYY0u0KHCASwgmCbnUZEPvb9ompQj0 4BMSdVmPA3iugPvsOvSODgFQ0on6nPEWifutar7yQ0b znnEZ0RGQRTxVQ1+BylhIQOHr5yaHiXJnzqzVJfQek3g 4EnIV4WeVdgR4tVKPvexlcJwApCMlrD0/w3P1Pnvy- cIB5D8J2Blrzz5uTI20LLsGc7CKpyQFnd3OwsoC3jSb8w B3aZ09OxM3f3f8sFDZtUVKMJNBKfKfwRtFm- NCwfJlAcWfMe7zJhahKxqBu98kDw1PCkCXp2m8Le52i eM1OLyEBaKD72cITJ0vMJ4j9bJnF/O53WqFMbFjVUfZ UV1fRQP8LaLKd3Ouj4JWTHnEmgiQjcE0t9IYM/AIDP- zOvMfK34w80yPMIS78O+cpJHyvCKdbSt4gdF8tSoo5v m4llw==</e:CipherValue> </e:CipherData> </e:EncryptedData> </s:Body> </s:Envelope>

Table 19.4

Message size increases considerably when adding WS-Addressing and even more by adding encryption. The actual message body is only 597 characters.

WCF allows you to specify increasing levels of message security at different levels of granularity. Attributes, such as the `ServiceContract`, `CapabilityContract` and several others, expose a `ProtectionLevel` property that controls security policies at a fine-grained level. You can set the property to `None`, `Sign` or `SignAndEncrypt`. However, `ProtectionLevel` only specifies the minimum level.

CASE STUDY EXAMPLE

Standard Mold's Catalog service is a great example of a service that transmits data that's neither sensitive nor confidential. Therefore, there is no business requirement to encrypt catalog data when responding to service requests. At the same time, Standard Mold architects want to ensure that catalog data is protected so that it remains accurate. They therefore deem encryption as unnecessary, but decide that digitally signing messages would ensure necessary message integrity.

The `CapabilityContract` attribute in WCF allows for the configuring of a service that can only accept signed messages and respond with a signed catalog response. With the `ProtectionLevel` property of `CapabilityContract` set to `Sign` and `WsHttpBinding` configured for message-layer security, messages were signed but not encrypted.

```
[ServiceContract(Namespace = "...")]
public interface ICatalogManager
{
  [CapabilityContract(ProtectionLevel =
    System.Net.Security.ProtectionLevel.Sign, Action = "...")]
  Catalog[] GetCatalogs(CatalogRequest catalogRequest);
  ...
}
```

Example 19.12

The configuration for the Catalog service is updated to turn off authentication. Setting the binding's security mode to `Message` and requiring signatures in the message contract definition through the `ProtectionLevel` property avoids the performance penalty associated with message encryption, but also guarantees message integrity to the message recipient.

The service's App.Config file shows the configuration for signatures only:

```
<configuration>
  <system.serviceModel>
    <services>
      <service
        behaviorConfiguration=
          "ServiceCredentialsBehavior"
        name="Catalog.CatalogServiceImpl">
        <endpoint address="..."
          binding="wsHttpBinding"
```

```
            bindingConfiguration="SignatureOnlyBinding"
            contract="Catalog.ICatalogManager" />
      </service>
    </services>
    <behaviors>
      <serviceBehaviors>
        <behavior name="ServiceCredentialsBehavior">
          <serviceCredentials>
            <serviceCertificate
              findValue="CN=example.org, O=StandardMold"
              storeLocation="CurrentUser"
              storeName="My"
              x509FindType="FindBySubjectDistinguishedName" />
          </serviceCredentials>
        </behavior>
      </serviceBehaviors>
    </behaviors>
    <bindings>
      <wsHttpBinding>
        <binding name="SignatureOnlyBinding">
          <security mode="Message">
            <transport clientCredentialType="None" />
            <message clientCredentialType="None"
              negotiateServiceCredential="false"
              establishSecurityContext="false" />
          </security>
        </binding>
      </wsHttpBinding>
    </bindings>
  </system.serviceModel>
</configuration>
```

Example 19.13

REST Service Message Sizes

Selecting REST over SOAP as the message format can reduce message size even further. REST does not require a SOAP envelope, which shaves off at least 107 protocol-related bytes of each transmitted message.

JSON encoding presents another opportunity to reduce the message size on the wire. JSON is less verbose than XML because message encoding resembles JavaScript notation. For example, it doesn't require opening and closing tags for each item in the message. Size reduction with JSON encoding can be significant for messages with lots of small data items.

WCF client bindings can decode JSON messages, but JSON is often targeted for consumption by JavaScript routines, which can be orders of magnitude slower to run than compiled C#.

REST can also provide performance benefits related to caching; however, you need to evaluate requirements for other service policies and transmitted content before selecting REST as an approach solely for performance improvement reasons. REST intentionally restricts services to HTTP transports, which also limits options for security, durable messaging, and other requirements.

Hardware Encryption

Delegating encryption to dedicated hardware is an interesting option to help boost performance. Encryption in hardware is generally much faster than software-based encryption solutions.

There are several hardware architectures for encryption acceleration:

- transport encryption (only with standard SSL accelerators)

- message encryption (with WS-Security-enabled Web service appliances)

- custom encryption (with an encryption utility service)

Again, it's important to understand the trade-offs between these solutions.

Transport Encryption

Transport encryption can leverage SSL accelerators, which are readily understood, widely deployed, and transparent to the services that they protect. The accelerator handles all encryption and decryption of outgoing and incoming messages.

However, SSL is designed for point-to-point HTTP communication, which is not suitable for service composition architectures that require multi-hop scenarios with routers and intermediaries. SSL servers always decrypt messages before passing them on, regardless of whether they carry SOAP, REST, or other types of messages. This leaves them vulnerable on intermediary servers as illustrated in Figure 19.18.

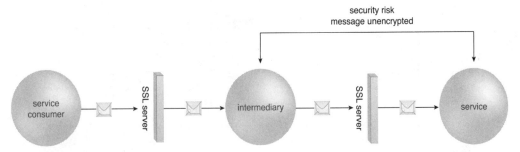

Figure 19.18
Transport-layer security with hardware accelerators does not provide end-to-end security.

The common belief is that you trade increased risk for performance and well understood infrastructure with transport-layer encryption. In this case, the performance hit of decrypting and re-encrypting messages along a multi-hop chain negates some, if not all of the advantages of a hardware accelerated SSL-solution. A message-layer security framework would encrypt the message at the originating server (hosting the initial sender) and then decrypt only at the ultimate receiver. Therefore, message-layer security provides an end-to-end solution without gaps and therefore does not require decryption and encryption cycles within each intermediary along a message path.

Message Encryption

Message encryption is the result of applying the Data Confidentiality [730] pattern. It is carried out with devices that encrypt messages compliant with WS-Security standards and the WS-I Basic Security Profile. This industry standards-based approach provides interoperability with contemporary Web service platforms. In contrast to SSL devices, dedicated Web service devices do not have to decrypt and re-encrypt on intermediaries. As a result, performance and security are higher compared to an SSL solution in environments where SOAP routers and intermediaries exist.

Also noteworthy is that these differences increase with the number of intermediaries. Figure 19.19 depicts a solution with appliances for encryption and decryption of messages.

Custom Encryption Solution

A custom encryption approach relies on a utility encryption service to encrypt sensitive parts of a message. Ideally, the utility service front-ends a hardware solution, such as a server with custom encryption hardware or a special appliance that performs all the cryptographic capabilities (Figure 19.20).

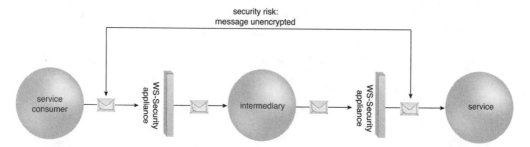

Figure 19.19

Web service appliances provide encryption along the entire transmission path.

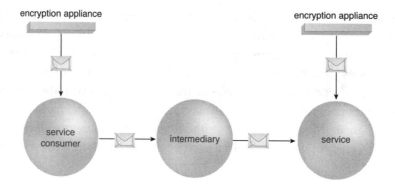

Figure 19.20

Custom encryption combined with encryption appliances provides a fast, but proprietary solution.

This utility service handles all performance intensive encryption and decryption algorithms and thus boosts overall performance. It does so at the expense of an additional remote service interaction and does not rely on open WS-Security industry standards.

While this approach allows for end-to-end encryption, you can't easily articulate which message parts are encrypted using WSDL or WS-Policy. Service and service consumer have to communicate to understand when and how to encrypt and decrypt messages. The benefit of this architecture is the reuse provided by the encryption utility service.

Whether or not a custom solution provides benefits for you depends on how frequently you perform encryption capabilities and if you can reuse an encryption utility service for other scenarios.

Table 19.5 summarizes the key arguments for the three architecture options.

	transport encryption	message encryption	custom encryption
standards-based	yes	yes	no
end-to-end	no	yes	yes
availability	high	low	low
reusable	no	no	yes

Table 19.5
A comparison of three performance solutions for encryption.

High Performance Transport

WCF, and therefore by extension BizTalk Server, offers alternative, more efficient transports than SOAP over HTTP. Bindings with names beginning with `Net`, such as `NetTcp-Binding` or `NetNamedPipesBinding`, provide efficiencies on the network by formatting messages in a binary format rather than text-based XML.

The performance advantages come from the binary representation of the message and more efficient connection management. However, the performance gain in situations where messages are secured can be small compared to the hardware-assisted solutions.

More importantly, bindings like the `NetTcpBinding` recognize that TCP is originally intended for stateful connections, not the single-call model associated with HTTP over TCP. `NetTcpBinding` includes optimizations to reduce the number of times connections between the service and the consumer are closed to avoid the performance hit of establishing a new connection for every service capability.

The impacts of this optimization are tighter coupling, a proprietary communication protocol, and the loss of the ability to load balance service calls across multiple servers. You can work around these issues by, for example, implementing the Dual Protocols [739] pattern with multiple endpoints tied to the same service. You can also solve load balancing issues by randomizing the service endpoint a consumer connects to for the initial call that establishes the connection. You could, for example, obtain an endpoint reference from a look-up service that hands out different addresses in a round-robin fashion.

CASE STUDY EXAMPLE

Standard Mold architects focused on a fine-grained interface when they designed the service contract for the internal Catalog Creation service. The service capabilities mirrored the steps catalog designers went through when creating a catalog.

Shortly after the service was put into production, users of the Catalog Creation service voiced concerns about performance and complained about noticeable latency whenever the service would communicate with other services. The service was configured with WsHttpBinding because some users were working remotely and needed to connect over the Internet. However, most users were accessing the service from inside Standard Mold's network.

The XML-based encoding and the connectionless nature of HTTP had impacted performance considerably. Furthermore, the service configuration required authentication because the service was externally accessible. The authentication requirement further impacted performance.

Architects identify that WCF offers an option to alleviate some of the performance problems without having to redesign the consumer or the service. A second service endpoint that provides communication over NetTcpBinding reduces the performance impact of re-establishing network connections and processing user credentials.

The resulting configuration for the two service endpoints is shown here:

```xml
<configuration>
  <system.serviceModel>
    <services>
      <service name="Catalog.CatalogServiceImpl">
        <endpoint
          address="http://localhost:8089/services/ws/catalog"
          binding="wsHttpBinding"
          bindingConfiguration="secuerWs"
          contract="Catalog.ICatalogManager" />
        <endpoint
          address="net.tcp://localhost:9000/services/catalog"
          binding="NetTcpBinding"
          bindingConfiguration="secureNet"
          contract="Catalog.ICatalogManager" />
      </service>
    </services>
    ...
```

```
    </system.serviceModel>
</configuration>
```

Example 19.14

Redesigning the service contract to remove all unnecessary communication over the network would have delivered greater performance improvements, but performance over `NetTcpBinding` was adequate for the majority of users.

MTOM Encoding

The original XML specification requires base64 encoding of all binary data inside an XML document. Similar to encryption, encoding is a separate processing step that takes extra time. In addition, the base64 encoding algorithm increases message sizes by 33%. That means the transmission time over the wire will also increase by 33%, unless we use some form of compression.

The MTOM industry standard aims to avoid base64 encoding of binary data in XML documents. Instead, SOAP messages are transmitted as multi-part MIME messages. The first MIME part contains the XML message, but all message parts of type `byte[]` only contain pointers to subsequent parts of the MIME message.

These subsequent parts only hold the raw binary data to avoid the processing overhead of base64 encoding and decoding as well as the bloat of the message. The MIME protocol adds a little bit of extra overhead, but it's small compared to the 33% increase of base64 encoding, and only significant when the binary data is less than 1KB in size.

The MTOM encoder in WCF analyzes an array of sizes to determine the smaller encoding format. The encoder encodes binary data in the base64 format if the amount of binary information is less than 1KB. Otherwise the encoder chooses the MTOM format.

You can select the MTOM encoder simply by configuring the binding's `messageEncoding` or setting the `MessageEncoding` property programmatically. Example 19.15 shows `basicHttpBinding` configured for MTOM encoding:

```
<system.ServiceModel>
  <bindings>
    <basicHttpBinding>
      <binding name="..." messageEncoding="Mtom" />
      ...
```

```
    </basicHttpBinding>
  </bindings>
</system.ServiceModel>
```

Example 19.15

CASE STUDY EXAMPLE

Standard Mold's Catalog service publishes images that can be stored and displayed
in procurement applications that access the service. Since these images are comprised
of binary data, they have to be base64 encoded to be transmitted within messages.

The service contract for the Catalog service defines `CatalogItem` entities through the
following WCF code:

```
[DataContract(Namespace =
  "http://www.example.org/SellFast/2007/1/15")]
public class CatalogItem
{
  [DataMember]
  public string VendorSku;
  [DataMember]
  public string ProductName;
  [DataMember]
  public byte[] ProductImage;
  [DataMember]
  public DateTime DisplayUntil;
  [DataMember]
  public string Description;
}
```

Example 19.16

The `ProductImage` byte array in the `CatalogItem` contains the image data and would
have to be base64 encoded for standard XML/text encoded messages. Standard Mold
architects check the image inventory and find that all images are well over 1KB in
size. They therefore decide to rely on MTOM encoding to reduce message size and
increase performance.

Although MTOM is widely supported, the architects decide to play it safe and add an
additional service endpoint that does not require MTOM encoding for WS-I BasicProfile compliance.

The following example shows how these two endpoints differ only in the message encoding in the WCF configuration snippet:

```
<system.serviceModel>
  <services>
    <serivce name="CatalogServiceImpl">
      <endpoint
        address="http://localhost:8089/services/catalog"
        binding="basicHttpBinding"
        bindingConfiguration="MtomBinding"
        contract="CatalogServices.ICatalogManager" />
      <endpoint
        address="http://localhost:8089/services/text/catalog"
        binding="basicHttpBinding"
        bindingConfiguration="TextBinding"
        contract="CatalogServices.ICatalogManager" />
    </serivce>
  </services>
  <bindings>
    <basicHttpBinding>
      <binding
        name="TextBinding"
        messageEncoding="Text" />
      <binding
        name="MtomBinding"
        messageEncoding="Mtom" />
    </basicHttpBinding>
  </bindings>
</system.serviceModel>
```

Example 19.17

NOTE

MTOM encoding makes transfer of large binary data more viable than transmitting it as an XML document. However, you need to examine if transmitting large binary objects in one message itself is actually a realistic approach. Transferring large binary objects in one swoop is more likely to fail on unreliable networks and can then require full re-transmission in case of failure. A chunked transmission approach is more resilient to network failure and can resume transmission at the point of failure.

Performance Considerations for Service Contract Design

There are many settings you can tweak to increase performance after you have deployed a service. Ideally, you should identify services with high performance requirements and design service contracts accordingly rather than relying on your ability to tune performance later. Contract design probably has the biggest impact on performance of all the options we've discussed so far.

However, in practice, you have to make some hard trade-off decisions between performance, reusability, and maintainability of a service contract. Optimizing only for reuse often results in service capabilities that return large amounts of data to make the response relevant to a larger range of service consumers.

When performance matters, however, service capabilities can do as little processing as needed. Because requirements can vary between consumers, how much processing is necessary is best decided by the individual consumer. This is where Contract Denormalization [728] can provide an effective means of accommodating multiple service consumers with the same service contract by providing intentionally redundant service capabilities optimized for different consumer types.

It's important to give consumers options to select how much processing the service is going to perform and how much data it is going to return. A Customer entity service, for example, could let the consumer decide if it requires results in a concise or detailed format. With Contract Denormalization, you can design contracts with this type of flexibility.

In general, you can follow a loosely coupled approach or you can opt for a more strongly-typed, deterministic approach when defining individual service capabilities within a contract. The loosely coupled approach will tend to involve weaker typed capabilities that may rely on the use of parameters. The deterministic approach, on the other hand, can be easier to apply with Visual Studio, where you derive .NET classes from the service's WSDL definition.

> **NOTE**
>
> The official series text book for service contract design and optimization techniques is *Web Service Contract Design & Versioning for SOA*.

CASE STUDY EXAMPLE

Standard Mold's Catalog service already utilizes MTOM encoding to reduce message size, but its customers still complain about slow response times. Architects discuss scenarios with their service consumers and realize that not all of the customers need the product image at all times. It would be perfectly acceptable for the service to respond with core data, such as SKU, name, and description.

Standard Mold quickly makes a change to the service contract definition by adding the `IsRequired` property to the `DataMember` attribute. This indicates to consumers that the `CatalogItem` type may or may not contain the `ProductImage`.

```
[DataContract(Namespace =
  "http://www.example.org/SellFast/2007/1/15")]
public class CatalogItem
{
  [DataMember]
  public string VendorSku;
  [DataMember]
  public string ProductName;
  [DataMember(IsRequired=false)]
  public byte[] ProductImage;
  [DataMember]
  public DateTime DisplayUntil;
  [DataMember]
  public string Description;
}
```

Example 19.18

Now consumers of the service have the choice to request core data only. The service architects also add the `IncludeImages` parameter to the `CatalogRequest` message definition that lets consumers specify whether they want images in the response message:

```
[DataContract(Namespace =
  "http://www.example.org/SellFast/2007/1/15")]
public class CatalogRequest
{
  [DataMember]
  public int CustomerNumber;
  [DataMember]
```

```
    public bool IncludeImages;
    [DataMember]
    public string RequestType;
    [DataMember]
    public int CatalogNumber;
    [DataMember]
    public DateTime PublicationStartDate;
    [DataMember]
    public DateTime PublicationEndDate;
}
```

Example 19.19

It's technically not necessary to mark reference types, such as the byte array in Example 19.19, as `IsRequired=false` for WCF or ASMX services because reference types are by default optional.

The default XML Schema representation for the `ProductImage` element without an `IsRequired` property or with `IsRequired=false` is:

```
<xs:element
  minOccurs="0"
  name="ProductImage"
  nillable="true"
  type="xs:base64Binary" />
```

Example 19.20

Specifying `IsRequired=true` on the other hand does force the presence of the element in the message:

```
<xs:element
  name="ProductImage"
  nillable="true"
  type="xs:base64Binary" />
```

Example 19.21

The `minOccurs="0"` statement that marks the element as optional content is no longer present in the schema.

NOTE
If transmitting large amounts of unnecessary data is hurting performance of a service you can also choose to layer another service over the first service to trim the data flowing to the service consumer. This is only effective if the data transmission is the cause of a performance problem. In some cases, generating the response is more of a performance concern than the actual message transmission. Introducing another service layer also introduces additional overhead that can further decrease the effectiveness of this approach. Multi-Channel Endpoint [755] may prove to be a more appropriate means for reducing message sizes.

Impact on Service-Orientation Principles

We've discussed a number of different techniques for how to architect services for performance. Let's now study how these techniques can impact the application of service-orientation principles. Tables 19.6 and 19.7 summarize these impacts.

	Standardized Service Contract (693)	Service Loose Coupling (695)	Service Abstraction (696)
Caching	no impact, transparent to the service	no impact, transparent to the service	possible impact when requiring cache keys in the contract
Reducing Contention	no impact, optimization inside the service	no impact, optimization inside the service	no impact, optimization inside the service
Throttling	no impact, transparent to the service	no impact, transparent to the service	no impact, transparent to the service
Scaling Out	no impact, infrastructure change only	no impact, infrastructure change only if contracts are designed for scale out	no impact, infrastructure change only
Coarse Service Contracts	no impact, coarse contracts are still contracts	possible impact if refactored contract changes MEPs	possible impact, coarse contracts could expose fewer internal details and raise abstraction

continues

	Standardized Service Contract (693)	Service Loose Coupling (695)	Service Abstraction (696)
Hosting Models	possible impact, in-process hosted service interfaces may not be defined as contracts	possible impact, co-hosting and direct consumption can lead to tight coupling	possible impact, contracts for co-hosted services do not need platform agnostic abstractions
Selective Encryption	no impact, policy change only	no impact, policy change only	no impact, policy change only
Hardware Encryption	no impact, infrastructure change only	no impact, infrastructure change only	no impact, infrastructure change only
Reducing Transport Overhead	no impact, policy change only	tighter coupling through platform dependency, possibly stateful connection	no impact, infrastructure change only
MTOM Encoding	no impact, policy change only	no impact, policy change only	no impact, infrastructure change only
Flexible Interfaces	possible impact, contracts may not be as expressive as fine grained contracts	possible positive impact, flexible interfaces are less specific, but could lead to looser coupling	raised level of abstraction

Table 19.6

Performance optimization techniques impact on the three service-orientation principles focused primarily on the service contract design.

	Service Reusability (697)	Service Autonomy (699)	Service Statelessness (700)	Service Composability (704)
Caching	no impact, when implemented transparent to the service	decreased autonomy (possible dependency on local cache database)	some services are technically still stateless, but the cache could be considered state	none— contracts don't change
Reducing Contention	no impact unless service contract changes	increased autonomy if contention reduced by changing dependencies	no impact, optimization inside the service	no impact, optimization inside the service
Throttling	no impact, transparent to the service	no impact, transparent to the service	no impact, transparent to the service	some impact to the number of consumers to the service
Scaling Out		no impact, infrastructure change only	stateless design required or Service Grid [777] pattern with state synchronization necessary	positive impact, higher number of consumers possible with infrastructure change only
Coarse Service Contracts	fine grained contracts are typically more reusable	no impact, contract change doesn't change autonomy	possible impact, contracts refactoring may eliminate or introduce statelessness	reduced composability due to reduced number of capabilities
Hosting Models	possible impact. co-hosted services are only reusable when they are accessible via Dual Protocol [739]	possible impact, co-hosting reduces autonomy	no impact, hosting model does not change state requirement	possible impact, co-hosted services are only reusable when they are accessible via Dual Protocol [739].

continues

	Service Reusability (697)	Service Autonomy (699)	Service Statelessness (700)	Service Composability (704)
Selective Encryption	no impact, policy change only as long as consumers support selective encryption	no impact, policy change only	no impact, policy change only	no impact, policy change only as long as consumers support selective encryption
Hardware Encryption	no impact, policy change only	dependency on additional, shared hardware	no impact, infrastructure change only	no impact, infrastructure change only
Reducing Transport Overhead	no impact, infrastructure change only	no impact, policy change only	no impact, infrastructure change only	use of proprietary transport may reduce number of consumers
MTOM Encoding	no impact, policy change only	no impact, policy change only	no impact, infrastructure change only	no impact, infrastructure change only
Flexible Interfaces	improving performance could increase reusability because the service meets the needs of more consumers	no impact, interface design does not affect autonomy	no impact, interface design does not change state requirements	depends on implementation

Table 19.7

Performance optimization techniques impact on service-orientation principles focused on the service implementation, behavior, and service contract design.

SUMMARY OF KEY POINTS

- There are numerous techniques for optimizing service architectures, several of which leverage caching and throttling technology.

- Techniques will vary depending on the service hosting platform, which itself will have performance implications.

19.3 Service Composition Performance Optimization Techniques

All of the challenges and techniques discussed so far apply equally to service compositions simply because they are comprised of services. However, when focusing specifically on inter-service design, there are additional performance issues and techniques that need to be considered (Figure 19.21).

The remaining sections in this chapter provide further strategies for optimizing service composition architectures.

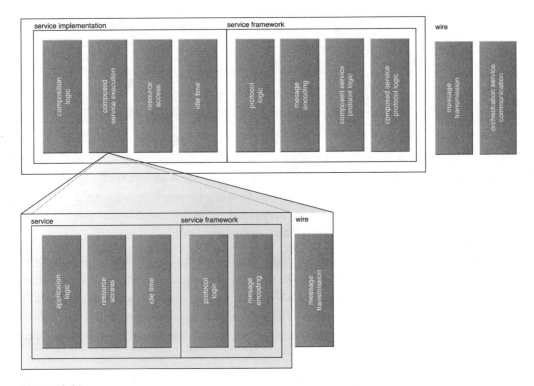

Figure 19.21

The performance model for service compositions reflects the challenges of communicating across service boundaries.

Transformation Avoidance and Caching

Applying the Data Model Transformation [732] is not inexpensive. Transformations of data can actually make up for a good bit of runtime processing logic in a service composition (Figure 19.22).

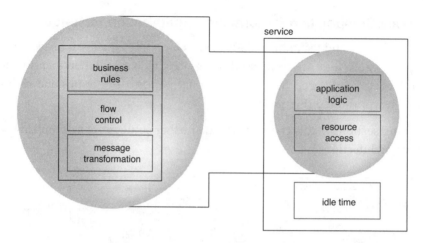

Figure 19.22

The application logic part of the service implementation includes the implementation of business rules, control of flow logic, and logic to transform messages.

The best way to avoid data transformation is to apply Canonical Schema [718], as already explained in Chapter 9. However, when you are in a situation where you must carry out transformation, you will likely need to consider working with XSLT. While it is the most common technology used to carry out data model transformations, XSLT can also be one of the most processing-intensive technology choices.

The XSLT programming model differs considerably from procedural or object-oriented programming. Orchestration engines like BizTalk Server that embrace XML technologies at the core make extensive use of XSLT. Because environments like BizTalk make XSLT transformations accessible and hide much of its mapping complexity, it's important to understand that performance is the price to pay for flexibility and developer productivity.

To alleviate the performance impact of XSLT, you can investigate the use of hardware appliances specifically for XSLT processing, especially if your message schemas are complex or if transformations are hard to express programmatically. Figure 19.23 depicts an environment with a hardware accelerated transformation service.

In some cases it may be possible to avoid performing the actual transformations. For example, if your service frequently transforms the same input document into the same output document, you could leverage some of the previously discussed caching techniques to cache not just the compiled transformation, but also the transformation results.

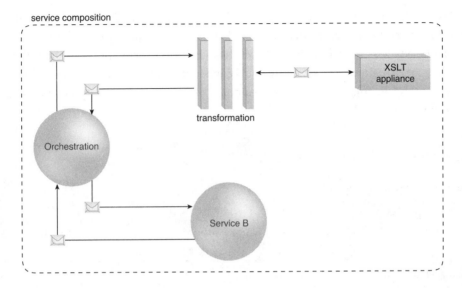

Figure 19.23

XSLT appliances can provide considerable performance improvements. A utility transformation service can front-end the appliance to make it accessible to service compositions.

Asynchronous Interactions

Designing inter-service message exchanges using asynchronous message exchange patterns allows for the optimization of service activities. Frameworks like ASMX and WCF enable asynchronous interactions even with synchronous service interfaces. Orchestration tools like BizTalk, on the other hand, don't even offer programming constructs for synchronous communication even with synchronous services where sending service requests is always decoupled from receiving the responses. You have to be explicit if you want the composition to wait for a response and potentially tie up resources like server threads while waiting for that response.

When you build compositions without an orchestration tool, such as BizTalk, you can still interact asynchronously with synchronous request-response service capabilities. There are several ways to create proxy classes to consume services in the .NET environment. Visual Studio, for example, has the "Add Web Reference" and "Add Service Reference" features (Figure 19.24) to create ASMX or WCF proxy classes. The command-line tools Wsdl.exe and SvcUtil.exe offer the same functionality outside of the IDE.

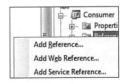

Figure 19.24

The Visual Studio Add Reference and Add Web Reference options.

Add Web Reference always generates ASMX proxy classes with methods to call synchronous service capability asynchronously. The SvcUtil.exe tool for WCF proxy classes creates a proxy class with functions to call the synchronous capability in the following example synchronously and asynchronously when you specify the /async switch. The service contract in this example exposes one synchronous capability called GetPublishedCatalogs:

```
[ServiceContract]
public interface ICatalogManager
{
  [CapabilityContract]
  CatalogResponseMessage
    GetPublishedCatalogs(
      CatalogRequestMessage catalogRequest);
}
```

Example 19.22

When you run SvcUtil.exe /async the generated proxy class includes not only a synchronous method GetPublishedCatalog, but also two extra methods (BeginGetPublishedCatalogs and EndGetPublishedCatalogs) to enable asynchronous interaction:

```
public Catalog[] GetPublishedCatalogs
  (CatalogRequest Request);
public System.IAsyncResult BeginGetPublishedCatalogs
  (CatalogRequest Request,
    System.AsyncCallback callback,
    object asyncState);
public Catalog[] EndGetPublishedCatalogs
  (System.IAsyncResult result);
```

Example 19.23

The Advanced tab on the Add Service Reference dialog allows creating asynchronous methods for synchronous service capabilities into Visual Studio. Checking the "Generate asynchronous capabilities" box adds serveral methods to the proxy class to call the service asynchronously and invoke callback capabilities when the response message is received:

```
public void GetPublishedCatalogsAsync
  (CatalogRequest Request);
public void GetPublishedCatalogsAsync
  (CatalogRequest Request, object userState);
public System.IAsyncResult BeginGetPublishedCatalogs
  (CatalogRequest Request, System.AsyncCallback callback,
    object asyncState);
public CatalogResponseMessage EndGetPublishedCatalogs
  (System.IAsyncResult result);
public Catalog[] EndGetPublishedCatalogs
  (System.IAsyncResult result);
```

Example 19.24

The option to communicate with the remote service asynchronously can increase the scalability of your compositions and in some cases reduce their execution time. That is, as long as you're able to perform other processing while waiting for a response instead of sitting idle. The capacity of your service may also be improved as you may be able to start processing several new requests while waiting for responses from composed services.

Service compositions in orchestration engines are well suited to deal with the challenges of asynchronous message exchanges. In concert with the constructs for parallel execution of process logic, orchestration tools help you to reduce idle waiting time and thus develop processes with increased efficiency.

Parallelize Where Possible

There is always overhead involved when communicating with remote services. This overhead can result in a lot of idle CPU cycles while your composition is waiting for a response. If you exploit parallelism and multi-threading, your composition can continue executing instead of waiting. Parallelizing tasks in a service composition is easier when you compose service contracts with asynchronous message patterns. Orchestration tools like those provided by BizTalk Server and WF make implementing parallelism pretty straightforward.

Parallel Activity in WF

The `ParallelActivity` class in WF simplifies implementing parallel execution of a service composition. Figure 19.25 shows the WF process designer with a workflow that has two parallel branches of execution.

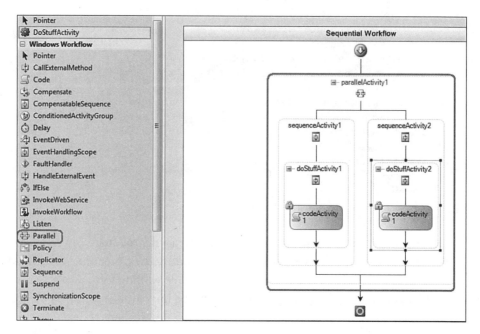

Figure 19.25

The Windows Workflow Foundation development tools visualize parallel execution branches in an intuitive manner.

It's important to note that these branches do not truly execute in parallel, even on a multi-processor or multi-core computer. The WF runtime only executes activities inside a workflow on a single thread. The executing branch has to enter a waiting state (for example, a `Delay` activity or a `WebServiceReceive` activity) for another branch to execute. That's a performance improvement by our definition of speeding up average execution time.

True parallelism might improve performance even more, but it also complicates the programming model and can lead to synchronization issues. The single-threaded approach keeps the programming model substantially simpler because there is no need to synchronize access to properties on the workflow class.

There are still a couple of ways to execute workflow logic truly in parallel on multi-processor servers. For one, you could factor parallel activities in their own workflows and start them from the `CallWorkflowActivity`. The new workflow executes on a different thread than the original workflow and could execute on a different CPU or core. There are currently no activities that allow you to communicate with the spawned child workflow or wait for it to finish, but you could easily build a custom activity to listen for those events. You could also build a custom parallel activity that does schedule execution of parallel branches on separate threads.

In both cases you're on the hook for synchronizing concurrent access to shared properties to avoid dead-locks, race conditions, and inconsistent data.

Parallel Execution in BizTalk Server

BizTalk Server has a parallel shape to code concurrent business logic, and just like its counterpart in WF, it's not a truly parallel execution of each branch. The branches execute on the same thread and the runtime determines when one branch yields execution to another branch. Figure 19.26 shows an orchestration with three parallel branches.

Figure 19.26

The parallel shape allows coding parallel logic. The CallOrchestration and StartOrchestration shapes invoke other orchestrations synchronously or asynchronously.

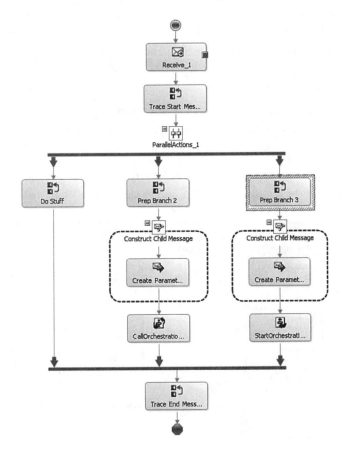

If you need true parallelism, you can factor code into separate orchestrations and start parallel orchestrations with the Start Orchestration shape. Now both the parent and the child orchestration can execute in parallel if there are CPUs available. There's no implicit connection between the parent and the child orchestration after you started the child. You have to communicate between the two orchestrations over regular BizTalk ports.

Note that BizTalk also provides a Call Orchestration shape, which invokes another orchestration synchronously on the same thread as the calling orchestration. In that case, the two orchestrations do not execute in parallel. Though unlike Windows Workflow Foundation, BizTalk Server does not provide the extensibility interfaces to create a custom shape to exercise more control over how shapes are executed.

Either solution can improve performance of your orchestrations. Parallel branches, even without starting child orchestrations, can reduce execution time as long as you can fill idle time from Receive, Delay or Listen shapes with other logic a process needs to execute in order to complete the process.

Replicator Activity in WF

The ReplicatorActivity in WF allows you to execute a set of activities either sequentially or in parallel. Just like in other parallel scenarios you can exploit idle time while waiting for responses from other services or take advantage of multi-CPU and multi-core hardware.

You configure the ReplicatorActivity to run in parallel by setting the `ExecutionType` property to `Parallel` as shown in the Figure 19.27.

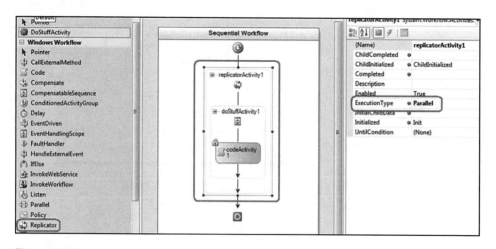

Figure 19.27
The ReplicatorActivity can execute workflow activities in parallel.

Again, the activities inside the replicator execute on the same thread, which follows the same threading model as the parallel activity we discussed earlier.

The ReplicatorActivity greatly simplifies changing the execution of a set of tasks from sequential to parallel execution. However, that doesn't mean you gain performance improvement every time you switch from sequential to parallel, even when you have a multi-core CPU. You have to determine if the tasks inside the `ReplicatorActivity` are easily parallelizable, for example, if there are no dependencies between results of individual iterations and if there are good opportunities in the workflow to yield control to another parallel branch.

Thus, configuring activities that primarily perform in-memory computation functions to run in parallel may not reduce average execution time of a service capability at all. Activities like in-memory XML parsing do not benefit from parallelizing because the context switches are necessary to switch between activities and can actually slow down the execution. Only workflows where you can fill idle time with actual processing benefit from parallelization.

Consider Co-Hosting When Necessary

Service invocations that require network hops are costly. They add latency that you simply cannot reduce. Sometimes you can architect a service composition to work around the latency of network calls, for example by parallelizing activities, but the only way to architect for performance is to avoid the delays associated with network communications as much as possible. Architecturally, you could follow the Composition Autonomy [725] pattern and co-host a composition controller and the composed services in the same application container, such as inside BizTalk Server. In that case, service invocations can turn into very fast, in-process function calls. Even co-hosting on the same server opens up possibilities for faster communication, over transports like named pipes or shared-memory for example. Figure 19.28 shows the improvements in the performance model.

If you co-host orchestrations inside the same BizTalk application host, for example, you can take advantage of the `CallOrchestration` and `StartOrchestration` shapes or follow the solution approaches outlined in Chapter 14 for invoking orchestrations in the same container.

WCF-based service compositions can take advantage of changing transports from HTTP to high performance alternatives, such as named pipes, as discussed in the *High Performance Transport* section of this chapter.

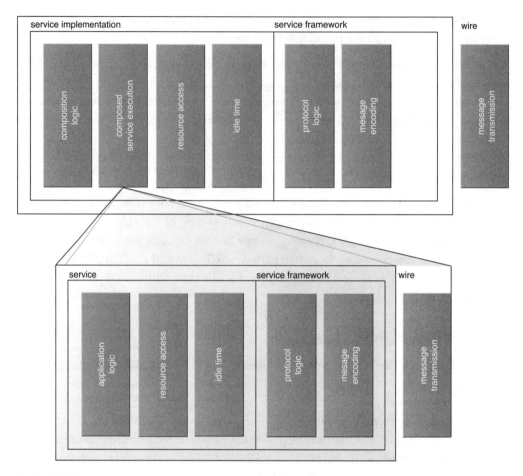

Figure 19.28

Co-hosting services and compositions eliminates costly message encoding transmission steps.

A third option for co-hosting is to bypass the services layer altogether and reference the service implementation classes directly in an application. An ASP.NET Web application co-hosted in IIS with a Web service that it calls could just instantiate the service implementation object directly rather than instantiating a proxy object that makes a call through the network layer.

For example, you have a class `CatalogServiceImpl` that's exposed as a WCF service:

```
ServiceHost host =
  new ServiceHost(typeof(CatalogServiceImpl));
host.AddServiceEndpoint(
```

```
  typeof(CatalogServices.ICatalogManager),
  new BasicHttpBinding(),
  "http://localhost:8089/services/catalog" );
host.Open();
```

Example 19.25

You could access the service through a proxy object, which would cause serialization of the request message to an XML InfoSet. This encodes the message according to the selected binding and puts the message on the wire. The receiver then deserializes the message, processes it, serializes, encodes and sends the response message. Finally, the consumer receives and deserializes the response message.

The consumer code with a dynamic proxy could look something like this:

```
ChannelFactory<ICatalogManager> factory =
  new ChannelFactory<ICatalogManager>
  (new BasicHttpBinding(),
   new EndpointAddress("...")));
ICatalogManager proxy = factory.CreateChannel();
CatalogRequestMessage request = new CatalogRequestMessage();
CatalogResponseMessage response = new CatalogResponseMessage();
response = proxy.GetPublishedCatalogs(request);
```

Example 19.26

You could simply avoid all this serialization and deserialization and the communication over the wire, if you co-hosted the consumer and the service and changed the first line of code in Example 19.26 to:

```
Service.CatalogServiceImpl catalog =
  new Service.CatalogServiceImpl();
```

Example 19.27

The latter example instantiates the service implementation directly instead of going through a proxy object.

Before you co-host a service and its consumer, you need to ask yourself why you factored out the logic into a service in the first place. If you intended the service to be reusable on its own, then why do you sacrifice autonomy and co-host the service and the application and the service together on the same server? If the service is not intended to be re-usable, then why is it built as a service and not as a class library?

The trade-off to consider when deciding on co-hosting services and service compositions is between decreased autonomy and increased performance. Service autonomy is an important criterion to shield services from the impact of load on other, co-hosted services. Co-hosting can improve performance if the combined resource consumption of both the service and the composition does not exceed the capacity of the server.

The next questions to answer are about the roadmap for the consuming application and the service. Is the number of users of the application and the service projected to grow significantly? Are you impacting the application's ability to scale out in the future by co-hosting them now?

The scalability concerns and sacrificing service autonomy make co-hosting a solution for applications where services were designed specifically to support a single application rather than following the design guidelines for reusable, loosely coupled services.

Other trade-off considerations could factor into the decision to co-host as well. For example, the service may benefit from an orchestration container's natural ability to realize Dual Protocol [739]. Thus allowing fast, local invocations to composition controllers and, at the same time, enabling remote access for other consumers. You have to determine if the benefits outweigh the increase in complexity and the reduced autonomy.

Compose High Performance Services

We may be restating the obvious, but it's extremely important that you understand the performance characteristics of a service before you aggregate it into a service composition. For example, you should carefully review service level agreements offered up by the service provider to see if it is in line with your performance expectations and your needs for availability. Communicating the load you expect to add on the service will help the provider's capacity planning and ensure that your service level expectations, including performance, are met continuously.

Sometimes you can architect a composition around poor performance characteristics with the approaches discussed so far, but in general you're bound by the service with the poorest performance in a composition. The more optimized the aggregated services are for performance, the better your composition performs.

Impact on Service-Orientation Principles

Tables 19.8 and 19.9 summarize the effect each of the strategies has on service-orientation principles. You will notice that many of the performance optimization strategies we discussed do not have much of an impact.

	Standardized Service Contract (693)	Service Loose Coupling (695)	Service Abstraction (696)
Avoiding Transformations	no impact, optimization inside the service	no impact, optimization inside the service	no impact, optimization inside the service
Asynchronous Message Exchange	no impact, contracts can express asynchronous patterns	possible impact, asynchronous service interfaces can lead to looser coupling	no impact, MEP does not alter abstraction
Parallel Task Execution (WF Parallel Activity)	no impact, implementation detail does not change contract definition	no impact, implementation detail does not change coupling characteristic	implementation detail does not change abstraction
Parallel Task Execution (WF Replicator)	no impact, implementation detail does not change contract definition	no impact, implementation detail does not change coupling characteristic	implementation detail does not change abstraction
Parallel Task Execution (BizTalk Server)	no impact, implementation detail does not change contract definition	no impact, implementation detail does not change coupling characteristic	implementation detail does not change abstraction
Co-Hosting	possible impact, WF workflows do not require formal contract definition when called internally/BTS orchestrations expose typed interfaces, but do not require WSDL contracts when called internally	possible impact, reduced, co hosting increases coupling between service and composition/no impact between composition and consumer	possible impact, contracts for co-hosted services do not need platform agnostic abstractions
Aggregate High Performance Services	no impact, implementation detail only	reduced when services optimize implementation and choose higher performing, proprietary transport or message format	no impact, implementation detail only

Table 19.8

Performance optimization techniques impact on the three service-orientation principles focused primarily on the service contract design.

	Service Reusability (697)	Service Autonomy (699)	Service Statelessness (700)	Service Composability (704)
Avoiding Transformations	no impact, optimization inside the service	no impact, optimization inside the service	no impact, transformations only affect transient flow	possible positive impact, Canonical Schema [718] can increase composability
Asynchronous Message Exchange	possible impact, asynchronous contracts may be more reusable	no impact, message exchange pattern does not alter autonomy	possible impact, service may require maintaining state between asynchronous request and responses	no impact, MEP does not alter composability
Parallel Task Execution (WF Parallel Activity)	no impact, implementation detail does not change reusability	no impact, implementation detail does not change autonomy	implementation detail does not change state requirements	implementation detail does not change composability
Parallel Task Execution (WF Replicator)	no impact, implementation detail does not change reusability	no impact, implementation detail does not change autonomy	implementation detail does not change state requirements	implementation detail does not change composability
Parallel Task Execution (BizTalk Server)	no impact, implementation detail does not change reusability	no impact, implementation detail does not change autonomy	implementation detail does not change state requirements	implementation detail does not change composability

	Service Reusability (697)	Service Autonomy (699)	Service Statelessness (700)	Service Composability (704)
Co-Hosting	possible impact, co-hosted services are only reusable when they are accessible via Dual Protocol [739]	possible impact, reduced, co-hosting the composition and the service(s) introduces dependencies on the same hardware	no impact, co-hosting model does not change state requirement	possible impact, co-hosted services are only reusable when they are accessible via Dual Protocol [739]
Aggregate High Performance Services	no impact, implementation detail only	possible impact if co-hosting is the strategy for achieving high performance	no impact, implementation detail only	no impact, implementation detail only

Table 19.9

Performance optimization techniques impact on service-orientation principles focused on the service implementation, behavior, and service contract design.

SUMMARY OF KEY POINTS

- Compositions face significant performance challenges when aggregating remote services.

- Asynchronous messaging and parallelism avoid costly idle time.

- Performance of aggregated services greatly impacts performance of service compositions.

- Message transformations are costly and can be avoided by applying the Canonical Schema [718] pattern and the Standardized Service Contract (693) principle.

Chapter 20

SOA Metrics with BAM

20.1 SOA Metric Types

20.2 Introducing BizTalk BAM

20.3 Activities and Views

20.4 BAM APIs

20.5 Managing BAM

etrics collection for services and service-oriented solutions are often overlooked in the absence of a proper governance plan. Project teams sometimes get lost in the rush to get services deployed, and it is only later that questions start being asked about how exactly these services are being utilized.

This chapter is specifically focused on the metrics collection features provided by the BizTalk Server Business Activity Monitoring (BAM) mechanism and how these features pertain to metrics for individual and composed services and their surrounding infrastructure.

20.1 SOA Metric Types

Within a service-oriented enterprise, metrics can be collected at different levels. Specifically, common metric types correspond to SOA types as follows:

- infrastructure metrics (apply to service inventory architecture)

- service metrics (apply to service architecture)

- business metrics (apply to service composition architecture)

Infrastructure metrics are all about server health in that they are concerned with monitoring the operation and CPU usage of a server. These kinds of statistics are typically provided by tools like Microsoft's System Center or Microsoft Operations Manager (MOM). MOM enables the monitoring of specific performance counters, and, among other things, allows for previously-scripted corrective actions to be invoked once certain events (such as a server outage) have occurred. Because this relates more to standard server administration, we do not explore infrastructure metrics in this chapter.

Service metrics is all about instrumenting the individual services in a given service inventory. The kinds of metrics that may be gathered here can include service latency, method invocation quantity, and quantity of exceptions. Depending on the toolset and the environment, there may be some cross-over with governance tools that require service metrics in order to determine service level agreement (SLA) compliance.

Business metrics allow you to gain visibility into the runtime execution of business processes, as they are automated by service compositions. Business metrics can provide powerful trend analysis and highlight business problems before they become a crisis. In addition, having deep business metrics could also lead to the discovery of new service and process utilization opportunities that may otherwise have gone unnoticed. A well-planned business process metrics solution can ensure that timely information is provided to business decision makers.

Before we explore how to collect and assess these metrics, let's briefly look at them from a business perspective. Whereas a CIO or IT manager would be concerned with infrastructure and service metrics, business metrics would be of interest to all managers and stakeholders. This metric essentially provides a window into business operation; the vista point from which business performance can be captured. Providing a world-class service-oriented solution to address business problems will enable business automation, but providing stakeholders with visibility into how automated business processes are being utilized and executed can provide profound insights into the inner workings of an organization.

20.2 Introducing BizTalk BAM

BizTalk BAM is a mechanism to generically externalize the tracking of business process data and metrics, isolating tracking from process.

BizTalk and BAM

BizTalk BAM was designed as an independent mechanism, and could just have easily been marketed as a standalone product. Business activity monitoring systems in other vendor platforms, in fact, are commonly sold as separate products. Even though Microsoft decided to bundle BAM with BizTalk Server, the licensing is such that it can also be used to instrument solutions beyond BizTalk environments. This means that it can be positioned as the foundation for business activity monitoring within an entire service inventory, regardless of whether the service inventory architecture incorporates BizTalk Server.

NOTE

For simplicity's sake, we'll be referring to BizTalk BAM as just *BAM* from hereon in this chapter. We will reference its relationship with BizTalk Server when required.

BAM's sole responsibility is to capture data. As we will explore in this chapter, there are several ways of accomplishing this. Fundamentally, BAM relies on either SQL Server or on SQL Analysis Services to capture and make data available for rendering. Once the data has been collected, how it is rendered or used is your decision.

In earlier times, a conventional approach to capturing data may have involved tracking data points in state tables associated with a solution. For example, a Web service operation may register the fact that it has been invoked. If a credit check fails, perhaps a table outside of the process is updated. However, these approaches are tightly bound to the underlying implementations. Should we need to change the metrics we are tracking, it would entail a corresponding code-level (implementation-level) change.

In contrast, BAM uses an observation model, whereby events that occur are noticed by interceptors that track data points. The tracking of metrics is isolated from the service, and the tracking can be modified without any code changes to the service implementation. In the case of a BizTalk solution, it is possible to deploy the aggregated services and then, some time later, deploy BizTalk BAM metrics tracking without redeploying or in any way changing the solution implementation. Whereas this provides a relatively "touch-free" means of instrumentation for native BizTalk solutions, it becomes less touch-free when you start instrumenting non-BizTalk solutions or work with the BAM APIs.

BAM Solution Architecture

The BAM environment includes system services, such as SSIS and DTS packages, that move data. Ultimately, the tracked data is available to be queried, either from SQL Server tables or from SQL Analysis Services OLAP cubes.

Two types of data are tracked:

1. business data values (such as "Order Amount" and "Customer Account")

2. the date and time of process milestones (such as "Order Received" and "Order Shipped")

A single metrics monitoring application could include data from one or more of the following sources:

- BizTalk process automation solutions (orchestrations)

- BizTalk messaging-only integration solutions

- WCF interceptors

- WF interceptors

- calls to BAM APIs

Figure 20.1 shows a logical model of the common participants in a metrics tracking solution.

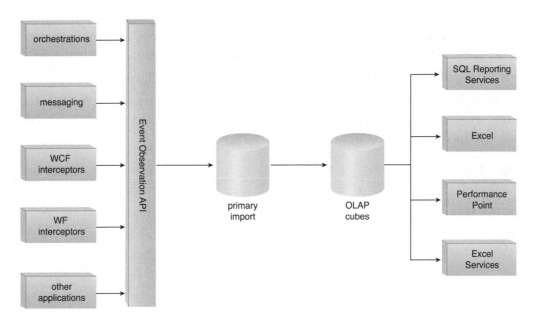

Figure 20.1

The metrics sources (left) are the BizTalk applications, BizTalk messaging, or other applications that are generating business data and process milestones events. The event observation layer (interceptors) captures data and stores it in SQL Server tables. The interceptors can be created programmatically, or through the tools provided with BizTalk.

There is nothing proprietary about the data formats. If you are querying against the SQL Server tables you can do so using anything capable of establishing a data connection, such as Excel, or a SharePoint Web part. If you are querying against the OLAP cubes, then any OLAP tool will work, including Excel, Performance Point, or various OLAP tools.

> **NOTE**
>
> With SQL Server 2005, BAM real-time aggregations will collect data in SQL Server tables. As of SQL Server 2008, real-time aggregations automatically take advantage of real-time cube updates where data is kept in SQL Server Analysis Services and is migrated there automatically. In

addition to enabling enhanced querying mechanisms, this also means that larger data sets can be retained before there are performance repercussions. Either way, it is always a good practice to set the RTA time windows to only retain what you really need in order to streamline performance.

When building a BAM solution, we essentially need to establish a "tool chain" for which we need to determine a metrics capture model. This can be accomplished programmatically with the BAM API, but is more commonly done using Excel (see BAM.xlsx part of the sample BAM solution architecture in Figure 20.2).

By using Excel, the metrics collection system can be established by non-technical users, such as business analysts. The types of activities and views that can be created in this manner are discussed later in this chapter.

Figure 20.2

A sample BAM solution driven by a human using Excel.

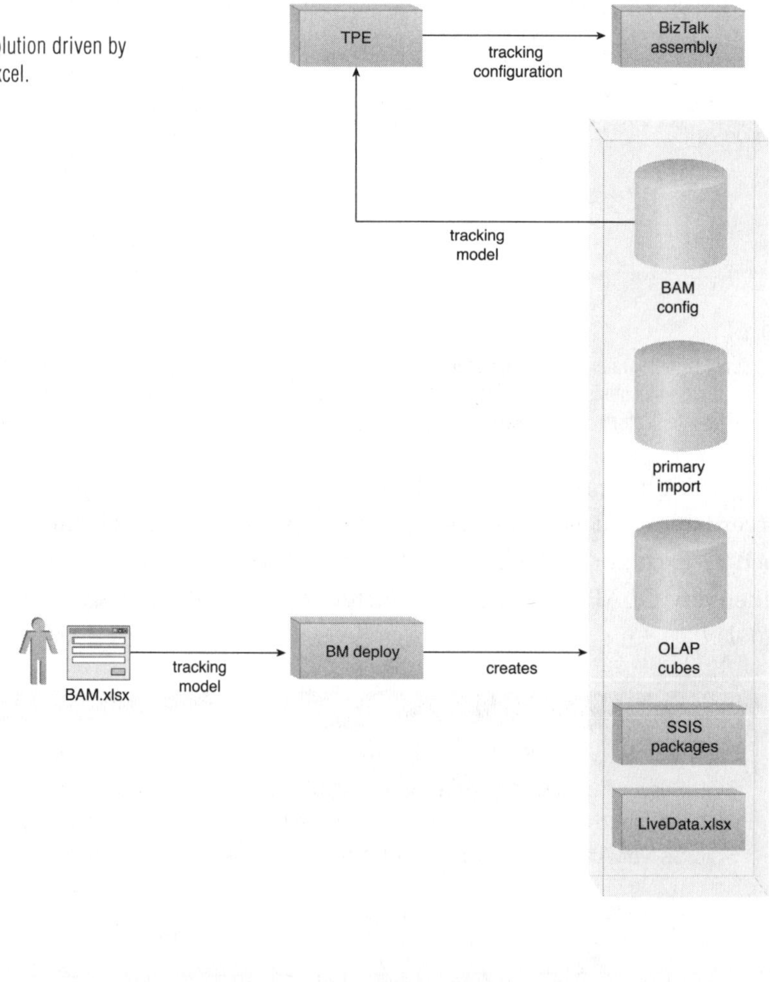

Before we get into using BAM to collect meters for services and service compositions, let's briefly describe a few primary BAM components.

The BAM Management Utility

The BAM Management utility (BM.EXE) command line tool does a lot of the "heavy lifting" required to create the following artifacts used in a metrics tracking solution:

- it creates the primary import tables (including the creation of triggers if real-time aggregations are used)

- it creates the SSIS packages required for scheduled aggregations to move data from the primary import table to the OLAP cubes

- if using scheduled aggregations, it creates the OLAP cubes

- if using real-time aggregations, it creates an RTA table in the primary import database

- if using SQL Server 2005 or 2008, it creates the real-time cubes with default update settings

- if using real-time aggregations, it creates a "LiveData" spreadsheet to view the data (the spreadsheet is stamped with a connection string to your primary import table)

- it deploys information about the activity and views to the BAM configuration tables (which are also in the BAMPrimaryImport database)

After this utility has been used, we will have defined a logical model and created the containers and transports for the data. If all metrics data come from WF or WCF interceptors or API calls, then we are done. If the metrics data originates in a BizTalk process or messages flowing through BizTalk Server, then we have an additional step, which is to map the logical model to the physical implementation in the BizTalk environment.

The Tracking Profile Editor (TPE)

The Tracking Profile Editor (TPE) is the tool that allows us to link the logical model to the physical implementation in BizTalk Server. It visually shows the logical model and implementation, allowing you to establish the link and create a *tracking profile*.

Once the tracking profile has been defined, it is "applied" to an assembly. You can only have one tracking profile per assembly and it is tied to the version of the assembly. In a development environment, this can be done directly from inside the TPE.

It is important to note that although the SSIS packages for scheduled aggregations are created, they will not be automatically scheduled to run. Scheduling them is the final step and is typically performed by the person doing the deployment.

When working with the TPE, you can choose the type of event source you would like to use:

- *orchestration schedule* – a BizTalk orchestration (which includes access to active messages that flow through the orchestration)

- *message payload* – contents of a message flowing through BizTalk (in a messaging-only solution, such as content-based routing)

- *context property* – allows tracking of context properties of messages flowing through BizTalk (includes the default context properties every message in BizTalk has, as well as any that you may have defined through an associated property schema)

- *messaging property* – allows tracking of system-level messaging properties of messages flowing through BizTalk (such as `MessageId`, `InterchangeId`, etc.)

NOTE

In a production environment, the TPE will not be available. This is because when BizTalk Server is installed, it detects whether Visual Studio is present. If not, it will not install the TPE because it is considered a development tool. In order to apply the tracking profile in a production environment, you need to export the tracking profile from the TPE as a BTT file, and then use the `BTTDeploy` command line utility to apply it.

Real-Time vs Scheduled Aggregations

BAM supports both scheduled aggregations and real-time aggregations, each of which is used differently to aggregate metrics data.

Real-time aggregations allow you to obtain up-to-the-minute metrics. A business example of this would be having a large shipment of perishable goods sitting on a loading dock that needs to be processed before it spoils. Perhaps the goods cannot be processed because the automation solution responsible for processing the order document has not been functioning properly. With a real-time aggregation, the administrator could generate a snapshot view of all services exceptions captured within the past 12 hours.

Scheduled aggregations can support a large number of dimensions, measures, and data, as they exist in SQL Analysis Services. It is more suitable for tracking metrics for the purpose of trend analysis over time. Although scheduled aggregations are not real-time, they can be *near* real-time, which will often be sufficient.

If you want to track activity in an order process over an extended period, you're looking at a multi-month or multi-year data set. In this case, having 12 hour old data may be perfectly acceptable. For example, perhaps you want to chart service capability invocation by service consumers over the past six months for trend analysis.

The data in a scheduled aggregation is as current as the last run of the SSIS or DTS package, so you can control the currency of the data by adjusting the frequency of package execution. If you have multiple scheduled aggregations, the update frequency can be defined by aggregation, so you could have some data sets more current than others. One final key benefit is that as all the data is being collected into OLAP cubes, it can be viewed in multiple ways, with a wide range of tools, so it is possible that you could create new views into this data months after collection was started.

SUMMARY OF KEY POINTS

- Even though it is bundled with BizTalk Server, BAM exists and can be used as a standalone metrics collection mechanism.

- There are several moving parts to a given BAM implementation; however, the output data is ultimately non-proprietary and can be accessed and used by a variety of programs.

- The BAM Management utility and the Tracking Profile Editor are important tools when configuring BAM solutions.

20.3 Activities and Views

The first step in creating a service or process instrumentation is to define the logical model that determines what metrics will be tracked. Two tools can be used to develop this model: Excel and the Orchestration Designer for Business Analysts. The functionality is largely the same, although using Excel does provide a wider range of relevant capabilities. With both tools, you first model an activity and then model views into that activity.

An activity defines two types of entities:

- business milestones (for example, the date or time an event occurred)

- business data (extracted from a message in flight or the data contract of a service contract or the metadata associated with a message)

Figure 20.3 shows a screenshot of a monitoring activity modeled in an Excel spreadsheet using the BizTalk BAM add-on. Once you have an activity defined, the next step is to create one or more views into the activity.

Figure 20.3

A screenshot of the BAM add-on for Excel.

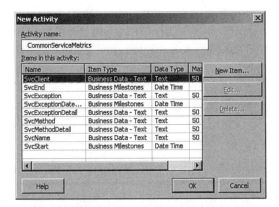

NOTE

If you are using real-time aggregations and SQL Server 2005, you are limited to 14 dimensions. This is significant, as a date/time value will decompose into multiple dimensions. The number of dimensions depends on the time resolution. Each element (year, month, day, hour, minute) is a dimension. This limitation is by design in order to ensure optimal performance. This does not apply to scheduled aggregations that are housed in SQL Analysis Services.

Roles-based Views for Service Governance

When structuring views for individual services, a good rule of thumb is to create one view for each role that needs visibility. For example, you may want to provide different views for an Order service, such as views for sales, manufacturing, and accounting.

Taking a roles-based approach like this also makes it easier to ultimately secure the views so that a service custodian can be granted a broader, more detailed view of a service than different types of service consumer designers that may only need to access (or may only be permitted to access) a subset of the service's available metrics.

Roles-based views also allow for a more granular approach to scheduling necessary OLAP updates.

Creating Views

The view creation process is wizard-driven. Here's a sample sequence of steps that we may have to complete in order to define a view:

1. Select the activity items.

2. Specify which data items are included in the view.

3. Define how the data items are stored.

4. Define the measures and dimensions of the data.

At this stage we determine the structure of the OLAP cubes in SQL Analysis Services, as well as any real-time aggregations with SQL Server tables (Figure 20.4).

Figure 20.4

The Business Activity Monitoring View Creation dialog.

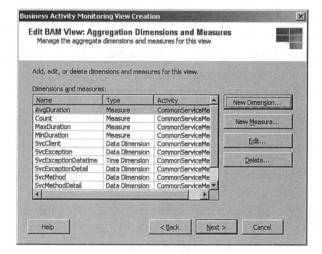

We will then be presented with a choice of the following dimensions:

- *progress dimension* – This is a virtual dimension that allows you to create stages in a process, which means that you can divide data into groups. Ultimately, you could use a progress dimension to produce a pie chart showing relative percentages of orders at different defined stages.

- *data dimension* – This dimension retrieves business data as it has been defined in the activity.

- *numeric range dimension* – A numeric range dimension groups data items into buckets. For example, we can specify service duration ranges, such as fast ("less than 1 second"), medium ("1–10 seconds"), or slow ("more than 10 seconds"). These ultimately allow for the creation of a pie chart showing the relative percentage of service duration ranges (for example, "50% of durations are fast").

- *time dimension* – This is essentially a timestamp for a milestone or a milestone group, which means we would specify the time resolution.

For the time dimension, it is a best practice to define only the granularity that is actually required. For example, if you do not need to track the hour and minute a milestone occurred, do not select it (Figure 20.5). During the data migration to the SQL Analysis Services process, there is a stage that will pre-populate the time dimension for a year. If you have specified fine granularity down to the minute, this part of the process will take longer, and the cube structure will be larger than it needs to be.

Note that the base data items available will change with the aggregation type. For example, a sum of dates makes no sense, but a minimum and maximum may. Count is normally always present in a view, as

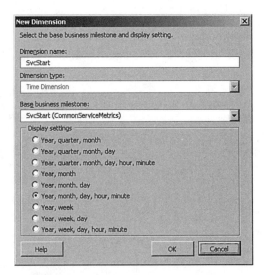

Figure 20.5

The levels of granularity at which a time dimension can be defined.

this is the count of the instances of the activity. If you are using scheduled aggregations, then ultimately you will have the ability to perform drill-through analysis such as minimum/maximum values over a month, average number of items per day, etc.

20.4 BAM APIs

As is the case with most parts of BizTalk, there is an exposed API that can be invoked to interact with the BAM tracking infrastructure. This allows you to extend a BAM-based instrumentation process beyond BizTalk solutions.

Event Streams

Registering events with BAM involves the use of an EventStream. There are four types of EventStream APIs, as described in the following sections. Regardless of which API is used, the ultimate result is the same—data will be captured (by default) in the BAMPrimaryImport database.

DirectEventStream (DES)

The DirectEventStream is a synchronous call. There is no latency, once you register an event it will be immediately available in the BAMPrimaryImport tables. However, being a synchronous operation, this is not a good choice if you are dealing with agnostic services that are being subjected to a large amount of concurrent reuse and surges in message volumes. Because this is a blocking operation, it can become a bottleneck in this situation. This is the only API that writes directly to the BAMPrimaryImport database.

BufferedEventStream (BES)

In most cases, for an external service that needs to call into the BAM tracking infrastructure, this is usually the correct API to use. It is an asynchronous operation that writes data to a temporary spooling table, and in time, the Tracking Data and Decoding Service (TDDS) will move those into the BAMPrimaryImport table. When you use the Tracking Profile Editor to link your activity model to an orchestration or message, it is creating interceptors that use the BufferedEventStream.

OrchestrationEventStream (OES)

The OrchestrationEventStream is similar to the BufferedEventStream, in that it is asynchronous and well suited to volatile event volumes. It is specifically intended to be used in those cases where you are calling the API from inside an orchestrated task service or from within centralized orchestration logic. In this case, events can participate in orchestration transactions.

When an orchestration transaction commits, the BAM data will be written out, and if a transaction is rolled back, so is the tracked data, ensuring synchronization between actions and tracked data. To minimize database latency, data is persisted in the MessageBox database, and is migrated into the BAMPrimaryImport database by the TDDS service.

IPipelineContext Interface

The IPipelineContext interface exposes a GetEventStream method that returns a MessagingEventStream object. This is an asynchronous API for use in pipeline components and participates in pipeline transactions. So when a pipeline transaction commits, the BAM data is persisted.

Abstracted APIs for Service Metrics

Most of the BAM APIs require some knowledge of the underlying activity definition. It is therefore sometimes suitable to shield developers from these details by creating a higher level abstraction layer that makes BAM easier to use.

The API for tracking service metrics essentially has to fulfill three tasks:

1. Track the service start.

2. Track the service end.

3. Track exception information.

In order to maintain continuity, we need some way to tie a service end or service exception back to its corresponding start. In order to do that, the service start method will return a GUID that we will then present to the other two methods.

Note that the maintenance tasks would need to be configured in such a way that any incomplete instances (such as a service start occurs, but there is a failure that prevents the service end from running) are removed at some point.

The `TrackServiceStart` method is overloaded, as shown here:

```
public class ServiceTracker
{
  const string ACTIVITY_NAME = "CommonServiceMetrics";
  const string CONNECTION_STRING = "Integrated
    Security=SSPI;Persist Security Info=False;
  Initial Catalog=BizTalkMsgBoxDb";
  public static Guid TrackServiceStart
    (string serviceName,
     string methodName,
     string client)
  {
    return TrackServiceStart(serviceName,
      methodName, client, "");
  }
  public static Guid TrackServiceStart
    (string serviceName,
     string methodName,
     string client,
     string methodDetails)
  {
    Guid guid = Guid.NewGuid();
    BufferedEventStream strm =
    new BufferedEventStream();
    strm.ConnectionString = CONNECTION_STRING;
    strm.BeginActivity(ACTIVITY_NAME, guid.ToString());
    strm.UpdateActivity(ACTIVITY_NAME, guid.ToString(),
      "SvcStart", DateTime.Now,
      "SvcName", serviceName,
      "SvcMethod", methodName,
      "SvcClient", client,
      "SvcMethodDetail",
      methodDetails);
    strm.Flush();
    return guid;
  }
}
```

Example 20.1

Assuming no exception is thrown, the next call to the API would be to the `TrackSer-viceEnd` method:

```
public static void TrackServiceEnd(Guid guid)
{
  BufferedEventStream strm = new BufferedEventStream();
  strm.ConnectionString = CONNECTION_STRING;
  strm.UpdateActivity(ACTIVITY_NAME, guid.ToString(),
    "SvcEnd", DateTime.Now);
  strm.EndActivity(ACTIVITY_NAME, guid.ToString());
  strm.Flush();
}
```

Example 20.2

If an exception occurs, we would log the exception:

```
public static void TrackServiceException
  (Guid guid,
   string exceptionType,
   string exceptionDetail)
{
  BufferedEventStream strm = new BufferedEventStream();
  strm.ConnectionString = CONNECTION_STRING;
  strm.UpdateActivity(ACTIVITY_NAME, guid.ToString(),
    "SvcExceptionDatetime", DateTime.Now,
    "SvcException", exceptionType,
    "SvcExceptionDetail", exceptionDetail);
  strm.Flush();
}
```

Example 20.3

With these three simple methods and the activity definition we created earlier, we now have a wide range of reports we can generate around service usage, including:

- successful versus failed service invocations over time (which could be useful for trend analysis to see increasing failure rates)

- service latency over time (which could be useful to spot service degradation that may not otherwise be noticed before it became critical)

- which capabilities inside a service are being called over time (which could help decide which services and capabilities may be candidates for retirement)

- a percentage breakdown of exceptions being tracked

This API is by no means presented as an alternative to more comprehensive third-party service monitoring products that can provide broader features, such as service SLA monitoring.

Metrics for Service Compositions

Although in the examples shown so far we are focused on metrics for individual services, we will often need to take a more holistic view of metrics on service compositions and service interactions. This will require generating reports that look beyond just individual service invocations in order to represent a broader view of cross-service usage and cross-service interaction patterns.

Reporting on metrics for service compositions poses an interesting dilemma, as within the potentially loosely coupled and asynchronous composition dynamics you need to be able to recognize that a given service invocation is part of a specific aggregate; and, you further need to be able to correlate the corresponding aggregate data.

To do this, we need some form of correlation identifier. In most cases, when composing service invocations, such a unique identifier will already be available. For example, in an order process, you would likely have an order number that can be used as the correlation value. However, if your business logic cannot provide you with a correlation identifier, you will need to add it to the service interface and metrics capturing model. Either way, by using a unique correlation identifier, you will be able to subsequently capture service composition-specific metrics by filtering or grouping on that identifier value.

A common metric that pertains to service composition processing is cross-service usage patterns; for example, the quantity of concurrent invocations that occur or the amount of concurrent invocations exceeding a pre-set limit determined in service SLAs. With the generic, service-level metrics we have outlined so far, it is easy to extract this type of data. It only entails the creation of an appropriate report or dashboard indicator that can derive the metric from the raw metrics data that is already being collected.

You may recall that earlier in the *SOA Metric Types* section we established service composition architecture as being primarily associated with business metrics. This, of course, is still valid when we want to capture metrics that pertain to the overall business process and workflow being collectively automated by a composition's participating services. However, a key consideration to keep in mind when designing and working with metrics for service compositions is that you will be able to create a metrics solution with greater flexibility and efficiency if it is based on service-level metrics. This is because BAM allows for these metrics to be aggregated in alignment with how services are aggregated as part of a composition.

WCF and WF Interceptors

BizTalk Server provides the ability to use interceptors to track data flowing through WWF processes and through WCF services. This allows service-oriented solutions based on those platforms to leverage BAM infrastructure.

Prior to the introduction of interceptors, you had to call the BAM API, which would have resulted in a more tightly coupled tracking solution. Alternatively, the API also provides the ability to create interceptors programmatically. While this is less tightly-coupled in general, it is still more tightly-coupled than a runtime configuration change.

Working with interceptors is comparable to working with the BAM API. The biggest difference is that instead of using the TEP to map from the activity definition to the actual implementation, you use configuration to add behaviors.

There is no front-end tool for creating interceptors. You need to work with interceptor configuration schemas. BAM provides three schemas: common, WCF, and WF. You need to incorporate them with the Visual Studio schema folder or by using Visual Studio's XmlSchema option. The latter approach provides you the benefit of IntelliSense when creating interceptor configuration files. This is a suggested best practice, as the files can become somewhat complex and IntelliSense will allow you to validate the schema document before you deploy it.

Notifications

Perhaps the most common and critical metric that needs to be tracked for agnostic services is usage thresholds. Agnostic services (such as entity and utility services) are designed for reuse and, when made available for discovery by new consumers, their concurrent usage can increase dramatically.

BAM supports event notifications that allow you to set alerts based on threshold values. For example, should service latency exceed a predefined value, you can have it issue an alert. This can help service custodians better manage and even refactor service implementations before thresholds are actually reached.

The BAM portal includes a mechanism that allows you to create alerts and manage alert subscribers. The alerting transport can be either an email or a file emitted into a folder. The folder option enables you to have BizTalk listening to the destination folder and perhaps launch a compensating business process in response to an alert event.

> **NOTE**
>
> With BizTalk Server 2006 R2 and BizTalk Server 2009 using SQL 2005 as the data store, the alerting mechanism is implemented using SQL Server 2005 Notification Services. With BizTalk Server 2009, if you are using SQL Server 2008 as the data store, a separate download is required to obtain notification capabilities.

Rapid Prototyping

There are times where it can be advantageous to start capturing metrics early in the development cycle, perhaps before services you want to monitor have been written.

Some situations where advanced service metrics development makes sense are:

- you want to develop your tracking metrics so you can begin the portal construction process and show stakeholders what a final product may look like

- your process relies on other services that have not yet been implemented (or, for any other reason, are not available)

- you need to work with creative personnel and give them examples of metrics presentation

- you want to show stakeholders the value that effective instrumentation will provide (service and process instrumentation ties directly back to business values, and as such is generally understood by non-technical stakeholders)

Using BAM it is possible to take a "metrics-first" approach to process and service instrumentation.

Recall that everything in BAM begins with a logical model created in Excel or the Orchestration Designer for Business Analysts. Once we have that logical model, we can use the BM.EXE tool to create the database artifacts required to track that activity. With a service or process to instrument, we don't have a physical representation to map to our logical model, so we cannot at that point use the TPE to create that link.

However, once we've used the BM.EXE tool, the stored procedures that will insert tracking data will exist. Normally, in a fully constructed and deployed BAM tracking infrastructure, these stored procedures would be called by the interceptors; however, there's nothing to stop us from calling them directly. This is an extremely effective way to approach rapid prototyping of BAM instrumentation.

SUMMARY OF KEY POINTS

- BAM provides four types of EventStream APIs used for registering events: DirectEventStream, BufferedEventStream, OrchestrationEventStream, IPipelineContext Interface.

- It is often suitable to create an abstracted API for use by developers in order to avoid the complexity of native BAM APIs.

- WCF and WF interceptors can be leveraged by BAM to collect runtime metrics.

- Notifications can be used to keep service custodians apprised of service usage patterns, especially in relation to thresholds.

20.5 Managing BAM

Provided in this section is a series of tips for managing BAM solutions in support of collecting and maintaining metrics for services and service compositions.

Database Outages

When tracking a service that is shared by multiple compositions, encountering a database outage within the metrics solution environment will impact the metrics collection of multiple business processes. It is therefore important to understand when a database outage is considered critical or non-critical.

The TDDS service is responsible for moving data into the BAMPrimaryImport database. This runs as a sub-process of a BizTalk host and is enabled by specifying that a host is a *tracking host*.

If you are using any of the asynchronous APIs, an outage of the BAMPrimaryImport database is non-critical, as data will continue to be collected in the MessageBox database. Once the BAMPrimaryImport database becomes available again, data will migrate into it. By contrast, an outage of the BAMPrimaryImport database when using the synchronous API is a critical failure and will result in an exception being thrown.

Security

It is important to remember that BAM is about tracking data and that means you can potentially also track sensitive data. Appropriate security measures must therefore be taken to ensure that the confidentiality of any sensitive metrics data is maintained.

As discussed earlier in this chapter, BAM security is managed by role membership. You can secure views by restricting access to only certain groups. This can be done by grouping tracked data into one view per group and then restricting membership in that group.

There are common security levels associated with common SOA project roles:

- service analysts and service architects typically require access to metrics data of already implemented services that may need to be composed with new services being modeled or designed

- service custodians typically receive access to all metrics data for general governance purposes

- schema and policy custodians often require access to service exception data, especially pertaining to exceptions raised as a result of validation or compliance failure

- service consumer designers often will request access to current service usage data in order to determine usage patterns that may impact the design of their consumer programs (although the release of this data is not always recommended as it will typically be subject to change)

Depending on how you render data for users, there may be further security options you can explore. If, for example, you are using SQL Server Reporting Services hosted in a SharePoint site, you could make use of the additional provided security mechanisms to further restrict and control visibility.

Scripting Deployment

Seasoned BAM developers often use scripted batch files to deploy and un-deploy parts of BAM infrastructure. The reason for this is twofold. First, developing the tracking infrastructure is generally an iterative process, with multiple iterations occurring until the logical model aligns with the physical implementation to the point where you can extract the required metrics. Secondly, un-deploying and re-deploying the tracking profile enables you to remove any collected data and "re-set" the environment to a clean state.

The syntax will vary with operating systems, but the following provides an example of a typical development-time deployment script:

```
@ECHO OFF
color a0
ECHO Deploying Common Service Metrics Tracking
rem :: delims is a TAB followed by a space
```

```
FOR /F "tokens=2* delims= " %%A IN ('REG QUERY
"HKEY_LOCAL_MACHINE\SOFTWARE\Microsoft\BizTalk Server\3.0" /v
InstallPath') DO SET InstPath=%%B
echo Using BAM Manager from BizTalk installation path '%InstPath%'
"%InstPath%\Tracking\bm" update-all -
DefinitionFile:"CommonServiceMetrics.xls"
```

Example 20.4

The script needs to call the BAM Manager tool (BM.EXE) located in the "tracking" folder where BizTalk was installed. Note that no tracking profile is applied here. In this development environment that would either be done using the TPE or, if using API calls or interceptors, it would not be required at all.

The use of the `color` command changes the background of the command window, which can be an effective means of visually indicating the type of task (deploy or un-deploy) being performed.

By contrast, the following is an example of a typical deployment script for a QA or production environment:

```
@ECHO OFF
mode con cols=120
color a0
cls
ECHO ** Please note that you must have BizTalk Administrator rights to
run this script.
:: delims is a TAB followed by a space
FOR /F "tokens=2* delims= " %%A IN ('REG QUERY
"HKEY_LOCAL_MACHINE\SOFTWARE\Microsoft\BizTalk Server\3.0" /v
InstallPath') DO SET InstPath=%%B
echo Using BAM Manager from BizTalk installation path '%InstPath%'
echo [[ Deploying activities... ]]
"%InstPath%\Tracking\bm" update-all -
DefinitionFile:"CommonServiceMetrics.xml"
echo.
echo [[ Deploying tracking profile... ]]
echo.
"%InstPath%\Tracking\bttdeploy" "CommonServiceMetrics.btt"
```

Example 20.5

You'll notice a couple of key differences from the development script. In this script, we are giving the BM.exe utility an XML file as an activity definition rather than an Excel spreadsheet. This is because, as a QA or production machine, Excel will presumably not be installed. This XML file was created from the BAM toolbar menu inside the spreadsheet.

Secondly, we are using BTTDeploy to apply the tracking profile (create the interceptors). Because the TPE is considered a development tool, it will likely not be available to us in these environments.

The corresponding undeployment script for development would be:

```
@ECHO OFF
color e0
ECHO Undeploying CommonServiceMetrics
rem :: delims is a TAB followed by a space
FOR /F "tokens=2* delims=   " %%A IN ('REG QUERY
"HKEY_LOCAL_MACHINE\SOFTWARE\Microsoft\BizTalk Server\3.0" /v
InstallPath') DO SET InstPath=%%B
echo Using BTTDeploy from BizTalk installation path '%InstPath%'
"%InstPath%\Tracking\bm.exe"  remove-all -
DefinitionFile:"CommonServiceMetrics.xls"
Pause
```

Example 20.6

And, lastly, the corresponding undeployment script for QA or Production could be something along these lines:

```
@ECHO OFF
mode con cols=120
color e0
cls
```

Example 20.7

```
ECHO ** Please note that you must have BizTalk Administrator rights to
run this script.
:: delims is a TAB followed by a space
FOR /F "tokens=2* delims=   " %%A IN ('REG QUERY
"HKEY_LOCAL_MACHINE\SOFTWARE\Microsoft\BizTalk Server\3.0" /v
InstallPath') DO SET InstPath=%%B
echo Using BAM Manager from BizTalk installation path '%InstPath%'
```

```
echo [[ Removing tracking profile... ]]
"%InstPath%\Tracking\bttdeploy.exe" /remove "CommonServiceMetrics.btt"
echo [[ Removing activities... ]]
"%InstPath%\Tracking\bm" remove-all -
DefinitionFile:"CommonServiceMetrics.xml"
```

Example 20.8

As was the case with the previous script, here too we use the XML version of the activity definition file and BTTDeploy.

Reporting

Tracking data about service invocation and business processes is a vital part of any SOA governance strategy, but it is meaningless without an effective rendering mechanism.

BizTalk Server includes an optional BAM Portal that exists as an ASP.NET site that provides a generic way for surfacing data that has been tracked by BAM. It allows for ad-hoc queries and rendering charts using the basic Office Web Controls. This BAM portal can be useful during the development cycle, but may not be suitable beyond the development environment.

Fortunately, because BAM stores metrics data in OLAP cubes (scheduled aggregations using SQL Server Analysis Services or real-time aggregations using SQL Server) or in SQL Server tables, the data can be queried and rendered with a range of additional tools. A common choice is to use a combination of SharePoint and SQL Server Reporting Services.

Using SharePoint as a host for reports allows you to leverage its identity management and present data at a departmental portal level. This enables you to secure access to those departmental sites based on domain group membership.

SQL Server Reporting Services allows you to create textual reports on data. The chart control for SQL Server Reporting Services is a chart control that provides 3D rendering capabilities, as well as fine-grained control for developers to implement "drill through" features. Also, with the reports being generated within SQL Server Reporting Services, you can leverage the native report subscription model so that reports can be generated at predefined intervals and e-mailed to subscribers.

Various other reporting options exist, including numerous customization opportunities for rendering data to users. In addition, metrics data can also be used to drive business intelligence applications, such as PerformancePoint.

SUMMARY OF KEY POINTS

- Common considerations when managing BAM solutions include accommodating BAM database outages, setting appropriate security roles, and working with scripts to better control deployment and undeployment of BAM components.

- Although BAM offers basic metrics reporting features, the open BAM storage architecture allows you to use more sophisticated reporting, charting, and rendering tools.

CASE STUDY EXAMPLE

Subsequent to deployment, a group is assigned responsibility of owning the Order service and ensuring its on-going governance. This group of service custodians, comprised of one enterprise architect and one systems administrator, is aware of the fact that, as an agnostic entity service central to several business processes, reuse of the Order service will continue to increase.

Standard Mold's IT infrastructure personnel need visibility into all service metrics in order to ensure that services are functioning within acceptable limits, and also for trend analysis that may allow them to respond to problem conditions. Because the service inventory platform is already based on BizTalk Server, the Order service custodians opt to use BizTalk BAM as a foundation for their metrics solution.

After some deliberation, the team defines a common profile of the metrics they would like to track. They then proceed with a project to wrap a class library around the BAM API as a layer of abstraction. This will require the Order service to call into the API to register events. This API will be for use on machines that do not have BizTalk installed but can still support asynchronous communication. Therefore, the API will be based on the `BufferedEventStream` class.

For auditing, they would like to implement simple tracking that uses real-time aggregation to capture a list showing information about orders (buyer name, customer number and order amount). They use SQL Server Reporting Services to display a running list in a portal.

Rather than embedding tracking points in their service, they want to implement this using the interceptors for WCF. Even though it is possible to have multiple activities in a single interceptor configuration file, they only create a single activity called OrderActivity. They proceed with the creation of the interceptor configuration file, as follows:

They assign a symbolic name that can be used later in the definition and further specify the fully-qualified assembly they will be tracking. Next, they define a BamActivity that will contain filter conditions and logic determining what they want to track.

Shown in the following two examples are the configuration file contents:

```
<ic:InterceptorConfiguration
  xmlns:ic="http://schemas.microsoft.com/..."
  xmlns:wcf="http://schemas.microsoft.com/...">
  <ic:EventSource Name="OrderEventSource"
    Technology="WCF"
    Manifest ="Soanet.Contracts.IOrderManager,
      ServiceContracts, Version=1.0.0.0,
      Culture=neutral, PublicKeyToken=null">
    <wcf:NamespaceMappings>
      <wcf:Namespace Prefix="a"
        Uri="http://example.org/sellfast/2007/1/1"/>
    </wcf:NamespaceMappings>
  </ic:EventSource>
  <ic:BamActivity Name="OrderActivity">
    <ic:OnEvent Name="SubmitOrder"
      Source="OrderEventSource"
      IsBegin="true" IsEnd="true">
      <ic:Filter>
        <ic:Expression>
          <wcf:Operation Name="GetOperationName"/>
          <ic:Operation Name="Constant">
            <ic:Argument>SubmitOrder</ic:Argument>
          </ic:Operation>
          <ic:Operation Name="Equals"/>
          <wcf:Operation Name="GetServiceContractCallPoint"/>
          <ic:Operation Name="Constant">
            <ic:Argument>ServiceRequest</ic:Argument>
          </ic:Operation>
          <ic:Operation Name="Equals"/>
          <ic:Operation Name="And"/>
        </ic:Expression>
      </ic:Filter>
      <ic:CorrelationID>
        <ic:Expression>
          <wcf:Operation Name="AutoGenerateCorrelationToken"/>
        </ic:Expression>
      </ic:CorrelationID>
      ...
```

Example 20.9

The `filter` construct (red) is used to establish a filter so that only the SubmitOrder capability of the service is tracked. The `CorrelationID` construct (bold) then assigns the activity ID value. (The remainder of this example is continued in the next example section.)

The final section in the interceptor configuration file specifies which fields they want to update. Most of this code is self-explanatory as they are using XPath expressions to reach into the message and retrieve specific values.

```
    ...
    <ic:Update DataItemName="CustomerNumber" Type="NVARCHAR">
      <ic:Expression>
        <wcf:Operation Name ="XPath">
          <wcf:Argument>//a:CustomerNumber</wcf:Argument>
        </wcf:Operation>
      </ic:Expression>
    </ic:Update>
    <ic:Update DataItemName="BuyerName" Type="NVARCHAR">
      <ic:Expression>
        <wcf:Operation Name ="XPath">
          <wcf:Argument>//a:BuyerName</wcf:Argument>
        </wcf:Operation>
      </ic:Expression>
    </ic:Update>
    <ic:Update DataItemName="OrderTotsl" Type="INT">
      <ic:Expression>
        <wcf:Operation Name ="XPath">
          <wcf:Argument>//a:OrderTotal</wcf:Argument>
        </wcf:Operation>
      </ic:Expression>
    </ic:Update>
  </ic:OnEvent>
 </ic:BamActivity>
</ic:InterceptorConfiguration>
```

Example 20.10

The `Update` constructs identify the tracked fields to update. Note that the namespace used was declared as part of the EventSource.

In this configuration file the filter expression specifies that they are looking for a WCF OperationName of SubmitOrder. The GetServiceContractCallPoint indicates when the custodians want to capture the data. In this case it is as the service receives the request, but it could have been when the service returns its response as well.

The `CorrelationID` element is used to house the activity ID in the BAM infrastructure. They are asking for a new key (a GUID) to be generated, but they could have just as easily used something in the message for this (such as an order number).

> **NOTE**
>
> The operators `Equals` and `And` show that operations in an interceptor configuration file are implemented using reverse Polish notation. In Reverse Polish Notation, operators follow all of the operands, meaning "2 + 2" is expressed as "2 2 +", "3 + 4 – 9" is expressed as "3 4 9 + -" and so forth.

With their metrics solution in place, the service custodians use SQL Server Reporting Services to generate their metrics reports. In addition, because Standard Mold's IT division already uses Microsoft SharePoint Server as their intranet solution, the custodians can use the enterprise SharePoint sites as a "host" for the reports. They proceed to use a Dundas Chart for SQL Server Reporting Services. Figures 20.6 and 20.7 show how this renders the metrics as chart data.

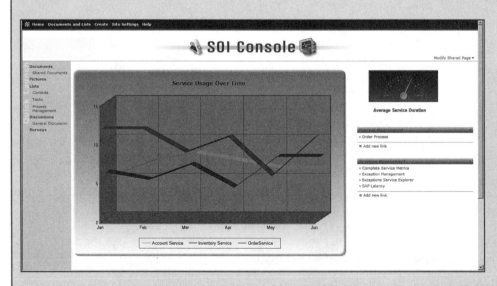

Figure 20.6
A metrics report rendered in SharePoint.

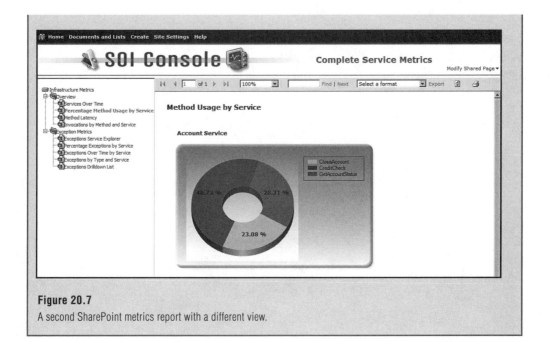

Figure 20.7
A second SharePoint metrics report with a different view.

Part IV

Appendices

Appendix A: Case Study Conclusion

Appendix B: Industry Standards Reference

Appendix C: Service-Orientation Principles Reference

Appendix D: SOA Design Patterns Reference

Appendix E: The Annotated SOA Manifesto

Appendix F: Additional Resources

Appendix A

Case Study Conclusion

Standard Mold project teams accomplished their original goals of improving the automation of internal business processes and data exchanges with business partners, namely Superior Stamping. Through their exploration of the Microsoft technology platform, they identified numerous additional opportunities to build new services and optimize existing service-oriented solutions. Furthermore, they were able to leverage advances in virtualization and infrastructure that helped them establish scalable and reliable inventories of services.

The ultimate results are improvements in responsiveness while further increasing the cost effectiveness of their overall IT enterprise. They have reached a stage where they feel they can better maneuver within the increasingly competitive global market, while retaining their business goals and without compromising their business philosophy.

In part due to their partnership with Standard Mold, but primarily due to their internal SOA adoption efforts, Superior Stamping has succeeded in streamlining several business tasks, while positioning services to help accommodate anticipated business change within their individual business units.

Appendix B

Industry Standards Reference

The following is an alphabetical list of industry standards and specifications referenced in this book. To access the corresponding specifications, visit www.soaspecs.com.

- ATOM Publishing Protocol

- Component Object Model (COM)

- Distributed Component Object Model (DCOM)

- Extensible Access Control Markup Language (XACML)

- Extensible Markup Language (XML)

- Hypertext Transfer Protocol (HTTP)

- JavaScript Object Notation (JSON)

- Security Assertion Markup Language (SAML)

- SOAP (formerly the Simple Object Access Protocol)

- Universal Description, Discovery, and Integration (UDDI)

- Web Application Description Language (WADL)

- Web Services Description Language (WSDL)

- WS-AtomicTransaction

- WS-Basic Profile

- WS-BPEL

- WS-BusinessActivity

- WS-Coordination

- WS-Discovery

- WS-Eventing

- WS-Federation

- WS-I Basic Security Profile

- WS-MetadataExchange

- WS-Policy

- WS-PolicyAttachments

- WS-ReliableMessaging

- WS-SecureConversation

- WS-Security

- WS-Trust

- XML Encryption

- XML Key Management Specification (XKMS)

- XML Schema Definition Language (XSD)

- XML Signature

- XML Transformations (XSLT)

- XPath

Appendix C

Service-Orientation Principles
Reference

This appendix provides profile tables for the eight design principles that are documented in *SOA Principles of Service Design*, a title that is part of this book series. Each principle that is referenced in this book is suffixed with the page number of its corresponding profile table in this appendix.

Every profile table contains the following sections:

- *Short Definition* – A concise, single-statement definition that establishes the fundamental purpose of the principle.

- *Long Definition* – A longer description of the principle that provides more detail as to what it is intended to accomplish.

- *Goals* – A list of specific design goals that are expected from the application of the principle. Essentially, this list provides the ultimate results of the principle's realization.

- *Design Characteristics* – A list of specific design characteristics that can be realized via the application of the principle. This provides some insight as to how the principle ends up shaping the service.

- *Implementation Requirements* – A list of common prerequisites for effectively applying the design principle. These can range from technology to organizational requirements.

Note that these tables provide only summarized content from the original publication. Information about service-orientation principles is also published online at www.soaprinciples.com.

Standardized Service Contract	
Short Definition	*"Services share standardized contracts."*
Long Definition	*"Services within the same service inventory are in compliance with the same contract design standards."*
Goals	• To enable services with a meaningful level of natural interoperability within the boundary of a service inventory. This reduces the need for data transformation because consistent data models are used for information exchange. • To allow the purpose and capabilities of services to be more easily and intuitively understood. The consistency with which service functionality is expressed through service contracts increases interpretability and the overall predictability of service endpoints throughout a service inventory. Note that these goals are further supported by other service-orientation principles as well.
Design Characteristics	• A service contract (comprised of a technical interface or one or more service description documents) is provided with the service. • The service contract is standardized through the application of design standards.
Implementation Requirements	The fact that contracts need to be standardized can introduce significant implementation requirements to organizations that do not have a history of using standards. For example: • Design standards and conventions need to ideally be in place prior to the delivery of any service in order to ensure adequately scoped standardization. (For those organizations that have already produced ad-hoc Web services, retro-fitting strategies may need to be employed.) • Formal processes need to be introduced to ensure that services are modeled and designed consistently, incorporating accepted design principles, conventions, and standards.

- Because achieving standardized Web service contracts generally requires a "contract first" approach to service-oriented design, the full application of this principle will often demand the use of development tools capable of importing a customized service contract without imposing changes.

- Appropriate skill-sets are required to carry out the modeling and design processes with the chosen tools. When working with Web services, the need for a high level of proficiency with XML schema and WSDL languages is practically unavoidable. WS-Policy expertise may also be required.

These and other requirements can add up to a noticeable transition effort that goes well beyond technology adoption.

Table C.1

A profile for the Standardized Service Contract principle.

Service Loose Coupling	
Short Definition	*"Services are loosely coupled."*
Long Definition	*"Service contracts impose low consumer coupling requirements and are themselves decoupled from their surrounding environment."*
Goals	By consistently fostering reduced coupling within and between services we are working toward a state where service contracts increase independence from their implementations and services are increasingly independent from each other. This promotes an environment in which services and their consumers can be adaptively evolved over time with minimal impact on each other.
Design Characteristics	• The existence of a service contract that is ideally decoupled from technology and implementation details. • A functional service context that is not dependent on outside logic. • Minimal consumer coupling requirements.
Implementation Requirements	• Loosely coupled services are typically required to perform more runtime processing than if they were more tightly coupled. As a result, data exchange in general can consume more runtime resources, especially during concurrent access and high usage scenarios. • To achieve the right balance of coupling, while also supporting the other service-orientation principles that affect contract design, requires increased service contract design proficiency.

Table C.2

A profile for the Service Loose Coupling principle.

Service Abstraction	
Short Definition	*"Non-essential service information is abstracted."*
Long Definition	*"Service contracts only contain essential information and information about services is limited to what is published in service contracts."*
Goals	Many of the other principles emphasize the need to publish *more* information in the service contract. The primary role of this principle is to keep the quantity and detail of contract content concise and balanced and prevent unnecessary access to additional service details.
Design Characteristics	• Services consistently abstract specific information about technology, logic, and function away from the outside world (the world outside of the service boundary). • Services have contracts that concisely define interaction requirements and constraints and other required service meta details. • Outside of what is documented in the service contract, information about a service is controlled or altogether hidden within a particular environment.
Implementation Requirements	The primary prerequisite to achieving the appropriate level of abstraction for each service is the level of service contract design skill applied.
Web Service Region of Influence	The *Region of Influence* part of this profile has been moved to the *Types of Meta Abstraction* section (in the book *SOA Principles of Service Design*) where a separate Web service figure is provided for each form of abstraction.

Table C.3

A profile for the Service Abstraction principle.

Service Reusability
Short Definition	*"Services are reusable."*
Long Definition	*"Services contain and express agnostic logic and can be positioned as reusable enterprise resources."*
Goals	The goals behind Service Reusability are tied directly to some of the most strategic objectives of service-oriented computing: • To allow for service logic to be repeatedly leveraged over time so as to achieve an increasingly high return on the initial investment of delivering the service. • To increase business agility on an organizational level by enabling the rapid fulfillment of future business automation requirements through wide-scale service composition. • To enable the realization of agnostic service models. • To enable the creation of service inventories with a high percentage of agnostic services.
Design Characteristics	• *The service is defined by an agnostic functional context*—The logic encapsulated by the service is associated with a context that is sufficiently agnostic to any one usage scenario so as to be considered reusable. • *The service logic is highly generic*—The logic encapsulated by the service is sufficiently generic, allowing it to facilitate numerous usage scenarios by different types of service consumers. • *The service has a generic and extensible contract*—The service contract is flexible enough to process a range of input and output messages. • *The service logic can be accessed concurrently*—Services are designed to facilitate simultaneous access by multiple consumer programs.

Implementation Requirements	From an implementation perspective, Service Reusability can be the most demanding of the principles we've covered so far. Below are common requirements for creating reusable services and supporting their long-term existence:
	• A scalable runtime hosting environment capable of high-to-extreme concurrent service usage. Once a service inventory is relatively mature, reusable services will find themselves in an increasingly large number of compositions.
	• A solid version control system to properly evolve contracts representing reusable services.
	• Service analysts and designers with a high degree of subject matter expertise who can ensure that the service boundary and contract accurately represent the service's reusable functional context.
	• A high level of service development and commercial software development expertise so as to structure the underlying logic into generic and potentially decomposable components and routines.
	These and other requirements place an emphasis on the appropriate staffing of the service delivery team, as well as the importance of a powerful and scalable hosting environment and supporting infrastructure.

Table C.4

A profile for the Service Reusability principle.

Service Autonomy	
Short Definition	*"Services are autonomous."*
Long Definition	*"Services exercise a high level of control over their underlying runtime execution environment."*
Goals	• To increase a service's runtime reliability, performance, and predictability, especially when being reused and composed. • To increase the amount of control a service has over its runtime environment. By pursuing autonomous design and runtime environments, we are essentially aiming to increase post-implementation control over the service and the service's control over its own execution environment.
Design Characteristics	• Services have a contract that expresses a well-defined functional boundary that should not overlap with other services. • Services are deployed in an environment over which they exercise a great deal (and preferably an exclusive level) of control. • Service instances are hosted by an environment that accommodates high concurrency for scalability purposes.
Implementation Requirements	• A high level of control over how service logic is designed and developed. Depending on the level of autonomy being sought, this may also involve control over the supporting data models. • A distributable deployment environment, so as to allow the service to be moved, isolated, or composed as required. • An infrastructure capable of supporting desired autonomy levels.

Table C.5

A profile for the Service Autonomy principle.

Service Statelessness	
Short Definition	*"Services minimize statefulness."*
Long Definition	*"Services minimize resource consumption by deferring the management of state information when necessary."*
Goals	• To increase service scalability. • To support the design of agnostic service logic and improve the potential for service reuse.
Design Characteristics	What makes this somewhat of a unique principle is the fact that it is promoting a condition of the service that is temporary in nature. Depending on the service model and state deferral approach used, different types of design characteristics can be implemented. Some examples include: • Highly business process-agnostic logic so that the service is not designed to retain state information for any specific parent business process. • Less constrained service contracts so as to allow for the receipt and transmission of a wider range of state data at runtime. • Increased amounts of interpretative programming routines capable of parsing a range of state information delivered by messages and responding to a range of corresponding action requests.
Implementation Requirements	Although state deferral can reduce the overall consumption of memory and system resources, services designed with statelessness considerations can also introduce some performance demands associated with the runtime retrieval and interpretation of deferred state data. Here is a short checklist of common requirements that can be used to assess the support of stateless service designs by vendor technologies and target deployment locations: • The runtime environment should allow for a service to transition from an idle state to an active processing state in a highly efficient manner.

- Enterprise-level or high-performance XML parsers and hardware accelerators (and SOAP processors) should be provided to allow services implemented as Web services to more efficiently parse larger message payloads with less performance constraints.

- The use of attachments may need to be supported by Web services to allow for messages to include bodies of payload data that do not undergo interface-level validation or translation to local formats.

The nature of the implementation support required by the average stateless service in an environment will depend on the state deferral approach used within the service-oriented architecture.

Table C.6

A profile for the Service Statelessness principle.

Service Discoverability	
Short Definition	*"Services are discoverable."*
Long Definition	*"Services are supplemented with communicative meta data by which they can be effectively discovered and interpreted."*
Goals	• Services are positioned as highly discoverable resources within the enterprise. • The purpose and capabilities of each service are clearly expressed so that they can be interpreted by humans and software programs. Achieving these goals requires foresight and a solid understanding of the nature of the service itself. Depending on the type of service model being designed, realizing this principle may require both business and technical expertise.
Design Characteristics	• Service contracts are equipped with appropriate meta data that will be correctly referenced when discovery queries are issued. • Service contracts are further outfitted with additional meta information that clearly communicates their purpose and capabilities to humans. • If a service registry exists, registry records are populated with the same attention to meta information as just described. • If a service registry does not exist, service profile documents are authored to supplement the service contract and to form the basis for future registry records. (See Chapter 15 in *SOA Principles of Service Design* for more details about service profiles.)

Implementation Requirements	• The existence of design standards that govern the meta information used to make service contracts discoverable and interpretable, as well as guidelines for how and when service contracts should be further supplemented with annotations. • The existence of design standards that establish a consistent means of recording service meta information outside of the contract. This information is either collected in a supplemental document in preparation for a service registry, or it is placed in the registry itself. You may have noticed the absence of a service registry on the list of implementation requirements. As previously established, the goal of this principle is to implement design characteristics within the service, not within the architecture.

Table C.7

A profile for the Service Discoverability principle.

Service Composability	
Short Definition	*"Services are composable."*
Long Definition	*"Services are effective composition participants, regardless of the size and complexity of the composition."*
Goals	When discussing the goals of Service Composability, pretty much all of the goals of Service Reusability (697) apply. This is because service composition often turns out to be a form of service reuse. In fact, you may recall that one of the objectives we listed for the Service Reusability (697) principle was to enable wide-scale service composition.
	However, above and beyond simply attaining reuse, service composition provides the medium through which we can achieve what is often classified as the ultimate goal of service-oriented computing. By establishing an enterprise comprised of solution logic represented by an inventory of highly reusable services, we provide the means for a large extent of future business automation requirements to be fulfilled through…you guessed it: service composition.
Design Characteristics for Composition Member Capabilities	Ideally, every service capability (especially those providing reusable logic) is considered a potential composition member. This essentially means that the design characteristics already established by the Service Reusability (697) principle are equally relevant to building effective composition members.
	Additionally, there are two further characteristics emphasized by this principle:
	• The service needs to possess a highly efficient execution environment. More so than being able to manage concurrency, the efficiency with which composition members perform their individual processing should be highly tuned.
	• The service contract needs to be flexible so that it can facilitate different types of data exchange requirements for similar functions. This typically relates to the ability of the contract to exchange the same type of data at different levels of granularity.

The manner in which these qualities go beyond mere reuse has to do primarily with the service being capable of optimizing its runtime processing responsibilities in support of multiple, simultaneous compositions.

Design Characteristics for Composition Controller Capabilities	Composition members will often also need to act as controllers or sub-controllers within different composition configurations. However, services designed as designated controllers are generally alleviated from many of the high-performance demands placed on composition members.

These types of services therefore have their own set of design characteristics:

- The logic encapsulated by a designated controller will almost always be limited to a single business task. Typically, the task service model is used, resulting in the common characteristics of that model being applied to this type of service.

- While designated controllers may be reusable, service reuse is not usually a primary design consideration. Therefore, the design characteristics fostered by Service Reusability (697) are considered and applied where appropriate, but with less of the usual rigor applied to agnostic services.

- Statelessness is not always as strictly emphasized on designated controllers as with composition members. Depending on the state deferral options available by the surrounding architecture, designated controllers may sometimes need to be designed to remain fully stateful while the underlying composition members carry out their respective parts of the overall task.

Of course, any capability acting as a controller can become a member of a larger composition, which brings the previously listed composition member design characteristics into account as well.

Table C.8

A profile for the Service Composability principle.

Appendix D

SOA Design Patterns Reference

This appendix provides profile tables for all 85 patterns that are documented in *SOA Design Patterns*, a title that is part of this book series. Each pattern that is referenced in this book is suffixed with the page number of its corresponding profile table in this appendix.

Every profile table contains the following sections:

- *Requirement* – A requirement is a concise, single-sentence statement that presents the fundamental requirement addressed by the pattern in the form of a question. Every pattern description begins with this statement.

- *Icon* – Each pattern description is accompanied by an icon image that acts as a visual identifier. The icons are displayed together with the requirement statements in each pattern profile as well as on the inside book cover.

- *Problem* – The issue causing a problem and the effects of the problem. It is this problem for which the pattern is expected to provide a solution.

- *Solution* – This represents the design solution proposed by the pattern to solve the problem and fulfill the requirement.

- *Application* – This part is dedicated to describing how the pattern can be applied. It can include guidelines, implementation details, and sometimes even a suggested process.

- *Impacts* – This section highlights common consequences, costs, and requirements associated with the application of a pattern and may also provide alternatives that can be considered.

- *Principles* – References to related service-orientation principles.

- *Architecture* – References to related SOA architecture types (as described in Chapter 3).

Note that these tables provide only summarized content from the original publication. All pattern profile tables in this book are also published online at SOAPatterns.org.

Agnostic Capability

How can multi-purpose service logic be made effectively consumable and composable?

Problem	Service capabilities derived from specific concerns may not be useful to multiple service consumers, thereby reducing the reusability potential of the agnostic service.
Solution	Agnostic service logic is partitioned into a set of well-defined capabilities that address common concerns not specific to any one problem. Through subsequent analysis, the agnostic context of capabilities is further refined.
Application	Service capabilities are defined and iteratively refined through proven analysis and modeling processes.
Impacts	The definition of each service capability requires extra up-front analysis and design effort.
Principles	Standardized Service Contract (693), Service Reusability (697), Service Composability (704)
Architecture	Service

Agnostic Context

How can multi-purpose service logic be positioned as an effective enterprise resource?

Problem	Multi-purpose logic grouped together with single purpose logic results in programs with little or no reuse potential that introduce waste and redundancy into an enterprise.
Solution	Isolate logic that is not specific to one purpose into separate services with distinct agnostic contexts.
Application	Agnostic service contexts are defined by carrying out service-oriented analysis and service modeling processes.
Impacts	This pattern positions reusable solution logic at an enterprise level, potentially bringing with it increased design complexity and enterprise governance issues.
Principles	Service Reusability (697)
Architecture	Service

Agnostic Sub-Controller

How can agnostic, cross-entity composition logic be separated, reused, and governed independently?

Problem	Service compositions are generally configured specific to a parent task, inhibiting reuse potential that may exist within a subset of the composition logic.
Solution	Reusable, cross-entity composition logic is abstracted or made accessible via an agnostic sub-controller capability, allowing that subset of the parent composition logic to be recomposed independently.
Application	A new agnostic service is created or a task service is appended with an agnostic sub-controller capability.
Impacts	The addition of a cross-entity, agnostic service can increase the size and complexity of compositions and the abstraction of agnostic cross-entity logic can violate modeling and design standards established by Service Layers [779].
Principles	Service Reusability (697), Service Composability (704)
Architecture	Composition, Service

Asynchronous Queuing

By Mark Little, Thomas Rischbeck, Arnaud Simon

How can a service and its consumers accommodate isolated
failures and avoid unnecessarily locking resources?

Problem	When a service capability requires that consumers interact with it synchronously, it can inhibit performance and compromise reliability.
Solution	A service can exchange messages with its consumers via an intermediary buffer, allowing service and consumers to process messages independently by remaining temporally decoupled.
Application	Queuing technology needs to be incorporated into the surrounding architecture, and back-up stores may also be required.
Impacts	There may be no acknowledgement of successful message delivery, and atomic transactions may not be possible.
Principles	Standardized Service Contract (693), Service Loose Coupling (695), Service Statelessness (700)
Architecture	Inventory, Composition

Atomic Service Transaction

How can a transaction with rollback capability be propagated across messaging-based services?

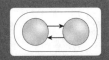

Problem	When runtime activities that span multiple services fail, the parent business task is incomplete and actions performed and changes made up to that point may compromise the integrity of the underlying solution and architecture.
Solution	Runtime service activities can be wrapped in a transaction with rollback feature that resets all actions and changes if the parent business task cannot be successfully completed.
Application	A transaction management system is made part of the inventory architecture and then used by those service compositions that require rollback features.
Impacts	Transacted service activities can consume more memory because of the requirement for each service to preserve its original state until it is notified to rollback or commit its changes.
Principles	Service Statelessness (700)
Architecture	Inventory, Composition

Brokered Authentication

By Jason Hogg, Don Smith, Fred Chong, Tom Hollander, Wojtek Kozaczynski, Larry Brader, Nelly Delgado, Dwayne Taylor, Lonnie Wall, Paul Slater, Sajjad Nasir Imran, Pablo Cibraro, Ward Cunningham

How can a service efficiently verify consumer credentials if the consumer and service do not trust each other or if the consumer requires access to multiple services?

Problem	Requiring the use of Direct Authentication [736] can be impractical or even impossible when consumers and services do not trust each other or when consumers are required to access multiple services as part of the same runtime activity.
Solution	An authentication broker with a centralized identity store assumes the responsibility for authenticating the consumer and issuing a token that the consumer can use to access the service.
Application	An authentication broker product introduced into the inventory architecture carries out the intermediary authentication and issuance of temporary credentials using technologies such as X.509 certificates or Kerberos, SAML, or SecPAL tokens.
Impacts	This pattern can establish a potential single point of failure and a central breach point that, if compromised, could jeopardize an entire service inventory.
Principles	Service Composability (704)
Architecture	Inventory, Composition, Service

Canonical Expression

How can service contracts be consistently understood and interpreted?

Problem	Service contracts may express similar capabilities in different ways, leading to inconsistency and risking misinterpretation.
Solution	Service contracts are standardized using naming conventions.
Application	Naming conventions are applied to service contracts as part of formal analysis and design processes.
Impacts	The use of global naming conventions introduces enterprise-wide standards that need to be consistently used and enforced.
Principles	Standardized Service Contract (693), Service Discoverability (702)
Architecture	Enterprise, Inventory, Service

Canonical Protocol

How can services be designed to avoid protocol bridging?

Problem	Services that support different communication technologies compromise interoperability, limit the quantity of potential consumers, and introduce the need for undesirable protocol bridging measures.
Solution	The architecture establishes a single communications technology as the sole or primary medium by which services can interact.
Application	The communication protocols (including protocol versions) used within a service inventory boundary are standardized for all services.
Impacts	An inventory architecture in which communication protocols are standardized is subject to any limitations imposed by the communications technology.
Principles	Standardized Service Contract (693)
Architecture	Inventory, Service

Canonical Resources

How can unnecessary infrastructure resource disparity be avoided?

Problem	Service implementations can unnecessarily introduce disparate infrastructure resources, thereby bloating the enterprise and resulting in increased governance burden.
Solution	The supporting infrastructure and architecture can be equipped with common resources and extensions that can be repeatedly utilized by different services.
Application	Enterprise design standards are defined to formalize the required use of standardized architectural resources.
Impacts	If this pattern leads to too much dependency on shared infrastructure resources, it can decrease the autonomy and mobility of services.
Principles	Service Autonomy (699)
Architecture	Enterprise, Inventory

Canonical Schema

How can services be designed to avoid data model transformation?

Problem	Services with disparate models for similar data impose transformation requirements that increase development effort, design complexity, and runtime performance overhead.
Solution	Data models for common information sets are standardized across service contracts within an inventory boundary.
Application	Design standards are applied to schemas used by service contracts as part of a formal design process.
Impacts	Maintaining the standardization of contract schemas can introduce significant governance effort and cultural challenges.
Principles	Standardized Service Contract (693)
Architecture	Inventory, Service

Canonical Schema Bus

By Clemens Utschig-Utschig, Berthold Maier, Bernd Trops, Hajo Normann, Torsten Winterberg, Thomas Erl

While Enterprise Service Bus [741] provides a range of messaging-centric functions that help establish connectivity between different services and between services and resources they are required to encapsulate, it does not inherently enforce or advocate standardization.

Building upon the platform established by Enterprise Service Bus [741], this pattern positions entry points into the logic, data, and functions offered via the service bus environment as independently standardized service contracts.

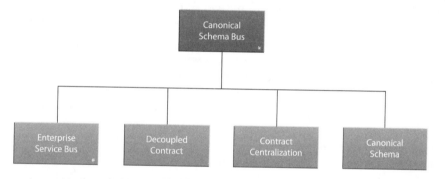

Canonical Schema Bus is comprised of the co-existent application of Enterprise Service Bus [741], Decoupled Contract [735], Contract Centralization [727], and Canonical Schema [718].

Canonical Versioning

How can service contracts within the same service inventory be versioned with minimal impact?

Problem	Service contracts within the same service inventory that are versioned differently will cause numerous interoperability and governance problems.
Solution	Service contract versioning rules and the expression of version information are standardized within a service inventory boundary.
Application	Governance and design standards are required to ensure consistent versioning of service contracts within the inventory boundary.
Impacts	The creation and enforcement of the required versioning standards introduce new governance demands.
Principles	Standardized Service Contract (693)
Architecture	Service, Inventory

Capability Composition

How can a service capability solve a problem that requires logic outside of the service boundary?

Problem	A capability may not be able to fulfill its processing requirements without adding logic that resides outside of its service's functional context, thereby compromising the integrity of the service context and risking service denormalization.
Solution	When requiring access to logic that falls outside of a service's boundary, capability logic within the service is designed to compose one or more capabilities in other services.
Application	The functionality encapsulated by a capability includes logic that can invoke other capabilities from other services.
Impacts	Carrying out composition logic requires external invocation, which adds performance overhead and decreases service autonomy.
Principles	All
Architecture	Inventory, Composition, Service

Capability Recomposition

How can the same capability be used to help solve multiple problems?

Problem	Using agnostic service logic to only solve a single problem is wasteful and does not leverage the logic's reuse potential.
Solution	Agnostic service capabilities can be designed to be repeatedly invoked in support of multiple compositions that solve multiple problems.
Application	Effective recomposition requires the coordinated, successful, and repeated application of several additional patterns.
Impacts	Repeated service composition demands existing and persistent standardization and governance.
Principles	All
Architecture	Inventory, Composition, Service

Compatible Change
By David Orchard, Chris Riley

How can a service contract be modified without impacting consumers?

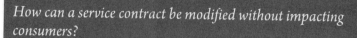

Problem	Changing an already-published service contract can impact and invalidate existing consumer programs.
Solution	Some changes to the service contract can be backwards-compatible, thereby avoiding negative consumer impacts.
Application	Service contract changes can be accommodated via extension or by the loosening of existing constraints or by applying Concurrent Contracts [726].
Impacts	Compatible changes still introduce versioning governance effort, and the technique of loosening constraints can lead to vague contract designs.
Principles	Standardized Service Contract (693), Service Loose Coupling (695)
Architecture	Service

Compensating Service Transaction

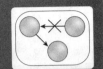

By Clemens Utschig-Utschig, Berthold Maier, Bernd Trops, Hajo Normann, Torsten Winterberg, Brian Loesgen, Mark Little

How can composition runtime exceptions be consistently accommodated without requiring services to lock resources?

Problem	Whereas uncontrolled runtime exceptions can jeopardize a service composition, wrapping the composition in an atomic transaction can tie up too many resources, thereby negatively affecting performance and scalability.
Solution	Compensating routines are introduced, allowing runtime exceptions to be resolved with the opportunity for reduced resource locking and memory consumption.
Application	Compensation logic is pre-defined and implemented as part of the parent composition controller logic or via individual "undo" service capabilities.
Impacts	Unlike atomic transactions that are governed by specific rules, the use of compensation logic is open-ended and can vary in its actual effectiveness.
Principles	Service Loose Coupling (695)
Architecture	Inventory, Composition

Composition Autonomy

How can compositions be implemented to minimize loss of autonomy?

Problem	Composition controller services naturally lose autonomy when delegating processing tasks to composed services, some of which may be shared across multiple compositions.
Solution	All composition participants can be isolated to maximize the autonomy of the composition as a whole.
Application	The agnostic member services of a composition are redundantly implemented in an isolated environment together with the task service.
Impacts	Increasing autonomy on a composition level results in increased infrastructure costs and government responsibilities.
Principles	Service Autonomy (699), Service Reusability (697), Service Composability (704)
Architecture	Composition

Concurrent Contracts

How can a service facilitate multi-consumer coupling requirements and abstraction concerns at the same time?

Problem	A service's contract may not be suitable for or applicable to all potential service consumers.
Solution	Multiple contracts can be created for a single service, each targeted at a specific type of consumer.
Application	This pattern is ideally applied together with Service Façade [776] to support new contracts as required.
Impacts	Each new contract can effectively add a new service endpoint to an inventory, thereby increasing corresponding governance effort.
Principles	Standardized Service Contract (693), Service Loose Coupling (695), Service Reusability (697)
Architecture	Service

Contract Centralization

How can direct consumer-to-implementation coupling be avoided?

Problem	Consumer programs can be designed to access underlying service resources using different entry points, resulting in different forms of implementation dependencies that inhibit the service from evolving in response to change.
Solution	Access to service logic is limited to the service contract, forcing consumers to avoid implementation coupling.
Application	This pattern is realized through formal enterprise design standards and the targeted application of the Service Abstraction (696) design principle.
Impacts	Forcing consumer programs to access service capabilities and resources via a central contract can impose performance overhead and requires on-going standardization effort.
Principles	Standardized Service Contract (693), Service Loose Coupling (695), Service Abstraction (696)
Architecture	Composition, Service

Contract Denormalization

How can a service contract facilitate consumer programs with differing data exchange requirements?

Problem	Services with strictly normalized contracts can impose unnecessary functional and performace demands on some consumer programs.
Solution	Service contracts can include a measured extent of denormalization, allowing multiple capabilities to redundantly express core functions in different ways for different types of consumer programs.
Application	The service contract is carefully extended with additional capabilities that provide functional variations of a primary capability.
Impacts	Overuse of this pattern on the same contract can dramatically increase its size, making it difficult to interpret and unwieldy to govern.
Principles	Standardized Service Contract (693), Service Loose Coupling (695)
Architecture	Service

Cross-Domain Utility Layer

How can redundant utility logic be avoided across domain service inventories?

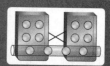

Problem	While domain service inventories may be required for independent business governance, they can impose unnecessary redundancy within utility service layers.
Solution	A common utility service layer can be established, spanning two or more domain service inventories.
Application	A common set of utility services needs to be defined and standardized in coordination with service inventory owners.
Impacts	Increased effort is required to coordinate and govern a cross-inventory utility service layer.
Principles	Service Reusability (697), Service Composability (704)
Architecture	Enterprise, Inventory

Data Confidentiality

By Jason Hogg, Don Smith, Fred Chong, Tom Hollander, Wojtek Kozaczynski,
Larry Brader, Nelly Delgado, Dwayne Taylor, Lonnie Wall, Paul Slater,
Sajjad Nasir Imran, Pablo Cibraro, Ward Cunningham

How can data within a message be protected so that it is not disclosed to unintended recipients while in transit?

Problem	Within service compositions, data is often required to pass through one or more intermediaries. Point-to-point security protocols, such as those frequently used at the transport-layer, may allow messages containing sensitive information to be intercepted and viewed by such intermediaries.
Solution	The message contents are encrypted independently from the transport, ensuring that only intended recipients can access the protected data.
Application	A symmetric or asymmetric encryption and decryption algorithm, such as those specified in the XML-Encryption standard, is applied at the message level.
Impacts	This pattern may add runtime performance overhead associated with the required encryption and decryption of message data. The management of keys can further add to governance burden.
Principles	Service Composability (704)
Architecture	Inventory, Composition, Service

Data Format Transformation

By Mark Little, Thomas Rischbeck, Arnaud Simon

How can services interact with programs that communicate with different data formats?

Problem	A service may be incompatible with resources it needs to access due to data format disparity. Furthermore, a service consumer that communicates using a data format different from a target service will be incompatible and therefore unable to invoke the service.
Solution	Intermediary data format transformation logic needs to be introduced in order to dynamically translate one data format into another.
Application	This necessary transformation logic is incorporated by adding internal service logic, service agents, or a dedicated transformation service.
Impacts	The use of data format transformation logic inevitably adds development effort, design complexity, and performance overhead.
Principles	Standardized Service Contract (693), Service Loose Coupling (695)
Architecture	Inventory, Composition, Service

Data Model Transformation

How can services interoperate when using different data models for the same type of data?

Problem	Services may use incompatible schemas to represent the same data, hindering service interaction and composition.
Solution	A data transformation technology can be incorporated to convert data between disparate schema structures.
Application	Mapping logic needs to be developed and deployed so that data compliant to one data model can be dynamically converted to comply to a different data model.
Impacts	Data model transformation introduces development effort, design complexity, and runtime performance overhead, and overuse of this pattern can seriously inhibit service recomposition potential.
Principles	Standardized Service Contract (693), Service Reusability (697), Service Composability (704)
Architecture	Inventory, Composition

Data Origin Authentication

By Jason Hogg, Don Smith, Fred Chong, Tom Hollander, Wojtek
Kozaczynski, Larry Brader, Nelly Delgado, Dwayne Taylor, Lonnie Wall,
Paul Slater, Sajjad Nasir Imran, Pablo Cibraro, Ward Cunningham

*How can a service verify that a message originates from a known
sender and that the message has not been tampered with in transit?*

Problem	The intermediary processing layers generally required by service compositions can expose sensitive data when security is limited to point-to-point protocols, such as those used with transport-layer security.
Solution	A message can be digitally signed so that the recipient services can verify that it originated from the expected consumer and that it has not been tampered with during transit.
Application	A digital signature algorithm is applied to the message to provide "proof of origin," allowing sensitive message contents to be protected from tampering. This technology must be supported by both consumer and service.
Impacts	Use of cryptographic techniques can add to performance requirements and the choice of digital signing algorithm can affect the level of security actually achieved.
Principles	Service Composability (704)
Architecture	Composition

Decomposed Capability

How can a service be designed to minimize the chances of capability logic deconstruction?

Problem	The decomposition of a service subsequent to its implementation can require the deconstruction of logic within capabilities, which can be disruptive and make the preservation of a service contract problematic.
Solution	Services prone to future decomposition can be equipped with a series of granular capabilities that more easily facilitate decomposition.
Application	Additional service modeling is carried out to define granular, more easily distributed capabilities.
Impacts	Until the service is eventually decomposed, it may be represented by a bloated contract that stays with it as long as proxy capabilities are supported.
Principles	Standardized Service Contract (693), Service Abstraction (696)
Architecture	Service

Decoupled Contract

How can a service express its capabilities independently of its implementation?

Problem	For a service to be positioned as an effective enterprise resource, it must be equipped with a technical contract that exists independently from its implementation yet still in alignment with other services.
Solution	The service contract is physically decoupled from its implementation.
Application	A service's technical interface is physically separated and subject to relevant service-orientation design principles.
Impacts	Service functionality is limited to the feature-set of the decoupled contract medium.
Principles	Standardized Service Contract (693), Service Loose Coupling (695)
Architecture	Service

Direct Authentication

By Jason Hogg, Don Smith, Fred Chong, Tom Hollander, Wojtek Kozaczynski,
Larry Brader, Nelly Delgado, Dwayne Taylor, Lonnie Wall, Paul Slater,
Sajjad Nasir Imran, Pablo Cibraro, Ward Cunningham

How can a service verify the credentials provided by a consumer?

Problem	Some of the capabilities offered by a service may be intended for specific groups of consumers or may involve the transmission of sensitive data. Attackers that access this data could use it to compromise the service or the IT enterprise itself.
Solution	Service capabilities require that consumers provide credentials that can be authenticated against an identity store.
Application	The service implementation is provided access to an identity store, allowing it to authenticate the consumer directly.
Impacts	Consumers must provide credentials compatible with the service's authentication logic. This pattern may lead to multiple identity stores, resulting in extra governance burden.
Principles	Service Composability (704)
Architecture	Composition, Service

Distributed Capability

How can a service preserve its functional context while also fulfilling special capability processing requirements?

Problem	A capability that belongs within a service may have unique processing requirements that cannot be accommodated by the default service implementation, but separating capability logic from the service will compromise the integrity of the service context.
Solution	The underlying service logic is distributed, thereby allowing the implementation logic for a capability with unique processing requirements to be physically separated, while continuing to be represented by the same service contract.
Application	The logic is moved and intermediary processing is added to act as a liaison between the moved logic and the main service logic.
Impacts	The distribution of a capability's logic leads to performance overhead associated with remote communication and the need for new intermediate processing.
Principles	Standardized Service Contract (693), Service Autonomy (699)
Architecture	Service

Domain Inventory

How can services be delivered to maximize recomposition when enterprise-wide standardization is not possible?

Problem	Establishing an single enterprise service inventory may be unmanageable for some enterprises, and attempts to do so may jeopardize the success of an SOA adoption as a whole.
Solution	Services can be grouped into manageable, domain-specific service inventories, each of which can be independently standardized, governed, and owned.
Application	Inventory domain boundaries need to be carefully established.
Impacts	Standardization disparity between domain service inventories imposes transformation requirements and reduces the overall benefit potential of the SOA adoption.
Principles	Standardized Service Contract (693), Service Abstraction (696), Service Composability (704)
Architecture	Enterprise, Inventory

Dual Protocols

☑ + ☑

How can a service inventory overcome the limitations of its canonical protocol while still remaining standardized?

Problem	Canonical Protocol [716] requires that all services conform to the use of the same communications technology; however, a single protocol may not be able to accommodate all service requirements, thereby introducing limitations.
Solution	The service inventory architecture is designed to support services based on primary and secondary protocols.
Application	Primary and secondary service levels are created and collectively represent the service endpoint layer. All services are subject to standard service-orientation design considerations and specific guidelines are followed to minimize the impact of not following Canonical Protocol [716].
Impacts	This pattern can lead to a convoluted inventory architecture, increased governance effort and expense, and (when poorly applied) an unhealthy dependence on Protocol Bridging [764]. Because the endpoint layer is semi-federated, the quantity of potential consumers and reuse opportunities is decreased.
Principles	Standardized Service Contract (693), Service Loose Coupling (695), Service Abstraction (696), Service Autonomy (699), Service Composability (704)
Architecture	Inventory, Service

Enterprise Inventory

How can services be delivered to maximize recomposition?

Problem	Delivering services independently via different project teams across an enterprise establishes a constant risk of producing inconsistent service and architecture implementations, compromising recomposition opportunities.
Solution	Services for multiple solutions can be designed for delivery within a standardized, enterprise-wide inventory architecture wherein they can be freely and repeatedly recomposed.
Application	The enterprise service inventory is ideally modeled in advance, and enterprise-wide standards are applied to services delivered by different project teams.
Impacts	Significant upfront analysis is required to define an enterprise inventory blueprint and numerous organizational impacts result from the subsequent governance requirements.
Principles	Standardized Service Contract (693), Service Abstraction (696), Service Composability (704)
Architecture	Enterprise, Inventory

Enterprise Service Bus
By Thomas Erl, Mark Little, Thomas Rischbeck, Arnaud Simon

An enterprise service bus represents an environment designed to foster sophisticated interconnectivity between services. It establishes an intermediate layer of processing that can help overcome common problems associated with reliability, scalability, and communications disparity.

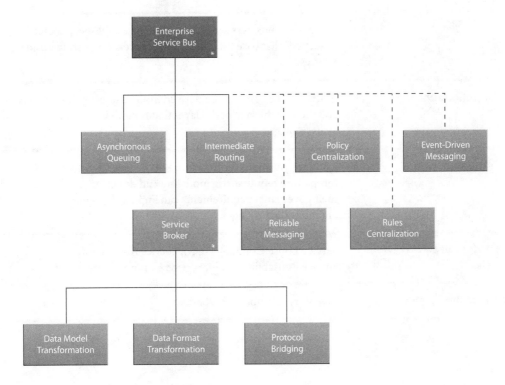

Enterprise Service Bus is fundamentally comprised of the co-existent application of Asynchronous Queuing [712], Intermediate Routing [748], and Service Broker [771], and can be further extended via Reliable Messaging [767], Policy Centralization [761], Rules Centralization [768], and Event-Driven Messaging [743].

Entity Abstraction

How can agnostic business logic be separated, reused, and governed independently?

Problem	Bundling both process-agnostic and process-specific business logic into the same service eventually results in the creation of redundant agnostic business logic across multiple services.
Solution	An agnostic business service layer can be established, dedicated to services that base their functional context on existing business entities.
Application	Entity service contexts are derived from business entity models and then establish a logical layer that is modeled during the analysis phase.
Impacts	The core, business-centric nature of the services introduced by this pattern require extra modeling and design attention and their governance requirements can impose dramatic organizational changes.
Principles	Service Loose Coupling (695), Service Abstraction (696), Service Reusability (697), Service Composability (704)
Architecture	Inventory, Composition, Service

Event-Driven Messaging

By Mark Little, Thomas Rischbeck, Arnaud Simon

How can service consumers be automatically notified of runtime service events?

Problem	Events that occur within the functional boundary encapsulated by a service may be of relevance to service consumers, but without resorting to inefficient polling-based interaction, the consumer has no way of learning about these events.
Solution	The consumer establishes itself as a subscriber of the service. The service, in turn, automatically issues notifications of relevant events to this and any of its subscribers.
Application	A messaging framework is implemented capable of supporting the publish-and-subscribe MEP and associated complex event processing and tracking.
Impacts	Event-driven message exchanges cannot easily be incorporated as part of Atomic Service Transaction [713], and publisher/subscriber availability issues can arise.
Principles	Standardized Service Contract (693), Service Loose Coupling (695), Service Autonomy (699)
Architecture	Inventory, Composition

Exception Shielding

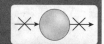

By Jason Hogg, Don Smith, Fred Chong, Tom Hollander, Wojtek
Kozaczynski, Larry Brader, Nelly Delgado, Dwayne Taylor, Lonnie Wall,
Paul Slater, Sajjad Nasir Imran, Pablo Cibraro, Ward Cunningham

How can a service prevent the disclosure of information about its internal
implementation when an exception occurs?

Problem	Unfiltered exception data output by a service may contain internal implementation details that can compromise the security of the service and its surrounding environment.
Solution	Potentially unsafe exception data is "sanitized" by replacing it with exception data that is safe by design before it is made available to consumers.
Application	This pattern can be applied at design time by reviewing and altering source code or at runtime by adding dynamic sanitization routines.
Impacts	Sanitized exception information can make the tracking of errors more difficult due to the lack of detail provided to consumers.
Principles	Service Abstraction (696)
Architecture	Service

Federated Endpoint Layer

Federation is an important concept in service-oriented computing. It represents the desired state of the external, consumer-facing perspective of a service inventory, as expressed by the collective contracts of all the inventory's services.

The more federated and unified this collection of contracts (endpoints) is, the more easily and effectively the services can be repeatedly consumed and leveraged.

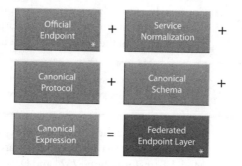

The joint application of Official Endpoint [757], Service Normalization [781], Canonical Protocol [716], Canonical Schema [718], and Canonical Expression [715] results in Federated Endpoint Layer.

File Gateway

By Satadru Roy

How can service logic interact with legacy systems that can only share information by exchanging files?

Problem	Data records contained in flat files produced by a legacy system need to be processed individually by service logic, but legacy systems are not capable of directly invoking services. Conversely, service logic may need to produce information for the legacy system, but building file creation and transfer functionality into the service can result in an inflexible design.
Solution	Intermediary two-way file processing logic is positioned between the legacy system and the service.
Application	For inbound data the file gateway processing logic can detect file drops and leverage available broker features to perform Data Model Transformation [732] and Data Format Transformation [731]. On the outbound side, this logic intercepts information produced by services and packages them (with possible transformation) into new or existing files for consumption by the legacy system.
Impacts	The type of logic provided by this pattern is unsuitable when immediate replies are required by either service or legacy system. Deployment and governance of two-way file processing logic can further add to operational complexity and may require specialized administration skills.
Principles	Service Loose Coupling (695)
Architecture	Service

Functional Decomposition

*How can a large business problem be solved without having
to build a standalone body of solution logic?*

Problem	To solve a large, complex business problem a corresponding amount of solution logic needs to be created, resulting in a self-contained application with traditional governance and reusability constraints.
Solution	The large business problem can be broken down into a set of smaller, related problems, allowing the required solution logic to also be decomposed into a corresponding set of smaller, related solution logic units.
Application	Depending on the nature of the large problem, a service-oriented analysis process can be created to cleanly deconstruct it into smaller problems.
Impacts	The ownership of multiple smaller programs can result in increased design complexity and governance challenges.
Principles	n/a
Architecture	Service

Intermediate Routing
By Mark Little, Thomas Rischbeck, Arnaud Simon

How can dynamic runtime factors affect the path of a message?

Problem	The larger and more complex a service composition is, the more difficult it is to anticipate and design for all possible runtime scenarios in advance, especially with asynchronous, messaging-based communication.
Solution	Message paths can be dynamically determined through the use of intermediary routing logic.
Application	Various types of intermediary routing logic can be incorporated to create message paths based on message content or runtime factors.
Impacts	Dynamically determining a message path adds layers of processing logic and correspondingly can increase performance overhead. Also the use of multiple routing logic can result in overly complex service activities.
Principles	Service Loose Coupling (695), Service Reusability (697), Service Composability (704)
Architecture	Composition

Inventory Endpoint

How can a service inventory be shielded from external access while still offering service capabilities to external consumers?

Problem	A group of services delivered for a specific inventory may provide capabilities that are useful to services outside of that inventory. However, for security and governance reasons, it may not be desirable to expose all services or all service capabilities to external consumers.
Solution	Abstract the relevant capabilities into an endpoint service that acts as a the official inventory entry point dedicated to a specific set of external consumers.
Application	The endpoint service can expose a contract with the same capabilities as its underlying services, but augmented with policies or other characteristics to accommodate external consumer interaction requirements.
Impacts	Endpoint services can increase the governance freedom of underlying services but can also increase governance effort by introducing redundant service logic and contracts into an inventory.
Principles	Standardized Service Contract (693), Service Loose Coupling (695), Service Abstraction (696)
Architecture	Inventory

Legacy Wrapper
By Thomas Erl, Satadru Roy

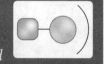

How can wrapper services with non-standard contracts be prevented from spreading indirect consumer-to-implementation coupling?

Problem	Wrapper services required to encapsulate legacy logic are often forced to introduce a non-standard service contract with high technology coupling requirements, resulting in a proliferation of implementation coupling throughout all service consumer programs.
Solution	The non-standard wrapper service can be replaced by or further wrapped with a standardized service contract that extracts, encapsulates, and possibly eliminates legacy technical details from the contract.
Application	A custom service contract and required service logic need to be developed to represent the proprietary legacy interface.
Impacts	The introduction of an additional service adds a layer of processing and associated performance overhead.
Principles	Standardized Service Contract (693), Service Loose Coupling (695), Service Abstraction (696)
Architecture	Service

Logic Centralization

How can the misuse of redundant service logic be avoided?

Problem	If agnostic services are not consistently reused, redundant functionality can be delivered in other services, resulting in problems associated with inventory denormalization and service ownership and governance.
Solution	Access to reusable functionality is limited to official agnostic services.
Application	Agnostic services need to be properly designed and governed, and their use must be enforced via enterprise standards.
Impacts	Organizational issues reminiscent of past reuse projects can raise obstacles to applying this pattern.
Principles	Service Reusability (697), Service Composability (704)
Architecture	Inventory, Composition, Service

Message Screening

By Jason Hogg, Don Smith, Fred Chong, Tom Hollander, Wojtek
Kozaczynski, Larry Brader, Nelly Delgado, Dwayne Taylor, Lonnie Wall,
Paul Slater, Sajjad Nasir Imran, Pablo Cibraro, Ward Cunningham

How can a service be protected from malformed or malicious input?

Problem	An attacker can transmit messages with malicious or malformed content to a service, resulting in undesirable behavior.
Solution	The service is equipped or supplemented with special screening routines that assume that all input data is harmful until proven otherwise.
Application	When a service receives a message, it makes a number of checks to screen message content for harmful data.
Impacts	Extra runtime processing is required with each message exchange, and the screening logic requires additional, specialized routines to process binary message content, such as attachments. It may also not be possible to check for all possible forms of harmful content.
Principles	Standardized Service Contract (693)
Architecture	Service

Messaging Metadata

How can services be designed to process activity-specific data at runtime?

Problem	Because messaging does not rely on a persistent connection between service and consumer, it is challenging for a service to gain access to the state data associated with an overall runtime activity.
Solution	Message contents can be supplemented with activity-specific metadata that can be interpreted and processed separately at runtime.
Application	This pattern requires a messaging framework that supports message headers or properties.
Impacts	The interpretation and processing of messaging metadata adds to runtime performance overhead and increases service activity design complexity.
Principles	Service Loose Coupling (695), Service Statelessness (700)
Architecture	Composition

Metadata Centralization

How can service metadata be centrally published and governed?

Problem	Project teams, especially in larger enterprises, run the constant risk of building functionality that already exists or is already in development, resulting in wasted effort, service logic redundancy, and service inventory denormalization.
Solution	Service metadata can be centrally published in a service registry so as to provide a formal means of service registration and discovery.
Application	A private service registry needs to be positioned as a central part of an inventory architecture supported by formal processes for registration and discovery.
Impacts	The service registry product needs to be adequately mature and reliable, and its required use and maintenance needs to be incorporated into all service delivery and governance processes and methodologies.
Principles	Service Discoverability (702)
Architecture	Enterprise, Inventory

Multi-Channel Endpoint
By Satadru Roy

How can legacy logic fragmented and duplicated for different delivery channels be centrally consolidated?

Problem	Legacy systems custom-built for specific delivery channels (mobile phone, desktop, kiosk, etc.) result in redundancy and application silos when multiple channels need to be supported, thereby making these systems burdensome to govern and difficult to federate.
Solution	An intermediary service is designed to encapsulate channel-specific legacy systems and expose a single standardized contract for multiple channel-specific consumers.
Application	The service established by this pattern will require significant processing and workflow logic to support multiple channels while also coordinating interaction with multiple backend legacy systems.
Impacts	The endpoint processing logic established by this pattern often introduces the need for infrastructure upgrades and orchestration-capable middleware and may turn into a performance bottleneck.
Principles	Service Loose Coupling (695), Service Reusability (697)
Architecture	Service

Non-Agnostic Context

How can single-purpose service logic be positioned as an effective enterprise resource?

Problem	Non-agnostic logic that is not service-oriented can inhibit the effectiveness of service compositions that utilize agnostic services.
Solution	Non-agnostic solution logic suitable for service encapsulation can be located within services that reside as official members of a service inventory.
Application	A single-purpose functional service context is defined.
Impacts	Although they are not expected to provide reuse potential, non-agnostic services are still subject to the rigor of service-orientation.
Principles	Standardized Service Contract (693), Service Composability (704)
Architecture	Service

Official Endpoint

As important as it is to clearly differentiate Logic Centralization [751] from Contract Centralization [727], it is equally important to understand how these two fundamental patterns can and should be used together.

Applying these two patterns to the same service realizes the Official Endpoint [757] compound pattern. The repeated application of Official Endpoint [757] supports the goal of establishing a federated layer of service endpoints, which is why this compound pattern is also a part of Federated Endpoint Layer [745].

The joint application of Logic Centralization [751] and Contract Centralization [727] results in Official Endpoint.

Orchestration
By Thomas Erl, Brian Loesgen

An orchestration platform is dedicated to the effective maintenance and execution of parent business process logic. Modern-day orchestration environments are especially expected to support sophisticated and complex service composition logic that can result in long-running runtime activities.

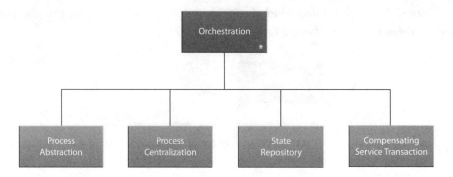

Orchestration is fundamentally comprised of the co-existent application of Process Abstraction [762], State Repository [785], Process Centralization [763], and Compensating Service Transaction [724], and can be further extended via Atomic Service Transaction [713], Rules Centralization [768], and Data Model Transformation [732].

Partial State Deferral

How can services be designed to optimize resource consumption while still remaining stateful?

Problem	Service capabilities may be required to store and manage large amounts of state data, resulting in increased memory consumption and reduced scalability.
Solution	Even when services are required to remain stateful, a subset of their state data can be temporarily deferred.
Application	Various state management deferral options exist, depending on the surrounding architecture.
Impacts	Partial state management deferral can add to design complexity and bind a service to the architecture.
Principles	Service Statelessness (700)
Architecture	Inventory, Service

Partial Validation

By David Orchard, Chris Riley

How can unnecessary data validation be avoided?

Problem	The generic capabilities provided by agnostic services sometimes result in service contracts that impose unnecessary data and validation upon consumer programs.
Solution	A consumer program can be designed to only validate the relevant subset of the data and ignore the remainder.
Application	The application of this pattern is specific to the technology used for the consumer implementation. For example, with Web services, XPath can be used to filter out unnecessary data prior to validation.
Impacts	Extra design-time effort is required and the additional runtime data filtering-related logic can reduce the processing gains of avoiding unnecessary validation.
Principles	Standardized Service Contract (693), Service Loose Coupling (695)
Architecture	Composition

Policy Centralization

How can policies be normalized and consistently enforced across multiple services?

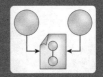

Problem	Policies that apply to multiple services can introduce redundancy and inconsistency within service logic and contracts.
Solution	Global or domain-specific policies can be isolated and applied to multiple services.
Application	Up-front analysis effort specific to defining and establishing reusable policies is recommended, and an appropriate policy enforcement framework is required.
Impacts	Policy frameworks can introduce performance overhead and may impose dependencies on proprietary technologies. There is also the risk of conflict between centralized and service-specific policies.
Principles	Standardized Service Contracts (693), Service Loose Coupling (695), Service Abstraction (696)
Architecture	Inventory, Service

Process Abstraction

How can non-agnostic process logic be separated and governed independently?

Problem	Grouping task-centric logic together with task-agnostic logic hinders the governance of the task-specific logic and the reuse of the agnostic logic.
Solution	A dedicated parent business process service layer is established to support governance independence and the positioning of task services as potential enterprise resources.
Application	Business process logic is typically filtered out after utility and entity services have been defined, allowing for the definition of task services that comprise this layer.
Impacts	In addition to the modeling and design considerations associated with creating task services, abstracting parent business process logic establishes an inherent dependency on carrying out that logic via the composition of other services.
Principles	Service Loose Coupling (695), Service Abstraction (696), Service Composability (704)
Architecture	Inventory, Composition, Service

Process Centralization

How can abstracted business process logic be centrally governed?

Problem	When business process logic is distributed across independent service implementations, it can be problematic to extend and evolve.
Solution	Logic representing numerous business processes can be deployed and governed from a central location.
Application	Middleware platforms generally provide the necessary orchestration technologies to apply this pattern.
Impacts	Significant infrastructure and architectural changes are imposed when the required middleware is introduced.
Principles	Service Autonomy (699), Service Statelessness (700), Service Composability (704)
Architecture	Inventory, Composition

Protocol Bridging

By Mark Little, Thomas Rischbeck, Arnaud Simon

How can a service exchange data with consumers that use different communication protocols?

Problem	Services using different communication protocols or different versions of the same protocol cannot exchange data.
Solution	Bridging logic is introduced to enable communication between different communication protocols by dynamically converting one protocol to another at runtime.
Application	Instead of connecting directly to each other, consumer programs and services connect to a broker, which provides bridging logic that carries out the protocol conversion.
Impacts	Significant performance overhead can be imposed by bridging technologies, and their use can limit or eliminate the ability to incorporate reliability and transaction features.
Principles	Standardized Service Contract (693), Service Composability (704)
Architecture	Inventory, Composition

Proxy Capability

How can a service subject to decomposition continue to support consumers affected by the decomposition?

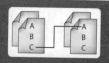

Problem	If an established service needs to be decomposed into multiple services, its contract and its existing consumers can be impacted.
Solution	The original service contract is preserved, even if underlying capability logic is separated, by turning the established capability definition into a proxy.
Application	Façade logic needs to be introduced to relay requests and responses between the proxy and newly located capabilities.
Impacts	The practical solution provided by this pattern results in a measure of service denormalization.
Principles	Service Loose Coupling (695)
Architecture	Service

Redundant Implementation

How can the reliability and availability of a service be increased?

Problem	A service that is being actively reused introduces a potential single point of failure that may jeopardize the reliability of all compositions in which it participates if an unexpected error condition occurs.
Solution	Reusable services can be deployed via redundant implementations or with failover support.
Application	The same service implementation is redundantly deployed or supported by infrastructure with redundancy features.
Impacts	Extra governance effort is required to keep all redundant implementations in synch.
Principles	Service Autonomy (699)
Architecture	Service

Reliable Messaging
By Mark Little, Thomas Rischbeck, Arnaud Simon

How can services communicate reliably when implemented in an unreliable environment?

Problem	Service communication cannot be guaranteed when using unreliable messaging protocols or when dependent on an otherwise unreliable environment.
Solution	An intermediate reliability mechanism is introduced into the inventory architecture, ensuring that message delivery is guaranteed.
Application	Middleware, service agents, and data stores are deployed to track message deliveries, manage the issuance of acknowledgements, and persist messages during failure conditions.
Impacts	Using a reliability framework adds processing overhead that can affect service activity performance. It also increases composition design complexity and may not be compatible with Atomic Service Transaction [713].
Principles	Service Composability (704)
Architecture	Inventory, Composition

Rules Centralization

How can business rules be abstracted and centrally governed?

Problem	The same business rules may apply across different business services, leading to redundancy and governance challenges.
Solution	The storage and management of business rules are positioned within a dedicated architectural extension from where they can be centrally accessed and maintained.
Application	The use of a business rules management system or engine is employed and accessed via system agents or a dedicated service.
Impacts	Services are subjected to increased performance overhead, risk, and architectural dependency.
Principles	Service Reusability (697)
Architecture	Inventory

Schema Centralization

How can service contracts be designed to avoid redundant data representation?

Problem	Different service contracts often need to express capabilities that process similar business documents or data sets, resulting in redundant schema content that is difficult to govern.
Solution	Select schemas that exist as physically separate parts of the service contract are shared across multiple contracts.
Application	Up-front analysis effort is required to establish a schema layer independent of and in support of the service layer.
Impacts	Governance of shared schemas becomes increasingly important as multiple services can form dependencies on the same schema definitions.
Principles	Standardized Service Contract (693), Service Loose Coupling (695)
Architecture	Inventory, Service

Service Agent

How can event-driven logic be separated and governed independently?

Problem	Service compositions can become large and inefficient, especially when required to invoke granular capabilities across multiple services.
Solution	Event-driven logic can be deferred to event-driven programs that don't require explicit invocation, thereby reducing the size and performance strain of service compositions.
Application	Service agents can be designed to automatically respond to predefined conditions without invocation via a published contract.
Impacts	The complexity of composition logic increases when it is distributed across services, and event-driven agents and reliance on service agents can further tie an inventory architecture to proprietary vendor technology.
Principles	Service Loose Coupling (695), Service Reusability (697)
Architecture	Inventory, Composition

Service Broker

By Mark Little, Thomas Rischbeck, Arnaud Simon

Although all of the Service Broker patterns are used only out of necessity, establishing an environment capable of handling the three most common transformation requirements can add a great deal of flexibility to a service-oriented architecture implementation, and also has the added bonus of being able to perform more than one transformation function at the same time.

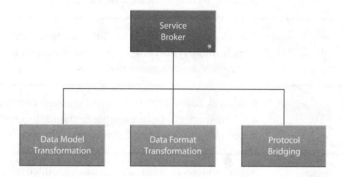

Service Broker is comprised of the co-existent application of Data Model Transformation [732], Data Format Transformation [731], and Protocol Bridging [764].

Related Patterns in Other Catalogs

Broker (Buschmann, Henney, Schmidt, Meunier, Rohnert, Sommerland, Stal)

Related Service-Oriented Computing Goals

Increased Intrinsic Interoperability, Increased Vendor Diversification Options, Reduced IT Burden

Service Callback

By Anish Karmarkar

How can a service communicate asynchronously with its consumers?

Problem	When a service needs to respond to a consumer request through the issuance of multiple messages or when service message processing requires a large amount of time, it is often not possible to communicate synchronously.
Solution	A service can require that consumers communicate with it asynchronously and provide a callback address to which the service can send response messages.
Application	A callback address generation and message correlation mechanism needs to be incorporated into the messaging framework and the overall inventory architecture.
Impacts	Asynchronous communication can introduce reliability concerns and can further require that surrounding infrastructure be upgraded to fully support the necessary callback correlation.
Principles	Standardized Service Contract (693), Service Loose Coupling (695), Service Composability (704)
Architecture	Inventory, Service, Composition

Service Data Replication

How can service autonomy be preserved when services require access to shared data sources?

Problem	Service logic can be deployed in isolation to increase service autonomy, but services continue to lose autonomy when requiring access to shared data sources.
Solution	Services can have their own dedicated databases with replication to shared data sources.
Application	An additional database needs to be provided for the service and one or more replication channels need to be enabled between it and the shared data sources.
Impacts	This pattern results in additional infrastructure cost and demands, and an excess of replication channels can be difficult to manage.
Principles	Service Autonomy (699)
Architecture	Inventory, Service

Service Decomposition

How can the granularity of a service be increased subsequent to its implementation?

Problem	Overly coarse-grained services can inhibit optimal composition design.
Solution	An already implemented coarse-grained service can be decomposed into two or more fine-grained services.
Application	The underlying service logic is restructured, and new service contracts are established. This pattern will likely require Proxy Capability [765] to preserve the integrity of the original coarse-grained service contract.
Impacts	An increase in fine-grained services naturally leads to larger, more complex service composition designs.
Principles	Service Loose Coupling (695), Service Composability (704)
Architecture	Service

Service Encapsulation

How can solution logic be made available as a resource of the enterprise?

Problem	Solution logic designed for a single application environment is typically limited in its potential to interoperate with or be leveraged by other parts of an enterprise.
Solution	Solution logic can be encapsulated by a service so that it is positioned as an enterprise resource capable of functioning beyond the boundary for which it is initially delivered.
Application	Solution logic suitable for service encapsulation needs to be identified.
Impacts	Service-encapsulated solution logic is subject to additional design and governance considerations.
Principles	n/a
Architecture	Service

Service Façade

How can a service accommodate changes to its contract or implementation while allowing the core service logic to evolve independently?

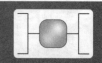

Problem	The coupling of the core service logic to contracts and implementation resources can inhibit its evolution and negatively impact service consumers.
Solution	A service façade component is used to abstract a part of the service architecture with negative coupling potential.
Application	A separate façade component is incorporated into the service design.
Impacts	The addition of the façade component introduces design effort and performance overhead.
Principles	Standardized Service Contract (693), Service Loose Coupling (695)
Architecture	Service

Service Grid

By David Chappell

How can deferred service state data be scaled and kept fault-tolerant?

Problem	State data deferred via State Repository or Stateful Services can be subject to performance bottlenecks and failure, especially when exposed to high-usage volumes.
Solution	State data is deferred to a collection of stateful system services that form a grid that provides high scalability and fault tolerance through memory replication and redundancy and supporting infrastructure.
Application	Grid technology is introduced into the enterprise or inventory architecture.
Impacts	This pattern can require a significant infrastructure upgrade and can correspondingly increase governance burden.
Principles	Service Statelessness (700)
Architecture	Enterprise, Inventory, Service

Service Instance Routing

By Anish Karmarkar

How can consumers contact and interact with service instances without the need for proprietary processing logic?

Problem	When required to repeatedly access a specific stateful service instance, consumers must rely on custom logic that more tightly couples them to the service.
Solution	The service provides an instance identifier along with its destination information in a standardized format that shields the consumer from having to resort to custom logic.
Application	The service is still required to provide custom logic to generate and manage instance identifiers, and both service and consumer require a common messaging infrastructure.
Impacts	This pattern can introduce the need for significant infrastructure upgrades and when misued can further lead to overly stateful messaging activities that can violate the Service Statelessness (700) principle.
Principles	Service Loose Coupling (695), Service Statelessness (700), Service Composability (704)
Architecture	Inventory, Composition, Service

Service Layers

How can the services in an inventory be organized based on functional commonality?

Problem	Arbitrarily defining services delivered and governed by different project teams can lead to design inconsistency and inadvertent functional redundancy across a service inventory.
Solution	The inventory is structured into two or more logical service layers, each of which is responsible for abstracting logic based on a common functional type.
Application	Service models are chosen and then form the basis for service layers that establish modeling and design standards.
Impacts	The common costs and impacts associated with design standards and up-front analysis need to be accepted.
Principles	Service Reusability (697), Service Composability (704)
Architecture	Inventory, Service

Service Messaging

How can services interoperate without forming persistent, tightly coupled connections?

Problem	Services that depend on traditional remote communication protocols impose the need for persistent connections and tightly coupled data exchanges, increasing consumer dependencies and limiting service reuse potential.
Solution	Services can be designed to interact via a messaging-based technology, which removes the need for persistent connections and reduces coupling requirements.
Application	A messaging framework needs to be established, and services need to be designed to use it.
Impacts	Messaging technology brings with it QoS concerns such as reliable delivery, security, performance, and transactions.
Principles	Standardized Service Contract (693), Service Loose Coupling (695)
Architecture	Inventory, Composition, Service

Service Normalization

How can a service inventory avoid redundant service logic?

Problem	When delivering services as part of a service inventory, there is a constant risk that services will be created with overlapping functional boundaries, making it difficult to enable wide-spread reuse.
Solution	The service inventory needs to be designed with an emphasis on service boundary alignment.
Application	Functional service boundaries are modeled as part of a formal analysis process and persist throughout inventory design and governance.
Impacts	Ensuring that service boundaries are and remain well-aligned introduces extra up-front analysis and on-going governance effort.
Principles	Service Autonomy (699)
Architecture	Inventory, Service

Service Perimeter Guard

By Jason Hogg, Don Smith, Fred Chong, Tom Hollander, Wojtek Kozaczynski, Larry Brader, Nelly Delgado, Dwayne Taylor, Lonnie Wall, Paul Slater, Sajjad Nasir Imran, Pablo Cibraro, Ward Cunningham

How can services that run in a private network be made available to external consumers without exposing internal resources?

Problem	External consumers that require access to one or more services in a private network can attack the service or use it to gain access to internal resources.
Solution	An intermediate service is established at the perimeter of the private network as a secure contact point for any external consumers that need to interact with internal services.
Application	The service is deployed in a perimeter network and is designed to work with existing firewall technologies so as to establish a secure bridging mechanism between external and internal networks.
Impacts	A perimeter service adds complexity and performance overhead as it establishes an intermediary processing layer for all external-to-internal communication.
Principles	Service Loose Coupling (695), Service Abstraction (696)
Architecture	Service

Service Refactoring

How can a service be evolved without impacting existing consumers?

Problem	The logic or implementation technology of a service may become outdated or inadequate over time, but the service has become too entrenched to be replaced.
Solution	The service contract is preserved to maintain existing consumer dependencies, but the underlying service logic and/or implementation are refactored.
Application	Service logic and implementation technology are gradually improved or upgraded but must undergo additional testing.
Impacts	This pattern introduces governance effort as well as risk associated with potentially negative side-effects introduced by new logic or technology.
Principles	Standardized Service Contract (693), Service Loose Coupling (695), Service Abstraction (696)
Architecture	Service

State Messaging

By Anish Karmarkar

How can a service remain stateless while participating in stateful interactions?

Problem	When services are required to maintain state information in memory between message exchanges with consumers, their scalability can be comprised, and they can become a performance burden on the surrounding infrastructure.
Solution	Instead of retaining the state data in memory, its storage is temporarily delegated to messages.
Application	Depending on how this pattern is applied, both services and consumers may need to be designed to process message-based state data.
Impacts	This pattern may not be suitable for all forms of state data, and should messages be lost, any state information they carried may be lost as well.
Principles	Standardized Service Contract (693), Service Statelessness (700), Service Composability (704)
Architecture	Composition, Service

State Repository

How can service state data be persisted for extended periods without consuming service runtime resources?

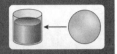

Problem	Large amounts of state data cached to support the activity within a running service composition can consume too much memory, especially for long-running activities, thereby decreasing scalability.
Solution	State data can be temporarily written to and then later retrieved from a dedicated state repository.
Application	A shared or dedicated repository is made available as part of the inventory or service architecture.
Impacts	The addition of required write and read functionality increases the service design complexity and can negatively affect performance.
Principles	Service Statelessness (700)
Architecture	Inventory, Service

Stateful Services

How can service state data be persisted and managed without consuming service runtime resources?

Problem	State data associated with a particular service activity can impose a great deal of runtime state management responsibility upon service compositions, thereby reducing their scalability.
Solution	State data is managed and stored by intentionally stateful utility services.
Application	Stateful utility services provide in-memory state data storage and/or can maintain service activity context data.
Impacts	If not properly implemented, stateful utility services can become a performance bottleneck.
Principles	Service Statelessness (700)
Architecture	Inventory, Service

Termination Notification
By David Orchard, Chris Riley

How can the scheduled expiry of a service contract be communicated to consumer programs?

Problem	Consumer programs may be unaware of when a service or a service contract version is scheduled for retirement, thereby risking runtime failure.
Solution	Service contracts can be designed to express termination information for programmatic and human consumption.
Application	Service contracts can be extended with ignorable policy assertions or supplemented with human-readable annotations.
Impacts	The syntax and conventions used to express termination information must be understood by service consumers in order for this information to be effectively used.
Principles	Standardized Service Contract (693)
Architecture	Composition, Service

Three-Layer Inventory

This compound pattern is simply comprised of the combined application of the three service layer patterns. Three-Layer Inventory exists because the combined application of these three patterns results in common layers of abstraction that have been proven to complement and support each other by establishing services with flexible variations of agnostic and non-agnostic functional contexts.

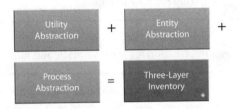

The joint application of Utility Abstraction [791], Entity Abstraction [742], and Process Abstraction [762] results in Three-Layer Inventory.

Trusted Subsystem

By Jason Hogg, Don Smith, Fred Chong, Tom Hollander, Wojtek
Kozaczynski, Larry Brader, Nelly Delgado, Dwayne Taylor, Lonnie Wall,
Paul Slater, Sajjad Nasir Imran, Pablo Cibraro, Ward Cunningham

*How can a consumer be prevented from circumventing a service
and directly accessing its resources?*

Problem	A consumer that accesses backend resources of a service directly can compromise the integrity of the resources and can further lead to undesirable forms of implementation coupling.
Solution	The service is designed to use its own credentials for authentication and authorization with backend resources on behalf of consumers.
Application	Depending on the nature of the underlying resources, various design options and security technologies can be applied.
Impacts	If this type of service is compromised by attackers or unauthorized consumers, it can be exploited to gain access to a wide range of downstream resources.
Principles	Service Loose Coupling (695)
Architecture	Service

UI Mediator

By Clemens Utschig-Utschig, Berthold Maier,
Bernd Trops, Hajo Normann, Torsten Winterberg

*How can a service-oriented solution provide a consistent,
interactive user experience?*

Problem	Because the behavior of individual services can vary depending on their design, runtime usage, and the workload required to carry out a given capability, the consistency with which a service-oriented solution can respond to requests originating from a user-interface can fluctuate, leading to a poor user experience.
Solution	Establish mediator logic solely responsible for ensuring timely interaction and feedback with user-interfaces and presentation logic.
Application	A utility mediator service or service agent is positioned as the initial recipient of messages originating from the user-interface. This mediation logic responds in a timely and consistent manner regardless of the behavior of the underling solution.
Impacts	The mediator logic establishes an additional layer of processing that can add to the required runtime processing.
Principles	Service Loose Coupling (695)
Architecture	Composition

Utility Abstraction

How can common non-business centric logic be separated, reused, and independently governed?

Problem	When non-business centric processing logic is packaged together with business-specific logic, it results in the redundant implementation of common utility functions across different services.
Solution	A service layer dedicated to utility processing is established, providing reusable utility services for use by other services in the inventory.
Application	The utility service model is incorporated into analysis and design processes in support of utility logic abstraction, and further steps are taken to define balanced service contexts.
Impacts	When utility logic is distributed across multiple services it can increase the size, complexity, and performance demands of compositions.
Principles	Service Loose Coupling (695), Service Abstraction (696), Service Reusability (697), Service Composability (704)
Architecture	Inventory, Composition, Service

Validation Abstraction

How can service contracts be designed to more easily adapt to validation logic changes?

Problem	Service contracts that contain detailed validation constraints become more easily invalidated when the rules behind those constraints change.
Solution	Granular validation logic and rules can be abstracted away from the service contract, thereby decreasing constraint granularity and increasing the contract's potential longevity.
Application	Abstracted validation logic and rules need to be moved to the underlying service logic, a different service, a service agent, or elsewhere.
Impacts	This pattern can somewhat decentralize validation logic and can also complicate schema standardization.
Principles	Standardized Service Contract (693), Service Loose Coupling (695), Service Abstraction (696)
Architecture	Service

Version Identification

By David Orchard, Chris Riley

How can consumers be made aware of service contract version information?

Problem	When an already-published service contract is changed, unaware consumers will miss the opportunity to leverage the change or may be negatively impacted by the change.
Solution	Versioning information pertaining to compatible and incompatible changes can be expressed as part of the service contract, both for communication and enforcement purposes.
Application	With Web service contracts, version numbers can be incorporated into namespace values and as annotations.
Impacts	This pattern may require that version information be expressed with a proprietary vocabulary that needs to be understood by consumer designers in advance.
Principles	Standardized Service Contract (693)
Architecture	Service

Appendix E

The Annotated SOA Manifesto

The SOA Manifesto was authored and announced during the 2nd Annual International SOA Symposium in Rotterdam by a working group comprised of 17 experts and thought leaders from different organizations. Four of the SOA Manifesto Working Group members (John deVadoss, Brian Loesgen, Herbjörn Wilhelmsen, and Thomas Erl) are co-authors of this book.

The original SOA Manifesto is published at www.soa-manifesto.org. You are encouraged to visit this site and enter your name on the *Become a Signatory* form to show your support for the values and principles declared in the manifesto.

Subsequent to the announcement of the SOA Manifesto, Thomas Erl authored an annotated version that supplements individual statements from the original manifesto with additional commentary and insights. The Annotated SOA Manifesto is published at www.soa-manifesto.com and has been further provided as a supplementary resource in this appendix.

The Annotated SOA Manifesto

Commentary and Insights about the SOA Manifesto from Thomas Erl

Service-orientation is a paradigm that frames what you do. Service-oriented architecture (SOA) is a type of architecture that results from applying service-orientation.

From the beginning it was understood that this was to be a manifesto about two distinct yet closely related topics: the service-oriented architectural model and service-orientation, the paradigm through which the architecture is defined. The format of this manifesto was modeled after the Agile Manifesto, which limits content to concise statements that express ambitions, values, and guiding principles for realizing those ambitions and values. Such a manifesto is not a specification, a reference model or even a white paper, and without an option to provide actual definitions, we decided to add this preamble in order to clarify how and why these terms are referenced in other parts of the manifesto document.

We have been applying service-orientation...

The service-orientation paradigm is best viewed as a method or an approach for realizing a specific target state that is further defined by a set of strategic goals and benefits. When we apply service-orientation, we shape software programs and technology architecture in support of realizing this target state. This is what qualifies technology architecture as being service-oriented.

...to help organizations consistently deliver sustainable business value, with increased agility and cost effectiveness...

This continuation of the preamble highlights some of the most prominent and commonly expected strategic benefits of service-oriented computing. Understanding these benefits helps shed some light on the aforementioned target state we intend to realize as a result of applying service-orientation.

Agility at a business level is comparable to an organization's responsiveness. The more easily and effectively an organization can respond to business change, the more efficient and successful it will be to adapting to the impacts of the change (and further leverage whatever benefits the change may bring about).

Service-orientation positions services as IT assets that are expected to provide repeated value over time that far exceeds the initial investment required for their delivery. Cost-effectiveness relates primarily to this expected return on investment. In many ways, an increase in cost-effectiveness goes hand-in-hand with an increase in agility; if there is more opportunity to reuse existing services, then there is generally less expense required to build new solutions.

"Sustainable" business value refers to the long-term goals of service-orientation to establish software programs as services with the inherent flexibility to be continually composed into new solution configurations and evolved to accommodate ever-changing business requirements.

...in line with changing business needs.

These last six words of the preamble are key to understanding the underlying philosophy of service-oriented computing. The need to accommodate business change on an on-going basis is foundational to service-orientation and considered a fundamental over-arching strategic goal.

Through our work we have come to prioritize:

The upcoming statements establish a core set of values, each of which is expressed as a prioritization over something that is also considered of value. The intent of this value system is to address the hard choices that need to be made on a regular basis in order for the strategic goals and benefits of service-oriented computing to be consistently realized.

Business value over technical strategy

As stated previously, the need to accommodate business change is an overarching strategic goal. Therefore, the foundational quality of service-oriented architecture and of any software programs, solutions, and eco-systems that result from the adoption of service-orientation is that they are business-driven. It is not about technology determining the direction of the business, it is about the business vision dictating the utilization of technology.

This priority can have a profound ripple effect within the regions of an IT enterprise. It introduces changes to just about all parts of IT delivery lifecycles, from how we plan for and fund automation solutions, to how we build and govern them. All other values and principles in the manifesto, in one way or another, support the realization of this value.

Strategic goals over project-specific benefits

Historically, many IT projects focused solely on building applications designed specifically to automate business process requirements that were current at that time. This fulfilled immediate (tactical) needs, but as more of these single-purpose applications were delivered, it resulted in an IT enterprise filled with islands of logic and data referred to as application "silos." As new business requirements would emerge, either new silos were created or integration channels between silos were established. As yet more business change arose, integration channels had to be augmented, even more silos had to be created, and soon the IT enterprise landscape became convoluted and increasingly burdensome, expensive, and slow to evolve.

In many ways, service-orientation emerged in response to these problems. It is a paradigm that provides an alternative to project-specific, silo-based, and integrated application development by adamantly prioritizing the attainment of long-term, strategic business goals. The target state advocated by service-orientation does not have traditional application silos. And even when legacy resources and application silos exist in environments where service-orientation is adopted, the target state is one where they are harmonized to whatever extent feasible.

Intrinsic interoperability over custom integration

For software programs to share data they need to be interoperable. If software programs are not designed to be compatible, they will likely not be interoperable. To enable interoperability between incompatible software programs requires that they be integrated. Integration is therefore the effort required to achieve interoperability between disparate software programs.

Although often necessary, customized integration can be expensive and time consuming and can lead to fragile architectures that are burdensome to evolve. One of the goals of service-orientation is to minimize the need for customized integration by shaping software programs (within a given domain) so that they are natively compatible. This is a quality referred to as intrinsic interoperability. The service-orientation paradigm encompasses a set of specific design principles that are geared toward establishing intrinsic interoperability on several levels.

Intrinsic interoperability, as a characteristic of software programs that reside within a given domain, is key to realizing strategic benefits, such as increased cost-effectiveness and agility.

Shared services over specific-purpose implementations

As just explained, service-orientation establishes a design approach comprised of a set of design principles. When applied to a meaningful extent, these principles shape a software program into a unit of service-oriented logic that can be legitimately referred to as a service.

Services are equipped with concrete characteristics (such as those that enable intrinsic interoperability) that directly support the previously described target state. One of these characteristics is the encapsulation of multi-purpose logic that can be shared and reused in support of the automation of different business processes.

A shared service establishes itself as an IT asset that can provide repeated business value while decreasing the expense and effort to deliver new automation solutions. While there is value in traditional, single-purpose applications that solve tactical business requirements, the use of shared services provides greater value in realizing strategic goals of service-oriented computing (which again include an increase in cost-effectiveness and agility).

Flexibility over optimization

This is perhaps the broadest of the value prioritization statements and is best viewed as a guiding philosophy for how to better prioritize various considerations when delivering and evolving individual services and inventories of services.

Optimization primarily refers to the fulfillment of tactical gains by tuning a given application design or expediting its delivery to meet immediate needs. There is nothing undesirable about this, except that it can lead to the aforementioned silo-based environments when not properly prioritized in relation to fostering flexibility.

For example, the characteristic of flexibility goes beyond the ability for services to effectively (and intrinsically) share data. To be truly responsive to ever-changing business requirements, services must also be flexible in how they can be combined and aggregated into composite solutions. Unlike traditional distributed applications that often were relatively static despite the fact that they were componentized, service compositions need to be designed with a level of inherent flexibility that allows for constant augmentation. This means that when an existing business process changes or when a new business process is introduced, we need to be able to add, remove, and extend services within the composition architecture with minimal (integration) effort. This is why service composability is one of the key service-orientation design principles.

Evolutionary refinement over pursuit of initial perfection

There is a common point of confusion when it comes to the term "agility" in relation to service-orientation. Some design approaches advocate the rapid delivery of software programs for immediate gains. This can be considered "tactical agility," as the focus is on tactical, short-term benefit. service-orientation advocates the attainment of agility on an organizational or business level with the intention of empowering the organization, as a whole, to be responsive to change. This form of organizational agility can also be referred to as "strategic agility" because the emphasis is on longevity in that, with every software program we deliver, we want to work toward a target state that fosters agility with long-term strategic value.

For an IT enterprise to enable organizational agility, it must evolve in tandem with the business. We generally cannot predict how a business will need to evolve over time and therefore we cannot initially build the perfect services. At the same time, there is usually a wealth of knowledge that already exists within an organization's existing business intelligence that can be harvested during the analysis and modeling stages of SOA projects.

This information, together with service-orientation principles and proven methodologies, can help us identify and define a set of services that capture how the business exists and operates today while being sufficiently flexible to adapt to how the business changes over time.

That is, while we value the items on the right, we value the items on the left more.

By studying how these values are prioritized, we gain insight into what distinguishes service-orientation from other paradigms. This type of insight can benefit IT practitioners in several ways. For example, it can help establish fundamental criteria that we can use to determine how compatible service-orientation is for a given organization or IT enterprise. It can further help determine the extent to which service-orientation can or should be adopted.

An appreciation of the core values can also help us understand how challenging it may be to successfully carry out SOA projects within certain environments. For example, several of these prioritizations may clash head-on with established beliefs and preferences. In such a case, the benefits of service-orientation need to be weighed against the effort and impact their adoption may have (not just on technology, but also on the organization and IT culture).

The upcoming guiding principles were provided to help address many of these types of challenges.

We follow these principles:

So far, the manifesto has established an overall vision as well as a set of core values associated with the vision. The remainder of the declaration is comprised of a set of principles that are provided as guidance for adhering to the values and realizing the vision.

It's important to keep in mind that these are guiding principles specific to this manifesto. There is a separate set of established design principles that comprise the service-orientation design paradigm and there are many more documented practices and patterns specific to service-orientation and service-oriented architecture.

Respect the social and power structure of the organization.

One of the most common SOA pitfalls is approaching adoption as a technology-centric initiative. Doing so almost always leads to failure because we are simply not prepared for the inevitable organizational impacts.

The adoption of service-orientation is about transforming the way we automate business. However, regardless of what plans we may have for making this transformation effort happen, we must always begin with an understanding and an appreciation of the organization, its structure, its goals, and its culture.

The adoption of service-orientation is very much a human experience. It requires support from those in authority and then asks that an IT culture adopt a strategic, community-centric mindset. We must fully acknowledge and plan for this level of organizational change in order to receive the necessary long-term commitments required to achieve the target state of service-orientation.

These types of considerations not only help us determine how to best proceed with an SOA initiative, they further assist us in defining the most appropriate scope and approach for adoption.

Recognize that SOA ultimately demands change on many levels.

There's a saying that goes: "Success is being prepared for opportunity." Perhaps the number one lesson learned from SOA projects carried out so far is that we must fully comprehend and then plan and prepare for the volume and range of change that is brought about as a result of adopting service-orientation. Here are some examples.

service-orientation changes how we build automation solutions by positioning software programs as IT assets with long-term, repeatable business value. An upfront investment is required to create an environment comprised of such assets and an on-going commitment is required to maintain and leverage their value. So, right out of the gate, changes are required to how we fund, measure, and maintain systems within the IT enterprise.

Furthermore, because service-orientation introduces services that are positioned as resources of the enterprise, there will be changes in how we own different parts of systems and regulate their design and usage, not to mention changes to the infrastructure required to guarantee continuous scalability and reliability.

The scope of SOA adoption can vary. Keep efforts manageable and within meaningful boundaries.

A common myth has been that in order to realize the strategic goals of service-oriented computing, service-orientation must be adopted on an enterprise-wide basis. This means establishing and enforcing design and industry standards across the IT enterprise so as to create an enterprise-wide inventory of intrinsically interoperable services. While there is nothing wrong with this ideal, it is not a realistic goal for many organizations, especially those with larger IT enterprises.

The most appropriate scope for any given SOA adoption effort needs to be determined as a result of planning and analysis in conjunction with pragmatic considerations, such as the aforementioned impacts on organizational structures, areas of authority, and cultural changes that are brought about.

These types of factors help us determine a scope of adoption that is manageable. But for any adoption effort to result in an environment that progresses the IT enterprise toward the desired strategic target state, the scope must also be meaningful. In other words, it must be meaningfully cross-silo so that collections of services can be delivered in relation to each other within a pre-defined boundary. In other words, we want to create "continents of services," not the dreaded "islands of services."

This concept of building independently owned and governed service inventories within domains of the same IT enterprise reduces many of the risks that are commonly attributed to "big-bang" SOA projects and furthermore mitigates the impact of both organizational and technological changes (because the impact is limited to a segmented and managed scope). It is also an approach that allows for phased adoption where one domain service inventory can be established at a time.

Products and standards alone will neither give you SOA nor apply the service-orientation paradigm for you.

This principle addresses two separate but very much related myths. The first is that you can buy your way into SOA with modern technology products, and the second is the assumption that the adoption of industry standards (such as XML, WSDL, SCA, etc.) will naturally result in service-oriented technology architecture.

The vendor and industry standards communities have been credited with building modern service technology innovation upon non-proprietary frameworks and platforms. Everything from service virtualization to cloud computing and grid computing has helped advance the potential for building sophisticated and complex service-oriented solutions. However, none of these technologies are exclusive to SOA. You can just as easily build silo-based systems in the cloud as you can on your own private servers.

There is no such thing as "SOA in a box" because in order to achieve service-oriented technology architecture, service-orientation needs to be successfully applied; this, in turn, requires that everything we design and build be driven by the unique direction, vision, and requirements of the business.

SOA can be realized through a variety of technologies and standards.

service-orientation is a technology-neutral and vendor-neutral paradigm. Service-oriented architecture is a technology-neutral and vendor neutral architectural model. Service-oriented computing can be viewed as a specialized form of distributed computing. Service-oriented solutions can therefore be built using just about any technologies and industry standards suitable for distributed computing.

While some technologies (especially those based on industry standards) can increase the potential of applying some service-orientation design principles, it is really the potential to fulfill business requirements that ultimately determines the most suitable choice of technologies and industry standards.

Establish a uniform set of enterprise standards and policies based on industry, de facto, and community standards.

Industry standards represent non-proprietary technology specifications that help establish, among other things, consistent baseline characteristics (such as transport, interface, message format, etc.) of technology architecture. However, the use of industry standards alone does not guarantee that services will be intrinsically interoperable.

For two software programs to be fully compatible, additional conventions (such as data models and policies) need to be adhered to. This is why IT enterprises must establish and enforce design standards. Failure to properly standardize and regulate the standardization of services within a given domain will begin to tear at the fabric of interoperability upon which the realization of many strategic benefits relies.

This principle not only advocates the use of enterprise design standards, it also reminds us that, whenever possible and feasible, custom design standards should be based upon and incorporate standards already in use by the industry and the community in general.

Pursue uniformity on the outside while allowing diversity on the inside.

Federation can be defined as the unification of a set of disparate entities. While allowing each entity to be independently governed on the inside, all agree to adhere to a common, unified front.

A fundamental part of service-oriented architecture is the introduction of a federated endpoint layer that abstracts service implementation details while publishing a set of endpoints that represent individual services within a given domain in a unified manner. Accomplishing this generally involves achieving unity based on a combination of industry and design standards. The consistency of this unity across services is key to realizing intrinsic interoperability.

A federated endpoint layer further helps increase opportunities to explore vendor-diversity options. For example, one service may need to be built upon a completely different platform than another. As long as these services maintain compatible endpoints, the governance of their respective implementations can remain independent. This not only highlights that services can be built using different implementation mediums (such as EJB, .NET, SOAP, REST, etc.), it also emphasizes that different intermediary platforms and technologies can be utilized together, as required.

Note that this type of diversity comes with a price. This principle does not advocate diversification itself—it simply recommends that we allow diversification when justified, so that "best-of-breed" technologies and platforms can be leveraged to maximize business requirements fulfillment.

Identify services through collaboration with business and technology stakeholders.

In order for technology solutions to be business-driven, the technology must be in synch with the business. Therefore, another goal of service-oriented computing is to align technology and business. The stage at which this alignment is initially accomplished is during the analysis and modeling processes that usually precede actual service development and delivery.

The critical ingredient to carrying out service-oriented analysis is to have both business and technology experts working hand-in-hand to identify and define candidate services. For example, business experts can help accurately define functional contexts pertaining to business-centric services, while technology experts can provide pragmatic input to ensure that the granularity and definition of conceptual services remains realistic in relation to their eventual implementation environments.

Maximize service usage by considering the current and future scope of utilization.

The extent of a given SOA project may be enterprise-wide or it may be limited to a domain of the enterprise. Whatever the scope, a pre-defined boundary is established to encompass an inventory of services that need to be conceptually modeled before they can be developed. By modeling multiple services in relation to each other we essentially establish a blueprint of the services we will eventually be building. This modeling exercise is critical when attempting to identify and define services that can be shared by different solutions.

There are various methodologies and approaches that can be used to carry out service-oriented analysis stages. However, a common thread among all of them is that the functional boundaries of services be normalized to avoid redundancy. Even then, normalized services do not necessarily make for highly reusable services. Other factors come into play, such as service granularity, autonomy, state management, scalability, composability, and the extent to which service logic is sufficiently generic so that it can be effectively reused.

These types of considerations guided by business and technology expertise provide the opportunity to define services that capture current utilization requirements while having the flexibility to adapt to future change.

Verify that services satisfy business requirements and goals.

As with anything, services can be misused. When growing and managing a portfolio of services, their usage and effectiveness at fulfilling business requirements need to be verified and measured. Modern tools provide various means of monitoring service usage, but there are intangibles that also need to be taken into consideration to ensure that services are not just used because they are available, but to verify that they are truly fulfilling business needs and meeting expectations.

This is especially true with shared services that shoulder multiple dependencies. Not only do shared services require adequate infrastructure to guarantee scalability and reliability for all of the solutions that reuse them, they also need to be designed and extended with great care to ensure their functional contexts are never skewed.

Evolve services and their organization in response to real use.

This guiding principle ties directly back to the "Evolutionary refinement over pursuit of initial perfection" value statement, as well as the overall goal of maintaining an alignment of business and technology.

We can never expect to rely on guesswork when it comes to determining service granularity, the range of functions that services need to perform, or how services will need to be organized into compositions. Based on whatever extent of analysis we are able to initially perform, a given service will be assigned a defined functional context and will contain one or more functional capabilities that likely involve it in one or more service compositions.

As real world business requirements and circumstances change, the service may need to be augmented, extended, refactored, or perhaps even replaced. service-orientation design principles build native flexibility into service architectures so that, as software programs, services are resilient and adaptive to change and to being changed in response to real world usage.

Separate the different aspects of a system that change at different rates.

What makes monolithic and silo-based systems inflexible is that change can have a significant impact on their existing usage. This is why it is often easier to create new silo-based applications rather then augment or extend existing ones.

The rationale behind the separation of concerns (a commonly known software engineering theory) is that a larger problem can be more effectively solved when decomposed into a set of smaller problems or concerns. When applying service-orientation to the separation of concerns, we build corresponding units of solution logic that solve individual concerns, thereby allowing us to aggregate the units to solve the larger problem in addition to giving us the opportunity to aggregate them into different configurations in order to solve other problems.

Besides fostering service reusability, this approach introduces numerous layers of abstraction that help shield service-comprised systems from the impacts of change. This form of abstraction can exist at different levels. For example, if legacy resources encapsulated by one service need to be replaced, the impact of that change can be mitigated as long as the service is able to retain its original endpoint and functional behavior.

Another example is the separation of agnostic from non-agnostic logic. The former type of logic has high reuse potential if it is multi-purpose and less likely to change. Non-agnostic logic, on the other hand, typically represents the single-purpose parts of parent business process logic, which are often more volatile. Separating these respective logic types into different service layers further introduces abstraction that enables service reusability while shielding services, and any solutions that utilize them, from the impacts of change.

Reduce implicit dependencies and publish all external dependencies to increase robustness and reduce the impact of change.

One of the most well-known service-orientation design principles is that of service loose coupling. How a service architecture is internally structured and how services relate to programs that consume them (which can include other services) all comes down to dependencies that are formed on individually moving parts that are part of the service architecture.

Layers of abstraction help ease evolutionary change by localizing the impacts of the change to controlled regions. For example, within service architectures, service facades can be used to abstract parts of the implementation in order to minimize the reach of implementation dependencies.

On the other hand, published technical service contracts need to disclose the dependencies that service consumers must form in order to interact with services. By reducing internal dependencies that can affect these technical contracts when change does occur, we avoid proliferating the impact of those changes upon dependent service consumers.

At every level of abstraction, organize each service around a cohesive and manageable unit of functionality.

Each service requires a well-defined functional context that determines what logic does and does not belong within the service's functional boundary. Determining the scope and granularity of these functional service boundaries is one of the most critical responsibilities during the service delivery lifecycle.

Services with coarse functional granularity may be too inflexible to be effective, especially if they are expected to be reusable. On the other hand, overly fine grained services may tax an infrastructure in that service compositions will need to consist of increased quantities of composition members.

Determining the right balance of functional scope and granularity requires a combination of business and technology expertise, and further requires an understanding of how services within a given boundary relate to each other.

Many of the guiding principles described in this manifesto will help in making this determination in support of positioning each service as an IT asset capable of furthering an IT enterprise toward that target state whereby the strategic benefits of service-oriented computing are realized.

Ultimately, though, it will always be the attainment of real world business value that dictates, from conception to delivery to repeated usage, the evolutionary path of any unit of service-oriented functionality.

—*Thomas Erl (November 22, 2009)*
www.soa-manifesto.com

Appendix F

Additional Resources

Following is a list of resource Web sites that provide supplementary content for books in this series. If you'd like to be automatically notified of new book releases, new supplementary content for this title, or key changes to these Web sites, send a blank e-mail to notify@soabooks.com.

www.soabooks.com

The official site of the *Prentice Hall Service-Oriented Computing Series from Thomas Erl*. Numerous resources are provided, including sample chapters from available books and updates and corrections.

www.soamag.com

This site is the home of *The SOA Magazine*, a monthly publication officially associated with this book series. This magazine is dedicated to publishing specialized articles, case studies, and papers that explore various aspects of service-oriented computing.

www.soaglossary.com

A master glossary for all books in the *Prentice Hall Service-Oriented Computing Series by Thomas Erl* is hosted by this site. This site is constantly growing as new titles are developed and released.

www.soaspecs.com

This Web site establishes a convenient central portal to industry standards and specifications covered or referenced by titles in this book series.

www.soapatterns.org

The official site of the master catalog of SOA design patterns. This site allows for the online submission and community review of candidate patterns proposed for inclusion in the master patterns catalog.

www.serviceorientation.com, www.soaprinciples.com, www.whatissoa.com

These sites provide papers, book excerpts, and various content dedicated to describing and defining the service-orientation paradigm, associated principles, and the service-oriented technology architectural model.

Consuming Services with WCF

by Herbjörn Wilhelmsen
Published: September 25, 2009 (SOA Magazine Issue XXXII: September 2009)
http://www.soamag.com/I32/0909-4.php

Introduction

Microsoft's Windows Communication Foundation (WCF) is an effective framework for implementing services as well as service consumers. Whenever you deal with WCF communication objects, you need to pay attention to the disposal of the resources that these objects hold. However, these disposal mechanisms are not that straightforward and are very much related to how resources need to be cleaned up. The how and why of cleaning up service resources is the topic of this article.

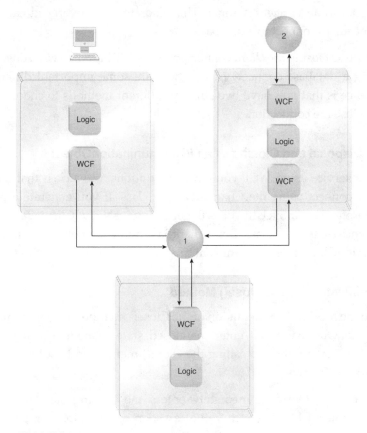

Figure F.1
WCF can be used to receive requests and send response messages in services. It can also be used to send requests to and receive response messages from services.

Cleaning Up Resources

Cleaning up resources is something that has been important for as long as programming has existed. In unmanaged languages, cleaning up memory resources is essential as it would otherwise lead to memory leaks that could eventually prevent your program from working properly or even bring down an entire machine. Another area where cleaning up resources is considered critical is in the world of database access. Closing database connections is a proven practice that nobody questions since omitting to do so could overpower the database server as it can only keep a limited number of connections open at any given time. One technique that has been developed over the years to optimize connection handling is connection pooling. Each client pools all of its connections as a common resource. As required, an application pulls a connection out of the pool. Once you are finished with the connection it is put back into the pool. If you do not close your connection before releasing it, the connection will not be put back into the connection pool in an efficient manner. This leads to extra overhead each time your application needs to connect to a database.

In several respects closing the client connection in a WCF based service consumer is similar to closing a database connection. But there are some important differences. One major difference is that you have two slightly different methods to choose from when you want to close the connection.

The Proper Disposal and Closing of an ICommunicationObject

To consume a service using WCF you have two options: use a class that inherits from ClientBase or connect using the ChannelFactory class. If you generate a proxy using Add Service Reference or SvcUtil you will get a [ServiceName]Client class that inherits from the ClientBase generic class. Both ClientBase and ChannelFactory implement the ICommunicationObject interface which in turn specifies a Close() method.

The ICommunicationObject.Close() Method

According to the MSDN documentation of the Close() method, the object implementing ICommunicationObject will not enter the closed state immediately after the Close() method has been called. Instead calling the Close() method will start a graceful transition that works as follows:

The ICommunicationObject immediately enters the Closing state (defined by the CommunicationState.Closing enum value) as soon as the Close() method has been called. It will remain in that state while unfinished work, such as sending or receiving buffered messages, is completed. Upon the completion of this work the state of the

ICommunicationObject will be changed to the Closed state (defined by the CommunicationState.Closed enum value) and then the Close() method returns.

Another very interesting property of the Close() method is that it may throw exceptions. Documented exceptions are

- TimeoutException; will be thrown if the close timeout has elapsed before the Close() method returned.

- CommunicationObjectFaultedException; will be thrown if the Close() method was called on an ICommunicationObject that is in the Faulted state (defined by the CommunicationState.Faulted enum value).

Apart from these two exceptions, the work that was initiated could throw exceptions, too. This flow of events is illustrated in Figure F.2.

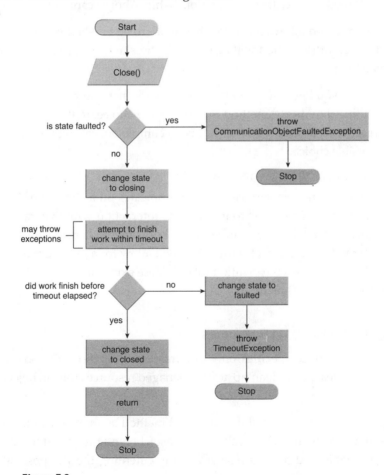

Figure F.2

The ICommunicationObject.Abort() Method

The ICommunicationObject interface also specifies an Abort() method, using this method is obviously somewhat different from using the Close() method. Abort() will also transition an ICommunicationObject to the Closed state. However, this transition will not be graceful, as in the case of the Close() method, instead any unfinished work is ignored or terminated and the state will be changed to Closed before the method returns.

Abort() versus Close()

In practice there are only two differences between calling the Abort() and Close() methods:

1. The Close() method may throw exceptions while Abort() cannot throw exceptions.

2. The Close() method allows for unfinished work to be finished within a specified timeout, the Abort() method will cause any unfinished work to be aborted immediately.

This means that if you know for sure that all the work that you have initiated has completed then calling the Abort() method may be a good choice. It also means that if there is a chance that some of your work has not been completed, calling the Close() method is the more sensible choice.

It is fairly easy to create a service that clearly demonstrates the difference between Close() and Abort(). Create a service that communicates on a WS-SecureConversation channel and a client that connects to it. Trace the interaction with SvcTraceViewer and see what happens after calling the Close() and Abort() methods respectively. When you call the Close() method, the graceful transition will allow for a few more messages to be sent in order to remove the conversation token. These extra messages will not be sent if you instead call the Abort() method.

IDisposable for Cleaning Up Resources

The IDisposable interface specifies only one method: Dispose(). The sole purpose of this method is to release and clean up any unmanaged resources that an object has made use of.

A proven practice is to always call the Dispose() method as soon as you finish working with a class that implements IDisposable. The reason behind this is that the implementer of the class probably had a good reason for implementing the IDisposable interface.

Typically classes that implement the IDisposable interface make use of unmanaged resources like memory or connections and providing a way of easily disposing of these resources is meant to make it easier for you to write code that uses these classes without getting into trouble. In some cases you may know for sure that the Dispose() method doesn't implement anything (e.g. by inspecting the source code with Red-Gate's .Net Reflector) but even in these cases you are still recommended to call the Dispose() method from your code. Doing so allows you to easily upgrade your program to make use of a newer version of the class with a minimum of fuss. The new version may use resources that need to be disposed of and therefore actually have logic implemented inside the Dispose() method. If you have not called the Dispose() method, you may get a lot of unforeseen problems with the newer version.

IDisposable and Its Relation to ClientBase and ChannelFactory

In its very first incarnation the ICommunicationObject interface implemented the IDisposable interface, but in its current version it does not. However, both ClientBase and ChannelFactory do implement the IDisposable interface. So, both ClientBase and ChannelFactory need to call either the Abort() method or the Close() method from inside their Dispose() method implementations. As a matter of fact, the WCF team has attempted calling both methods in different versions of the WCF framework.

In a very early release of WCF (at that time WCF went by the name of Indigo) the Abort() method was called from inside the Dispose() method. According to the Indigo team this was the first and foremost complaint on Beta 1 of WCF as it lead to cached messages not being sent. To mitigate this, the Indigo team attempted to make the Dispose() method smarter by calling the Close() method if the state of the ICommunicationObject was in the Opened state (defined by the CommunicationState.Opened enum value), and otherwise calling the Abort() method. Unfortunately, this way of implementing resource disposal lead to a situation where the Dispose() method could throw exceptions but would not always let you know if something went wrong!

Their ultimate decision was to remove the IDisposable interface from the ICommunicationObject interface, let ClientBase and ChannelFactory implement IDisposable and let both classes call the Close() method from inside their Dispose() methods. The end result is that the Dispose() method of the ClientBase and ChannelFactory classes can throw exceptions. The MSDN documentation for the Dispose() method clearly states that objects that implement the IDisposable interface should ensure that all held resources are freed, but as our discussion below will show this is not always the case with ClientBase and ChannelFactory.

Cleaning Up Resources with the Using Block

A very convenient way of making sure that you do not inadvertently forget to call the Dispose() method, e.g. due to an exception being thrown, is to use a using block. The using block is a short hand for writing a try-finally block. The two following code snippets show semantically identical code.

```
using (myObject)
{
    //some code here
}

myObject;
try
{
    //some code here
}
finally
{
    if (myObject != null)
    {
        myObject.Dispose();
    }
}
```

The using block internally emits IL-code that essentially wraps your code in a try-finally block. In the finally block the Dispose() method will be called. This is actually exactly what you want in the normal case as it means that the Dispose() method will be called even if an exception is thrown from your code inside the using block.

The beauty of the using block syntax is that it is compact and that if you use it you do not have to worry about the disposal of your resources. Unfortunately this also leads to many developers following the proven practice and wrapping ClientBase and ChannelFactory objects in using statements. They are used to writing code like this for their database connections and assume that it will work equally well for ClientBase and ChannelFactory. The problem is that calling the Close() method (remember that the Dispose() methods of both ClientBase and ChannelFactory call the Close() method) of an ICommunicationObject may result in an exception being thrown. This leads to two separate problems: The worst of them is that the connection may not be closed in some situations. The other is that if a CommunicationObjectFaultedException exception is thrown it will hide the exception that was originally thrown from inside your using block. To avoid these problems ClientBase and ChannelFactory objects should not be wrapped by a using block.

Cleaning Up Resources with the Try-Catch-Finally-Abort Pattern

A better way to handle the closing of an ICommunicationObject is to wrap the logic in a try block and to call the Close method from inside the try block. If something goes wrong in the try block, the Abort method should be called from inside a finally block. This approach is sometimes referred to as try-close-finally-abort and is very similar to the way the using block works. The code snippet below shows what this pattern looks like.

```
var finallyClient = new OrganizationClient();
try
{
    //method calls
    finallyClient.Close();
}
finally
{
    if (finallyClient.State != CommunicationState.Closed)
    {
        finallyClient.Abort();
    }
}
```

Please note that the proper criteria for calling the Abort() method is that the state of the channel is something other than Closed. If the channel has another state, it means that something went wrong (an exception was thrown) either before the Close() method was called or during the execution of the Close() method. In both cases you want to call the Abort() method, in any other case you should not call the Abort() method.

To make this approach as efficient as possible, you should try to include only WCF code and code that is necessary for WCF calls to proceed as planned in the try block. Attempt to place other code before and/or after the try block where possible. Ideally the code inside the try block should only consist of a call to the Open() method, calls to the service, and finally a call to the Close() method. When the .NET runtime exits the try block you will have either finished all the work you need to get done or something went wrong with the calls that went via WCF and your work cannot be completed.

If everything went well you are home free. If something went wrong you can call the Abort() method knowing that you did as much as you could to complete the calls to the composed services.

This code will essentially defer any exception handling code until you have properly disposed of your resources, which is what you want for most scenarios. If it is not what you want, a slightly different approach is needed.

Handling Exceptions and Cleaning Up Resources with the Try-Close-Catch-Abort Pattern

The call to the Abort() method can be wrapped inside a catch block instead of in a finally block. If you need exception handling to take place before closing the channel, this is the correct choice. If you do not need exception handling before closing then the try-close-finally-abort pattern is more suitable as resources will be disposed of before any exception handling occurs. Whenever an exception is caught, an exception stack has to be built; this is a time-consuming task. Put slightly differently, if you place the call to the Abort() method inside a catch block you have to wait for the exception stack to be built before you can release your resources.

The following code snippet shows how this can be done.

```
var catchClient = new OrganizationClient();
try
{
    //method calls
    catchClient.Close();
}
catch (Exception)
{
    //code that handles the exception
    catchClient.Abort();
}
```

A variation of this is also possible for cases when you have exception handling code that depends on the exact exception as illustrated in the next code snippet.

```
var catchClient = new OrganizationClient();
try
{
    //method calls
    catchClient.Close();
}
catch (ApplicationException)
{
    //code that handles ApplicationException
}
catch (Exception)
{
    //code that handles all other exceptions
}
finally
{
```

```
    if (catchClient.State != CommunicationState.Closed)
{
        catchClient.Abort();
    }
}
```

Although this pattern is used by quite a few systems, we find that in practice it is hard to find circumstances that justify prioritizing exception handling over resource disposal. It should only be considered if the channel needs to be used as a part of the exception handling or directly after it.

Cleaning Up Resources in a Convenient Way

Adding code for closing channels to all your WCF calls is tedious and error prone. It also defies the DRY (Don't-Repeat-Yourself) principle. As the behavior is essentially the same each and every time you call a service using WCF, this is a good opportunity to write a utility method that encapsulates the required behavior. The proposed utility methods will enable you to write code that looks and feels very similar to the kind of code you would write if you could wrap WCF calls in a using block. The code listing below shows a utility class called WcfClient.

```
public static class WcfClient
{
/// <summary>
/// Performs the action on the client (a <see cref="ICommunicationOb-
ject"/>) using the try-close-finally-abort pattern
/// </summary>
/// <typeparam name="TClient">The type of client</typeparam>
/// <param name="client">The client</param>
/// <param name="action">The action to perform on the client</param>
public static void Using<TClient>(TClient client, Action<TClient>
action) where TClient : ICommunicationObject
{
    if (client == null)
    {
        throw new ArgumentNullException("client");
    }
    if (action == null)
    {
        throw new ArgumentNullException("action");
    }

    try
    {
```

```
        client.Open();
        action(client);
        client.Close();
    }
    finally
    {
        if (client.State != CommunicationState.Closed)
        {
            client.Abort();
        }
    }
}


/// <summary>
/// Creates a WCF client channel using a <see cref="ChannelFactory"/>
and performs the action on the channel using the try-close-finally-
abort pattern
/// </summary>
/// <typeparam name="TChannel">The type of channel</typeparam>
/// <param name="channelFactory">The channel factory</param>
/// <param name="action">The action to perform on the created
channel</param>
public static void Using<TChannel>(ChannelFactory<TChannel>
channelFactory, Action<TChannel> action) where TChannel : class
{
    if (channelFactory == null)
    {
        throw new ArgumentNullException("channelFactory");
    }
    if (action == null)
    {
        throw new ArgumentNullException("action");
    }

    TChannel clientChannel = channelFactory.CreateChannel() ;
    try
    {
        channelFactory.Open();
        action(clientChannel);
        channelFactory.Close();
    }
    finally
    {
        if (channelFactory.State != CommunicationState.Closed)
```

```
    {
        channelFactory.Abort();
    }
    clientChannel = null;
    }
}
}
```

All you need to do in order to properly dispose of your ICommunicationObjects is then to write code such as this (if you use a generated WCF client):

```
GetUsersResponse response = null;
WcfClient.Using(new OrganizationClient(), client =>
{
    response = client.GetUsers(new GetUsersRequest());
});
```

Please note that you are able to use any WCF specific classes that need to be used after the channel has been opened. For instance OperationContextScope as discussed in the Idempotency section of Chapter 10.

```
GetUsersResponse response = null;
WcfClient.Using(new OrganizationClient(), client =>
{
    using (new OperationContextScope(client.InnerChannel))
    {
        OperationContext.Current.OutgoingMessageHeaders.MessageId =
        messageId;
        response = client.GetUsers(new GetUsersRequest());
    }
});
```

If you prefer to use the generic ChannelFactory class, instead your code would look similar to this:

```
GetUsersResponse response = null;
WcfClient.Using(new ChannelFactory("WSHttpBinding_IOrganization"),
client =>
{
    response = client.GetUsers(new GetUsersRequest());
});
```

How to Handle Connections when Consuming Services Using WCF

Handling and closing connections when you consume services using WCF is obviously an important matter as our discussion above has shown. However, its importance is related to the type of binding that is used.

Different bindings use different protocols. For some protocols it is very important to close the connection, this pertains to connection-full protocols. In such protocols subsequent calls to your consumed service will happen on the same connection. To make this possible a transport session is maintained between calls. But this is not so for http as it is a stateless or connectionless protocol meaning that the connection is destroyed automatically. In early versions of http the connection was destroyed after each call, but since then it has been optimized to actually keep the connection alive so that multiple response/requests can be transmitted without renegotiation. From this it follows that closing the connection is not critical from the perspective of handling resources when you consume a service over http.

On the other hand, WCF allows you to configure which binding you want to use when you consume a service, and when you do so you may also change the protocol. If you were to consume a WCF service over http and not close your client connection, you would experience no problems at all. However, say that you get the opportunity to consume this service over TCP, which has considerably less overhead than http. You, or someone else several years later for that matter, change the configuration and verifies that the service still works. And it does! Great. But then after a short while you get strange problems. You may soon reach a threshold where the number of open channels blocks your application.

To avoid these kinds of problems, it seems wise to always close the connection as that will enable you to change the configuration and consume a service over different protocols as required without having to worry about changing your code.

There is one exception though: REST services. REST services are built upon principles that define how to use web standards and are per definition connection-less. The only relevant standards that are available today for implementing REST are http and URIs. A REST service built with http will most likely always use http. More to the point: You cannot merely change your configuration to consume a REST service over another protocol than http. Http is an indispensable part of a REST service, not just a transport protocol.

So here at last comes a recommendation: Make sure that you close your client connection whenever you consume a service using WCF, except when you consume a REST service.

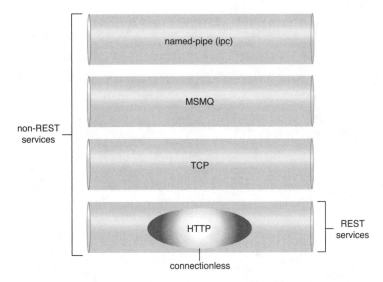

Figure F.3
The protocols supported by standard WCF bindings. REST services always use the
http protocol which is connectionless.

Conclusion

Efficient disposal of resources is important and the importance of getting this right
should be reflected in your code. Generally, the using block is a great way to ensure that
resources are disposed of, but not so in the case of consuming services with the ICommunucationObject. Instead, you need to write custom code to call the Close() or Abort()
methods as appropriate. Ideally you should dispose of resources before any exception
handling code is executed.

The resources you release from your ICommunucationObject are the resources of the
underlying channel. Some protocols (stateless or connectionless) do not mandate that
you close your client connection so this can be safely omitted when you consume REST
services over HTTP.

About the Authors

David Chou

David Chou is a technical architect at Microsoft and is based in Los Angeles. His focus is on collaborating with enterprises and organizations in such areas as cloud computing, SOA, Web, distributed systems, and security. His involvement supports decision makers in helping them to define the appropriate evolutionary strategies in their architecture development. Drawing from his extensive experience at previously held positions with Sun Microsystems and Accenture, David enjoys helping his clients and customers create value by using objective and pragmatic approaches to create definitive IT strategies, roadmaps, and solution architectures. Find David and his blog at blogs.msdn.com/dachou.

John deVadoss

John deVadoss leads the Patterns & Practices team at Microsoft and is based in Redmond, WA. Patterns & Practices is the trusted source for guidance on the Microsoft platform; John and his team are chartered with creating, collating, and disseminating proven practices to enable productive, predictable development on the Microsoft .NET platform. John's experience spans 15 years in the software industry. 10+ years have been with Microsoft—all of it in the enterprise space as a consultant, a program manager in the distributed applications platform division, an architect working with some of Microsoft's key partners, a director of architecture strategy and, most recently, as the leading technical strategist for the all-up application platform. Prior to Microsoft, John spent a number of years as a technology consultant in Silicon Valley working on large-scale middleware and distributed systems design and development. His areas of interest are broadly in distributed application architectures, data and metadata, systems management and currently on edge architectures (both service/cloud and experience), but most of all in creating business value from technology investments. John holds a BE in Computer Engineering, and an MS in Computer Science. Both degrees were awarded by the University of Massachusetts at Amherst where he also did graduate work towards a PhD in Computer Science.

Thomas Erl

Thomas Erl is the world's top-selling SOA author, series editor of the *Prentice Hall Service-Oriented Computing Series from Thomas Erl* (www.soabooks.com), and editor of the *SOA Magazine* (www.soamag.com). With more than 120,000 copies in print worldwide, his books have become international bestsellers and have been formally endorsed by senior members of major software organizations, such as IBM, Microsoft, Oracle, Sun, Intel, SAP, CISCO, and HP. Two of his five books, *SOA Design Patterns* and *SOA Principles of Service Design*, were authored in collaboration with the IT community and have contributed to the definition of the service-oriented architectural model and service orientation as a distinct paradigm. In cooperation with SOASchool.com™, Thomas has helped develop the curriculum for the internationally recognized SOA Certified Professional accreditation program (www.soaschool.com), which has established a series of formal, vendor-neutral certifications in the areas of service-oriented computing. Thomas is also the founder of SOA Systems Inc. (www.soasystems.com), the founding member of the SOA Manifesto Working Group (www.soa-manifesto.org), a member of the SOA Education Committee (www.soacommittee.org), and oversees the SOAPatterns.org initiative, a community site dedicated to the on-going development of a master pattern catalog for SOA. Thomas has toured more than 20 countries as a speaker and instructor for public and private events, and regularly participates in events, such as the SOA Symposium (www.soasymposium.com) and Gartner conferences. More than 100 articles and interviews by Thomas have been published in numerous publications, including the *Wall Street Journal* and *CIO Magazine*. For more information, visit www.thomaserl.com.

Nitin Gandhi

Nitin Gandhi is an enterprise architect and an independent software consultant, based in Vancouver, BC. His extensive background in service-oriented architecture (SOA), SOA Governance, Enterprise Service Bus (ESB), and message-oriented middleware (MOM) has seen him work on server products and technologies including, .NET, Windows Communication Foundation (WCF), Microsoft BizTalk Server, SQL Server, Workflow Foundation (WF), Service Virtualization technologies, J2EE/JMS, Oracle, and

TIBCO products. He has completed several large projects in insurance, utilities, financial-services, government and healthcare. Nitin is an author, book reviewer and member of several architecture groups. He holds a Bachelor's of Engineering in Electronics (with honors) and a Post Graduate diploma in Management. Find Nitin at ngandhi@shaw.ca.

Hanu Kommalapati

Hanu Kommalapati is a Principal Platform Strategy Advisor for a Microsoft Developer and Platform Evangelism team based in North America. His current focus is working with Microsoft's top enterprise customers in North America in evangelizing software + services and Cloud Computing. Hanu received his M.S. in Engineering from the Indian Institute of Technology—a top engineering school in India—and has 18 years experience in the IT Industry working with PriceWaterHouseCoopers and Microsoft. His career began as a software engineer at Hindustan Aeronautics Ltd., a fighter jet manufacturer solely owned by the Indian Defense Department; he also programmed on HP Apollo workstations, Unix mini computers and IBM mainframes. Hanu frequently speaks at customer and industry events, writes articles in technology magazines and has written papers for internal consumption on various industry trends, including Service Oriented Architecture and Cloud Computing.

Brian Loesgen

Brian Loesgen is a Principal SOA Architect with Microsoft, based in San Diego. His extensive experience includes building sophisticated enterprise, ESB and SOA solutions. Brian is a 6-time Microsoft MVP for BizTalk Server, and has been involved with BizTalk since before the release of BizTalk Server 2000 beta; he was a key architect/developer of the "Microsoft ESB Guidance," initially released by Microsoft in Oct. 2006. A speaker at numerous major technical conferences worldwide, Brian is a co-founder and past-President of the International .NET Association (ineta.org), and past-President of the San Diego .NET user group, where he continues to lead the Connected Systems SIG, and is a member of the Editorial Board for the .NET Developer's Journal. Brian was also a member of the Microsoft Connected Systems Division Virtual Technical Specialist Team pilot, and is part of Microsoft's Connected Systems Advisory Board. Brian has authored technical white papers for Intel, Microsoft and others; is a co-author of the SOA Manifesto, as well as the co-author of 7 books, including this one, and is the lead author on the upcoming *BizTalk Server 2009 R2 Unleashed* title. Find Brian and his blog at: blog.BrianLoesgen.com.

Christoph Schittko

Christoph Schittko is an architect for Microsoft, based in Texas. His focus is to work with customers to build innovative solutions that combine software + services for cutting edge user experiences and the leveraging of service-oriented architecture (SOA) solutions. Prior to joining Microsoft, Christoph assisted companies with the adoption of service orientation and the delivering of Software-as-a-Service (SaaS) solutions. Christoph holds an advanced degree in Electrical Engineering from the Friedrich-Alexander University Erlangen-Nürnberg. His extensive experience in developing and architecting software solutions in a wide variety of industries allows him to write and to speak at various conferences on Web services and XML.

Herbjörn Wilhelmsen

Herbjörn Wilhelmsen is a consultant at Forefront Consulting Group, based in Stockholm, Sweden. His main areas of focus are Service-Oriented Architecture, Cloud Computing and Business Architecture. Herbjörn has many years of industry experience working as a developer, development manager, architect and teacher and has worked with customers in several fields of operations such as telecommunications, marketing, payment industry, healthcare and public services. Herbjörn is the acting chair of the SOA Patterns Review Committee (www.soapatterns.org) and also leads the Business 2 IT group within the Swedish chapter of the IASA.

Mickey Williams

Mickey Williams leads the Technology Platform Group at Neudesic, based in Laguna Hills, CA. As a member of that team, he oversees technical leadership, strategy, and enablement across all of Neudesic's practice areas, and manages a team of architects that have a national role at Neudesic. Mickey has extensive experience building mission-critical applications on a wide variety of platforms, ranging from large telecommunication networks to desktop clients, and his work with .NET extends back to the earliest public release. Mickey's academic interests revolve around ensuring the reliability of high-performance distributed systems. Mickey is a Microsoft MVP, has written numerous books on Windows development, and is a frequent speaker at conferences and other events.

About the Contributors

Scott Golightly

Scott Golightly is currently an Enterprise Solution Strategist with Advaiya, Inc; he is also a Microsoft Regional Director with more than 15 years of experience helping clients to create solutions to business problems with various technologies. Scott is an experienced speaker and trainer. He has taught classes around the globe on various technical and business related topics. Scott has presented at numerous code camps, Tech Ed break out sessions, and Tech Ready. Scott holds many certifications, including: Certified Power-Builder Developer, Certified Sybase Instructor, MCP, MCSD, and MCT.

Darryl Hogan

Darryl Hogan is an architect with more than 15 years experience in the IT industry. Darryl has gained significant practical experience during his career as a consultant, technical evangelist and architect. During an 11-year tenure with Microsoft, Darryl delivered presentations to many large local Microsoft technology events and internal technical readiness conferences. Darryl currently works as an architect with a major marketing company where he is responsible for product architecture and emerging technology adoption.

Kris Horrocks

As a Senior Technical Product Manager at Microsoft, Kris works with customers, partners, and industry analysts to ensure the next generation of Microsoft technology meets customers' requirements for building distributed, service-oriented solutions. Currently, that work centers around several middleware technologies including BizTalk Server, Windows Server AppFabric, and Windows Azure AppFabric. Prior to joining Microsoft, Kris was an independent consultant focused on distributed systems development, B2B integration, and web services interoperability.

Jeff King

Jeff King has been working with the Windows Azure platform since its first announcement at PDC 2008 and works with Windows Azure early adopter customers in the Windows Azure TAP. Within the Microsoft community, Jeff is a worldwide Windows Azure subject matter expert who continues to mentor in ongoing Windows Azure training programs. Jeff currently consults for Microsoft Services. He has expert knowledge in designing and implementing large-scale integration and SOA solutions by leveraging Microsoft technologies and products (.NET, WCF, BizTalk Server, ESB Toolkit, etc.). He also helped develop the first publicly available version of the Enterprise Service Bus Toolkit (then, it was called the ESB Guidance), particularly the Exception Management Framework.

Scott Seely

Scott Seely is co-founder of Tech in the Middle, www.techinthemiddle.com, and president of Friseton, LLC, www.friseton.com. He is an active member of the .NET community in the Chicago area, helping organize the Lake County .NET Users' Group, organize Code Camps, and speaking at user groups throughout the region.

About the Foreword Contributors

David Chappell

David Chappell is Principal of Chappell & Associates (www.davidchappell.com) in San Francisco, California. Through his speaking, writing, and consulting, he helps people around the world understand, use, and make better decisions about new technology. He has been the keynote speaker for many conferences and events on five continents, and his seminars have been attended by tens of thousands of developers, architects, and decision makers in more than forty countries. David's books have been published in a dozen languages and used regularly in courses at MIT, ETH Zurich, and other universities.

S. Somasegar

As senior vice president of the Developer Division at Microsoft, S. Somasegar leads the teams responsible for providing tools and developer platform technologies targeted at developers, designers and teams involved in software development. This includes the Microsoft .NET developer platform that provides a consistent programming model spanning client, Web, server, device and services platform, Silverlight, the Visual Studio family of products, and Expression Studio. Somasegar is also responsible for the Web server platform including Internet Information Services (IIS), Media Server and Commerce Server. His team also owns MSDN and TechNet online properties to enable a deep connection with the developer and IT professional audience. In addition, Somasegar oversees the Microsoft India Development Center (IDC) in Hyderabad, India, and the Microsoft Canada Development Center (MCDC) in Vancouver, British Columbia.

Somasegar joined Microsoft in 1989, and worked on eight different operating system releases before heading up the Developer Division. Before joining Microsoft, Somasegar was a graduate student in computer engineering at the State University of New York in Buffalo. He holds a master's degree in computer engineering from Louisiana State University and a bachelor's degree in electronics and communication engineering from Guindy Engineering College, Anna University, Chennai, India. In November 2006, Somasegar was awarded an honorary doctorate (honoris causa) by Anna University, India. In February 2008, he was awarded the Asian American Engineer of the Year Award. Somasegar and his wife have two daughters. He frequently shares his thoughts via his blog, blogs.msdn.com/somasegar.

Index

A

Abort() method
(ICommunicationObject), 814
abstracted APIs (BizTalk BAM),
666-669
Access Control, 548-553
    cross-domain access control in
        cloud computing, 544
    service authorization scenarios,
        553-554
    Standard Mold case study, 555-556
    in Windows Azure, 528
access tokens, requesting, 551
activation types in .NET Remoting,
58, 60
Active Directory Federation Services
(ADFS), 539
activities (in WF), 172-175, 662
ad hoc discovery, 141, 143-144
adapter providers (ESB Toolkit),
478-479
adapters (BizTalk Server), 199-200
address attribute (service endpoints),
88-89
ADFS (Active Directory Federation
Services), 539
administration management tools
(WCF), 151

Agnostic Capability design pattern,
169, 334, 709
Agnostic Context design pattern, 169,
182, 332-333, 377, 710
agnostic logic, 32
Agnostic Sub-Controller design
pattern, 711
alerts, 165, 670-671
ambient transactions, 69
analysis, inventory analysis cycle,
337-338
Annotated SOA Manifesto, 796-808
AppFabric. See Windows Azure
platform AppFabric, Windows
Server AppFabric
Application Blocks, 182-183
application container (Windows
Azure), 216-217. See also hosting
models
application domains, 109
application integration models,
467-470
ASMX (XML Web services), 71, 73
    code generation, 302-304
    industry standards supported by, 70
    programming model for WF
        orchestrations, 397
    publishing workflows as, 399-407

**ASP.NET, caching REST responses,
599-601**
assemblies, history of, 51
asynchronous interactions, 639-641
**Asynchronous Queuing design
pattern, 712**
**Atomic Service Transaction design
pattern, 127, 388, 435, 458, 713**
attachments (SOAP), 701
authentication. *See also* **Brokered
Authentication design pattern;
Direct Authentication design pattern**
brokered authentication, 519
defined, 122
direct authentication, 518-519
mutual authentication, 520
Service Bus security, 508-509
authorization
claims-based authorization,
524-529, 546-547
defined, 122
role-based authorization, 520-524
service authorization scenarios
(Access Control), 553-554
WCF security, 125-126
AuthorizationContext class, 527
Azure. *See* **Windows Azure**

B
backup lists, 139
**BAM (Business Activity
Monitoring), 194**
abstracted APIs, 666-669
capturing data, 655-656
EventStream APIs, 665-666
interceptors, 670
management
database outages, 672
reporting, 676

scripting deployment, 673-676
security, 672-673
notifications, 670-671
rapid prototyping, 671
real-time versus scheduled
aggregations, 660-661
service composition metrics, 669
solution architecture, 656-659
Standard Mold case study, 677-680
Tracking Profile Editor (TPE),
659-660
**BAM Management utility
(BM.EXE), 659**
base activity library (WF), 174
behaviors
defining for routing services, 136
WCF, 104-105
**binding attribute (service endpoints),
89-92**
bindings, cleaning up resources, 822
BizTalk BAM. *See* **BAM (Business
Activity Monitoring)**
**BizTalk Operations service (ESB
Toolkit), 471**
BizTalk Server, 193
adapters, 199-200
architecture, 193-195
context properties, 200-201
ESB Toolkit. *See* ESB Toolkit
hosts, 481
hub-bus integration model, 469-470
messaging, 193, 196
pipelines, 197-198
ports and locations, 199
orchestration and, 193, 388-391,
443-445
*Compensating Service
Transaction design pattern,
456-461*

exception management,
202-203
itineraries, 201
orchestrated task service
contracts, 445-447
Process Centralization design
pattern, 450-451, 454
State Repository design pattern,
455-456
Superior Stamping case study,
448-449
WS- support, 447-448*
parallelism in, 643-644
productivity tools in, 194
request throttling, 607-608
selecting hosting models, 611-612
blobs in Windows Azure Storage, 239,
242-243
block blobs in Windows Azure
Storage, 242
BM.EXE (BAM Management utility),
659
books, related to this book, 4-6, 41-42
bootstrapper, 574
brokered authentication
mechanism, 519
Brokered Authentication design
pattern, 126, 714
BufferedEventStream API (BizTalk
BAM), 665
Business Activity Monitoring. *See* BAM
(Business Activity Monitoring)
business activity services (BizTalk
Server), 194
business metrics, 655
business processes, human intervention
in, 450-451

business rules in Windows Workflow
Foundation (WF), 180-181
business rules engine (BizTalk
Server), 194

C

cache hit ratio, 601
cache keys, computing, 593-594
caching, 587-591
cache keys, computing, 593-594
implementation technologies,
592-593
in-memory application cache
(Windows Server AppFabric),
190-191
intercepting messages, 589
at caching utility service, 590
comparison of techniques, 591
at intermediary, 589
at service proxy, 590
in service container, 589
monitoring cache efficiency, 601
REST responses, 599-601
Standard Mold case study, 594-596
Superior Stamping case study,
597-599
caching utility service, intercepting
messages, 590
Canonical Expression design pattern,
78, 147, 280
profile, 715
service capability naming
conventions, 281-282
service naming conventions, 280
Canonical Protocol design pattern, 274
component implementation,
278-279
dual protocols, 279-280

named pipes, 279

profile, 716

REST services implementation, 277-278

Web services implementation, 275-277

Canonical Resources design pattern, 249, 717

Canonical Schema Bus compound pattern, 719

Canonical Schema design pattern, 78, 82, 84, 217, 251, 253, 404, 445-446, 638

    creating schemas, 254, 256-258

    DataContract library, 264-267

    generating .NET types, 258-264

    profile, 718

Canonical Versioning design pattern, 720

CAO (client-activated objects), 58

Capability Composition design pattern, 374-375, 721

capability granularity, 38, 308-313

Capability Recomposition design pattern, 374-376, 722

capturing data, 655-656

case studies background, 16-19. *See also* code examples

case studies conclusion, 686. *See also* code examples

channel bindings, 148

channel layer, 149

channel layer extensibility (WCF), 150

channel stack, 149

ChannelFactory class, 119-120, 815

chapters, described, 6, 8-11

chatty interface, 311

claim sets, 526

claims, 534, 546

    accessing, 527

    designing custom, 529

    generating, 525

    passport example, 525

    processing, 526

claims-based authorization, 524-529, 546-547

ClaimSet class, 527

classes in .NET Remoting, 56

cleaning up resources, 811-812

    Abort() method (ICommunicationObject), 814

    based on bindings, 822

    ClientBase and ChannelFactory classes, 815

    Close() method (ICommunicationObject), 812-814

    Dispose() method (IDisposable), 814-815

    try-catch-finally-abort block, 817

    try-close-catch-abort block, 818-819

    using block, 816

    utility methods, 819, 821

client connections, closing, 822

client-activated objects (CAO), 58

client-server architecture, 44-45

client-side hybrid itineraries, 474

client-side itineraries, 474

ClientBase class, cleaning up resources, 815

clients, 537

Close() method (ICommunicationObject), 812-814

closing
> client connections, 822
> database connections, 812
> ICommunicationObject. *See*
> > cleaning up resources

cloud computing. *See also*
> **Windows Azure**
> cloud deployment models, 208
> > *community cloud, 209*
> > *dedicated cloud, 209*
> > *hybrid cloud, 209*
> > *intercloud, 209*
> > *private cloud, 208*
> > *public cloud, 208*
> > *Windows Azure and, 210*
> ESB with Windows Azure, 483
> > *receiving messages from Service Bus, 484-485*
> > *sending messages to Service Bus, 485-486*
> explained, 206-208
> security, 543-547
> service delivery models, 210-212

Cloud Computing & SOA, 6

cloud service projects, creating (Hello World example), 224

cloud-to-cloud authorization model (Access Control), 554

co-hosting, 645-648

coarse-grained service contracts, 608-610

code examples
> accessing claims, 527
> activities calling REST services, 424
> adding discovery endpoints, 142
> adding services to runtime, 414
> address attribute (service endpoints), 88

ambient transactions, 69

ASP.NET role provider authentication, 523

AspNetCacheProfile attribute, 599

aspNetCompatibilityEnabled attribute, 600

AspNetCompatibilityRequirements attribute, 600

asynchronous interactions, 640-641

asynchronous interfaces for workflows, 402

authorization, 126

backup lists, 139

behaviors (WCF), 105

binding configuration, 418

binding workflows to WCFcontracts, 409

bootstrapper setup, 574-575

bootstrapping workflow instances, 424

cache creation in Windows Server AppFabric, 191

caching (Standard Mold case study), 595-596

caching (Superior Stamping case study), 597-599

caching profile, 601

channel layer extensibility, 150

ChannelFactory class, 119-120

claim processing, 526

client-activated objects, 60

CLR type serialization, 83

co-hosting, 647

coarse-grained service interface, 312

communication protocols in .NET Remoting, 61

component implementation, 279

configuration file contents (ASMX services), 407

configuring REST endpoints, 421

configuring Send/Receive activities for REST services, 423

configuring service behaviors, 432

consuming RESTful services directly, 96

contract-first development, 411

converting service operations, 94

creating filter tables for routing services, 138

creating message queues, 64

custom discovery metadata, 143

data model transformations, 269

DataContract library, 266

declarative authorization, 524

defining behaviors for routing services, 136

defining endpoints for routing services, 136

defining message filters for routing services, 137

defining target endpoints for routing services, 137

defining workflow contract, 416

deleting message queues, 65

development-time deployment script, 674

development-time undeployment script, 675

Diagnostic Monitor, 229

Discovery Proxies, 146

documentation (Standard Mold case study), 351

durable services, 131

dynamically loading modules, 580-581

elements in SOAP messages, 413

endpoint element, 87

exception shielding, 319-321

exceptions for MSMQ message processing, 66

exporting BizTalk orchestrations to WS-BPEL, 452

façade creation, 306-307

fault contracts, 99-100

filter rules referencing backup lists, 140

fine-grained component interface, 310

Flexible Strategy (versioning), 103

GUID extraction (Standard Mold case study), 345

high performance transports (Standard Mold case study), 627

IIdentity interface, 522

IIS hosting, 113-114

imperative authorization, 524

implicit programming model (System.Transactions library), 69

implicit service discovery, 147-148

importing types into XML schemas, 289

in-line documentation, 322

interface for request-response operation, 400

internal endpoint definition for IRC, 223

internal endpoint listings for IRC, 223

internal endpoint specification for IRC, 222

IOrderService in REST services, 237

IOrderService interface contract, 231

IPrincipal interface, 521

JSON encoding, configuring contracts for, 422

launching svcutil, 294

LINQ-to-XML mapping, 272

listener configuration for service announcements, 145

logging and diagnostic APIs, 229

managed Windows services, 112

meeting notes (Standard Mold case study), 363

message contracts, 85

message contracts, changing parameters, 85

message logging, 153

message schema, 291

messaging queues (Standard Mold case study), 348-350

module creation, 565, 575-577

MTOM encoding, 628

MTOM encoding (Standard Mold case study), 629

multiple service endpoints, 87

namespaces in generated services, 404

.NET type generation, 264

.NET API interaction (Standard Mold case study), 341

notification properties (Standard Mold case study), 347

object-to-object mapping, 271

operation attributes for transactions, 128

orchestration and BizTalk Server (Superior Stamping case study), 449

Order data contract, 231

output of IOrderService interface contract and Order data contract, 232

passing data to workflows, 416

passing parameters to workflow instances, 178

performance policies (Standard Mold case study), 621

persistence service parameter list, 430

persistence services, attaching to workflow runtime, 428

probe queries, 144

probe request management, 142

production deployment script, 674

production undeployment script, 675-676

Query Notification (SQL Server), 165

raw messages in SOAP, 412

receiving MSMQ messages, 66

region/view association, 578

regions in shells, 564

relying parties, developing, 542

request throttling (Superior Stamping case study), 607

request throttling with WCF, 605

REST-based Service Bus contracts, 514

REST contracts in WCF, 420

REST service creation (Standard Mold case study), 355-356

REST service hosting, 116

REST service implementation, 278

REST service XML output (Standard Mold case study), 358

retrieving XML (Standard Mold case study), 364

returning data from services, 82

returning parameters from workflow instances, 178-179

RoutingService class, 133-134

saving messages (Standard Mold case study), 346

self-hosted services, 111-112

sending MSMQ messages, 65

sending service announcements, 144

service attributes for transactions, 129

Service Broker (SSB) implementation, 163-164

Service Bus configuration file, 510

Service Bus contract definition, 506

Service Bus contract implementation, 507

Service Bus message buffer creation, 516

Service Bus service configuration, 508

Service Bus service host configuration, 512

Service Bus service publication, 512

service consumer code creation (Standard Mold case study), 359-360, 362

service consumer code XML output (Standard Mold case study), 361, 363

service contract behavior attributes, 80

service contract creation, 80

service contract definition, 79

service contract design (Standard Mold case study), 631-632

service contract implementation, 107-108

service contracts (Standard Mold case study), 628

service contracts, changing default name and namespace, 80

service definition (ASMX services), 403

service endpoint attributes, 81

Service Metadata Tool usage, 117

ServiceConfiguration.cscfg, 228

ServiceDefinition.csdef, 228

ServiceFault data contract, 99

ServiceHost class, 109

shell control setup, 573-574

shell implementation, 561-562

signing messages (Standard Mold case study), 620

SingleCall objects, 59

Singleton objects, 59

SOAP messages, 85-86

SQL Server endpoint creation, 158

SQL Server stored procedure creation, 158

Standard Mold case study metrics, 678-679

stateful interactions, 131

.svc file for compiled workflow, 418

.svc file for REST contracts, 421

svcutil-generated code, 296

throttling controls, 105

timestamps (Standard Mold case study), 365

tracing, 152

tracing listener creation, 230

TrackServiceEnd method, 668

TrackServiceException method, 668

TrackServiceStart method overload, 667

transactions, 53

TransactionTimeout attribute, 130
try-catch block for fault contracts, 100
try-catch blocks, 98
updating configuration settings, 230
updating database information (Standard Mold case study), 366-367
updating OrderService.svc file for REST services, 238
updating WCF behavior in REST services, 238
updating Web role service configuration file, 233
UriTemplate attribute (REST services), 96-98
validation abstraction, 316-318
verifying metadata compatibility, 146
view creation, 577
view definition, 562
WCF interface (Standard Mold case study), 344
WCF security (Standard Mold case study), 532-533
Web service implementation, 276-277
WebGet attribute (REST services), 93
WebInvoke attribute (REST services), 95
WebRole.cs, 227
WebService attribute, 72
@WebService directive, 71
WF programming model, 177
Windows Authentication binding for a service, 522
workflow host associations, 432
workflow persistence (with AppFabric), 190

workflow persistence (with WF), 171
workflows as ASMX services, 404
writing proxy class, 118-119
WSCF.blue-generated code, 301
WSCF.classic-generated code, 304
WSDL definition, 293
XML schema creation with Visual Studio, 255-257
XSLT transformation, 273
COM, history of, 48-49
COM+ services
    history of, 49, 51
    hosting .NET Remoting components, 57
Command design pattern, 568
Common Object Request Broker Architecture (CORBA), 47
communication protocols
    in .NET Remoting, 60
communication with host container, 171-172
community cloud deployment model, 209
Compatible Change design pattern, 102, 316, 723
Compensating Service Transaction design pattern, 132, 387, 434
    BizTalk Server, 456-461
    creating compensations, 434-435
    profile, 724
    triggering compensations, 435
components
    as service implementation option, 278-279
    services as, 29
Composite Application Library for WPF and Silverlight. See Prism Library
Composite design pattern, 568

Composite View design pattern, 568

composite views (Prism Library), 562

composition. *See* service composition

Composition Autonomy design
  pattern, 645, 725

composition controller, 377

composition controller capabilities,
  design characteristics, 704-705

composition initiator, 377

composition member, 377

composition member capabilities,
  design characteristics, 704

composition sub-controller, 377

compound patterns. *See also* design
  patterns
    Canonical Schema Bus, 719
    Enterprise Service Bus, 136, 194,
      219. *See also* ESB (enterprise
      service bus)
        mapping ESB to, 490, 492
        profile, 741
    Federated Endpoint Layer, 249, 745
    Official Endpoint, 757
    Orchestration, 169, 194, 382, 395,
      443, 758
    Service Broker, 136, 160-164, 771
    Three-Layer Inventory, 378, 788

Concurrent Contracts design pattern,
  102, 226, 307-308, 726

confidentiality, defined, 122

configuration
    router services, 135-139
    Service Bus, 504-512
        authentication, 508-509
        contract definition, 505-506
        contract implementation,
          506-507
        end-to-end security, 509

service configuration, 508
service host configuration,
  511-512
service publication, 512
SQL Express, 224

connections, closing
    client connections, 822
    database connections, 812

connectivity fabric, Service Bus as,
  494-496

connectivity models (Service Bus), 499
    Eventing, 500
    Service Remoting, 501
    Tunneling, 501-502

console applications, hosting .NET
  Remoting components, 57

constraint granularity, defined, 38

consumer-to-contract coupling, 286

consumer-to-implementation
  coupling, 286

consumer-to-logic coupling, 310

consumers. *See* service consumers (WCF)

contention, 603-604

context properties (BizTalk Server),
  200-201

context property, 660

contract attribute (service
  endpoints), 92

Contract Centralization design pattern,
  286, 288, 727

Contract Denormalization design
  pattern, 313, 630, 728

contract-first development,
  250-252, 694

contract-to-functional coupling, 286

contract-to-implementation
  coupling, 286

contract-to-logic coupling, 285

contract-to-technology coupling, 286
conversation group identifier, 161
conversation groups, 161
CORBA (Common Object Request Broker Architecture), 47
coupling. *See* Service Loose Coupling design principle
CREATEENDPOINT statement (SQL Server), 158-159
credentials, 123-125
cross-domain access control in cloud computing, 544
Cross-Domain Utility Layer design pattern, 182, 729
custom encryption, 623-625

D

data access in Windows Azure Storage, 241
Data Confidentiality design pattern, 125, 730
data contracts
    creating, 251
    DataContract attribute, 82-83
    defined, 78
    fault contracts, 98-100
    versioning, 102
data dimension, 664
Data Format Transformation design pattern, 200, 731
data granularity, 38
Data Model Transformation design pattern, 200, 267-269, 388, 446, 453, 637
    LINQ-to-XML mapping, 271-272
    object-to-object mapping, 269-271
    profile, 732
    XSLT transformations, 272-273

Data Origin Authentication design pattern, 125, 733
data serialization, 82-83
database connections, closing, 812
database outages, BizTalk BAM management, 672
databases. *See* SQL Azure; SQL Server
DataContract attribute (WCF), 82-83
DataContract library, 264-267
DCOM (Distributed Component Object Model), 47-49
declarative authorization, 524
Decomposed Capability design pattern, 734
Decoupled Contract design pattern, 81, 207, 217, 277, 288, 397, 399
    profile, 735
    svcutil utility program, code generation with, 294-297
    WSCF.blue, code generation with, 297-301
    WSCF.classic, code generation with, 302-304
    WSDL-first approach, 289-290, 292-294
dedicated cloud deployment model, 209
dependency injection container, 566, 571
Dependency Injection design pattern, 570-571
deployment models in cloud computing, 208
    community cloud, 209
    dedicated cloud, 209
    hybrid cloud, 209
    intercloud, 209
    private cloud, 208
    public cloud, 208
    Windows Azure and, 210

deployment scripting, BizTalk BAM
  management, 673-676
design patterns. *See also* compound
  patterns
    Agnostic Capability, 169, 334, 709
    Agnostic Context, 169, 182,
      332-333, 377, 710
    Agnostic Sub-Controller, 711
    Asynchronous Queuing, 712
    Atomic Service Transaction, 127,
      388, 435, 458, 713
    Brokered Authentication, 126, 714
    Canonical Expression, 78, 147, 280
      profile, 715
      *service capability naming
        conventions, 281-282*
      service naming conventions, 280
    Canonical Protocol, 274
      *component implementation,
        278-279*
      dual protocols, 279-280
      named pipes, 279
      profile, 716
      *REST services implementation,
        277-278*
      *Web services implementation,
        275-277*
    Canonical Resources, 249, 717
    Canonical Schema, 78, 82, 84, 217,
      251, 253, 404, 445-446, 638
      creating schemas, 254, 256-258
      DataContract library, 264-267
      generating .NET types, 258-264
      profile, 718
    Canonical Versioning, 720
    Capability Composition,
      374-375, 721

Capability Recomposition,
  374-376, 722
Command, 568
Compatible Change, 102, 316, 723
Compensating Service Transaction,
  132, 387, 434
    BizTalk Server, 456-461
    *creating compensations,
      434-435*
    profile, 724
    triggering compensations, 435
Composite, 568
Composite View, 568
Composition Autonomy, 645, 725
Concurrent Contracts, 102, 226,
  307-308, 726
Contract Centralization, 286,
  288, 727
Contract Denormalization, 313,
  630, 728
Cross-Domain Utility Layer,
  182, 729
Data Confidentiality, 125, 730
Data Format Transformation,
  200, 731
Data Model Transformation, 200,
  267-269, 388, 446, 453, 637
    *LINQ-to-XML mapping,
      271-272*
    *object-to-object mapping,
      269-271*
    profile, 732
    *XSLT transformations,
      272-273*
Data Origin Authentication,
  125, 733
Decomposed Capability, 734

Decoupled Contract, 81, 207, 217, 277, 288, 397, 399
  profile, 735
  svcutil utility program, code generation with, 294-297
  WSCF.blue, code generation with, 297-301
  WSCF.classic, code generation with, 302-304
  WSDL-first approach, 289-290, 292-294
  defined, 38-39
Dependency Injection, 570-571
Direct Authentication, 736
Distributed Capability, 737
Domain Inventory, 182, 337, 371, 738
Dual Protocols, 226, 279-280, 399, 625, 648, 739
Enterprise Inventory, 740
Entity Abstraction, 169, 336, 377-378
  with .NET REST service (Standard Mold case study), 351-367
  profile, 742
Event Aggregator, 570
Event-Driven Messaging, 165, 445, 743
Exception Shielding, 319-321, 529, 744
File Gateway, 746
Functional Decomposition, 169, 330-331, 445, 560, 747
Intermediate Routing, 133, 136, 748

inventory boundary patterns. *See* Domain Inventory design pattern
Inventory Endpoint, 749
inventory standardization patterns. *See* Canonical Protocol design pattern; Canonical Schema design pattern
inventory structure patterns
  Logic Centralization design pattern, 751
  Service Layers design pattern, 169, 377-378, 779
  Service Normalization design pattern, 781
Inversion of Control, 570
Legacy Wrapper, 750
Logic Centralization, 751
Message Screening, 529, 752
Messaging Metadata, 84, 201, 251, 753
Metadata Centralization, 147, 219, 325-326, 417, 754
Model-View-Controller, 568
Model-View-Presenter, 568
Model-View-View-Model, 568
modularity design patterns, 569-571
Multi-Channel Endpoint, 633, 755
Non-Agnostic Context, 169, 379-380, 756
Partial State Deferral, 456, 759
Partial Validation, 760
Passive View, 568
Plug-In, 570
Policy Centralization, 761

for presentation layer, 567
    modularity patterns, 569-571
    user interface patterns, 567-569
Presentation Model, 568-569
Process Abstraction, 169, 378, 380,
    382-385, 762
Process Centralization, 169,
    382-385, 425, 450
    human intervention in business
        processes, 450-451
    profile, 763
    workflow design in WF,
        425-426
    WS-BPEL support, 426,
        451, 454
Protocol Bridging, 136, 200,
    274, 764
Proxy Capability, 765
Redundant Implementation, 207,
    213, 766
reference notation, 12
Reliable Messaging, 160, 767
Rules Centralization, 181, 388, 768
Schema Centralization, 217, 251,
    253, 445, 769
Separated Interface, 570
Separated Presentation, 568-569
Service Agent, 133, 589, 770
Service Callback, 772
Service Data Replication, 190,
    218, 773
Service Decomposition, 774
Service Encapsulation, 169,
    332, 775
Service Façade, 304, 306-307, 776
Service Grid, 777
Service Instance Routing, 778
Service Layers, 169, 377-378, 779

Service Locator, 571
Service Messaging, 84, 780
Service Normalization, 781
Service Perimeter Guard, 529, 782
Service Refactoring, 217, 783
sources for information, 11-12
State Messaging, 456, 784
State Repository, 171, 207, 386,
    426-428
    BizTalk Server, 455-456
    persistence service and scaling
        out in WF 3.0, 429-431
    persistence service and scaling
        out in WF 4.0, 431-433
    profile, 785
Stateful Services, 190, 207, 213,
    456, 590, 786
Supervising, 568
Supervising Presenter, 569
Termination Notification, 102, 787
Trusted Subsystem, 789
UI Mediator, 568, 790
Uniform Contract, 282
user interface design patterns,
    567-569
Utility Abstraction, 169, 182, 335,
    377-378
    profile, 791
    with .NET Web service
        (Standard Mold case study),
        339-351
Validation Abstraction, 82, 217,
    315-318, 792
Version Identification, 102, 793
design principles
list of, 26-27
reference notation, 12
Service Abstraction, 26, 82, 84, 102,
    104, 207, 217, 313-314, 696

Service Autonomy, 27, 110, 190, 218, 699

Service Composability, 27, 125, 373, 560, 704-705

Service Discoverability, 27, 147, 219, 321, 417, 535
  implementation requirements, 703
  in-line documentation, 322
  profile, 702-703
  REST services, 323
  service profiles, 323-324

Service Loose Coupling, 26, 81-82, 84, 217, 285-286, 559
  design patterns and, 286
  profile, 695
  service capability granularity and, 308-313

Service Reusability, 26, 125, 329-330, 337, 339, 697-698, 704

Service Statelessness, 27, 171, 190, 700-701

sources for information, 11-12

Standardized Service Contract, 26, 78, 81-82, 84, 217, 250, 274, 340, 399
  contract-first development, 250-252
  design patterns and, 252
  profile, 693-694

dialogs, 161

digital identity, 534-536, 546

dimensions
  in real-time aggregations, 662
  types of, 664

direct authentication, 518-519

Direct Authentication design pattern, 736

direct connectivity model (Service Bus), 494-496

DirectEventStream API (BizTalk BAM), 665

discovering services, WCF Discovery, 140-141. *See also* Service Discoverability design principle
  discovery modes, 141-143
  Discovery Proxies, 146
  implicit service discovery, 147-148
  probe queries, 143-144
  sending/receiving service announcements, 144-146

discovery modes, 141-143

Discovery Proxies, 146

Dispose() method (IDisposable), 814-815

distributed architecture, explained, 45-47

Distributed Capability design pattern, 737

Distributed Component Object Model (DCOM), 47

distributed computing
  client-server architecture, 44-45
  distributed architecture, 45-47
  service-oriented architecture, 47

distributed ESBs, 482-483

distributed garbage collection, 49

distributed resource transactions, 67-68

Distributed Transaction Coordinator (DTC), history of, 52-53

distributed transactions, explained, 51

documentation, in-line, 322

Domain Inventory design pattern, 182, 337, 371, 738

domain service inventory, 34

DTC (Distributed Transaction Coordinator), history of, 52-53

Dual Protocols design pattern, 226, 279-280, 399, 625, 648, 739

durable services, WCF transactions, 131-132

dynamically loading user-interface modules, 579-581

E

elevated mode (Visual Studio), 223

encoding, MTOM, 627-629

encryption, 622-625

end-to-end security (Service Bus), 509

endpoint element, 86-87
    address attribute, 88-89
    binding attribute, 89-92
    contract attribute, 92

endpoints
    defining for routing services, 135-136
    SQL Server, creating, 158-160

Enterprise Service Bus compound pattern, 136, 194, 219. *See also* ESB (enterprise service bus)
    mapping ESB to, 490, 492
    profile, 741

enterprise single sign-on (BizTalk Server), 194

Enterprise Inventory design pattern, 740

entities in Windows Azure Storage, 240-241

Entity Abstraction design pattern, 169, 336, 377-378
    with .NET REST service (Standard Mold case study), 351-367
    profile, 742

entity group transactions in Windows Azure Storage, 241

entity service model, defined, 32

errors, fault contracts, 98-100

ESB (enterprise service bus), 466
    cloud-enabling with Windows Azure, 483
        receiving messages from Service Bus, 484-485
        sending messages to Service Bus, 485-486
    governance, 487
        monitoring, 488-489
        SLA enforcement, 488
        transition plans, 489
    high-availability architecture, 480
        distributed ESBs, 482-483
        scaling, 481-482
    mapping to Enterprise Service Bus compound pattern, 490, 492
    Microsoft and, 466-467

ESB Guidance, 467

ESB Toolkit, 470-471
    adapter providers, 478-479
    itineraries, 472-474
        lifecycle of, 475-476
        types of, 474
    resolvers, 476-478
    services provided by, 471

Event Aggregator design pattern, 570

Event Collector Service (Windows Server AppFabric), 192

event notifications, 165, 670-671

event sources, types of, 660

Event-Driven Messaging design pattern, 165, 445, 743

Eventing connectivity model (Service Bus), 500

EventStream APIs (BizTalk BAM),
665-666

exception management (BizTalk
Server), 202-203

Exception Management service (ESB
Toolkit), 471

Exception Shielding design pattern,
319-321, 529, 744

explicit programming model
(System.Transactions library), 68-69

extensibility

WCF

channel bindings, 148

channel layer extensibility, 150

layers, 149-150

Windows Workflow Foundation
(WF), 180

Extensible Application Markup
Language (XAML), 560

external cloud, 208

external identity providers, 546

ExternalDataExchange services,
publishing workflows via, 413-416

F

failover (in Windows Azure), 221

fault contracts, 98-100

fault tolerance, router services, 139-140

FaultContract attribute (WCF), 98-100

faults, Exception Shielding design
pattern, 319-321

Federated Endpoint Layer compound
pattern, 249, 745

federated ESBs, 482-483

federated identity, WCF security, 126

federation, 40

File Gateway design pattern, 746

filter tables, creating for routing
services, 138-139

Flexible strategy (versioning), 102

Functional Decomposition design
pattern, 169, 330-331, 445, 560, 747

G

GAT (Guidance Automation
Toolkit), 184

GAX (Guidance Automation
Extensions), 184

glossary Web site, 13, 810

governance, ESB, 487-489

granularity

capability granularity, 308-313

levels, list of, 37-38

performance tuning, 608-610

Guidance Automation Extensions
(GAX), 184

Guidance Automation Toolkit
(GAT), 184

H

hardware accelerators, 701

hardware encryption for performance
tuning, 622

custom encryption, 623-625

message encryption, 623-624

transport encryption, 622-623

HATEOAS (Hypermedia as the Engine
of Application State), 323

health and activity tracking tool
(BizTalk Server), 194

Hello World example. *See* Windows
Azure, Hello World example

high-availability ESB architecture, 480

distributed ESBs, 482-483

scaling, 481-482

host container, communication with, 171-172

host service, creating (Web service example), 233

hosted cloud, 209

hosting
co-hosting, 645-648
.NET Remoting components
in COM+ services, 57
in console applications, 57
in IIS, 57
in Windows services, 56
WCF services
IIS hosting, 113-114
managed Windows services, 112-113
REST service hosting, 115-116
selecting hosting environment, 108-110
self-hosted services, 110-112
Windows Activation Service (WAS), 114

hosting environment in Windows Server AppFabric, 188-189

hosting models, selecting, 610-612

hosts in BizTalk Server, 481

hub-and-spoke integration model, 468

hub-bus integration model, 469-470

human intervention in business processes, 450-451

hybrid cloud authorization model (Access Control), 553-554

hybrid cloud deployment model, 209

hybrid clouds, 545

Hypermedia as the Engine of Application State (HATEOAS), 323

I

IaaS (Infrastructure-as-a-Service), 210-212

ICommunicationObject, closing. *See* cleaning up resources

ICommunicationObject.Abort() method, 814

ICommunicationObject.Close() method, 812-814

Identity Metasystem, 533, 535

identity providers, 537
developing, 542-543

IDisposable interface, ClientBase and ChannelFactory classes, 815

IDisposable.Dispose() method, 814-815

IHttpHandler, REST service processing, 74

IIdentity interface, 522

IIS (Internet Information Service)
hosting .NET Remoting components, 57
selecting hosting models, 612

IIS hosting, 113-114

imperative authorization, 524

implementation requirements, service contracts, 693

implicit programming model (System.Transactions library), 68-69

implicit service discovery, 147-148

in-line documentation, 322

in-memory application cache in Windows Server AppFabric, 190-191

Increased Federation goal, 249-250

Increased Intrinsic Interoperability goal, 250, 285

Increased Organizational Agility goal, 285

Increased ROI goal, 285

Increased Vendor Diversification
Options goal, 249-250

industry standards, list of, 70, 688-689

InfoCard, 536-540

infrastructure metrics, 654

Infrastructure-as-a-Service (IaaS),
210-212

input endpoints, Windows Azure roles,
221-222

instancing (WCF), 105-106

instantiating services (Hello World
example), 226

integration models, 467-470

integrity, defined, 122

inter-organization service composition
security, 545-546

Inter-Role Communication (IRC),
222-223

intercepting messages, 589
at caching utility service, 590
comparison of techniques, 591
at intermediary, 589
in service container, 589
at service proxy, 590

interceptors, 670

intercloud deployment model, 209

interface contracts
creating, 252
defined, 78

intermediary, intercepting
messages, 589

Intermediate Routing design pattern,
133, 136, 748

internal cloud, 208

Internet Information Service (IIS),
hosting .NET Remoting
components, 57

interoperability, 40

interoperable bindings, 91

inventory analysis cycle, 337-338

inventory boundary design patterns. *See*
Domain Inventory design pattern;
Enterprise Inventory design pattern

Inventory Endpoint design pattern, 749

inventory standardization design
patterns. *See* Canonical Protocol
design pattern; Canonical Schema
design pattern

inventory structure design patterns
Logic Centralization design
pattern, 751
Service Layers design pattern, 169,
377-378, 779
Service Normalization design
pattern, 781

Inversion of Control design
pattern, 570

IPipelineContext interface (BizTalk
BAM), 666

IPrincipal interface, 521

IRC (Inter-Role Communication),
222-223

itineraries
BizTalk Server, 201
ESB Toolkit, 472-474
lifecycle of, 475-476
types of, 474

J

Java RMI (Java Remote Invocation
Call), 47

JIT resolution, 477

JSON encoding, configuring contracts
for, 421-422

just-in-time activation (JITA), 50

K–L

large binary objects, transferring, 629
Laws of Identity, 536
layers (WCF), 149-150
Legacy Wrapper design pattern, 750
LINQ-to-XML mapping, 271-272
listener adapters, 114
locations in BizTalk Server
    messaging, 199
logging messages (WCF), 153
Logic Centralization design pattern, 751
logic-to-contract coupling, 285
logical models for metrics, defining,
    661-662
loose coupling. *See* Service Loose
    Coupling design principle
Loose strategy (versioning), 102
loosely couple events, 50

M

manageability extensions (Windows
    Server AppFabric), 192
managed discovery, 141
managed Windows services, 112-113
management of BizTalk BAM
    database outages, 672
    reporting, 676
    scripting deployment, 673-676
    security, 672-673
management tools (WCF)
    administration tools, 151
    message logging tools, 153
    troubleshooting tools, 151-152
mappings
    LINQ-to-XML, 271-272
    Microsoft ESB to Enterprise Service
        Bus compound pattern, 490-492
    object-to-object, 269-271

memory resources, cleaning up, 812
message buffers, Service Bus, 496-497
    creating, 514-516
    REST and, 499
message contracts
    creating, 251
    defined, 79
    MessageContract attribute, 83-86
message encryption, 623-624
message filters, defining for routing
    services, 137
message formats in .NET Remoting, 60
message logging tools (WCF), 153
message payload, 660
message queues (MSMQ), 63-65
Message Screening design pattern,
    529, 752
message security mode, 123
message sizes (REST services), 621-622
MessageContract attribute (WCF),
    83-86
messages
    intercepting, 589
        at caching utility service, 590
        comparison of techniques, 591
        at intermediary, 589
        in service container, 589
        at service proxy, 590
    itineraries. *See* itineraries
    receiving from Service Bus, 484-485
    sending to Service Bus, 485-486
    MSMQ, sending/receiving, 65-66
messaging
    BizTalk Server, 193, 196
        pipelines, 197-198
        ports and locations, 199
    Service Broker (SSB), 160-164

Messaging Metadata design pattern, 84, 201, 251, 753

messaging property, 660

messaging-based middleware, 468

metadata

BizTalk Server context properties, 200-201

MEX endpoints, 100-101

Metadata Centralization design pattern, 147, 219, 325-326, 417, 754

metadata exchange (MEX), 101

metrics

BAM. *See* BAM

capturing data, 655-656

logical model definition, 661-662

service composition metrics, 669

Standard Mold case study, 677-680

types of, 654-655

views

creating, 663-664

role-based views, 662

MEX (metadata exchange), 101

MEX endpoints, 100-101

microflow, 472

Microsoft, ESB and, 466-467

Microsoft Messaging Queue. *See* MSMQ

Microsoft Operations Manager (MOM), 654

mixed mode security, 124

Model-View-Controller design pattern, 568

Model-View-Presenter design pattern, 568

Model-View-View-Model design pattern, 568

Modern SOA Infrastructure, 6

modularity design patterns, 569-571

modules (Prism Library), 565-566

in application lifecycle, 576

dynamically loading, 579-581

MOM (Microsoft Operations Manager), 654

monitoring ESB, 488-489

MSMQ (Microsoft Messaging Queue), 63

components of, 63

message queues, 64-65

messages, sending/receiving, 65-66

service-orientation and, 66

MTOM encoding, 627-629

Multi-Channel Endpoint design pattern, 633, 755

multi-tenant cloud, 208

mutual authentication, 520, 536

N

n-tier architecture, 45-47

named pipes, 279

naming conventions

service capabilities, 281-282

services, 280

Native XML Web Services (SQL Server), 157-160

.NET assemblies, history of, 51

.NET Enterprise Services, 156

history of

COM+ services, 49, 51

COM/DCOM, 48-49

Distributed Transaction Coordinator (DTC), 52-53

.NET assemblies, 51

service-orientation and, 53

.NET Remoting, 47, 54
   architecture of, 54, 56
   configurations, 57
      activation types, 58, 60
      communication protocols, 60
      message formats, 60
   hosting components
      in COM+ services, 57
      in console applications, 57
      in IIS, 57
      in Windows services, 56
   object lifetime management, 61
   service-orientation and, 61-62
.NET System.Transactions library, 67
   ambient transactions, 69
   distributed resource transactions,
      67-68
   explicit/implicit programming
      models, 68-69
.NET types, generating, 258-264
Non-Agnostic Context design pattern,
   169, 379-380, 756
non-agnostic logic, defined, 32
non-repudiation, 552
notification service for this book series,
   14, 810
notifications, 165, 670-671
numeric range dimension, 664

O

OAuth WRAP, 550
object lifetime management in .NET
   Remoting, 61
object-to-object mapping, 269-271
Official Endpoint compound
   pattern, 757

on-premise cloud, 208
On-ramp service (ESB Toolkit), 471
Open Authentication Web Resource
   Access Protocol, 550
operation attributes (WCF
   transactions), 127-128
operation contracts, defined, 78
OperationContract attribute (WCF),
   79-81
optimization. *See* performance tuning
orchestrated task service contracts in
   BizTalk Server, 445-447
orchestrated task services, 382-384,
   423-425
orchestration
   BizTalk Server and, 193, 388-391,
      443-445
      Compensating Service
         Transaction design pattern,
         456-461
      exception management,
         202-203
      itineraries, 201
      orchestrated task service
         contracts, 445-447
      Process Centralization design
         pattern, 450-451, 454
      State Repository design pattern,
         455-456
      Superior Stamping case study,
         448-449
      WS-* support, 447-448
   execution time, 385
   optional design patterns, 388
   versioning, 180

WF (Windows Workflow
Foundation) and, 388-391,
395-397
*ASMX services, publishing
workflows as, 399-407*
*Compensating Service
Transaction design pattern,
387, 434-435*
*ExternalDataExchange services,
publishing workflows via,
413-416*
history of, 397-398
*Process Abstraction design
pattern, 382-385*
*Process Centralization design
pattern, 382-385, 425-426*
*REST services, publishing
workflows as, 419-425*
*Standard Mold case study,
436-439*
*State Repository design pattern,
386, 426-433*
*WCF 3.5 activities, publishing
workflows via, 408-410*
*WCF 4.0 activities, publishing
workflows via, 410-413*
*WS-I BasicProfile support,
417-419*
Orchestration compound pattern, 169,
194, 382, 395, 443, 758
orchestration schedule, 660
OrchestrationEventStream API
(BizTalk BAM), 666
outbound-rendezvous relayed
connectivity model (Service Bus),
494, 496

P
PaaS (Platform-as-a-Service), 211-212
page blobs in Windows Azure
Storage, 243
parallelism, 641
in BizTalk Server, 643-644
iReplicatorActivity in WF, 644-645
in WF, 641, 643
parameters
passing to workflow instances, 178
returning from workflow instances,
178-179
Partial State Deferral design pattern,
456, 759
Partial Validation design pattern, 760
partition keys in Windows Azure
Storage, 240
Passive View design pattern, 568
patterns. *See* design patterns
performance policies, 612,
615-616, 621
performance tuning, 584
optimization areas, 585-586
service capabilities, 586
caching, 587-591
*caching implementation
technologies, 592-593*
*caching REST responses,
599-601*
*coarse-grained service contracts,
608-610*
computing cache keys, 593-594
hardware encryption, 622-625
monitoring cache efficiency, 601
MTOM encoding, 627-629
*performance policies, 612,
615-616, 619-621*

reducing resource contention,
  603-604
request throttling, 604-608
REST service message sizes,
  621-622
selecting hosting models,
  610-612
service contract design, 630-632
service-orientation principles,
  impact on, 633
Standard Mold case study,
  594-596
Superior Stamping case study,
  597-599
transports, 625-627
service compositions, 637, 648
  asynchronous interactions,
    639-641
  co-hosting, 645-648
  parallelism, 641, 643-645
  service-orientation principles,
    impact on, 648
  transformation avoidance,
    637-638
state management and, 700-701
persistence, workflow
  with AppFabric, 189-190
  in WF, 170-171
persistence service, 131
  in WF 3.0, 429-431
  in WF 4.0, 431-433
pipelines in BizTalk Server messaging,
  197-198
Platform-as-a-Service (PaaS), 211-212
Plug-In design pattern, 570
point-to-point integration channels, 467
policies, effect on performance, 612,
  615-616, 619-621

Policy Centralization design pattern, 761
PolicyActivity, 181
ports in BizTalk Server messaging, 199
Prentice Hall Service-Oriented
  Computing Series from Thomas Erl,
  13-14, 810
presentation layer
  design patterns, 567
    modularity patterns, 569-571
    user interface patterns, 567-569
  Prism Library, 559
    modules, 565-566
    regions, 563-564
    shared services, 566
    shell, 561-562
    views, 562-563
  service-oriented user interface
    example, 571
      dynamically loading modules,
        579-581
      project creation, 571-579
  weaknesses in traditional models,
    558-559
Presentation Model design pattern,
  568-569
Prism Library, 559
  modules, 565-566
  regions, 563-564
  service-oriented user interface
    example, 571
      dynamically loading modules,
        579-581
      project creation, 571-579
  shared services, 566
  shell, 561-562
  views, 562-563
private assemblies, 51
private cloud deployment model, 208

private components in COM+, 50

probe queries, 143-144

Process Abstraction design pattern, 169, 378, 380, 382-385, 762

process boundary (IIS), 113

Process Centralization design pattern, 169, 382-385, 425, 450

    human intervention in business processes, 450-451

    profile, 763

    workflow design in WF, 425-426

    WS-BPEL support, 426, 451, 454

production environment, tracking profiles in, 660

productivity tools in BizTalk Server, 194

programming model (WF), 176-177

progress dimension, 664

properties in Windows Azure Storage, 240-241

Protocol Bridging design pattern, 136, 200, 274, 764

protocol channels, 149

protocols

    Canonical Protocol design pattern, 274

        component implementation, 278-279

        dual protocols, 279-280

        named pipes, 279

        REST services implementation, 277-278

        Web services implementation, 275-277

    cleaning up resources, 822

Proxy Capability design pattern, 765

proxy classes, writing, 118-119

public cloud authorization model (Access Control), 554

public cloud deployment model, 208

publish-and-subscribe integration model, 468

publishing WF workflows

    as ASMX services, 399-407

    via ExternalDataExchange services, 413-416

    as REST services, 419-425

    via WCF 3.5 activities, 408-410

    via WCF 4.0 activities, 410-413

    WS-I BasicProfile support, 417-419

Q–R

Query Notification (SQL Server), 165

queued components, 50

queues

    message queues (MSMQ), 63-65

    in Windows Azure Storage, 239, 241-242

rapid prototyping, 671

real-time aggregations

    dimensions in, 662

    scheduled aggregations versus, 660-661

Receive activity, configuring for REST services, 422-423

receiving application (MSMQ), 63

receiving messages

    Service Bus, 484-485

    MSMQ, 65-66

recommended reading, 4-6, 41-42

Redundant Implementation design pattern, 207, 213, 766

regions (Prism Library), 563-564

Reliable Messaging design pattern, 160, 767

relying parties, 537, 541-542

remotable classes in .NET Remoting, 56

Remote Method Invocation (RMI), 47
Remote Procedure Calls (RPC), 47
remoting. *See* .NET Remoting
ReplicatorActivity in WF, 644-645
reporting (BizTalk BAM
    management), 676
request throttling, 604-605
    with BizTalk Server, 607-608
    Superior Stamping case study,
      606-607
    with WCF, 605-606
Resolver service (ESB Toolkit), 471
resolver strings for itineraries (ESB
    Toolkit), 475
resolvers (ESB Toolkit), 476-478
resource contention, reducing, 603-604
REST responses, caching, 599-601
REST services, 92-93
    Access Control (AppFabric) and,
      552-553
    cleaning up resources, 822
    discoverability, 323
    dispatcher system in WCF, 77
    entity abstraction with (Standard
      Mold case study), 351-367
    hosting, 115-116
    message sizes, 621-622
    processing, 74
    publishing workflows as, 419-425
    resource naming conventions, 282
    Service Bus contracts, defining,
      513-514
    Service Bus message buffers
      and, 499
    as service implementation option,
      277-278
    services as, 31
    UriTemplate attribute, 96-98

WCF-Custom adapter provider
    and, 479
WebGet attribute, 93-95
WebInvoke attribute, 95-96
in Windows Azure, 235
    addressing, 235
    creating, 236-239
REST-based service consumers in
    Service Bus, 499
REST-based service design in Service
    Bus, 498
reusability. *See* Service Reusability
    design principle
RMI (Remote Method Invocation), 47
role-based authorization, 520-524
role-based security in COM+, 50
role-based views, 662
roles, 520
    Azure roles, 219
      input endpoints, 221-222
      Inter-Role Communication
        (IRC), 222-223
      virtual machines, 220-221
      Web roles, 220
      worker roles, 220
    composition roles, 377
    selecting (Hello World
      example), 224
router services (WCF Router), 132-133
    fault tolerance, 139-140
    routing configuration, 135-139
    routing contracts, 134-135
    RoutingService class, 133-134
routing contracts, 134-135
RoutingService class, 133-134
row keys in Windows Azure Storage, 241
RPC (Remote Procedure Calls), 47
Rules Centralization design pattern,
    181, 388, 768

S

SaaS (Software-as-a-Service), 211
SAML, 126
SAO (server-activated objects), 58
scalability, 700
scaling ESB architecture, 481-482
scaling out, 608
    in WF 3.0, 429-431
    in WF 4.0, 431-433
scheduled aggregations, real-time
    aggregations versus, 660-661
Schema Centralization design pattern,
    217, 251, 253, 445, 769
schemas. *See* XML schemas
scripting deployment (BizTalk BAM
    management), 673-676
security
    BizTalk BAM management,
        672-673
    in COM+, 50
    Exception Shielding design pattern,
        319-321
    performance tuning, 612-621
    Service Bus authentication, 508-509
    terminology, 122
    WCF security, 122-123
        authorization, 125-126
        brokered authentication, 519
        claims-based authorization,
            524, 526-529
        direct authentication, 518-519
        federated identity, 126
        mutual authentication, 520
        role-based authorization,
            520-524
        security modes, 123-125
        Standard Mold case study, 530,
            532-533

    Windows Azure security, 543
        Access Control (AppFabric),
            548-554
        cloud computing, 543-547
        Standard Mold case study,
            555-556
    Windows Identity Foundation
        (WIF), 533
        Active Directory Federation
            Services (ADFS), 539
        digital identity, 534-536
        identity providers, developing,
            542-543
        programming model, 540-541
        relying parties, developing,
            541-542
        Windows Cardspace, 536-539
security modes, 123-125
security principal, 521-522
Security Token Service (STS), 535, 546
security tokens, 525, 534
self-hosted services, 110-112
Send activity, configuring for REST
    services, 422-423
sending application (MSMQ), 63
sending messages
    MSMQ, 65-66
    to Service Bus, 485-486
Separated Interface design pattern, 570
Separated Presentation design pattern,
    568-569
sequential workflows, 169
serializable classes in .NET
    Remoting, 56
serialization, 82-83
server-activated objects (SAO), 58
server-side itineraries, 474

Service Abstraction design principle,
26, 82, 84, 102, 104, 207, 217,
313-314, 696
Service Agent design pattern, 133,
589, 770
service announcements, sending/
receiving, 144-146
service attributes (WCF transactions),
129-130
service authorization scenarios (Access
Control), 553-554
service autonomy, 98
Service Autonomy design principle, 27,
110, 190, 218, 699
Service Broker compound pattern, 136,
160-164, 771
Service Bus, 494
configuration, 504-512
authentication, 508-509
contract definition, 505-506
contract implementation,
506-507
end-to-end security, 509
service configuration, 508
service host configuration,
511-512
service publication, 512
as connectivity fabric, 494-496
connectivity models, 499
Eventing, 500
Service Remoting, 501
Tunneling, 501-502
creating, 503
message buffers, 496-497
creating, 514-516
REST and, 499
receiving messages from, 484-485
REST-based contracts, defining,
513-514

REST-based service
consumers, 499
REST-based service design, 498
sending messages to, 485-486
service registry, 497-498
Service Callback design pattern, 772
service candidates, 35, 251
service capabilities
naming conventions, 281-282
performance tuning, 586
caching, 587-591
caching implementation
technologies, 592-593
caching REST responses,
599-601
coarse-grained service contracts,
608-610
computing cache keys, 593-594
hardware encryption, 622-625
monitoring cache efficiency, 601
MTOM encoding, 627-629
performance policies, 612,
615-616, 619-621
reducing resource contention,
603-604
request throttling, 604-608
REST service message sizes,
621-622
selecting hosting models,
610-612
service contract design, 630-632
service-orientation principles,
impact on, 633
Standard Mold case study,
594-596
Superior Stamping case study,
597-599
transports, 625-627

Service Composability design principle,
  27, 125, 373, 560, 704-705
service composition
  Capability Composition design
    pattern, 374-375
  Capability Recomposition design
    pattern, 374-376
  defined, 33-34
  inter-organization service
    composition security, 545-546
  Non-Agnostic Context design
    pattern, 379-380
  performance tuning, 637, 648
    asynchronous interactions,
      639-641
    co-hosting, 645-648
    parallelism, 641, 643-645
    service-orientation principles,
      impact on, 648
    transformation avoidance,
      637-638
  Process Abstraction design
    pattern, 380
  roles, 377
  Service Composability design
    principle, 373
  Service Layers design pattern,
    377-378
  service-orientation and, 371-373
  task services, 380
service composition metrics, 669
service consumers (WCF), 116-117
  ChannelFactory class, 119-120
  Service Metadata Tool, 117-118
  writing proxy class, 118-119
service container, intercepting
  messages, 589

service contracts, 704
  defined, 36-37, 78
  implementation example, 106-108
  performance tuning, 630-632
  ServiceContract and
    OperationContract attributes,
    79-81
  versioning, 102-103
  WF support, history of, 397-398
Service Data Replication design
  pattern, 190, 218, 773
Service Decomposition design
  pattern, 774
service delivery models in cloud
  computing, 210-212
Service Discoverability design
  principle, 27, 147, 219, 321, 417, 535
  implementation requirements, 703
  in-line documentation, 322
  profile, 702-703
  REST services, 323
  service profiles, 323-324
Service Encapsulation design pattern,
  169, 332, 775
service endpoints
  attributes, 81
  defined, 79
  endpoint element, 86-87
    address attribute, 88-89
    binding attribute, 89-92
    contract attribute, 92
Service Façade design pattern, 304,
  306-307, 776
service framework processing, 586
Service Grid design pattern, 777
service granularity, defined, 37

service hosting (WCF)
   IIS hosting, 113-114
   managed Windows services,
     112-113
   REST service hosting, 115-116
   selecting hosting environment,
     108-110
   self-hosted services, 110-112
   Windows Activation Service
     (WAS), 114
service implementation options, 274
   components, 278-279
   REST services, 277-278
   Web services, 275-277
service implementation processing, 585
Service Instance Routing design
   pattern, 778
service inventory, defined, 34
service inventory blueprints, 34
Service Layers design pattern, 169,
   377-378, 779
service level agreement (SLA)
   enforcement, 488
Service Locator design pattern, 571
Service Loose Coupling design
   principle, 26, 81-82, 84, 217,
   285-286, 559
   design patterns and, 286
   profile, 695
   service capability granularity and,
     308-313
Service Messaging design pattern,
   84, 780
Service Metadata Tool, 117-118
service metrics, 654
service model layer, 149
service modeling, 251
service models, defined, 31-32

service namespace, 503, 551
Service Normalization design
   pattern, 781
service package (Web service example)
   creating and deploying, 233
   promoting to production, 234
Service Perimeter Guard design
   pattern, 529, 782
service profiles, discoverability,
   323-324
service proxy, intercepting
   messages, 590
Service Refactoring design pattern,
   217, 783
service registry (Service Bus), 497-498
Service Remoting connectivity model
   (Service Bus), 501
Service Reusability design principle, 26,
   125, 329-330, 337, 339, 697-698, 704
Service Statelessness design principle,
   27, 171, 190, 700-701
service-orientation
   defined, 25-27
   history of .NET Enterprise Services
     and, 53
   MSMQ and, 66
   .NET Remoting and, 61-62
   service composition and, 371-373
service-orientation principles, impact
   of performance tuning, 633, 648
service-oriented analysis, defined,
   34-35
Service-Oriented Architecture: Concepts,
   Technology, and Design, 5
service-oriented architecture. *See* SOA
service-oriented computing
   defined, 25
   goals of, 40-41

service-oriented design, defined, 35-36

service-oriented user interface
example, 571
   dynamically loading modules,
      579-581
   project creation, 571-579

service-related granularity, defined,
   37-38

service-types, 81

ServiceContract attribute (WCF),
   79-81

services
   as components, 29
   defined, 28-29
   instantiating (Hello World
      example), 226
   naming conventions, 280
   protection patterns, 529
   as REST services, 31
   scalability, 700
   WCF. *See* WCF
   as Web services, 30

shared assemblies, 51

shared services (Prism Library), 566

shell (Prism Library), 561-562

silo-based applications, 467

Silverlight, 560. *See also* service-
   oriented user interface example

SingleCall objects, 58

Singleton objects, 59

SLA enforcement, 488

SOA (service-oriented architecture)
   defined, 27
   explained, 47

SOA Certified Professional (SOACP),
   14. *See also* www.soaschool.com

SOA Design Patterns, 5

SOA Governance, 6

SOA Magazine, The Web site, 14, 810

SOA Manifesto, 27
   annotated version, 796-808
   original version, 796

SOA Principles of Service Design, 5, 11

SOA with Java, 6

SOA with REST, 6

SOACP (SOA Certified Professional),
   14. *See also* www.soaschool.com

SOAP
   attachments, 701
   message contracts, 83-86
   processors, 701

SOAP Faults, 99

SOAP service in COM+, 50

Software Factories, 184
   Guidance Automation Extensions
      (GAX), 184
   Guidance Automation Toolkit
      (GAT), 184
   Web Services Software Factory,
      184-186

Software-as-a-Service (SaaS), 211

Software-plus-Services, 206

specifications, 70, 688-689

SQL Azure, 217-218

SQL Express configuration, 224

SQL persistence services
   in WF 3.0, 429-431
   in WF 4.0, 431-433

SQL Server, 156-157
   Query Notification, 165
   Service Broker, 160-164
   Web services support, 157-160
   XML support, 165-166

SQL Server Service Broker Adapter, 200

Standard Mold case study. *See* case
   studies; code examples

Standardized Service Contract design
principle, 26, 78, 81-82, 84, 217, 250,
274, 340, 399
  contract-first development, 250-252
  design patterns and, 252
  profile, 693-694
standards, 70, 688-689
state machine workflows, 169
state management, 700-701
State Messaging design pattern,
456, 784
State Repository design pattern, 171,
207, 386, 426-428
  BizTalk Server, 455-456
  persistence service and scaling out
    in WF 3.0, 429-431
  persistence service and scaling out
    in WF 4.0, 431-433
  profile, 785
Stateful Services design pattern, 190,
207, 213, 456, 590, 786
storage services
  creating (Web service example), 233
  in Windows Azure, 239-240
    blobs, 242-243
    queues, 241-242
    tables, 240-241
    Windows Azure Drive, 243
Strict strategy (versioning), 102
STS (Security Token Service), 535, 546
subjects. See clients
Superior Stamping case study. See case
  studies; code examples
Supervising design pattern, 568
Supervising Presenter design
  pattern, 569
svcutil utility program, 258
  code generation with, 294-297

symbols
  color in, 13
  legend, 13
synchronization, 50
system-provided bindings, 90
System.Transactions library, 67
  ambient transactions, 69
  distributed resource transactions,
    67-68
  programming models,
    explicit/implicit, 68-69
Systems Center Operations Manager
  Management Pack for BizTalk
  Server, 481

T

tables in Windows Azure Storage,
  239-241
target endpoints, defining for routing
  services, 136-137
task service model, defined, 31
task services, 380. See also orchestrated
  task services
Termination Notification design
  pattern, 102, 787
Three-Layer Inventory compound
  pattern, 378, 788
throttling. See request throttling
throttling controls, 105
time dimension, 664
timestamps in Windows Azure
  Storage, 241
tokens, 546, 551
TPE (Tracking Profile Editor),
  659-660
tracing (WCF), 151-152
tracking host, 672
Tracking Profile Editor (TPE),
  659-660

tracking profiles, 659-660

TransactionAutoComplete
attribute, 128

TransactionAutoCompleteOnSession-
Close attribute, 130

TransactionFlow attribute, 128

TransactionIsolationLevel
attribute, 129

transactions, 50. *See also*
System.Transactions library
ambient transactions, 69
distributed resource transactions,
67-68
explained, 51
in Windows Azure Storage, 241
WCF, 127
durable services, 131-132
operation attributes, 127-128
service attributes, 129-130

TransactionScopeRequired
attribute, 128

TransactionTimeout attribute, 130

Transformation service
(ESB Toolkit), 471

transformations. *See also* Data Model
Transformation design pattern
avoiding, 637-638
XSLT transformations, 272-273

transition plans for ESB, 489

transport channels, 149

transport encryption, 622-623

transport security mode, 123

transports, performance tuning,
625-627

troubleshooting management tools
(WCF), 151-152

trust, 546

trust boundaries, 122

Trusted Subsystem design pattern, 789

try-catch-finally-abort block, cleaning
up resources, 817

try-close-catch-abort block, cleaning up
resources, 818-819

tuning. *See* performance tuning

Tunneling connectivity model (Service
Bus), 501-502

U

UDDI, 325-326

UI Mediator design pattern, 568, 790

Uniform Contract design pattern, 282

Uniform Resource Identifiers (URIs),
explained, 88

UriTemplate attribute (REST services),
96-98

user interface design patterns, 567-569

user interface example. *See* service-
oriented user interface example

using block, cleaning up resources, 816

Utility Abstraction design pattern, 169,
182, 335, 377-378
profile, 791
with .NET Web service (Standard
Mold case study), 339-351

utility logic (Application Blocks),
182-183

utility methods, cleaning up resources,
819, 821

utility service model, defined, 32

V

Validation Abstraction design pattern,
82, 217, 315-318, 792

vendor diversification, 40

version control systems, 698

Version Identification design pattern,
102, 793

versioning
    orchestrations, 180
    service contracts, 102-103
view discovery, view injection versus, 563
view injection, view discovery versus, 563
views
    creating, 663-664
    Prism Library, 562-563
    role-based views, 662
virtual machines, Windows Azure roles, 220-221
virtual private cloud, 209
Visual Studio
    creating schemas, 254, 256-258
    elevated mode, 223

W

WAS (Windows Activation Service), 114, 612
WATs (Windows Azure Tables), 240-241
WCF (Windows Communication Foundation)
    administration management tools, 151
    behaviors, 104-105
    cleaning up resources, 811-812
        Abort() method (ICommunicationObject), 814
        based on bindings, 822
        ClientBase and ChannelFactory classes, 815
        Close() method (ICommunicationObject), 812-814
        Dispose() method (IDisposable), 814-815
        try-catch-finally-abort block, 817
        try-close-catch-abort block, 818-819
        using block, 816
        utility methods, 819, 821
    data contracts
        DataContract attribute, 82-83
        defined, 78
        fault contracts, 98-100
    extensibility
        channel bindings, 148
        channel layer extensibility, 150
        layers, 149-150
    instancing, 105-106
    interceptors, 670
    interface contracts, defined, 78
    message contracts
        defined, 79
        MessageContract attribute, 83-86
    message logging tools, 153
    MEX endpoints, 100-101
    operation contracts, defined, 78
    overview, 76-77
    programming model for WF orchestrations, 397
    request throttling, 605-606
    REST services, 92-93
        UriTemplate attribute, 96-98
        WebGet attribute, 93-95
        WebInvoke attribute, 95-96
    security, 122-123
        authorization, 125-126
        brokered authentication, 519
        claims-based authorization, 524, 526-529

direct authentication, 518-519
federated identity, 126
mutual authentication, 520
role-based authorization,
    520-524
security modes, 123-125
Standard Mold case study, 530,
    532-533
service consumers, 116-117
ChannelFactory class, 119-120
Service Metadata Tool,
    117-118
writing proxy class, 118-119
service contracts
defined, 78
implementation example,
    106-108
ServiceContract and
    OperationContract
    attributes, 79-81
versioning, 102-103
service endpoints
address attribute, 88-89
binding attribute, 89-92
contract attribute, 92
defined, 79
endpoint element, 86-87
service hosting
IIS hosting, 113-114
managed Windows services,
    112-113
REST service hosting, 115-116
selecting hosting environment,
    108-110
self-hosted services, 110-112
Windows Activation Service
    (WAS), 114
terminology, 78-79

transactions, 127
durable services, 131-132
operation attributes, 127-128
service attributes, 129-130
troubleshooting management tools,
    151-152
WCF 3.5 activities, publishing
    workflows via, 408-410
WCF 4.0 activities, publishing
    workflows via, 410-413
WCF Adapter, 200
WCF Discovery, 140-141
discovery modes, 141-143
Discovery Proxies, 146
implicit service discovery, 147-148
probe queries, 143-144
sending/receiving service
    announcements, 144-146
WCF Router, 132-133
fault tolerance, 139-140
routing configuration, 135-139
routing contracts, 134-135
RoutingService class, 133-134
WCF-Custom adapter provider, REST
    services and, 479
WCF-to-WCF bindings, 91
Web roles (Windows Azure), 220
Web Service Contract Design and
    Versioning for SOA, 5, 294
Web Service Enhancements (WSE), 73
Web service example. See Windows
    Azure, Web service example
Web services. See also services
ASMX (XML Web services), 71, 73
as service implementation option,
    275-277
services as, 30

SQL Server support for, 157-160

WSE (Web Service Enhancements), 73

Web Services Adapter, 199

Web Services Software Factory, 184-186

Web sites

www.serviceorientation.com, 810

www.sliverlight.net, 560

www.soa-manifesto.com, 5, 796

www.soa-manifesto.org, 27, 796

www.soabooks.com, 6, 13-14, 42, 810

www.soaglossary.com, 5, 13, 24, 42, 810

www.soamag.com, 14, 810

www.soapatterns.org, 5, 810

www.soaprinciples.com, 5, 42, 810

www.soaschool.com, 14

www.soaspecs.com, 5, 13, 70, 141, 560, 688, 810

www.whatissoa.com, 5, 41, 810

Web-oriented architecture (WOA), 207

WebGet attribute (REST services), 93-95

WebInvoke attribute (REST services), 95-96

WebMethod attribute, 72

WebService attribute, 71-72

WF (Windows Workflow Foundation), 76, 166

activities, 172-175

architecture, 167-168

business rules, 180-181

extensibility, 180

host container communication, 171-172

interceptors, 670

orchestration and, 388-391, 395-397

ASMX services, publishing workflows as, 399-407

Compensating Service Transaction design pattern, 434-435

ExternalDataExchange services, publishing workflows via, 413-416

history of, 397-398

Process Abstraction design pattern, 382-385

Process Centralization design pattern, 382-385, 425-426

REST services, publishing workflows as, 419-425

Standard Mold case study, 436-439

State Repository design pattern, 386, 426-433

WCF 3.5 activities, publishing workflows via, 408-410

WCF 4.0 activities, publishing workflows via, 410-413

WS-I BasicProfile support, 417-419

parallelism in, 641, 643-645

passing parameters to workflow instances, 178

programming model, 176-177

returning parameters from workflow instances, 178-179

versioning orchestrations, 180

workflow designer, 169-170

workflow persistence, 170-171

workflow runtime environment, 175

workflow types, 168-169

workflow-enabled services, 179

WF 3.0, persistence service and scaling out, 429-431

WF 4.0, persistence service and scaling out, 431-433

WIF (Windows Identity Foundation), 533

    Active Directory Federation Services (ADFS), 539

    digital identity, 534-536

    identity providers, developing, 542-543

    programming model, 540-541

    relying parties, developing, 541-542

    Windows Cardspace, 536-539

WIF (Windows Identity Framework), 76

Windows Activation Service (WAS), 114, 612

Windows Azure. *See also* **cloud computing**

    access control in, 528

    application container, 216-217

    cloud deployment models and, 210

    cloud-based services, categories of, 215-216

    ESB and, 483

        receiving messages from Service Bus, 484-485

        sending messages to Service Bus, 485-486

    Hello World example, 223

        cloud service project, creating, 224

        roles, selecting, 224

        service, instantiating, 226

        solution, creating, 225

    platform overview, 213-216

REST services, 235

    addressing, 235

    creating, 236-239

roles, 219

    input endpoints, 221-222

    Inter-Role Communication (IRC), 222-223

    virtual machines, 220-221

    Web roles, 220

    worker roles, 220

SQL Azure, 217-218

storage services, 239-240

    blobs, 242-243

    queues, 241-242

    tables, 240-241

    Windows Azure Drive, 243

Web service example, 227-232

    Diagnostic Monitor, 229

    host service and storage service, creating, 233

    IOrderService interface contract, 231

    logging and diagnostic APIs, 229

    Order data contract, 231

    output of IOrderService interface contract and Order data contract, 232

    service package, creating and deploying, 233

    service package, promoting to production, 234

    ServiceConfiguration.cscfg, 228

    ServiceDefinition.csdef, 228

    tracing listener creation, 230

    WebRole.cs, 227

Windows Azure Drive in Windows Azure Storage, 239, 243

Windows Azure Fabric Controller, 214

Windows Azure platform AppFabric, 218. *See also* Access Control; Service Bus

Windows Azure security, 543

    Access Control (AppFabric), 548-553

        service authorization scenarios, 553-554

        Standard Mold case study, 555-556

    cloud computing, 543-547

Windows Azure Tables (WATs), 240-241

Windows Cardspace, 76, 536-541

Windows Communication Foundation. *See* WCF

Windows Identity Foundation (WIF), 533

    Active Directory Federation Services (ADFS), 539

    digital identity, 534-536

    identity providers, developing, 542-543

    programming model, 540-541

    relying parties, developing, 541-542

    Windows Cardspace, 536-539

Windows Identity Framework (WIF), 76

Windows Management Instrumentation (WMI), 151

Windows Presentation Foundation. *See* WPF

Windows Server AppFabric, 187

    configurable hosting environment, 188-189

    Event Collector Service, 192

    in-memory application cache, 190-191

    manageability extensions, 192

    service namespaces, creating, 503

    workflow persistence, 189-190

Windows services, hosting .NET Remoting components, 56

Windows Workflow Foundation. *See* WF

wire transmission processing, 586

WMI (Windows Management Instrumentation), 151

WOA (Web-oriented architecture), 207

worker roles (Windows Azure), 220

workflow design, 425-426

workflow designer (in WF), 169-170

workflow instances

    passing parameters to, 178

    returning parameters from, 178-179

workflow persistence

    AppFabric, 189-190

    WF, 170-171

workflow runtime environment (in WF), 175

workflow-enabled services, 179

workflows. *See also* WF (Windows Workflow Foundation)

    history of, 397-398

    publishing

        as ASMX services, 399-407

        via ExternalDataExchange services, 413-416

        as REST services, 419-425

        via WCF 3.5 activities, 408-410

        via WCF 4.0 activities, 410-413

        WS-I BasicProfile support, 417-419

    types of, 168-169

WPF (Windows Presentation
    Foundation), 76
    Prism Library, 559
        modules, 565-566
        regions, 563-564
        shared services, 566
        shell, 561-562
        views, 562-563
WS-AtomicTransaction, 127, 458
WS-BPEL, 385, 426, 451, 454
WS-Coordination, 127
WS-Discovery, 140
WS-I Basic Security Profile, 125
WS-I Basic Profile, 417-419
WS-MetadataExchange, 101, 417, 536
WS-Policy, 694
WS-SecureConversation, 125
WS-Security, 125, 536
WS-SecurityPolicy, 125, 536
WS-Trust, 125
WSCF.blue, code generation with,
    297-301
WSCF.classic, code generation with,
    302-304
WSDL, 77, 694
WSDL-first design approach, 289-294
    svcutil utility program, code
        generation with, 294-297
    WSCF.blue, code generation with,
        297-301
    WSCF.classic, code generation
        with, 302-304
WSE (Web Service Enhancements),
    70, 73

X–Z
XAML (Extensible Application Markup
    Language), 560
XML parsers, 701
XML support in SQL Server, 165-166
XML Schema Definition Language, 82,
    253, 694
XML schemas
    creating, 254, 256-258
    WSDL-first design approach,
        289-294
        svcutil utility program, code
            generation with, 294-297
        WSCF.blue, code generation
            with, 297-301
        WSCF.classic, code generation
            with, 302-304
XML serializers, 82-83
XML Web services (ASMX), 71, 73
XML-Encryption, 125
XML-Signature, 125
xsd.exe utility program, 264
XSLT, 638, 272-273

FREE Online Edition

Your purchase of **SOA with .NET and Windows Azure** includes access to a free online edition for 45 days through the Safari Books Online subscription service. Nearly every Prentice Hall book is available online through Safari Books Online, along with more than 5,000 other technical books and videos from publishers such as Addison-Wesley Professional, Cisco Press, Exam Cram, IBM Press, O'Reilly, Que, and Sams.

SAFARI BOOKS ONLINE allows you to search for a specific answer, cut and paste code, download chapters, and stay current with emerging technologies.

Activate your FREE Online Edition at
www.informit.com/safarifree

> **STEP 1:** Enter the coupon code: TNSTQGA.

> **STEP 2:** New Safari users, complete the brief registration form.
> Safari subscribers, just log in.

If you have difficulty registering on Safari or accessing the online edition, please e-mail customer-service@safaribooksonline.com

Addison Wesley AdobePress ALPHA Cisco Press FT Press FINANCIAL TIMES IBM Press lynda.com Microsoft Press New Riders

O'REILLY Peachpit Press QUE Redbooks SAMS SAS Publishing Sun microsystems Wharton School Publishing WILEY

Direct Authentication [736] How can a service verify the credentials provided by a consumer?

 Distributed Capability [737] How can a service preserve its functional context while also fulfilling special capability processing requirements?

 Domain Inventory [738] How can services be delivered to maximize recomposition when enterprise-wide standardization is not possible?

 Dual Protocols [739] How can a service inventory overcome the limitations of its canonical protocol while still remaining standardized?

 Enterprise Inventory [740] How can services be delivered to maximize recomposition?

Enterprise Service Bus [741]

 Entity Abstraction [742] How can agnostic business logic be separated, reused, and governed independently?

 Event-Driven Messaging [743] How can service consumers be automatically notified of runtime service events?

 Exception Shielding [744] How can a service prevent the disclosure of information about its internal implementation when an exception occurs?

Federated Endpoint Layer [745]

 File Gateway [746] How can service logic interact with legacy systems that can only share information by exchanging files?

 Functional Decomposition [747] How can a large business problem be solved without having to build a standalone body of solution logic?

 Intermediate Routing [748] How can dynamic runtime factors affect the path of a message?

 Inventory Endpoint [749] How can a service inventory be shielded from external access while still offering service capabilities to external consumers?

 Legacy Wrapper [750] How can wrapper services with non-standard contracts be prevented from spreading indirect consumer-to-implementation coupling?

 Logic Centralization [751] How can the misuse of redundant service logic be avoided?

 Message Screening [752] How can a service be protected from malformed or malicious input?

 Messaging Metadata [753] How can services be designed to process activity-specific data at runtime?

 Metadata Centralization [754] How can service metadata be centrally published and governed?

 Multi-Channel Endpoint [755] How can legacy logic fragmented and duplicated for different delivery channels be centrally consolidated?

 Non-Agnostic Context [756] How can single-purpose service logic be positioned as an effective enterprise resource?

Official Endpoint [757]

Orchestration [758]

 Partial State Deferral [759] How can services be designed to optimize resource consumption while still remaining stateful?

 Partial Validation [760] How can unnecessary data validation be avoided?

 Policy Centralization [761] How can policies be normalized and consistently enforced across multiple services?

 Process Abstraction [762] How can non-agnostic process logic be separated and governed independently?

 Process Centralization [763] How can abstracted business process logic be centrally governed?

 Protocol Bridging [764] How can a service exchange data with consumers that use different communication protocols?